Family Counseling and Therapy

Family Counseling and Therapy

THIRD EDITION

ARTHUR M. HORNE

University of Georgia

AND CONTRIBUTORS

THOMSON

BROOKS/COLE

Australia • Canada • Mexico • Singapore • Spain • United Kingdom • United States

Edited by John Beasley
Production supervision by Kim Vander Steen
Designed by Jeanne Calabrese Design
Composition by Point West, Inc.
Printed and bound by Sheridan Books

ISBN: 0-87581-423-9
Library of Congress Catalog Card No. 98-68539

Wadsworth/Thomson Learning
10 Davis Drive
Belmont CA 94002-3098
USA

For information about our products, contact us:
Thomson Learning Academic Resource Center
1-800-423-0563
http://www.wadsworth.com

For permission to use material from this text or product,
submit a request online at http://www.thomsonrights.com

Any additional questions about permissions can be
submitted by email to thomsonrights@thomson.com

Printed in the United States of America
10 9 8 7 6 5 4 3 2

This book is dedicated to Merle M. Ohlsen and to:

The families of our past who contributed to making us who we are today;

To the families of our present who provide our lives with meaning and happiness;

To the families of our future who offer hope for continued meaning and happiness.

OUTLINE OF THE BOOK

The "Introduction" (Chapter 1) of *Family Counseling and Therapy* presents an overview of the book, including an explanation for the selection of topics within the book. The second chapter, "Working from a Family Focus," provides a historical context for understanding the development of family systems theory and family therapy interventions. Chapter 3, "Common Elements in Family Therapy Theory and Strategies," identifies core components of family therapy and explains how many of the methods used have universality across models and specific applications in some approaches. The final chapter of the book, "The Ethical Practice of Marriage and Family Therapy," provides a review of current ethical principles as well as professional and legal standards for practitioners of family therapy.

The chapters between 3 and 19 present theoretical models of marriage and family therapy. The authors followed a common outline, resulting in the table above, which may be used to compare common elements of the models, for in previous editions of the book readers have reported enjoying being able to compare approaches through use of such a table.

Contents

Preface

When the first edition of *Family Counseling and Therapy* was published in 1982, several changes in American society were identified that affected families, including:

- The move from a rural to an urban environment;
- Changing from a predominantly extended family system to a nuclear family arrangement;
- A breakdown of the nuclear family as defined in popular literature, changing to more diverse family forms including single-parent, multiple adult figures in the household, gay or lesbian parent families, and communal formats;
- Smaller family sizes;
- A changing emphasis on life skills education from the family to schools and other community agencies; and
- Power shifts from a patriarchal-dominated to more democratically oriented family structures.

Besides the structural differences, a number of other family changes were identified that also tax individual and family resources:

- People are living longer, needing emotional and financial support for extended periods of time.
- Mobility has provided freedom of travel but has increased contacts outside the family and has resulted in the separation of families.
- Mass media has influenced the family, defining new patterns of behavior and interactions our ancestors never experienced.
- Minority rights have resulted in changing family expectations and stresses, and multicultural issues have developed that were not a factor in family management in previous generations.
- The feminist movement has drastically altered family functioning.
- Changing sexual practices—particularly oral contraceptives—have influenced families by providing for smaller family size and greater sexual freedom and impacting levels of commitment to family expectations.
- New and emerging diseases, such as herpes, AIDS, and other sexually transmitted diseases, have led to family stress.
- Drugs, including alcohol and illicit drugs, have led to increased family tension and conflict.

A decade and a half later, most of the changes and stressors identified in 1982 are still with us and have become even more pronounced. There is a continued evolving of the family, from the nuclear "traditional family" often written about in the past to families with much greater diversity of makeup and structure. In fact, increased diversity throughout American society has resulted in many of the models and approaches to understanding families requiring considerable review and revision. The country has experienced enormous growth in wealth and opportunity, and with the changing American scene, the basic form of living—the family—has continued to evolve and change. Change always results in stress and some measure of difficulty.

The cumulative effect of the stressors just identified has impacted individuals, families, and communities, resulting in concern from many elements of society. Unlike our scientific and economic progress, families have not learned to adapt rapidly enough to cope effectively with the changes. It may be that the lack of progress in helping families is due more to the inability to disseminate new knowledge about improved family living than to a lack of knowledge of what services are helpful. In the scientific fields, dissemination of knowledge used to require years, whether it was the development and ultimate use of a hybrid corn or the implementation of electronic developments; today the time from invention to utilization has decreased to months. Such is not the case in the social sciences. The period for development to testing to large-scale implementation is still thought of in terms of years, or even generations, within the social sciences.

Family therapy has attempted to provide the support and direction that families have needed as a result of the stressors and additional pressures that have accrued with rapid changes. But just as there is not a clear picture of what the family is today, so there is not a single definition of family therapy. The hallmark of family therapy, though, is the belief that problems experienced by individuals indicate trouble within that individual and within the social system of that individual—usually the family.

The combining of societal stresses, marriage of people with diverse learning experiences in early family life situations, and developmental phases through which families go—courtship, marriage, children, moving, job changes, retirement—can lead to dysfunction within the family unit. However, families very seldom seek out family counseling or therapy. Generally, an identified patient is selected, often a child, and serves as the ticket of admission into therapy for the whole family. This may be the case for the mother who wants marriage counseling and fears asking for it, the alcoholic husband who wants help but doesn't know how to seek it, or the teenager who needs assistance developing into an autonomous individual. They enter family therapy through an individual who is identified as the patient; but in most such situations the family, not the individual, is treated as dysfunctional.

The chapters presented in this book represent a broad array of methods and approaches for treating troubled families, but all have as their emphasis a focus on the family, a definition of family interactions as the locus of problems for the individuals involved. Since publication of the first and second editions of this book, several new chapters have been added. There has been an attempt to address the common core elements of family therapy, to address ethical and professional issues within the field, and to represent the increased recognition that particular models have received. Several chapters from the first two editions have been omitted because either the models they described have received less emphasis within the field or, more likely, their major tenets have been incorporated into other models that continue to evolve and develop. Some chapters have undergone only minor revisions because the contributors have determined that, whereas the approach remains popular and relevant, little new knowledge in the form of development of new techniques or refinement of research or theory has occurred. Other chapters have been drastically revised to represent the activity level of the theorists and clinicians of that particular orientation.

Family Counseling and Therapy provides an introductory overview of the current status of family therapy. The chapters are more relevant to and cognizant of the greater diversity of American culture. The text does not, however, attempt to provide material of a specific nature (e.g., family therapy addressing specific problem areas such as substance abuse). The material presented, though, is an excellent introduction to the world of family therapy and counseling.

Acknowledgments

This book is the third edition of *Family Counseling and Therapy*. The first was coedited with Indiana State University Professor Emeritus Merle Ohlsen, who provided leadership and enthusiasm for the project. Without his creative and energetic leadership, the book would never have been. Merle has been a dear friend and mentor, and I thank him for leading the way professionally and personally. The second edition of the book was coedited with Indiana State University Professor J. Laurence Passmore, who provided creativity and vision and was a strong source of support in the project. Laurie has been a valued friend and colleague throughout my professional career, and I thank him for his support.

The contributors to this book were cooperative and helpful at all stages; they gave their time, energy, and resources to help bring their work to the readers. Their willingness to participate—to make the sacrifices necessary to meet deadlines, provide revisions, and do the detail work needed to complete each contribution—is greatly appreciated. They are a fine group of professionals who have given unselfishly.

Ted Peacock of F. E. Peacock Publishers, Inc., provided encouragement for the first edition and has remained a person of constant support. Richard Welna of F. E. Peacock has been of wonderful assistance and a source of encouragement for the completion of this edition of *Family Counseling and Therapy*. Ted and Dick, with their encouraging enthusiasm and continued prodding, led to this revision of the book. John Beasley and Kim Vander Steen have provided excellent editorial assistance. The contributions of all the Peacock staff have been extremely helpful and are highly appreciated.

The colleagues and students at Indiana State University were very supportive during the development of the first two editions of this book; the same has been true of the faculty and students of the University of Georgia for this current edition. Throughout the months of work they continued to give support and encouragement, and I thank them.

Finally, Gayle Horne has tolerated the long hours spent at the desk rather than in other activities, and yet maintained an ability to be accepting and loving. Thank you.

Contributors

JAMES ROBERT BITTER is Professor of Counseling at East Tennessee State University in Johnson City. A nationally certified counselor and marriage and family counselor, he worked and studied with Virginia Satir during the last 10 years of her life. Together, they published chapters and articles on the human validation process model, family reconstruction, and parts parties for couples. Dr. Bitter has been instrumental in integrating Satir's model with Adlerian counseling. He is a member of the AVANTA Network and was a member of its governing council for six years.

JANICE T. CALLAWAY, PharmD, MSW, is a doctoral candidate at the University of Georgia School of Social Work. Dr. Callaway completed her research and practice internship at the McPhaul Marriage and Family Clinic at the University of Georgia and is currently an instructor with the School of Social Work. Her research interests include medical family therapy, family violence, and spirituality.

JORGE COLAPINTO trained as a psychologist in Argentina and as a family therapist at the Philadelphia Child Guidance Clinic, where he was Associate Director of Training when he wrote the chapter on structural family therapy for this book. Since then he has continued practicing and teaching structural family therapy and extending its application to the work with larger systems, particularly at the interface between low-income families and social service agencies. He is the author of numerous articles and book chapters, and coauthor (with Patricia and Salvador Minuchin) of *Working with Families of the Poor* (Guilford, 1998). Currently, Mr. Colapinto is on the faculty of the Ackerman Institute for the Family, where he directs the Foster Care Project.

JOHN C. DAGLEY is an Associate Professor in the Department of Counseling and Human Development Services at the University of Georgia. He is a licensed psychologist, a licensed professional counselor, and a nationally certified career counselor. He has maintained a counseling practice for over three decades, working with adults, children, families, couples, schools, and corporations.

ALBERT ELLIS is the President of the Albert Ellis Institute in New York. He has practiced family counseling and therapy for 55 years and is the founder of rational-emotive behavior therapy, the pioneering cognitive behavior therapy dating from 1955. He has published over 400 articles and 65 books and monographs on psychotherapy and marriage and family counseling.

JERRY E. GALE is an Associate Professor in the Department of Child and Family Development at the University of Georgia. He is Director of the doctoral Marriage and Family Therapy Program. He is a clinical member and approved supervisor of the American Association of Marriage and Family Therapy and a member of American Family Therapy Association. Dr. Gale's clinical and research interests focus on narrative therapy and collaborative language systems, therapist-client discourse, mediation, and social constructionism.

ALICIA M. HOMRICH is an Assistant Professor in the Counseling program at Rollins College in Winter Park, Florida. She is a licensed psychologist with a specialization in family therapy. Her clinical practice is based on brief therapy and solution-oriented methods.

ARTHUR M. HORNE is a Professor of Counseling Psychology and a member of the faculty of the Certificate Program in Marriage and Family Therapy at the University of Georgia. He is a licensed psychologist, a clinical member of the American Association of Marriage and Family Therapy, and a fellow of the Divisions of Counseling Psychology, Group Psychology and Psychotherapy, and the Division of Family Psychology of the American Psychological Association. His practice and research have focused upon treatment of behavior-disordered children in the family and school context.

JAMES KEIM is a popular workshop presenter, author, and clinician. The former Director of Training for Jay Haley and Cloe Madanes at the Family Therapy Institute of Washington, D.C., he is currently an Adjunct Professor with the Department of Social Work of Colorado State University. He is completing his second book, a guide to therapy with oppositional children in the home, school, and research contexts.

DAVID V. KEITH, M.D., is Professor of Psychiatry, Family Medicine, and Pediatrics and Director of Family Therapy at S.U.N.Y. Health Science Center, Syracuse.

ALLIE C. KILPATRICK is Professor Emeritus in the School of Social Work at the University of Georgia. She is an approved Supervisor and Site Visitor for the American Association of Marriage and Family Therapy and has served as the Coordinator of the Pre-Professional Graduate Certificate Program in Marriage and Family Therapy at the University of Georgia. Dr. Kilpatrick is a Diplomate in Clinical Social Work and a member of the Academy of Certified Social Workers and is licensed in Georgia as a clinical social worker and as a marriage and family therapist. She has published extensively in the areas of family, social work practice, and instruction in refereed journals of national and international standing, and is the author of five books and numerous book chapters.

EBB G. KILPATRICK, JR., is a clinical member and approved supervisor of the American Association of Marriage and Family Therapy and is licensed in Georgia as a marriage and family therapist, retired. Having served as a chaplain in the Georgia National Guard and Army Reserve for 27 years, Chaplain Kilpatrick holds the rank of Lieutenant Colonel, retired. He was a clinical chaplain in the Mental Health System of Georgia for 21 years and is a retired member of the American Association of Pastoral Counselors. He has taught family courses in the School of Social Work at the University of Georgia, has supervised marriage and family therapy students at Mercer University School of Medicine, and has seen families in private practice for the past 24 years. Chaplain Kilpatrick has published articles in professional journals, presented papers on the family, and is a popular speaker on family issues.

STEVEN M. KOGAN is a doctoral candidate in the Department of Child and Family Development, Marriage and Family Therapy Program at the University of Georgia. He is a licensed marriage and family therapist and a clinical member of the American Association of Marriage and Family Therapy. His research and practice have focused on communication processes in marital therapy, language and therapy, and critical theory.

WILLIAM C. NICHOLS, EdD, ABPP, is currently with the Nichols Group, Inc.—consultants to business and organizations on family and human development issues. He has taught and supervised marital and family therapists at the doctoral, postdoctoral, master, and postmaster levels at Florida State University, the Merrill-Palmer Institute, and elsewhere, and was in full-time private practice for 22 years. A Diplomate in Clinical Psychology with the American Board of Professional Psychology, he also is a Fellow of the American Psychological Association, the American Psychological Society, and the American Association of Marriage and Family Therapy and is an approved supervisor of the AAMFT. He is currently president of the International Family Therapy Association and was president of both the National Council on Family Relations and the AAMFT. Editor of *Contemporary Family Therapy* since 1986, he also edited *Family Relations* and was the founder and first editor of the *Journal of Marital and Family Therapy*. His latest book is *Treating People in Families: An Integrative Framework* (Guilford, 1998). He is Adjunct Professor of child development and family relations at the University of Georgia.

KATHRYN L. NORSWORTHY is an Associate Professor in the Graduate Studies Program in Counseling, Rollins College, Winter Park, Florida, and a licensed psychologist. Her practice and research interests include feminist applications in family therapy, global perspectives in feminist psychology, and multicultural/diversity as foundational principles in counseling and psychotherapy.

DANIEL V. PAPERO is Clinic Director and Faculty Member of the Georgetown Family Center, Washington, D.C. He is a Board Certified Diplomate in Clinical Social Work and associate editor of *Family Systems*.

VIRGINIA M. SATIR died on September 10, 1989. She was one of the pioneers of family therapy, sometimes called the "Christopher Columbus of family therapy." For many years she was the lone woman to have developed a family therapy model. Having originally earned a Master of Social Work from the University of Chicago, she would eventually receive numerous doctorates for her work with families and for humanity. She was the founder of AVANTA, a training network of therapists and community leaders who were devoted to her human validation process model. She wrote more than a dozen books, with *Peoplemaking* and *Conjoint Family Therapy* the most widely read. Together her publications have appeared in more than 25 different languages.

THOMAS V. SAYGER is an Associate Professor and Director of Training in Counseling Psychology at the University of Memphis. He is a licensed psychologist and a member of the Division of Family Psychology of the American Psychological Association and the International Association of Marriage and Family Counselors. Dr. Sayger's research and clinical practice focuses upon prevention, early intervention, and family–school collaborative programs for behavior-disordered children and their families.

JOSEPH J. SCALISE is a licensed marriage and family therapist, an American Association of Marriage and Family Therapy Approved Supervisor, a licensed professional counselor, and a national certified counselor in private practice in Athens, Georgia, and has over 30 years of experience in counseling individuals, groups, couples, and families. He is currently an Adjunct Associate Professor and member of the graduate faculty in the Department of Counseling and Human Development Services and is a member of the faculty of the Pre-Professional Graduate Certificate Program in Marriage and Family Therapy at the University of Georgia. Dr. Scalise has recently completed six years as a member of the Georgia Composite Board of Professional Counselors, Social Workers and Marriage and Family Therapists (Marriage and Family Therapy Standards Committee). During his two terms, Dr. Scalise was elected to serve as Chair and Vice-Chair of the Board.

LOUIS THAYER is a Professor in the Department of Leadership and Counseling at Eastern Michigan University, Ypsilanti. Dr. Thayer is a member of Division 17 (Counseling Psychology) of the American Psychological Association, the American Counseling Association, the Association for the Development of the Person-Centered Approach, and Phi Delta Kappa. He has also served as president of the Association for Humanistic Education and Development. Dr. Thayer's teaching, learning, and research interests focus on person-centered theory and practice for counseling/therapy, education, and leadership. He seeks to develop unique ways of integrating experience-based and humanistic approaches into counseling/learning environments, and his research interests include the use of life teaching stories in university teaching/learning, couple and family counseling, T'ai Chi Ch'uan and Taoist philosophy, the use of storytelling, and imagery awareness in counseling/learning processes. Dr. Thayer received his doctorate from the University of Illinois and later completed a year of postdoctoral studies as a Visiting Fellow at the Center for Studies of the Person in La Jolla, CA. He has published two books on experiential learning.

ROBERT E. WUBBOLDING is a Professor of Counseling at Xavier University in Cincinnati, director of the Center for Reality Therapy, and a senior faculty member and Director of Training for The William Glasser Institute. He is a psychologist, a licensed professional clinical counselor, and a member of the American Psychological Association, the American Counseling Association, the Academy of Family Psychology, the American Association of Marriage and Family Therapists, and the International Association of Marriage and Family Counselors. Dr. Wubbolding is an internationally known teacher, author, and practitioner of Reality Therapy—emphasizing multicultural aspects of the approach—in North America, Europe, and Asia.

CHAPTER 1

Introduction

ARTHUR M. HORNE

Recently a third-grade boy was referred to our center. The referring complaint was of high-rate aggressive behavior, including teasing, name-calling, shoving and pushing, and several recent taunting incidents—the characteristics of bullying behavior. When the referral was received, we requested that the parents come with the boy for the initial interview. Though they were reticent for both to come in, and they indicated they just wanted help for their son, when it was explained that we needed information from each parent, they agreed to come to the intake session.

During the intake, Jess, the identified patient, appeared angry and bordered on being belligerent. He was not very cooperative with the intake process and moved about a great deal. The father, Ray, seemed irritated as well, and was quite short with his responses. The mother, Renee, appeared to be quite nervous and apprehensive about the process and she began to cry during the interview. After preliminary discussions with Jess, he was excused to go to a playroom where he spent time with toys under the supervision of another intake worker.

While Jess was out of the room the intake interviewer began asking about family interactions and about the parents' relationship. Ray became quite annoyed with the discussion and began telling Renee that this questioning was why he had not wanted to come, that people always jumped on the parents when a child refused to behave, and that he wasn't responsible for the problems, that it was a mother's responsibility to manage children. Renee appeared to be hurt by the comments, but whipped back with comments about Ray's not being available to

This chapter is based upon Chapter 1, "Introduction," by J. L. Passmore and A. M. Horne, in *Family Counseling and Therapy*, 2nd edition. The significant contributions of Laurie Passmore are valued and appreciated.

help raise Jess, and that the problem wasn't a boy who was acting out, but rather a father who was never around. Within minutes, the couple had moved into acrimonious accusations about fault and responsibility, blame and attempts at shame.

The intake interviewer indicated he would like some time alone with each of the parents, and asked Renee to go to the waiting room for a few minutes while he interviewed Ray. When alone, Ray admitted that he was not as available as he should be, that he had made major commitments to work rather than the family. At first he tried to explain his decision as an issue of responsibility and that he was a bit of a martyr for his extensive work hours, so expended that his family could be financially secure. It became clear, though, that Ray also found the work environment more attractive than the home situation. When asked more about that, Ray explained that the relationship had been stressful from the beginning and had grown worse after Jess was born. Ray said that much of the problem revolved around sexual incompatibility, and that Renee was not at all interested in sex, whereas it was on his mind all the time. He found it easier to be at work, where he attended to other things, than to be at home, where he thought of sex a lot but knew any attempts would be to no avail.

Ray went to the waiting room and Renee came in. When asked about the issue Ray had raised, the sexual incompatibility, she began crying. She said that, yes, Ray was right, that there was a clear difference in their interests about sex and that it had been there from the beginning. She told the intake interviewer that she had always had a sense of disgust related to sex and that she participated only when she thought she absolutely had to in order to keep Ray. The interviewer asked if there had been some earlier sexual experience that had led to Renee's having the attitude she did toward sex. Renee said that as a young adolescent, 13 years old, she had been gang-raped by her cousin and several of his friends. He had again raped her several more times over the next year. When Renee had tried talking to her mother about it, the mother said she didn't want to hear talk about "that kind of thing" because that's just what men did to women and Renee had better learn to live with it. Further, Renee was told to not talk with others about it because it was "family business" and no one else's affair. Renee's mother did talk with the cousin, and the physical contact stopped; but for years there was still taunting, teasing, and threats of further sexual attacks by the cousin whenever they were together. Renee said that Ray did not know about the past events, and he had always been gentle with her, but that she had such repulsion over the powerful images that returned every time he touched her sexually that she would pull away.

The interviewer called the family together and explained that their situation would be reviewed and that the center staff would be getting back with them for an appointment and recommendations for how therapy would proceed. After the family left, the intake interviewer began writing up notes and preparing a presentation of the family to the center staffing, scheduled for the next day.

In preparing the presentation for the center staffing, the therapist began detailing what led to the family's seeking help. What was happening? Who agreed to the problem? Why now? Who initiated the call? Who came for the interview? Who participated, and in what way? The therapist also reviewed the presentation of the problem that led to the intake, the additional information given by the father, and the further explanation by the mother. Who has the problem, and where does it reside? With Jess? Ray? Renee? With the parent-child interactions? Or the couple's communication and dynamics? Is it a whole family issue, or does it reside as individual pathology?

In examining the situation, one's orientation becomes apparent. When therapists have been trained in an individual approach, they tend to perceive individual problems. When they have been trained in a particular theoretical model, they begin to recognize how the model will be overlaid on this particular situation. Behavior therapists may be thinking of how the bullying behavior was learned and is maintained through a reinforcement paradigm. Narrative therapists may be attempting to understand the story from the narrator's perspective. A family systems therapist will begin looking for the family rules and exploring how there may be a lack of homeostatic balance in the present moment. Therapists who operate out of a medical setting are likely to begin looking for organic processes to help explain the current happenings.

Defining the problem is a process that is based upon one's theoretical orientation, background and training in therapy, and experience in and breadth of awareness of family dynamics. There is no "right answer" to how to define the problem, the patient/client, or the intervention. Rather the therapist's orientation and experience determine the answers. Conceptualization of the problem depends upon one's definitions of theory and practice.

This book is about the range of approaches to family therapy, and in the following pages authors present their orientations following a structured format that includes Definition, Historical Development, Tenets of the Model, Application, Case Example, and Evaluation.

DEFINITION

Each contributor to the book was asked to provide a definition of the model being presented—the theory, and the definition of family, and the counseling and therapy model.

THEORY

Scientific theory has a number of formal properties that may lead to its being proved or disproved. For this text, theory is not assumed to be a rigorous model that may be experimentally tested, but rather is a presentation of the conceptual framework of the model. It is a cognitive map that guides the practitioner through the complexities of understanding human behavior, family dynamics, and processes of therapy.

As will become evident, the theoretical foundations of many of the models presented in this book are based upon the individual experiences of the person(s) developing the approach. In that sense, the theory is both personal and projective, and constitutes a set of projected beliefs, observations, and constructs that are variously related or connected. Theory points us in directions and helps us identify what we are to attend to, what data to collect, what information is important.

Most of the theoretical models presented in this book were developed by practitioners, people who were working as therapists and who explored what worked and did not work, what explanations made sense, which ones did not.

They looked for the patterns of presentation of problems, consistency in how clients managed—or mismanaged—their lives, how family structures were formed and the impact those structures had upon the members of the family. They examined the therapist–patient relationship. Out of the observations grew written descriptions that the therapists used to communicate their understanding of family therapy processes to other therapists. The written word cannot capture all of what a person does in therapy, and therefore the theory presented in text form may be far removed from the actual practice of the person who developed the theory. What we have in text form is the "map of the territory" (Johnson, 1946), a representation of what the approach presents to the viewer, but the reader must be aware that, just as a description of a scene is not the same as seeing the scene itself, so the description of the model is not the practice of the model itself. Rather, it is as close a description as the writer can present.

FAMILY

In the first edition of this book there was an acknowledgment that families did not always fit the two-parent, three-child, never-divorced, middle-class model that many family therapy models describe. In the nearly two decades since that first edition, family structure has continued to become less narrowly defined, to take on many forms and structures. For the family of today—the family described in the following chapters—the term *relationship therapy* is more likely to be appropriate than *family therapy*, for the focus is upon the relationship of people, the interactions of those who in one way or another have defined themselves as "family." The nuclear family is included—the family that has two parents, has children, and resides together. The extended family is also included in our family orientation—the family members who may not reside together but are connected by marriage, birth, or choice. The extended family includes cousins, aunts, uncles, and so forth. Also included is the multi-generational family, and, in fact, the levels of the generations are a focus of several family therapy models. Understanding the current family in the context of several generations is the object of particular approaches.

But the families of today—with a high divorce rate, with many eschewing the bonds of matrimony, and with some electing very intense but less formal arrangements—represent the need to focus upon the relationships and dynamics of the people interinvolved rather than insisting that services be provided to persons engaged in the formal definition of family. Today, we are much more likely to be providing therapy to single-parent families, blended families, and families consisting of adults of the same gender, with the increase in gay and lesbian couples. The theories presented in this text focus upon the generic application of the approach to relationships rather than addressing the variety of ways of structuring the relationships of members who live together. Readers interested in specific applications of models to unique family structures, though, will need to go to the recommended readings and other sources.

Another change that has occurred in the United States is the tremendous increase in diversity of the citizenry. It seemed that many of the models of family therapy treatment developed in the '50s and '60s had an implied orientation to white, middle-class families. Today's families that present for therapy may be of European ancestry, but they may be from many other cultural backgrounds as well. There has been a tremendous growth in interest in working with families of diverse cultural backgrounds, and this edition of the book has included a greater focus on diversity throughout. There can be no preconceived assumptions about the cultural orientation of families coming to our offices, for even if we know some information about their racial or ethnic identity, we must also be cognizant that the "within" differences—the differences people have from one another within their own culture—are as important as the "between" differences—the differences that exist among people of different cultural groups.

Whole books on family therapy are written on the importance of cultural sensitivity and different therapeutic approaches for different cultural groups, and this topic is beyond the scope of this book. The reader is reminded, though, that sensitivity to cultural variation is a very important issue as is the need to learn more about how to apply the approaches to family therapy among different cultures. Many professional organizations now have specific guidelines governing culturally sensitive ethical and professional training and therapy.

COUNSELING AND THERAPY

For Jess, Renee, and Ray and their presenting problem(s): Will they be provided counseling or therapy? Why or why not? The title of this book is *Family Counseling and Therapy*, a title selected with purpose, indicating that the models presented are appropriate for family counseling and therapy, but how is one to decide which? The answer to the question of what is the difference between counseling and therapy has been discussed at length for more than three decades.

Counseling and therapy have often been differentiated by the locations in which they are applied. For example, seldom is therapy done in schools, for therapy implies therapeutic application of knowledge and skills to a condition that is wrong; perhaps there is an illness, and a school application would imply that school personnel treat illness as a school function. Likewise, persons who go to religious settings for assistance with family concerns generally expect to receive counseling service, not therapy, for the church, synagogue, mosque, or similar setting is seen as a place for counsel, for wisdom, for guidance, and not the treatment of sickness. Hospitals and medical settings, on the other hand, more likely offer therapeutic services, the sense of healing that which is wounded or sick. Insurance and other third-party payment sources are not inclined to provide financial support for nontherapeutic endeavors, and they generally pay for therapy, but not for counseling.

Another way counseling and therapy have been distinguished is by level of hierarchy—or status quotient. Within the mental health field there has been a hierarchy of prestige, based upon the level of service provided. Thus, in order of status quotient, we have traditionally had psychoanalysis, psychotherapy, therapy, counseling, psychoeducation, and, finally, guidance or advising. Often titles of service delivery persons reflect this hierarchy, with psychiatrists and some psychologists providing psychoanalysis, usually, doctoral- or master's-level practitioners providing psychotherapy or therapy, or clinicians providing counseling and psychoeducational services, and bachelor's-level practitioners providing guidance and advising. While there are exceptions, there is clear status hierarchy by degree and professional discipline.

Related to the difference in therapy and counseling by discipline and status is the level of treatment services provided. Generally the depth of treatment is considered to differentiate the two, with the deepest to shallowest being: personality restructuring, altered lifestyle, second-order family systems change, symptom removal, first-order family systems change, skills training, and education. Also related to the depth of treatment is the time frame being treated. Therapy is more often considered to be the orientation when one works with the distant past, whereas counseling is considered when the time frame of treatment is the recent past or present.

In this text, the terms *counseling* and *psychotherapy* are used interchangeably. Both denote processes for aiding individuals and families in changing in identified and agreed upon ways. The selection of a term to describe the process will be determined by the needs of the setting, the practitioner, and the family involved.

Readers should attend to what the authors say about the models presented in the definition section. The theories vary considerably in focus on the role of the therapist/counselor and the expectations of family members, ranging from highly engaged to less engaged. Further, there are considerable differences on emphasis on emotions (affect), actions (observable behaviors), and thoughts and beliefs (cognitions). Some place considerable interest in intrapsychic events (within the individuals involved), interpersonal events (between dyads of people involved), and family events (among all involved in the family). Finally, attention to medical conditions, economic conditions, and the sociopolitical milieu—albeit important—is beyond the scope of the present text.

HISTORICAL DEVELOPMENT

How did a particular approach come to be? Just as no description of an elephant describes the whole elephant, so the description of a model of family therapy does not describe all of family therapy. All of the descriptions of an elephant begin to provide a picture of the whole animal, just as all of the descriptions of family therapy begin to describe the field. Yet, each model presented began with a person or persons who had particular experiences, and understanding those experiences helps us to understand how they came to describe their particular part of the contribution to the larger picture. Theoretical models develop within a context, based upon experiences, and reflect the circumstances of the time, the situation, and the person who developed the model. Thus, understanding the historical development of each of the models is important for understanding its evolving role in treating families. Each presenter describes how early life experiences, family life, professional training, particular clientele, or contributions from other models influenced the development of the model in its current state.

EARLY EXPERIENCES AND FAMILY LIFE

The early life experiences of many of the developers of family therapy models were very influential in shaping how that person developed and provided family therapy services as well as the concepts that were used to share with others in describing the therapy. Virginia Satir, Carl Rogers, Carl Whitaker, Albert Ellis, and others describe how their personal life experiences shaped and determined the theories they developed. Satir *was* her theory—there was little differentiation in Satir the person and Satir the therapist; the personal, experiential aspect of her life was the focus of her therapy, and it shows in her writing. As you read each historical development section, observe how the life experiences of the developer of the model shaped the theory that evolved from those experiences.

TYPES OF CLIENTS

Theoretical models do not develop in a vacuum. Notice the specific clientele served as a particular model was being developed: Who was the recipient of the services? In the early work by Minuchin, treatment was provided to highly disorganized inner-city youth. Social learning family therapy was developed as a response to the need to treat acting out and aggressive youth. Glaser, the founder of reality therapy, worked in a school for delinquent girls and needed structure provided with support, which influenced the steps of treatment.

RESEARCH

What is the role of research in each of the models? Some models seem to place a great emphasis on the importance of research and tie the acceptance of the theory to validation by experimental research methods. The behavior therapy approach to family, for example, has always been integrally connected to a research paradigm in which the efficaciousness of the model has been regularly tested. Brief family therapy and strategic family therapy both incorporate theory from cybernetics, communications theory, and biological systems, and research has been an indispensable aspect of model development. Other models have eschewed research as not relevant or applicable, particularly when therapy is addressed more as an experiential art form than as a scientific process that can be dissected and analyzed. Art and experience cannot be studied under a magnifying glass to determine why they are so powerful—they can only be taken at the experiential level. Whereas our current move toward managed care is forcing more attention on evaluating outcomes of therapy, there is still a strong emphasis and recognition that not all things that are therapeutic can be measured.

TENETS OF THE MODEL

Tenets are principles that one considers to be true. In the description of the models presented in this text, they are also central concepts. The authors present their central concepts as they describe their view of the nature of pathology or problem definition, and how those problems may be explained. In a sense, the authors present their "world view"—their perception of why and how problems develop within the family system. What is the nature of the development of problems, and why?

A second component to examine as you read the tenets is the explanation given for why members of a family have the problem they have: For a behavior therapy approach, the explanation may be because of learned behavior. For a person-centered approach, the family members may learn of the distress characterizing relationships that do not honor all the members of the family. For those who perceive family problems in the context of the extended or the cross-generational framework, patterns of family rules are examined. Theorists present their models combining philosophical premises with clinical assumptions. Each presents with a schema—an explanation for how clients happen to be in the circumstances, the conditions, they are in. This schema guides the therapist, and is expected to provide structure and guidance for the family members.

Each model's tenets address the client—the affective, behavioral, cognitive, and interpersonal aspects of all persons involved in the family. Clients present when they are demoralized, distressed, or fail to see any way to alter their circumstances without help. Clients' very acts of asking for help imply an inability to manage their own lives, and so the writers, in describing their tenets, will also be describing their world view of health and resiliency, of unhealthiness and methods of therapy.

Another aspect of understanding the tenets of a model includes how the therapist and client relate—what is the process of therapy between the therapist and the family members? Some of the authors go to considerable detail describing the importance of a therapeutic environment. Some describe an environment that addresses power and authority, while others provide little structure and refuse to be problem-focused, electing instead to attend to interactional sequences and experiential activities. It is at this point that the reader may be making decisions about which models seem to "fit" and which ones seem so foreign that they lack applicability to the readers' experience.

APPLICATION

The application section bridges the gap between the theoretical constructs and tenets and the actual practice of family therapy. This is the section that moves from describing the constructs of the model to describing the "how" of the model. How is therapy done from this orientation?

- What are the roles and responsibilities of the client?
- What types of clients with what types of problems are best treated from this orientation?
- What are the goals of treatment?
- What are the roles and responsibilities of the therapist?
- What specific techniques have been identified as effective?

Strupp (1973) identified three basic components of therapy: the client–therapist relationship; the motivation of the client; and techniques of influence or change used by the therapist. The first two components are essential to all models of therapy, for although there is a difference in emphasis among the models, they all acknowledge the importance of a positive therapeutic relationship and the necessity of family members who are motivated to change and receptive to therapy. The third component, the techniques, varies considerably among the therapeutic models, though Strupp indicated that the first two aspects of therapy are the significant factors for change.

Prochaska (1984) has developed a model for categorizing models of therapy. He indicates that *consciousness raising* is a process activated by feedback in which family members monitor their own behavior and through the process achieve awareness of a need for change. This may include an educational experience and may be an important step in such models of family therapy as behavior therapy, brief therapy, and reality therapy.

Catharsis, a second change process described by Prochaska, has been described by a number of therapeutic approaches as a corrective emotional experience—an experience in which the person comes into contact with his or her affective state and experiences emotional relief through the sharing of the experience. Catharsis may occur as a result of the interaction of the therapist and client, or may be stimulated by other environmental circumstances, such as the client's identifying with the experiences of others—say in a song, a movie, a book, or a play—and having a strong emotional reaction as a result of that identification with the character.

Choosing is the third process Prochaska defines as common in verbal therapies. In this process, the client or family members have become conscious of the problem and the need for change (consciousness raising), have had a corrective emotional happening(s) in which the pain they have experienced has been expressed, and then they have become aware of the opportunity of choosing to make a change in their lives. In choosing, the family members are electing to change the patterns they have lived by, to make a choice not to continue in the maladaptive patterns and practices that resulted in their needing therapy. Choosing requires courage and support.

As you read the chapters and review the theories, attend to how the differing authors address the three conditions described by Strupp, as well as the mechanisms for change described by Prochaska: How are the points addressed in each model?

CASE EXAMPLE

Each author selected what was considered to be a good representative case describing the theoretical model being presented. There are considerable differences in the settings described, the clients who come for therapy, the relationship that is developed, and the methods that are used by the therapist to elicit change. Again, the "map is not the territory" so what is presented is a representation of the model, not the model itself. Videotape or filmed presentations would more powerfully illustrate the cases, but these are not available in most of the cases presented.

As you read the chapters, attempt to identify the theoretical constructs and tenets that have been described: Is there fidelity of the treatment to the theory? Does the map illustrate the territory well?

EVALUATION

The age of managed care has brought evaluation much closer to the forefront of consideration of theoretical models of mental health service delivery. The question is asked: Is family therapy effective? While it currently appears that no one form of therapy is better than others (Hazelrigg, Cooper, & Borduin, 1987), the following generalization may be made: Persons receiving individual, group, and family therapy benefit in several respects when compared to no-treatment control group members or people who are placed on a waiting list for treatment.

For the most part, family therapy evaluations are based much more upon subjective evaluations by clinicians and clients than by standardized objective measures. Further, the theories are by and large developed from clinical experiences, not research, and so the evaluation process relies also upon clinical evaluations rather than research standards. Managed care and third-party payment sources are demanding a greater accountability of outcome evaluations in return for payment for services. This emphasis on measured change for service fees provided is resulting in a gradual shift to more rigorous evaluation models, but as was true with the first two editions of this text, this book includes little evaluation that is quantitative in nature. Should there be more? That depends upon what the reader requires as evidence of effectiveness. As one of the contributors said to me: "I don't have to have numbers to tell me what my eyes can see." Others are more critical and judgmental and look toward validation of the process through objective measures. Haley (1986), for example, has indicated that up to 60% of families may appear to get better from therapy but really improve because their life circumstances change, and therapy was unrelated to the change—a condition called spontaneous recovery.

INTEGRATION OF THEORY: THEORETICAL PLURALISM

We are moving toward less of an emphasis on adherence to an individual theoretical model, and are becoming more accepting of theoretical pluralism, or an integrated model of therapy (Norcross & Goldfried, 1992). There are models that may be very helpful for guiding practitioners in their understanding of dynamics of the family and the role that developmental and dynamic influences play in the lives of family members. Object relations family therapy is an example. There are other models that place a strong emphasis on "what to do" and much less of an emphasis on the intrapsychic issues that are so important to people: Behavior therapy is an example. A hybrid approach that integrates the understanding and theoretical depth of object relations with the well-established interventions and processes of behavior therapy would demonstrate the approach that many are taking today. Just as no one part of a description of an elephant describes the elephant, so no one model of therapy adequately explains all the territory covered by family therapy. Readers need to become familiar with the array of orientations and identify what they believe will work for them, considering their case load in their practices, and given the restraints of accountability, ethical responsibility, and professional standards. It is important that the well-grounded practitioner goes beyond the family therapy literature as well, becoming well read in group theory and therapy, learning theory, social psychological theories, and other related disciplines.

SUMMARY

Before reading further, go back to the presenting problem: Jess, Renee, and Ray. How would you define the problem with which they have presented? Who is the client? What is the nature of the problem—individual, couples, parent–child, family? Is there a diagnosis, and does it fit traditional mental health nomenclature? Where do you begin, and what do you do? How do you know when you are through? How do you know how successful you are? It would be good to record answers to these questions before additional reading, then to review the answers later. Good reading.

REFERENCES

Haley, J. (1986). *The power tactics of Jesus Christ and other essays.* Rockville, MD: The Triangle Press.

Hazelrigg, M. D., Cooper, H. M., & Borduin, C. M. (1987). Evaluating the effectiveness of family therapies: An integrative review and analysis. *Psychological Bulletin, 101,* 428–442.

Johnson, W. (1946). *People in quandaries.* New York: Harper and Row.

Norcross, J. C., & Goldfried, M. R. (1992). *Handbook of psychotherapy integration.* New York: Basic Books.

Prochaska, J. (1984). *Systems of psychotherapy: A transtheoretical analysis.* Pacific Grove, CA: Brooks/Cole.

Strupp, H. (1973). On the basic ingredients of psychotherapy. *Journal of Consulting and Clinical Psychology, 41,* 1–8.

CHAPTER 2

Working from a Family Focus

The Historical Context of Family Development and Family Systems

THOMAS V. SAYGER, ALICIA M. HOMRICH, AND ARTHUR M. HORNE

Family therapy as an organized profession has a relatively short history, dating back only a few decades. Although historical roots for acknowledging the impact of family dynamics and processes on its members can be traced back to the early work of theoreticians, clinicians, and researchers in the fields of psychology, psychiatry, and social work, incorporating these dynamics and processes into the therapeutic process is a more recent phenomenon. This chapter will chronicle the historical and theoretical beginnings of family development and the impact of family systems on human development.

Theory shapes our definitions and expectations of family life. How we answer the question "What is family?" depends in part on how we think about families—their similarities and their differences. What we know about families is also based on theories that guide our research because our theory determines what questions we will study, and the theoretical perspectives one adopts are influenced by historical developments of the time, ideological beliefs, and personal experiences (Ingoldsby & Smith, 1995). Today, some would argue that the American family is being destroyed by a general lack of commitment to family values, while others may argue that the family is simply being redefined—as society understands families—from a culturally sensitive and accepting perspective. However one chooses to label the changes in family structures and systems, clearly change is happening. Multiracial families, single-parent families, parents-in-later-life families, same-gender parent families, dual-career families, teen-parent families, families with nontraditional gender role expectations, and stepfamilies are just a few examples of the changing phenomenon called "family." Whom the family identifies as a family member, how the family defines the roles and expectations of individual members, and how the family places value on individuality versus family conformity all play a role in how society must change its definition of family. Today, families are less likely to be composed of two, ever-married parents, and are more likely to represent a collage of diversity that makes up American society.

Berg-Cross (1988) suggested that a "family" has such characteristics as: a group in the service of the individual; a group being bound by philosophical, religious, or other convictions; a group of common ancestry; a group living under one roof; and a basic biosocial unit having at its nucleus two or more adults living together and cooperating in the care and rearing of their own or adopted children. However, psychological family members may also exist who are not biologically related. Berg-Cross (1988) noted that lifelong friends or honorary relatives may be considered family members, neighbors or coworkers may also hold psychological ties to a family system, and people may choose others to form a family though there may be no apparent ties other than a mixture of fate, interest, and choice.

Olson and DeFrain (1997) noted that single-parent families with children under the age of 18 are increasing dramatically. In 1994, 30% of children lived in single-parent households (U.S. Bureau of the Census, 1994). This rate varies by ethnic group with a rate of 25% for whites, 35% for Latinos, and 63% for African Americans (U.S. Bureau of the Census, 1994). In nearly 30% of U.S. families, both parents work full-time outside the home. In an additional 16% of households, the father works full-time and the mother works part-time outside the home.

Family systems change, as do the expectations of each family member. The developmental life cycle of families is not a static process or one that seems to have clear stages of passage. In fact, both family systems thinking and family life-cycle development theory have been strongly criticized for failing to address issues of gender, sexual orientation, cultural and ethnic diversity, and intra-individual dynamics. These criticisms will be more fully addressed later in this chapter.

HISTORICAL DEVELOPMENT OF FAMILY THERAPY

The practice of family therapy in the United States began to grow in the late 1940s and early 1950s and was, consequently, influenced greatly by the approaches of several early theorists and emerging influences. These include the individual theorists, such as Sigmund Freud and Carl Rogers, the understanding of small-group dynamics, the child guidance movement associated with the work of Alfred Adler and Rudolf Dreikurs, the field of social work, concomitant research on family dynamics and the etiology of schizophrenia within the psychiatric community, and the marriage counseling movement. Each of these influences provided a unique contribution to the understanding of families and their impact on individual family members. However, none of these influences, in and of themselves, provided the in-depth knowledge necessary for a comprehensive understanding of family functioning. It was not until clinicians and researchers began to tie the previous ideas and approaches together and, in a very nonsystematic manner, to address the processes of family systems as they affect individual family member development that our current understanding of families and family therapy began to develop.

CONTEXTUAL INFLUENCES ON FAMILY THERAPY

If one examines the development of family therapy in a historical context, it becomes apparent that family therapy emerged in parallel with other major changes in society. It arose at a time when industrialization, urbanization, and advances in communication technology were expanding, all accompanied by increased mobility and separation of extended family members (Seaburn, Landau-Stanton, & Horwitz, 1995). Most family therapists turn to the 1950s as the period when researchers, followed by practitioners, turned their attention to the family's role in creating and maintaining psychological problems in one or more family members (Goldenberg & Goldenberg, 1996). Goldenberg and Goldenberg (1996) identify five apparently independent scientific and clinical developments that together set the stage for the emergence of family therapy. These are: (1) the extension of psychoanalytic treatment to a full range of emotional problems, eventually including work with whole families; (2) the introduction of general systems theory with its emphasis on exploring relationships between parts that make up an interrelated whole; (3) the investigation of a family's role in the development of schizophrenia in one of its members; (4) the evolution of the fields of child guidance and marital counseling; and (5) the increased interest in clinical techniques such as group therapy (p. 54). We also add to this list a growing acceptance of others in the role of professional counselor and therapist, moving from the peer support of family members, friends, and religious advisors to the insitutionalization of helping. While family researchers were moving toward a systemic and ecological understanding of families, clinicians were moving toward greater specialization and treating families as entities apart from their community and cultural setting.

CONCOMITANT PSYCHOLOGICAL THEORY AND PRACTICE Psychoanalysts and person-centered therapists operated on the assumption that psychological problems developed from dysfunctional interactions with others. Therapeutic practice, however, remained individually focused and was maintained through individual client and therapist relationships. Freudians acknowledged the importance of the social environment in the development of the superego, which contained the ideas of morality and what was considered right or wrong. The battles between the superego and the id often created unconscious conflict, which if left unresolved (or inadequately mediated by the ego), would result in psychological disturbance. Although psychoanalysts acknowledged the importance of the social environment, therapy was a one-on-one interaction between client and therapist that attempted to bring these unconscious conflicts into the client's conscious awareness so they could be resolved. Thus, the family was seen as only a contributor to the development of the disturbance, but it was not thought necessary by analysts to involve other family members physically in the therapeutic relationship since the disturbance was judged to be maintained by the individual psyche of the client.

Carl Rogers also emphasized the importance of the social environment in terms of its impact on the development and resolution of psychological concerns. A basic premise of client-centered therapy is the assertion that the provision of a therapeutic environment, characterized by empathic understanding, positive regard, and genuineness, assists the client in achieving resolution of his or her problems. In essence, Rogers emphasized the importance of a positive social environment in healthy human development and functioning. Like psychoanalysts, however, client-centered therapists utilized a one-on-one therapeutic approach to assist clients. The assumption was that such a positive environment was not in existence in the client's world; thus, the extant family would derail attempts of the client to move toward self-actualization. Once the client had been involved in a positive interaction with a therapist, he or she would then be more prepared to seek out such a relationship in real life experience.

GENERAL SYSTEMS THEORY General systems theory (von Bertalanffy, 1950) emerged during the 1940s from the biological sciences and has developed, as a general concept, focusing on the relationship between elements rather than on the elements themselves. Based on this theory, the mutual interaction among component parts, in the form of relationships, is the foundation of a system. Organization and wholeness are keys to how systems operate, and form the context for viewing individual functioning. A family represents a system, in which the member components are organized into a group, forming a whole that transcends the sum of its separate parts (Goldenberg & Goldenberg, 1996; Satir, 1964). In the world of systems theory, linear causality does not exist. Instead, there is an emphasis placed on reciprocity, recursion, and shared responsibility. Person A and Person B exist in the context of a relationship in which each influences the other and both are equally responsible for the cause and effect of each other's behavior. Over time, Persons A and B establish patterns characteristic of their particular relationship. Becvar and Becvar (1996), in comparing individual psychology to family theories, drew the following conclusions: Family systems theories (1) emphasize *what* instead of *why*; (2) assess reciprocal causality instead of linear cause/effect; (3) are holistic instead of dualistic (subject-object); (4) are dialectical rather than dichotomous; (5) are subjective and perceptual rather than value-free science; (6) emphasize freedom of choice and proactivity rather than determinism and reactivity; (7) explore patterns instead of the laws of external reality; (8) utilize a here-and-now focus rather than a historical focus; (9) are relational versus individualistic; (10) are contextual instead of reductionistic; and (11) are relativistic rather than absolutistic. Becvar and Becvar (1996) additionally noted that the term *family therapy* may be a misnomer, and since family therapy is built on the assumptions of systems theory, a more appropriate label would probably be relationship therapy.

SCHIZOPHRENIA RESEARCH AND FAMILY DYNAMICS Research on family dynamics and the etiology of schizophrenia played a major role in the understanding and treatment of families. Such researchers as Gregory Bateson (Mental Research Institute in Palo Alto, California), Theodore Lidz (Yale University), and Lyman Wynne (National Institute of Mental Health) contributed to our understanding of the family dynamics in families of schizophrenic patients. Early exploration of the impact of families on hospitalized patients set the stage for examining the interpersonal, social, and contextual influences on such disorders as schizophrenia. Researchers and clinicians discovered that improvement in one family member often resulted in dysfunctional behaviors in another. Even though current research findings regarding the etiology of schizophrenia have defocused the role of family dynamics in the development or maintenance of the disorder in favor of biological factors, the contributions this early clinical work made to the evolving theory of systemic processes and the development of the field of family therapy remain.

CHILD GUIDANCE MOVEMENT Rudolf Dreikurs expanded the child guidance movement, based on the theory of child development devised by Alfred Adler, to the United States from Europe in the 1920s. This movement was based on the belief that emotional and psychological disorders began in childhood; thus, the prevention of mental illness in adulthood could occur if psychological problems were treated in childhood. Child guidance centers were established throughout the United States as laboratories examining the interlocking relationships of family members, especially the interactions between parents and their children, as they related to principles of Adlerian psychology (Dreikurs & Soltz, 1964). The goal of the child guidance movement was to teach parents how to understand their children and help them cope with their behaviors with loving and effective discipline.

MARRIAGE COUNSELING The influence of marriage counseling on the family therapy movement was first felt in the 1930s and took place outside the realm of psychiatry, which had been, to this point in time, the primary discipline exploring the impact of family dynamics on individuals. This movement developed as a part-time endeavor for psychologists, physicians, ministers, social workers, and others who became involved in assisting couples with marital dilemmas as a secondary profession. In 1932, there were three functioning marriage counseling centers in the United States, eventually prompting the initiation of the American Association of Marriage Counselors, formed in 1942, which proposed a set of guidelines for members.

GROUP DYNAMICS AND THERAPY Interest in working with the patient's family naturally led clinicians to study and incorporate small-group dynamics into their work with families. James Bell, a psychologist who was an early practitioner of this approach, wrote about his work involving the whole family in patient intervention. His initial work with families as a group began in 1953, after a visit to the Tavistock Clinic in London (described in Broderick & Schrader, 1981). Group dynamics seemed to provide a good base for understanding the process in which individual personalities interacted with the overall entity. Practitioners who valued the concept of systems theory considered the context of the individual when working with clients or patients, and applied group dynamics techniques in managing family interactions.

THE FIELD OF SOCIAL WORK The influence of social work is readily apparent in the field of family therapy. From the beginning of the social work profession in 1877, social workers were concerned in working with the family as both a critical social unit and a focus for intervention. Despite efforts in the early 1920s by the field of psychiatry to redirect the family focus of casework activities, social workers are the only professionals who have consistently conceptualized couples and families as a substantial aspect of individual functioning, and designed their clinical practice accordingly (Broderick & Schrader, 1981).

CHRONOLOGICAL TIMELINE OF FAMILY THERAPY DEVELOPMENT

The pioneers of family therapy, as an organized treatment modality, are many and diverse. John Bell, the Palo Alto Group (Gregory Bateson and Don Jackson), Murray Bowen, Nathan Ackerman, Carl Whitaker, Ivan Boszormenyi-Nagy, Salvador Minuchin, and Virginia Satir were all groundbreakers in the field of family therapy. In the 1940s, the family therapy movement was begun by a varying group of researchers and theorists from differing disciplines who were early explorers in the area of cybernetics. The field of cybernetics was concerned primarily with the organization, pattern, and process of information rather than the matter, material, and content (Becvar & Becvar, 1996). By focusing on feedback mechanisms, information processing, and patterns of communication, cybernetic scientists began to study and compare inanimate machines with living organisms to understand and control complex systems.

During the 1950s, an emphasis on the observation of the family from a research-oriented perspective, rather than a clinical approach, led to the development of theories of family dynamics and their impact on the symptomatic family member. During the 1960s, emphasis was placed on clinical applications of family therapy. In 1960, the first family therapy institute, now known as the Ackerman Institute of Family Therapy in New York, was opened. By emphasizing human interaction as the basis for therapeutic intervention, clinicians began to look for family patterns of interaction that exacerbated dysfunctional systems. Two years later, Nathan Ackerman and Don Jackson founded the first journal in the field of family therapy. *Family Process* was first edited by Jay Haley, a proponent of human communication theory, and thus a framework for the sharing of ideas between family therapists and researchers was established. In 1967, James Framo convened the first family therapy conference (Hayes, 1991).

The techniques of family therapy have often preceded sound theoretical bases. The 1970s found a proliferation of family therapy techniques, including multiple family therapy, milieu therapy, network therapy, and family crisis therapy. Family therapists noted that their primary goals were to improve family communication, improve autonomy and individuation, improve empathy, develop more flexible leadership, improve role agreement, reduce conflict, improve individual family members' symptoms, and improve individual task performance (Group for the Advancement of Psychiatry [GAP], 1970).

In the 1980s, family therapy came into its own as a profession. The number of professional journals increased dramatically, the number of family therapy institutes grew to over 300, several professional organizations became established representatives of the family therapy profession (i.e., American Association for

Marriage and Family Therapy [AAMFT]; American Family Therapy Association [AFTA], which is now the American Family Therapy Academy; the Division of Family Psychology of the American Psychological Association; and the International Association of Marriage and Family Counselors of the American Counseling Association). A seminal issue of *Family Process* in 1982 shook the foundation of family therapy. In this issue, several authors took to task the field of family therapy and questioned the profession's theoretical foundations, research models, and clinical practice (Allman, 1982; Dell, 1982; Keeney & Sprenkle, 1982).

As the field of family therapy has developed over the past several decades, the initial movement toward distinct schools of thought has given way to integration of these major modes of thinking into a general systemic perspective on family functioning. While early pioneers spoke of their particular approaches as a certain type of truth, the trend toward constructivist thinking has led toward greater acceptance of the family's unique reality (truth) and a flexible inclusion of contrasting points of view (Hanna & Brown, 1995). The 1990s have found clinicians integrating ideas and techniques from a variety of theories in an eclectic manner. Though therapists may ascribe to a particular model or theory of family therapy, they may borrow techniques from other approaches as the clinical problem demands. The constructivist epistemology has led to the examination of assumptions of previous generations of family therapists. For example, current theorists question whether family therapists are objective observers of family interactions or whether they are participants in the construction of the family's reality. Maturana (1978) suggested that each family member has his or her own version of reality determined by various psychological and biological factors. If this is true, then there are as many realities regarding the family as there are members of the family, with each bringing his or her own unique perspective that must be addressed during the therapeutic process. This constructivist epistemology has led many family therapists to focus on language and meaning in clinical work with families, in the tradition of cybernetics.

CONCEPTUAL INFLUENCES ON FAMILY THERAPY

Family therapy is a psychotherapeutic approach that focuses on altering interactions between a couple, within a nuclear family or extended family, or between a family and other interpersonal systems. The goal is to alleviate problems initially presented by individual family members, family subsystems, the family as a whole, or other referral sources (Wynne, 1988). How families are conceptualized by therapists influences their practice—their approach to therapy. Conceptual influences on the field of family therapy include structural functionalism, symbolic interactionism, social exchange theory, human ecology theory, family systems theory, cybernetics, power and control, Satir's humanizing effect, Bowen and differentiation of self, family life cycle, feminist theory, the Milan revolution, and constructivism. Many of these influences are discussed in greater detail below.

STRUCTURAL FUNCTIONALISM Like all other social systems, if the family were to survive, it had to develop the mechanisms to meet certain functions. The structural functionalists view society as an organism that strives to resist change and maintain itself in some sort of balance or equilibrium. The social patterns that maintain the larger social system are functional requisites. In every society, some arrangement of biologically related persons, which is the family, has had the primary function of recruiting new members through reproduction and socialization.

SYMBOLIC INTERACTIONISM This theory defines families as a unit of interacting personalities. Symbolic interactionism proposes that humans create symbolic worlds through their interactions, and that these in turn shape human behavior. Humans act toward things based on the meaning these things have for them. Meanings are based on cultural symbols and social values, which are expressed through verbal and nonverbal interactions. Individuals consciously use verbal and nonverbal behavior to perform a role and form an identity. Simultaneously, they interpret and assign meaning to others' responses. Through these social interactions, individuals gauge the appropriateness of their behavior in particular settings and align themselves with cultural expectations expressed by the other person. This process of aligning actions helps to explain how cultural values are understood and responded to at the individual level.

The symbolic interaction framework focuses on symbols based on shared meaning, and interactions, which are based on verbal and nonverbal communication. A role is the expected behavior of a person or group in a given social category (e.g., husband, wife, child). Roles are learned in society by role-taking, the process by which people learn how to play roles correctly by practicing and getting responses from others. Role-making involves creating new roles or revising existing roles. One assumption is that meaning arises in the process of interaction between people, and shared meaning helps people understand each other and learn how to play various roles. Another important concept is definition of the situation. Each person subjectively interprets a given situation, and different people will interpret an interaction or situation in different ways. Another assumption is that people learn about themselves and develop a self-concept based on their interaction with others. The "looking-glass self" concept suggests that people learn about themselves based on the responses received from others who are reacting to their behavior.

SOCIAL EXCHANGE MODEL Social relationships are considered markets in which individuals act out of self-interest, with the goal of maximizing profits. Rewards include personal attraction, social acceptance, social approval, instrumental services, prestige, and power. Resources are any commodity such as love, status, services, goods, information, and money. Costs include punishments experienced because of a certain exchange, or rewards that have been forgone due to engaging in one behavior or course of action rather than another. Relationships are generally viewed as satisfying when partners make about equal contributions and receive about equal positive outcomes. Under these conditions, a relationship meets expectations of fairness. When individuals do not believe the relationship outcomes are fair, they can reduce their investments in the relationship or try to increase their profits by attempting to change the other person's behavior. Another major consideration is whether exchanges are considered mutually responsive or reciprocal. Reciprocity refers to conditions in which individuals negotiate exchanges that not only benefit themselves but also are mutually rewarding and take each other's needs into account. Exchange theory gives us basic concepts with which to analyze the cognitive factors involved in the development, maintenance, and change of intimate relationships. In close relationships, the relative levels of partners' resources, dependence, and attraction impact the interaction, including intimacy, satisfaction, and stability.

HUMAN ECOLOGY THEORY Human ecology theory focuses on human–environment linkages. The theory is built on the concept of ecology, designed as the study of interrelationships between organisms and the environment, both organic and inorganic. The family is conceived as a life-support system dependent on the natural environment for physical sustenance and on the social environment for human contact and meaning. A premise of human ecology theory that differs from other systems theories of families is that all human populations are interdependent with the Earth's resources, so human quality of life cannot be considered apart from the health of the world's ecosystem. The human ecosystem is composed of the natural physical-biological environment (e.g., climate, animals, social, water, plants); the social-cultural environment, including social networks of humans (e.g., neighbors and community); cultural constructions (e.g., laws, values, norms) and social and economic institutions; and the human-built environment (e.g., roads, farms, cities). A family ecosystem comprises these environments with which a family interacts. Human ecology theory assumes that families, despite their structure, ethnic or national origin, social class, or life stage, take in energy and information and make necessary adaptations to the environment. They do this not only through communication and decision making but also through managing the physical and material resources and technologies available to them as they carry out their daily activities. Human development takes place in the family context and is influenced by the reciprocal interactions with the other three types of environments. This theory has the capacity to be a useful framework for multicultural family studies because it:

1. Accepts diverse family structures and inclusive definitions of family.

2. Assumes that cultural diversity may affect family interaction and human development.

3. Presents individual and family problems in relationship to the larger society (education, employment, and housing are related to structural factors such as discrimination and poverty).

4. Emphasizes environmental resources. (Bubolz & Sontag, 1993)

COMMUNICATION THEORIES The conceptualization of what a person does, what motives drive his or her behavior, and how behavior change occurs is directly related to the broader context in which that person functions. From this perspective, dysfunctional behavior is seen as the product of a struggle between persons, not simply the result of intra-individual forces (Haley, 1963). If dysfunctional behavior is, therefore, seen as the result of a flawed relationship, then the relationship becomes the focus of intervention rather than the individual (Goldenberg & Goldenberg, 1996). From a cybernetic perspective, the therapist conducting family therapy must acknowledge that several individuals are present, each with an individual view of reality and sense of family (Slovik & Griffith, 1992).

FAMILY SYSTEMS Family theories are based on systems concepts—family systems, human ecology, and family development. The basic systems concept is that the family is an organic system striving to maintain balance as it confronts external pressures.

1. Family members are considered interdependent parts of a larger whole; each family member's behavior affects all other family members.

2. To adapt, human systems take in information, make decisions about alternatives, try out a response, get feedback about its success, and modify behavior as needed.

3. Families maintain permeable boundaries, such as separate residences, family rituals, and inside jokes, that establish them as distinct from other social groups.

4. Like other social organizations, families must accomplish certain tasks to survive, such as physical sustenance, economic maintenance, reproduction (through birth or adoption) of family members, socialization for family and work roles, and emotional nurturance. Family systems theory emphasizes the family rather than individuals within the system. The theory emphasizes family transactional patterns—recurring sequences of behavior among family members that can be observed over long periods of time.

FAMILY CHARACTERISTICS Berg-Cross (1988) suggested that family systems have a sense of mutual commitment, a sense of history and continuity, and the potential for an expectation of long-lasting relationships that are extensive and intense, and maintain social responsibility of the adults for the welfare and development of any children in the family. According to family systems theory, everything that happens to any family member has an impact on everyone else in the family because family members are interconnected and operate as a group. The following dynamics are inherent in the operation of a family as a unit.

1. Wholeness—the concept that the whole is more than the sum of its parts.

2. Interdependence of parts—the parts or elements of a system are interconnected in such a way that if one part changes, other parts are automatically affected.

3. Balance of openness to change and resistance to change—systems exhibit both stability and the capacity to change, depending on the circumstances.

4. Balance of separateness and connectedness—couples and family members need to find a balance between their separateness as individuals and connectedness as a system.

5. Feedback within the system—communication in the system is essential; no matter how hard one might try, one simply cannot not communicate.

6. Multiple levels—systems are embedded within other systems that influence the functioning of each other. (Berg-Cross, 1988)

These qualities are the foundations of family dynamics. They define what a family is, while at the same time describing what a family does in the process of functioning. Within the systemic perspective, dynamics such as feedback or balancing factors operate in ways that are unique to each individual family. These dynamics are often the context of either effective or conflictual functioning.

As systems, family dynamics, reflected in interactional patterns as well as values, influence effective functioning. The family strengths framework focuses on how families succeed rather than on how they fail (Stinnett, 1979). Qualities of strong families include:

1. Commitment—enduring value for promoting each other's happiness and welfare, dependability, and faithfulness to the family as a group.

2. Positive communication—willingness to openly and honestly share feelings and concerns, give compliments, avoid blame, and agree to compromise or mutual disagreement.

3. Spiritual orientation—belief in a higher power that fosters a sense of hope, faith, compassion, shared ethical values, and oneness with humankind.

4. Appreciation and affection—mutual caring for each other, friendship, respect for individuality, encouragement, playfulness, and shared humor.

5. Shared times together—willingness to create opportunities for quality time in great quantity in order to enjoy each other's company, share positive time together, talking, and joint problem solving.

6. Ability to cope with stress—joining together in times of adversity in ways that are adaptable, encountering crises as challenges and opportunities, growing through crises together, openness to change, and flexibility and resilience.

The family strengths perspective, accompanied by growing emphasis on the resiliency factors of individuals, is an emerging influence on the field of family therapy. The characteristics of strong families can create a framework from which practitioners may conceptualize family functioning and therapy treatment.

FAMILY DEVELOPMENTAL PROCESSES AND TASKS According to family development theory, families go through a predictable sequence of family life-cycle stages precipitated by family member's biological, social, and psychological needs (Rodgers & White, 1993). At each stage, family developmental tasks must be accomplished if families are to move on successfully to the next stage and to maintain internal balance.

Carlson, Sperry, and Lewis (1997) noted that the practice of couple and family therapy has traditionally been built on the unexamined assumption that a model of appropriate family life exists. Unfortunately, the notion of a "normal" family not only is impractical but also may be harmful. Family life today is characterized by a myriad of structures, including nuclear families, singles, nonmarital heterosexual and homosexual cohabiting partners, single-parent families, remarried and blended families, foster and adoptive families, childless families, and multi-adult households. The expanding diversity of family forms implies that individuals will experience more family transitions over their life cycles than was true of previous generations. Many of these transitions will be unique to the individual family form. Pessimists believe that changes in the American family are destructive and prevent the family from carrying out its functions of child-rearing and the provision of stability in adult life. Optimists, in contrast, view the family as an institution that is not declining but, rather, expanding in breadth and depth and showing its flexibility and resilience.

From the viewpoint of many family therapists, symptoms of dysfunction develop within the life-cycle process and represent a family's inability to successfully negotiate or adapt to these changes. Most theorists who adhere to a family development model note that families develop through stages and each stage presents transitions that must be addressed for the family to proceed in a functional manner.

Transition points, the periods when families are moving from one stage to the next, often become times of stress or crisis in families as they negotiate new horizons in functioning. Family development stages typically are noted as the formation of the couple, childbearing family, families with preschool children, families with school-aged children, families with adolescents, families launching children, middle-aged parent families, and families with aging members. The developmental model of understanding family processes and tasks has come under much scrutiny in recent years, as many contemporary family forms may not follow this "traditional" model of development. There are many examples of family structures that may proceed through a nontraditional developmental process or family life cycle. For example, some couples may opt to not have children or have children later in life, resulting in the convergence of traditionally separate stages such as having school-aged children during the later middle-aged years of career development. Divorce and other social phenomena (e.g., teen pregnancy, criminal activity, emphasis on career success versus family involvement) have led to an increase in single-parent families. As a result, extended family members (grandparents, aunts/uncles, cousins, and friends) are often considered nuclear family members. Remarriage or blended families have a unique pattern of development that creates issues that have a major influence on family functioning. Another example is the growing phenomenon of intercultural marriages, which have introduced the issue of understanding cultural diversity as a factor in the developmental processes of a family and expanded the scope of family developmental processes and tasks.

Goldenberg and Goldenberg (1996) noted that a comprehensive understanding of a family's development and current functioning must consider its cultural group's kinship networks, socialization experiences, communication styles, typical male/female interactive patterns, the role of the extended family, and similar culturally linked attitudinal and behavioral arrangements. Family therapists must try to distinguish between universal, transcultural, culture-specific, and idiosyncratic family patterns in any assessment of family functioning. For example, Native American family systems generally comprise extended networks, including several households. Family loyalty, unity, and honor—as well as family commitment, obligation, and responsibility—characterize most Hispanic/Latino American families. Filial piety—loyalty, respect, and devotion of children to their parents—is very important in traditional Asian families. And African Americans often value and rely on the involvement of grandparents and extended family members to help raise children.

LIFE-CYCLE STAGES The traditional family life cycle has been divided into a series of developmental stages. As discussed above, this model may not apply to all contemporary family forms but is considered relevant to most American families (McGoldrick, 1989a).

Stage 1—Single Adult. The unattached young adult who is autonomous and self-responsible. Tasks of this stage include differentiation of self in relation to the family of origin, development of intimate peer relationships, and establishment of self in work.

Stage 2—Formation of a Couple. The joining of two families, traditionally through marriage. Tasks of this stage include formation of a marital system and realignment of relationships with extended families and friends to include the spouse. The primary expectation associated with the formation of a couple is establishing a commitment to each other.

Stage 3—Childbearing Families. The primary task associated with this life-cycle stage is the development of parenting roles. Families from some cultures may proceed through this stage in a nontraditional manner. For example, grandparents in some families may play a greater role in child-rearing than in families from other cultures. Boyd-Franklin (1989) coined the term "nonevolved grandmothers" to reflect an American family system in which a mother who gave birth in her teens now has a daughter who gives birth in her teens. The grandmother is now in a mothering role to her grandchild, although she may have little experience as a mother because her grandmother mothered her and her biological mother was much more like a sibling than a parent. Additionally, more childbearing families are made up of single parents who either choose not to marry or who adopt or give birth via in vitro fertilization. Thus, both cultural/ethnic histories and social phenomena (single-parent, same-gender-parent, and stepparent families) create new scenarios for parents regarding identifying parenting roles and expectations.

Families with young children encounter tasks that include adjusting the marital system to make space for children, taking on parenting roles, and realignment of relationships with extended family to include parenting and grandparenting roles. Substages within this period in the family development cycle include varying tasks. For example, the primary responsibility traditionally associated with rearing preschool children is accepting the fact that the child has a unique personality of his or her own and that this child may now need to learn how to interact with other children with personalities unique to them. Families with school-aged children face the primary task of introducing the child to social institutions (e.g., schools, churches, sport groups).

Stage 4—Families with Adolescents. Accepting adolescents who are struggling with their personal identities and facing changes in social and sexual roles may be one of the most difficult life-cycle stages in family development. Negotiating a clear relationship that respects the individual identity of the adolescent and the need to experiment with the independence of late teens, yet maintains family cohesion, is a very challenging process for most families. For the family with adolescents, additional tasks include the shifting of parent/child relationships to permit adolescents to move in and out of the family system, as well as parents' refocusing on midlife marital and career issues and beginning the shift toward concerns for the older generation.

Stage 5—Families Launching Children. Accepting the child's independent adult role is often difficult for parents. After investing many years in the child's development, it can be emotionally difficult to see the child as an adult and to let him or her develop an individual life path. Middle-aged families experience the process of letting go of children, refocusing family energies on the couple relationship, or, at times, facing life as a single person with young adult children. This stage often presents families with the greatest emotional challenges of the family life cycle. On the other hand, what some refer to as the midlife crisis for parents can lead to a reevaluation of family and career life, looking for new directions, or enjoying past accomplishments—even a sense of freedom and independence. Tasks of this stage include renegotiating the marital system as a dyad, development of adult-to-adult relationships between grown children and their parents, realignment of relationships to include in-laws and grandchildren, and realignment related to disabilities and death of aging parents (or grandparents).

Stage 6—Aging Families. Accepting old age in a youth-oriented society can be very difficult. In many cultures, aging individuals are revered and respected; however, American society seems to place higher value on youthfulness. The family in later life must face a multitude of changes. These tasks may include maintaining individual and/or couple functioning and interests in face of physiological decline, exploration of new familial and social-role options, and support for a more central role for the middle generation. Often encountered in this stage are issues of loss. Families are called upon to support the older generation without overfunctioning for them, often encountering the resistance of family members who don't wish to forfeit their independence. Elders may also be dealing with the losses of a spouse, siblings, and other peers, and may additionally be faced with the preparation for their own deaths, which includes the tasks of life review and integration.

DEVELOPMENTAL CONSIDERATIONS FOR REMARRIED FAMILIES

Carter and McGoldrick (1989) noted additional issues for remarried families in their formation of a family system. The initial stage, entering the new relationship, entails recovery from the loss of the first marriage and a recommitment to marriage and to forming a family—with readiness to deal with the probable complexity and ambiguity. The second stage, conceptualizing and planning a new marriage and forming a new family, entails accepting one's own fears and those of the new spouse and children about remarriage and forming a stepfamily. Additionally, the second stage includes accepting the need for time and patience for adjustment to complexity and ambiguity of multiple new roles, boundaries (e.g., space, time, membership, and authority), and affective issues (e.g., guilt, loyalty conflicts, desire for mutuality, unresolvable past hurts). The third stage, remarriage and reconstitution of family, entails the final resolution of attachment to the previous spouse and letting go of the ideal of forever having an "intact" family. Acceptance of a different model of family with permeable boundaries is necessary for the successful blending of families. Issues of conflict and concern associated with the progression through these stages include:

1. Working on openness in the new relationships to avoid pseudomutuality.

2. Planning for maintenance of cooperative financial and coparental relationships with ex-spouses.

3. Planning to help children deal with fears, loyalty conflicts, and membership in two systems.

4. Realignment of relationships with extended family to include the new spouse and children.

5. Planning maintenance of connections for children with extended family of ex-spouse.

6. Restructuring family boundaries to allow for inclusion of new spouse-stepparent.

7. Realignment of relationships and financial arrangements throughout sub-systems to allow interweaving of several systems.

8. Making room for relationships of all children with biological (noncustodial) parents, grandparents, and other extended family members.

9. Sharing memories and histories to enhance stepfamily integration. (Carter & McGoldrick, 1989)

Identifying the kind of life-cycle struggle a family is going through can be invaluable both in understanding why the family presents as it does and also in determining treatment direction. It is always legitimate to ask why a family is appearing for treatment now rather than, for example, six months ago. A prime question that the family therapist must answer early in treatment is who should be included in the therapy. Once a therapist has identified the system of import, the life-cycle transition, and an appropriate point for intervening, the next decision revolves around what to do about it. What intervention should be used? Or is there a choice of several? Should one use a compression strategy—pushing certain members closer together—or a diversion approach—drawing firm boundaries. Should several techniques be used concomitantly (Stanton, 1988)? An understanding of the family's stage of development in the family life cycle—traditional or contemporary in structure—is an important consideration in determining the context of the family's functioning and the direction of treatment.

FEMINIST THEORY In general, feminist theories combine a focus on women and others who have traditionally been in subordinate roles in society with a commitment to ending that subordination. Feminist theory posits that existing gender relationships in families and society are considered ineffective and in need of correction through social change and political action. According to liberal feminism, women and men have the same rational and spiritual capabilities, and equality can be obtained if they have equivalent educational, economic, and political opportunities. Feminists believe that social and legal reforms will create these opportunities for individuals who are not members of the dominant culture by ending discrimination and stereotyping, and improving educational and employment opportunities. Radical feminism focuses on patriarchy as a source of oppression and proposes that patriarchy must be eliminated to create equality in social power across genders and cultures. Socialist or materialist feminism emphasizes the material base of subordination in capitalism as well as patriarchy. The emphasis is on the underlying economic relations that structure social interaction between men, women, and children, including family relations, and provide privilege to some members of society, such as white men, while devaluing the work of others, such as women and people of color. Feminists argue that equality is not possible in a class-based society and that radical social change, rather than reform, is necessary to overcome class-, culture-, and gender-based oppression. The feminist perspective views gender relations as being at the core of family life and asserts that it is almost universally true that women have the primary responsibility for family matters (Osmond & Thorne, 1993).

The feminist framework for understanding family functioning begins with the notion that women are exploited, devalued, and oppressed and that society should commit to empowering women and changing their oppressed condition (Olson & DeFrain, 1997). Feminists assume that women's experiences are valuable, not less important than those of men, and that gender must be explicitly used as a central focus. Feminist theories examine gender differences and how gender-based distinctions legitimize power differences between men and women in the context of family and couple functioning. They see the family as a dynamic, changing, and open system that should not restrict roles and opportunities. It encourages all family members to value and express their feelings, to share wage-earning responsibilities, and to focus both on their careers and on their children.

PHENOMENOLOGY Phenomenology assumes that because people construct their own social worlds, all things, including families, can have a variety of meanings, depending on the observer. Phenomenology emphasizes what is termed family discourse—the talk and practical reasoning about families. The focus of this work is on the interpretations people make about families, not the family structure as an entity. The theoretical concerns are less about defining who is part of the family and more on how people use family as an idea to specify their relations with others. The meanings people use to organize and interpret the world in understandable terms can be called culture. The focus of phenomenology is on the social construction of everyday life. The concept-of-life world refers to our experience of life, which we take for granted. Family matters can be defined on the basis of the following characteristics: (1) affectional—the quality of the relationship, particularly the love and attention given by one person to another; (2) custodial—the ties or bonds that link persons in caregiving relationships; and (3) durational—a sense of history of the relationship and of ongoing commitment to support through a family connection. Our interpretation of homelife is based on our stock of knowledge about the life world, which includes our images, theories, values, attitudes, and ideas about what constitutes family.

CONSTRUCTIVISM Constructivism asserts that reality does not exist "out there," but instead is a mental construction of the observer. The implications for therapy of the constructivist position are that therapists should not consider what they're seeing in families as existing in the family. Instead, they should understand that what they are seeing is the product of their assumptions—about people, families, and problems—and of their interactions with the family. Much as Adler argued that faulty thinking or cognitions were the important constructs to address in therapy, since the events could not be changed, the therapist should work on changing the client's thoughts or cognitions about the events. These cognitions may or may not be accurate, but are impeding the client's growth and, therefore, need to be changed to more growth-enhancing thoughts.

Instead of focusing on patterns of family interaction, constructivists shift the focus to exploring and reevaluating individual family members' assumptions about their problems. Meaning itself becomes the primary target. One clinical consequence of constructivism has been to make therapists humbler in their dealings with families. Therapists are expected to realize that they have their own meaning systems that can interfere with the therapeutic process, if not acknowledged, and their perceptions are not to be considered as "better" than the clients' own views of the situation. Rather than presupposing that family members' views are incorrect and in need of change, second-order therapists try to promote an understanding of everyone's private reality and to create an atmosphere of respect in which various points can be discussed nondefensively. Many constructivists have gravitated toward a kinder, gentler therapy in which they are more like collaborators with the family than experts or directors. The second-order teams have invented several techniques for engaging with families in conversations about their problems, during which the constructions of each member of the system, including therapist and team members, are examined and critiqued collectively and nonjudgmentally. The second-order groups are, in some ways, circling family therapy back toward a person-centered, nondirective position, although Carl Rogers gets little citation in their literature (Nichols & Schwartz, 1995).

Another concern about relativistic family therapies is that they do not deal with family denial. There is a tendency in many troubled families to deny that problems exist or that they are experiencing any pain. Fish (1993) claims that the relativistic assumption that every family member's story is equally valid maintains a politically conservative tendency to ignore or minimize the plight of those who are oppressed in families.

A fundamental assumption of the social constructionist is that all reality is constructed or generated by participants, rather than being objective, external, or given. From this perspective, stories and personal meaning become important aspects of a person's life because stories transmit meaning, their creation formulates coherent sequences, they shape one's identity, they organize values and explain choices, they are organized by plots and themes, and they involve choosing from alternative interpretations. Family functioning depends upon shared meanings. Meanings cannot be controlled from outside, and emphasis shifts from actions to meanings, from expertise to collaboration, and from diagnosis of problems to mutual creation of solutions. Clinical practice and the therapist's stance from this focus are demonstrated through a nonhierarchical relationship; shared explorations, offering new meanings and assumptions; bringing client themes and values into awareness, being the coauthor of a living story with them; and nurturing, supportive relationships that are not paternalistic. Some pitfalls of this approach include seeing any interpretation as being as good as any other, inattention to power differences in family and community regarding interpretations, and assuming that social constructionism has all the answers and that they are the best (Holland & Kilpatrick, 1995, p. 32).

SOCIAL INFLUENCES ON FAMILY THERAPY

INFLUENCE OF ETHNICITY DeGenova (1997) noted that American culture is a mixture of the arts, beliefs, customs, and all other products of human endeavor and thought created by many different ethnic groups. Billingsley (1993) stated that while superficially humans may be dissimilar, the essence of being human is very much the same for all of us. The paradox of human diversity is that we are all the same but in different ways. The Dalai Lama (1991) stated that "one thing I have noticed is an inclination for people to think in terms of 'black and white' and 'either, or,' which ignores the facts of interdependence and relativity. They have a tendency to lose sight of the grey areas which inevitably exist between two points of view" (p. 199).

McGoldrick (1989a) noted that ethnicity interacts with the family life cycle at every stage. Ethnicity gives patterns to thinking, feeling, and behaving in both obvious and subtle ways, although generally operating outside one's awareness. Ethnicity refers to a concept of a group's "peoplehood" based on a combination of race, religion, and cultural history, whether or not members realize their commonalities with each other. Americans are marrying out of their ethnic groups at an ever-increasing rate, yet intermarriage is feared because it threatens the survival of the group. Generally, the greater the difference in cultural background, the more difficulty spouses have in adjusting to marriage. As increasing numbers of families migrate to the United States, it is imperative that therapists gain a greater understanding of the disruption migration causes to the family system. McGoldrick (1989a) stated that migration should perhaps be considered another life-cycle stage that the family must negotiate. The readjustment to a new culture is a prolonged developmental process that will affect family members differently depending on the life-cycle phase they are in at the time of the transition.

Appreciation of cultural variability leads to a radically new conceptual model of clinical intervention. Restoring a stronger sense of identity may require resolving cultural conflicts within the family, between the family and the community, or in the wider context in which the family is embedded. Differentiation involves selecting from our ethnic traditions those values we wish to retain and carry on. Olson and DeFrain (1997) noted the following strengths for culturally diverse families:

1. White families. Strengths: commitment to family, time spent together, ability to cope with stress, spiritual well-being, positive communication, appreciation and affection. Challenges: maintaining an "expected" status quo.

2. African American families. Strengths: strong kinship bonds, strong work orientation, flexibility of family roles, strong motivation to achieve, strong religious orientation, caring parenting. Challenges: being judged as a financial risk, feeling powerless, building self-esteem, high risk of young men being killed, discrimination/racism, lack of education, violence against each other, lack of male role models, managing the effects of prejudice and stereotyping.

3. Hispanic/Latino families. Strengths: familialism (family is a major priority), high family cohesion, high family flexibility, supporting kin network system, equalitarian decision making, strong ethnic identity. Challenges: remaining family centered, maintaining traditions, gaining financial resources, overcoming the language barrier, overcoming economic discrimination, handling relocation issues, increasing education, acculturation across generations.

4. Asian American families. Strengths: filial piety (respect for elders), high value on education, well-disciplined children, extended family support, family loyalty. Challenges: high expectations for self, loss of ties with kin, emotional vulnerability, stigma against seeking help, distrust of those outside the group, excessive focus on work.

5. Native American families. Strengths: extended family systems, traditional beliefs, high family cohesion, respect for elders, bilingual language skills, tribal support system. Challenges: conflicting values of tribe and U.S. society, maintaining family traditions, staying cohesive and connected, lack of role models, improving education.

CHALLENGES FOR ALL ETHNIC FAMILIES

1. Marriage outside the group.

2. Assimilation (relinquishing old cultural traits and values and replacing them with those of the dominant culture).

3. Acculturation (cultural traits and values from one ethnic group become intermeshed with those of the dominant culture).

4. Segregation (ethnic group isolates itself or is forced into isolation within the dominant culture).

FEMINIST CRITIQUE Hare-Mustin (1978) criticized family therapists and systems theory specifically by noting that family therapy failed to consider the larger context when describing family dysfunction, adhering to the notion that all parties to a problem have contributed equally and thus share equal responsibility for that problem, continuing to view mothers as the source of pathology in families, and assuming a neutral stance vis-à-vis families. Advocates of the feminist perspective have suggested that the family therapist include discussions of gender-related issues in therapy, self-disclose regarding the therapist's biases, and place an emphasis on the strengths of women, their individual needs, and the ways in which women may be empowered (Avis, 1988). In order to avoid gender bias, Becvar and Becvar (1996) suggest that theorists—therapists and researchers—become conscious of their personal values and beliefs and recognize the degree to which the observer influences that which he or she observes. Nichols and Schwartz (1995) noted that the feminist critique of family therapy has emphasized the notion that family therapists are guilty of mother blaming, looking through the traditional lens of gender (patriarchy permeates all therapy), and blaming the victim in violent family situations.

The issue of women and the family life cycle has come under scrutiny as our understanding of gender roles, identities, and expectancies has become more informed. Clearly male and female development is both biologically and socially different. Women have historically defined themselves and judged themselves in terms of their ability to care and nurture. Though most theories have recognized the importance of individuation, the commitment to creating and maintaining family connections has been less valued. Basic to this systemic perspective is the belief that human identity is inextricably bound up in one's relationships with others and that complete autonomy is a fiction. Women's sense of self has been organized around being able to develop and maintain relationships with others, thus, the loss of a relationship is perceived as a loss of one's identity. The lack of recognition and respect for this role in the family systems and life-cycle literature has been a basis of concern to feminist theorists when examining gender-related values.

McGoldrick (1989b) suggests that family therapists shift toward gender-sensitive therapy. This approach would include paying attention to a variety of issues within a family system, including:

1. Income and work opportunities of the husband and for the wife, and implications for the balance of power in their relationship.

2. Relative physical strength of men and women in a family, and to the impact of any physical intimidation or incident of physical abuse as a regulator of the balance of power between spouses.

3. Examination by family members about what they like and do not like about being male or female.

4. Helping the family clarify the rules by which male and female roles in the family, in education, and in work are chosen and rewarded.

5. Helping the family clarify rules about who makes which decisions and who handles concerns such as finances, legal matters, emotional matters, caretaking arrangements, and upkeep of the home.

6. Helping the family place their attitudes toward male and female roles in context, clarifying the broader political, social, and economic issues of divorce, aging, and child-rearing, and encouraging families to educate themselves about these matters.

7. Validating women's focus on relationships while, at the same time, empowering them in the areas of work and money.

8. Being sensitive to the high price men may have to pay if they change their male orientation toward success and give higher priority to relationships and emotional expressiveness.

THINKING OF FAMILIES AS DIVERSE AND CHANGING SYSTEMS

Horne and Sayger (1990) noted that as the therapist works with the family in the initial stages of family therapy, it is important to develop an understanding of the systemic properties of how each family member's interactions impact the functioning of all other family members. Schwebel and Fine (1994) noted that the typical family unit performs the following basic tasks:

1. Providing shelter, food, clothing, and health care for its members.

2. Meeting family costs and allocating such resources as time, space, and facilities according to each member's needs.

3. Determining who does what in the support, management, and care of the home and its members.

4. Assuring each member's socialization through the internalization of increasingly mature roles in the family and beyond.

5. Establishing ways of interacting, communicating, and expressing affection and sexuality, within limits acceptable to society.

6. Bearing (or adopting) and rearing children, incorporating and releasing family members appropriately.

7. Relating to school, church, and community life; establishing policies for including in-laws, relatives, guests, and friends.

8. Maintaining morale and motivation, rewarding achievement, meeting personal and family crises, setting attainable goals, and developing family loyalties and values.

Family roles include, but may not be limited to:

1. Housekeeper roles: This entails completing the many and varied tasks required to keep the family's living quarters in order as well as the chores associated with keeping family members fed, their clothes clean and available, and so forth.

2. Provider roles: This involves earning the monetary and other material resources necessary to support the family members.

3. Child-care roles: This includes the physical and psychological maintenance of the children; activities such as keeping the child clean, fed, and warm as well as protected from physical dangers and frightening experiences.

4. Child-socialization roles: This covers those processes and activities within the family that contribute to developing the children into competent, social, and moral people.

5. Kinship roles: This involves the maintenance of relationships with extended family members through communication, participating in holiday gatherings, and so forth. Support and assistance are exchanged in the kinship relationships, and a sense of identity is developed.

6. Therapeutic roles: This involves assisting other family members in dealing with the day-to-day difficulties they encounter. The help-giver may engage in careful listening, offer sympathy or assistance, and express reassurance or affection.

7. Recreational roles: This includes organizing family members and involving them in leisure-time activities.

8. Sexual roles: This is unique in that it, alone, applies to the heads of the household, and it subsumes their exchange of affection and sexual gratification.

Sherman and Dinkmeyer (1987) stated a belief that each family member plays a fully equal part in the family system, despite age and intelligence, and that the system must formulate itself to accommodate his or her presence and existence. Family members can change their places in the family, or their behavior, at any time, eliciting new responses from others, thus changing the dynamic in the family. Sherman and Dinkmeyer (1987) noted that there are many issues faced by individuals in the creation of a family. First is a general readiness to move from a couple to a family. Couples often experience some confusion in establishing an identity, boundaries, common goals, and procedures. The second potential issue is conflict about having a child. Couples may disagree about whether or when to have children. Third, a couple may experience difficulty in conceiving; fourth, in integrating the child into the couple relationship; fifth, in deciding who should care for the child; sixth, in agreeing on child-rearing practices; seventh, in resolving differences in temperament and style between parents and child; and eighth, in agreeing on family goals and aspirations. According to Sherman and Dinkmeyer (1987), the ideal family uses a democratic process, is growth- and development-oriented, supports a feeling of social interest, and establishes and follows consistent rules.

Carter (1978) noted that the family experiences both "vertical" and "horizontal" stressors. The vertical stressors include patterns of relating and functioning (e.g., myths, secrets, legacies, attitudes, taboos, expectations, labels) that are transmitted from generation to generation of a family primarily through the mechanism of emotional triangling. Horizontal stressors include life-cycle transitions and unpredictable life events (e.g., untimely death, chronic illness, accidents) that occur as the family moves forward through time. If enough stress occurs during the family system's progression, any family may appear dysfunctional. One cannot overlook the stress that comes from being in a particular place at a particular moment in time. Thus all levels of a system must be considered when assessing families (e.g., individual, nuclear family, extended family, community [work, friends], social/cultural/political/economic [gender, religion, ethnicity]). One simply cannot ignore the social, economic, and political context and its impact on families moving through different phases of the life cycle at each point in history. All these factors influence the system of family functioning.

Hoffman (1989) noted that the family life cycle is characterized by discontinuous change. It is argued that families need a symptom to maintain family homeostasis; however, a more correct interpretation may be that all parts of a system are engaged in whatever ordering of constancy or change is in question, in an equal and coordinate fashion. One must realize that a family is a living system in which self-organizing processes reach toward new evolutionary stages rather than equilibrium. The goal of therapy is to make available to a family that is becoming more like a homeostatically controlled piece of machinery the power inherent in all living systems—the ability to transcend the impasse and move to a different stage. One property that families share with other complex systems is that they change not in a smooth, unbroken line but in discontinuous leaps.

Fennell and Weinhold (1997) noted the following characteristics of healthy families:

1. Subsystem boundaries are clear and may be altered, as the family requires.
2. Family rules are clear and fairly enforced, and may change as family conditions change.
3. Family members have a clear understanding of their roles.
4. Individual autonomy is encouraged, and a sense of family unity is maintained.
5. Communication is clear and direct without being coercive.

Characteristics of dysfunctional families include:

1. Subsystem boundaries are rigid or very diffuse and are not subject to change.
2. Rules are unchanging and rigidly enforced, or the family has no rules or methods for organizing behavior.
3. Roles are rigid and may not be modified, or roles are not clearly defined and members are unsure what is required to meet expectations.
4. Individual autonomy is sacrificed for family togetherness or autonomy is required because of lack of family unity.
5. Communication is vague and indirect or coercive and authoritarian.

Family therapists who believe that the family-of-origin system can have a deep and pervasive effect on an adult's current behavior may use the genogram and family life space to understand the past and present of the family. People are seen as being influenced and controlled by the unachieved goals and unresolved problems of the parental and grandparental generations. Healthy personality development depends on the ability to separate oneself from these irrational, intense, emotional attachments to parents while retaining the capacity for warm, expressive, and positive interactions within the family of origin.

GAY AND LESBIAN FAMILIES

Gay and lesbian families are characterized by a lack of affirming role models and societal support. To provide affirming, empowering therapy, clinicians need to:

1. Acknowledge and be open to continuous understanding of their own unconscious and conscious homophobia.

2. Consider the impact of cultural and societal homophobia on socialized roles and expectations, and the related psychological development and well-being of individuals, couples, and families.

3. Keep abreast of developing scientific knowledge about homosexuality and concomitant issues (e.g., health, antigay violence) as well as with emerging life style models.

4. Study the most current literature about clinical issues.

5. Become familiar with local, state, and federal laws as well as community and psychoeducative resources.

Families need help with adjusting to the life-threatening diagnosis of AIDS, dealing with fears of contagion, accepting the sexual orientations of family members, and coping with discrimination stigma. As with most families, nontraditional ones also need assistance with managing conflict among family members and significant others, confronting reconciliation of relationships—especially when pushed with limited time, preparing for loss and bereavement, shifting family roles, and providing necessary care and negotiating with external systems

CURRENT TRENDS IN FAMILY THEORY

DIVERSITY

Family theories as a whole place some limitations on understanding family diversity.

1. The concentrated theoretical and empirical focus on white, Western, two-parent families has limited our understanding of other families and has resulted in an implicit or explicit model of comparison for all families, despite cultural, ethnic, racial, or class differences. As a result, diverse family patterns are overlooked, misunderstood, judged as deviant, or assumed to be on the same assimilative path to the nuclear family form.

2. The focus on the family unit as a cooperative, homeostatic group overlooks differences within the family, in individual interests, personal concerns, and access to resources. Due to the stratification of most societies and families along

gender and generational lines, the unequal distribution of resources and power tends to favor the interests of men over those of women and children.

3. A conceptual focus on individual processes and intrafamilial interactions tends to isolate families from the social context and limits our understanding of the influences of diverse social, cultural, and historical forces that affect family processes.

The original theories of racial identity do not consider gender, class, and environmental influences (Okun, 1996). To provide culturally sensitive family therapy, therapists must become aware of their own attitudes about people of different race and ethnicity and their own attitudes toward mixed marriages and families. They must also learn about cultural and experiential differences of clients within a sociopolitical context, develop therapeutic processes and goals that are consistent with and appropriate to the individual differences and cultural orientation of clients, be familiar with available community resources and support groups, understand racial identity development processes, and strengthen their capacity for creating a culturally sensitive climate of compassion, empathy, dignity, and respect for differences. Cross-cultural theorists suggest that clinicians can learn about effective helping strategies from other cultures, in addition to alternative normative values. For example, the meditation, imaging, and relaxation techniques from the Asian and Indian cultures can be useful complements to our Western techniques. The therapist who is most effective in working with diverse populations is the person who respects and covalues differences.

INDIVIDUALS AS SYSTEMS

The self reenters the system as family therapists begin to realize the importance of intrapsychic phenomena as they influence an individual's interaction within the family system. Okun (1996) argued that without understanding context, we cannot make meaning of people's concerns and behaviors. Without understanding clients' meaning and its implications, we cannot help people to understand what part of their difficulties can be attributed to intrapsychic, to interpersonal, and to larger social systems variables. Our notions of family need to be reassessed and broadened. Does a family have to have biological ties? May it be a committed group of people who care about each other? Must it be heterosexual? Of one race or culture? Does it require two parents? Does the primary parent have to be female? Is the critical factor in outcome the family structure or the adults' generative capacities to focus on children's needs and development? The larger ecological view of families includes (1) psychosociobehavioral consideration of the individual within the contexts of family of origin and current family systems; (2) consideration of families within larger sociocultural, political, and economic contexts; and (3) consideration of (1) and (2) as shaping and being shaped by gender, ethnicity, class, sexual orientation, and race.

Auerswald (1988) noted that there are five paradigms for understanding families:

1. A psychodynamic paradigm in which a family is defined as a group made up of the interlocking psychodynamics of its members who are at various developmental stages.

2.   A family systems paradigm, which defines a family as a system that operates independently, and from which individual psychodynamics, including those that create symptoms, emerge.

3.   A general systems paradigm in which a family is defined as a system that shares isomorphic characteristics with all systems, and which arranges systems in a hierarchy according to classes—from quarks to universe—and with higher systems containing those lower in the hierarchy (e.g., sociocultural systems contain families that contain individuals who contain a psyche, etc.).

4.   A cybernetic systems paradigm, which defines systems, including a family system, in terms of circular information flow and regulatory mechanisms.

5.   An ecological systems (or ecosytemic) paradigm, which defines a family as a coevolutionary ecosystem located in evolutionary time/space.

An important development in family therapy and family research is the redirection from a pathology-based focus on family deficits to a normality-based orientation (Walsh, 1995). Family systems therapists and researchers are becoming increasingly aware that all views of normality are socially constructed. Examples of commonly held perspectives on family functioning include:

1.   Normal families as asymptomatic. From this common clinical perspective, grounded in the medical model, a family is regarded as normal—and healthy—if there are no symptoms of disorder in any family member. The judgment of normality is based on the absence of pathology. This perspective points to the limitation of this approach. This deficit-based model fails to acknowledge the positive attributes of family well-being and assumes that an individual disorder is invariably a symptom of a family dysfunction.

2.   Normal families as average or typical. This approach seeks to identify typical patterns and traits. A family is viewed as normal if it fits a pattern or model that is common or prevalent in ordinary families. The negative connotations of deviance can lead to the pathologizing of a family that has a manner of functioning that is not congruent with the designated model. This perspective disengages the concepts of normality, health, and absence of symptoms. Family patterns that are common are not necessarily healthy and may even be destructive, such as problem drinking and violence. Because average families have occasional problems, the presence of a problem does not, in itself, signal family abnormality or pathology.

3.   Normal families as ideal or optimal. This approach seeks to define a healthy family in terms of ideal traits or characteristics. Social norms of the ideal family are culturally constructed values that prescribe how families ought to be. A certain range of conduct is deemed permissible, and particular family forms and traits are considered desirable according to prevailing standards in the dominant society. Ideals may vary in particular ethnic groups. Unconventional family arrangements that do not fit the standard deemed ideal may nevertheless be optimal for the functioning of a particular family. Such pathologizing of difference from the norm—both typical and ideal—continues to stigmatize families who do not conform to the invariant standard, such as dual-earner, single-parent, remarried, and gay and lesbian families.

4.   Normal families in relation to systemic transactional processes. This perspective is based on systems theory and considers both average and optimal functioning in terms of basic processes characteristic of human systems. This view pays specific attention to ongoing processes over time. Transactional processes support the integration and maintenance of the family unit and its ability to carry out essential tasks for the growth and well-being of its members. Family operations are governed by a relatively small set of patterned and predictable rules that serve as norms. What is normal, in terms of optimal family functioning, will vary with the different developmental demands and structural configurations. The family strengths perspective is based in this view of normal family functioning.

Individuals seek assistance with a wide range of difficulties, from problems of everyday living to severe mental illness; families seek assistance in resolving conflicts, in dealing with intergenerational issues, and in remaining viable units in the face of economic hardship. Because no one method is likely itself to be the key to resolving human problems, professionals who deal with human problems must have more than a passing acquaintance with the major representative types of behavior-change methods currently used (Vondracek & Corneal, 1995). The panoply of behavior change methods currently used creates the danger of being overinclusive and superficial. If one chooses to be selective, however, one risks missing the core objective of increasing the understanding of the diversity of behavior change methods available. Each method of intervention has unique theoretical constructs and unique conceptualizations of problems, and each often uses unique and sometimes idiosyncratic language to represent what it aims to accomplish and how it intends to accomplish those goals.

The enduring concepts and techniques of family therapy include the importance of the family context, family structure, psychopathology as serving a function in families, circular sequences of interaction, the family life cycle, and multigenerational patterns. The fundamental goals of treatment include contextualizing the problem, dealing with resistance, and changing family interaction.

ANNOTATED SUGGESTED READINGS

Becvar, D. S., & Becvar, R. J. (1996). *Family theory: A systemic integration* (3rd ed.). Boston: Allyn & Bacon.
>   Provides a thoughtful overview of the historical development of family therapy from the 1940s through its current status, including paradigm shifts, controversies, and understanding of family systems. Psychodynamic, experiential, structural, communications, strategic, behavioral, and emerging models of family intervention are reviewed.

Boss, P. G., Doherty, W. J., LaRossa, R., Schumm, W. R., & Steinmetz, S. K. (Eds.). (1993). *Sourcebook of family theories and methods: A contextual approach.* New York: Plenum.
>   Provides a sociohistorical approach to understanding the development of family therapy theory from its earliest philosophy through theory construction and methodology of the mid-twentieth century to its current emerging models. Chapters on specific family therapy theories outline their initial sociocultural milieu, historical development, core assumptions, major contemporary concepts in the theory, and theoretical limitations and research.

Carter, B., & McGoldrick, M. (Eds.). (1999). *The expanded family life cycle: Individual, family, and social perspectives* (3rd ed.). Boston: Allyn & Bacon.

> This book provides an extensive overview of various influences on the family life-cycle development model. The impact of culture, social class, gender, siblings, migration, death, and the creation of meaningful family rituals is discussed. Specific chapters are also provided on the challenges faced by African American families, single-adult families, lesbian and gay male families, divorced families, and remarried families, to name a few. Clinical applications are also reviewed with regard to the impact of chronic illness, violence, and substance abuse on family development and adjustment to life-cycle tasks.

DeGenova, M. K. (Ed.). (1997). *Families in cultural context: Strengths and challenges in diversity.* Mountain View, CA: Mayfield Publishing.

> This book offers an overview of issues of culture and values as they pertain to the development and implementation of family theory and therapy. Issues for the treatment of Native American families, African American families, families of Mexican origin, Chinese American families, Arab American families, and Cuban American families, among others, are discussed.

Ingoldsby, B. B., & Smith, S. (Eds.). (1995). *Families in multicultural perspective.* New York: Guilford Press.

> Family theory and a multicultural family perspective are discussed in relation to understanding the impact of cultural world view, values, traditions, and history on family development, structure, and system roles and functions. Issues such as mate selection, socialization of children, divorce, household division of labor, poverty, and public policy are addressed as they influence the understanding of family systems.

Wynne, L. C. (Ed.). (1988). *The state of the art in family therapy research: Controversies and recommendations.* New York: Family Process Press.

> This book emphasizes the issues and dilemmas in conducting research from a family systems perspective. Issues of identifying a conceptual framework for study, the selection of variables, designing effective outcome research, and data analysis are addressed.

REFERENCES

Allman, L. R. (1982). The aesthetic preference: Overcoming the pragmatic error. *Family Process, 21,* 43–56.

Auerswald, E. H. (1988). Epistemological confusion and outcome research. In L. C. Wynne (Ed.), *The state of the art in family therapy research: Controversies and recommendations* (pp. 55–72). New York: Family Process Press.

Avis, J. M. (1988). Deepening awareness: A private study guide to feminism and family therapy. In L. Braverman (Ed.), *A guide to feminist family therapy* (pp. 15–46). New York: Harrington Park Press.

Becvar, D. S., & Becvar, R. J. (1996). *Family therapy: A systematic integration.* Boston: Allyn & Bacon.

Berg-Cross, L. (1988). *Basic concepts in family therapy: An introductory text.* New York: Haworth.

Billingsley, R. (1993). Fostering diversity: Teaching by discussion. *The Teaching Professor, February,* 3–4.

Boyd-Franklin, N. (1989). *Black families in therapy.* New York: Guilford Press.

Broderick, C. B., & Schrader, S. S. (1981). The history of professional marriage and family therapy. In A. S. Gurman & D. P. Kniskern (Eds.), *Handbook of family therapy* (pp. 5–35). New York: Brunner/Mazel.

Bubolz, M. M., & Sontag, M. S. (1993). Human ecology theory. In P. B. Boss, W. J. Doherty, R. LaRossa, W. R. Schumm, & S. K. Steinmetz (Eds.), *Sourcebook of family theories and methods: A contextual approach* (pp. 419–448). New York: Plenum.

Carlson, J., Sperry, L., & Lewis, J. A. (1997): *Family therapy: Ensuring treatment efficacy.* Pacific Grove, CA: Brooks/Cole.

Carter, E. A. (1978). The transgenerational scripts and nuclear family stress: Theory and clinical implications. In R. R. Sager (Ed.), *Georgetown family symposium* (Vol. 3, 1975–1976). Washington, DC: Georgetown University.

Carter, B., & McGoldrick, M. (1989). Overview: The changing family life cycle—A framework for family therapy. In B. Carter & M. McGoldrick (Eds.), *The changing family life cycle: A framework for family therapy* (2nd ed., pp. 3–28). Boston: Allyn & Bacon.

Dalai Lama. (1991). *Freedom from exile.* Scranton, PA: Transaction Publishing.

DeGenova, M. K. (1997). Introduction. In M. K. DeGenova (Ed.), *Families in cultural context: Strengths and challenges in diversity* (pp. 1–13). Mountain View, CA: Mayfield Publishing.

Dell, P. F. (1982). Beyond homeostasis: Toward a concept of coherence. *Family Process, 21,* 21–42.

Dreikurs, R., & Soltz, V. (1964). *Children the challenge.* New York: Plume.

Fennell, D. L., & Weinhold, B. K. (1997). *Counseling families: An introduction to marriage and family therapy.* Denver: Love Publishing.

Fish, V. (1993). Poststructuralism in family therapy: Interrogating the narrative/conversational mode. *Journal of Marital and Family Therapy, 19,* 223–232.

Goldenberg, I., & Goldenberg, H. (1996). *Family therapy: An overview* (4th ed.). Pacific Grove, CA: Brooks/Cole.

Group for the Advancement of Psychiatry. (1970). *The field of family therapy* (Report No. 78). New York: Author.

Hanna, S. M., & Brown, J. H. (1995). *The practice of family therapy: Key elements across models.* Pacific Grove, CA: Brooks/Cole.

Haley, J. (1963). *Strategies of psychotherapy.* New York: Grune & Stratton.

Hare-Mustin, R. T. (1978). A feminist approach to family therapy. *Family Process, 17,* 181–194.

Hayes, H. (1991). A re-introduction to family therapy: Clarification of three schools. *Journal of Family Therapy, 12,* 27–43.

Hoffman, L. (1989). The family life cycle and discontinuous change. In B. Carter & M. McGoldrick (Eds.), *The changing family life cycle: A framework for family therapy* (2nd ed., pp. 91–105). Boston: Allyn & Bacon.

Holland, T. P., & Kilpatrick, A. C. (1995). An ecological systems social constructionism approach to family practice. In A. C. Kilpatrick & T. P. Holland (Eds.), *Working with families: An integrative model by level of functioning* (pp. 17–38). Boston: Allyn & Bacon.

Horne, A. M., & Sayger, T. V. (1990). *Treating conduct and oppositional defiant disorders in children.* Elmsford, NY: Pergamon.

Ingoldsby, B. B., & Smith, S. (Ed.). (1995). *Families in multicultural perspective.* New York: Guilford Press.

Keeney, B. P., & Sprenkle, D. H. (1982). Ecosystemic epistemology: Critical implications for the aesthetics and pragmatics of family therapy. *Family Process, 21,* 1–19.

Maturana, H. R. (1978). Biology of language: The epistemology of reality. In G. A. Miller & E. Lennenberg (Eds.), *Psychology and biology of language and thought.* New York: Academic Press.

McGoldrick, M. (1989a). Ethnicity and the family life cycle. In B. Carter & M. McGoldrick (Eds.), *The changing family life cycle: A framework for family therapy* (2nd ed., pp. 69–90). Boston: Allyn & Bacon.

McGoldrick, M. (1989b). Women and the family life cycle. In B. Carter & M. McGoldrick (Eds.), *The changing family life cycle: A framework for family therapy* (2nd ed., pp. 29–68). Boston: Allyn & Bacon.

Nichols, M. P., & Schwartz, R. C. (1995). *Family therapy: Concepts and methods* (3rd ed.). Boston: Allyn & Bacon.

Okun, B. F. (1996). *Understanding diverse families: What practitioners need to know.* New York: Guilford Press.

Olson, D. H., & DeFrain, J. (1997). *Marriage and the family: Diversity and strengths* (2nd ed.). Mountain View, CA: Mayfield Publishing.

Osmond, M. W., & Thorne, B. (1993). Feminist theories: The social construction of gender in families and society. In P. B. Boss, W. J. Doherty, R. LaRossa, W. R. Schumm, & S. K. Steinmetz (Eds.), *Sourcebook of family theories and methods: A contextual approach* (pp. 591–623). New York: Plenum.

Rodgers, R. H., & White, J. M. (1993). Family development theory. In P. B. Boss, W. J. Doherty, R. LaRossa, W. R. Schumm, & S. K. Steinmetz (Eds.), *Sourcebook of family theories and methods: A contextual approach* (pp. 225–254). New York: Plenum.

Satir, V. M. (1964). *Conjoint family therapy.* Palo Alto, CA: Science and Behavior Books.

Schwebel, A. I., & Fine, M. A. (1994). *Understanding and helping families: A cognitive-behavioral approach.* Hillsdale, NJ: Lawrence Erlbaum Associates.

Seaburn, D., Landau-Stanton, J., & Horwitz, S. (1995). Core techniques in family therapy. In R. H. Mikesell, D. Lusterman, & S. H. McDaniel (Eds.), *Integrating family therapy: Handbook of family psychology and systems theory* (pp. 5–26). Washington, DC: American Psychological Association.

Sherman, R., & Dinkmeyer, D. (1987). *Systems of family therapy: An Adlerian integration.* New York: Brunner/Mazel.

Slovik, L. S., & Griffith, J. L. (1992). The current face of family therapy. In J. S. Rutan (Ed.), *Psychotherapy for the 1990s.* New York: Guilford Press.

Stanton, M. D. (1988). The lobster quadrille: Issues and dilemmas for family therapy research. In L. C. Wynne (Ed.), *The state of the art in family therapy research: Controversies and recommendations* (pp. 7–31). New York: Family Process Press.

Stinnett, N. (1979). Strong families: A national study. In N. Stinnett, B. Chesser, & J. DeFrain (Eds.). *Building family strengths: Blueprints for action.* Lincoln: University of Nebraska Press.

U. S. Bureau of The Census. (1994). *Statistical abstract of the United States* (114th ed.). Washington, DC: U. S. Government Printing Office.

von Bertalanffy, L. (1950). An outline of general system theory. *British Journal of the Philosophy of Science, 1,* 134–165.

Vondracek, F. W., & Corneal, S. (1995). *Strategies for resolving individual and family problems.* Pacific Grove, CA: Brooks/Cole.

Walsh, F. (1995). From family damage to family challenge. In R. H. Mikesell, D. Lusterman, & S. H. McDaniel (Eds.), *Integrating family therapy: Handbook of family psychology and systems theory* (pp. 587–606). Washington, DC: American Psychological Association.

Wynne, L. C. (1988). An overview of the state of the art: What should be expected in current family therapy research. In L. C. Wynne (Ed.), *The state of the art in family therapy research: Controversies and recommendations* (pp. 249–266). New York: Family Process Press.

CHAPTER 3

Common Elements in Family Therapy Theory and Strategies

**THOMAS V. SAYGER AND
ARTHUR M. HORNE**

A unique aspect of conducting family therapy is that, even though there is a wide diversity of theoretical approaches, most family practitioners utilize a basic way of thinking (systemic) and core skills inherent in most therapeutic strategies. This chapter will highlight the primary premises that underlie clinical practice from a systemic point of view and the skills necessary to develop a positive therapeutic relationship with families in treatment.

FAMILY SYSTEMS THEORY AND CONCEPTS

Haley (1987), von Bertalanffy (1968), and Walsh (1982) have all referred to a family as an open system that functions in relationship to its sociocultural context and grows and evolves over the life cycle. From this perspective, individual pathology is seen as a symptom of family dysfunction even when the family member's behavior may be adaptively constructed to fit within the bounds of expectation for his or her particular family system. In essence, this pathological behavior helps to maintain the homeostatic state of the family. Fleischman, Horne, and Arthur (1983) asserted that no behavior is illogical or crazy, but rather is understandable within the contingencies and context of that individual family system. Therefore, psychopathology is a relationship problem, and since dysfunctional family systems reinforce the pathology, the relationship pattern must be altered to assist individuals in overcoming their concerns (Haley, 1987).

Families operate according to the same standards as all systems in maintaining their status quo and continued operations (Walsh, 1991). These operating constructs include circular causality, nonsummativity, equifinality, homeostasis, morphogenesis, and family communication.

CIRCULAR CAUSALITY

The concept of circular causality asserts that family members are interrelated individuals, and as a result, change in one member affects other members and the family group as a whole in generally predictable ways once the family's pattern of interacting is fully understood. In this circular chain of events, each action is also a reaction. For example, Andy yells at his brother Tom because he is angry that Tom broke one of his favorite toys. Andy's behavior was a reaction to a behavior exhibited by Tom. In fact, Tom's behavior was also a reaction to some other action in the family; perhaps Andy had broken one of Tom's favorite toys. It is easy to see that, from this viewpoint, attempts at faultfinding and blaming are counterproductive to the real issues facing such a family system. Since it would be difficult to identify the first action in the overall chain of events, the family therapist must focus on the overall patterns of interaction, and individual family members must take responsibility for altering their action/reaction within the circular chain of events. Many clinicians and researchers have criticized this concept—as a way of absolving the perpetrator of the negative behavior (e.g., batterers, abusers) and blaming the victim. However, if the perpetrator is held responsible for his or her behavior, yet is not the negative focus of blame and fault, the family can move on to the beginning of a better understanding of what has precipitated this behavior. Likewise, victims are in a better position of deciding if they wish to remain in this family system and discuss potential new patterns of interaction or to remove themselves from the system and move on to addressing their personal growth and well-being.

NONSUMMATIVITY

Perhaps consistent with the gestalt perspective, the concept of nonsummativity refers to the belief that the family system as a whole is greater than the sum of its parts. The behavior of members is interlocking and, therefore, one cannot describe the family just by describing characteristics of its individual members. Families function as interbehaving, intercommunicating, and interdependent systems that are affected by past family events, family-of-origin influences, society, and a multitude of other environmental or contextual influences. Therefore, families do not function in isolation and family members do not function as independent beings, because they are impacted by and impact other family members. Often families will wonder how they got in such a state of dysfunction; yet, it is understandable as interactions build upon interactions, as thoughts and feelings are altered by these interactions, and as perspectives and perceptions change over the course of day-in and day-out interaction. The family is often unaware of the metacommunication that exists within the system and the social influences imposed by larger social systems (e.g., school, neighborhood, government, work settings) as well as how these larger systems impact daily activity.

EQUIFINALITY

The term *equifinality* refers to the idea that the same etiological foundation may, in fact, lead to different or similar outcomes in family systems. Although no two sets of circumstances are identical, two families with very similar life situations may follow very different paths and, while one family system may function in very healthy and effective ways, the other family system operates within very dysfunctional patterns. Likewise, for two well-functioning families, one may have had a traumatic background, whereas the other may not. Watzlawick, Beavin, and Jackson (1967) refer to this concept as the erroneous genetic fallacy. One cannot assume that all children reared in homes of abusive, addicted, or disrupted families will grow up to be abusive, addicted, or otherwise dysfunctional. In fact, many children who are reared in such homes may develop into very responsible, emotionally healthy, and productive adults, as the research on resiliency in children and families has demonstrated. The task of researchers and clinicians is to determine what factors impede or exacerbate healthy human development in spite of highly dysfunctional home environments, or what leads to dysfunction in family members of healthy functioning families. Individual temperament, social-support networks, strong bonds with the healthy functioning family members, and opportunities to interact with healthy, functioning role models outside the family system may help individuals develop into effectively functioning human beings in spite of familial systemic or individual psychological problems.

HOMEOSTASIS

Family systems resist change through mechanisms intended to delimit and enforce norms. All family members contribute to this homeostatic balance through a reinforcing feedback loop in which desired behaviors are complemented or reciprocally reinforced and dysfunctional behaviors are coercively reinforced. These homeostatic mechanisms function to counteract any deviation from family norms and thus keep the family members bound together, even if in negative ways. Although homeostasis can work to maintain the family system and, perhaps, aid in the development of family cohesion or togetherness, it can also be a powerful force working against changes that may need to be made to ensure the continued healthy development of each family member and the family system. For example, families referred for disruptive child behavior may wish that the child could immediately change his or her behavior—without understanding that all family members must also change their behavior or mode of interacting. And this must occur even with the understanding that some family members may be content with the current interaction, since they may be able to have their needs met for attention, power, control, revenge, or some other motivator within the current pattern of behavior. Change within families is very painful, for as difficult as it may be to live in dysfunctional families, family members know their roles in their current situation and it may feel safer to be in a painful known role than to venture into an unknown role.

MORPHOGENESIS

Family systems must be able to cope with or adapt to many changing situations during the course of their lifetime. Families transition through such developmental states as coupling, childbirth, children in school, adolescence, leaving home, and aging. The ability to adapt flexibly to the changing roles and expectations as the members of the family system grow and develop is of primary importance to healthy family functioning. This required adaptation to internal and external changes in the family and to developmental stages of individual members and the family system as a whole provides the "moments of truth" for many families. Moreover, family systems that successfully address the challenges posed during these times of change stand the best chance of healthy development. For families and family members who are accustomed to interacting in very circumscribed ways and who hold rigid expectations of behaviors of their family members, the requisite changes posed during these transitional periods can be overwhelming. The first day a child goes to school, the rebellion of the searching adolescent, the leaving home of the "almost" adult child, the constant presence of a retired spouse, and the death of family members over the years pose moments of challenge to every individual and family. Will the family break apart or pull together? Will the family member succumb to depression or find other avenues of interest and growth? How these situations are addressed will help to determine both the short-term and long-term health and adaptability of the family and its members. While many will successfully negotiate these challenges to their satisfaction, others may continue to struggle to find their way. These latter families are the ones most likely to present for treatment as they find the struggle to adapt and cope overwhelming. In light of the fact that families are morphogenic in nature (i.e., constantly changing), the ability to cope provides the opportunity to develop in functionally effective ways.

FAMILY COMMUNICATION

Communication within a family system is of major importance to daily family operations and maintenance. All behavior transmits an interpersonal message, and each communication, either verbal or nonverbal, has two functions: the first, to provide information, feelings, and opinions; the second, to develop a relationship. This function of communication dictates how the information is to be interpreted and, consequently, defines the relationship between the individuals or system members communicating. Families develop stable relationships among members through mutual agreement and the development of family rules.

Family rules may be implicit and/or explicit as they organize family interaction and maintain a stable system by defining and limiting member's behavior (Watzlawick, Beavin, & Jackson, 1967). These family rules provide for the establishment and maintenance of role expectations for each family member and subsystem, the definition of acceptable and nonacceptable behaviors and actions, and the provision for positive or negative consequences for behaviors. Because of these rules, families tend to interact in repetitious ways, as interactions are governed by a small set of patterned and predictable rules. Watzlawick, Beavin, and Jackson (1967) refer to this repetitive nature of family interaction as the redundancy principle. In the therapeutic venture, clinicians attempt to assist the family in gaining awareness of these patterned interactions and alter the rules upon which these behaviors and expectations have been developed.

CHANGE ORDER

The systemic concepts just presented imply that there is stability to family systems, and that the system is maintained by the interactions of the members of the family. When problems develop within a family, members often attempt changes that are called first-order changes—they attempt to bring about change through solutions that include nagging, fussing, criticizing, and threatening. A first-order change attempt is exemplified by using a specific behavioral intervention to encourage change. A second-order change attempt, on the other hand, goes beyond the behavioral change intervention to address the nature of the interaction of the people involved. So, whereas fussing or nagging may be seen as first-order change, second-order change would involve identifying options that underlie change, that are more active and less verbal. To withhold privileges or pleasures, without argument or discussion, and a shift in who is responsible for carrying out the planned realignment within the family in response to inappropriate behavior would be examples.

GLOBAL ASSUMPTIONS ABOUT TREATING FAMILIES

Beavers and Hampson (1990) posited a number of assumptions regarding the treatment of families. These assumptions alert the clinician to possible pitfalls that may inhibit the successful completion of the therapeutic process. First, diagnosing the typology of a family is not as important as assessing the systematic qualities of relationships, communications, and exchanges within each family system. Every family system is unique, and to simply imply that all stepfamilies, single-parent families, multigenerational families, biological families, same-gender parent families, or intercultural families are alike and, therefore, experience the same problems overlooks the specific, idiosyncratic nature of each family—with their unique history, context, and mode of operations. Second, family competence ranges along a continuum from healthy functioning to severely dysfunctional. The clinician must assume that each family system has the potential for growth and adaptation. If the family does not have the ability to grow and change, then there would be no purpose to therapy. Third, families at the same point on the family competence continuum may have different styles of relating. To be healthy within the family system, families must balance and shift their functional styles as they are faced with varying developmental changes. Fourth, successful therapy involves understanding *this* family and subtly altering characteristics and rules that have exacerbated the family's dysfunction. The therapist joins the family and attempts to be the catalyst for its growth. Fifth, a successful therapist appreciates the hierarchical structure of interacting systems within and surrounding the family. Ignoring or failing to recognize these influences at any level from the intrapersonal through the larger social network will result in an ineffective therapeutic venture. Sixth, individual treatment for relationship problems is often ineffective and complicating; thus, interventions that emphasize the interactional nature of humn and family development may prove to be the most effective—although sometimes most complicated—form of therapeutic intervention.

CHARACTERISTICS OF HEALTHY FAMILIES

All family therapists view families in terms of interactions and relationships and focus on the system of the family. Clinicians perceive families along a continuum of healthy to unhealthy, and the determination of unhealthiness is generally based upon how effectively—or ineffectively—the family system functions to assist the family members individually and the family as a whole in accomplishing its goals. The concept of healthy family functioning is mostly hypothetical and abstract, with little empirical validation. However, in 1990, a group of family experts (Krysan, Moore, & Zill) identified nine characteristics of a strong, healthy family. These characteristics included:

* adaptability,
* a commitment to family (including individual members and the family as a unit),
* communication that is clear, open, and frequent,
* encouragement of individuals by providing both a feeling of belonging and support for their individual development,
* expression of appreciation,
* religious/spiritual orientation (but no consensus on what specific aspects of religion are important),
* social connectedness, which makes external resources available for adapting and coping,
* clear—yet flexible—roles, and
* shared time of sufficient quantity and quality.

Minuchin (1974) stated that healthy families have a strong family organization that is flexible enough to change, yet rigid enough to know who is in charge. Ultimately, the determination of healthy versus unhealthy family systems is based on how the family deals with problems. To this end, Minuchin and other family theorists are in agreement. Additional discussions of healthy families, as depicted by each theoretical model, are presented in later chapters.

THERAPIST CHARACTERISTICS

As in all therapy, certain characteristics of the clinician seem to contribute to the success of the therapeutic relationship and effective change on the part of clients (Fleischman, Horne, & Arthur, 1983; Horne & Sayger, 1990). Among these characteristics are:

- warmth and genuine concern,
- an unconditional regard for each member of the client family and the family as a whole,
- respect for the family's struggles and attempted solutions,
- encouragement and belief in the family's ability to successfully resolve their concerns and develop effective coping strategies,
- recognizing the value of utilizing and modeling a sense of humor in a respectful manner to assist the family in seeing the lighter side of their predicament and modeling that there is still room for laughter and joy in the family,
- being optimistic about the family's potential,
- being skillful in the exercise of therapeutic interventions, and
- being flexible and adaptive in the therapeutic endeavor, as seldom will events transpire as predicted. (Carlson & Lewis, 1991; Smith, 1991)

In summary, the successful therapist is characterized by the ability to listen in a supportive, caring manner and to provide the family with the encouragement to change, a sense that they are understood, and motivation to be hopeful.

CORE SKILLS

The competent implementation of core therapeutic skills is necessary in conducting any kind of therapy, and family therapy is no exception. These skills include rapport building, information gathering, information giving, structuring, reflecting content and feelings, summarizing, self-disclosure, confrontation, interpretation, behavior change, closure, dealing with resistance, tracking and determining patterns and sequences, and labeling and relabeling (Carlson, Sperry, & Lewis, 1997; Fennell & Weinhold, 1997).

- *Rapport building.* From the moment of the first telephone call to the final session of the therapeutic experience, the therapist is in the process of building a relationship with clients. Concern and interest, along with a positive interpersonal style, contribute to the building of rapport. A firm handshake, a pleasant smile, and the ability to communicate genuinely with the client family are the basic building blocks. In preparing the client family for successful therapy, the therapist attempts to appropriately normalize the family's concerns, accept the fact that all family members are doing the best they can (even though they must learn new ways of interacting), and make contact with each family member to communicate that each perspective on the family's concern is important. This is often referred to as "joining with the family."

- *Information gathering and giving*. The communication of information is a two-way street. The therapist tries to determine what each family member does, thinks, and feels; how they interact and communicate with each other; and how each sees the problem affecting him or her as well as what level of responsibility each is willing to own for the current patterns of interaction. Ultimately, the initial session must allow for all family members to have a chance to "tell their story" about what they believe is happening within their family system. The therapist must inform the family of what is acceptable and unacceptable behavior within session, what is the purpose of therapy, how the therapist will be working with them, what expectations the therapist holds for the family's participation, what the legal and ethical limits of therapy are, and reimbursement. Often the therapist will provide information regarding normal developmental tasks and expectations or obtain information about ways in which the family has addressed similar family concerns in the past.

- *Structuring*. Structuring the therapy interaction varies from theory to theory; however, it is important for the family to understand how the sessions will be structured and what will be expected of them. How long will sessions last? How many sessions will there be? Who will be expected to attend? This often includes serving as a stage director who provides directives to the family, hypothesizing about the problem and encouraging the family to identify steps necessary to solve the problem.

- *Reflecting content and feelings*. Communicating empathically is an underlying requirement for all forms of therapy. Being able to communicate to the client that you (the therapist) understand what is happening in the family's world and how that affects their feelings toward themselves and others is the first step in the helping process. Reflections must be able to tie together the emotional experience of the family with the actual events in their life, and to do this the therapist must be able to listen accurately and communicate to the family what is heard.

- *Summarizing*. Often families in therapy are multicrisis systems and, in this environment, the therapist must be able to summarize the series of problems outlined by the family and begin the process of prioritizing which concerns may need to be the initial focus of treatment.

- *Self-disclosure*. Self-disclosure often serves the purpose of making the therapist appear more "human." Usually families perceive therapists as experts and, therefore, ascribe to them a certain amount of power and control, with the sometimes exceptions of involuntary family members who participate only under duress. In self-disclosing, the therapist can bridge this gap to demonstrate humanness to the family. Self-disclosure, however, must be used cautiously and for the purposes of helping the family address their concerns and not for the purposes of conducting therapy for the therapist's sake. A guideline to follow is to self-disclose if the therapist believes it will aid the family in better understanding and ultimately resolving their concerns.

- *Confrontation*. Learning to challenge or confront a client is often the most anxiety-producing skill that an effective therapist must learn. In pointing out client incongruencies, whether through inconsistent verbal and nonverbal expressions or responding differentially to the same question, the therapist is primarily informing the family that he or she is seeing through their story. This confrontation can be very subtle or very direct, but often individuals will respond by saying "I never thought of it that way" or "Yes, but you misunderstood." In either case, the family is placed in a position where they must rethink their story to determine what parts are true and which have been distorted either knowingly or unknowingly.

- *Interpretation*. Interpretation attempts to get at the "why" of what is happening in the family's life. This is the point at which therapists call upon their theoretical understanding of family and human development to offer a suggestion as to why things may be occurring as they are in the family system.

- *Behavior change*. The goal of all therapy is to achieve change on the part of the family system, generally manifested in new or different behavioral manifestations. This behavior change may be initiated by changing the affective or cognitive state of the family, the context of the family, or the underlying motivations of the family; yet, the ultimate goal is for the family system to interact in different and healthier ways.

- *Closure*. Closure occurs when the family and the therapist believe the goals of the intervention have been achieved for a particular session or for the therapeutic venture. If the therapist has informed the family of the treatment plan, the measurement and achievement of goals, and the expectations of the intervention strategy, then the point of closure and termination will be clear to all parties involved in the experience. Closure for individual sessions during the treatment process involves the ability to summarize the primary topics discussed, identify areas for further discussion and attention, develop and suggest a homework plan to address current interactional problems, and acknowledge the family's progress to date.

- *Dealing with resistance*. Resistance is sometimes readily apparent as the client consistently refuses to actively participate in discussions or assignments, and sometimes resistance is so subtle that it is difficult to detect—as in the case of the family who agrees to everything but does little or nothing. Resistance can be most effectively addressed if the therapist understands what motivates it. Families may resist because they simply do not understand or agree with the suggested assignment, but defer to the "expert" instead of openly disagreeing. If the problem is one of understanding, then the therapist must review the task with the family until he or she is sure that the family understands. If the resistance still occurs, then it is likely that the family is resisting because they do not agree with the assigned task. In this case, the therapist must always remember to ask the family what they believe needs to be done and openly discuss the advantages and disadvantages of each alternative. Therapists and families are sometimes too quick to agree on a plan of action before they have looked at all of the alternatives and the benefits and consequences of each.

- *Tracking and determining patterns and sequences*. The therapist looks for sequential patterns of behavior in the family. Observing the family in action is the most effective method of viewing the ways in which the family structures their interaction. Families have well-defined and mutually accepted family patterns of interacting that can either lead to the continuation of ineffective functioning or be the groundwork for developing healthy functioning. In the process of tracking the family's patterns and sequences, the therapist is in a position to identify patterns that exacerbate the problems expressed by the family and sequences that aid in healthy functioning in some areas of family interaction. In tracking patterns and sequences, the therapist should be aware of who responds to which questions, who follows up on that response, what are the nonverbal signals being sent by other family members when one is talking, who aligns with whom, who seems to hold the power and control, who mindreads or speaks for others, and whose suggestion is ultimately adopted by the family, either in support or protest.

• *Labeling and relabeling.* Using terms to help family members understand the problem can be very helpful, though sometimes difficult to accept. In working with children who are high-rate stealers, for example, it is often necessary to label the behavior: "When you take other people's property, that is stealing. People who do that are called stealers." This is particularly useful with families who are in denial about internal problems. Another use of the process is to relabel in order to provide a more positive meaning. For example the "nagging mother" may be relabeled as "caring," and "anger blowouts" may be relabeled "desired attention" in order to provide a more positive connotation. At times, parents are encouraged to think of their adolescent child's behavior as "practicing for independence" rather than defiance and insolence.

INTERVENTION TECHNIQUES

Intervention may take many different forms and levels. It is generally assumed that while some families may be resistant and oppositional, many are not. Therefore it is often best to start with an approach that is straightforward and direct. Give instruction and directives to those families who lack the knowledge or understanding of how to be more effective in family roles. This psychoeducational approach is often beneficial to a large number of families. On the other hand, for those who are more resistant to change, more elaborate and involved approaches are needed.

Some authors (Seaburn, Landau-Stanton, & Horwitz, 1995) have categorized family therapy interventions into four categories: here-and-now, transgenerational, ecosystemic, and integrative. Although there is some differential employment of these according to theoretical model (i.e., structural, strategic, and transgenerational therapies look the most similar), the following techniques are fairly common across most major theoretical approaches.

TRANSGENERATIONAL INTERVENTIONS

Transgenerational interventions incorporate the work of therapy pioneers who addressed family dynamics across several generations; they generally held a background in psychodynamic theory. The past is seen as operating in the present.

The marital and parenting patterns of the presenting family are seen to have been heavily influenced by each parent's family of origin. Therefore, the gathering of information about the family of origin and relationships that each person today has with those of the past is important and serves as a starting point for therapy in the present.

1. *Genogram:* The genogram is an interview process with the family that is designed to develop an understanding of the family tree or family of origin. In the process, the therapist interviews the family to understand who has been, and currently is, in the family, what the lines of descent are, and what important events occurred at what points in the lives of the people (marriage, divorce, birth of children, leaving for war, and so on). Used early in therapy, the multigeneration genogram reveals the family's structure, demographics, functioning, patterns, and relationships, and serves the purpose of aiding both the therapist and the family to see the interconnectedness of family members, and to understand the multigenerational transmission of family values and beliefs. Generally, the therapist uses a form to assist in gathering the information. The genogram is most closely associated with the work of Murray Bowen, but has been adopted by nearly all of the current theoretical approaches (Bowen, 1989; Hall, 1991; McGoldrick & Gerson, 1985).

2. *Trips home:* Trips home literally means returning to the childhood home and spending time with family members, friends, and neighbors, and reestablishing contact with the home of origin. It involves interviewing family members and attempting to develop a rapprochement with parents and other relatives, as well as developing a context of understanding for how the past has influenced the present. Trips home assists the family members in gaining a better understanding of the behaviors, thoughts, and feelings that each brings to his or her new family system from the family of origin. Often family members will get in touch with feelings of disempowerment, connectedness, or disconnectedness, which impact their behavior in their present-day families. Trips home is associated with the work of James Framo (1992) and the family-of-origin therapy approach.

3. *Inclusion of extended family into treatment:* The belief that events from past generations and history impact current patterns of interacting may lead the therapist to invite extended family members into the treatment session or therapy process. This intervention allows the client to address unresolved issues with other family members within the safety and confines of the therapeutic endeavor. Also, in many cultural groups, the extended family is an integral part of the current family functioning and should not be overlooked in the therapeutic venture (Boyd-Franklin, 1989; Koss-Chioino & Vargas, 1992). Often grandparents are rearing grandchildren with the parent in the household, aunts and uncles may reside in the same home, or other family members in close proximity may bear great influence on the family in treatment.

4. *Symbolic inclusion of family of origin:* In situations where family members are deceased or geographically distant, the therapist may include them symbolically to accentuate their influence on the current family system. This task may be accomplished by an empty-chair technique consistent with gestalt approaches, a psychodramatic play, or a role play within the family session. Again, unresolved issues with the family of origin may be addressed as families better understand the emotional, behavioral, contextual, and cognitive impact of their respective families of origin on their current interactions.

5. *Family floor plan:* A family floor plan can provide information regarding the family of origin or the current family system. A family floor plan of the family of origin provides transgenerational information about family structure, patterns of communication, systems of conflict, and those included or excluded across the generations. A family floor plan for the current family system can reveal rules, subsystems, boundaries, level of cohesion, and the general structure and organization of the family in treatment.

HERE-AND-NOW INTERVENTIONS

The primary focus is on the present rather than the past, and that attention needs to be paid to the value of emotional expression as a part of the growth process of the individuals in the family and the family unit itself. There is a belief that family and social needs may cause individuals to suppress their individuality and self expression in order to "get along" in the family, but that in doing so they lose personal integrity and do not become fully known to the other members of the family. There is often a restricted range of emotional expression in the family, resulting in family members not being able to express themselves or seek the love and relationships they need.

1. *Reframing:* Reframing provides a perceptual shift for the family and is used to join with the family and offer different perspectives on old or recurring problems (Fisch, Weakland, & Segal, 1985; Madanes, 1984; Minuchin, 1984; Minuchin & Fishman, 1981). Specifically, reframing involves cognitively taking something out of its logical class and placing it in another category (Sherman & Fredman, 1986). By offering alternative explanations for behaviors or outcomes to the explanations the family has previously held, such as providing a positive connotation (Milan School) for what has usually been perceived negatively, or by ascribing noble intentions to what has previously been considered offensive, family members may develop a different mindset or understanding of the behavior. Reframing reinterprets the problem or symptom. For example, a child who nags a parent for attention may be seen by the parent as purposefully being a nuisance and a problem child, whereas a reframe may demonstrate to the parent that attention is important to the child as a way of showing love. Suggesting or creating a new meaning to old behaviors may produce new behaviors that are associated with the new meaning. In reframing a new understanding of the problem, a term such as "distant" becomes "pain or sorrow" and "left out" becomes "insecure." Family therapists must understand how the specific reframe will facilitate family change; thus, the reframe should have some truth in it and fit the situation of the client. Reframing is an experiment to develop a different view of the world and, as such, the therapist should try several scenarios and experiment to find a reframe that rings true for the family. Understanding that symptoms serve a purpose in the family system, reframing can place problems (intentions, motives, behaviors) in less severe light and provide a perception of more control over change and a more positive desire to change. Reframing addresses both family rigidity within the context of normal occurrences in the family's life-cycle stage and the prior developments associated to the symptom, and assists the therapist to avoid imposing shame and guilt while providing multiple, alternative views and creating hope.

2. *Tracking:* Listening intently and recording events and sequences related to the family's experience of the presenting problem helps the family and therapist gain insight into the day-to-day sequences of interaction within the family system. Does the presenting problem or other problems within the family result from the same circular or spiral sequence of events, or do the sequences vary according to the time, place, and people involved?

3. *Communication skill building:* Improving family communication may include teaching listening techniques, instruction in how to fight fair, assertiveness training, or the specific dos and don'ts of communicating effectively (Haley, 1987). Respecting personal space, maintaining appropriate eye contact, speaking one's piece, using "I" messages, being brief and clear, checking out that others are listening and finding out what they are thinking, asking questions when confused, demonstrating that one is listening, and stopping to let others know when communication is breaking down are important aspects of sending and receiving communication effectively. Open and effective communication is compromised when family members communicate via putdowns, blaming, denial, defensiveness, mind reading, sidetracking, talking for others, withholding, or giving up.

4. *Family sculpting:* Family sculpting is associated with the work of Virginia Satir (1983) and attempts to recreate the family system through the physical, visual representation of relationships to one another within the family at a particular point in time. The family members are asked to create a tableau or visual sculpture using themselves as the subjects, positioned in ways that represent their view of family interactions and dynamics. This is an effective strategy for uncovering different perspectives on the environment within the family system and how those within the system view its impact on their lives. It is also a useful and alternative form of expression for families or family members who are not as capable of articulating their experiences verbally.

5. *Family photos:* Sharing family photos can be an uplifting experience for families attempting to recapture a time in their lives when they were happy and involved in joyful activities. Photos can also create an opportunity for the family to discuss past events, which may have been traumatic or otherwise painful. Ultimately, the use of family photos provides information on the present and past functioning of the family systems as well as verbal recollections of different points in time and nonverbal information with regard to who is more actively participating in the family's life.

6. *Individual and team feedback:* The use of one-way mirrors and telephones is a common practice in the training of family therapists. Often the therapist working with a family may find it difficult to track the numerous interactions or nuances of the family's functioning. The use of a team—a group of therapists and therapists-in-training who observe the interactions via a one-way mirror—with the consent of the family, to provide immediate input may assist the therapist in intervening more efficiently to assist the family in achieving their goal of change (Burbatti & Formenti, 1988).

7. *Special days/outings, gift giving:* Many times families have forgotten how to have fun together, and suggesting that the family or a subsystem of the family spend some special time together in an activity that is fun for both may rekindle the positive feelings each has for the other. The therapist might suggest that the parents go out on a date, that the family go to the zoo, that the children spend a

weekend with extended family members, or that someone prepare a special meal as a gift. All of these suggestions provide opportunities for families to break the cycle of negative interaction, at least for as short period of time, and replace the painful times with caring activities of shared enjoyment.

8. *Contracting:* Contracts may be verbal or written, but they require a certain level of specificity so that those entering into the contract will know exactly what they will be getting and expected to give. The contracts may be between therapist and family: "I will meet with you weekly to review your progress and identify ways in which you may increase the positive ways of interacting within the family. You will keep daily data sheets of how interactions are going within the family and you will agree to use no physical punishment against one another." Or the contract may be between members of the family who contract with each other for what they want or expect. The basic format for a contract is "I will . . . if you . . . ." For example, "I will wash the dishes if you dry them." Or "I will let you watch a half-hour of television later if you do your homework before dinner." Putting agreements in a contractual form can be very powerful for helping family members make commitments that are public and verifiable. The point of doing them is to specify expectations and agreements in a manner that all in the room may understand and agree to.

9. *Empty chair:* This technique places an empty seat in the room that is identified to symbolically represent another person who is not present, or to represent a part of a person who is present so that it may be addressed by the person in the session. The subject of the empty chair may be absent either through refusal (a spouse who won't come to therapy) or impossibilities (a deceased family member for whom there is unfinished business, such as anger over childhood abuse). Or the subject may be other parts of the personality when there is a dualism operating (the "Angry Andy" that most people don't see, the "Scared Sarah" who is the other side of the confident-acting young woman). This allows the client to express feelings, participate in role plays, or carry on a dialogue with family members who are not present. In addressing this unfinished business clients learn more effective ways of communicating what they feel and how they will ultimately resolve any conflict they may have with other family members or part of their persona in question.

10. *Family choreography:* This technique is an extension of family sculpting and places the family sculpture into action. A typical question for beginning the family choreography would be "Remember coming home from school as a child and walking up to the door. Open the door, walk in, and tell us what typically happened." The family members then reenact the sequence of events behaviorally to learn more adaptive patterns. Choreography offers useful information to the therapist and may suggest possible strategies for changing the current pattern of interaction. The family may even be able to relive the reenactment in a more positive, desirable sequence.

11. *Family council meetings:* Associated most closely with the Adlerian approach to family intervention, the family council is a method of bringing the family together as a whole group at least once a week to share events and concerns, and to discuss issues that impact the entire family and each of its members. This is not intended to be a gripe session, but an information-sharing and problem-solving discussion of issues that incorporates and values the opinions and thoughts of all family members.

12. *Strategic alliances:* A strategic alliance technique is utilized to attempt to disrupt the circular system and behavior pattern that is keeping the family from focusing on solutions to their concerns. A strategic alliance involves the therapist's adopting or establishing an unexpected alliance or relationship with a member of the family. Alliances may be utilized to unbalance the system in such a way that differing points of view may be heard and alternative solutions to current problems can be offered. The therapist, for example, may adopt an alliance with a disruptive teenager in front of the whole family in order to develop a supportive relationship with the teenager and to give the parents the message that they may need to be more flexible: "I guess I've got to take your side on this; your family does sound boring the way it is so highly structured and with so many rules. I can see why you've been screwing up. Can you and I talk with your parents about this to see what we can swing in terms of backing off some?"

13. *Family sociogram:* The family sociogram is a drawing that the therapist uses to illustrate and identify family roles and participation of family members in the family unit. The family sociogram can identify family members who are left out of the loop in family decision making, who may align themselves with many family members to get their own way, or who may identify themselves as outcasts in the family system to garner sympathy or control specific aspects of family functioning.

14. *Family rituals:* Family rituals add needed structure to the family system by marking important developmental milestones in the family's history, adding to the family's cohesiveness and identity, and aiding the family's adaptation to change. Often, in times of stress, families forget, or decide to forgo, family rituals that may, in fact, assist in the healthy adaptation to a traumatic event such as divorce, death, or illness, or such a landmark as graduation or birth.

15. *Paradoxical intervention:* Paradoxical intervention involves attempts to block dysfunctional sequences by using indirect and seemingly illogical means. The method has been a part of therapy going back more than 70 years and has been included within psychodynamic, behavioral, and humanistic approaches. The theme has been consistent: If one practices the symptom, it will go away. It is sometimes referred to as "prescribing the symptom" and involves encouraging attention to the symptom rather than avoiding it. There are many paradoxical interventions with the intent to alter the current pattern of interaction within the family system (DiTomasso & Greenberg, 1989; Schotte, Ascher, & Cools, 1989). Prescribing indecision, an example of a paradoxical intervention, allows the family to more clearly understand the purpose of their current difficulty in making decisions and serves in maintaining the homeostasis of the family system. Putting the client in control of the symptom, or prescribing the symptom, is another paradoxical technique, which if used under highly specified circumstances, assists clients in coming to an understanding that they can have some control over the symptom that has brought them and their family into treatment. A spouse who behaves in a depressed manner in order to attract attention from the other spouse may be told that he seems to still be having some enjoyment in life, and that to be more effective he needs to be depressed all of the time, at which point both spouses will take steps to break the depression behavioral cycle. Another example includes talking with a recalcitrant family and telling them they may be so entrenched in their interactional style that they may not be able to change

and may, instead, have to be encouraged to learn to live with the pain of the conflict (to which families rebel and prove the therapist wrong).

16. *Reenactment/enactment:* In structural family therapy (Minuchin & Fishman, 1981), these techniques are utilized to encourage the family to act out the problem (enactment) they are experiencing and then, after discussing possible changes in the interactional pattern, to act out the situation using their newly acquired understanding of the problem and alternative behaviors (reenactment). In essence, this allows for a role play of current interaction, and how the family would like it to be.

17. *Defining the problem/establishing goals and action plans/assigning tasks/directives:* To measure client progress and make sure that everyone is working toward the same outcome, it is important that the problem be clearly defined and goals that are acceptable to all family members be clearly established. Based upon this information, a plan of action can be developed to address the current patterns and sequences of behaviors within the family system that exacerbate the problems and maintain the dysfunctional system interactions. Once the problems are defined, goals are established, and a plan of action is agreed upon, the family members can then focus on the assigned tasks that will help them develop a family system that functions in everyone's best interest. Depending upon the theoretical orientation of the family therapist, these tasks may be in the form of directives or may be agreed upon and suggested by family members.

18. *Family psychoeducation:* Often family members are not aware of the overall ramifications of particular dysfunctional behavior patterns or the impact of pathology on the family system. Family therapists are in a position to educate their clients about normal developmental processes and tasks, as well as deviations from those processes. The family may need to be educated about the impact of an illness on the family system and how the family has adjusted in healthy and unhealthy ways to address the needs of an individual family member. Likewise, the therapist may need to educate the family members about symptoms and characteristics of individuals with varying pathologies and ways that the family can effectively address the needs of the individual family member, of themselves, and of the family unit as a whole.

19. *Therapist's use of self with family:* The greatest tool a therapist brings to a therapy encounter is the self of the therapist. The therapist in being genuine, open, honest, caring, empathic, and attentive can establish an environment that will help the client openly address concerns and strive for a healthy solution. The therapist must be able to both observe and participate in the process of therapy, and when appropriate, share his or her perception of the therapeutic process with the family.

20. *Metaphors/storytelling/storymaking:* Often clients will use metaphors or tell stories to make their points, and therapists often use metaphors to describe what they are hearing from the family: "Your family life sounds like running the rapids in a kayak—full of fury and excitement, but absolutely exhausting. I'm wondering, aren't you ready to go sailing for a while instead, to have a life that is calmer, more relaxed, and with less stress?" The therapist needs to pay attention to the storytelling form of communication and utilize it in the process of therapy. Clients will paint pictures of how they feel, think, and/or behave in situations, and these pictures can provide the most powerful path for intervention as the therapist uses the clients' own words to assist them in understanding all of the details of their story. The clients who feel they have truly had the opportunity to tell their story and believe it

has been heard and understood by their therapist are the clients who are most likely to continue in therapy to seek solutions to their concerns.

ECOSYSTEMIC–INTEGRATIVE INTERVENTIONS

Ecosystemic or integrative models of family therapy combine the best elements of the various models of family therapy. They go beyond the traditional models, though, in that they also incorporate diversity issues reflective of American society today: gender, race, culture, life cycle, socioeconomic status, disability, and an appreciation for the uniqueness of world view that each person may have developed. There is an assumption that any given situation may be interpreted in many and different ways, none of which may be more "correct" or "true" than others, but which may serve to provide meaning to the family members. This constructivist approach then works to develop an understanding that the family's view of the problem is the most important point to consider, not what an "objective bystander" may see as the most important element of concern. Social constructionists believe that people develop a world view through dialogues, conversations, and interactions with others, and so the meaning a person has of a situation is a function of the social process rather than an isolated internal event.

1. *Sensitivity to extrafamilial factors in the development of problems:* The therapist needs to keep in mind that the family does not function in isolation, but is impacted by a variety of sociopolitical factors including governmental decisions, the general economic structure, and issues of employment, community issues, poverty, crime, and safety—just to mention a few. All of these external forces can both impact the family's ability to cope and exacerbate the continuation of the family's problems. Attending to the role that societal impact has on the family is important and involves the sensitivity of the therapist as to what issues such as racism, gender discrimination, and other social influences contribute to the stresses the family endures. It will be necessary for a sensitive therapist to incorporate that understanding and appreciation into communications with the family, and to help the family identify resources for addressing the influences.

2. *Utilization of larger systems resources in the assessment and treatment process:* Often the therapist may need to act as the family's advocate to make sure that they are receiving all of the services available to them. The therapist may connect them with local service and government organizations that can assist the family in getting job training, food, shelter, or other resources needed to meet their basic survival needs.

ECOSYSTEMIC-INTEGRATIVE PROCESSES

1. *Hypothesizing:* Through experience and solid grounding in theoretical principles, the skilled therapist will be able to develop a number of hypotheses to explain the interactions of the family in therapy. Patterns of interaction may be common across similar disorders, and finding similarities or deviations from these

suggested patterns may lead to various hypotheses about the family's functioning and what they are trying to achieve. As clinicians become more experienced they become more aware of the nuances of family functioning and the impact of specific events and disorders. Additionally, experience with a diverse client population assists the therapist in understanding populations that are culturally unique and thus aids in the development of culturally sensitive hypotheses. As clinicians become greater consumers and producers of research, their understanding of the internal systems of families will lead to more accurate hypotheses and efficient therapeutic intervention.

2. *Questioning:* The goal of questions is to elicit information that will bring about change. In general, the therapist will gain more information by using open-ended versus closed questions; however, questioning within the realm of family therapy may also be more complex, since many members of the same system may be present during the therapy session and have different responses to the same question. For many therapists, and specifically for those adhering to the Milan School (Burbatti & Formenti, 1988), questions are used to define the problem, determine the sequence of interactions within the family system, compare and classify the family system and its concerns with regard to similar family systems, and decide upon the appropriate method and approach to intervention. In addition, questioning can be utilized to look for exceptions to the pattern of interaction (i.e., when the family uses a sequence or pattern of interaction different from those patterns that brought them into therapy) and to identify the specifics of the family's interactions (e.g., How is the family influenced by the problem? How is the problem influenced by the family? How does the conflict affect the individual family member? What does the family member do?).

3. *Use of language:* Using language that is easily understood, but not condescending to the family, is very important in the treatment process. Listening for the words that clients use and then using them as part of the therapist's communication can be an effective way of establishing a relationship with the family. The words that the client uses may also help the therapist understand which interventions might be the most effective. If a client uses feeling words, then an intervention that begins with an emphasis on emotions may be more readily received. Likewise, for clients who use thinking or doing words, cognitive and behavioral methods, respectively, might be more readily accepted. Additionally, the therapist must be sure that all family members understand what is being discussed so that they can fully participate in the process. The use of language is also critical for immigrant families in which the command of English may be marginal or completely lacking. In many families where English is a second language, the therapist, in consultation with the family, must make a decision if a referral is necessary.

4. *Joining/mapping:* Joining the family and mapping out the family system assists the therapist in establishing rapport and gaining a better understanding of who is involved in and impacting the family system. Joining the family refers to making contact with each family member, gathering information about the role and expectations of each family member in the system, and assisting the family in getting to know more about the therapist, including qualifications, experience, and competencies. Mapping refers to the process of identifying family members, both present in the session and in the household, who directly impact the family

system on a daily basis. It also provides an opportunity to identify larger systems that may impact the family, including church members and officials, extended family, school, work setting, and the like.

5. *Assessing strengths and formulating the transitional perspective (life-cycle tasks):* Families come to therapy having spent many hours, days, weeks, months, and possibly years focusing upon the negative aspects of their family systems. The effective therapist will assist the family in identifying the strengths, assets, and resources that will aid them in coping with and adapting to the life-cycle tasks experienced by most family systems.

SYNTHESIS

Tracking interactional sequences is a strategy shared by all models of family therapy and, even though the therapeutic goals may be different, the ultimate goal of changing the family system's behavior is also common to all models. Some models have a therapeutic goal to achieve structural or interactional change within the family system and are primarily interested in how the family interacts (i.e., Who speaks to whom? For whom? Who answers? Is the symptom a metaphor? How does the system maintain the symptom? What functions does the symptom serve?). Other models may focus specifically on how to alter the behavior of specific family members or to aid the client in achieving some insight into the type of bonding experienced in the family of origin and its impact on current functioning. Intervention is an attempt to interrupt or change behavioral patterns that appear to be the family's response to a presenting problem and are being perpetuated by the homeostatic nature of family systems. Families are often assigned a task or ritual to be completed inside or outside the therapy room as a maneuver during therapy to direct interaction, clarify communication, or change behavior. A family therapist who is well-grounded in theoretical understanding of family systems operations, who demonstrates the basic skills of competency expected of all clinicians, and who keeps an open mind for further learning should find clinical practice to be both successful and rewarding.

ANNOTATED SUGGESTED READINGS

Brock, G. W., & Barnard, C.P. (1999). *Procedures in marriage and family therapy* (3rd ed.). Boston: Allyn & Bacon.

> Provides an overview of assessment, initial stage, middle stage, termination, and specialized treatment procedures. Also includes procedures for challenging clinical situations, referral and consultation, and risk management.

Carlson, J., Sperry, L., & Lewis, J. A. (1997). *Family therapy: Ensuring treatment efficacy.* Pacific Grove, CA: Brooks/Cole.

> This book outlines treatment goals, processes, and techniques for the primary theoretical approaches in family therapy. Additional information is provided on working with couples, work-family concerns, families under stress, the significance of culture, relapse prevention, and models for matching treatment protocols to client needs.

Kilpatrick, A. C., & Holland, T. P. (Eds.). (1999). *Working with families: An integrative model by level of need* (2nd ed.). Boston: Allyn & Bacon.

> This book provides theoretical and contextual bases for working with families according to four levels of need including basic survival issues; issues of structure, limits, and safety; problem-focused issues; and family and personal growth issues. A discussion of structural, social learning, solution-focused, family systems, narrative, and object relations family therapy models is provided.

Mikesell, R. H., Luster, D. D., & McDaniel, S. H. (Eds.). (1995). *Integrating family therapy: Handbook of family psychology and systems theory.* Washington, DC: American Psychological Association.

> This book discusses the clinical principles of family systems therapy, developmental issues in families, assessment and research, and future directions of family psychology and systems. Other chapters include gender and ethnic issues, medical systems, couples therapy, family-work and family-school interventions, domestic violence, cults, and family treatment for alcohol and other substance abuse.

Nichols, M. P., & Schwartz, R. C. (1998). *Family therapy: Concepts and methods* (4th ed.). Boston: Allyn & Bacon.

> An overview of the major theories of family therapy is provided including theoretical formulations, perspectives on normal family development, development of psychological disorders, goals of therapy, techniques, conditions for behavior change, and current evaluation of treatment effectiveness.

REFERENCES

Beavers, W. R., & Hampson, R. B. (1990). *Successful families: Assessment and intervention.* New York: Norton.

Bowen, M. (1989). *Family therapy in clinical practice.* Northvale, NJ: Jason Aronson.

Boyd-Franklin, N. (1989). *Black families in therapy: A multisystems approach.* New York: Guilford Press.

Burbatti, G. L., & Formenti, M. D. (1988). *The Milan approach to family therapy.* Northvale, NJ: Jason Aronson.

Carlson, J. C., & Lewis, J. A. (1991). An introduction to family counseling. In J. C. Carlson & J. Lewis (Eds.), *Family counseling: Strategies and issues* (pp. 3–11). Denver: Love Publishing.

Carlson, J. C., Sperry, L., & Lewis, J. A. (1997). *Family therapy: Ensuring treatment efficacy.* Pacific Grove, CA: Brooks/Cole.

DiTomasso, R. A., & Greenberg, R. L. (1989). Paradoxical intention: The case of the case study. In L. M. Ascher (Ed.), *Therapeutic paradox* (pp. 32–89). New York: Guilford Press.

Fennell, D. L., & Weinhold, B. K. (1997). *Counseling families: An introduction to marriage and family therapy.* Denver: Love Publishing.

Fisch, R., Weakland, J. H., & Segal, L. (1985). *The tactics of change: Doing therapy briefly.* San Francisco: Jossey-Bass

Fleischman, M. J., Horne, A. M., & Arthur, J. (1983). *Troubled families: A treatment program.* Champaign, IL: Research Press.

Framo, J. L. (1992). *Family-of-origin therapy: An intergenerational approach.* New York: Brunner/Mazel.

Haley, J. (1987). *Problem-solving therapy: New strategies for effective family therapy* (2nd ed.). San Francisco: Jossey-Bass.

Hall, C. M. (1991). *The Bowen family theory and its uses.* Northvale, NJ: Jason Aronson.

Horne, A. M., & Sayger, T. V. (1990). *Treating conduct and oppositional defiant disorders in children.* New York: Pergamon Press.

Koss-Chioino, J. D., & Vargas, L. A. (1992). Through the cultural looking glass: A model for understanding culturally responsive psychotherapies. In L. A. Vargas & J. D. Koss-Chioino (Eds.), *Working with culture: Psychotherapeutic interventions with ethnic minority children and adolescents* (pp. 1–22). San Francisco: Jossey-Bass.

Krysan, M., Moore, K. A., & Zill, N. (1990). *Identifying successful families: An overview of constructs and selected measures.* Washington, DC: Child Trends.

Madanes, C. (1984). *Strategic family therapy.* San Francisco: Jossey-Bass.

McGoldrick, M., & Gerson, R. (1985). *Genograms in family assessment.* New York: Norton.

Minuchin, S. (1974). *Family and family therapy.* Cambridge, MA: Harvard University Press.

Minuchin, S. (1984). *Family kaleidoscope.* Cambridge, MA: Harvard University Press.

Minuchin, S., & Fishman, H. C. (1981). *Family therapy techniques.* Cambridge, MA: Harvard University Press.

Satir, V. (1983). *Conjoint family therapy.* Palo Alto, CA: Science and Behavior Books.

Schotte, D. E., Ascher, L. M., & Cools, J. (1989). The use of paradoxical intention in behavior therapy. In L. M. Ascher (Ed.), *Therapeutic paradox* (pp. 17–31). New York: Guilford Press.

Seaburn, D., Landau-Stanton, J., & Horwitz, S. (1995). Core techniques in family therapy. In R. H. Mikesell, D. D. Luster, & S. H. McDaniel (Eds.), *Integrating family therapy: Handbook of family psychology and systems theory* (pp. 5–26). Washington, DC: American Psychological Association.

Sherman, R., & Fredman, N. (1986). *Handbook of structured techniques in marriage and family therapy.* New York: Brunner/Mazel.

Smith, R. L. (1991). Marital and family therapy: Direction, theory, and practice. In J. C. Carlson & J. Lewis (Eds.), *Family counseling: Strategies and issues* (pp. 13–34). Denver: Love Publishing.

von Bertalanffy, L. (1968). *General systems theory: Foundations, development, application.* New York: Braziller.

Walsh, F. (1982). Conceptualizations of normal family functioning. In F. Walsh (Ed.), *Normal family processes* (pp. 3–42). New York: Guilford Press.

Walsh, W. M. (1991). *Case studies in family therapy: An integrated approach.* Boston: Allyn & Bacon.

Watzlawick, P., Beavin, J., & Jackson, D. D. (1967). *Pragmatics of human communication.* New York: Norton.

CHAPTER 4

The Therapist and Family Therapy

Satir's Human Validation Process Model

VIRGINIA M. SATIR AND JAMES ROBERT BITTER

INTRODUCTION

Virginia M. Satir was one of the early pioneers in family therapy. She began working with families when it was considered by many in the helping professions to be a waste of time or even a detriment to clients. As a pioneer in a clinical field dominated by men as well as by therapeutic notions that pertained mostly to the individual, she worked with the families of schizophrenics, hospitalized patients, and other people who were extremely hard to help. Satir used her personal presence and touch, an absolute faith in human potential, a penchant for detective work, a unique communication model, and an understanding of systems shared by very few. And she was successful, making a difference in the growth of thousands of families all over the world.

A creative seeker and visionary, Satir moved with the courage and determination of the profoundly and happily unorthodox. She liked to think of herself as a "homemade" family therapist, because she had no formal training in family therapy. In the process of a life of discovery, Satir suggested that she simply "stumbled" on the possibility of working with the family as a treatment unit. To be sure, Satir was a role model for countless women in the helping professions. Indeed, she was a role model for all people who believed in the power of human contact and who, like herself, were more impressed with the potential for human health than the presence of human pathology.

Toward the end of her life, Satir dedicated much of her time and energy to promoting peace. The connected harmony that she knew was possible in families was a metaphor for the peace she sought in the world. She believed that people centered in personal congruence and connected to others who were at peace with themselves could change a planet.

In July 1988, she had just returned from a month of training seminars in the former Soviet Union; as she started her summer institute in Colorado, she became severely ill and was diagnosed with cancer of the pancreas and liver. Satir died September 10, 1988. She died as she had lived—at peace with herself and the world and full of wonder about all the possibilities in human life.

This chapter extends the original material Satir presented in the first edition of this text (Horne & Ohlsen, 1982) and adds some important material missing in the second edition (Horne & Passmore, 1991). While change and rearrangement are inevitable, every effort has been made to stay faithful to Satir's beliefs, values, and therapeutic approach. Where possible, her model is presented in her own words, as it was in the original text.

DEFINITION

Virginia Satir used a number of different names to define her therapeutic approach, each one reflecting a slightly different emphasis in her work. When she first published *Conjoint Family Therapy* (Satir, 1964), her emphasis was on making connections with and within families. She believed that an individual's self-esteem could be accessed through a supportive, nonjudgmental therapist's presence. It was the therapist's first task to reconnect people to the self-esteem inherent in the acknowledgment of their personal resources. Satir used her understanding of communication and metacommunication to help family members join with each other in the tasks of building a life together. Each connection added a piece to the whole and opened up possibilities that were blocked in the individual or the system. Therapeutic connections were the foundation of her work with families.

When Satir integrated posturing, sculpture, and movement into her therapy, the drama of families-in-change took center stage. She began to call her work "process therapy" (Satir, 1982), which highlights the dynamics of family interaction in a series of dramatic pictures—the system in the process of growth and evolution. Like a nurturing director of a play, the therapist is a guide, a leader in the process of change. The therapist and the family join forces to promote wellness. In Satir's model, the personhood of the therapist is more important than specific intervention skills. Therapists do not "cure" people or make change happen; they are process leaders in charge of the therapeutic experience, not the people in the experience.

During the last 10 years of her life, Satir wanted to emphasize the importance of nurturing the self-worth of people involved in the process of change. She began to call her work the "human validation process model" (Satir & Baldwin, 1983; Satir & Bitter, 1991; Satir, Banmen, Gerber, & Gomori, 1991). She knew that she would encounter individuals and families who were experiencing pain and difficulty, but her focus was on wellness and growth. Therapy proceeded from all of the confirming and validating interactions and transactions, translated into methods and procedures, that moved the individuals in the family as well as the family system from a symptomatic base toward one of wellness.

Satir knew that all systems were balanced. The question is: What price does each part of the system pay to keep it so? The rules governing a family system are derived from the ways parents maintain personal self-esteem and, in turn, form the context within which children grow and develop their own self-esteem. Communication and self-worth are the basic components of a family system and the building blocks of the human validation process model.

HISTORICAL DEVELOPMENT

PRECURSORS

Satir's early clinical training was essentially based on Freud's psychoanalysis. While she retained parts of this model (e.g., an acceptance of unconscious process in human behavior and defense mechanisms), she rejected its essence from the start of her professional work. Freud's emphasis on intrapsychic dysfunction and a deterministic model of pathology was essentially at odds with Satir's belief in human potential and human growth. While there is no evidence that Satir ever studied the approaches of Adler or Jung during her early training, later reviews noted parallels in her techniques to Adler's holistic orientation (Bitter, 1987, 1988, 1993) and the integrative possibilities with Jung's dynamic theory (Dodson, 1977).

Satir created her model largely from her phenomenal ability to learn from experience. Like all pioneers, she was charting unexplored territory, and she had to create a map at the same time that she entered the unknown. Undoubtedly, she was also influenced by some of her fellow travelers—contemporaries forging change in therapeutic process and conceptualization.

The similarity of Satir's emphasis on the power of congruent communication to the work of Carl Rogers (1980; Kirschenbaum & Henderson, 1989) is obvious. In addition, both of these practitioners shared a belief in the importance of the fully functional and fully human person as therapist.

Satir's systems approach with families developed separately from, but at the same time as, the methodology of Murray Bowen (1990). Gregory Bateson (1972, 1979) and Don Jackson (1968; Lederer & Jackson, 1968), however, had the most direct influences on her conceptualization and utilization of systems theory in therapy.

During her life, Satir interacted with a wide range of therapists and thinkers who contributed to her growth and to the development of her model. Among them were Fritz Perls (gestalt therapy); Eric Berne (transactional analysis); J. L. Moreno (psychodrama); Ida Rolf (life-posturing reintegration); Alexander Lowen (bioenergetics); Milton Erickson (hypnosis); Hans Selye (stress); and several New

Age theorists and practitioners (Satir, 1982). In turn, most of these people knew and were influenced by Satir, thus fostering a cross-fertilization of thought and process that changed the frontier of therapy. Also, as always, experience was her guide in the discovery of meaning.

Satir's development was a quest. It was always at once a person-to-person pursuit and a world-transforming mission to her. It is a story told best in her own words (Satir, 1982, pp. 13–22).

Long before I had professional training, I had to work my way up from being a child. When I was five, I decided to become a children's detective on parents. There was so much that went on between my parents that made little or no sense to me. Making sense of things around me, feeling loved, and being competent were my paramount concerns. I did feel loved, and felt I was competent, but making sense of all the contradictions, deletions, and distortions I observed both in my parents' relationship and among people outside in the world was heart-rending and confusion-making to me. Sometimes this situation raised questions about my being loved, but mostly it affected my ability to predict, to see clearly, and to develop my total being.

Becoming a detective meant becoming an observer. Naturally, I put all the clues I had together to make the best wholeness I could. This was my reality. The human brain has to make sense of what is going on, even if it is nonsense. In those days, faithful to the format of detective stories, I needed to find out who was the "bad guy," to catch the person, then punish him or her, and subsequently bring about reform. Sometimes the culprit would be me, or one or both of my parents.

I was curious about everything, including those things I was "too young for," or that "weren't for girls." Accordingly, I developed a capacity for storing secrets, presumably without giving any clues. I loved school, was an insatiable reader, and got "very high" on ideas, particularly on knowing how things work, and what made things what they were.

Every once in a while, I would put words to some of my observations, and would tell my parents about their behavior. I got varying reactions: dismay, shame, amusement, surprise, or sometimes silence. I never knew what went into each variation. The same oral observation would get different reactions from each parent at different times. I handled this by making jokes, behaving as if I were deaf and dumb, and, many times, I behaved as though I had my attention elsewhere. I had twin brothers, 18 months younger than myself, who were quite useful in this regard.

Somewhere there was a whole world (inside human beings) that I meant to investigate. I felt a deep connection with all children. They were my troops. They were my focus. I was nearly 30 years old before it dawned on me that all adults were just children grown big. If they hadn't learned anything since childhood, they would still be doing childish things. This bit of insight helped me to understand adults a lot better.

The natural thing for me "when I grew up" was to be a teacher of grade school children. My education to become a teacher taught me about how children learn (learning theory), gave me a special appreciation and respect for the human capacity, and provided some inklings about the influence of parents on children. I was fortunate to have a group of very gifted and very human instructors who inspired me to continue to observe, listen, and draw my own conclusions. At this point, I enlarged my scope of understanding. These instructors helped me to keep a nonjudgmental attitude toward human beings. I felt like a humanistic scientist in the laboratory of children's lives.

I wanted to be a "real live" expert on children instead of an "armchair expert," so I arranged my six years of teaching experience in five different schools which were in different economic and social groups in widely scattered geographical areas. Some children were physically and mentally handicapped. Some were gifted. Some were racially different, and some were the so-called "average" children.

When I started teaching, it seemed natural to me that, if I wanted to help children, I needed to know their parents. So I proceeded to visit one child's home every evening after school. This home visitation program helped me develop strong bonds with over 200 families during those six years.

Armed with a little more intellectual understanding from my undergraduate training, my observations became more focused. Through my contacts with individual family members, I soon began to put two and two together. For example, there was one youngster who seemed listless and uninterested in school and who looked like he needed help. When I got to know the family, I found that they were night owls. Everyone else could sleep late in the morning, but this lad had to get up early. I arranged a nap time for him and shared the situation with the family who then used their resources to help out. I know now that my nonjudgmental and human feelings drew them to helping me so I could help them. With their help, I was a better teacher to this little boy, and he was a better student with all of us helping.

…What I was learning at this early stage was that:

1. Parents can be assets to their children if we know how to enlist their help;
2. If children have problems, something is going on in the family or has happened in the past which affects the child;
3. Difficult problems can be solved if we trust that they can and if we create a trusting atmosphere and work at gaining access to the necessary human resources.

My detective work was giving me more pieces, but I still didn't understand how they fit together. I knew that success had something to do with what goes on inside people as well as outside. I heard about something called social work, where one could learn about people's insides. I made plans, after two years of teaching, to enter summer sessions, and four years later entered as a full-time student. I then got caught up in the excitement of pathology, and essentially forgot what I had learned about the growing potential in people.

In graduate school, I learned about the world existing within people, and especially about something I interpreted as drives within ourselves that become powerful factors in our behavior. Since these drives are out of our awareness, they are also out of our control, as well as our understanding. In social work school, I learned intellectually about these "pathological" parts. I learned also that to help someone necessitated having rapport and investigating feelings, really a new intellectual concept to me. All of this was very exciting.

Prior to and following my graduation, for about 10 years, I worked with delinquent girls in a setting where I followed the same course I had in teaching school—that is, I attempted to get in touch with the girls' families. This job wasn't so "clinical." There were many who were listed as having either no parents at all, or mothers but no fathers. It seemed important to find out who and where their parents were. I played detective again, and I discovered the whereabouts of most of the parents, some of whom were still living, and some who had already died. In the cases where the parents were dead, I took the girls to the cemetery. The search for the parents brought me in contact with the very, very ugly part of life—mental hospitals, dirty rooming houses, death under horrible circumstances, poverty, neglect, morgues, hospitals. Regardless of all that, I had hope for everyone. I set about trying to reach the "little self-worths" in each person, which by now I knew, without any question, were present. Most of the time I succeeded in not only helping the girls, but their parents too. I could enlist their help in their own behalf as well as that of their children.

I had developed a profound and unshakable belief that each human can grow. After 42 years, that belief is stronger than ever. My search is to learn how to touch it and show it to people so they can use it for themselves. That was, and still remains, the primary goal in my work. It means a special tailoring for each situation. I came to learn, upon starting clinical work, that that kind of detective work was called "diagnosis." What I had learned about awakening the hope in people was called "developing motivation."

In clinical work, I learned the psychiatric nomenclature. I could "diagnose" with confidence. This meant that I was "professional." It enabled me to talk "professionally" with my colleagues as well as to write impressive reports. It, however, did not always result in helping people very much.

Frequently, I felt that I was doing some kind of "name calling" when I diagnosed. My profession seemed to require it. The things in my clinical work that I was trained to look at were all negative. My sense told me that somewhere there had to be something positive. I certainly wasn't putting anything into anyone. I reached a point where I got a twinge every time I wrote a clinical diagnosis. It gradually dawned on me that it was because I was looking at only part of the picture. I began to understand why I felt so overwhelmed. I could not treat someone whom I labeled "paranoid" or "schizophrenic"; I could, however, help someone who felt empty and useless. It was the same person. By viewing that person as a person instead of a category, I could relate, and things would happen.

…In 1951, at the urging of a close psychiatrist friend, I went into private practice. Now I was on the firing line. Being nonmedical, there was no liability insurance nor third-party payments for me. If I were to survive financially, I needed to get results; and if I were to survive professionally, I had to do it without making people worse, or even more scary, having my patients threaten to commit suicide.

To compound the situation, the people who initially found their way to me were either people whom no one else would touch or people who were "long-time alcoholics," "chronic schizophrenics," extremely dependent, or who had undergone treatment from others who had given up on them; they were all high risk.

Two things happened. First, knowing that all the classical treatment regimes had been tried, I realized that there was no point in my repeating them. I laid aside, for the time being my "clinical professional self," and went back to my detective work of former years. Being a detective brought me back to observing, listening, and looking for health. Then one day, the second thing happened. After I had worked for six months successfully with a young girl who had been labeled "an ambulatory schizophrenic," I was called by her mother who threatened to sue me for "alienation of affection." That day, somehow, I heard two messages in her statement—a plea from her expressed in her voice tone, and a threat in her words. I responded to the plea and invited her in.

To my surprise, she agreed. I had been taught that she wasn't supposed to do that. When she came to join her daughter, lo and behold, the daughter was back at square one. When I got over my shock, I again began to observe and saw what I later came to know as the nonverbal cueing system, part of the double-level message phenomenon. This was the beginning of my Communication Theory (Satir, 1976, 1983, 1988; Satir & Baldwin, 1983). It became clear that words were one thing, and that body language was something else.

Eventually, it occurred to me that the mother might have a husband and the girl, a father. I inquired. (In child guidance practice, fathers were excluded. Women had charge of the family.) There was a father, and he was still living. I extended an invitation to the wife and daughter to have the husband-father join. They agreed, and he came. Now I was privy to a new phenomenon. Mother and daughter had been doing well. With father's coming, a very different drama unfolded. I was now dealing with what I later came to know as the primary survival triad. This is now a conceptual cornerstone of my work. We all start life in a triad. The way this primary triad is lived is what gives us our identity. Somehow it had been assumed and seemed to be taken for granted everywhere that a triad had to be potentially destructive. The best one could hope for was to manipulate it so that it was benevolent rather than malevolent. I now know that this triad is the source of the destructive and/or constructive messages children receive. I know that in successful family therapy, the outcome rests on accomplishing a "nourishing triad" (see Satir & Baldwin, 1983, pp. 170–175).

Thinking back to my brothers and sisters, I wondered one day whether there were other children in the family. Upon inquiring, I found there was a brother who turned out to be the "good guy" with his sister being the sick one. I was now in touch with what later I understood to be the family system (Satir, 1983). I was to see this particular form many times in the future.

I was observing a new phenomenon and, being the detective that I am, I kept watching and listening, hoping to find some connection with previous experience. I extended the learning I gained with this family to all my other "patients." I eventually worked with people who were delinquent, alcoholic, psychotic, or handicapped, physically or mentally. I began to see different variations of the same theme. In the interest of survival, people were conforming to something that worked against them. A child would lie so mother would continue to love her; family members would say "yes" when they felt "no," and so forth.

During this period, I had a great deal of experience with people who were somaticizing. Here, I learned about the powerful link between body, mind, and feeling. The body is willing to accommodate itself to the most destructive directions issued by the mind. I began to see that the body said what the mouth denied, projected, ignored, or repressed. I saw this manifested in back problems, gastrointestinal disturbances, asthma, skin eruptions, diabetes, tuberculosis, propulsive vomiting, bedwetting, and other ailments. I also began to see that the body parts became a metaphor for psychological meaning.

It was while I was observing the body-mind-feeling phenomenon that I developed the communication stances which were later incorporated into literal body postures; placating, blaming, super-reasonable, and irrelevant (Satir, 1976, 1983). Those stances gave a vivid picture of what was going on. When I put people into certain postures, I noticed they developed much more awareness. I know now that the physical act of posturing, which I extended into sculpting, activated the right brain experience so people could feel their experience with minimal threat. They were experiencing themselves, instead of only hearing about themselves. "Awareness" could be developed.

There are now many body therapies. I believe the body records all the experience one has. When the body is postured and sculpted, the old experience returns and has a chance for a new interpretation....The body, mind, and feelings form a triad, and I began to see that if what one feels is not matched by what one says, the body responds as if it has been attacked. The result is physical dysfunction accompanied by either disturbances of emotion or thought.

I learned that I could see this discrepancy in the way people communicated with one another. I watched for the discrepancy between verbal and nonverbal levels of communication. I began to see that all nonverbal messages were a statement of the *Now*. The verbal part could come from anywhere, past, present, or future. Often this verbal component reflected the "shoulds" of the inhuman rules one had. The forms of discrepancy were manifest in (1) what one felt but could not say (inhibition); (2) what one felt but was unaware of (repression) and only reacted to in another (projection); (3) what one consciously felt, but since it did not fit the rules, one denied its existence (suppression); and (4) what one felt but ignored as unimportant (denial).

Out of the clear blue, in January 1955, I got a phone call from a man who was then a stranger to me, a Dr. Kalman Gyarfas. He was heading an innovative training program for psychiatric training. This was the forerunner of the Illinois State

Psychiatric Institute, based in Chicago. Dr. Gyarfas was interested in the relationship between identified patients and their family members, and he asked me to become an instructor in family dynamics for his residents.

By now, I had completed four years of working with families. They numbered over 300. I had been busy working with exciting ideas and had been having good results. Now to teach, I had to conceptualize what I had been doing. In doing so, I was able to clarify what I had been learning. Indeed, as I taught it, I also learned more about what I meant, and I became aware of the glaring gaps in my theoretical base.

Dealing with the psychiatric residents' experiences and their questions helped me greatly to fill in the holes and to clear up my fuzziness. New possibilities were revealed. All this training was done with state hospital patients, who were a mixture of persons in both acute and chronic states.

Here, I formulated that I was using the interaction between family members to understand the meaning and the cause of the symptom. I saw how family members cued each other on levels outside of their awareness.

I saw the need for developing an overview to understand the process. I developed something called the Family Life Fact Chronology (Satir, 1983; Satir & Baldwin, 1983) which featured what happened to a person's family over three generations: when events occurred, with whom, who went out, who came in, and other details. This was based largely on events and outcomes. I stayed away from subjective, emotional reactions. I put this chronology in a time frame so I could see the outcomes of family members' coping over time.

This chronology started with the birth of the oldest grandparents, and succeeding events were brought up to the present. Since we live by time, I chronicled by time. Generally, most case and medical histories chronicled only the negative events which had emotional or medical impact.

…Previously, when I took histories, I would file separate pieces of information, such as "when I was five, I had several accidents." In one place, I might record: "in 1936, my brother was born," and in another place, I might read that "father lost his job when I was young," or that "mother became depressed and was hospitalized." When I put all of this into a specific time frame, it turned out "when I was 5, I had several accidents; it was also 1936. Mother was hospitalized shortly after the birth of my brother, and father lost his job at the same time." That makes a clearer picture of the stresses involved. I also began to see that outbreaks of symptoms often occurred around a clustering of stress factors.

All these facts produced a context in which one could better understand the meaning of the symptom. Instead of isolating facts, I put them in a time frame. Important new connections began to emerge. Patterns over generations became obvious. This also helped me to see people in the perspective of human life rather than only categories. Making a Family Life Fact Chronology became a requirement for those training with me. It aided them in coming to understand and appreciate the family as a context in which people lived, coped, and struggled as they responded to life events. It also provided them with a firmly documented background in which the current situations existed. This tool became the backbone of another basic technique called Family Reconstruction (Nerin, 1986, 1993; Satir, Banmen, Gerber, & Gomori, 1991; Satir & Baldwin, 1983; Satir, Bitter, & Krestensen, 1988). Family Reconstruction is now part of my therapeutic tool kit.

I was sitting in my office one day in 1956, and I became absorbed in an article entitled "Toward a Theory of Schizophrenia" (Bateson, Jackson, Haley, & Weakland, 1956). I remember the thrill of reading that other therapists' work affirmed what I had been seeing in my work with families. While I continued to have good relationships with my professional colleagues in Chicago, many of them later confided to me that what I was doing sounded "freaky" to them. Jackson and his associates were clearly supportive of what I was doing.

In the article, there was some information that helped me to understand better what I was doing and seeing, and some clues as to why it was working. I began combing the literature to provide a bibliography for the residents. I found a reference to Murray Bowen, Bob Dysinger, Warren Brodey, and Betty Baramania (Bowen et al., 1957), all M.D.'s who were engaged in research on schizophrenia that brought whole families to reside at the National Institute of Mental Health.

I immediately contacted Dr. Bowen. He graciously invited me to visit. He was probably as lonely as I was. At that time, working with families was unknown. When I visited Dr. Bowen I saw and heard so much that again validated what I had experienced and what I had conceptualized. Here was more support.

I taught the residents for three years. Since my instructorship was only part-time, I continued my private practice. I regarded private practice as a kind of laboratory which gave me material to feed into my teaching. Then there came a significant turning point.

In 1958, I moved to California for personal reasons. Remembering "Toward a Theory of Schizophrenia," it was natural for me to contact Don Jackson when I moved to the San Francisco bay area in California. I had hardly begun to tell him about my work with families when he invited me to present my findings to his group at the Veterans Administration Hospital in Menlo Park. That group was composed of Gregory Bateson, John Weakland, Jay Haley, Bill Fry, and a few others. That was February 19, 1959. Don asked be to come to Palo Alto and help him together with Dr. Jules Riskin to open an institute. On March 19, one month later, the Mental Research Institute was opened. It was originally conceived as an institute dedicated to researching the relationship of family members to each other, and how those relationships evolved into the health and illness of its members. The men involved agreed that family interaction seemed to behave like a system. Don Jackson and Gregory Bateson and their colleagues had studied one family in depth in which there was one "schizophrenic" member, and they had been able to conceptualize the rules of the family system and to dramatize them in a simulated family which, when heard on tape, sounded authentic. One of the rules of science is that when you replicate your experience you have discovered a new truth. Jules, Don, and I succeeded in getting a good research grant.

After a few months, I was keenly aware that research was boring to me. I felt I needed to develop a training program, and I took it on as my next project. It was completed and opened to students in the fall of 1959. To the best of my knowledge, this was the first formal training program in family therapy. Actually, I was building on the experience I had had at the Illinois State Psychiatric Institute.

In 1964, at the suggestion of Gregory Bateson, I became acquainted with Eastern thought through Alan Watts and S. I. Hayakawa, a leader and student of general semantics. These contacts led to my discovering Esalen, a growth center in Big Sur, California, which had a profound effect on my professional thinking. Here I learned about sensory awareness, gestalt therapy, transactional analysis, altered states of consciousness, and the so-called "touchy-feely" experiences: encounters, body therapies, and other nontraditional therapy modes.

Again, I found that the relationship between how one sees things, and how one interprets what one sees, determines the direction one takes.

I used to ask my students to state their views about (1) how growth takes place, (2) how growth becomes distorted or repressed, and (3) how the normal growth process is restored or established. The first question is related to healthy development, the second to symptom development, and the third to so-called "treatment."

I found, in the main, that most professional training had been based on pathology as being the center of attention, with health being a possible offshoot. Today, I see the strivings for health at the center with symptoms being a barrier or stumbling block to that health.

In my clinical training, I was taught to focus on ill health, which, if properly done, would result in the absence of a symptom. There was an underlying assumption that the absence of ill health was the same as the presence of health. I found this to be no more true than that the absence of hair on the female face was the same as the presence of beauty in that face.

While at Esalen, I was exposed to the concept of "affective domain" and the full use and experience of the senses. I began to understand that seeing, hearing, and touching are experiences in themselves, and are not confined to the objects to which they are related. The experience of seeing, hearing, and touching which, in turn, is related to feeling, thinking, and moving is the essence of life. I learned that it is quite possible for a person to be so focused on what he or she is seeing that the experience of seeing is quite overlooked. For example, one may not be aware of smelling and tasting food, but only of eating it. This is probably the case with people who overeat. I observed that it is possible to listen to the rhythm or lyrics of music without experiencing the music. I often heard people relate that they could wash their hands without the sensation of touching. I began to learn how to help people extend their awareness of their sensual reactions, and watched their sense of self-worth expand.

The central core of my theory is self-esteem. I now clearly see that without a direct link to the experience of the senses, there would be little change in feelings. Consequently, there would be little change in self-esteem, and therefore little real, dependable change in behavior.

This, of course, is a far cry from looking at individuals as masses of pathology. At this point, I was approaching a holistic model, the glasses through which I look at human beings. Since we were all born little, our concept of ourselves is made up of all the interactions around us, about us, toward us. We develop our concepts as a result of a system.

In 1964, I published *Conjoint Family Therapy*. I wrote about what I had learned when I continued to use my most up-to-date glasses to view new experiences. I was always able to change my glasses when I came upon new things. Along the way, I discovered that growth was an ongoing process of sorting, adding on, and letting go of that which no longer fit.

I am compelled and impelled to understand the nature of life: what happens to stymie life, and what happens to transform it? What process makes it move and change? What factors nourish it, and what factors deplete and damage it?

Originally, I was taught that therapy was concerned with that which damaged life, and finding ways to repair it. I now see therapy as an educational process for becoming more fully human. I put my energies and attention on what can be added to what is present. To explain it in an oversimplified way, I find that when one adds what is needed to one's life, that which is no longer needed disappears, including the symptom. I call this process the concept of transformation and atrophy. I pay attention to the damage, but with the emphasis on what will develop health, instead of merely trying to get rid of what is wrong.

Many questions continue to present themselves. Does there have to be destruction in the human condition? It is a precursor to developing strength? What are the best ways to restore health? The answers grow and change as my explorations of new possibilities continue. Exploring altered states, spiritual planes, and cosmic connections seem to be the next, natural steps to take in understanding the nature of life. What we learn may improve our day-to-day living experiences with ourselves, our intimates, and our society.

TENETS OF THE MODEL

The Human Validation Process Model is a communications/systems therapy that grew out of Satir's early work with families. Every part of Satir's approach is oriented toward growth, with a belief in and focus on what people can become. Human beings are seen as unique, complex, whole individuals who grow up and live the majority of their lives in various human and organizational systems.

Satir's approach to both individuals and systems is holistic. Parts are always seen in relation to and interacting with other parts to create a dynamically changing whole. Rules are generated within individuals and among members of a system to govern the process and interaction of the various parts.

Satir used the metaphor of the mandala to describe eight ways in which individuals grow and their life experiences can be accessed (Satir & Baldwin, 1983). The first four are really the structural components of human life: the physical body; the intellect (or left-brain experience); the emotions, including intuition (or right-brain experience); and the five senses. The last four aspects are experiential needs that individuals must satisfy for ongoing growth and development: interactional or social needs, nutritional needs, contextual or life-space needs, and spiritual needs. At the center of each person is the self, the organizing, interpreting (meaning-making and esteem-processing) summation of the eight evolving aspects of the human mandala. Self-esteem is intimately linked to the meaning and value that people associate with the whole of their personal mandalas.

The first task for all human beings is to survive. Indeed, survival is the main motivation for most of an infant's behavior. The first experiences of children are often characterized by alternating states of fear, satisfaction, want, helplessness, frustration, anger, striving, accomplishment, and joy. Their survival, however, is almost totally dependent on the care and nurturance provided by parents. Everything about parents (their words, tones, gestures, moods, attitudes, convictions, actions, etc.) takes on a special meaning to the baby, a survival meaning. It is the communication and posture of these important people that significantly affect the development of the child's self-esteem. Just as food, shelter, protection, and touch are essential for physical survival, parental validation nurtures the development of the self in the child.

The minute the child is born, a new system is created (Satir & Baldwin, 1983). The primary triad of mother-father-child is both an identity and a learning system for the child. Messages from parents about the child's self and behavior are interpreted and registered by the child as answers to "Who am I?" and "What am I worth?" Within the family system, the child also learns about other people, the larger community, and relationships of inclusion and exclusion (boundaries) with both.

As Caplow (1969) and Bowen (1974) note, dynamics within a family triad can often be described as a coalition of two and the exclusion or isolation of the third person. The coalitions and isolations within triads are always changing and fluid. Caplow and Bowen seem to attach distinctly negative connotations (two against one) to triads in families. Satir did not.

While Satir recognized that negative experience is always possible, she also noted that coalitions could be formed *for* a third person as well as against that person. Indeed, infant survival often depends on the nurturing coalition the parents form for the child. High self-esteem in the parents makes a nurturing coalition (dyad) possible and provides the basis for a positive, nourishing triad with the child (Satir & Baldwin, 1983). Within a nurturing family triad, the child can find a place and a balance between personal power and cooperative effort (shared connections). The child's primary motivation of survival is replaced by the motivating desire for growth and maturation.

Growth, of course, is a lifelong process. In the same sense that Maslow (1987) refers to self-actualization as the motivation for human development, Satir knew that everything a person does is geared toward ongoing growth, "no matter how distorted [behavior] may look" (Satir, 1983, p. 24). Maturation, on the other hand, need not take a lifetime to achieve. Satir's definition of maturity is a guide for functional process and involves the effectiveness of personal congruence.

> A mature person is one who, having attained his majority, is able to make choices and decisions based on accurate perceptions about himself, others, and the context in which he finds himself; who acknowledges these choices and decisions as being his; and who accepts responsibility for their outcomes. (Satir, 1983, p. 118)

Growth and maturation in the child are highly influenced by the levels of self-esteem attained by the parents. High self-esteem in a child is the result of parental validation of the child as masterful, unique, and capable-as-a-sexual-being. In a position similar to Bowen's (1990), Satir believed that people with similar levels of self-esteem tend to find each other and marry. When self-esteem is low, each person marries the other to "get": to get the other's esteem; to get qualities in the other experienced as a lack in oneself; to get a validation (in the form of sameness) for oneself; and to get the other to become the "good" parent the person never had. Each enters and maintains the marriage with "low self-esteem, high hopes, and little trust" (Satir, 1981, p. 248). Partners with low self-esteem tend to insist on "sameness" as evidence of a strong relationship; when sameness fails to produce the closeness each person desired, *different-ness* may be acknowledged, but *separateness* is still not allowed. Bitter fighting is often the result.

When a child is born to a dysfunctional union, the parents will expect the child to augment their self-esteem, to be an extension of themselves, and to relieve the pain inherent in the couple's relationship. Under such circumstances, little validation of the child is possible: growth and maturation are thwarted.

Marital partners with high self-esteem have learned to count on themselves, appreciate different-ness as additive to the relationship, and ask for help when help is needed; they can engage in self-care as well as other-care (Bernhard, 1975); they have high hopes and high trust. Such people as parents are able to validate the child and provide a model for functional relationships in the world. Parents validate child growth (1) when they recognize it, (2) communicate that they recognize it, and (3) provide the child with opportunities to demonstrate emerging abilities. Timing, developmental appropriateness, and consistency are all essential ingredients in parental validation processes (Satir, 1981).

Because so much of our self-esteem is related to gender awareness and validation as sexual beings, Satir suggest that:

> Sexual identification is the result of a three-person learning system. Parents validate a child's sexuality by how they treat him (or her) as a small sexual person. But they mainly validate it by serving as models of a functional, gratifying male-female relationship. (Satir, 1981, p. 254)

While Satir thought all children needed both male and female models in their lives, she also noted that children were experts at finding missing models in extended family and community (Satir, 1983). Children growing up with a single parent or in a family headed by a same-sex couple select or generate alternative models for the missing gender; and like children of a heterosexual couple, the *messages* they hear from significant adults have the greatest influence on the development of sexual identity. In the area of sexual development, children seek answers to three types of questions (Satir, 1981):

> *How do significant women (mother) treat me? How do significant men (father) treat me?*
>
> *How do women (mother) and men (father) treat each other?*
>
> *How do significant women (mother) tell me to treat men (father)? How do significant men (father) tell me to treat women (mother)?*

It is the model that the parents present in the primary triad that enhances or detracts from the child's possibilities for growth and maturation. A life without problems is as impossible as a system without stress. Within families, what is experienced as a problem by one member exists as stress within the system for everyone else. For Satir, however, problems and stress are never "the problem." Coping is the problem. Functional family process and personal maturation are characterized by many of the same aspects: an openness to change, flexibility of response, the generation of personal choices or system options, an awareness of resources, an appreciation for difference as well as similarity, equality in relationships, personal responsibility, reasonable risk, freedom to experience, freedom of expression, clarity, and congruent communication.

When individuals discover effective ways of handling certain problems, they tend to return to those methods again and again. These patterns of individual coping take on the force of a personal rule: "When this…, do this.…" Similarly, families develop rules that govern acceptable behavior and system process: rules about good, bad, right, and wrong; rules about inclusion and exclusion; rules about required activity; rules about personal coping within the family group; and most importantly, rules about communication.

In functional families, rules are small in number, humanly possible, consistently applied, and relevant in new situations. When rules become fixed and rigid or arbitrary and inconsistently applied, when rules are invented to keep family members the same or bolster low self-esteem in the parents, the system quickly becomes dysfunctional. Chaos results, and the system loses its ability to cope. The system is in distress (Selye, 1974).

Satir used communication process to access rules that exist within a family and to clarify the coping styles of individual members. Family members in distress are thrown back into survival mode; they invariably adopt communication patterns, defense positions, or postures that Satir described as "blaming," "placating," "super reasonable," and "irrelevant" (Satir, 1976, 1983, 1988; Satir & Baldwin, 1983; Satir, Stachowiak, & Taschman, 1975). *Blaming* is an effort to avoid fault and put others on the defensive; it is expressed as criticism, irritation, anger, or aggressive acting out. *Placating* is an effort to avoid rejection and to make others happy; it is conveyed as constant agreement, pleasing, acceptance of fault, anxiety, self-sacrifice, or a willingness to follow any directive. *Super reasonable* describes an effort to avoid personal involvement and to gain control; it is demonstrated as an assertion of rational principles or right answers. *Irrelevant* is an effort to avoid stress and deny problems; it is manifested as distraction, distortion, changing the subject, or refusing to focus or to take a stand. Each time a stance is used, the energy used to safeguard the self is diverted from the system's ability to handle problems. Still, a defensive stance is the family member's best effort at that time at coping with and surviving the distress in the system. It deserves acknowledgment and an initial respect.

Satir (1976, 1988) believed in the power of *congruence* to handle stress without experiencing it as distress. Congruence is expressed in words that accurately match personal feeling and experience. There is a personal integrity in the communication, and emotional honesty. The person is alert, balanced, sensitive, and in touch with personal resources. The communication and the metacommunication match; there are no second-level, double-bind messages. "Anything can be talked about; anything can be commented on; any questions can be raised; there is nothing to hold back" (Satir, Stachowiak, & Taschman, 1975, p. 49). Congruence is direct and clear; it frees energy in the system for generating options, problem solving, and creating new choices.

In its fullest sense, congruence is an expression of the personhood of the speaker. It is that personhood that Satir sought to access in every family member she encountered. Her goal was to help people find the resources they did not know they had and then to help them make full use of these new possibilities.

> I equate the evolving, healthy person with a beautifully made and finely tuned instrument. Our instrument is finely made. We need to learn how to tune it better. That means developing a philosophy and an approach that are centered in human value and use the power of the seed which is based on growth and cooperation with others. (Satir, 1987, p. 68)

APPLICATION

CLIENTS FOR WHOM THE MODEL IS ESPECIALLY EFFECTIVE

Even though this model grew out of work with clients who were extremely difficult to help and who were often highly disturbed, it is appropriate for everyone. All people start in a family. Their present outlooks reflect their early learnings in the family. Because the focus of Satir's work is on human validation and human communication, the therapist meets and works with family members as they present themselves. Whether the difficulties experienced are extreme or relatively minor, families who are in charge of their personal resources and connected to each other in a cooperative effort can face and handle whatever comes their way.

Adult life is often characterized by a striving to make *whole* that which was a *hole* in the individual's early understanding. People who have serious difficulties in their present are still trying to create wholeness or make up for their past. This concept is as applicable to pairs and systems as it is for individuals.

Because the family system is the context in which people are born, raised, and live, it is essential to work with all parts of the system, the whole family. If one part is removed and isolated from the rest of the system, that part becomes alien to the primary system. Even if an individual family member is helped to change and improve, the person must eventually return to the system in which he or she lives. Once this is done, the system will either require a return to former ways of being or reject the changed member who no longer fits. When an identified patient is treated in isolation from other family members, therapy generally makes matters worse—except in unusual circumstances.

A whole family, physically present, can become a support network for all members. For the most part, the family contains the resources that it needs. When accessed and transformed, these resources can heal the family.

People seek therapy through many avenues, with behaviors or physical complaints that serve as a call for help or through voluntary or involuntary referrals. They may exhibit some obvious deficiency or behavior that is destructive to themselves or to others. Commonly used terms to describe such persons are schizophrenic, depressed, suicidal, delinquent, criminal, alcoholic, drug abuser, slow learner, and poor and unmotivated; such people may be diagnosed with a clinical disorder, have relationship problems, or suffer organic difficulties (asthma, skin problems, back and intestinal problems, etc.).

People in pain may currently live in their families of origin, nuclear families, single-parent families, blended families (step, foster, adoptive), or communal or social families. The initial unit seen in therapy may be the individual, a marital pair, parental-filial pair, a whole family, or a group. The people may be children, adolescents, adults, or geriatrics. Whatever description is appropriate, the therapist is always facing human beings who started out as children and received knowledge through learning, no matter who they are.

Satir never doubted that change was always possible. She would take whomever she could get at the onset of a therapy session; she would depend on her skills to encourage those present to bring in the rest of the family. When individuals were able to collect other members of the system for therapy, they were often exercising resources they didn't know they had, and the process of change was well underway.

GOALS OF THE THERAPEUTIC PROCESS

The goals and the process of therapy parallel Satir's picture of the process of change. Indeed, in a simplified sense, the entire goal and process of therapy is the facilitation of desired change in the family system. Change is learning. The context for change can always be different, but the process is the same.

THE CHANGE PROCESS

THE STATUS QUO All people and all systems seek a balance, a homeostatic pattern of parts or transactions that allow people and systems to function in familiar ways. Once these patterns are established in the family, they become the status quo, the known and protected ways of being, participating, and belonging. Within the status quo, family members develop a set of assumptions, predictions, and expectations that help them handle life. They live and count on the predictions governing the status quo.

The status quo does not have to involve happiness or functionality. To the contrary, it all too often involves pain, personal and psychological stress, abuse, or dysfunction. Unfortunately, familiarity is stronger than comfort. A symptom, for example, allows a person or system to predict; it is just based on hardened assumptions.

The status quo is always in balance. The question is, what price does everyone pay to keep the balance? In a healthy balance, everyone gives and receives to meet the collective needs of individuals within the whole. The thrust for change often comes when one or two members are paying all or too much of the price required for continued balance.

THE INTRODUCTION OF A FOREIGN ELEMENT When anything happens to upset the balance of the system, a foreign element has been introduced. The foreign element is something new that cannot be ignored. It may be a personal or family crisis. It may be an illness or injury. It may be the intrusion of another system on the family. An initial meeting with a therapist is *always* the introduction of a foreign element into the family system.

A foreign element requires the system to address what will happen in new and largely unknown territory. At first, the system will attempt to expel the intruding element and return to the status quo. Failing this effort, a space, place, or context has to be made to help in receiving what is new to the family process. Most systems will attempt to integrate what is new into old and established patterns, as if nothing has really changed. A foreign element, however, changes everything.

CHAOS Anytime something new is added to the system, the whole configuration has to be rearranged. Family members experience this rearrangement as chaos, a highly vulnerable state characterized by fear and a loss of predictability. Everything seems out of balance and out of control. Chaos can last for a few seconds or much longer (days, even weeks or months).

Chaos is often experienced as being locked in an either-or (e.g., life-or-death) choice. Any movement seems at once absolutely necessary and dangerous. The resources needed to move effectively are not acknowledged or accessed within the person or the system. When confronted with or experiencing chaos, human beings first want to run to familiarity and safety. No change happens, however, without chaos. It acts as a demand on the person or system for coping. Seeing it through, with support and care, is the only chance people have for new possibilities.

NEW POSSIBILITIES New possibilities exist beyond the vulnerability of chaos. They arise out of personal inspiration, a reconnection with personal resources, or a different approach when a shared effort is realized. On rare occasions, they occur simply with the passage of time or changes in environmental opportunities.

New possibilities take the person and the system out of the either-or deadlock. Real choice exists when there are at least three options for handling problems. Any new choice generated is only a possibility. Implementation involves risk, planning, a willingness to be awkward during first steps, and lots of practice. There is hope in new possibilities, and even a little excitement, but the person or the system will experience a need for concentration and a dedicated effort.

NEW INTEGRATION New integration takes effect when the new possibilities implemented by the person or system become second nature. What was once new, awkward, and unfamiliar becomes with practice almost automatic. It is a recognized resource within the system. Change has occurred.

With a new integration, a new status quo is established. The system is in balance again, and predictability is newly restored. With a new integration, the person or the system experiences a state of rest and replenishment that lasts until a new foreign element requires another cycle of the change process.

With each successful cycle of the change process, the process itself becomes easier. Movement through the stages becomes known and somewhat predictable. The anxiety experienced when change is unfamiliar is less when change becomes an expected part of life.

Specific goals in therapy are related to the facilitation of the change process. The first goal is to generate hope and courage in the members of the family, to "reawaken old dreams or develop new ones" (Satir & Baldwin, 1983, p. 185). The second goal is to access, strengthen, enhance, or generate coping skills in family members. The third goal is to facilitate the development of choices and options, to develop health rather than merely eliminate symptoms, to unlock the energy that is bottled up by symptoms or symptomatic behavior, and to reorient that energy toward a positive outcome.

THERAPIST'S ROLE AND FUNCTION The therapist's role and function is to guide the person or the family through the process of change. In this role, the therapist's personhood and humanness are more important that any particular set of skills. Faith in the ability of people and in systems to grow and change is essential. The therapist must know that people have the resources they need within them. The therapist's focus is on the whole of the system; problems and tasks are viewed from multiple perspectives. There are no one-directional causes in family dysfunction. Mostly, the therapist must model congruence and respond to family communication and metacommunication in a completely human and nonjudgmental manner (Satir & Baldwin, 1983).

This therapeutic posture infuses every stage of therapy with nurturance, human validation, and safety. The therapist is in charge of the therapeutic process. That leadership must be evident from the first meeting as well as when traveling through chaos with the family on the way to a new integration.

MAKING CONTACT The first effort is to make real contact with the family via a meeting that demonstrates the feelings of value the therapist has for everyone involved in the process. This means the therapist shaking hands; focusing full attention on each person; and expressing a readiness to hear and listen, to be heard and be listened to, to see and be seen, to touch and be touched. This process sets the tone and the context for the human contact among the people who will work together.

Metaphorically, and sometimes literally, the therapist becomes a temporary companion, taking the hand of each family member and creating learning situations in which everyone can participate and benefit. This approach results in hope and trust, which in turn permits the risk of approaching life in a new or different way.

The therapist must trust that if people truly feel valued, they will allow themselves to be more fully seen. Initial contacts are aimed at engaging people as researchers of their own lives. In the beginning, the therapist may temporarily be the senior researcher. This approach counteracts the blaming that is so prevalent in families. Change in the family becomes like a puzzle—a puzzle that requires family members to become first-rate detectives, students of life, and experimenters.

Satir often visualized in images and made frequent use of metaphors. These images might be expressed directly to join with the family or be used as a basis for indirectly shifting focus. The therapist might say, "Right now, I feel as though I were a can of worms. Does anyone else feel that way?" Most of the time, some family members do. In another instance, the therapist might relate a "family story" that is similar to what has been presented in the session but that has an ending that offers hope and encouragement.

As soon as possible, the therapist will usually make body postures of the current family communication pattern, then sculptures of their movement. People seem to find this method relatively nonthreatening and are quicker to identify their underlying feelings. Within this frame, these sharings become more a statement of what is, rather than indictments of others.

Family therapy is experiential learning, a drama of real life, where many of the techniques of good theater are relevant. "I encourage people to come to know their masks and also to be comfortable enough to look at what is underneath, so they expand their universe of choice" (Satir, 1982, p. 24).

In one sense, people present themselves as being made up of bad stuff—blame, incompetencies, and irrelevancies—that they protect through excuses, rationalizations, projections, denials, and ignorance. The therapist adds the parts that are present but in the background: the wish to be loved and valued, the wish to belong, the wish to feel and express their feelings without being judged, the wish to matter and to make a difference in the family or even the world. The therapist reminds people of personal and family successes, however small. This expands the perspective so that background becomes more prominent in the foreground.

CHAOS Just describing the challenge (or foreign element) facing the family system can initiate the stage of chaos. The therapist may be able to create hope that change can happen at this stage, but the family will not see any of the possibilities yet. Faith must come totally from the therapist–leader. It is important never to promise any specific outcome but to be willing to look for possibilities.

No matter how strong the desire in the family for retreat at this stage, the therapist–leader must not run. Chaos is an opportunity for the leader to be vulnerable, to touch and be touched, to cope from a congruent position. It is important to breathe and stay grounded, to relax and find strength in the humanness and human resources present. Chaos is the leader's signal for a renewed openness to present, here-and-now experience.

When a person or system is in chaos, it is important to make no decision "that cannot be carried out in the next 10 to 15 seconds" (Satir & Baldwin, 1983, p. 219). It is not a time to decide about marriage or divorce, hospitalization, moving, changing jobs, or any other major event. In chaos, the survival fears or anxieties that people experienced as children may resurface. The risk of sharing fears, hurt, or worries—of speaking the unspeakable—is always a breakthrough in the journey through chaos.

INTEGRATION When someone experiences something new, the therapist may look around and note that no one has dropped dead. Life is reaffirmed; new possibilities are highlighted; hope is being realized. To be sure, practice lies ahead, but the stage of integration is largely a time for temporary closure and emotional rest. It is also time for celebration and the warmth of human connection.

A family is at once the weaver and the tapestry of the system's life. Working with a family is like weaving a new tapestry out of an old and cherished one. The therapist takes the threads from the used one, adds new ones, lets go of out-of-date ones, and together with the family's master weavers creates a new design.

PRIMARY TECHNIQUES USED IN TREATMENT

Family therapists must work through their own life experiences; professional skills and knowledge must emanate from a sense of well-being, of being grounded. Part of this groundedness relates to an attitude toward life and a commitment to use oneself to help clients discover wellness within themselves.

It is important to remember that therapists are people, too, who may have faced difficulties and pain in their own lives similar to the people they are trying to help. This humanness is a significant awareness for the therapist, and it may even be important to share with family members. All of the therapist's ideals, values, and assumptions about family life get thoroughly tested when working with other families. When tested, the skills of the detective are especially important. What is going on and what would people like to have working better? What is present but not acknowledged? What change is possible? What resources are available? What wisdom is available in the therapist? How can the therapist join with the family in a human way? What skills, experiences, or techniques will make a difference? (Satir & Baldwin, 1983). Observation and intuition will usually point the therapist in an effective direction.

Throughout her life, Satir developed many tools and techniques to help her facilitate change in families. Most of her therapeutic interventions were created as spontaneous reactions to the special needs of the families or family members. Some of the techniques she developed (or used in a special way) for assessment or intervention are listed and described next.

SYMPTOM ASSESSMENT Any symptom signals a cessation in growth and has a survival connection to a system requiring blockage and distortion of growth in order to maintain a balance. The form differs in each individual and in each family, but the essence is the same.

ROPES Perhaps Satir's most unique intervention is her use of ropes to highlight process in family systems (Satir & Baldwin, 1983). Ropes can be used to manifest concretely the binds and pulls in the system and the many different ways in which family ties can be perceived. The feelings experienced by family members during this process are often similar to those they have in daily life.

SELF-ESTEEM AND THE MANDALA Human beings have all the resources they need to flourish. Therapy helps people gain access to their nourishing potentials and learn how to use them. This is what creates a growth-producing system. The mandala represents eight levels of access: physical, intellectual, emotional, sensual, interactional, contextual, nutritional, and spiritual.

FAMILY MAPS Family maps are diagrams or visual representations of family structure over three generations. Similar to genograms (McGoldrick & Gerson, 1985), a set of circles and lines is used to represent people and their relationships within the family. Three maps are used during family therapy: (1) father's family of origin, (2) mother's family of origin, and (3) the current family.

FAMILY LIFE FACT CHRONOLOGY (FLFC) FLFC is a holistic family history, a chronological listing of all significant events in the family starting with the birth of the oldest grandparents and proceeding through time to the present (Satir, Bitter, & Krestensen, 1988).

SCULPTURE The use of sculpture often is paired with stress positions to illustrate family interactions and the ballet of the family system. People take physical postures, together with components of distance and closeness, that demonstrate their communication and relationship patterns.

Sculpture involves having all the people present (in spirit, if not in body) who impact one another. This may include, in addition to the nuclear family, the family of origin (grandparents and in-laws); significant others; household help; pets; and even, in a fitting way and at the relevant time, ex-spouses. When working with families or in groups, family members or role players can stand in for absent members. Satir's friend and colleague, Bunny Duhl (1983) provides an excellent integration of sculpture and metaphor.

METAPHOR Metaphor is an indirect, often parallel communication, used to speak to families symbolically or without threat. Because the metaphor creates a certain distance between the family and a threatening situation, the message is more easily heard. Metaphor may be used to convey an idea or feeling, to teach, or to suggest options that are not readily apparent (Satir & Baldwin, 1983).

DRAMA Drama puts family metaphors, sculpture, stories, and events into motion. Through drama, the therapist is able to help family members reexperience and fully examine significant events or developments in the family's life. The process is especially important in helping children understand events that happened before they were born (e.g., their parents' first meeting or life in each parent's family of origin). "This allows them to look at the situation with new eyes and enables them to achieve new insights and develop new connections with the people they relate to" (Satir & Baldwin, 1983, p. 246).

REFRAMING Reframing is often used to create a shift in the perceptions of family members. The therapist may use reframing to restructure a session away from a symptomatic focus and toward growth and change. Reframing may be used to create options or to defuse the potential for blame. "The therapist decreases threat of blame by accentuating the idea of puzzlement and the idea of good intentions" (Satir, 1983, p. 142).

HUMOR Humor is an opportunity to develop perspective on ourselves, others, and events. A careful look a the human condition suggests that tragedy and comedy are often part of the same event. What is the tragedy of today can, when properly viewed, become the comedy of tomorrow.

Humor can add friendliness and relaxation to initial human contacts. It can be used to modify the intensity of difficult or confrontational situations; in such situations, humor often reduces the need for defensive reactions. By deliberately understating or overstating a perception, humor clarifies intent, nudges a family member in a new direction, or encourages a little movement or change. Natural humor emerges from everyday family interactions. It serves as a strengthening agent for families, giving them a new way to experience their joint difficulties.

TOUCH Touch is probably one of the most healing and truly human aspects of therapy. For too long, helpers have tied their hands because too much of society associated touch only with sex and aggression. The power of touch in caregiving has been ignored. Through the use of hands, the therapist can give and receive information and provide comfort, reassurance, nurturance, and encouragement.

Satir developed two therapeutic processes specifically designed for multiple-family group therapy, each relying heavily on many of the techniques just described:

FAMILY RECONSTRUCTION Family reconstruction is a psychodramatic reenactment of significant events in three generations of family life. Based on the information generated through family maps and the FLFC, the experience is designed to clarify the source of old learnings and add a human perspective to parents who grew up in a different generation (Nerin, 1986, 1993; Satir & Baldwin, 1983; Satir, Banmen, Gerber, & Gomori, 1991; Satir, Bitter, & Krestensen, 1988).

PARTS PARTY A parts party is a drama that can be used to access and highlight the resources and characteristics of individuals within the family. Characters representing different parts of the individual are invited to a simulated party. The experience often dramatizes the inner conflicts that shackle and constrict the person's best efforts. The goal of a parts party is to acknowledge conflicting parts and transform them into a harmonious whole.

EXAMPLE OF TECHNIQUES

A short excerpt from a family reconstruction group demonstrates many of the interventions listed above, including a culturally embedded mandala, drama, touch, metaphor, sculpture, and reframing. A Satir-trained therapist is working with a 35-year-old Native American woman who is part of a family reconstruction group. Her family map and FLFC are loaded with pain and heartache. Several people have died, including her mother when the woman was very young. The family and her culture have known great poverty, and there have been multiple cases of abuse, which the woman, herself, has experienced. Hence, life is not safe to her. Out of more than 30 people in her family map, only one has avoided chronic difficulties with alcohol, and that person is less than five years of age.

She, too, has struggled with alcohol abuse, eating too much, lack of purpose, low self-esteem, and self-depreciation. She finished high school, and she has an opportunity to go to college, but it means leaving her family, leaving the culture and the reservation she calls home, breaking with traditions that have meant survival for her people for hundreds of years.

Although the Satir-trained therapist is from a different culture, as was Satir, he lets the individual who is the star of this drama guide him in helping her. The symbol of the medicine circle or wheel is used, but it is transformed into the woman's family mandala. In this session, the group members have absorbed her family information and cultural processes so much that their intuitive responses are filled with meaning for the drama's star.

Therapist (TH): In your culture, what is the symbol of health? Of well-being?

Native American Woman (W): The medicine circle. It is like a wheel. In it is safety and peace of the spirit.

TH: If you were to use this circle in your life, how would the process go?

W: I would draw a large circle on the ground, like this. (Taking a stick, she traces the circle in the dirt.) At the north end, here, is the wind; here to the South is the sun, fire, warmth, and heat; here to the West is rain, for cleansing and growth; and from the East enters the great spirit, to signify new beginnings.

TH: Pick someone to be the wind and to stand at the north end of your circle. (She picks a strong, stout man to stand there.) I want you to look at this man you have chosen. If you close your eyes and see him there, who else does he remind you of?

W: My father.

TH: Yes, let both the wind and your father be there. Now pick someone to be the sun, warmth.

(Again, she picks a man, a younger man, who also represents her son. In turn, she picks a woman for the West—rain—who also represents her mother; she picks another woman for the East—spirit—who reminds her of the medicine woman—healer—from her community.)

TH: Are you allowed inside of the circle?

W: Yes.

TH: Who will bring you into the circle?

W: The wind; my father.

(Without guidance, the man representing the wind takes her hand, and she, almost involuntarily, closes her eyes. She is led into the center of the circle.)

TH: I wonder if you can allow my voice to be with you?

W: Yes, I want you here.

TH: How old do you feel at this moment?

W: About 12, I guess.

TH: What is the ceremony that should take place for you at this time?

W: I should be given my name, my adult name.

TH: What is the name, and who would give it to you?

W: I was never given a name. My father never took me through the ceremony.

TH: What would he call you if he had?

W: I would want to be called something like Bluebell Standing in Snow. Something beautiful and strong, that perseveres.

TH: I want you to hear father's words to you now, spoken through the wind, and bestowing on you your name.

The Wind: I see you are Bluebell Standing in Snow. It is not a name I give you or that you have earned; it has always been your name and your spirit. It is who you are.

(She stands silently with her eyes still closed, in the middle of the circle. The therapist brings the hands of the wind to rest gently on her shoulders.)

TH: What does the sun say to you about your name?

W: The sun is proud of me. He says he will shine on me and help me grow.

TH: You will feel the wind release you now, and the sun will take your hands. What says the sun?

The Sun: I am always here, and I need you as much as you need me.

W: Whatever I do, I have to do for both of us. You will never be far from me or out of my heart. Wherever I go, I take you with me.

TH: You will feel the sun release you, and the rain will touch your right shoulder. What says the rain?

The Rain: I am here to wash you clean, to give you a new beginning. I, too, am always with you; I have always known you. You are my daughter, and I am very proud. (The woman turns toward the rain, opens her eyes and embraces her. She takes in fully the experience of being held, and she feels the warmth of the hug fully in her body.)

TH: I want you to look fully at the rain. She is also your mother. What word do you use to describe her.

W: Wisdom.

TH: Now turn to the sun. What word describes him?

W: Courage.

TH: And the wind, who is also your father?

W: Strength.

TH: Now turn to the East, to this spirit healer from your community. What word describes her?

W: Creation. Creator. She makes everything possible.

TH: Ask her what is in your heart.

W: What do you have to say to me?

The Spirit Healer: What you have always known, but have been afraid to hear. You will go. You will follow your dream. You will return. And you will go again, never to return. You will leave a small part of you here. You will return for what matters. You will take all of us with you when going is all that is left. (While others have been talking, the Wind-Father has stepped away and picked a blue flower, still growing though it is somewhat cold outside. When he returns, the therapist is talking.)

TH: One last time today, I want you to really feel the power of this circle in your life. Allow yourself to stand there, to feel the warmth and courage of the sun; the wisdom of cleansing rain; the strength of the wind; the message of the spirit-healer, the creator of possibilities. They are all with you. I want you to feel their hands on your shoulders. They are all part of you; they imprint you in ways you will always feel. They are you. (The woman turns and fully looks at each one, smiling: they are all smiling. And when, at last, she looks at her Wind-Father, he places the flower in her hand.)

CASE EXAMPLE

The following case example is an edited typescript of a session Satir conducted with a blended family in 1968. The family is composed of Elaine, age 34, the wife and mother; Jerry, age 46, the husband and stepfather; Tim, age 16, the son; and Tammy, age 12, the daughter.

A year prior to this interview, the family decided to send the son to live with his biological father [Buddy]. His situation deteriorated to the point where he got all F's academically. The parents decided to bring the son back to this family unit. At the time of the interview, the new school year had been in progress for a month and a half. The boy refused to go to school or, when forcibly dropped at school, he refused to stay. The family was in the early stages of therapy at the time Virginia saw them. (Golden Triad Films, 1968, p. 11)

When the typescript begins, Satir has already met and greeted everyone in the family. She and the family are seated in chairs arranged in a circle.

Satir: Well, tell me: When you came here today, what did you hope would happen for you? (Turning to Jerry) Jerry, what did you hope would happen for you?

Jerry: I hoped that someone would give us more insight on what was going on, and I thought it would be to our benefit to be able to talk to you.

Satir: When you ask about some insight, it means to me that you have a puzzle of some sort that isn't very clear to you; and I wonder what that is for you, Jerry?

Jerry: Well, the insight I was talking about was, you know, the problem we're having with Tim.

Satir: Could you tell me as explicitly as possible what it is that you see Tim doing or not doing that gives you a problem?

Jerry: Well, number 1: not going to school. Number 2: not wanting to work. And number 3: I can't…beyond my wildest dreams, I can't believe a boy not wanting a car. He had the opportunity to have a car if he went to school, but he chose not to do that. The only other way to have a car is to work, but he chose not to do that. I don't care whether he goes to college or not, but I think it's very important to have a minimum education. There's not too much that you can even do with that today.

Satir: Let me see if I can understand Tim not wanting a car. Were you saying that if he wanted a car badly enough that he would work or go to school? And since he isn't working or going to school, he must not want a car?

Jerry: Yes.

Satir: Well, the two might be related or not, but I think you are asking for something that you would like to see Tim have for his life somehow, that you feel he isn't doing. Is that right?

Jerry: Absolutely.

Satir: What would you like to have him have in his life that you're afraid he isn't going to get?

Jerry: I'm not sure what makes him happy, but you have to have a minimum of comforts to make you happy. Given the route he's going right now, he's not going to be able to afford them. In fact, he's not going to be able to support himself.

Satir: I picked up that you said you didn't know what made him happy. You've known Tim about six years? And what I hear you say is, "I haven't learned yet or found out how Tim lives inside himself, what has meaning to him."

Jerry: That's correct. I haven't.

Satir: Would you like to know that?

Jerry: I sure would.

Satir: Tammy, when you came today, what had you hoped would happen for you?

Tammy: Well, I think he should be going to school.

Satir: OK. Now when your dad talked about it, that was a piece of it, but what he really came to was wanting to know what made Tim happy. Do you know what makes Tim happy?

Tammy: No.

Satir: You don't? Would you like to know?

Tammy: Yeah.

Satir: Do you know what makes Jerry happy, what makes him bubble inside and feel good about living? Do you know what makes Elaine, your mother, feel good?

Tammy: No.

Satir: So maybe in this family, people don't know how to find out what makes people happy. I don't know. Well, let's see. If you could find some ways to know what made Jerry, Elaine, or Tim happy, would you want to learn those ways?

Tammy: Yes.

Satir: Do you know what makes you happy?

Tammy: Usually.

Satir: Could you say one of the things you know for sure that when it happens you're really happy, bubbling inside with "Oh, isn't it great to be alive!"

Tammy: When I get an "A" on a test.

Satir: When you get an "A" on a test! Oh, there it is: I get an "A" on a test, and I feel, "Boy, I'm really OK." (Turning to Elaine) Well, when you came here today, Elaine, what did you hope would happen for you?

Elaine: I hoped that as a family we might get some insight. Right now, I don't want to turn down any possibility of any kind of help.

Satir: For…?

Elaine: For all of us, Tim especially.

Satir: Well, let's see. You said all of us. What more would you like to find out or get in your relationship with Jerry?

Elaine: Maybe a better understanding of the best way to deal with the children.

Satir: Now, does that mean that you've noticed some ways that Jerry talks to or deals with Tim or Tammy that you wish he'd do differently?

Elaine: Jerry is basically a disciplinarian. He's very strict. Sometimes, I feel maybe a little too strict. So I maybe have a tendency not to be strict enough to maybe make up for it occasionally.

Satir: Would it go something like this? Jerry would say to Tim, "All right, Tim, I want you to do this or that." Then, you would go over to Tim and say, "Now wait. Come on, Jerry, don't be so hard on him." Is that a picture that might happen?

Elaine: Not directly to Tim. I wouldn't stand up and counteract whatever Jerry had done in front of Tim—and probably a lot of times, I wouldn't say anything. I would feel that it was too strict, but not necessarily say anything.

Satir: So here you would be with your feelings, and you would think, "Gosh, Jerry is so hard on those kids (I may be exaggerating a bit), but I can't tell him that I feel that way, because I don't want Jerry's image put down, but I feel that way anyway." Is that kind of how it goes?

Elaine: Uh huh.

Satir: Is there any special area, any way Jerry handles situations in relation to Tim or Tammy, that you could let him know how you feel?

Elaine: Sometimes, they don't mind as well as they should. They're supposed to do, obviously, their rooms and clean up after themselves. They don't always do that, and Jerry gets very, very upset with those types of things.

Satir: Well, let's see. Would you like your house nice and clean?

Elaine: Yes.

Satir: So would you just wait longer? Or how would you handle it differently than Jerry?

Elaine: I would probably wait longer.

Satir: So you'd like some way to get a little more clear or have Jerry hear you more about where you are on this?

Elaine: Uh huh.

Satir: Now, what changes would you like with Tammy?

Elaine: Yes. Tammy is getting a little mouthy lately. I haven't really had a problem with her in terms of discipline until Tim came back. She sees some of the things that Tim does, and I'm getting the "Well, Tim does it" or "Tim gets away with it." I really haven't had a problem with her before.

Satir: When my mother used to tell me I was "mouthy," she meant I was disagreeing with her. Is that what you're saying about Tammy?

Elaine: Talking back. Yes, disagreeing, I guess.

Satir: I have a feeling that you want to have the best-developed, best-equipped kids that they can be for life.

Elaine: Yes.

Satir: And one of the things they need to know is when and how to disagree. We could get into something sticky here if we aren't careful, couldn't we? Something about how Tammy talks to you that makes you afraid?

Elaine: Maybe afraid of losing control.

Satir: So is it like this? "If Tammy doesn't listen to me, then she doesn't have very good judgment, and she might do some things that she would be sorry for." Is it something like that that gets into your fears?

Elaine: Yes.

Satir: OK. Is there something now that you're worried about: something that Tammy might do that you think would hurt her for life, or something like that, that you want desperately to stop her from doing?

Elaine: No, nothing that desperate right now. She's doing well in school. For the most part, it's her attitude, defying. She knows she's not supposed to leave the neighborhood, and she's done that a few times.

Satir: That's where the scary part comes in? What's happening to her? Do you get into that?

Elaine: Yes.

Satir: Have you ever talked with Tammy and shared with her about two things: you're scared when you don't know where she is and your worried about how she makes judgments about how to take care of herself?

Elaine: I've let her know the reasons that I don't want her out after dark. Things could happen to her; so, yes, I've talked with her.

Satir: Do you think she hears you? And if she hears you, does she share the same fears you have?

Elaine: I don't think she probably shares the same fears, but I think she listens.

Satir: So that's a very important piece. You feel she listens to you. When you were growing up, and you were struggling with finding your own freedom, was there something similar that went on between you and your mother that goes on between you and Tammy?

Elaine: No, I don't think so. Mother worked quite a bit, and I started working when I was 14, so mother didn't really share a whole lot with me.

Satir: So maybe it was like Tammy not knowing what made you happy. You didn't know what would make your mother happy—maybe not even what made her sad, only maybe what made her angry.

Elaine: Uh huh.

Satir: You didn't want to make her angry, I guess, so you learned how to say, "yes," oftentimes, when you meant "no"?

Elaine: Uh huh.

Satir: Are you still doing that in this family? Is that true here?

Elaine: Probably.

Satir: Would you like to change it?

Elaine: Yes.

Satir: OK. Now, what about Tim? We've talked about what you would like to have differently with Jerry and Tammy. What about Tim?

Elaine: I would like for Tim to go back to school. I think it's important that he get an education and prepare himself for life. At this point, he thinks that he would like to be out on his own.

Satir: Do you know what that could feel like? At 16, that feeling: "I'd just love to be out on my own!" Do you know what that feels like? Have you ever had that feeling?

Elaine: Yes, to a certain extent. I think that the difference is that I was working, and I'm not sure that Tim really knows at this point what he wants.

Satir: Could be. Could be. What I'm getting is that if you knew something about what Tim would want, you'd probably try to help him get it. Would you?

Elaine: Yes.

Satir: (Turning to Tim) Well, Tim, when you came here today, what did you want for you?

Tim: I didn't want to come.

Satir: You didn't want to come. But you got here.

Tim: I had to.

Satir: Somebody would be angry if you didn't come? Who would be angry?

Tim: Them…all of them.

Satir: And if somebody in the family gets angry at you, what happens for you?

Tim: I won't be able to go anywhere.

Satir: So if you can learn how to do what people in the family ask you to do, you'll get some privileges. Is that kind of how it goes?

Tim: I guess.

Satir: How does that feel to you? To feel that the only way you'll be able to get something is to do what other people tell you to do? It never went over very well with me when I was a kid. How does it feel for you? Maybe these are too hard to talk about. (Tim makes no response.) So at this point in time, am I to understand that you would like to work it out some way so that you could be more a part of the family and have more things to say about what happens to you? (Tim shrugs his shoulder slightly.) From the way you lifted your shoulder, I have a hunch that you feel it wouldn't matter what you wanted. There wouldn't be any use; it wouldn't matter. That's the feeling I got. (Turning to Jerry) Is that anything you know about, Jerry? The feeling that if I asked for something, it wouldn't matter anyway.

Jerry: Well, I think one of the problems is that he's had too much.

Satir: Too much what?

Jerry: Of everything. Whatever he wanted at the time, whether it would be from his mother or his grandparents. Up until he went to live with his father, he had everything he wanted.

Satir: Could you help me out, at least from your point of view, Jerry? What did you think would be helpful for Tim if he went to live with his father?

Jerry: Well, if it had turned out like Tim thought, and I thought it might, you know…(Pause) My son came to live with us when he was 17, OK? And I'm not sure that a son doesn't need a father more at that age than he does a mother. I don't know, but I think that he could probably relate to a father better.

Satir: So you thought that maybe you could be helping Tim if he lived with his father a little bit, to support that idea?

Jerry: Well, I don't know whether it was that or whether I was just happy to see Tim go.

Satir: So were there already some ways in which you and Tim weren't seeing eye to eye by that time?

Jerry: Oh, I don't think Tim and I have ever seen eye to eye.

Satir: So it would be new if you ever did, huh?

Jerry: Yes.

Satir: Do you have at this moment any kind of clues at all about what stops you and Tim from being able to see eye to eye, except your height?

Jerry: What prevents it?

Satir: Yeah. What do you think as you look with grown-up eyes?

Jerry: Tim is a taker, and unfortunately, I'm a giver. There's never any giving on his side that I've ever seen.

Satir: So you kind of feel that you've been putting out your gifts, and you're not getting anything in return. Is that it?

Jerry: Yes.

Satir: (Turning to Elaine) Did you know that was happening when you and Jerry were thinking about how to team up in a relationship? Because you must have had some hopes about what could happen between Jerry and Tim.

Elaine: I had hoped that Jerry would be a very positive influence on Tim.

Satir: In your experience, were you afraid that Tim didn't have a strong enough influence from a man? Is that what you worried about? Because, let's see, when you came together, he was only 10. Just a young man, a very young man. But you were worried about that?

Elaine: Yes.

Satir: (Turning to Jerry) Did you know what it was that Elaine was hoping about you coming in to father Tim.

Jerry: Well, I thought so at the time. I'm not sure anymore. As I see it, Elaine got married very young. She had a very domineering mother-in-law, who said "Jump!" and everybody would jump. And from the things that Elaine and the family have told me, Elaine had no support from Buddy as far as discipline is concerned. So I thought when she turned it over to me, and she will admit that she turned over to me the discipline of the children, that what she wanted was discipline, because they had not had any before. And I think it worked on Tammy.

Satir: So are you saying now that you feel that maybe Elaine didn't mean that you should take it so seriously?

Jerry: I think that she did not participate, and it was left to me. She may have had feelings, but she didn't express them. And I don't do windows or read minds.

Satir: So you felt you were kind of off in left field.

Jerry: Yes.

Satir: (To Elaine) Is this a new idea that you are hearing from Jerry?

Elaine: No.

Satir: When you heard him just now, what went on inside you?

Elaine: It's basically true. It was kind of a relief for me to say, "Here are these two kids, and you kind of take over the responsibility as far as the discipline for a while." But on the other hand, I wanted it to be one, big, happy family.

Satir: I want to look at something. (To Elaine) Would you get up on this chair for me? (Virginia helps Elaine to stand on a chair.) Now, Jerry, would you stand up. I want you, Elaine, to look at Jerry, because it must be a long time that you've been looking up to him. And now I know that you are a little taller than he is, but I want you to look at him from up here. Tell me, Elaine, at this moment in time, what's your feeling toward this beautiful man in front of you.

Elaine: Warm.

Satir: OK. Would you take a little bit of a risk and tell me what it is that you think Jerry is feeling as he's looking at you up here? Because he hardly ever sees people at his eye level.

Elaine: I think he's feeling the same.

Satir: Ask him. Would you check it out?

Elaine: (Turning to Jerry) How are you feeling?

Jerry: I feel the same.

Satir: We only have a short time together, and I want to share a hunch, OK? I heard Jerry say, "I did everything I knew to help you. And I did it in such a way, I think, that a boy I wanted to make friends with, I didn't succeed in making into a friend." (To Jerry) Is that true?

Jerry: Yes.

Satir: "And I feel bad about it at this point." (To Elaine) How do you feel hearing that from him?

Elaine: A little hurt.

Satir: OK, now, I'd like you to be aware that you, like Tim, like Tammy, like me and Jerry, at the moment we do something, it's the best we can do, or we'd do something different. What I'm hearing is that when you married Jerry, you needed so much, and you hoped for so much, I'd just like you to give yourself a forgiving message at this moment. You don't have to berate yourself. So right now, as you look at Jerry, can you think of telling him what you would like from him in relation to how he could be with Tim?

Elaine: (To Jerry) I would like you to be friends.

Jerry: And so would I.

Satir: Could you and would you be willing to remove from Jerry at this point the requirement that he be the only one who tries to give Tim help?

Elaine: I can try.

Satir: What does it feel like if you allow that to happen?

Elaine: Scared.

Satir: What do you get scared about?

Elaine: That I couldn't handle it.

Satir: Let's go step by step. Could you imagine asking Jerry to be a consultant to you, and you being a consultant to Jerry, and you and Jerry and Tim all becoming consultants to each other on how to make friends with each other where friends haven't existed for a while? Could you imagine that?

Elaine: Yes.

Satir: OK. I would like you to look at Jerry and see if you really feel you have a solid teammate.

Elaine: (Looking at Jerry) Yes, I do.

Satir: A few minutes ago, I remember you saying you'd like Jerry to do things differently with Tim in some respects. Do you remember that?

Elaine: Yes.

Satir: Look at him now and tell him how you would like him to be different in relation to Tim.

Elaine: Well, I think you made one step this week when you took Tim golfing, and I appreciated that.

Satir: Did you tell that to Tim?

Elaine: No.

Satir: Could you tell him that now? Because he may not know what in this family people appreciate and what they don't appreciate. Could you come down and tell him? (Virginia helps Elaine off the chair.) Just come close to him.

Elaine: (Sitting close to Tim, Elaine reaches to touch Tim's knee. He pulls it away from her.) I appreciated that you all went golfing together. (Tim says nothing.)

Satir: How does it feel to say that to Tim?

Elaine: It was fine.

Satir: How did you feel about Tim's response to you?

Elaine: It hurt.

Satir: What did you notice? What did he do that made you feel hurt?

Elaine: He pulled away when I touched him.

Satir: I saw you move toward his knee. I heard the feeling about it, and I saw him pull his leg away, but what did you make of that?

Elaine: He doesn't really want me around or near him.

Satir: He doesn't really want you around him. OK. Let's use that as a first working hypothesis. Could it be that at this moment Tim doesn't know whether to trust what's going on? Do you think that could be?

Elaine: Well, maybe.

Satir: Let's think of that as a possibility. Could we make another possibility: that Tim would also like to participate in the choice of whether someone would touch him or not. Is that another possibility?

Elaine: Yes.

Satir: If you start thinking about those possibilities, what happens to your feeling of being hurt by Tim?

Elaine: Maybe it was understandable.

Satir: Could you look at Tim as he is right now, and think of Tim as he is—as somebody who needs help along the road; and before we give people help, we have to know what kind they need. (Elaine nods.) And one of the funny things is that we sometimes offer help that we think other people need, but it may not be what they need. Has that ever happened to you? Maybe someone like your mother-in-law. "I know what you need, Elaine." Ever have that experience?

Elaine: Uh huh.

Satir: What did you feel like when your mother-in-law knew what you needed?

Elaine: I thought, "You don't know what you're talking about."

Satir: Can you imagine Tim feeling that way sometimes? "I don't know what she's talking about. How could she be asking that of me?" And when that thought comes to you, what are you aware of feeling?

Elaine: That he's probably confused.

Virginia now turns to Tammy to check in with her. It becomes clear that in the absence of a positive feeling from Tammy, Elaine feels responsible for not being with her daughter.

Satir: I think that's been going on for you a long time. You have to be everywhere at once. I want to show you something I'm seeing. Will you get up? (They rise, and Virginia gets Jerry and Tim to stand on opposite sides of Elaine, holding her arms out and pulling.) Is that something you've ever felt in this family? (Elaine nods.) Now, when you felt like this, what did you want to do?

Elaine: Hide.

Satir: OK. I want you to look over here. (Virginia takes her face and gently moves it.) My husband. My son. (Virginia reaches for a tissue and dabs the tears on Elaine's face.) What I was hearing earlier was that you were trying to bring your husband and your son together. Now, I want you to look at Jerry and say to him—we'll try this on for size—"Right now, Jerry, I want to turn all my attention to Tim." See what happens in your body when you say it.

Elaine: (To Jerry) I want to turn all my attention to Tim now.

Satir: (Virginia takes Elaine's hand from Jerry.) Now, tell me how it feels to make this choice at this moment?

Elaine: Kind of cut off.

Satir: What do you think Jerry feels at this moment?

Elaine: Left out.

Satir: So if you gave your attention to Tim at a time when you were supposed to be with Jerry, you would feel cut off from him. And probably what Jerry would do is turn around (Virginia turns Jerry's back to Elaine), and he'd say he's not going to have anything more to do with you.

Elaine: Yes.

Satir: Now that's a very important thing to find out whether that's really true. Would you ask him if that's really true?

Elaine: Is it true?

Jerry: No.

Satir: Now look at him. Look at those eyes. Look at his shoulders. Look at what goes on in his face. Do you believe him?

Elaine: Yes.

Satir: Now, turn your full attention to Tim, and tell him that you're here.

Elaine: I'm here. (Tim smiles and turns head slightly away.)

Satir: What does it feel like to make that decision, because there are times when that decision needs to be made?

Elaine: It felt good.

Satir: Good. I want you to look at Tim and know that Tim and his relationship to you is a decision you make at a moment in time, and you don't lose Jerry.

Virginia now repeats the process with Jerry receiving Elaine's full attention when she turns away from Tim. Virginia continues to support the idea that Elaine can have a relationship with each man without getting in the way of her relationship with either.

When Tammy is asked where she fits in the family, she slowly takes a place between her mom and Jerry. Again, Elaine worries that Tim will feel left out.

Satir: Now isn't it funny. That's a worry you had. If you can't be with everyone, you'll leave somebody out, and you'll be to blame. But you know what? You can't go to the toilet that way. (Everyone laughs.) Are you ready to go beyond that now? You notice you only have two hands.

Virginia now leads the family through all the possible triads in their system. She shifts the focus to looking at the dyads that are possible when any two people turn their full attention to each other. Finally, she asks:

> *Satir:* Is it OK for people in this family at a moment in time to have their own special space? Can you imagine, Elaine, that you, Jerry, Tim, and Tammy can all have something, their own private space? Is that possible?
>
> *Elaine:* Yes. I don't think it has been in the past.

In the last moments of the session, Virginia notes that the family will be continuing some work with their therapist:

> *Satir:* I recommend this very strongly, because what I heard you say is that in the interest of trying to help each other, you've lost each other a bit.
>
> *Jerry:* Yes.
>
> *Satir:* And Tim has got to be in charge, so to speak, without meaning to be. And I'd just like you to be in touch with that.

Virginia ends the session by expressing the closeness she's feeling for the family and by asking if she could share a hug with them. When she comes to Tim at the end, she asks:

> *Satir:* I would like to hug you too, Tim. Are you ready for that? (Tim smiles and gets up slowly to hug Virginia.) I really appreciate that.

EVALUATION

Satir worked with more than 5,000 families during her lifetime. The families came in nearly every shape, form, nationality, race, income group, religious orientation, and political persuasion. She measured her effectiveness phenomenologically and clinically, using feedback from the families she helped. Like any therapist, she would meet a family from time to time with whom she could not facilitate meaningful change. These families were few and far between, especially toward the end of her career. Her personal presence and skill at human contact as well as a tenacious determination to enhance self-worth contributed to an extremely high rate of family engagement and completion of therapy.

Satir did a phenomenal amount of work in public, often before audiences of professional therapists and lay people numbering in the hundreds—even thousands. Her public work provided a certain accountability through visibility. The human common sense of her approach was validated by the multitudes who were drawn to her presentations, demonstrations, and training programs.

Perhaps because of the tedium she associated with the pragmatics of research, Satir eschewed all but one formal study of her model and methods. In 1980, she joined the Family Research Project (Winter, 1989, 1993) in Richmond, Virginia. This project sought to assess the effectiveness of the models proposed by Bowen, Haley, and Satir. While these giants in the field of family therapy participated as consultants within the project, the delivery of family therapy services was left to practitioners specifically trained in the models under investigation. Satir chose members of her Avanta Network* to implement her model.

More than 185 families were referred to practitioners working within the project. Sixty-four families were referred to the Satir group. Satir's practitioners engaged 59 families (92% of referrals) in therapy, of which 57 families (97%) completed therapy, both significantly high rates of involvement in family therapy. Families in the Satir group were seen for less than 10 hours of therapy each. Satir's practitioners used multiple-family group therapy as well as working with individual family units.

In general, the effectiveness of Satir's family therapy model was confirmed. Multiple measures of effectiveness and family change (improvement) were developed and used. Families who completed therapy made significant gains. Families who engaged in multiple-family group therapy improved more than families seen only as an individual unit. In some families, there were some differential results for individuals within the system. In the study, the differences in improvement in individuals are attributed in part to the brevity of treatment.

In 1995, Sharon S. Armstrong (personal communication, October 15, 1996) began a project, funded by the AVANTA Network, to test the effectiveness of using a Satir-based multifamily group program with families who had at least one member recently released from prison. The initial groups included a Samoan father and his daughter, an African American mother and her two children, and a Native American lesbian couple with their young son. The goals of this project include enhancing understanding among and self-esteem within family members; facilitating family cohesion; addressing family conflict and couples satisfaction in parolee families; and a reduction in recidivism of parolees. The initial participant evaluations have been quite positive: including, "family maps brought up a lot of issues"; "learning to listen was helpful"; and "maps, sculpting, and listening exercises all worked well together." This project is still in progress, with more formal results due.

SUMMARY

The human validation process model grew out of Virginia Satir's lifelong quest to unlock the potential and self-esteem she know was bottled up in every family system. There was always a detective in her who wanted to make sense out of the clues that people presented about themselves and the worlds in which they lived. Some of her training and all of her experience convinced her that a nurturing, nonjudgmental approach would unlock the meaning in human transactions and release the full potential and health of individuals.

Within this model, the therapist and the family members join forces to promote wellness. The heart of the human validation process model is the therapist's use of self as a leader of the change process and a facilitator of the family's movement from a symptomatic base to wellness.

*The Virginia Satir Network is composed of human-service providers from various disciplines. Most of the trainers actually worked and trained with Satir. For more information about the training programs offered through AVANTA, write to: Margarita Suarez, Director, 310 Third Avenue NE, Suite 126, Issaquah, WA 98027; telephone: (206) 391-7310; e-mail: AVANTAN@AOL.COM.

All people are geared toward growth. A symptom is an indication that the freedom to grow is stalled by the rules in the family system, a blockage that limits the family's creative use of the context. The rules governing the family system are derived from the ways in which parents maintain their self-esteem.

These rules in turn form the context within which the children grow and develop their self-esteem. Communication and metacommunication are the human vehicles by which rules are transmitted in the system and identity formation is affected and affirmed. Communication and self-worth are the foundation of the family system.

Functional family process and personal maturation are characterized by many of the same aspects. Among the most important are an openness to change, flexibility of response, the generation of personal choices or system options, an awareness of resources, an appreciation for difference as well as similarity, equality in relationships, personal responsibility, reasonable risk, freedom of experience and expression, clarity, and congruent communication.

When parents have high self-esteem, they can create an open context and a nurturing triad in which children can grow and learn to handle life. A life without problems is as impossible as a system free from stress. Within families, what is experienced as a problem by one member exists as stress within the system for everyone else. Problems and stress, however, are never the problem. Coping is the problem.

Low self-esteem will be reflected in defensive coping stances and communication patterns. Satir (1976, 1988) identified four dysfunctional communication patterns common in families: blaming, placating, super reasonable, and irrelevant. Congruence is the road to change within the family and the communication process that makes an open system possible.

The process of change always starts with a recognition of and an appreciation for the elements that constitute the status quo. The power of the status quo is its familiarity and predictability. Most often, change is motivated by the introduction of a foreign element that cannot be ignored (e.g., a family crisis, an illness or problem facing a family member, or even a session with a family therapist). A foreign element throws a person or a system into chaos and acts as a demand for a coping response. When people are helped to move through chaos, it is possible to generate new options for coping, growth, and development. With practice, these new possibilities can become fully integrated as a natural part of the person or the system.

Satir's therapeutic model is designed to facilitate and lead people through the process of change. The first task of the therapist is to make full contact with the individuals who make up the family, to build safety and hope, and to assess the status quo. When chaos surfaces, the leadership of the therapist is tested. A focus on the here and now and congruent communication are used to access the hidden family resources that are needed to create new possibilities. Integration is facilitated through practice, human validation, family celebration, and encouragement. As new and stronger processes are incorporated into the system, the family will be able to let go of what no longer fits.

The primary tool of the therapist is the full presence of self, the complete use of one's senses, and the total interest of the "observer-detective." As the therapist engages the family, he or she may choose to assess any symptoms present for meaning; access self-esteem; explore rules and family process through an assessment of communication and metacommunication; or examine the family system through maps, a family life fact chronology, ropes, or sculpture. Throughout the process, metaphor, drama, reframing, humor, touch, family reconstruction, and parts parties can be used to promote change and free human resources.

The effectiveness of the model has been demonstrated in one major research project involving 57 families who completed therapy with the Satir group (Winter, 1989, 1993). It has also been validated clinically and phenomenologically with the thousands of families seen by Satir and members of her Avanta Network.

ANNOTATED SUGGESTED READINGS

Baldwin, M., & Satir, V. M. (Eds.). (1987). *The use of self in therapy.* New York: Haworth.
    A collection of noted family therapists present their personal approaches to the use of self in therapy.

Bandler, R., Grinder, J., & Satir, V. M. (1976). *Changing with families.* Palo Alto, CA: Science and Behavior Books.
    A collaboration on patterns of communication and the process of therapy. Bandler and Grinder later developed their concepts under the title "neurolinguistic programming."

Bateson, G. (1972). *Steps to an ecology of mind.* New York: Chandler.
    The papers and essays that first influenced Satir to adopt a systems perspective in her work, including classic works on schizophrenia.

Jackson, D. D. (Ed.). (1968). *Communication, family, and marriage.* Palo Alto, CA: Science and Behavior Books.
    A collection of papers and research generated by the Mental Research Institute group in the 1960s, including papers by Satir, Jackson, and Haley.

Nerin, W. F. (1986). *Family reconstruction: Long day's journey into light.* New York: Norton.
    Satir's family reconstruction process presented in detail with a foreword written by Satir.

Nerin, W. F. (1993). *You can't grow up till you go back home: A safe journey to see your parents as human.* Gig Harbor, WA: Magic Mountain Publishing.
    Nerin's 1995 AAMFT/AVANTA-Satir Award winning second work on Satir's family reconstruction process with plenty of case examples.

Satir, V. M. (1976). *Making contact.* Millbrae, CA: Celestial Arts.
    Satir's communication model written for families and lay people.

Satir, V. M. (1978). *Your many faces.* Millbrae, CA: Celestial Arts.
    Satir's mandala and routes to self-esteem presented for families and lay people.

Satir, V. M. (1983). *Conjoint family therapy* (3rd ed.). Palo Alto, CA: Science & Behavior Books. (Original work published 1964; 2nd ed., 1967)
    The primary source for Satir's approach to family therapy that includes an essential chapter on how she met people and another on how she worked with larger systems.

Satir, V. M. (1988). *The new peoplemaking.* Palo Alto, CA: Science & Behavior Books.
    An update of the original *Peoplemaking* (1972) and the last book Satir published before she died. An account of universal factors in families is presented simply to increase appreciation of what families are all about. This book is published in 27 different languages.

Satir, V. M. & Baldwin, M. (1983). *Satir: Step by step.* Palo Alto, CA: Science & Behavior Books.

>   The human validation process model is presented. Part I is a typescript of a family therapy session with commentary added; Part II is theory.

Satir, V. M., Banmen, J., & Gerber, J. (Eds.). (1985). *Meditations and inspirations.* Berkeley, CA: Celestial Arts.

>   A collection of Satir's favorite meditations.

Satir, V. M., Bitter, J. R., & Krestensen, K. K. (1988). Family reconstruction: The family within—A group experience. *The Journal for Specialists in Group Work, 13(4),* 200–208.

>   A complete presentation in journal form of the theory, tools, and process of family reconstruction. Satir's last published article.

Satir, V. M., Stachowiak, J., & Taschman, H. A. (1975). *Helping families to change.* New York: Jason Aronson.

>   Based on presentations by the authors during a set of workshops, the book contains two chapters by Satir: one on a simulated family with whom Satir worked, and one presenting an interview with her.

REFERENCES

Bateson, G. (1972). *Steps to an ecology of mind.* New York: Chandler.

Bateson, G. (1979). *Mind and nature.* New York: Bantam.

Bateson, G., Jackson, D. D., Haley, J., & Weakland, J. H. (1956). Toward a theory of schizophrenia. *Behavioral Science, 1*(4), 251–264.

Bernhard, Y. (1975). *Self-care: In and out of bed.* Brookline, MA: BFI Publications.

Bitter, J. R. (1987). Communication and meaning: Satir in Adlerian context. In R. Sherman & D. Dinkmeyer (Eds.), *Systems of family therapy: An Adlerian integration* (pp. 109–142). New York: Brunner/Mazel.

Bitter, J. R. (1988). Family mapping and family constellation: Satir in Adlerian context. *Individual Psychology, 44*(1), 106–111.

Bitter, J. R. (1991). Satir's parts party with couples. In T. Nelson & T. Trepper (Eds.), *101 Interventions in family therapy* (pp. 132–136). New York: Haworth.

Bitter, J. R. (1993). Communication styles, personality priorities, and social interest: Strategies for helping couples build a life together. *Individual Psychology, 49*(3/4), 328–350.

Bowen, M. (1974). Toward the differentiation of self in one's family of origin. In F. Andres & J. Lorio (Eds.), *Georgetown family symposium papers, I* (ch. 21). Washington, DC: Georgetown University Press.

Bowen, M. (1990). *Family therapy in clinical practice.* Northvale, NJ: Jason Aronson. (Original work published in 1978.)

Bowen, M., Dysinger, R. H., Brodey, W. M., & Basamania, B. (1957, March). *Study and treatment of five hospitalized families, each with a psychotic member.* Paper presented at the meeting of the American Orthopsychiatric Association, Chicago, IL.

Caplow, T. (1969). *Two against one: Coalitions in triads.* Englewood Cliffs, NJ: Prentice-Hall.

Dodson, L. S. (1977). *Family counseling: A systems approach.* Muncie, IN: Accelerated Development.

Duhl, B. S. (1983). *From the inside out and other metaphors: Creative and integrative approaches to training in systems thinking.* New York: Brunner/Mazel.

Golden Triad films, Inc. (1968). *Study guide for teaching tapes featuring Virginia Satir.* Kansas City, MO: Author.

Horne, A. M., & Ohlsen, M. M. (Eds.). (1982). *Family counseling and therapy.* Itasca, IL: F. E. Peacock.

Horne, A. M., & Passmore, J. L. (Eds.). (1991). *Family counseling and therapy* (2nd ed.) Itasca, IL: F. E. Peacock.

Jackson, D. D. (Ed.). (1968). *Communication, family, and marriage.* Palo Alto, CA: Science and Behavior Books.

Kirschenbaum, H., & Henderson, V. L. (Eds.). (1989). *The Carl Rogers reader.* Boston: Houghton Mifflin.

Lederer, W. J., & Jackson, D. D. (1968). *The mirages of marriage.* New York: Norton.

Maslow, A. H. (1987). *Motivation and personality* (3rd ed., rev. by R. Frager, J. Fadiman, C. McReynolds, & R. Cox). New York: Harper and Row.

McGoldrick, M., & Gerson, R. (1985). *Genograms in family assessment.* New York: Norton.

Nerin, W. F. (1986). *Family reconstruction: Long day's journey into light.* New York: Norton.

Nerin, W. F. (1993). *You can't grow up till you go back home: A safe journey to see your parents as human.* Gig Harbor, WA: Magic Mountain Publishing.

Rogers, C. R. (1980). *A way of being.* Boston: Houghton Mifflin.

Satir, V. M. (1964). *Conjoint family therapy.* Palo Alto, CA: Science and Behavior Books.

Satir, V. M. (1976). *Making contact.* Millbrae, CA: Celestial Arts.

Satir, V. M. (1981). Self-esteem, mate selection, and different-ness. In R. J. Green & J. L. Framo (Eds.), *Family therapy: Major contributions* (pp. 235–261). Madison, CT: International Universities Press.

Satir, V. M. (1982). The therapist and family therapy: Process model. In A. M. Horne & M. M. Ohlsen (Eds.), *Family counseling and therapy* (pp. 12–42). Itasca, IL: F. E. Peacock.

Satir, V. M. (1983). *Conjoint family therapy* (3rd ed.). Palo Alto, CA: Science and Behavior Books. (Original work published 1964; 2nd ed., 1967).

Satir, V. M. (1987). Going behind the obvious: The psychotherapeutic journey. In J. K. Zeig (Ed.), *The evolution of psychotherapy* (pp. 58–74). New York: Brunner/Mazel.

Satir, V. M., (1988). *The new peoplemaking.* Palo Alto, CA: Science and Behavior Books.

Satir, V. M., & Baldwin, M. (1983). *Satir: Step by Step.* Palo Alto, CA: Science and Behavior Books.

Satir, V. M., Banmen, J., Gerber, J., & Gomori, M. (1991). *The Satir model: Family therapy and beyond.* Palo Alto, CA: Science and Behavior Books.

Satir, V. M., & Bitter, J. R. (1991). The therapist and family therapy: Satir's human validation process model. In A. M. Horne & J. L. Passmore (Eds.), *Family counseling and therapy* (2nd ed., pp. 13–45). Itasca, IL: F. E. Peacock.

Satir, V. M., Bitter, J. R., & Krestensen, K. K. (1988). Family reconstruction: The family within—A group experience. *The Journal for Specialists in Group Work, 13*(4), 200–208.

Satir, V. M., Stachowiak, J., & Taschman, H. A. (1975). *Helping families to change.* New York: Jason Aronson.

Selye, H. (1974). *Stress without distress.* New York: J. B. Lippincott.

Strauss, A., & Corbin, J. (1990). *Basics of qualitative research.* Newberry Park, CA: Sage Publications.

Whitaker, C. (1942). Without psychosis: Chronic alcoholism. *Psychiatric Quarterly, 16,* 373–392

Whitaker, C. (1966). Family treatment of a psychopathic personality. *Comprehensive Psychiatry, 7,* 397–402.

Winter, J. E. (1989). *Family research project: treatment outcomes and results.* Unpublished manuscript.

Winter, J. E. (1993). *Selected family therapy outcomes with Bowen, Haley, and Satir* (Doctoral dissertation, The College of William and Mary, 1993). *Dissertation Abstracts International, 54* (07B), AAG9326240.

CHAPTER 5

Symbolic Experiential Family Therapy

DAVID V. KEITH

DEFINITION

Symbolic experiential family therapy is essentially clinical. It has evolved from an effort to intensify the family's organization and assertive competence so that they can better handle their own relationship to the community—both as a whole and in reference to a particular member, whether one of the children or one of the parents. It is not anchored in any specific theory. It is not guided by research, nor is it organized around the community's demands.

We presume it is experience, not education, that changes families. Most of our experience goes on outside of our consciousness. We gain best access to experience symbolically. For us, "symbolic" implies that something or some process has more than one meaning, and the meaning is linked to emotion. While education can be emotionally helpful, the covert process of the family is the one that contains the most power for potential changing.

HISTORICAL DEVELOPMENT

The background of our style of family therapy can be understood by the evolution of Carl Whitaker's career, so richly summarized in *From Psyche to System* (Neill & Kniskern, 1982). His nontheoretical, experience-based learning is a model for the clinically based learning that is implicit in our thinking about how to learn family therapy.

This history highlights some of the essentials of learning from clinical experience—*learning by doing*, with full responsibility for outcome. This pattern departs dramatically from graduate training in psychotherapy, which is part of the reason this model is unlikely to be found in graduate school curricula. A crucial component is learning by engaging with patients in a variety of situations, placing a high value on the subjective experience of both patients and therapists.

Whitaker left private practice in 1965 to become a professor of psychiatry at the University of Wisconsin Medical School in Madison. At this point he defined himself as a family therapist. Gus Napier and I arrived at Madison by different pathways and became interested in Whitaker's style of family therapy. Each of us worked closely with him but in different ways. Neither Napier nor I had the advantage of insufficient training, enjoyed by Whitaker. In 1978, Napier completed *The Family Crucible* with Whitaker—an in-depth, book-length review of psychotherapy with the family. When I met Whitaker in the early '70s, psychiatry was coming full circle. The culture was attempting to modulate itself after the romantic craziness of the Age of Aquarius. At the time, psychiatrists were fairly creative and attuned to community and relationship issues as important components of health.

But the tolerance for ambiguity soon began to shrink, and a movement called the remedicalization of psychiatry gradually began to gain momentum, supported by advances in psychopharmacology, including antipsychotic and antidepressant drugs with fewer side effects. Lithium arrived on the scene, and for a while all kinds of human deviances could be explained as affective disorders or masked affective disorders, treatable with lithium. The previously clumsy diagnostic and statistical manual of psychiatric disorders was refined, emerged as the DSM III, and gained considerable influence as a political document that categorized, pathologized, and labeled human experience. For all intent and purposes, the DSM series had ignored the implications of an ecosystemic or family systems view of human experience. We thought of the DSM series as a catalog of overextended metaphors for the pain of living. In form, it is a nineteenth-century document, and in that sense a regression backward from ecosystemic thinking. In this simplified historical perspective, family therapy gradually turned into a whimsical antique in the psychiatric context and became the property of academic training programs. Family therapy, which has origins in an effort to correct the orthodox methods of psychiatry and psychoanalysis, was pushed into a role as adjunct to these more linear, orthodox methods. Symbolic experiential family therapy remains, in a covert way, a comment on the depersonalization of mental health care and mental health practitioners. For some reason we (our culture) like solutions that make our problems nonpersonal ("chemical imbalance," "genetic problem"). Why is it that parents are relieved to discover that their child has a neurological disorder, instead of one that may be explained by interpersonal experience?

My point here is that I was well trained in psychiatric methods; I find myself wary of the way in which modern psychiatry has evolved. Symbolic experiential family therapy gives irrevocable freedom to be creative, but it insists that the therapist be a careful clinical observer—meaning that you attempt to say what you see even when you do not understand it fully. It is a family therapy pattern that supports the freedom to be inventive, simultaneously insisting that you take full responsibility for what you do. Symbolic experiential family therapy is a therapeutic pattern that has evolved out of working with families in a wide variety of clinical settings. One of the distinguishing characteristics of this pattern is its emphasis on clinical experience; this makes it somewhat more like a medical practice system as opposed to an academic discipline. It is based on a mixture of methods from medical office practice, which is guided by a blend of knowledge of physiology and pathophysiology coupled with extensive experience. There is no overriding theory. However, psychiatry may have become an exception in this regard, in that a metaphorical theory of "chemical imbalance" eclipses the value of clinical methods. The patient comes in, and with the clinician's help describes the pain and its context. When the pain or anxiety disappears or diminishes, the patient stops coming; the family decides when it has had enough treatment. It is not the clinician's job to make them feel comfortable, or to seduce them—or a subset of them—into a long-term relationship. Learn to see with your own eyes, not with someone else's.

There are several important themes behind the evolution of Whitaker's career in psychotherapy: (1) the use of cotherapy in clinical work, as well as in teaching and writing; (2) the use of symbolic, nonverbal methods or play; (3) a steady effort to depathologize human experience by giving human experience a positive valence (where there is caring, all pathology is sharing); and (4) a pragmatic nontheoretical approach to psychotherapy.

TENETS OF THE MODEL

The foundation for symbolic experiential family therapy can be understood from two dialectical but harmonizing perspectives. In essence, we believe that health is related to a person's belonging to a family. Health is a constant tension between belonging and autonomy, in which autonomy increases with belongingness. So our thinking about psychotherapy is based on (1) a look at both the healthy or normally crazy family and the growth-inhibiting or abnormally normal family, and (2) a dichotomy between the socially adapted self, the one we know best, and another, undefinable, essential self—one we do not know well, the one we see through a glass, darkly. I am an adult playing the duplicitous social word games of adulthood. Calling them games is not to trivialize them. Psychotherapy is one of the games. Writing about psychotherapy is another of the games. I play some of these games with passion and energy, some with awkwardness and discomfort, and others, because of my ineptitude, I avoid completely. In my role as parent, I teach my children to play these games of social adaptation. Being a good player is crucial to survival and growing. But I am also an unadapted self.

I am also a printout of earlier programming. The software was installed at my core by my family during my preverbal, infancy years, when I was a passive "victim" of their nurturing. I have no memory of this time or these experiences. I had no veto power. I believe the program that was installed at that time has not been, nor can it be, altered. I was the "victim" of those who cared for me. Their loving and nurturing were the basis for my self-esteem. But it was also the time when I was irreparably wounded by what they did to me, and also by what they were unable to do for me out of their own anxiety, their fears, and their feelings of inadequacy. I was marked by their disappointments in me and the ways I shattered their fantasies and stressed their relationships. This program is the basis for my integrity, my personhood, my beingness. Whitaker commented often that "we are all schizophrenic." The chief symptom is the nighttime dreams that we forget during the daytime. I speak like a poet when I suggest that this early pre-verbal period is where the chronic undifferentiated schizophrenic in me lives. I believe there is such a thing as a healthy schizophrenic, someone with great access to this crazy side of himself but who has the wisdom to know when to share it, where to expose it, and with whom. This creative component of me refuses to adapt, seeks freedom, and is devoted to independence (Live free or die!).

Somewhere past the age of two and a half I learned to play peek-a-boo and to say "NO!" This was the beginning of my preparation for the adult world. Memory appears along with veto power. This socialization process was in full swing by the time I was three. Here I was taught how to suppress my jealous rages, what to do about my wish-you-would-drop-dead envy, how to act innocent, how to keep my clothes on, when to kiss whom, when to be polite, and when to praise the emperor's new clothes. So there are these two components of me: this social self—the one I know the most about—and a true self, which is the basis of my personhood.

Most psychotherapy today is about social adaptation; that is, how to be a healthy sociopath. But the therapy that interests us most in the world of symbolic experiential family therapy is related to gaining more access to this initial programming and helping these germ cells of personality to be more responsive to the pressures of the world. Health leads to the constant expansion of the self, so I gain more and more experience and maturity, I have access to more and more of the adequate parts of myself. Sticking with our software analogy, when I learned to use my computer I used only the word processor system. Other experiences made me learn how to use the modem, how to use the financial balance sheet, how to utilize the Internet. The point is, experience forced me to gain access to more of the computer's potential. But to erase the fantasy of orderliness, this therapy is based on experiences that may feel chaotic and profoundly frustrating at the time.

THE SYMPTOMS OF A HEALTHY FAMILY

Health is a process of perpetual becoming. When Warkentin (Warkentin, Felder, Malone, & Whitaker, 1961) coined the term *growing edge therapy*, he pictured an open wound healing from both sides. The operation of a family, healthy or not, is covert and implicit. Their rules and regulations are not expressed in any formal manner; they develop out of the operation of the family. The rules are largely expressed in living rather than words. Health has neither a past nor a future. Most important in the healthy family is the sense of an integrated whole. Health is rooted in the group morale of the family. The healthy family is neither a fragmented nor a congealed group. The whole functions as the leader and the control system both in supporting the family security and in inducing change. The healthy family will utilize constructive input and handle negative feedback with power and comfort. The group is also therapist to the individual, rotating the security blanket and serving as a goad when needed by persons or subgroups.

> The Martins had been in therapy off and on for three years. Treatment had begun with a serious depression in the father, who made a dangerous suicide attempt. The father, a successful attorney, had dominated the family for 18 years with his depression, which gave him great freedom to scold and criticize. The group became more healthy through several courses of family therapy, but the father tended to remain an outsider. Therapy had been suspended for four months, when the children—17, 15, and 12—prevailed upon the mother to make another appointment because of their being upset with the father. (The children had been opposed to therapy initially.) During the interview the children complained about the father to me and to him. They were upset at his being mean and his constant complaining that no one cared about him. Mother and the three children were united, they were both confronting and tender. They were saying, in effect, "Look, Dad, we are tired of your blaming us for your bad moods. Did it ever occur to you that you are a major cause of your unhappiness? How can we be nice to you when you are so rude to us?" This is an example of a family being therapeutic to itself.

The family is a longitudinally integrated, three-to-four-generation whole. The family, the subgroups, and the individual members relate to an intrapsychic unit of three generations. Interaction within the extended family is related to this sense of their historical ethos. This three-to-four-generation intrapsychic family is like a reference library that helps define the family image and informs decision making (Keith & Whitaker, 1988).

GENERATIONAL BOUNDARIES The healthy family maintains a separation of the generations. The mother and father are not children, and the children are not parents. The two generations function in these two separate role categories. Members of the same generation have equal rank. Both parents are five-star generals and neither can boss the other around. However, there is a massive freedom of choice in periodic role selection, and each role is available to any member. The father can be a five-year-old, the mother can be a three-year-old, the three-year-old can be the father, and the father can be the mother, depending on the situation. Each family member is protected by an implicit "as-if" clause.

"AS-IF" The basic characteristic of all healthy families is the availability of this "as-if" structure. Play characterizes at metacommunication. For example, the six-year-old son says to the father, "Can I serve the meat tonight?" and Daddy says, "Sure, you sit over on this chair and serve the meat and potatoes and I'll sit over in your place and complain." Dad does this and probably gets more out of making believe he's six than the son does out of pretending he's Mother's husband, the father of the family, and an adult man. Metacommunication is considered to be an experimental process, an offer of participation that implies the clear freedom to return to an established role security rather than to be caught in the tongue-in-cheek, as-if microtheater. That trap is the context that pushes the son into vandalizing the neighborhood or the daughter into incest with her father while the mother plays the madam. The whimsy and creativity of the family can even be extended to family subgroups in which individuals are free to be nonrational and crazy.

POWER IN FAMILIES The power distribution within the healthy family is flexible, with a casualness evolved through the freedom to express individual differences, to renegotiate role structure and role expectations, and to reevaluate past experience. There is great freedom of choice in each individual's right to be himself or herself. The individual may develop uniquely with encouragement from the family and very little counterpressure. This freedom for either aloneness or belongingness is protected by the group.

MANAGING CONFLICT The normal family does not reify stress. Some families stay connected by such weird rituals as the evening meal fight. The healthy family is one that continues to grow in spite of whatever troubles come their way. The family lives with the fact of their inconsistency and acknowledges the passing of time. The healthy family always seeks to expand their experience. All families have myths; myths are part of the definition of a family. One of the problems for dysfunctional families is that they are unable to tolerate changes in their myths. In contrast, the healthy family has evolving myths. The evolving myths permit them to travel through the cycles of regression and reintegration. Symptoms are not absent from the healthy family; rather, they are a way to increase the family's experience and thereby growth.

FAMILY ROLES Roles are defined by a panorama of conditions in the family: past history (e.g., the family of origin), present history (e.g., age of the kids), and ideas about the future (e.g., the mother's plan to return to teaching). The family roles are further defined by interactions with each family member, with the extended family demands, and with the culture. The roles are also defined by the individuals' own growth experiences. The guiding myth evolves; it is not fixed. Sometimes roles are defined by covert needs of the parents, determined before the child's birth, in order to reestablish for the parents a sense of being back at home in their family of origin, whether that was a good or a bad world; home is home. I believe roles are defined interactionally in vivo, not by deliberate decision making. The mother's needs for the comforting of her mother may establish the role of the first child. Or the role of the first child may be defined by the mother's need to care for the real, live three-year-old fantasy dolly with the daddy. As the mother becomes more involved with taking care of the later children, the third child or the fourth child may be given the role of the father's girlfriend or the father's mother as his need and the mother's need are integrated. A friend of mine says, "We get the children we need."

Some of this may sound silly, but it is experientially powerful. These are amoral patterns I am describing. They contribute to health when protected by the playful as-if clause. They are bad and they are toxic when they are reified; that is, the daughter becomes Dad's girlfriend because Mother is excluded or unavailable. Is it possible that the immoral therapist fails to say what he or she sees and hides behind social convention—that is, what is socially "appropriate"?

FAMILY PROBLEM MANAGEMENT Problems are solved in the normal family by marshalling customs, myths, family rules, hopes, taboos, and facts. There are many covert assumptions and some overt rationalizations, but basically problems develop as impasses and get resolved by the standard process of thesis, antithesis, and synthesis. Father wants a new convertible; Mother says, "We can't afford it." Time resolves this, and they buy a less expensive car with a tape deck in it.

Problem solving is often accomplished by realigning the gestalt. The realigning is accomplished in a complex systems way. The family's process of deciding is similar to that of each of us. Decision making by family members is based on those factual realities brought to bear on the situation and the methodologies that worked in the past. These decisions may be impulsive, irrational, ambivalent, and dependent; children may be strongly influenced on a covert level by watching the mother and father make decisions, or by watching schoolteachers or others who have been important to them. Living problems are like calculus problems with multiple variables. The constants are the long-term family values of both spouses. The decisions include influences from the next-door neighbor, the parents' work situation, and each child's school situation. These cultural influences, language-bound limitations, restrictions, and processes from the families of origin of the two parents result in a compromise end point, with many pressures of varying quantitative effect in an algebraic summation of taboos, rules, mythologies, and realities. All of this sounds complex and ponderous, but the human mind and its combinations in the family operate with computer-like precision, handling an infinite variety of stimuli.

ACCOMMODATING TO THE FAMILY LIFE CYCLE The family life cycle is a great model of evolution in a system, changing while simultaneously maintaining its integrity. The clearest markers in the family life cycle are birth, death, and marriage. The developmental periods of the children in large part define family process. For example, the new baby pulls all three generations together, whereas adolescents push the parents into middle age. Some other life-cycle markers include changes in income, family moves, Father quitting drinking, and Mother turning religious. These are important events that the family therapist must listen and watch for. They are frequently understated and underestimated in significance; however, it is common for important life events to cluster in the family history. We learn from families that life-cycle stress is cumulative within the system as a whole. For example, Father's effort to maintain a good relationship with his mother may produce tension in the marriage, which causes depression in the wife, manifested by somatic symptoms and school phobia in the nine-year-old son. The clearest example of cumulative stress in the family life cycle occurs in the family with adolescent children. The kids are individuating and in an identity crisis, the parents are frequently suffering a midlife crisis, and the grandparents are in an old-age crisis related to retirement, illness, or another change in self-image. The healthy family acknowledges the stress in all members and does not concretize it in one of them.

Another way to look at the family life cycle is as serial impasses. The primary "we" of courtship is ruptured; the secondary "we" of living together emerges and develops stress. The stress is resolved either by repression, by struggling through it in the open, or by various other means such as accidents or change of focus; thus, we-ness is reestablished. The stress between unification and separation of the individuals is repeatedly erupting and resolving.

The healthy family becomes increasingly strong as a group, therapeutic in its role to itself and its components, and flexible, casual, and covert. Organic functioning of the whole resembles physical skills, like the psychomotor stage of cognitive development. Coordination is confused by the long circuiting of aware-ness. The high level of affect that is established in the beginning gradually be-comes part of the fiber of the family, and individual freedom to separate and return crystallizes an increasing wholeness within the family. The component parts contribute to the whole, and the whole contributes to the component parts.

The healthy family changes through identity crisis (self-doubt, illness, struggling with the children). Frustration is a useful enzyme for accelerating change. The processes are assimilation and accommodation. On another scale, the process is regression then reintegration, falling apart then reorganizing. Episodes of laughing, crying, and other orgasmic equivalents serve that function in individuals.

Passion and sexuality are the current in a family system. When the flow is free, things go well. When the flow is impeded, the system heats up and the pos-sibility of damage is always present. Passion describes our sense of the "feeling juices" in the family. *Passion* arises out of a Greek word meaning "to struggle"; thus, it defines a process and not a state. It includes sadism and hatred as well as lovingness. The kernel of affective energy at the center of family living process is the core of psychosomatic living; an undifferentiated germ plasma. The behavior in the family is an emanation, always with interpersonal and metaphorical com-ponents. In effect, we assume the biological basis of family therapy. The culture thinks of a healthy family as one with a lot of positive affect. We agree, but we also think that children hate and ought to know that they are hated (Winnicott, 1949). The failure to have an easy flow of affect often results in at least migraine headaches, if not peptic ulcer or high blood pressure.

Feelings in the family in whatever form or degree are handled in nonverbal and symbolic pulses, mediated by the as-if clause noted earlier. The as-if clause makes it possible for the mother and child or the father and child to play out quasi-sexual roles. Mother and son may go on a date while Dad stays home, com-plaining jealously and insisting that Junior bring Mom home before 10 p.m. Fa-ther and his daughter go to the grade school dance. Father catches himself being absurd in a temper tantrum and switches to playing a roaring buffoon. The healthy family knows the difference between murder and play murder, between sexual play and intercourse. This as-if clause was demonstrated dramatically when one child-abusing family began to play-fight with rubber bats in our office. The whole family had great fun with a symbolic slugfest, transcending the danger of real murder.

Love, sexuality, and hatred are lived out through touching, nonverbal inti-macy, fighting and making up, subgrouping and regrouping, triangulation and de-triangulation, teaming, and fantasies.

Bob and Harriet completed therapy just before the birth of their first child. They asked for another appointment when the baby was four months old. Bob felt Harri-et had grown cold toward him, and Harriet said he was too distant and mechanical with her. He was frustrated with her constant refusal to make love. But he was also sympathetic with her feelings about herself, with her fatigue and her attachment to the new baby. He reported the following in the second interview. On Sunday afternoon, the baby was napping. Bob felt loving toward Harriet and attempted to arouse her, but she stayed indifferent. He went to the kitchen to get something to eat, discovered how angry he was, and returned to the bedroom to tell her off. She was sitting on the bed, her back to him, thumbing through a magazine. He was startled when he had a visual image of himself bashing her ribs in with his fists. He said nothing, relaxed, changed his shirt, and went out and mowed the lawn. The conscious experience of this fantasy, and Bob's then telling it to us, facilitated an existential shift in his head. It permitted him more open, less demanding lovingness. You might say he grew up a small bit. Does this bit of experience make sense? No, it only describes an experience, and experience is nonrational.

It is the physical sexuality combined with lifetime commitment that makes marriage a unique, nearly biological relationship. We think the whole family is involved in the family sex life in one way or another. Sex is more open and fun if it involves all the generations. One of the best methods is by sexual joking. In the early marital years, half of a couple's sex life is their fighting about it, but, unfortunately, we don't learn that until after we are married. Family sexuality is obviously conveyed in a preverbal, experiential manner. Middlefort (personal communication, 1976) says that sex education does not occur in the schools; it is not a vocabulary course. Real sex education is in the parents' eyes. When the mother in a pseudomutual family declares that their sex life is "just lovely," the therapist thinks of a funeral parlor visitation where the lady is saying that the corpse is "just lovely."

In this section on the healthy family, we have emphasized that family process is covert and nonverbal. In our method of doing psychotherapy, we distrust communication training methods because they often cool (acting out) rather than increase (acting in) interpersonal stress. In our method of therapy, affective expression is a natural process that is allowed or invited rather than taught.

Increases in intimacy and separateness must go hand in hand. Neither can increase without an increase in the other. One can only be as close as one can be separate, and one can only be as separate as one can be close. Family rules define the tolerable degree of this pressure, and the unspoken family barometer is very accurate. In a healthy family, a wide range of intimacy and separateness levels is found. The levels are also movable without inducing panic in a healthy family. The size of the family space bubble and of each individual's space bubble is determined by experience and the historical perspective that the family has inherited via their "social genes" (Grinker, 1971).

Real dependency is linked to real autonomy in the same way that intimacy and separateness are linked. A symbiotic relationship is one in which there is a fixed emotional distance. Each member is dependent on the other not to alter the distance; the relationship controls the two persons. Thus, two married persons may appear to be quite autonomous, but if the relationship heats up in some way, such as having a child or one member's becoming ill, the other member may experience quite a bit of stress because he or she relies on this relationship's remaining distant. In a marriage, the wife may appear dependent while the husband appears autonomous and independent. However, on the covert side it may be quite different; the wife carries a lot of power, while the husband is really a little boy whose power is in his tantrums or his good behavior. Extended family relationships are troublesome when they are not updated—in other words, if extended family relationships are in-the-head projections left over from when the kids were 12 and the parents were 40. Therapeutic family conferences are excellent ways to arrange to update the projections so that all generations are seen in their current ages.

Bob and Gloria had been married for 23 years. The marriage was unsatisfactory but stable. Gloria stayed at home, took care of kids, and seemed quite dependent. Bob was a successful businessman who spent a lot of time away from home and characterized himself as being strongly independent. During the marriage, he maintained a close relationship with his mother, who lived nearby. The couple divorced one year after his mother's death. We assume that the marriage was not able to absorb his covert dependency needs.

The healthy family is a subculture established over several generations. The power of this subculture is well structured, and the subculture filtering down from the mother's family of origin is gradually integrated, sometimes with a struggle, with the power of the subculture handed down from the father's family of origin.

Relationships with extended families, however, are secondary to the healthy nuclear family. It is possible to visit the extended family of origin without double-crossing the nuclear family. Troubles develop when there is a fixed relationship with someone in the extended family—for example, two sisters having a closer relationship between themselves than either has with her husband. In the healthy family, the relationships are also variable and responsive to specific needs. Grandma may be able to take care of the kids once in a while if the second generation needs it, but she is also free to turn them down. The 40-year-old son is able to go home to take care of his mother after she falls and strains her hip, but he does not double-cross his wife in doing this.

The boundaries of the family are flexible, and here custom and historical perspectives are as important as they are in family dynamics. Information regarding who is allowed in, when, under what conditions, for how long, and on whose OK is all programmed covertly. The interdigitating of the two family cultures evolves over time and after endless experiences in vivo. The family is in a constant flux between the culture of the two families, modified by reality stresses and their resolution.

The healthy family has the capacity for outside relationships and the ability to move in and out without counterbalancing family struggles. That is, the wife may choose to play golf on Wednesday evenings because she like to play golf, not to get even with her husband. Members need not have joint access to non-family members. The husband need not share in all of his wife's relationships, and vice versa.

THE PATHOLOGICAL OR DYSFUNCTIONAL FAMILY

Our general orientation toward pathological functioning is related to the concept of craziness, which can be colored pink by calling it "creativity." We include Minuchin's (1974) concepts of both disengaged families and enmeshed families in this category—that is, the family with excessive calluses and no craziness but massive inhibitions, and the family with "nobody in it" in which the family members live back-to-back. The dysfunctional family is characterized by a very limited sense of the whole. In a more specific way, it is frequently true that the only person who believes in the spirit of the family is the family scapegoat who may, of course, be either the black sheep, the delinquent, or the member who is crazy or disorganized in some way that stresses the family. On the other hand, she or he may be the "white knight" or the socially overadapted family hero, often a workaholic and the one used by the family to cover up their anxiety and extol their health.

Family craziness is denoted in the same way as individual craziness—that is, through a nonrational process that may show up as silliness, fun, or chaos. This psychoticogenic family is dedicated to a state of chaos, which generally becomes worse when the therapist falls into the common trap of attempting to induce organization. But like individuals who are crazy, these families *disconnect themselves from the social structure*. Some other families are creatively exciting and are *more socially adapted and integrated*. The summation of these two adaptations to creativity is one way of measuring the dysfunction. Indications for lack of integration are expressed by way of fixed triangles and fixed subgroups. When the family has unresolved oedipal triangles or a feud between the males and females, the functioning of the family as a whole is disrupted. The dysfunctional relationships disrupt the marriage and, many times, even more the relationship of the two extended families from which the dysfunction originated. Families that are inclined to develop more serious psychiatric illness, psychosomatic illness, and anorexia nervosa have an implicit rule that does not allow members to comment on behavioral processes or behavioral sequences. Pathological functioning in a family is largely a nonverbal process (psychosomatic), and we assume that the verbalization is mostly a facade, a sociopolitical campaign for the community.

Craziness in the family may be compared to several of the individual diagnostic categories. The catatonic family imitates the New England patterns of rigidity and emotional constriction; there are paranoid families who are profoundly suspicious, very much as the lower socioeconomic "have nots" are about the "haves." A surprising number of families operate like the simple schizophrenic in that they make decisions without any content and in a very fogbound manner. They roam into decisions; their behavior apparently has no basic understructure that is perceptible or even intellectually available to them. This living style is more common in families in which members have serious mental illness, anorexia nervosa, or other psychosomatic illnesses. A common symptom of covert destructive craziness in the family is as follows. We make a practice of asking who the children in the family are patterned after. A healthy family oftentimes has some fantasy of who the kids are modeled after: "Oh, he's just like my brother," or "He's just like grandfather was when he was a young man." It is symptomatic of a chaotic family when they say, "We don't think that way. We believe each is their own person." This is a symptom of a family who has little capacity for as-if, who has little capacity for play. Literal-mindedness is a form of dishonesty.

The craziness of the individual can be divided easily into three general categories. First, there is the *driven crazy*, the individual who has been driven outside the family and is trying to find a primary process mother in the community. Another type of craziness we call *going crazy*, that is, craziness that emerges out of the profound acceptance, or unconditional positive regard, that Carl Rogers (1980) spoke of. Falling in love can be a metaphor for this process. This is identical with a therapeutic psychosis, a kind of intensified version of the therapeutic neurosis. A third variety of craziness, many times misidentified, is *acting crazy*. This pattern comes about when one who has been crazy is faced with an intolerable anxiety and regresses into crazy behavior. It is not a process craziness but a reactive craziness, in the same sense that there is process schizophrenia and reactive schizophrenia.

CAUSES AND DEVELOPMENT OF FAMILY DYSFUNCTION

We think that dysfunction is related to the struggle over whose family of origin the new family is going to model itself after. One way to view etiology assumes there is no such thing as marriage; it is merely an arrangement whereby scapegoats are sent out by two families in an effort to re-create themselves. There are also family growth impasses that lead to dysfunction—the arrival of a new child, the death of a family member, invasion from the outside culture, corporate depersonalization, developmental dynamics relating to the growth of children, aging of parents, or other natural phenomena related to time.

Dysfunction also arises following the father's retirement, one child leaving for college, or other time or space wars. Time and space conflicts can produce stress without becoming apparent to those involved. Who gets the nicest bedroom as the children come along, who occupies the living room or the parent's bedroom, to what degree do friends belong in the family living space, and who has territorial rights to the car, the garage, and so forth? These decisions may be important literally and as symbolic expressions of family power dynamics.

GOAL SETTING

The goals of family therapy are to establish the member's sense of belongingness and simultaneously to provide the freedom to individuate. In our system of therapy, social adaptation is not a goal; we seek to increase the creativity (what we call craziness or right-brained living) of the family and of the individual members.

These goals are accomplished by the aggregate effect of the following subgoals:

1. *Increase the interpersonal stress.* We assume that all families can tolerate any increase in anxiety. The homeostatic power of the family is massive in comparison with the therapist's input. Raising stress can be accomplished in several ways. One way is to convert individual symptoms into systems problems that increase the interpersonal stress. As an example, a young mother had a phobia about being dangerous to her husband and daughter. She refused to describe the content, and she never acted anything out. We said that if she was so selfish with her crazy thoughts we could not stand working with her. The problem was not her intrapsychic thoughts but her depriving the family of excitement. The second method is to expose another unacknowledged problem, such as the father's obesity or the mother's tearfulness. In other words, the anxiety is not expanded in the same territory as the presenting symptom but is expanded horizontally.

2. The family's administrative competence and power emerge from shared anxiety in the *development of a family nationalism.* The family becomes more of who they are, a team with increased morale.

3. We push to *expand the family's relationships with the extended family.* This relationship has a psychic introjection of at least three generations, probably more.

4. We push to *expand the family's relationship to the culture and the community members.* In this way, the family establishes an interface with the culture,

accentuating their sense of belonging to the culture and simultaneously maintaining the freedom to move in and out of it.

5. We push for a *sense of the family boundaries* with joint understanding of, and connection with, family expectations.

6. An effort to *separate the generations* is critical. Although the mother and father should be able to play at being children from time to time and the children should be able to play at being adults, there are real differences between the generations and a separate structure for each. Especially dangerous are cross-generational triangles, because they disrupt the separation between the generations. When the child carries the delusion that he is Mother's peer or when Mother completely deserts her adult role and becomes a bonded partner with her son against her husband, it is more dangerous than the triangle between three children, between the father, mother, and her sister, or between the father, mother, and his secretary.

7. Simultaneously with the clearer structure, *the family must learn how to "play."* This goal sounds simple, but family groups often have great difficulty with it. To be more specific, families need to differentiate between playful sadism and real murder. They need to differentiate between sexual intercourse and flirting. Play is universal; it must be present to maintain health and facilitate growth (Winnicott, 1971). One manifestation of playfulness is the role availability in the family. All roles should be available to each person, depending on the situation and with the family's agreement.

8. We strive to develop a we-they union between the therapeutic team and the family with the *constant cycle of separation and rejoining.* In this way we model the we-ness of the children to the parents, and model for the parents a relationship to their own two families of origin.

9. We want to *explode the myth of individuality.* We want the family to believe in themselves as a unit, but it is important that this belief be flavored with a strong sense of the absurdity of the belief.

10. Each family member ought *to be more of who they are,* with added access to themselves.

The more specific ultimate goals involved in work with a family tend to evolve out of the process of the therapy. That is, they are often established without any verbal definition by the cotherapists, evolving out of their interaction with the family. Those goals established by the cotherapist nonverbally have an advantage because the usual intellectual thinking tends, in both the family and the cotherapy team, to divert, dilute, and avoid change. Methods that bypass this intellectual game-playing are more effective. As parents need to maintain their roles, cotherapists assumedly will remain faithful to their role responsibilities, while at the same time using the self to the fullest possible effect.

The goals of treatment are evolved by the therapist and the family, both jointly and separately. Many are largely unconscious and can be acknowledged only in retrospect. The family usually has goals that vary from those to which the therapist aspires. The therapist's early goals are usually covert but dominant. For example, the therapist may merely try to help the patients stay in treatment, or he or she may elect to invade greatly in hopes of accomplishing what is needed within the first few interviews. In essence, our goal as therapists is to become more human in the context of the family.

The piano teacher metaphor is useful in defining the family's ongoing expectations and interests. The pupil may come the first time just because her parents send her, or she may stay on for a brief time to learn a few techniques and then decide she does not want to know anything about piano. On the other hand, she may gradually change from being a reluctant victim of her mother's interest to becoming an enthusiastic student, even going on to playing Beethoven. This metaphor accurately describes the range of what is available in our style of family therapy. The differences in goals between therapists and families are often resolved in a mutual experience of learning one another's language in the process of the therapist highlighting significant interpersonal events. In some way with each family, we try to create a new culture or a new family, with us as grandparents. We work at developing a dream gestalt with the family. However, it is valuable for the family to know explicitly the personal agenda of the therapist. The most honest way of revealing the therapist's personal agenda is to admit that we do family therapy as a way for us to aid our own growth. We do not operate altruistically out of any saintly inner wish to help the patients change in order to counterbalance the gargantuan pressures of the culture.

Usually the family's painful symptom is only a ticket of admission. Symptom relief is certainly valuable in itself or as a cultural goal, but we assume there is always a more serious distress. Relief of the symptom too soon may prevent a more adequate handling of the hidden stress. For example, one patient came in for treatment of sexual impotence. His symptom disappeared when the therapist exposed a delusion that he would get the Nobel prize. As a result, the interpersonal lifestyle that generated the two symptoms was not modified, only diverted.

Our goal is to bring about change in the patient so that we can thereby alter ourselves. Psychotherapy, like a courtship, demands some understanding of the investment the therapist has, the personal vulnerability he or she hopes to establish, the respect for both the family's rights and his or her own rights. The goals of the therapist should be overt because therapy is a test of the teaming established between the family and the therapist. Any deliberate dishonesty tends to weaken that bond. The way we discuss goals depends on the developmental age of the family. If we give the family objective information at the beginning or end of the first interview, we often find later that they have completely forgotten it. We usually discuss goals when the family asks for them. We don't always respond in the frame of their question. Sometimes we define goals in a double-binding way or invent a Zen-style koan, or paradox. A family in which the father had long-term neck and back pain without much change over 12 years was seeing one of us. After the third interview the father asked what the therapist was trying to do. The therapist told him he was trying to teach him how to suffer. He was trying to help him outgrow the delusion that he could ever be pain-free.

The impression may have been given here that we refuse to talk straight about goals, but that is not the case. We do wait until the family asks, and we respond according to the terms in which they ask. The terms, of course, have both verbal and nonverbal components, with the nonverbal carrying the greatest importance. As much as possible, our goals are established in metaphorical language—a language that incorporates more than one level of meaning, that expands meaning rather than narrowing it. Thus, another goal is to reactivate metaphors in the family process, to use expanded meanings. The use of metaphorical language and visual or pictorial metaphors is most valuable because they can be left incomplete. Overextended metaphors may lose their power for stimulating creativity. The open gestalt or the nonverbal component in any metaphor makes it less easy for the family to memorize it and then dismiss it, making it one more thing they recognize but don't learn from. An incomplete gestalt makes for learning rather than recognition only.

APPLICATION

The main contraindication to family therapy is the absence of a family therapist. There is also a relative contraindication—the absence of a family, that is, the absence of relatives. (Clinicians will understand this humor.) Our method of clinical practice is family therapy. *We do not simply do family therapy, we are family therapists.* Any psychotherapy venture ought to begin with a family interview. If the whole family is not available, then someone from the patient's world should be there for the first interview. This someone might include old therapists, caseworkers, or friends. The presenting problem is not what determines the suitability for family treatment. Suitability depends on the extent to which the family shares our implicit belief that the world works best with people who believe in families and less well with people who do not believe in families.

FAMILIES WITH SUSCEPTIBILITY TO THIS APPROACH

The following types of families are most likely to experience successful experiential/symbolic therapy:

1. Crazy families who are in for fun and/or involved in a dilemma that is multifaceted and multipersonal.

2. Families with therapists who would like a family therapy experience or families with psychological sophistication.

3. Nonsubjective families with psychological problems. The system is based not on intellectual understanding but rather on interactive process in the family, metaphorical language, and personal interaction between therapists and family members.

4. Families in crisis.

5. Families with a serious scapegoat—for example, a member with schizophrenia (preschizophrenia, acute schizophrenia, or chronic schizophrenia) or one experiencing juvenile delinquency.

6. Families with young children: They seem to get more from working with us. We become parents to these new families.

7. Families with multilevel problems.

8. High-powered or VIP families.

9. Families with a psychosomatic problem.

10. Families who are disorganized by the culture—for example, a family who has a probation officer, a social worker, or an alcoholic counselor over-attached to them. Our effort is to increase the family's unity so that they can get rid of intruders.

FAMILIES IMMUNE TO INFECTION

The families for whom there is no stake in experiential/symbolic therapy are idiosyncratic. We have no way of predicting a priori what families will and will not work well. The approach has developed in work with biologically intact families and operates best when all three generations are available. It works less well when members are not available by reason of death, distance, or a simple refusal to come. We assume a denial of participation to be a family ploy. We adapt our work to all sorts of situations, but the likelihood of a therapeutic connection is reduced by compromise. When compromise is necessary we announce our skepticism at the outset. We work with extended families, social networks, divorcing couples having simultaneous affairs, divorced couples with a child in crisis, and gay and lesbian couples. Still, families who seem immune to infection by this method of family therapy are:

1. Those who are panicked by spontaneous feelings, such as postdivorce situations where wounds are still healing and are too tender for re-exploration.

2. Those with long-standing pathology and no strong inducement to change.

3. Those in which the scapegoat is an adopted child.

4. Those in which the identified patient has had long-term individual therapy.

5. Families where important members are involved in some cultural campaign such as feminism, gay rights, or alliance for the mentally ill; any person who belongs to a group that must be protected from irony or suffers from irony deficiency.

"NO TREATMENT" ADVISED

There are families for whom therapy is not recommended. Based upon our clinical experience, we have found that the following situations are predictive of therapy not working.

1. When there has been a completed treatment case, the family has had a therapeutic experience and has ended it. When a new symptom emerges or an old one reemerges, we have the family come back for a single-visit consultation. If there is excitement in the whole family and they are handling the symptom well, then it is not useful to reactivate treatment. These situations are like fire drills. The family is testing the members' ability to respond to a crisis and is checking out our availability.

2. Families who have had too much therapy, so-called professional patients, are advised that they should stop looking for treatment. They are to come in if a crisis arises.

3.   Families who are seeing a good therapist and come to us out of a negative transference response are sent back with the suggestion that we act as consultants if the therapist so desires.

There are some situations in which we are not likely to continue or to begin treatment, but not because treatment is not indicated. If the family is only willing to send a segment—that is, the husband and one child, husband and wife, or husband, wife, and one child only—then we suggest they find someone else. If the father is against psychotherapy, we would rather not be involved. The family is free to do whatever they want with our refusal. We leave the opportunity open to return to family therapy at any time the father may decide that he is willing. The same is true if there is not enough anxiety in the family to make psychotherapy worthwhile. Then it is our preference to decline the referral rather than to try to carry their part of the anxiety load.

RESPONSIBILITY OF PATIENTS

Somehow, patient responsibility is not an important issue for us. We expect patients to grow up and leave home. They have responsibility for their own living and for changing. Whether they change or not has to do with their level of desperation, which must outweigh the pressure for homeostatis or remaining the same.

Patients are responsible for their own secrets. They may expose them or continue with them as they see fit. We do not look for additional background information from other sources. We let the family describe the problem and their needs. If they say they do not need therapy, we take their word for it and terminate immediately.

As the therapist sees more patients and gains confidence, the question of the client's responsibility diminishes. The family is more and more free to come to the office and regress, like the grown-up adolescent who returns home for a weekend.

ROLE OF THE THERAPIST

In order for therapists to determine what they are attempting to do, it is helpful to define a metaphorical model for what they are doing and then to follow it out. The therapist is like a coach. The coach is different from a referee because the coach wants his or her team to win, but the coach stays on the sidelines. The coach does not play in the game. It is unusual for a good coach to fraternize with the players. We like to think of ourselves as being like foster mothers. The family comes to us when their present living situation isn't working well. They are welcome to live with us but they have to follow our rules, or else find somewhere else to live. If we find a way of loving them we will probably be helpful. If we are successful they will grow up and take responsibility for their lives back into their own hands. If they don't like the foster home or the rules of the foster home they can run away. We won't chase them.

The therapist is like both a coach and a surrogate grandparent. Both roles demand structure, discipline, and creativity, as well as caring and personal availability. Balance among these components is established through experience. Our availability is different from that of the biological parent in that it does not involve the whole self of the therapist.

We are very active as therapists. We don't exclude being directive; on the other hand, we may use silence as one unusual activity for increasing anxiety. The therapist overtly controls the first few sessions of family therapy. He or she is active, both in infiltrating the family and in exposing anxiety-laden territory, but usually without being directive. We expect to be part of the family's interaction. Although we do not forbid family members to talk to each other, we assume the main process to come from the family's interaction with the therapeutic team.

We always prefer to work as cotherapists. (Cotherapy is discussed in detail in the next section.) The therapeutic team is modeled after a marriage with children. The family is seen as a new baby who, with luck, grows to be a child, an adolescent, and finally leaves home. The two "parents" ordinarily assume the complementary roles described in the small-group literature as executive or educational director (father) and the supportive or nurturant individual (mother). These roles with the family can be stabilized, but ordinarily they alternate during a single interview or from the early part of therapy to the later part. The third therapist, the cotherapy "we" (or, from the other side, the paranoid "they"), functions as a decision-making discussion center.

The evolving role of the therapy team moves through several stages. In the early part of therapy, the parental team is all-powerful, but they quickly define themselves as impotent, unable to push the whole family around. The therapeutic team declines all efforts to be regarded as magic or possessing supraknowledge of how that family should live. We assume that each family has a unique culture style and that our function is to help perfect it and give it more explicit and specific direction, defined by the family's own functional patterning. It is like teaching tennis to an advanced player. The entire game cannot be made over; rather, the player's strong points are consolidated and emphasized, the weak points are corrected.

In the second interview, the family says, "What should we talk about?" One therapist replies, "I don't know. What do you want to change?" "Well, we told you last time." "I know, but that has probably altered since then. You carry the ball, and we'll be glad to try to help."

In the midphase of therapy, the parental therapeutic team functions as a stress activator, a growth expander, and a creativity stimulator. In this phase, when the family is secure, the therapist may say, "By the way, Jane, when you spoke like that to your husband, you sounded like you were talking to your mother or your father. I wonder if you really want to let him get away with that." This implies that it is a joint arrangement between the two spouses. She is being infantile not only because she wants to be but also because the husband needs her to be infantile.

In the adolescent or late phase, the team has no function except to be there and watch. They provide a time and place for the family to get together. Of course, they are available for deeper involvement as needed. The therapists depend on the family to carry all of the initiative, and they do not try to interfere even if they see they can contribute. In this later phase, the therapeutic team functions as a proud parent, watching the family while mitigating their own role. This follows the patterning of parents' relationship to a late adolescent who is about ready to leave home. Parents who try to continue educating their children at this late stage are making a serious mistake. The adolescent's independent functioning should be more than respected—it should be revered. The therapeutic team needs to do this with a late-stage family. For example, the mother says to the father, "I think I may end up divorcing you." Cotherapists are tempted to say, "You've never done it all these 18 years; we don't see why you think you could do it now," or, conversely, "It looks like you two are more loving; we cannot see why you talk about divorce." These comments are helpful in the early or midphase of therapy, but not in the late phase.

We often use self-disclosure, sharing minutia in a metaphorical manner, imposing on ourselves the limits of our own role models. We use it in specific ways, usually sharing fragments or facets of our lives that we have worked on in our own therapy or through our living. Going beyond the role model must be carefully monitored by the therapist to avoid a role change in which he or she becomes an organizing educator while the family is not allowed full opportunity for its own initiative. We use personal disclosure not as a model for how the family should live but often as a fragment of how we have struggled so that we are modeling personal experiential growth. Personal disclosure is used to increase the interpersonal focus or to shatter a gestalt that is becoming too set, never to diminish anxiety.

Later in therapy, cotherapists' participation can at times be increased, moving toward fragments of their fantasy, experiencing bits of the personal history as they occur during the interview. As the family becomes more secure in handling the input, the therapist can feel free to be increasingly nonrational, free associative, fantasy organized, confronting, or paradoxical in any one of many different models. For example, "Dad, I don't think you have to worry about the family getting along so much better. It's not going to last anyway. They'll go back to isolating you and beating on Mother by next week or at least the week after." Or, on another occasion, "Mary, I'm certainly glad I'm not married to you the way you take off after your husband. I think I would run for the hills if you were my wife." Or, to one of the kids, "Hey, you know the way your father looks at you when he tells you to either clean up your room or he's going to paddle your behind, I would be tempted to head for San Francisco and probably get on drugs just to get back at him." Noting physical responses to interactions can be extremely powerful. "The way you glared at me just then gave me a prickly feeling in the back of my neck."

Another method of self-disclosure that we use is interaction between the cotherapists. It may be in the form of a private joke or a comment about our outside life. We may share a childhood recollection with our cotherapists, or we may ask the cotherapists if we are being too judgmental.

Therapists do not have a choice about joining the family. If the family continues to come to the clinic, they do so because they have given the therapist some role. We actively join the family. We assume our transference to them to be the anesthesia that enables them to tolerate the anxiety precipitated later in the middle phase. Ongoing therapy demands both joining and distancing sequences. That is, therapists must be able to leave the role by their own initiative and later to reenter it. It's as though the cotherapists take turns jumping over Wynne's (Wynne et al., 1958) "rubber fence" into the family, holding hands with the partner, and jumping back. They thus take turns being "in" and "out." They model the basic problem in family growth. The process of uniting and individuating is both a group stress and the fluctuating experience of individual members as well as family subsystems. The cotherapy team joins the family and in so doing forms a therapeutic suprafamily of which they are a subgroup.

The sequence of joining and distancing is important. It is a lot like being with children. A father can get furious with his kids one minute, then be loving the next. We take the same stance with families. If the therapist gets angry, he or she does not hold onto it; if the therapist jokes with the son about his flirtation with the mother, he or she simultaneously retains the freedom to empathize with the father's sadness about being left out. Don Juan, Carlos Castaneda's teacher (Castaneda, 1975), is a good model. Don Juan is described in a number of quasi-real, quasi-metaphorical situations in which he moves close and then away, then disappears and suddenly reappears. This is a nice model for the family therapist. The joining/distancing sequence is a difficult, advanced technique for the therapist to master. Less experienced therapists often do not have a sense of when they are in and when they can afford to withdraw. There is a difference in the way that the two of us, David Keith and Carl Whitaker, handle this. Whitaker was able to allow himself to be disinterested, then suddenly become involved deeply with a family member, then just as suddenly change the topic or dissociate himself. There therapist's role changes throughout therapy; with developing thought processes, the role changes with each family and with the therapist's career. In the beginning, the therapist is a kindergarten teacher/shepherd. Within the therapy, he or she moves from being this dominant, all-giving parent of the infant to being the as-if pal, an age-mate of the young child, then to being the advisor and resource person of the older child, and eventually, the retired parent of an adult. As the family becomes more independent, the therapist team can become more personal, more educational, and more outside the family as such. When a family moves toward ending therapy, we respect it as a real initiative, not a symbolic one. We always stand ready to end with them. We do not look at reasons why the family wants to leave but begin to help planning the termination as soon as it's mentioned.

COTHERAPY AND CONSULTATION

Cotherapy is a regular component of our work. However, it has become more difficult to do in the climate of modern psychotherapy practice. Usually, two therapists join together in a professional marriage to provide ongoing treatment; however, we use alternatives. A therapist may work alone but use a colleague as consultant along the way. The consultant comes into interviews on call. We also get together as therapists to share case fragments and problems.

There are a number of reasons for operating as a team:

1. Teaming allows more creativity and variability in functioning. At root this gives more power to the cotherapy team.

2. Psychotherapy is anticultural, and it is important to have a close colleague in order not to pay the price of being depersonalized. When two professionals are present in the name of therapeutic change, the spiritual power increases exponentially. When subjective perceptions are shared by two members, they are less easily disregarded.

3. The therapists' pathology intrudes less. When there is a cotherapist, the family is under less pressure to take care of the therapist. This component may be less important if the therapist uses a structured method of working. In

cotherapy, each therapist may use himself or herself and his or her subjectivity, with a colleague there for counterbalance.

4. Cotherapy offers the freedom to think, thus enhancing our growth as therapists. While one therapist is working actively with the family, the second therapist may sit back, look at what is happening from a distance, think over what is said, and arrive at some differing conceptions.

5. Cotherapy helps prevent the therapist from stealing one family member to be a therapeutic helper. Either the black sheep or the white knight, when used in this way, distorts the process of family unity and further isolates the scapegoat of the family.

6. We believe that cotherapy reduces affect spilling outside the interview. There is less chance of therapists being aloof during the interview and taking their affect out in a supervisory or curbstone consultation with another therapist, or on a spouse or some unrelated person.

7. Cotherapy decreases the sense of loss at the family's leave-taking. Protective withdrawal of the individual therapist from the next patient and the grieving that might distort the family's leave-taking are minimized. When the family ends, the therapists have each other. Therapists' professional development, increasing competence, and growing enjoyment of family therapy is thus enhanced. More simply, it is much easier for two therapists to avoid compromising their integrity or their goals because of the impending departure of the family.

8. Finally, it is possible in the cotherapy setting for one therapist and one patient to have an extended experience in a one-to-one relationship while the family is present and still to avoid feeling extruded. This may take place either in a single interview or over a period of interviews. Such special empathy and interaction between one team member and one family member will not distort the therapeutic process as it does when one therapist wears several hats.

There are obvious disadvantages in working as cotherapists. It costs the patients more, there are more scheduling problems with a whole family, it reduces each therapist's grandiosity, and interpersonal complications between the therapists can arise. We use marriage as a metaphor to guide our work as cotherapists. At the heart of a prosperous marriage is the struggle between the two spouses to remain autonomous I's and at the same time to join in a dependent we. This same struggle is at issue for both the family and the cotherapy team. Working as co-therapists is an art in which the enrichment of cotherapeutic work increases with experience. It is our belief that the therapy project is much more therapeutic in a shorter period of time when there are two therapists.

TECHNIQUES OF FAMILY THERAPY

We noted earlier that structuring in our therapy sessions is implicit. The first interview includes developing a systems history of the family. We actively attempt to learn about the family emotional system: What is the pain like? Where are the stressors located? Who has had symptoms? What are the individual character structures? What about past stress episodes? What attempts to repair the problem have failed? Why are you here now?

We follow a pattern in our first interview. The family is told that we will talk with each member singularly to get a multifaceted view of what is going on with the group. We start with the member who is psychologically most distant, most often the father. After the father, we go around to the different siblings, saving the mother for last. In most cases, the mother knows what is going on and is most available to be a symptom bearer. This style of interviewing may seem awkward and may go against the instincts of many therapists, but the interactions that develop around it and the messages that are sent often result in a big therapeutic payoff.

If other family members interrupt the talking person, we politely ask them to wait their turn and tell them that they will have their chance. If an argument breaks out that sounds like an ongoing one, we ask them to hold it because we are not trying to cause trouble but to find out what is up with the family. While we get the history, we are continually restructuring what the family says by their deciding who talks—minimizing some information, and highlighting other areas.

JOINING THE FAMILY

The family therapist must develop a basic empathy with the family. We hope his or her transference feelings will include an identification, a feeling of pain, and a sense of the family's desperate efforts to self-heal.

We work hard to capture the family in the first interviews. If the therapist can develop a liaison with the father, there is a good chance that the family will continue in therapy; if not, chances are they will drop out. Additionally, the chance of losing the family increases if the therapist gets overinvolved with the mother too soon. The overinvolvement can happen in several ways: (1) sexually tinged seduction, (2) taking her on as the identified patient and thus stealing her from the family, or (3) making her angry.

Another way the therapist gains membership in the family is by the bilateral transference. We adopt some of their language, a softer accent, or a special rhythm. The therapist's posture may be the same as someone else's in the family. We listen for the metaphorical set and attempt to make use of it.

Playing with the children is another important way to join the family. The play need not be explicitly significant, but often it turns out that way by surprise.

SPECIFIC TECHNIQUES

One of our standard early techniques is to precipitate in the family a taboo against the bilateral pseudotherapy that develops in every marriage. We give the parents full credit for what they have accomplished in straightening each other out. However, we declare an end to that therapy, because it is failing, and demand that they turn the therapeutic function over to us. They are to allow no further crying on shoulders and no further talking about illness, symptoms, or their relationship except during the interview. Isolating the metacommunication to the interview setting induces a great reality to the home-edited interpersonal communication. The parentification typical of the ordinary marriage is interrupted. Blocking the parental (therapeutic) function in the spouses undercuts the secondary gain they accrued as each took a turn at being infantile. The technique is most ably activated in the middle of the first interview. When the father says, "You see, Mary, that's exactly what I was saying to you," the therapist may say, "Shut up! This is my project, I don't want you helping. You'll just make things worse. And think of the joy of not having to listen to her whining any more." This kind of specific interdiction models what we hope will happen outside the interview.

Changes in the family structure many times result from the therapist invading the family dynamic operation. We tend to emphasize noneducational, noninsightful patterns, such as paradoxical intention, the posing of dissonant models, teasing, deriding or reversing a family's statements, or presenting ego-syntonic arguments. For example, if the mother says, "I am unhappy with my husband," the therapist suggests that the next time she should get a younger man since she looks more energetic than her husband. Maybe she could pick a professional athlete who likes a lot of exercise. She could consider taking all this husband's money and going to Chicago, where life is very exciting and the possibility of happiness much greater.

We like to use personal confrontations, even presenting our own boredom. "Mrs. Zilch, the way you responded to your husband just then made me have the nicest feeling that I am not married to you. I don't know whether I would cringe and leave the house or move to counterattack, but it certainly was upsetting to me, and I'm just a visitor here." In like manner, if the mother, for example, is talking about how weak she feels in the family, we tease her by presenting contrary evidence. She has raised five children who were born a year apart, her husband was absent most of that time, and it is a wonder that she is not flat on her back with battle fatigue or a psychosis.

Our intent with these techniques is to produce transcendent experiences—that is, to help the individual members or even the family as a whole move above their pain and stress to savor the laughable situations the therapist verbalizes, or to help them enjoy the experience of looking from a completely different frame. We hope to attain the kind of existential shift that Ehrenwald (1966) presents. Similarly, we call patients on praxis—that is, the accommodation the husband makes to the wife's projection. For example, she wants a mother and looks up to him, and he very obligingly agrees to play the mother game, even though both agree that she gets pseudomothering.

With our emphasis on the power of the experience in the therapy hour itself, it is not surprising that homework is rarely used, except to interdict the generation flip as described above. We collapse their pseudotherapy work on each other. We also advise getting the extended family into the therapy and exert pressure until this is accomplished. We may suggest that each person visit the home of origin without the other so as to regress in the service of that family's ego. If the extended family cannot come in and a home visit is not possible, we suggest that the members of the marriage send empty audiocassettes to their families. The instructions are for the parents to dictate tapes describing their lives up until the kids were born.

These techniques are used gently and early in therapy to test out the family's tolerance. Later on, we push them more specifically. A partial list and discussion of the techniques we consider important follow.

SYMPTOMS ARE REDEFINED AS EFFORTS FOR GROWTH We then increase the pathology and implicate the whole family scene. The family scene is converted into an absurd one. Our effort is to depathologize human experience. The wife is complaining that her husband is trying to get rid of her. "He's never loved me, you know," she says. "He said once that he would cut me up. Another time he threatened me with a gun." The therapist replies, "How can you say he doesn't love you? Why else would he want to kill you?" Psychosis in one of the family members can be defined as an effort to be Christlike: "I'll be a nobody so that you and Father will be saved." Or the desperation felt by one member of the family can be redefined as a hopeful sign because it means the family cares enough. Just a mild tongue-in-cheek quality must be included with this technical play so that the confrontation will not be too painful.

WE MODEL FANTASY ALTERNATIVES TO REAL-LIFE STRESS A woman who has attempted suicide can be pushed to a fantasy. "If you were going to murder your husband, how would you do it?" or, "Suppose when you got suicidal you decided you were going to kill me. How would you do it? Would you use a gun or a knife or cyanide?" In a family with a schizophrenic son, the daughter's conversation with her father was understood by the therapist as a sexual pass. The family was embarrassed and perplexed by that. At the end of the hour, however, the father tenderly held his daughter and rocked her in his arms. Thus, teaching the use of fantasy permits expansion of the emotional life without the threat of real violence or real sexual acting out.

WE SEPARATE INTERPERSONAL STRESS AND INTRAPERSONAL FANTASY STRESS For example, the patient who has attempted suicide can be encouraged to talk with the group about whom her husband would marry if she killed herself, how soon he would marry, how long he would be sad, how long the children would be sad, who would get the insurance, how her mother-in-law would feel, what they would do with her personal belongings, and so forth. This conversion of intrapersonal fantasy stress to an interpersonal framework is valuable since it contaminates the fantasy. It allows the family a new freedom in communication among themselves since they discover that such frightening words do not mean the end of the world.

PRACTICAL BITS OF INTERVENTION ARE ADDED In one-to-one therapy these moves would be inappropriate. In the context of an operational suprafamily, they are safe, since the family will utilize what it wants and is perfectly competent in discarding what is not useful. For example, the husband whose wife is having headaches can be offhandedly offered the possibility that, if he were to spank her, the headaches might go away. Or the wife who is driven up the wall by her children's nagging or Dad's aloofness can casually be offered in the presence of the whole family the idea that she would run away to her mother's for a week and let the family make their own meals.

WE AUGMENT THE DESPAIR OF A FAMILY MEMBER The family will then unite around that person. This technique is usually most efficient when used with a scapegoat. For instance, we might say to a schizophrenic son, "If you give up and become a nobody and spend the rest of your life in a state hospital, do you really think your mother and father will be happy with each other 20 years from now, or will they be at each other's throats as they are now and you will have given up your life for nothing?" Or the therapist might say, "I do not worry about the situation being worse, I'm worried that the same thing will be going on 20 years from now."

WE USE AFFECTIVE CONFRONTATION This is the kind of event that takes place vis-à-vis the parents, most often in defense of the children. It is the change in tone that occurs when the child in play therapy goes from knocking over a pile of blocks to throwing a block at a window pane. An eight-year-old boy and the therapist were mock fighting during a family interview. The parents viewed it as a distraction and continually interrupted as though the boy were the initiator, when it was clearly the therapist. After several minutes of listening to the parents complaining to the boy, the therapist got angry and told them to bug off. He said he was playing with their son, and did not want to be interrupted by them.

WE TREAT CHILDREN LIKE CHILDREN AND NOT LIKE PEERS Younger children at times like to tease us or to fight us physically. We enjoy taking them on and always overpower them. We are willing to be supportive and understanding of teenagers, but we also set strong limits with them. Despite our usual openness and acceptance, we can be very moralistic when chewing out a teenager for pushing us around.

CASE EXAMPLE

BACKGROUND

The Cashman family was referred to us by an attorney. The son, Mike, aged 15, had run away from home 10 months before our first contact. While on the run, he was involved in a car theft. After being apprehended, he went to boys' training school for six months, then was paroled to custody of his father, a senior executive in a well-known local firm. The parents had divorced 12 years prior. Negotiating the first appointment was difficult. The mother, who had recently received an MBA, did not want to attend the therapy sessions. There was also a 17-year-old daughter, Carol.

In the first interview, all the family members filed in and sat down. The therapists sat in their usual seats, side by side, at the north end of the room. The father and Mike sat at opposite ends of a sofa on the south end, while the mother and Carol were perpendicular to them on a sofa on the west side of the room.

Keith: The first questions are how can we help, and what is it that you want from us? How about if you start us off, Dad?

Father: Well, my ex-wife knows more of the details, why…

Keith: I know, it's always true that mothers know the most about families, but I like to pick on fathers, so why don't *you* say how it looks to you.

Father: Well, I should have some hard and fast answers for this, I guess, let's see, ah…

Whitaker: (Interrupting) Or maybe some tricky questions instead. (His voice was challenging, yet indifferent.)

The father shifted gears in his head. He had started under the guise of a confused buffoon; the slight pressure of Whitaker's challenge now caused him to organize his thinking.

Father: My son, Mike, came to live with me. I'm scared to dert…ah …death that it's going to fail and I'd like to…ah…avoid failure. I want to make sure I can provide a good home and avoid the distance we feel right now. Right now our relationship is fragile. I want to find out how to make it work better.

Whitaker: (While rummaging in his desk drawer) Just like that, huh?

Carol, the daughter, was working on a three-dimensional puzzle. It was made of clear plastic in the shape of an egg. No one addressed her, but at the pause in the father's speech several people in the room turned their attention to her.

Carol: (Defensively) I didn't take it all apart.

Keith: The question is how far to go with it.

Carol: I'm afraid to go much further or else it will all fall apart, and I would die of embarrassment if I couldn't get it back together.

Keith: So go ahead and take it apart some more. If you die, it won't be a big problem. I know the hospital mortician personally; I could call him, and he would come over right away so that you wouldn't have to lie here long. (Then addressing the father) Can you tell us more how the family operates?

The father then related more of the family's unstable, dissonant history.

Father: Since all of this trouble, we've been back together more than ever.

Keith: (Directing his questioning to Carol) From the way your dad describes it, it sounds like an impossible situation. It's not very clear to me what you want from us. Do you think it would help if we taught your brother how to run away and not get caught?

Carol: I don't know what's needed. It's Mom and Dad's ball game right now.

Whitaker: (Still fumbling in his desk drawer) Just because you play second base, you don't count?

Carol: No, I'm more of a spectator.

Whitaker: How can you be a spectator on your own baseball team?

Keith and Whitaker are working as a team here. Keith has the job of a straight man. Whitaker moves in and out of the interview, putting questions in a metaphorical frame of reference and dissociating himself as he rummages in his desk drawer.

The interview plodded on, not gaining any momentum of its own. We reviewed the history as we described earlier. We distorted the dynamics and made primary process observations and interpretations. It was a flat, tiresome interview. In rummaging, Whitaker had found four steel ball bearings that he began to roll Queeglike in his hand as we talked.

As we neared the end of the hour, there was a prolonged silence of perhaps two minutes. Whitaker broke it: "The whole thing sounds discouraging from here. Sounds like a war over the size of the table. Nobody wants to negotiate, and everybody's afraid to put his cards on the table. Nobody is willing to put demands on the table. Everybody plays his cards so close to the vest, he isn't even sure if they're playing bridge or poker." There was another long silence. Nobody said anything. Whitaker's steel balls clicked in the silence.

Keith leaned back in his chair, reached over, and held the arm of Whitaker's chair as he said to Whitaker, "The other possibility is that they're afraid it's going to get worse."

> *Whitaker:* I think they ought to be afraid of that. (Then to Mike) Would you go to the men's reformatory at Quebec Falls next time? Or do you think you would go back to Viroqua School for Boys again? Viroqua is kind of kid stuff, but they do treat you nice there. How was the food, by the way?
>
> *Mike:* Oh, it wasn't very good.
>
> *Keith:* I don't suppose it's very good at Quebec Falls, either. You could get a job in the kitchen. But even than I suppose most of the good food goes to the more experienced criminals in the kitchen. Maybe you could go crazy first, then you wouldn't have to go to jail. You could get off on a plea of innocent by reason of insanity. Then you would have to come back and see us, and it would be worse because the court would make you come. (There was more silence. The family was thinking; they weren't looking at each other or at the therapists. Their eyes seemed to be turned inward.)
>
> *Father:* I think we have to figure out what game we're playing.
>
> *Keith:* I doubt that you'll ever figure it out. So far it sounds like a game of secrets. (Another short silence)
>
> *Whitaker:* To say it more straight, it seems to us that the only time a family changes is when everybody is scared, and it doesn't feel like anybody is really very scared in this family.
>
> *Keith:* It seems like you're concerned, but the concern is of such low voltage.
>
> *Father:* It may appear that way, but I don't believe it.
>
> *Whitaker:* I don't *believe* it either, but if the pain is hidden, it's hard to summate enough to make any difference. And worse than that, you can't find it if you run away from each other.
>
> *Father:* I feel a sense of isolation. I tiptoe around in my house because I'm afraid of too much noise.
>
> *Whitaker:* That's what I'm talking about. It feels like all four of you are tiptoeing around in here lest something happen.

That ended the first interview. The cross sections that we selected for use here represent portions in which we attempt to increase anxiety, while the history segments are not included. From here we will summarize the case as it continued. We picked it in advance with the conviction that we would report wherever it went. It is one of the psychotherapies that cannot be regarded as a success or a failure; more accurately, it is a combination of both.

The Cashmans returned for two very flat interviews that were, in essence, continuations of the first interview. Then the mother moved to another city, as planned, to take on a high-level job, leaving the father and son to suffer with one another. Another appointment was not scheduled because the father planned to take Mike on a business trip to North Carolina. Two months elapsed before the father called back, essentially because things had gone sour between them and he was getting fed up.

The father was upset because he could not keep track of Mike. He had complaints from Mike's school and the probation officer. Additionally, he was being psychologically tortured as only an adolescent can torment a parent. Mike would leave the house in a mess and never clean up after himself. His father's stereo was badly damaged by Mike's misuse.

One day the front door was locked, so Mike kicked it in. Mr. Cashman complained that he had to pay to get it fixed. We told Mike that he should kick in the back door and the side door too, just to keep his old man from getting uppity. They were an odd couple—this youthful, energetic, bright, 43-year-old executive and the cynical, indifferent, 15-year-old son. They made up a kind of Cain and Abel twosome.

We liked Mr. Cashman. He was quite lively and hated to act like an old fuddy-duddy. His father had been too strict with him, and he was dedicated to being a more lenient father than his had been. On the other hand, when he joined the second generation, he felt weak and impotent. He was afraid that Mike was headed for more trouble somewhere, although he didn't really have many facts at his disposal.

Mike: (Furious with his father) You interfere with everything. You want me to live like you do.

Keith: (To Mike) Do you think he's trying to map out your life?

Father: (Joining in) That's probably true, I would like to map out his life because I'm afraid that he's going to let himself go down the drain.

Keith: The only problem with that is that he sounds like he's got a different map.

Father: I suppose I am being a nursemaid.

Whitaker: Not so much a nursemaid. I had a picture of a St. Bernard running to the rescue whenever Junior gets in a jam.

Father: I guess so. I'm a faithful friend alright. I'm always waiting for the alarm to go off. Then I go to offer my expert help, and he gets mad about it. What is it that St. Bernards carry around in that little barrel?

Whitaker: Brandy, I think.

Father: Yeah, that's it, brandy. I suppose I should just sit down in a snowbank and drink it myself.

Whitaker: That's an even better idea. You could become an alcoholic. Do you think you could be any good at it?

The hour ended shortly thereafter. We elaborated the plans for how helpful it would be if the father became an alcoholic. Then he wouldn't be expected to take care of this twerp son of his; in fact, if he was lucky, the Social Services would intervene and take the boy away. Or they could make him go back to the mother; that way the father could kill two birds with one stone. He could get rid of his son and torture his wife simultaneously.

Father: (As he was headed out the door) So you think I ought to be an alcoholic?

Keith: We think it's one way that you could help your son, but remember that it could be dangerous to your health. It's mainly a question of how self-sacrificial you want to be.

The father thought we were nuts to make a suggestion like that, but on the other hand, our distortion helped him to see some of the absurdity in the strange struggle he was having with his son.

The next interview began in silence. Mike tossed one of the Nerf Frisbees to Keith, who tossed it back to the father and then it went back to Whitaker. The four of us tossed it around a few more times.

Father: Things haven't changed much. I haven't become an alcoholic, but I've been sort of upset with the idea that you think I'm a St. Bernard. I think I'm upset because it seems pretty accurate, but I can't think what the next step is. In some ways it is easy to turn my back on what he is doing, but I'm afraid to. How can I stop worrying about him? He is my kid.

Whitaker: (Comfortingly) Of course you can't stop worrying. He is your son, and you're stuck with the problem of worrying about him. But worrying is different from giving him your map for his life. I don't think parents ever get over worrying. In fact, yesterday afternoon we saw a family with 65-year-old parents, and the father is still worrying about his 40-year-old daughter and the path that her life had taken.

The father visibly relaxed. It looked as if he had shifted gears inside his head, as if he had suddenly settled the problem of how to be responsible and still not responsible for his son. He was still worried but not too worried. It would be simple to say that he was now able to laugh at himself, but there was more to it than that.

We had started therapy by being confrontational with him, implicating the father in the family situation, laughing at his naivete and impotence. We had developed what we think of as a therapeutic double-bind. We cared about him and his life's predicament, encouraged him to try harder, but snickered when he did. He found himself in a logically impossible situation—a little like a Zen student who is shown a stick and asked, "What is it? If you tell me it is a stick, I'll hit you; if you tell me it is not a stick, I'll hit you; if you don't tell me anything, I'll hit you."

The therapy continued uncertainly with all the grace of a trained circus bear riding a bicycle. The father would say things such as, "I don't know what he's doing. I'm worried about him, but it's very clear to me that I can't make him do what I want him to."

Mike remained a kind of mystery for all of us adults, but he was cleared from probation. However, the father made no progress at all at becoming an alcoholic.

We met every other week or so for an hour. Once Mike had been off of probation for a month, the father began to get frustrated again. He came in one day without Mike. The father had been 10 minutes late to pick him up at school, and Mike did not wait. The father said, "God, I've had it with that little shit. I feel like he is constantly working to outmaneuver me. I want him to do better, so I'm always suckered out of position when he suggests that he is going to do something constructive. I don't know what I should do."

Whitaker: Maybe you ought to get Mike's mother up here.

Father: What would she do?

Keith: I'm not sure what she'd do, but at least you would have a team. You're outmaneuvered because you're all by yourself. With a twosome you might have more luck.

Father: (Thinking for a moment, then speaking) But she's got a job, and I hear that it is going well, and I don't think that she'd come back. But I have been thinking of something. I've been thinking of having my father come up here with us. I'm very certain that he wouldn't take any of this bullshit from Mike.

Whitaker: That sounds like a good idea to us. Single parenting is virtually impossible. From what you say it sounds like your father would make a good choice behind your ex-wife. It would also probably go partway to upsetting this very careful dance that you and your son do with one another.

The father left the office again. He said he was going to think some more about having his dad come up. There, in midair, is where the situation is suspended.

EVALUATION

EFFECTIVENESS OF THE APPROACH

Whitaker's first publication described his role as a researcher (Whitaker, 1942, cited in Whitaker, 1989). He designed a cross-sectional longitudinal study that investigated the progress of hospitalized alcoholic patients. The study involved conducting interviews with patients and/or their families four years after discharge. In the study of 158 alcoholics, adequate follow-up information was procurable on 26 patients. The present adjustment of the 26 patients was found to be: 39% improved; 46% relatively static or worse; 8% relieved but with poor adjustment; 5% did not respond; and 2% deceased.

As a researcher in this study, Whitaker experienced difficulty separating himself from the data. He stated, "It must be admitted that the personal equation is present. Yes, it must be admitted that it is paramount" (Whitaker, 1942, p. 6, cited in Whitaker, 1989). He believed the subjective experience of the researcher correlating case studies, interviews, and personal reactions into a panoramic view of the process was a valid way to represent experimental data. He stated, "The interviewer can obtain information in the field which cannot be obtained through statistical studies with their fixation on the objective experimental approach" (p. 19). This "trend approach" (p. 7) is congruent with that of a qualitative researcher in that it permeates all future evaluations of this symbolic experiential therapy pattern.

In the 1950s, Whitaker coauthored *The Roots of Psychotherapy* (Whitaker & Malone, 1953). This was Whitaker's first attempt to identify crucial components of the change process that occurs in symbolic experiential therapy. This is the first step in conducting task analysis, a qualitative method, to identify and evaluate critical components within various schools of psychotherapy (Heatherington & Friedlander, 1990).

In *The Roots of Psychotherapy*, Whitaker and Malone provided the first detailed description of how an experiential therapist intervenes in and changes symbolic processes. The therapist facilitates movement and treatment by shifting from reality to the symbolic by a mutual sharing of fantasies, free association, and stories, which results in the clients gaining access to primary process. Through primary process play the client then relives transference experiences with the therapist, who is a more adequate "parental figure" (Whitaker & Malone, 1953, p. 194). The client experiences himself or herself differently within the context of the therapeutic relationship, and change occurs intrapsychically and interpersonally.

In *The Roots of Psychotherapy*, the authors use inductive methods to first observe the therapy and *then* to develop a model of change. They believe practitioners need to spend more time recording their observations. Hypotheses about the therapy process could then be generated inductively based on the data observed. The authors believed this did not occur often enough because most researchers were taught to use traditional methods in which observations were made only after "certain initial hypotheses had been made and certain inferences drawn" (Whitaker & Malone, 1953, p. 8). It is of interest to note again that these criticisms and suggestive methods of studying the change process are similar to the method of a qualitative researcher.

In 1955, Whitaker began experimenting with couples therapy. He studied 30 couples treated between 1955 and 1957 and reported his observations (Whitaker, 1958). He discovered that although one spouse presented with overt symptomatology, the level of dysfunction seemed equal in both spouses. Their interlocking dynamics were a result of protective identification. Just as Whitaker helped shape our thinking about the role of the therapist, his early work with couples contributed to a new way of viewing interpersonal relationships that came to be known as "systems theory."

In 1966, Whitaker provided a framework for evaluating techniques. Techniques could be rated on a continuum in four areas, including verbal openness, affective openness, psychological empathy, and area beyond techniques. The extent to which the therapist relied on the use of self when implementing techniques was related. Verbal openness involved the willingness to confront the client regarding areas of growth. Affective openness involved the willingness of the therapist to share feelings related to the therapy process. Psychological empathy involved attending to psychosomatic responses to therapy, such as headaches, and sharing them with the client. Finally, the area beyond techniques included those moments that were not preplanned but were experienced as therapeutic in terms of the emotional interchange between the therapy participants.

Whitaker struggled throughout his career with the notion of how to measure change. Change is seen as always being embedded in a family's interactional process, but is idiosyncratic to each family based on their unique requirements, interpersonal needs, and living patterns. Whitaker and Napier described what they perceived to be change in one couple: "We began to see some highly significant little things; they glanced at each other more often; they sat together; occasionally their hands touched. They did not do anything dramatically different; they were different" (Napier & Whitaker, 1978, p. 265). Similarly, Keith and Whitaker (1988) wrote about another client in family therapy: "Bill left the interview room in a different way. It was our sense that he had been hooked that day. He parted with a warm handshake. Bill never allowed himself to be touched before, let alone offering his own hand. It was the offering of his hand and the warmth in his eyes that was suggestive of change" (p. 151).

Since 1994, Connell and Mitten have been conducting a fascinating qualitative research project to identify core variables of symbolic experiential therapy (Connell, Bumberry, & Mitten, 1999). Based on methods of grounded theory, as described by Strauss and Corbin (1990), the following conceptual categories of therapy states were inductively derived: (1) generating an interpersonal set; (2) creating a super system, including the therapist and the family; (3) stimulating a symbolic context; (4) activating stress within the system; (5) creating symbolic experiences through associative communication; and (6) moving out of the system.

Through a constant comparative method, the study further organizes intervention strategies into the conceptual category in which they occur most frequently. For example, symbolic interventions such as expanding the symptom, getting at cross-generational influences, and amplifying effectively loaded issues are various intervention strategies used to *generate an interpersonal set*. Two symbolic interventions are relied on to stimulate a symbolic context, including expanding fantasies and using double-entendres. The findings of this study present an overall conceptual framework about how Whitaker accessed, communicated with, and intervened in symbolic processes over the course of therapy.

Future research needs to continue to build upon the conceptual framework identified by Connell and Mitten. There is a need to isolate therapeutic processes that facilitate a deeper level of second-order change based upon symbolic communication. Task-analysis procedures should be employed to analyze how symbolic interventions affect the problem-solving strategies of families in therapy if the grounding conceptual framework is utilized to provide a broader guide in order to grasp the gestalt of symbolic experiential therapy credibility.

THE TRAINING OF FAMILY THERAPISTS

Learning family therapy occurs in three different stages: (1) learning *about* family therapy, which is probably best done in seminars and workshops; (2) learning *to do* family therapy, with requires the pressure of clinical experience; and (3) *being* a family therapist, which involves orienting one's clinical work around families, a reorientation in which the therapist comes to believe in families rather than individuals.

The first stage has to do with who should do family therapy. It is important that the persons have a background of some powerful existential experience—some kind of Zenlike explosion, a brief episode of craziness, individual therapy, or some other identity crisis or confrontation with himself or herself. These might include therapy, an extended work experience outside of psychotherapy, or perhaps military service. One characteristic of such experience is that the person loses the sense of uniqueness while retaining fascination with his or her complexity.

A background of clinical experience is essential. The people who make the best use of training include frustrated physicians or battle-experienced social workers who have come to the point of giving up without becoming nonsubjective. These people have an experiential sense of systems and have learned to work through and within experience more than ideas. They are acquainted with but not frightened by their own impotence. We think that the symbolic experimental method of family therapy is best practiced by professional psychotherapists. The discipline of the therapist is not critical, but discipline is required.

There are problems with professionally qualified people attempting to learn family therapy. Physicians have difficulty because of their specificity of functioning and their training, which focuses on the person in pain. Persons with graduate training have trouble switching to family therapy because of their mind lock into research methodology, which forces a need to stay with linear thinking. Likewise, training programs that focus on theory construction often lose their clinical perspective. The theory takes up so much room in the office that there is not enough room for the family.

LEARNING ABOUT FAMILY THERAPY Learning is best initiated by reading, attending seminars, and observing clinical work (either live or by videotape). All of these combine to introduce therapists to a new language and thinking paradigm that goes with family work. Exposure to the language also stimulates their thinking and helps interest them in conceptualizing about families and family therapy.

Some clinical experience is necessary in order to learn about family therapy. Experience can be acquired in several ways—such as by watching an experienced family therapist work or by seeing families in a context such as inpatient psychiatry service, a medication clinic, or a social agency. These experiences provide a look into the back window of family therapy. There is no great demand for change in the families seen in these contexts, but it is a way to learn about the power and functioning of the family.

LEARNING TO DO FAMILY THERAPY Therapists learn to do family therapy best in an outpatient setting. A person who is capable of doing family therapy should be able to do the following:

1. Take a family system history.
2. Understand basic systems thinking and the ways in which it complements and is related to clinical work in mental health areas.
3. Assess family structure and process.
4. Provide crisis intervention for couples and families.
5. Do long-term couples therapy.
6. Organize and construct a family conference around a crisis in a family or an illness in a family.
7. Know the potential use of family systems methods in general psychiatric and medical practices, for example, in doing medication checks or in seeing patients with psychosomatic illness.
8. Utilize consultation in the practice of psychotherapy.

BEING A FAMILY THERAPIST This is a more complex, long-range process. Our impression is that fewer and fewer people practice family therapy today. This is true because of the demands that the culture places on therapists to describe what they are doing in linear, cause–effect language. Those components of the culture that have the most power have little tolerance for the circular, non-rational thinking that goes with more serious work with families. As a discipline, family therapy attempted to sell itself to the culture. The effort was partially successful, but the culture bought only parts of family therapy, and in this new marketplace thinking about psychotherapy, the customer is always right. But as we indicated earlier, psychotherapy is a countercultural process, and the demand to serve the needs of the customer results in a therapy for social adaptation. "Why *can't* we all ride together and be cowboy buckaroos?"

Another reason why few practice family therapy today is that families are powerful. And therapists are injured by families, become frightened, and presume that the feeling of being in over their heads is a measure of their incompetence when it comes to working with the whole (multigenerational) family.

As background, it should be understood that marital therapy is a unigenerational, psychosocial process and family therapy is a multigenerational, biopsychosocial process. Thus, the voltage is higher, the problems more difficult, and the pressures much greater in practicing family therapy. Individual therapy is also biopsychosocial, but it operates from an intrapsychic framework dealing with introjects. The model we believe in for learning family therapy utilizes cotherapy. The cotherapy team should be embedded in a cuddle group of other cotherapy teams. Our ideal sequencing of clinical experiences in becoming a family therapist is as follows:

1.   We like to think that the process of learning begins with a cotherapy team treating a marital couple. This opportunity is really a play at psychotherapy. The actual process is to supervise the bilateral pseudotherapy between the husband and wife, who are already deeply transferred to each other.

2.   The cotherapy team treats a couples group. Here the process moves from the husband/wife supporting each other to a later effort to offer themselves as patients. The couples group also must resolve the male–female subgroup and thereafter the emotional triangulation that challenges each couple.

3.   The next stage in training to be a family therapist is for the cotherapy team to treat an individual, preferably an individual who has been in treatment with his or her family by another therapist. The patient could be someone from a family therapy success who wants to go on in intrapsychic development; it may be a person who is working through a divorce and who is now alone; or it might be an older adolescent who is individuated after family therapy and is living at a distance from the family.

4.   The final stage is cotherapy with a family. With this stage completed, the trainee can go back through the whole process in several different patterns: (1) with a peer for cotherapist or (2) without a cotherapist but with a consultant who comes in on the second interview and is available from time to time to evaluate and help clarify the situation in therapy. Thus, the trainee should learn couples therapy first, individual therapy later, and family therapy last. Individual treatment also gives therapists new to psychotherapy a way to learn about therapeusis (mutually therapeutic relationships). A family therapist without exposure to individual therapy runs the risk of being too strategic, too technique addicted. At this point, I can't resist an observation from Whitaker: "Techniques are something to use while waiting for the therapist to arrive."

Learning individual therapy should include individual therapy with children, using the model we described earlier. It is difficult to become a family therapist without an extended experience with children. Doing therapy with children teaches the therapist nonverbal methods as well as extensive work with the use of fantasy and communication.

Therapy for the therapist is crucial. We don't think one is prepared to do psychotherapy until one has had the experience of being a patient. When I am working with a difficult case in the psychiatric world I am inclined to stick with psychotherapy when the situation becomes difficult. I would not do this if it were not for my experience as a patient and the impact that it had on me. The family therapist should start his or her investment by having marital therapy and then family therapy with three generations. Where family therapy is not available, a useful substitution is to do a study of one's own family with a group of colleagues involved in the same project. After work with the therapists, one may decide to go into extensive intrapsychic therapy to increase access to his or her own creativity.

The reason for family therapy for therapists and the study of the therapist's own family is not only to get them individuated out of their families but also to help them develop more belongingness to their family. They need to gain a sense of the flexibility of the triangles in their own families. Jung (1961) said of people who leave their families that their development ceases at the point at which they depart. This developmental arrest is profoundly damaging to the family therapist.

We would like to expand some of the ideas generated earlier in this chapter. First of all, we are dedicated to cotherapy as the primary model of training. We operate our cotherapy training as peers. Some think that cotherapy should not be done except between equal and heterosexual peers. This is ideal but not always available. We think that any cotherapy team develops a model for pairing that has therapeutic value to the family. When we, two males, are together, we talk about being a father and a mother, and families often tease us about that playful symbolic pattern. Much of our cotherapy with trainees works out something like an older man's marriage to a young wife. The less experienced member of the cotherapy team tends to follow the lead of the more experienced.

For example, when a learner works with a teacher, the learner is much more likely to follow the teacher's lead. On the other hand, the teacher can use the learner's working time as a time to pull away from the family so that he or she may reenter at a different point. When the cotherapy team is made up of peers of the same generation and experience, the functioning is always much more mixed and provides more security and more freedom for each person. It takes time to develop a cotherapy team so that each member can work together and trust each other. One learns the most about cotherapy when working with the same cotherapist in different treatment settings.

The cotherapy method for training is especially useful when family therapists are advanced in their training. Consider how a surgeon learns to do surgery: The resident performs surgery with the professor. There is a strong tradition for this model in medicine, which may have to do with why we prefer it. The method has much to do with an identification with the teacher. The Hippocratic oath suggests that the professor and student will live together as father and son. It is very clear to us that our investment in a learner has to do with his or her learning and vice versa. Many trainees ask if they can see a family; they do, then drift away. Others become more invested in the work, and we naturally become more invested in them.

The core of our training is organized around the use of cotherapy. Regardless of where the trainee is in his or her experience, we operate our cotherapy training as peers. We do not invite the trainee in as a cotherapist so that we can provide him or her with an experience; we invite the trainee in because we need him or her. The best model for the cotherapy team is the marital relationship, in which the therapists function both as two separate I's and as a we. As teachers, we form cotherapy units with the trainees, the trainees develop cotherapy teams with each other, and we meet weekly as a group to discuss cases and conceptual issues. This cuddle group of therapists provides us a way to gain more personally from our psychotherapy work. It is here that we can celebrate our wins and mourn our losses. It also gives us a way to develop conceptually the basis of psychotherapy work.

It is important to mix up methods of training so that the therapist does not end up programmed to a set pattern. It is useful to watch and be watched from behind a one-way mirror and to use videotape so that the therapist can review the session after the fact.

Something more needs to be said about the importance of using couples groups in training family therapists. It is a unique, valuable experience, especially when working with couples who may have been consulting with the therapist previously. In the beginning, it is best if couples are selected who are not too disturbed. Cotherapy with a couples group allows the trainee and supervisor to take part with other couples but simultaneously to operate in an administrative role and to lose themselves in or utilize personal involvement. The dynamics of the individuals supporting their spouses gradually weakens, and the war goes on between the males and the females. Once the battle of the sexes has been worked through, triangles between husband 1, his wife, and wife 2; or wife 1, husband 1, and husband 2 preoccupy the couples group. The therapist has the opportunity to live through the experience of these family dynamics.

Does a family therapist need to have full child therapy training? We do not think so. As noted above, the more that the therapist knows about children, the better. He or she can also learn about children from having his or her own or from working part-time in a child-related agency such as a school or other treatment facility. The important factor is that the therapist learns how to relate to children, that he or she learns the importance of children and the special stresses that they generate and are exposed to in any multigenerational group.

SUMMARY

In this presentation of one method for helping families develop a quality change in their living pattern, we have not been able to describe fully the reciprocal effects of such efforts on the therapist as a person. Interaction obviously impacts on each interactor. As a father in a family so accurately put it at their ending interview, "Overall, I've really enjoyed coming here…but something must happen to you guys in all this too. I mean, even if you just sat there, you would have to get something personal out of it."

Like becoming a parent in the nuclear family, the qualitative effects of becoming a family therapist are often dramatic. Treating families is both painful and deeply moving. Working with families changes the definition of competence, and success and failure become more ambiguous (Keith & Whitaker, 1980). Doing psychotherapy is change-inducing in its symbolic effect on the therapist. The power of the family, like that of the infant, is seductive and threatening. The therapist and the conceptual framework that emanates from his or her work live between the pressure for constrictive narrowing toward more specific definition and the need for openness and vulnerability that lead to growth and reparative experience.

ANNOTATED SUGGESTED READINGS

Campbell, J., & Robinson, H. M. (1961). *A skeleton key to* Finnegan's Wake. New York: Viking Press.
> Campbell and Robinson's masterful review of Joyce's classic is a useful guided tour into the murky terrain of primary process language. The book provides an artful introduction to the schizophrenic lurking in each of us.

Connell, G. M., Bumberry, W. M., & Mitten, T. J. (1999). *Reshaping family relationships: The symbolic therapy of Carl Whitaker.* New York: Brunner/Mazel.
> A detailed analysis of Carl Whitaker's therapeutic methodology. Two of the authors worked closely with Dr. Whitaker and know his work intimately. The authors divide the therapeutic process into six stages and describe experiential therapeutic techniques in each stage. They bring a new ordering to this pattern of therapeutic work without disrupting its highly subjective quality.

García-Márquez, G. (1971). *One hundred years of solitude.* New York: Avon Books.
> A fictionalized family chronicle weaving between history and dream in the way that we think families in treatment do. The images in this book are vivid and frequently come to mind when seeing families in the clinic.

Haley, J. (1973). *Uncommon therapy.* New York: Norton.
> A series of brilliant case reports from Milton Erickson's work. We think that it teaches best how to make creative yet pragmatic interventions in common but complex clinical situations.

Neill, J. R., & Kniskern, D. P. (Eds.). (1982). *From psyche to system. The evolving therapy of Carl Whitaker.* New York: Guilford Press.
> A finally crafted review of Carl Whitaker's work from the '50s to the late '70s. Salvador Minuchin compared it to a retrospective exhibit of an artist's work.

Napier, A., & Whitaker, C. A. (1978). *The family crucible.* New York: Harper and Row.
> A review of a family's therapy experience in a case where Napier and Whitaker work as cotherapists. *The Family Crucible* complements this chapter perfectly.

Whitaker, C. A. (1989). *Midnight musings of a family therapist* (M. Ryan, Ed.). New York: Norton.
> This is a unique book. It was prepared with the editorial help of M. Ryan. Dr. Whitaker took a collection of notes accumulated over 20 years. The content is deeply subjective, poetic reflections on family psychotherapeutic work. It is something of a meditation/creativity stimulus for psychotherapists, to be read at random and in small doses.

Whitaker, C. A., & Bumberry, W. M. (1988). *Dancing with families: A symbolic experiential approach.* New York: Brunner/Mazel.

This book reviews a brief intensive course of therapy with a family. It contains reflections on families, marriage, children, sex, death, the role of the therapist, and the person of the therapist. There are extended interview transcripts with comments by Drs. Whitaker and Bumberry. The book was published with an accompanying instructive 60-minute videotape, "Dancing with the Family," which an edited summary of the family interviews with Bumberry interviewing Whitaker about the therapy interposed.

Whitaker, C. A., & Malone, T.P. (1981). *The roots of psychotherapy* (2nd ed.). New York: Brunner/Mazel.

A reissue of the book first published in 1953. The book develops the experiential component of psychotherapy and adds historical depth to the ideas presented in this chapter.

REFERENCES

Castaneda, C. (1975). *Tales of Power.* New York: Simon & Schuster.

Connell, G. M., Bumberry, W. M., & Mitten, T. J. (1999). *Reshaping family relationships: The symbolic therapy of Carl Whitaker.* New York: Brunner/Mazel.

Ehrenwald, J. (1966). *Psychotherapy: Myth and method, an integrative approach.* New York: Grune & Stratton.

Grinker, R. R., Sr. (1971). Biomedical education on a system. *Archives of General Psychiatry, 24,* 291–297.

Heatherington, L., & Friedlander, M. L. (1990, July). Couple and family therapy alliance scales: Empirical considerations. *Journal of Marital & Family Therapy, 16*(3), 299–306.

Jung, C. G. (1961). *Memories, dreams, reflections.* (A. Jaffe, Ed.). New York: Pantheon.

Keith, D. V., & Whitaker, C. A. (1988). *The presence of the past: Continuity and change in the symbolic structure of families.* New York: Guilford Press.

Minuchin, S. (1974). *Families and family therapy.* Cambridge, MA: Harvard University Press.

Napier, A., & Whitaker, C. A. (1978). *The family crucible.* New York: Harper and Row.

Neill, J. R., & Kniskern, D. P. (Eds.). (1982). *From psyche to system: The evolving therapy of Carl Whitaker.* New York: Guilford Press.

Rank, O. (1936). *Will therapy.* New York: Alfred A. Knopf.

Rogers, C. R. (1980). *A way of being.* Boston: Houghton Mifflin.

Warkentin, J., Felder, R. E., Malone, T. P., & Whitaker, C. A. (1961). The usefulness of craziness. *Medical Times, 89.* 587–590.

Whitaker, C. A. (Ed.). (1958). *Psychotherapy of chronic schizophrenia.* Boston: Little, Brown.

Whitaker, C. A., & Malone, T. P. (1953). *The roots of psychotherapy.* New York: Blakiston.

Winnicott, D. W. (1949). Hate in the countertransference. *The International Journal of Psychoanalysis, 30,* 69–74.

Winnicott, D. W. (1971). *Playing and reality.* New York: Basic Books.

Wynne, L. C., Ryckoff, I. N., Day, J., & Hirsch, S. I. (1958). Pseudomutuality in the family relations of schizophrenics. *Psychiatry, 21,* 205–220.

CHAPTER 6

Structural Family Therapy

JORGE COLAPINTO

DEFINITION

Structural family therapy is a model of treatment based on systems theory that was developed primarily at the Philadelphia Child Guidance Clinic, under the leadership of Salvador Minuchin. The model's distinctive features are its emphasis on structural change as the main goal of therapy, which acquires preeminence over the details of individual change, and the attention paid to the therapist as an active agent in the process of restructuring the family.

HISTORICAL DEVELOPMENT

Structural family therapy was the child of necessity, or so the student may conclude in tracing the origins of the movement back to the early 1960s, to the time when Minuchin was doing therapy, training, and research at the Wiltwyck School for Boys in New York. Admittedly, our historical account does not need to start precisely there, but the development of a treatment model—no less than the development of an individual or a family—can only be told by introducing a certain punctuation and discarding alternative ones.

We could choose a more distant point in time and focus on Minuchin's experience in the newborn Israel, where families from all over the world converged carrying their bits of common purpose and their lots of regional idiosyncrasies, and found a unique opportunity to live the combination of cultural universals and cultural specifics. Or, reaching further back, we could think of Minuchin's childhood as the son of a Jewish family in the rural Argentina of the 1920s and wonder about the influence of this early exposure to alternative cultures—different rules, different truths—on his conception of human nature. Any of these periods in the life of the developer of structural family therapy could be justified as a starting point for an account of his creation. The experiences provided by both are congruent with philosophical viewpoints deeply rooted in the architecture of the model—for instance, that we are more human than otherwise, that we share a common range of potentialities that each of us displays differentially as a function of our specific context.

But the Wiltwyck experience stands out as a powerful catalyst of conceptual production because of a peculiar combination of circumstances. First of all, the population of Wiltwyck consisted of delinquent boys from disorganized, multi-problem, poor families. Traditional psychotherapeutic techniques, largely developed to fulfill the demands of verbally articulate, middle-class patients besieged by intrapsychic conflicts, did not appear to have a significant impact on these youngsters. Improvements achieved through the use of these and other techniques in the residential setting of the school tended to disappear as soon as the child returned to his family (Minuchin, 1961). The serious concerns associated with delinquency, from both the point of view of society and of the delinquent individual himself, necessarily stimulated the quest for alternative approaches.

The second circumstance was the timing of the Wiltwyck experience: It coincided with the consolidation of an idea that emerged in the 1950s—the idea of changing families as a therapeutic enterprise (Haley, 1971). By the early '60s, family therapy thinking had become persuasive enough to catch the eye of Minuchin and his colleagues in their anxious search for more effective ways of dealing with juvenile delinquency. Finally, a third fortunate circumstance was the presence at Wiltwyck of Braulio Montalvo, whom Minuchin would later recognize as his most influential teacher (Minuchin, 1974, p. vii).

The enthusiastic group shifted the focus of attention from the intrapsychic world of the delinquent adolescent to the dynamic patterns of the family. Special techniques for the diagnosis and treatment of low socioeconomic–level families were developed (Minuchin & Montalvo, 1967), as well as some of the concepts that would become cornerstones in the model exposed a decade later.

Approaching delinquency as a family issue proved more helpful than defining it as a problem of the individual; but it should not be inferred that Minuchin and his collaborators discovered the panacea for juvenile delinquency. Rather, they experienced the limitations of therapeutic power, the fact that psychotherapy does not have the answers to poverty and other social problems (Malcolm, 1978, p. 70). Nowadays, *Families of the Slums* (Minuchin, Montalvo, Guerney, Rosman, & Schumer, 1967), the book that summarizes the experience at Wiltwyck, will more likely be found in the sociology section of the bookstore than in the psychotherapy section. But the modalities of intervention developed at Wiltwyck, and even the awareness of the limitations of therapy brought about by their application, have served as an inspirational paradigm for others. Harry Aponte, a disciple of Minuchin, has worked on the concept of bringing organization to the underorganized family through the mobilization of family and network resources (Aponte, 1976).

From the point of view of the historical development of Minuchin's model, the major contribution of Wiltwyck has been the provision of a nurturant and stimulating environment. The model spent its childhood in an atmosphere of permissiveness, with little risk of being crushed by conventional criticism. Looking retrospectively, Minuchin acknowledges that working in "a no man's land of poor families," inaccessible to traditional forms of psychotherapy, guaranteed the tolerance of the psychiatric establishment, which had not accepted Nathan Ackerman's approach to middle-class families (Malcolm, 1978, p. 84).

The possibility to test the model with a wider cross section of families came in 1965, when Minuchin was appointed director of the Philadelphia Child Guidance Clinic. The facility was at the time struggling to emerge from a severe institutional crisis—and, as Minuchin himself likes to remind us, the Chinese ideogram for "crisis" is made of "danger" and "opportunity." In this case the opportunity was there to implement a systemic approach in the treatment of a wide variety of mental health problems, and also to attract other system thinkers to a promising new pole of development for family therapy. Braulio Montalvo also moved from New York, and Jay Haley was summoned from the West Coast.

Haley's own conceptual framework differs in significant aspects from that of Minuchin, but undoubtedly the ideas of both men contributed a lot to the growth and strengthening of each other's models—sometimes through the borrowing of concepts and techniques, many times by providing the contrasting pictures against which the respective positions each became better defined. Together with Montalvo, Haley was a key factor in the intensive training program that Minuchin wanted and had implemented at the Philadelphia Child Guidance Clinic. The format of the program, with its emphasis on live supervision and videotape analysis, facilitated the discussion and refinement of theoretical concepts and has continuously been a primary influence on the shaping of the model. The preface to *Families and Family Therapy* (Minuchin, 1974) acknowledges the seminal value of the author's association with Haley and Montalvo.

While Minuchin continued his innovative work in Philadelphia, the clinical and research data originating in different strains of family therapy continued to accumulate, up to a point at which alternative and competitive theoretical renderings became possible. The growing drive for a systemic way of looking at behavior and behavior change had to differentiate itself from the attempts to absorb family dynamics into a more or less expanded version of psychoanalysis (Minuchin, 1969, pp. 179–187). A first basic formulation of Minuchin's own brand of family therapy was almost at hand; it only needed a second catalyst, a context comparable to Wiltwyck.

The context was provided by the association of the Philadelphia Child Guidance Clinic with the Children's Hospital of Philadelphia, which brought Minuchin to the field of psychosomatic conditions. The project started as a challenge, in many ways similar to the one posed by the delinquent boys of Wiltwyck. Once again the therapist had to operate under the pressures of running time. The urgency, of a social nature at Wiltwyck, was a medical one at the hospital. The patients who first forced a new turn of the screw in the shaping of Minuchin's model were diabetic children with an unusually high number of emergency hospitalizations for acidosis. Their conditions could not be explained medically and would not respond to classical individual psychotherapy, which focused on improving the patient's ability to handle his or her own stress. Only when the stress was understood and treated in the context of the family could the problem be solved (Baker, Minuchin, Milman, Liebman, & Todd, 1975). Minuchin's team accumulated clinical and research evidence of the connection between certain family characteristics and the extreme vulnerability of this group of patients. The same characteristics—enmeshment, overprotectiveness, rigidity, lack of conflict resolution—were also observed in the families of asthmatic children who presented severe, recurrent attacks and/or a heavy dependence on steroids (Liebman, Minuchin, & Baker, 1974a, 1974b, 1974c; Liebman, Minuchin, Baker, & Rosman, 1976, 1977 [pp. 153–171]; Minuchin, Baker, Rosman, Liebman, Milman, & Todd, 1975).

The therapeutic paradigm that began to evolve focused on a push for clearer boundaries, increased flexibility in family transactions, the actualization of hidden family conflicts, and the modification of the (usually overinvolved) role of the patient in them. The need to *enact* dysfunctional transactions in the session (prescribed by the model so that they could be observed and corrected) led therapists to deliberately provoke family crises (Minuchin & Barcai, 1969, pp. 199–220), in contrast with the supportive, shielding role prescribed by more traditional approaches. If the underorganized families of juvenile delinquents invited the exploration of new routes, the hovering, overconcerned families of psychosomatic children led to the articulation of a first version of structural family therapy.

In an early advance of a new conceptual model derived from the principles of general systems theory (Minuchin, 1970), the clinical material chosen as illustration is a case of anorexia nervosa. Although Minuchin's involvement with this condition was practically simultaneous with his work with diabetics and asthmatics, anorexia nervosa provided a special opportunity because in this case the implementation of the model aims at eliminating the disease itself, while in the other two cases it cannot go beyond the prevention of its exacerbation. In both diabetes and asthma, the emotional link is the triggering of a somatic episode, but it operates on a basic preexistent physiological vulnerability—a metabolic disorder, an allergy. Thus, the terms *psychosomatic diabetic* and *psychosomatic asthmatic* do not imply an emotional etiology for either of the two conditions. In anorexia nervosa, on the other hand, the role of such vulnerability is small or nonexistent. Emotional factors can be held entirely responsible for the condition, and then the therapeutic potential of the model can be more fully assessed. Clinical and research experience with anorexia is the most widely documented of the model's application (e.g., Liebman, Minuchin, & Baker, 1974a, 1974b; Minuchin, Baker, Liebman, Milman, Rosman, & Todd, 1973; Rosman, Minuchin, & Liebman, 1975; Rosman, Minuchin, Liebman, & Baker, 1976, 1977 [pp. 341–348]).

During the first half of the 1970s, with the Philadelphia clinic already established as a leading training center for family therapists, Minuchin continued his work with psychosomatics. In 1972, he invited Bernice Rosman, who had worked with him at Wiltwyck and coauthored *Families of the Slums*, to join the clinic as director of research. Minuchin, Rosman, and the pediatrician Lester Baker became the core of a clinical and research team that culminated its work six years later with the publication of *Psychosomatic Families* (Minuchin, Rosman, & Baker, 1978).

Also in 1972, Minuchin published the first systematic formulation of his model in "Structural Family Therapy" (Minuchin, 1972). Many of the basic principles of the current model are already present in this article: the characterization of therapy as a transitional event, where the therapist's function is to help the family reach a new stage; the emphasis on present reality as opposed to history; the displacement of the locus of pathology from the individual to the system of transactions, from the symptom to the family's reaction to it; the understanding of diagnosis as a constructed reality; the attention paid to the points of entry that each family system offers to the therapist; the therapeutic strategy focused on the realignment of the structural relationships within the family, on a change of rules that will allow the system to maximize its potential for conflict resolution and individual growth.

During this same period of time, the clinical experience supporting the model went far beyond the psychosomatic field. Under Minuchin's leadership, the techniques and concepts of structural family therapy were being applied by the clinic's staff and trainees to school phobias, adolescent runaways, drug addictions, and the whole range of problems typically brought for treatment to a child clinic. The model was finally reaching all sorts of families from all socioeconomic levels and with a variety of presenting problems.

In 1974, Minuchin presented structural family therapy in book form (Minuchin, 1974), and the Philadelphia Child Guidance Clinic moved to a modern, larger building complex together with Children's Hospital. A process of fast expansion started: The availability of services and staff increased dramatically, and a totally new organizational context developed. The visibility of the Philadelphia Child Guidance Clinic, which reached international renown, brought a new challenge to the model in the form of increasing and not always positive attention from the psychiatric establishment. In 1975, Minuchin chose to step down from his administrative duties and to concentrate on the teaching of his methods and ideas to younger generations, at the specially created Family Therapy Training Center.

This move signaled the beginning of the latest stage in the development of the model, a period of theoretical creation driven by the need to develop a didactically powerful body of systemic concepts consistent with the richness of clinical data. The current status of structural family therapy (Minuchin & Fishman, 1981) is characterized by an emphasis on training and theoretical issues. In the delivery of training, increasing attention is being paid to the therapist's epistemology—concepts, perspectives, goals, attitudes—as a "set" that conditions the learning of techniques. In the development of theory, the trend is to refine the early systemic concepts that served as foundations of the model by looking into ideas developed by systems thinkers in other fields.

TENETS OF THE MODEL

Structural family therapy is primarily a way of thinking about and operating in three related areas: the family, the presenting problem, and the process of change.

THE FAMILY

The family is conceptualized as a living open system. In every system, the parts are functionally interdependent in ways dictated by the supraindividual functions of the whole. In a system AB, A's passivity is read as a response to B's initiative (interdependence), while the passivity–initiative pattern is one of the ways in which the system carries on its functions (e.g., the provision of a nurturant environment for A and B). The set of rules regulating the interactions among members of the system is its structure.

As an *open* system the family is subjected to and impinges on the surrounding environment. This implies that family members are not the only architects of their family shape; relevant rules may be imposed by the immediate group of reference or by the culture in the broader sense. When we recognize that Mr. Brown's distant relationship to Jimmy is related to Mrs. Brown's overinvolvement with Jimmy, we are witnessing an idiosyncratic family arrangement as well as the regulating effects of a society that encourages mothers to be closer to children and fathers to keep more distance.

Finally, as a *living* system the family is in constant transformation: Transactional rules evolve over time as each family group negotiates the particular arrangements that are more economical and effective for any given period in its life as a system. This evolution, as any other, is regulated by the interplay of homeostasis and change.

Homeostasis designates the patterns of transactions that assure the stability of the system, the maintenance of its basic characteristics as they can be described at a certain point in time; homeostatic processes tend to keep the status quo (Jackson, 1957, 1965). The two-way process that links A's passivity to B's initiative serves a homeostatic purpose for the system AB, as do the father's distance, the mother's proximity, and Jimmy's eventual symptomatology for the Browns. When viewed from the perspective of homeostasis, individual behaviors interlock like the pieces in a puzzle, a quality that is usually referred to as *complementarity*.

Change, on the other hand, is the reaccommodation that the living system undergoes in order to adjust to a different set of environmental circumstances or to an intrinsic developmental need. A's passivity and B's initiative may be effectively complementary for a given period in the life of AB, but a change to a different complementarity will be in order if B becomes incapacitated. Jimmy and his parents may need to change if a second child is born. Marriage, births, entrance to school, the onset of adolescence, going to college or to a job are examples of developmental milestones in the life of most families; loss of a job, a sudden death, a promotion, a move to a different city, a divorce, or a pregnant adolescent are special events that affect the journey of some families. Whether universal or idiosyncratic, these impacts call for changes in pattern and in some cases—for example, when children are added to a couple—dramatically increase the complexity of the system by introducing differentiation. The spouse subsystem coexists with parent–child subsystems and eventually a siblings subsystem, and rules need to be developed to define who participates with whom and in what kind of situations, and who is excluded from those situations. Such definitions are called *boundaries*; they may prescribe, for instance, that children should not participate in adults' arguments, or that the oldest son has the privilege of spending certain moments alone with his father, or that the adolescent daughter has more rights to privacy than her younger siblings.

In the last analysis, homeostasis and change are matters of perspective. If one follows the family process over a brief period of time, chances are that one will witness the homeostatic mechanisms at work and the system in relative equilibrium.

Moments of crisis in which the status quo is questioned and rules are challenged are relative exceptions in the life of a system; when crises become the rule, they may be playing a role in the maintenance of homeostasis. Now if one steps back so as to visualize a more extended period, the evolvement of different, successive system configurations becomes apparent, and the process of change comes to the foreground. But by moving further back and encompassing the entire life cycle of a system, one discovers homeostasis again: The series of smooth transitions and sudden reaccommodations of which change is made presents itself as a constant attempt to maintain equilibrium or to recover it. Like the donkey that progresses to reach for the carrot that will always be out of reach, like the aristocrats in Lampedusa's *The Leopard* who wanted to change everything so that nothing would change, families fall for the bait that is the paradox of evolution. They need to accommodate in order to remain the same, and accommodation moves them into something different.

This ongoing process can be arrested. Families can fail to respond to a new demand from the environment or from their own development: They will not substitute new rules of transactions for the ones that have been patterning their functioning. AB finds it impossible to let go of the passivity–initiative pattern even if B is now incapacitated; Jimmy and his mother find it impossible to let go of a tight relationship that was developmentally appropriate when Jimmy was two but not now that he is 18. Maybe Jimmy started showing trouble in school when he was 12, but the family insisted on the same structure with the mother monitoring all communications around Jimmy and the school, so that Jimmy was protected from his father's anger and the father from his own disappointment.

When families get stagnated in their development, their transactional patterns become stereotyped. Homeostatic mechanisms exacerbate as the system holds tightly to a rigid script. Any movement threatening a departure from the status quo is swiftly corrected. If the father grows tougher on Jimmy, the mother will intercede and the father will withdraw. Intergenerational coalitions that subvert natural hierarchies (e.g., the mother and son against the father), triangular patterns where parents use a child as a battleground, and other dysfunctional arrangements serve the purpose of avoiding the onset of open conflict within the system. Conflict avoidance, then, guarantees a certain sense of equilibrium but at the same time prevents growth and differentiation, which are the offspring of conflict resolution. The higher levels of conflict avoidance are found in *enmeshed* families—where the extreme sense of closeness, belonging, and loyalty minimize the chances of disagreement—and, at the other end of the continuum, in *disengaged* families, where the same effect is produced by excessive distance and a false sense of independence.

In their efforts to keep a precarious balance, family members stick to myths that are very narrow definitions of themselves as a whole and as individuals—constructed realities made by the interlocking of limited facets of the respective selves, which leave most of the system's potentials unused. When these families come to therapy, they typically present themselves as a poor version of what they really are. For example, the white area in the center of Figure 6.1 represents the myth, "I am this way and can only be this way, and the same is true for him and for her, and we cannot relate in any other way than our way," while the shaded area contains the available but as yet not utilized alternatives.

FIGURE 6.1 | **A MODEL OF STRUCTURAL FAMILY THERAPY**

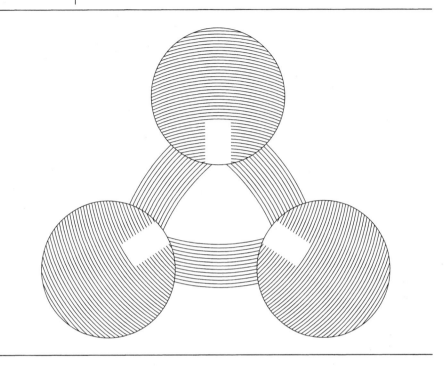

THE PRESENTING PROBLEM

Structural family therapy conceptualizes the problem behavior as a partial aspect of the family structure of transactions. The complaint, for instance, that Jimmy is undisciplined and aggressive needs to be put in perspective by relating it to the context of Jimmy's family.

For one thing, the therapist has to find out the position and function of the problem behavior: When does Jimmy turn aggressive? What happens immediately before? How do others react to his misbehavior? Is Jimmy more undisciplined toward his mother than toward his father? Do the parents agree on how to handle him? What is the homeostatic benefit from the sequential patterns in which the problem behavior is imbedded? The individual problem is seen as a complement of other behaviors, a part of the status quo, a token of the system's dysfunction; in short, the system as it is supports the system.

The therapist also has to diagnose the structure of the family's perceptions in connection with the presenting problem. Who is more concerned about Jimmy's lack of discipline? Does everybody concur that he is aggressive? That his behavior is the most troublesome problem in the family? What are the other, more positive facets in Jimmy's self that go unnoticed? Is the family exaggerating in labeling as "aggressive" a child that maybe is just more exuberant than his siblings? Is the family failing to accommodate their perceptions and expectations to the fact that Jimmy is now 18 years old? Does the system draw a homeostatic gain from perceiving Jimmy primarily as a symptomatic child? An axiom of structural family therapy, illustrated by Figure 6.1, is that a vast area of Jimmy's self is out of sight for both his relatives and himself, and that there is a systematic support for this blindness.

So the interactional network knitted around the motive of complaint is the real presenting problem for the structural family therapist. The key element in this view is the concept of systemic *support*. The model does *not* claim a direct causal line between system and problem behavior; the emphasis is on maintenance rather than on causation. Certainly, one sometimes observes families and listens to their stories and can almost see the pathways leading from transactional structure to symptomatology. But even in these cases, the model warns us that we are dealing with current transactions and current memories as they are organized *now*, after the problem has crystallized. Thus, instead of a simplistic, one-way causal connection, the model postulates an ongoing process of mutual accommodation between the system's rules and the individual's predispositions and vulnerabilities. Maybe Jimmy was born with a "strong temperament" *and* to a system that needed to pay special attention to his temper tantrums, to highlight his negative facets while ignoring the positive ones. Within this context, Jimmy learned about his identity and about the benefits of being perceived as an aggressive child. By the time he was nine, Jimmy was an expert participant in a mutually escalating game of defiance and punishment. These mechanisms—selective attention, deviance amplification, labeling, counterescalation—are some of the ways in which a system may contribute to the etiology of a "problem." Jimmy's cousin Fred was born at about the same time and with the same "strong temperament," but he is now a class leader and a junior tennis champ.

Discussions around etiological history, in any case, are largely academic from the perspective of structural family therapy, whose interest is focused on the *current* supportive relation between system and problem behavior. The model shares with other systemic approaches the radical idea that knowledge of the origins of a problem is largely irrelevant for the process of therapeutic change (Minuchin & Fishman, 1979). The identification of etiological sequences may be helpful in *preventing* problems from happening to families, but once they have happened and are eventually brought to therapy, history has already occurred and cannot be undone. An elaborate understanding of the problem history may in fact hinder the therapist's operation by encouraging an excessive focus on what appears as *not* modifiable.

THE PROCESS OF THERAPEUTIC CHANGE

Consistent with its basic tenet that the problems brought to therapy are ultimately dysfunctions of the family structure, the model looks for a therapeutic solution in the modification of such structure. This usually requires changes in the relative positions of family members; more proximity may be necessary between the husband and wife, more distance between the mother and son. Hierarchical relations and coalitions are frequently in need of a redefinition. New alternative rules for transacting must be explored. The mother, for instance, may be required to abstain from intervening automatically whenever an interaction between her husband and son reaches a certain pitch, while the father and son should not automatically abort an argument just because it upsets Mom. Frozen conflicts have to be acknowledged and dealt with so that they can be solved, and the natural road to growth reopened.

Therapeutic change is then the process of helping the family to outgrow their stereotyped patterns, of which the presenting problem is a part. This process transpires within a special context, the *therapeutic system*, that offers a unique chance to challenge the rules of the family. The privileged position of the therapist allows him or her to request from the family members different behaviors and to invite different perceptions, thus altering their interaction and perspective. The family then has an opportunity to experience transactional patterns that have not been allowed under their prevailing homeostatic rules. The system's limits are probed and pushed, and its narrow self-definitions are questioned; in the process, the family's capacity to tolerate and handle stress or conflict increases, and their perceived reality becomes richer, more complex.

In looking for materials to build this expansion of the family's reality— alternative behaviors, attitudes, perceptions, affinities, expectations—the structural family therapist has one primary source from which to draw: the family. The model contends that beyond the systemic constraints that keep the family functioning at an inadequate level, there exists an as yet underutilized pool of potential resources (see Figure 6.1, shaded areas). Releasing these resources so that the system can change, and changing the system so that the resources can be released, are simultaneous processes that require the restructuring input of the therapist. The therapist's role will be discussed at some length in the following section.

APPLICATION

In discussing the practical applications of structural family therapy, the first point to be made is that the model is not just a cluster of techniques with specific indications, but rather a consistent way of thinking and operating, derived from the basic tenet that human problems can only be understood and treated in context. As such, the model is in principle applicable to any human system in need of change.

The family, however, presents some unique characteristics that make it a comparatively accessible and rewarding field of application. A natural group with a history and a future, family members tend to remain associated even under circumstances that would be lethal for the fate of other human groups—such as high levels of ongoing conflict, extreme negative feelings, and ultimate dysfunctionality—and can then be expected (more than as members of other groups) to endure the challenges of therapy. Families usually have the motivation to invest time, money, energy, and affection for the sake of one of their members. They also offer a prospect of continuity for the changes initiated during therapy.

In actual practice, structural family therapy has been mostly applied to—and has grown from—families where a son or daughter is the identified patient. This context offers some additional advantages, in that cultural expectations define the family as a most relevant environment for a child, and the parents as directly responsible for his or her well-being. The extent of the bias, if any, built into the model's current formulations by virtue of the specifics of child psychotherapy will only be measurable on extensive application of structural family therapy to "adult" problems.

There are no specific requirements that families or problems should meet for the model to be applicable. True, the family needs to be motivated and resourceful, but a systemic understanding implies that any family can be motivated and no family is resourceless—otherwise the point of meeting the therapist would never have been reached. Similarly, the problem must be a transactional one, but this, according to systems thinking, is a matter of how the problem is defined, described, or framed. In addition to the work with low socioeconomic–level families, delinquency, and psychosomatic illness (already mentioned in connection with the historical development of the model), the literature on structural family therapy includes case material from many different origins. School-related problems (Aponte, 1976; Berger, 1974; Moskowitz, 1976), drug abuse (Stanton, 1978; Stanton & Todd, 1979; Stanton et al., 1978), mental retardation (Fishman, Scott, & Betof, 1977), specific symptoms such as elective mutism (Rosenberg & Lindblad, 1978), and encopresis (Andolfi, 1978) are some examples. Although not a complete list, these cases give an idea of the variety of clinical contexts to which the model has been applied.

While it is difficult to imagine a family problem that could *not* be approached from structural family therapy, there are nonetheless certain contexts, of a different sort, that limit the applicability of the model. Hospitalization of the identified patient, for instance, hinders the efforts to restructure the family because of the unnatural isolation of a key member, the confirmation of the family's definition of the problem, and the naturalization of a crucial source of energy for family change. By artificially removing stress from the family's reality, hospitalization tends to facilitate and reinforce the operation of homeostatic mechanisms; the resulting therapeutic system is one in which the therapist's power to challenge stereotyped transactional rules effectively is greatly diminished. A similar constraint is typically associated with medication and generally with any condition that appeases crisis and takes the motivation for change away from the system.

Another crucial variable in determining the applicability of structural family therapy is the therapist's acceptance of the goals set by the model for the therapeutic enterprise and of the function prescribed for him or her. These are areas in which structural family therapy departs considerably from some other approaches, as will be described in the following discussion.

GOALS AND FUNCTION OF THERAPY

The basic goal of structural family therapy is the restructuralization of the family's system of transactional rules, such that the interactional reality of the family becomes more flexible, with an expanded availability of alternative ways of dealing with each other. By releasing family members from their stereotyped positions and functions, this restructuralization enables the system to mobilize its underutilized resources and to improve its ability to cope with stress and conflict. Once the constricting set of rules is outgrown, individual dysfunctional behaviors, including those described as the presenting problem, lose their support in the system and become unnecessary from the point of view of homeostasis. When the family achieves self-sufficiency in sustaining these changes without the challenging support of the therapist, therapy comes to an end.

This statement of goals may appear as too ambitious an objective; after all, the presenting problem was perhaps originally characterized as one aspect in the behavior of one out of seven family members. But from the model's point of view, the structural relationship between system and problem behavior is not just a far-fetched conceptual connection—it is an observable phenomenon. Whenever the "problem" is enacted in a session, the structure of related transactions is set in motion with the regularity of clockwork. Again, the presenting problem ultimately is the structure of relationships, and each occurrence of the problem behavior or symptom provides a metaphor for the system. Changing one of the terms in this equation implies changing the other, not as a prerequisite but as a co-variation. In structural family therapy, it is not necessary to postpone consideration of the original complaint in order to pursue structural change. On the contrary, it is possible, and frequently inescapable, to weave the fabric of the one with the threads of the other.

The therapist's function is to assist the family in achieving the necessary re-structuralization. The position prescribed for him or her by the model is similar to that of a midwife helping in a difficult delivery. Once change is born and thriving, the therapist must withdraw and resist the temptation to rear the "baby." Some therapists are specially vulnerable to this temptation because of the tradition in psychotherapy that calls for a complete, ultimate "cure" of the client—an improbable goal whose equivalent cannot be found in other health disciplines (an internist will hardly tell a patient that he or she will never need a doctor again). The concept of an ultimate cure is unthinkable in structural family therapy, which emphasizes constant growth and change as an essential feature of the family system. Hence, the structural family therapist is encouraged to limit his or her participation to the minimum that is necessary to set in motion the family's natural healing resources.

It certainly may happen that as a result of the therapist's intervention the family is helped not only to change but also to metachange—that in addition to overcoming the current crisis, the family will also be better able to deal with future events without external help. This high level of achievement is, of course, desirable, but that does not mean that other, more modest accomplishments are valueless. A restructuralization that allows Danny to go back to school while Dad takes care of Mom's depression and emptiness may be a perfectly legitimate outcome, even if the family comes back four years later when Jenny runs into adolescent trouble. From the point of view of structural family therapy, this prospect is more sensible, natural, and economic than the protracted presence of a therapist accompanying the family for years, unable to separate because of a need to make sure that things are developing in a satisfactory way.

In yet another sense, the therapist's role as prescribed by structural family therapy runs contrary to psychotherapy tradition. Much of the confessor-like behavior encouraged by other approaches is here regarded as therapeutically irrelevant, and mostly contraindicated. The therapist is not there primarily to listen to and answer sympathetically the clients' fantasies, secrets, fears, and wishes, but to assist in the development of a natural human context that can and should provide that kind of listening. He or she is not there to provide extensive one-to-one reparative experience for this and that family member but rather to operate an intensive tune-up of the natural healing system.

By limiting the duration and depth of the therapist's incursion into the family system, the model places restrictions on the therapist's curiosity and desire to be helpful, and ultimately on his or her power to control events. This loss of control is an inevitable consequence of the broadening of the therapist's scope (Minuchin, 1970).

THERAPIST'S ROLE

The therapist's role, as prescribed by the structural therapy model, includes an element of paradox. The therapist is asked to support while challenging, to attack while encouraging, to sustain while undermining. A crucial conceptual distinction is necessary here to protect the therapist from confusion or hypocrisy: He or she is requested to be *for* the people in need of help and *against* the system of transactions that cripples them.

The first task for the structural family therapist is to enter the system that needs change and to establish a working relationship. This requires a certain degree of accommodation to the system's rules—but not up to a point at which the therapist's leverage to promote change is lost. Too much challenge to the system's rules at the entry stage would lead to the therapist's dismissal; too much accommodation would void his or her input by absorbing it into homeostasis. The therapist has to find the right equation of accommodation/challenge for each particular family through a process of probing, advancing, and withdrawing that guides his or her entrance while at the same time providing clues about the family structure.

So the therapist is actively engaged in a dance with the family right from the beginning of their contact. There is little room in this model for neutral listening or floating attention. The therapist approaches the family with a series of initial hypotheses built on the basis of minimal intake information and proceeds to test, expand, and correct those hypotheses as he or she joins the family. Attention is selectively oriented toward process and away from content; he or she is more interested in how people relate than in what they have to say, listening to content mostly as a way of capturing the language of the family, the metaphors that will help catch the ears of the clients. As processes and themes unravel, the therapist's selective attention privileges some of them and discards the others. A map of the family depicting positions, alliances, hierarchies, and complementary patterns begins to emerge.

Soon the dancer turns into the stage director, creating scenarios where problems are played according to different scripts. The embedding of the symptom in family transactions is explored and highlighted. Family members are invited to talk to each other or are excluded from participation. Distances and positions are prescribed, alternative arrangements tried. The therapist–director uses whatever knowledge he or she is gaining about the actors to create situations that will uncover hidden resources or confirm suggested limitations. He or she is looking for the specific ways in which this system is keeping its homeostasis in order to disrupt them and force a new equilibrium at a higher level of complexity. But the therapist is also searching for the systems strengths that will indicate possible directions to follow. The stage director is out to make trouble for the cast.

While the model prescribes activity, initiative, and directiveness, it also warns against centrality. The therapist is supposed to organize a scenario and start the action, but then to sit back as a spectator for a while. If he or she becomes too central, the system cannot fully display its limitations and potentialities; the therapist may get trapped in a stereotyped position and will most probably be absorbed by homeostasis. The therapist needs to be mobile, to redefine his or her position constantly, displacing himself or herself from one role to another, from one alliance to another, from one challenge to the next—while at the same time maintaining a focus, a thread, a relevant theme connecting all of the moves together and to the presenting problem. Now the structural family therapist resembles a camera director in a television studio who decides to air the close-up take from one of the cameras. Far from indulging in self-praise for the beauty of the achieved picture, he or she is already planning the next take—knowing also that from time to time the total picture will be needed to remind the audience what it is all about.

In short, the role of the therapist is to move around within the system, blocking existing stereotyped patterns of transactions and fostering the development of more flexible ones. While constantly negotiating the immunological mechanisms of the family organism in order to be accepted, the therapist behaves as a strange body to which the organism must accommodate by changing and growing.

PRIMARY TECHNIQUES

Over the years, structural family therapists have developed and adapted a variety of techniques to help themselves carry out their function as prescribed by the model. The techniques can be classified, according to their main purpose, into (1) those that are primarily used in the formation of the therapeutic system and (2) the larger group of techniques more directly aimed at provoking disequilibrium and change.

JOINING TECHNIQUES

Joining is the process of coupling that occurs between the therapist and the family and that leads to the formation of the therapeutic system. In joining, the therapist becomes accepted as such by the family and remains in that position for the duration of treatment. Although the joining process is more evident during the initial phase of therapy, the maintenance of a working relationship to the family is one of the constant features in the therapist's job.

Much of the success in joining depends on the therapist's ability to listen, capacity for empathy, genuine interest in the clients' dramas, and sensitivity to feedback. But this does not exclude a need for technique in joining. The therapist's empathy, for instance, needs to be disciplined so that it does not hinder his or her ability to keep a certain distance and to operate in the direction of change. Contrary to a rather common misunderstanding, joining is not just the process of being accepted by the family; it is being accepted *as a therapist*, with a recognition of leadership. Sometimes a trainee is described as "good at joining, but not at pushing for change"; in this case, what in fact happens is that the trainee is *not* joining well. The trainee is accepted by the family, yes, but at the expense of relinquishing his or her role and being swallowed by the homeostatic rules of the system. Excessive accommodation is not good joining.

Maintenance is one of the techniques used in joining. The therapist lets himself or herself be organized by the basic rules that regulate the transactional process in the specific family system. If a four-generation family presents a rigid hierarchical structure, the therapist may find it advisable to approach the great-grandmother first and then proceed downward. In so doing, the therapist may be resisting his or her first empathic wish—perhaps to rescue the identified patient from verbal abuse—but by respecting the rules of the system, he or she will stand a better chance to generate a therapeutic impact.

However, in order to avoid total surrender, the therapist needs to perform maintenance operations in a way that does not leave him or her powerless; the therapist does *not* want to follow the family rule that Kathy should be verbally abused whenever somebody remembers one of her misdoings. As with any other joining techniques, maintenance entails an element of challenge to the system. The therapist can, for instance, approach the great-grandmother respectfully but say, "I am very concerned because I see all of you struggling to help, but you are not being helpful to each other." While the rule "great-grandma first" is being respected at one level, at a different level the therapist is creating a position one up in relation to the entire system, including the great-grandmother. The therapist is joining the rules to his or her own advantage.

While maintenance concentrates on process, the technique of *tracking* consists of an accommodation of the therapist to the content of speech. In tracking, the therapist follows the subjects offered by family members in the same way as a laser disc is read. This enables the therapist not only to join the family culture but also to become acquainted with idiosyncratic idioms and metaphors that he or she will use later to endow directive statements with additional power—by phrasing them in ways that have a special meaning for the family or for specific members.

At times the therapist will find it necessary to establish a closer relation with a certain member, usually one that positions himself or herself or is positioned by the family in the periphery of the system. This may be done through verbal interventions or through *mimesis*, a nonverbal response where the therapist adopts the other person's mood, tone of voice, or posture, or imitates his or her behavior—crossing legs, removing a jacket, lighting a cigarette. In most of the occasions, the therapist is not aware of the mimetic gesture itself but only of his or her disposition to get closer to the mimicked member. In other cases, however, mimesis is consciously used as a technique; for instance, the therapist wants to join the system via the children and accordingly decides to sit on the floor with them and play.

TECHNIQUES FOR DISEQUILIBRATION

The second, larger group of techniques encompasses all interventions aimed at changing the system. Some of them, like enactment and boundary making, are primarily employed in the creation of a different sequence of events, whereas others, like reframing, punctuation, and unbalancing, tend to foster a different perception of reality.

Reframing is putting the presenting problem in a perspective that is different from what the family brings and more workable. Typically this involves changing the definition of the original complaint from a problem of one to a problem of many. In a consultation (Minuchin, 1980) with the family of a five-year-old girl who is described by her parents as "uncontrollable," Minuchin waits silently for a couple of minutes as the girl circles noisily around the room and the mother tries to persuade her to behave, then he asks the mother, "Is this how you two run your lives together?" If the consultant had asked something such as "Is this the way *she* behaves usually?" he would be confirming the family's definition of the problem as located in the child. By making it a matter of two persons, the consultant is beginning to reframe the problem within a structural perspective.

In this example, the consultant is feeding into the system his own reading of an ongoing transaction. Sometimes a structural family therapist uses information provided by the family as the building materials for a frame. Minutes later in the session, the mothers comments, "But we try to make her do it," and the father replies, "I make her do it." Minuchin then highlights this brief interchange by commenting on the differences that the family is presenting: Mother cannot make her do it, Father can. The initial "reality" described just in terms of the girl's "uncontrollability" begins to be replaced by a more complex version involving an ineffective mother, an undisciplined child, and maybe an authoritarian father.

The consultant is reframing in terms of *complementarity*, a typical variety of the reframing technique in which any given individual's behavior is presented as contingent on somebody else's behavior. The daughter's uncontrollability is related to her mother's ineffectiveness, which is maintained by the father's taking over, which is triggered by the mother's ineffectiveness in controlling the daughter. Another example of reframing through complementarity is the question, "Who makes you feel depressed?" addressed to a man who claims to be "the" problem in the family because of his depression.

As with all other techniques employed in structural family therapy, reframing is based on an underlying attitude on the part of the therapist. He or she needs to be actively looking for structural patterns in order to find them and use them in communicating with the family. Whether the therapist will read the five-year-old's misbehavior as a function of her own "uncontrollability" or of a complementary pattern depends on his or her perspective. Also, the therapist's field of observation is so vast that he or she cannot help but be selective in perception. Whether he or she picks up that "I make her do it" or lets it pass by unnoticed amid the flow of communication depends on whether his or her selective attention is focused on structure or not. As with joining and unbalancing, reframing requires from the therapist a "set" without which the technique cannot be mastered.

The reframing attitude guides the structural family therapist in the search of structural embeddings for "individual" problems. In one case involving a young drug addict, the therapist took advantage of the sister's casual reference to the handling of money to focus on the family's generosity toward the patient and the infantile position in which he was being kept. In another case, involving a depressed adolescent who invariably arrived late at his day treatment program, the therapist's reframing interventions led to the unveiling of a pattern of overinvolvement between the mother and son: She was actually substituting for his alarm clock. In an attempt to help him, she was instead preventing him from developing a sense of responsibility.

The intended effect of reframing is to render the situation more workable. Once the problem is redefined in terms of complementarity, for instance, the participation of every family member in the therapeutic effort acquires a special meaning for them. When they are described as mutually contributing to each other's failures, they are also given the key to the solution. Complementarity is not necessarily pathological; it is a fact of life, and it can adopt the form of family members helping each other to change. Within such a frame, the therapist can request the family members to enact alternative transactions.

Enactment is the actualization of transactional patterns under the control of the therapist. This technique allows the therapist to observe how family members mutually regulate their behaviors and to determine the place of the problem behavior within the sequence of transactions. Enactment is also the vehicle through which the therapist introduces disruption in the existent patterns, probing the system's ability to accommodate to different rules and ultimately forcing the experimentation of alternative, more functional rules. Change is expected to occur as a result of dealing with the problems rather than talking about them.

In the case of the uncontrollable girl, the consultant, after having reframed the problem to include the mother's ineffectiveness and the father's hinted authoritarianism, sets up an enactment that will challenge that "reality" and test the family's possibilities of operating according to a different set of assumptions. He asks the mother whether she feels comfortable with the situation as it is—the grown-ups trying to talk while the little girl runs in circles screaming and demanding everybody's attention. When the mother replies that she feels tense, the therapist invites her to organize the situation in a way that will feel more comfortable, and he finishes his request with "Make it happen," which will be the motto for the following sequence.

The purpose of this enactment is multileveled. At the higher, more ambitious level, the therapist wants to facilitate an experience of success for the mother, and the experience of a successful mother for the rest of the family. But even if the mother should fail to make it happen, the enactment will at least fulfill a lower-level goal: It will provide the therapist with an understanding of the dysfunctional pattern and of the more accessible routes to its correction.

In our specific example, the mother begins to voice orders in quick succession, overlapping her own commands and hence handicapping her own chances of being obeyed. The child seems deaf to what she has to say, moving around the room and only sporadically doing what they are being asked to do. The consultant takes special care to highlight those minisuccesses, but at the same time he keeps reminding the mother that she wanted something done and "it is not happening—make it happen." When the father, following the family rule, attempts to add his authority to the mother's, the consultant blocks his intervention. The goal of the enactment is to see that the mother makes it happen by herself; for the same reason, the consultant ignores the mother's innumerable violations to practically every principle of effective parenting. To correct her, to teach her how to do it, would defeat the purpose of the enactment.

The consultant keeps the enactment going on until the mother eventually succeeds in organizing the girl to play by herself in a corner of the room, and then the adults can resume their talk. The experience can later be used as a lever in challenging the family's definition of their reality.

If the mother had not succeeded, the consultant would have had to follow a different course—typically one that would take her failure as a starting point for another reframing. Sometimes the structural family therapist organizes an enactment with the purpose of helping people to *fail*. A classic example is provided by the parents of an anorectic patient who undermine each other in their competing efforts to feed her. In this situation, the therapist may want to have the parents take turns in implementing their respective tactics and styles, with the agenda that they should both fail and then be reunited in their common defeat and anger toward their daughter—now seen as strong and rebellious rather than weak and hopeless.

Whether it is aimed at success or at failure, enactment is always intended to provide a different experience of reality. The family members' explanations for their own and each other's behaviors, their notions about their respective positions and functions within the family, their ideas about what their problems are and how they can contribute to a solution, and their mutual attitudes are typically brought into question by these transactional microexperiences orchestrated by the therapist.

Enactments may be dramatic, as in an anorectic's lunch (Rosman, Minuchin, & Liebman, 1977, pp. 166–169), or they can be almost unnoticeably launched by the therapist with a simple "Talk to your son about your concerns; I don't know that he understands your position." If this request is addressed to a father who tends to talk to his son through his wife, and if mother is kept out of the transaction by the therapist, the structural effects on behavior and perception may be powerful, even if the ensuing conversation turns out to be dull. The real power of enactment does not reside in the emotionality of the situation but rather in the very fact that family members are being directed to behave differently in relation to each other. By prescribing and monitoring transactions, the therapist assumes control of a crucial area—the rules that regulate who should interact with whom, about what, when, and for how long.

Boundary making is a special case of enactment, in which the therapist defines areas of interaction deemed open to certain members but closed to others. When Minuchin prevents the husband from "helping" his wife to discipline the girl, he is indicating that such specific transaction is for the mother and daughter to negotiate and that the father has nothing to do at this point. This specific way of making boundaries is also called *blocking*. Other instances of boundary making consist of prescriptions of physical movements: A son is asked to leave his chair (in between his parents) and go to another chair on the opposite side of the room so that he is not "caught in the middle"; a grandmother is brought next to the therapist and far from her daughter and granddaughter, who have been requested to talk; the therapist stands up and uses his or her body to interrupt visual contact between father and son; and so forth.

Boundary making is a restructuring maneuver because it changes the rules of the game. Detouring mechanisms and other conflict avoidance patterns are disrupted by this intervention; underutilized skills are allowed and even forced to manifest themselves. The mother of the five-year-old is put in the position of accomplishing something without her husband's help; the husband and wife can and must face each other without their son acting as a buffer; the mother and daughter continue talking because grandma's intervention, which usually puts an end to their transactions, is now being blocked; the father and son cannot distract one another through eye contact.

As powerful as the creation of specific events in the session may be, their impact depends to a large extent on how the therapist punctuates those events for the family.

Punctuation is a universal characteristic of human interaction. No transactional event can be described in the same terms by different participants because their perspectives and emotional involvements are different. A husband will say that he needs to lock himself in the studio to escape his wife's nagging; she will say that she cannot help protesting about his aloofness. They are linked by the same pattern, but when describing it they begin and finish their sentences at different points and with different emphases.

The therapist can put this universal to work for the purposes of therapeutic change. In structural family therapy, punctuation is the selective description of a transaction in accordance with the therapist's goals. In our example of enactment, the consultant organized a situation in which the mother was finally successful, but it was the consultant himself who made the success "final." Everybody—the mother included—expected at that point that the relative peace achieved would not last, but the consultant hastened to put a period—punctuate— by declaring the mother successful and moving to a different subject before the girl could misbehave again. If he had not done so, if he had kept the situation open, the usual pattern in which the girl demanded the mother's attention and the mother became incompetent would have repeated itself, and the entire experience would have been labeled a failure. Because of the facts of punctuation, the difference between success and failure may be no more than 45 seconds and an alert therapist.

Later in the same session, the consultant asked the parents to talk without allowing interruptions from their daughter. The specific prescription was that the father should make sure that his wife paid attention only to him and not to the girl. Given this context for the enactment, whenever the mother was distracted by the girl, the therapist could blame the *father* for the failure—a different punctuation from what would have resulted if the consultant had just asked the mother to avoid being distracted.

A variety of punctuation is *intensity*, a technique that consists of emphasizing the importance of a given event in the session or a given message from the therapist, with the purpose of focusing the family's attention and energy on a designated area. Usually the therapist magnifies something that the family ignores or takes for granted as another way of challenging the reality of the system. Intensity is achieved sometimes through repetition: One therapist put the question about 80 times to a patient who had decided to move out of his parents' home and did not do so: "Why didn't you move?" Other times the therapist creates intensity through emotionally charged interventions ("It is important that you all listen, because your sister can die.") or confrontation ("What your father did just now is very disrespectful."). In a general sense, the structural family therapist is always monitoring the intensity of the therapeutic process, so that the level of stress imposed on the system does not become either unbearable or too comfortable.

Unbalancing is a term that could be used to encompass most of the therapist's activity since the basic strategy that permeates structural family therapy is to create disequilibrium. In a more restricted sense, however, unbalancing is the technique in which the weight of the therapist's authority is used to break a stalemate by supporting one of the terms in a conflict. Toward the end of the consultation with the family of the "uncontrollable" girl, Minuchin and the couple discuss the wife's idea that her husband is too harsh on the daughter:

Minuchin: Why does she think that you are such a tough person? Because I think she feels that you are very tough, and she needs to be flexible because you are so rigid. I don't see you at all as rigid, I see you actually quite flexible. How is it that your wife feels that you are rigid, and not understanding?

Husband: I don't know; a lot of times I lose my temper I guess, right? That's probably why.

Wife: Yeah.

Minuchin: So what? So does she. I have seen you playing with your daughter here, and I think you are soft and flexible, and that you were playing in a rather nice and accepting way. You were not authoritarian, you had initiative, your play engaged her....That is what I saw. So why is that she sees you only as rigid and authoritarian, and she needs to defend the little girl from you (Punches father's knee)? I don't see you that way at all.

Husband: I don't know; like I say, the only thing I can think of, really, is because I lose my temper with my wife and daughter.

Wife: Yes, he does have a short fuse.

Minuchin: So what? So do you.

Wife: No, I don't.

Minuchin: Oh you don't. OK, but that doesn't mean that you are authoritarian, and that doesn't mean that you are not understanding. Your play with your daughter here was full with warmth and you entered very nicely, and as a matter of fact she enjoyed the way in which you entered to play. So, some way or other your wife has a strange image of you and your ability to understand and be flexible. Can you talk with her? How is it that she sees that she needs to be supportive and defending of your daughter? I think she is protecting the girl from your short fuse, or something like that. Talk with her about that, because I think she is wrong.

Wife: That's basically what it is. I'm afraid of you really losing your temper on her, because I know how bad it is, and she is little, and if you really hit her with a temper you could really hurt her; and I don't want that, so that's why I go the other way, to show her that everybody in the house doesn't have that short fuse.

Husband: Yes, but I think when you do that, that just makes it a little worse because that makes her think that she has somebody backing her, you know what I mean?

Minuchin: (Shakes husband's hand) This is very clever, and this is absolutely correct, and I think that you should say it again because your wife does not understand that point.

In this sequence, the consultant unbalances the couple through his support of the husband. His focus organizes him to disregard the wife's reasons, which may seem unfair at first sight. But it is in the nature of unbalancing to be unfair. The therapist unbalances when he or she needs to punctuate reality in terms of right and wrong, victim and villain, actor and reactor, in spite of knowing that all the comings and goings in the family are regulated by homeostasis and that each person obliges with his and her own contribution, because the therapist also knows that an equitable distribution of guilts and errors would only confirm the existing equilibrium and neutralize change potentialities.

While unbalancing is admittedly and necessarily unfair, it is not arbitrary. Diagnostic considerations dictate the direction of the unbalancing. In the case of our example, the consultant chooses to support the husband rather than the wife because in so doing he is challenging a myth that *both* spouses share; initially the husband agrees to his wife's depiction of him, and it is only through the intensity of the consultant's message that he begins to challenge it. At different points in the same session, the consultant supports the wife as a competent mother and questions the idea of her unremitting inefficiency—again, a myth defended not only by her husband but by herself as well. In the last analysis, unbalancing—like the entire structural approach—is a challenge to the system rather than an attack on any member.

CASE EXAMPLE

The Murphy family is composed of Joe, the father, 33 years old; Connie, the mother, 30; Jenny, seven; and Kevin, four. On the telephone, Connie stated that Kevin is very aggressive, throws toys at his sister, and screams for no apparent reason. Last week he pushed Jenny and caused her to injure her eye. Connie's sister Pat, 28 years old, who lives in the same apartment building and is a schoolteacher, has always thought Kevin to be hyperactive, and some time ago she arranged for a neurological examination. The test found nothing wrong with Kevin. The Murphys own a small grocery store where both work.

When the family (including Pat) enters the room for the first interview, Kevin and Jenny (who has a patch on her right eye) go directly to the toys; the therapist follows them and starts his joining by inquiring about Jenny's condition. He finds out that the lesion is not serious and also that Pat intervenes frequently in the dialogue with the children—adding to or correcting the information provided by them. It turns out that Kevin pushed Jenny while playing, and then Jenny hit a counter corner. As the therapist stands up from the floor and sits on a chair, the children quickly organize themselves to play; Kevin does not—and will not—show any of the typical signs of hyperactivity. The therapist proceeds then to explore the family structure and to reframe the problem.

> *Therapist:* So you had a scare.
>
> *Connie:* Yes. Thank God she is going to be OK, but I still—I don't know, it is scary, the things that can happen, and I—(Looks at Pat).
>
> *Pat:* Yes, well, I was the one who started this I guess, so maybe I should say something. (Connie nods.) You know, I had been noticing, like Kevin was always too active, and I wondered whether I should say something, but then Connie came up with the same thing and—
>
> *Therapist:* Connie? What did you come up with?
>
> *Connie:* Like she said, he was always difficult, but then he started to give more and more trouble and it got to a point—he is impossible. One minute he can be playing, and the next thing you know he is yelling and he will not stop. I don't know, the doctor says he doesn't need any medicine but I—

Therapist: You can't control him, eh? (After some exploration, Jenny has started to build a tower with blocks; Kevin follows her leadership.)

Pat: He is really uncontrollable when it comes to it.

Therapist: So Connie and Pat find Kevin difficult. How about you, Joe?

Joe: I don't know, he does get on his mother's nerves, but he doesn't give me any trouble.

Pat: Well, but you—you are different.

Joe: Yeah, maybe, but...well, I don't know.

Therapist: You think you are different?

Pat: He is more patient.

Therapist: Are you?

Joe: I don't know, she says that but... (The therapist signals that he should talk to Pat.) You say that I don't pay them enough attention.

Pat: It's not that. (To therapist) I feel it's easier for Joe because he can turn himself off, like when Kevin is hyper.

Therapist: (To Connie) What do you think?

Connie: Pardon?

Therapist: Your sister is saying something about your husband.

Connie: Is it easier for him? Yes, in a way I think it is easier. Like, the kids can be playing rough and it is like OK with him, he doesn't care, he says kids are kids. But I cannot see them going on like that; someone has to stop them, or everybody gets crazy.

Therapist: Everybody or just you?

Connie: Everybody. You know, Mr. Murphy here has his temper too.

Therapist: Then you stop them, eh? You mean you need to help him to keep his patience? Are you making things easier for him?

Connie: I guess, yes, I guess I am.

Therapist: That must be a hell of a lot of work. Is your sister helpful?

Connie: What do you mean?

Therapist: I mean, it must be very difficult to protect your husband's patience if he has a temper. Does your sister help you with that?

Connie: Well, she helps with the kids, they listen to her—that helps, a lot.

Thearpist: That helps with Jenny but not with Kevin, because you two together cannot cope with him, right? It takes your husband's temper to control Kevin?

Connie: Well yes, when it gets real bad he is the only one.

Therapist: And I bet Kevin knows that, Kevin? Your daddy is tough? Is he tougher than Mommy? (Kevin nods and goes back to his play with Jenny.) So you have a nice arrangement here. You two take care of Joe's patience, and Joe only intervenes when it is really necessary. Only that then (To Joe), maybe sometimes Kevin has to get tougher if he wants you rather than Connie or Pat?

During this sequence the therapist has had a chance to assess the extent of Pat's involvement in the life of the Murphys. He is not challenging her interferences;

rather, he is accepting the rules of communication of the family. At the same time, the therapist has been reframing the problem from a complaint about Kevin into a situation involving at least four people. Now the therapist is ready to initiate his challenge to the family's arrangement.

He sets the stage for an enactment by asking the parents to bring Jenny to talk with the grown-ups but to leave Kevin playing. At this point he thinks that Jenny also has a function in keeping Kevin busy and that the separation of the children will trigger Kevin's "hyperactivity." When Kevin, as expected, begins to protest loudly about the unfair discrimination, the therapist asks Connie to protect Joe's patience.

> *Connie:* You stay there playing for a while, Kevin; the doctor wants to talk to Jenny.
>
> *Kevin:* No! (Stands up and moves toward his mother)
>
> *Connie:* No Kevin, I told you to stay there. You cannot come here now.
>
> *Pat:* (To Kevin) It is only for a while.
>
> *Kevin:* Is he going to see her eye?
>
> *Pat:* No, I don't think so. (Pat looks at the therapist who looks at the ceiling. Kevin leans on Pat.)
>
> *Connie:* (To therapist) Is it OK if he stays here?
>
> *Therapist:* I don't know. (To Joe) Is it OK that he should disobey your wife? She just told him to stay there.
>
> *Joe:* Yeah, but that is it, you see, they keep doing it. Connie and Pat, they do it all the time.
>
> *Therapist:* Tell that to your wife.
>
> *Joe:* But I tell her. I tell you, don't I?

Joe and Connie now initiate a rather low-key discussion about what should be done when Kevin does not respond to their requests, with Joe espousing a more stern position and Connie advocating for more understanding. Pat alternates between trying (not too forcefully) to send Kevin back to the toys and listening to the couple's dialogue. Jenny watches silently. After a minute or two, the therapist interrupts the sequence and steps up the challenge.

> *Thearpist:* You are not going to get anywhere because you are asking your wife to send Kevin back but she can't do it.
>
> *Joe:* Yes, I know. Well, I wasn't—
>
> *Therapist:* But you know why? You know why your wife can't do it? Because she does not have Kevin right now, Pat does.
>
> *Joe:* How do you mean?
>
> *Pat:* He means I'm stealing your son, like we used to say—
>
> *Therapist:* No, you are not stealing anything; you are trying to help. But you are not being helpful, because all the time that you take care of Kevin they don't have to agree. You see, they can't finish this argument, they don't need to, because you are protecting them from Kevin, and Kevin from them.

Pat: But I am not keeping him.

Therapist: Oh yes you are, by being so available. I'll tell you what, I'll ask you to take a rest.

The therapist then invites Pat to move her chair next to him and spend the next minutes observing her relatives. So Pat is being defined as a well-meant, helpful person—which she most probably is—but the boundaries are being set all the same.

The therapist is also punctuating the triadic relationship by placing the emphasis of his description on Pat's helpfulness toward the Murphys. The same transaction could alternatively have been described as the Murphys helping Pat to feel useful, or as the two women forming a coalition against Joe, or as Connie being the middlewoman between her husband's and her sister's demands, and so forth. In fact, these different versions of the same reality are equally true and will eventually be emphasized in later sessions. At this point, however, the therapist chooses the angle that seems to be less threatening for Pat, because he has assessed the power held by the sister in the family.

The rest of the first session is employed in discussing the differences in personality between Jenny and Kevin and other issues in which the children are the focus of attention. Joe is asked to "interview" the children for the therapist, in a move that anticipates the direction of the unbalancing that will be initiated in the second interview. At the end of the session, Pat is invited to share her observations with her family.

The Murphys were in treatment for a total of 18 weekly sessions. The early scene in which Joe and Connie fruitlessly disagreed while Kevin clung to Pat could be used as an illustration for different stages of the treatment—provided the scene was photographed from many different angles and with many different lenses, so that it could render a variety of themes. The first therapeutic goal was to make room for an unobstructed relationship between Joe and Kevin. They should be able to establish their own rules without interference from Connie or Pat. This objective was made difficult by the myth that Joe was unable, either because of his temper or his indifference, to sustain such a relationship. The therapist had to unbalance by pushing Joe to exercise his rights and obligations, challenging Connie's opinion and maintaining Pat as a non-participating observer.

As Joe gained in assertiveness, he began to bring his own challenges into the picture. He insisted that Kevin should go to nursery school and successfully refuted his wife's objections. (Kevin had been spending most of his days with Connie at the store, a small place that constrained his activity and where Jenny's accident occurred.) The complaints about Kevin's behavior gradually disappeared, and, simultaneously, Pat began to lose interest in the sessions and even missed some. The therapist decided to temporarily excuse the children from attending the sessions and to shift the focus toward her.

Pat, the younger of the two sisters, was single and divided her life mostly between her job as a teacher and the Murphys. She and Connie talked a lot, mostly about the children and probably about Joe as well. Pat was also the family's favorite baby-sitter. With Joe assuming a new role in the family, the pattern of coalitions underwent a change: Connie moved closer to her husband and away from her sister. Pat began to feel depressed and to withdraw even from the children, which brought about a reversal in the sisters' relationship. While before Pat had been the knowledgeable teacher and Connie the troubled mother, now Connie was being the fulfilled family woman and Pat the lonely single. Connie grew solicitous about Pat, which only helped to increase Pat's feelings of depression and inadequacy.

The therapist introduced his own framing in this arrangement by pointing out that Connie was being intrusive; Pat had a right to her own privacy, including the right to feel depressed and lonely without interference. Connie could indicate that she would be available if Pat needed company or advice, but she should not impose herself on her sister. At Pat's own request, the therapist held a couple of individual sessions with her alone.

The content of those two sessions is not nearly as important as the fact that they took place, reinforcing the message of differentiation. Following them—and although the subject had not been discussed between Pat and the therapist—Pat announced in a somewhat solemn manner her "resignation" as the Murphy's baby-sitter. The Murphys, particularly Connie, were distressed at the possibility that Pat could be acting out of a feeling of rejection; the therapist supported Pat in her stand that she was just making what she thought was a good decision for her.

The last sessions, in which the children were again included, were devoted to monitoring the adjustment of the Murphy family to the new set of rules. At that point, Kevin was doing well in nursery school (after a somewhat difficult start), while at home he did not present any problem that his parents could not handle. The parents had reopened a discussion about the future of their grocery store, an issue on which they had conflicting points of view. Dealing with the conflict had been impossible before because of Connie's fears of making Joe feel incompetent and his fears of upsetting her; now, from their new perceptions of each other, a conflict-solving approach was possible. Finally, Pat's private life remained wrapped in a mystery that the therapist had to respect because his restructuring intervention had come to an end.

However, eight months later, the therapist called for a follow-up, and, according to Connie, the only news worth mentioning was that Pat was dating somebody whom she—Connie—did not like at all. "But," she hastened to add, "Joe keeps telling me it's her life and it's none of my business. And I tell him if I don't like the guy, I'm sorry, I don't like him, and that's none of *his* business either."

EVALUATION

Treatment models tend to resist evaluation, not only because of the methodological difficulties that plague the definition and control of relevant variables, but mainly because of the decisive effect of value judgments on the selection and interpretation of data. Outcome criteria, which are crucial in assessing the efficacy of treatment, ultimately reflect the ethical choices of a culture or subculture; "empirical evidence" is just a relative truth (Colapinto, 1979).

Structural family therapy enjoys in this respect a comparatively enviable status, because one of its areas of application—psychosomatic illness—facilitates the formulation of objective criteria for the evaluation of outcome. Symptom remission is a more precise indicator when the issue is labile diabetes than when we are talking about a depressive reaction. In the first case, it is possible to count the number of hospitalizations, whereas in the second, one has to rely more on subjective reports.

Minuchin and his collaborators have periodically published their research findings in the field of psychosomatics (see, e.g., Baker et al., 1975; Liebman, Minuchin, & Baker, 1974c; Minuchin et al., 1975; Rosman et al., 1976, 1977). The most complete report (Rosman, Minuchin, Liebman, & Baker, 1978) summarizes information on 20 cases of labile diabetes, 53 cases of anorexia, and 17 cases of intractable asthma.

In the case of labile diabetes (operationally defined as severe, relapsing ketoacidosis, chronic acetonuria, and/or extreme instability in diabetic control), 88% of the subjects (aged 10 to 18 years) recovered—this meaning that no hospital admissions for ketoacidosis occurred after treatment and/or that diabetic control stabilized within normal limits. The remaining 12% showed moderate improvement: Some symptomatology persisted after treatment, but there was a marked reduction in the number of hospital admissions and/or a more stable diabetic control. The diabetic group was in therapy for periods ranging from 3 to 15 months, with a median of 8 months, and was followed up for 2 to 9 years, with a median of 4.5 years.

Of the 53 anorectics (aged 9 to 21 and with a median weight loss of 30%), 86% achieved normal eating patterns and body weight stabilized within normal limits; 40% gained weight but continued suffering the effects of the illness (borderline weight, obesity, occasional vomiting); and 10% showed little or no change or relapsed. Treatment lasted between 2 and 16 months, with a median of 6, and follow-up was done between 1.5 and 7 years, with a median of 2.5 years.

Finally, the 17 asthmatics (suffering severe attacks with regular steroid therapy or an intractable condition with steroid dependency, aged 7 to 17 years), achieved recovery (little or no school days lost, moderate attacks with occasional or regular use of bronchodilator only) in 82% of the cases. An additional 12% improved moderately (weeks of school lost, prolonged and severe attacks, and some use of steroids but with symptomatic improvement), and the remaining 6% stayed unimproved (more than 50% school loss, need for special schooling, persistent symptoms, dependency on regular steroid therapy). Duration of treatment was between 2 and 22 months, with a median of 8, and follow-up was done between 1 and 7 years later, with a median of 3.

Psychosocial assessment of the 90 cases, based on the degree of adjustment to family, school, or work, and social and peer relationships, showed results that paralleled these data.

The systematic and sustained application of the model in the Philadelphia Child Guidance Clinic over the last 25 years—in which thousands of families were served—provides an additional, although admittedly indirect, indication of its validity. The same applies to the sustained enrollment in the training programs offered at the clinic by the Family Therapy Training Center. In addition to workshops and other continuous education activities, the center offers an eight-month extern program, where an average of 40 family therapists are trained each year, and three summer practica, which provide an intensive experience to another 70 professionals. The intensive use of live supervision and videotapes encourages and facilitates the evaluation of treatment process.

SUMMARY

Structural family therapy is a model of treatment primarily characterized by its emphasis on structural change and on the therapist as an active agent of change. Its origins can be traced back to Salvador Minuchin's work with delinquent boys from poor families at the Wiltwyck School in the early 1960s. Its consolidation coincided with Minuchin's tenure at the Philadelphia Child Guidance Clinic, where he was appointed director in 1965. The successful application of the model to the treatment of psychosomatic conditions, documented through research, was primarily responsible for the interest aroused by Minuchin's approach; but structural family therapy can be and has been applied to the entire range of emotional disorders.

The model conceptualizes the family as a living open system whose members are interdependent and that undergoes transformation of an evolutionary nature. Family process is regulated by the multilevel interplay of homeostasis and change, and it can be arrested—in which case the family fails to adjust its rules to changing environmental or intrinsic demands, and homeostasis becomes dominant. Intergenerational coalitions, triangulations, conflict avoidance, and lack of growth and differentiation characterize these families, which then come to therapy as caricatures of themselves.

The problem behavior is seen as a partial aspect of this family stagnation. The diagnostic endeavor consists of assessing the transactional and perceptual structure that is supporting (rather than "causing") the symptom. Accordingly, therapeutic change depends on the modification of the family structure: Positional changes, increases and reductions in distances, redefinition of hierarchical relations, exploration of new alternative rules, and conflict resolution are required so that the natural road to growth can be reopened. A special context, the therapeutic system, is created to this effect, where the therapist pushes the system limits in a quest for its potential strengths and underutilized resources.

The therapist, whose function is to assist the family in restructuralization, participates subject to boundaries in terms of both depth and time. In a paradoxical role, he or she needs to find the right equation of accommodation and challenge. At different times, the therapist's role can be compared to the job of a dancer, a stage director, a camera director, and a strange body in the family organism. The model provides the therapist with techniques for forming the therapeutic system and for creating disequilibrium and change: joining techniques such as maintenance, tracking, and mimesis; and disequilibrating techniques such as reframing, enactment, boundary making, punctuation, and unbalancing.

Structural family therapy has been validated directly through research in the fields of psychosomatics and indirectly through its application to thousands of families presenting all sorts of different problems. The sustained demand for training from mental health practitioners provides another indirect measure of the model's validity.

ANNOTATED SUGGESTED READINGS

Minuchin, S. (1974). *Families and family therapy*. Cambridge, MA: Harvard University Press.
  The first systematic presentation of structural family therapy. It discusses the basic concepts in the model and their implications for therapy, with the help of excerpts and transcriptions from interviews with normal and problem families.

Minuchin, S., Montalvo, B., Guerney, B. G., Rosman, B. L., & Schumer, R. (1967). *Families of the slums*. New York: Basic Books.
  A summary of the experience at Wiltwyck. It reports on research focused on the structure and dynamics of poor and disorganized families with more than one delinquent child, and it includes some of the early instruments developed by the group to assess family interaction.

Minuchin, S., & Fishman, H. C. (1981). *Family therapy techniques*. Cambridge, MA: Harvard University Press.
  An updated account of the model that draws from the experience accumulated in the course of several years of teaching at the Family Therapy Training Center. Emphasis is on the analysis of techniques and the theoretical and philosophical rationale behind the techniques.

Minuchin, S., Rosman, B. L., & Baker, L. (1978). *Psychosomatic families: Anorexia nervosa in context*. Cambridge, MA: Harvard University Press.
  Presents the specifics of psychosomatic disorders, including the characterization of the psychosomatic family, the treatment program, and the outcome, with a special emphasis on anorexia nervosa. It also includes long excerpts from family sessions.

Umbarger, C. C. (1983). *Structural family therapy*. New York: Grune & Stratton.
  Beginning family therapists will find in this book a simple yet not oversimplified step-by-step explanation of the major moves and interventions in structural family therapy, preceded by a coherent presentation of the underlying concepts. Provides an excellent introduction to Minuchin's own writing.

REFERENCES

Andolfi, M. (1978). A structural approach to a family with an encoprectic child. *Journal of Marriage and Family Counseling, 41*, 25–29.

Aponte, H. J. (1976). Underorganization and the poor family. In P. Guerin (Ed.), *Family therapy: Theory and practice*. New York: Gardner Press.

Baker, L., Minuchin, S., Milman, L., Liebman, R., & Todd, T. C. (1975). Psychosomatic aspects of juvenile diabetes mellitus: A progress report. In *Modern problems in pediatrics* (Vol. 12). White Plains, NY: S. Karger.

Berger, H. (1974). Somatic pain and school avoidance. *Clinical Pediatrics, 13*, 819–826.

Colapinto, J. (1979). The relative value of empirical evidence. *Family Process, 18*, 427–441.

Fishman, H. C., Scott, S., & Betof, N. (1977). A hall of mirrors: A structural approach to the problems of the mentally retarded. *Mental Retardation, 15*, 24.

Haley, J. (1971). A review of the family therapy field. In J. Haley (Ed.), *Changing families*. New York: Grune & Stratton.

Jackson, D. D. (1957). The question of family homeostasis. *Psychiatric Quarterly Supplement, 31*, 79–90.

Jackson, D. D. (1965). The study of the family. *Family Process, 4*, 1–20.

Liebman, R., Minuchin, S., & Baker, L. (1974a). An integrated treatment program for anorexia nervosa. *American Journal of Psychiatry, 131,* 432–436.

Liebman, R., Minuchin, S., & Baker, L. (1974b). The role of the family in the treatment of anorexia nervosa. *Journal of the American Academy of Child Psychiatry, 13,* 264–274.

Liebman, R., Minuchin, S., & Baker, L. (1974c). The use of structural family therapy in the treatment of intractable asthma. *American Journal of Psychiatry, 131,* 535–540.

Liebman, R., Minuchin, S., Baker, L., & Rosman B. L. (1976). The role of the family in the treatment of chronic asthma. In P. Guerin (Ed.), *Family therapy: Theory and practice.* New York: Gardner Press.

Liebman, R., Minuchin., S., Baker, L., & Rosman, B. L. (1977). Chronic asthma: A new approach to treatment. In M. E. McMillan & S. Henao (Eds.), *Child psychiatry treatment and research.* New York: Brunner/Mazel.

Malcolm, J. (1978, May 15). A reporter at large: The one-way mirror. *The New Yorker,* pp. 39–114.

Minuchin, S. (1961). *The acting-out child and his family: An approach to family therapy.* Paper presented at the William Alanson White Institute, New York.

Minuchin, S. (1969). Family therapy: Technique or theory? In J. H. Masserman (Ed.), *Science and psychoanalysis* (Vol. 14). New York: Grune & Stratton.

Minuchin, S. (1970). The use of an ecological framework in the treatment of a child. *International yearbook of child psychiatry* (Vol. 1). New York: Wiley.

Minuchin, S. (1972). Structural family therapy. In G. Caplan (Ed.), *American handbook of psychiatry* (Vol. 2). New York: Basic Books.

Minuchin, S. (1974). *Families and family therapy.* Cambridge, MA: Harvard University Press.

Minuchin, S. (1980). *Taming monsters* [videotape]. Philadelphia: Philadelphia Child Guidance Clinic.

Minuchin, S., Baker, L., Liebman, R., Milman, L., Rosman, B. L., & Todd, T. (1973). Anorexia nervosa: Successful application of a family approach. *Pediatric Research, 7,* 294.

Minuchin, S., Baker, L., Rosman, B. L., Liebman, R., Milman, L., & Todd, T. C. (1975). A conceptual model of psychosomatic illness in children. *The Archives of General Psychiatry, 32,* 1031–1038.

Minuchin, S., & Barcai, A. (1969). Therapeutically induced family crisis. In J. H. Masserman (Ed.), *Science and psychoanalysis* (Vol. 14). New York: Grune & Stratton.

Minuchin, S., & Fishman, H. C. (1979). The psychosomatic family in child psychiatry. *Journal of the American Academy of Child Psychiatry, 18* (1), 76–90.

Minuchin, S., & Fishman, H. C. (1981). *Family therapy techniques.* Cambridge, MA: Harvard University Press.

Minuchin, S., & Montalvo, B. (1967). Techniques for working with disorganized low socioeconomic families. *American Journal of Orthopsychiatry, 37,* 380–387.

Minuchin, S., Montalvo, B., Guerney, B. G., Rosman, B. L., & Schumer, F. (1967). *Families of the slums.* New York: Basic Books.

Minuchin, S., Rosman, B. L., & Baker, L. (1978). *Psychosomatic families: Anorexia nervosa in context.* Cambridge, MA: Harvard University Press.

Moskowitz, L. (1976). Treatment of the child with school-related problems. *Philadelphia Child Guidance Clinic Digest, 5,* 1.

Rosenberg, J. B., & Lindblad, M. (1978). Behavior therapy in a family context: Treating elective mutism. *Family Process, 17,* 77–82.

Rosman, B. L., Minuchin, S., & Liebman, R. (1975). Family lunch session: An introduction to family therapy in anorexia nervosa. *American Journal of Orthopsychiatry, 45*, 846–853.

Rosman, B. L., Minuchin, S., & Liebman, R. (1977). Treating anorexia by the family lunch session. In C. E. Schaefer & H. L. Millman (Eds.), *Therapies for children: A handbook of effective treatments for problem behavior.* San Francisco: Jossey-Bass.

Rosman, B. L., Minuchin, S., Liebman, R., & Baker, L. (1976). Input and outcome of family therapy in anorexia nervosa. In J. C. Claghorn (Ed.), *Successful psychotherapy.* New York: Brunner/Mazel.

Rosman, B. L., Minuchin, S., Liebman, R., & Baker, L. (1977). A family approach to anorexia nervosa: Study, treatment, outcome. In R. A. Vigersky (Ed.), *Anorexia nervosa.* New York: Raven Press.

Rosman, B. L., Minuchin, S., Liebman, R., & Baker, L. (1978, November). *Family therapy for psychosomatic children.* Paper presented at the annual meeting of the American Academy of Psychosomatic Medicine, Atlanta, GA.

Stanton, M. D. (1978). Some outcome results and aspects of structural family therapy with drug addicts. In D. Smith, S. Anderson, M. Buxton, T. Chung, N. Gottlieb, & W. Harvey (Eds.), *A multicultural view of drug abuse: Selected proceedings of the national drug abuse conference—1977.* Cambridge, MA: Shenkman.

Stanton, M. D., & Todd, T. C. (1979). Structural family therapy with drug addicts. In E. Kaufman & P. Kaufman (Eds.), *The family therapy of drug and alcohol abuse.* New York: Gardner Press.

Stanton, M. D., Todd, T. C., Heard, D. B., Kirschner, S., Kleiman, J. I., Mowatt, D. T., Riley, P., Scott, S. M., & Van Deusen, J. M. (1978). Heroin addiction as a family phenomenon: A new conceptual model. *American Journal of Drug and Alcohol Abuse, 5*, 125–150.

CHAPTER 7

Strategic Family Therapy

The Washington School

JAMES KEIM

DEFINITION

The Washington School of strategic therapy is an extraordinarily pragmatic model of family therapy born of an unusual mixture of anthropology, psychiatry, and systems theory. Descended from the work of Milton Erickson, Gregory Bateson, and Don Jackson, the Washington School was organized by Jay Haley and Cloe Madanes in the mid-1970s. The approach is now represented by a range of practice and practitioners. Clinical flexibility, pragmatism, and an interactional view remain central to the model, whereas other aspects have evolved and changed.

The term *strategic therapy* was popularized by Haley's publication of the books *Strategies of Psychotherapy* (1963) and *Uncommon Therapy: The Psychiatric Techniques of Milton Erickson, M.D.* (1973). The term *Washington School* was first used in the 1990s to specifically refer to the strategic therapy of Haley and Madanes, as the term *strategic* is sometimes applied to a number of related approaches, including that of the Mental Research Institute (MRI).

For the Washington School of strategic therapy, therapy is thought to begin when the clients initiate contact to hire a therapist to help facilitate change. The therapist and clients work together to create an empowering description of the desired change and, in the context of a carefully created and strong therapist–client relationship, to experiment with actions and discussions that will help the desired change occur. Sometimes the ideas for these experiments are primarily inspired by the therapist. At other times, the ideas are mainly the inspiration of the clients. In either case, the therapist encourages the clients to experiment with efforts to create change.

It may be necessary for the therapist to help to negotiate difficulties between clients who have different ideas about how to proceed or who have difficulty talking to one another. The process of therapy is different for each case, and an individual approach is developed for each client group. Usually, the clinician will work with a natural social group such as a family, but, depending on individual attributes of the case, the therapist may work with an individual, a couple, a family, or another social unit. However, in all cases, the therapist thinks interactionally and pays careful attention to issues of sequence, hierarchy, and metaphor (these terms will be defined later).

HISTORICAL DEVELOPMENT

The Washington School has distinct oral and written histories. The written history is widely known and incudes powerful contributions from the Bateson Project, MRI, the Philadelphia Child Guidance Clinic, and other groups with whom Haley and/or Madanes have been associated. Less well known is the rich oral history that plays an intimate role in strategic training. Part of the socialization of the Washington School therapist involves exposure to a plethora of historical and legendary tales involving key figures and events; it is through these stories that the Washington School passes on a profound humanitarian, multidisciplinary, and intellectual tradition.

The Washington School is described as having six developmental stages. The first, from 1953 to 1960, can be viewed as a phase dominated by research and experimentation in clinical practice. Clinical interests began to take precedence over research interests during the second stage, 1961 to 1967. The third stage, 1968 to 1973, marks the development of a cohesive approach to clinical practice and training. The fourth developmental stage, 1974 to 1983, began as Haley and Madanes started their own institute in Washington, D.C.; this stage marks the beginning of a distinctly identifiable Washington School. The fifth developmental stage, from 1984 to 1991, is characterized by evolution in training concepts and by advances in the treatment of abuse and violence. The sixth and present stage, which began in 1992, is characterized by contributions from a new generation of Washington School figures and by collaboration with other schools of therapy.

STAGE ONE (1953–1960): THE RESEARCH PHASE

The following piece of strategic oral history describes an incident that, on one level, exemplifies the dangers of cultural ignorance. On another level, it is the tale of how an odd incident involving a Native American spurred the West Coast beginnings of family therapy and perhaps the book *One Flew Over the Cuckoo's Nest*, as well. I originally heard part of this story on a videotaped conversation between

John Weakland and Haley entitled "Remembering Bateson," and pursued it further in personal conversation with Weakland.

> In the late 1940s or early 1950s, an American Indian was arrested in California on drunk and disorderly charges. The Indian, upon awakening in a jail cell, refused to speak to anyone and sat motionless. Suspected of being a catatonic schizophrenic, he was shipped off to a veterans hospital psychiatric ward where he continued to refuse to speak and sat much of the time motionless.
>
> An anthropologist happened to be visiting the psychiatric unit and thought he recognized the Indian as perhaps belonging to a tribe that the anthropologist had studied. The anthropologist walked over to the patient and tried speaking to him in an Indian dialect. The patient replied immediately and began in an angry, energetic voice to tell his story. After chatting with the Indian for a bit, the anthropologist went to the hospital director and said, "I've studied the tribe that this gentleman belongs to. He's not catatonic; his silence is a sign of tremendous anger and contempt. He's just acting like a typical member of his tribe."
>
> The California VA Hospital administration was horrified at this mistake and, to prevent future incidents of cultural misunderstanding, set out to hire two ethnologists on a part-time basis. Gregory Bateson was hired to fill one of the part-time positions, and it was understood that he could also pursue his own research and could use VA facilities towards this end (thus, Gregory's octopi collection ended up in the VA morgue, but that is a different story).
>
> Although Bateson's communication research [Bateson and associates] initially was focused on animals and normal human communication, a VA hospital physician was able to interest them in observing emotionally disturbed patients. This led to a shift in the research project's primary focus to pathological communication. The shift led to the West Coast birth of family therapy.
>
> The mistakenly hospitalized Indian not only helped to spur one of the major movements in family therapy; it is thought by some that another VA Hospital employee, Ken Kesey, was similarly influenced by the story and used it as the basis for a central character (the Chief) and a theme in his book, *One Flew Over the Cuckoo's Nest* (1962).

The Research Phase (1953–1960) is dominated by the work of a group that became known as the Bateson Project. In 1952, Bateson received a grant from the Rockefeller Foundation to study paradoxes in communication. John Weakland was the first research assistant hired, followed by Haley in January of 1953. In 1954, the project members received a grant to investigate schizophrenic communication, and the group was joined by psychiatrists William Fry and Don Jackson. The focus of the research became the confusion of logical types in schizophrenic communication. In 1956, the project published what is perhaps the single most important paper in the history of family therapy, "Toward a Theory of Schizophrenia," in *Behavioral Science* (Bateson et al., 1956). This paper described the etiology and nature of schizophrenia from the perspective of a communication theory.

The concept of the double bind, presented in "Toward a Theory of Schizophrenia," did not turn out to be clinically empowering; it never directly became a successful model of therapy for schizophrenia. Rather, the paper marked a major advance in the creation of a systemic language and galvanized unprecedented energy and interest in interactional studies and therapy. By drawing attention to family and systems issues, the Bateson Project indirectly helped to draw attention to the work of other systems researchers and theorists such as Theodore Lidz, Lyman Wynne, and Margaret Singer.

The Washington School maintains Bateson's sensitivity to levels of communication and learning, paradox, metaphor, and interactional sequences. The Bateson Project became oriented toward triangles in its final years (Weakland, 1960), and strategic therapy shares this emphasis as well. However, the concept of the double bind was not found to be useful in the treatment of schizophrenics (Haley, 1980). The double bind concepts are, however, manifest in the modern practice of strategic therapy in the form of paradoxical interventions, a subject that will be addressed later in this chapter.

The contributions of the Bateson Project to the Washington School, described above, consist of analytical and conceptual tools but do not include intervention theory. In order to understand how the Washington School developed a theory of how to inspire change in the context of therapy, one must understand the impact of Milton Erickson and Don Jackson.

STAGE TWO (1961–1967): MILTON ERICKSON, DON JACKSON, MRI, AND FAMILY PROCESS

The final years of the Bateson Project (1958–1962) were marked by increasing focus by Haley and Weakland on clinical work. Previously, both had been supervised as therapists by Erickson and Jackson, but it was not until the 1960s that Haley and Weakland began to speak with a more authoritative voice on their own practice of psychotherapy. The publication of *Strategies of Psychotherapy* (Haley, 1963) made it apparent that Haley and Weakland had combined Bateson's sensitivity to paradox and levels of communication with the clinical artistry and pragmatism of Jackson and Erickson.

During this second stage, Haley became the founding editor of the first family therapy journal, *Family Process*, which gave him the broadest possible exposure to the emerging field of family therapy. Madanes, toward the end of this period, worked as a research assistant at MRI and also for Margaret Singer, a well-known researcher who, with Lyman Wynne, pioneered important studies on deviant family communication.

MILTON ERICKSON Bateson introduced Haley and Weakland to Erickson in 1953 because the researchers wanted to study hypnotic communication. But it was the whole range of Erickson's therapy (which sometimes involved formal trance and at other times did not) which came to fascinate Haley and Weakland. By the late 1950s, Haley had set up a practice as a brief therapist and consulted with Erickson.

In contrast to the standard psychiatric practice of the time, Erickson's therapy was directive (which is to say that sometimes he would give overt directives and sometimes not), carefully planned, and often brief. Depending on the unique qualities of each case, he might see an individual or some combination of family members (in the 1950s, Erickson professionally advertised himself not only as a psychiatrist and hypnotist but also as a family adviser). Unlike most other clinicians of his period, Erickson believed that change could be sudden and discontinuous (Haley, 1973), and his ideas formed the basis for most modern brief therapy models. Erickson also believed that a clinician must have a broad range of skills in order to be able to work with a broad range of people, and he refused to be bound by convention. Using teaching stories to illustrate his points, he was a very effective mentor and supervisor.

There was a great degree of similarity in the pursuits of Bateson and Erickson. Both were extremely interested in paradox and in the multiple levels involved in human communication. But while Bateson was more interested in the pathological aspects of these issues, Erickson's focus was on their therapeutic potential. Erickson and Bateson were thus often interested in different sides of the same coin.

Bateson was interested in how paradox could contribute to schizophrenia; Erickson was interested in how paradox might allow patients to free themselves of symptoms, and he prescribed paradoxical interventions. In the context of therapy, an intervention is paradoxical "when it contains two messages that qualify each other in conflicting ways" (Madanes, 1981, p. 7). For example, a man with insomnia was asked to wake up even earlier than usual to start waxing his floor, a chore he despised but needed to do (Haley, 1984). In this specific case, the patient began to "oversleep" by accident and in doing so recovered from the insomnia. Paradox will be defined in greater detail later in this chapter.

Bateson was interested in how conflict between levels of communication could create pathology. Erickson was interested in how clinical use of multiple levels of communication could make therapy more effective. For example, in order to talk about sex with a client who was highly embarrassed, Erickson might talk about the steps involved in a good meal on one level and, on another level, provide suggestions to improve the person's sex life.

The fundamental tools of Erickson's therapy were thus the very same aspects of communication that, in their pathological form, so fascinated Bateson. Erickson's focus on the positive use of paradox and other concepts helped Haley and Weakland develop a more optimistic view of human potential and change.

DON JACKSON In response to the question "Who started family therapy?" the prominent textbook authors Nichols and Schwartz note that the honor is probably shared by Don Jackson and three others (Nichols & Schwartz, 1998, p. 37). Jackson's influence on strategic therapy is profound, but his untimely death in 1968 robbed him of much credit that he might otherwise have received. It was rumored that Jackson had committed suicide; however, the understanding of this author is that the autopsy determined that a heart arrhythmia was the cause of death. The rumor of suicide to some degree dampened interest in Jackson's contributions which, at the time of his death in the late 1960s, had become so anonymously standard that they seemed more like common sense.

Jackson's contributions are too many to mention in this chapter. One must at least, however, note that he gave form to many of family therapy's early concepts—such as homeostasis, family rules, quid pro quo relationship rules, and complementary and symmetrical relationships. Clinically, Jackson was one of the pioneers who moved family therapy from theory to clinical application. In the 1950s, he was using a one-way mirror not only for research but also to train Haley and Weakland in many standard family therapy techniques such as circular questioning. Jackson also joins Minuchin among the originators of systemic optimism—the belief that a clinician needs to be optimistic and believe that humans have tremendous potential to live normally if their social context can be changed to allow it.

STAGE THREE (1968–1973): THE PHILADELPHIA CHILD GUIDANCE CLINIC YEARS

Salvador Minuchin brought Jay Haley to the Philadelphia Child Guidance Clinic in the late 1960s. Haley soon became involved in the training of therapists and spent much time with Minuchin and Braulio Montalvo behind one-way mirrors. The Philadelphia group created one of the first coherent approaches to family therapy training and clinical intervention, called structural therapy. Madanes joined the staff of the Child Guidance Clinic in the 1970s.

Haley and Madanes integrated many ideas from the Child Guidance Clinic including hierarchy, training techniques, and approaches to working with urban poor. Many of the more commonly used Washington School interventions were first perfected during these years in Philadelphia. Also absorbed was the idea that a well-trained therapist should have a range of clinical skills, including the ability, should the need arise, to passionately engage or challenge clients.

In practice, the Washington School of strategic therapy and structural therapy bear many similarities. In the 1990s there would be discussions among clinicians as to whether the differences between the two models still warranted their being considered distinct schools.

STAGE FOUR (1974–1983)

In 1974, Madanes and Haley opened the Family Therapy Institute of Washington, D.C. In one decade of publications, workshops, and live supervision, the Washington School developed a large following and became one of the most influential movements in brief and family therapy. Haley's *Problem-Solving Therapy* (1976) and Madanes's *Strategic Family Therapy* (1981) were the two most influential books published by the authors during this period. This chapter is devoted to describing the current practice of the model of therapy organized in this stage.

STAGE FIVE (1984–1991)

This stage is characterized by a clinical focus on treating physical and sexual abuse. A 16-step approach for treating sexual abuse was developed by Madanes (1990), and workshops on this subject may perhaps have been some of the more widely attended in the United States.

This period is also characterized by the beginning of the collapse of intensive (one or more years) live supervision programs in the United States under the financial strains of managed care. Managed care started a severe financial contraction in the therapy world, and training was usually one of the first aspects of individual and institutional budgets to be cut. The end result was that one- and two-day workshops became a much more dominant mode of brief and family therapy training. Replacing small-scale training in which the trainer and clinicians held a two-way conversation were short workshops characterized by clinicians as merely audience members.

During the 1980s, the brief and family therapy world was swept by a trend toward greater sensitivity to sexism and other prejudices. Structural and strategic training institutes sometimes led and sometimes followed the development toward awareness of therapy's potential role in perpetuating sexism, racism, and other prejudices.

STAGE SIX (1992–PRESENT)

A new generation of strategic therapists came to prominence in the 1990s, and their publications mark a broadening of range in the Washington School of strategic therapy. They include David Grove, coauthor with Haley of *Conversations on Therapy* (1993); James Keim, coauthor with Dinah Smelser and Madanes of *The Violence of Men* (1995); Jerry Price, author of *Power and Compassion* (1996); Marilyn Wedge, author of *In the Therapist's Mirror* (1996); Richard Whiteside, author of *The Art of Using and Losing Control* (1998), and coauthor with Frances Steinberg of *Whispers from the East* (1999); and Anthony Yeo, author of *Counseling: A Problem-Solving Approach* (1993).

During this stage, the humanistic elements of strategic work began to receive more attention. Price coined the term *strategic humanism*, which embodies a more explicit emphasis on the therapeutic relationship and on clinical utilization of warmth, love, and soothing. Central to strategic humanism is the idea that a therapy that can offer both directive and nondirective approaches to clients is most likely to respect and increase client self-determination (Price & Keim, 1993).

The current stage of Washington School evolution also emphasizes collaboration with other schools of psychotherapy. In 1993, a conference was held at the National Institutes of Health on the integration of structural and strategic therapy that featured Minuchin, Madanes, and Haley. In 1995, Pat Emard of MRI and James Keim, then Director of Training under Haley and Madanes, organized a gathering of prominent brief therapy figures in honor of terminally ill Weakland. The theme of the meeting was collaboration between approaches. Weakland summarized the gathering's message in a letter to the *Family Therapy Networker*: "The emphasis on having things 'my way' and needing something new each year has distracted us from serious and useful dialogue about what aids people in distress and facilitates change" (1995, p. 16).

The final advance of this stage of evolution relates to the more collaborative stance that the Washington School has assumed. In the past decades, the therapeutic relationship had not received much attention, and there were not sufficient safeguards to sensitize clinicians to avoidance of being overly directive and patriarchal. One reason for this neglect is that Washington School trainees had, on average, been already trained in two previous models of therapy and tended to arrive with psychodynamic and Rogerian skills intact and well developed. The challenge until the 1980s was helping passively trained former analysts and the like to give advice when appropriate and to offer experiments that might catalyze change in a family. By the 1980s, a less humanistic group of students was appearing, and they needed restraint and sensitivity training.

TENETS OF THE MODEL

CONSTRUCTIVISM

The Washington School follows in the constructivist tradition of Erickson and Jackson; its theory is an acknowledged oversimplification designed only to facilitate change in the context of therapy. This constructivism was expressed among strategic therapists in the 1970s with the popular saying "the map is not the territory." Clinical theory is a guide in the same sense that a road map is. It would be a mistake to believe that the land and roads exactly resemble those on the map; the color and sizes of roads are changed to make navigation easier. Similarly, clinical theory is not in any way an exact map of human behavior; it is artificially colored, and many features are exaggerated in size in order to provide orientation and guidance.

THE MAP: PUSH

The core problem description used by the Washington School to characterize presenting problems is known as PUSH. PUSH is a point of view that empowers therapists, but the clinician does not attempt to force this map on the client; it is expected and healthy for clients and therapists to have different maps.

PUSH is an acronym developed by Haley that stands for:

*P*rotection

*U*nit

*S*equence

*H*ierarchy

These are the tools with which a strategic therapist dissects a problem that is the focus of therapy.

PROTECTION It is human nature always to have a theory about the motivations of others. A therapist's theory of motivation should be deliberately chosen. It is important to have a theory that allows the therapist to start with a positive view of clients and their situations. Protection refers to the theory that family members try in unhelpful ways to help other family members (Madanes, 1981). For example, an adolescent who perceives difficulties in her parents' marriage might misbehave with the probably unconscious motivation of bringing her parents together. Bringing parents together might take the form of the adolescent's provoking the parents to unite against her. The hypothesis of protection is a starting point in therapy, even though it is not always the best way to look at a problem. (The hypothesis of protection is not usually applied to sexual abuse or certain other types of abuse.) Of all theories that impact a therapist's attitude toward clients, the hypothesis of protection is the most important. A therapist who believes in loving motivation finds loving interventions. A therapist who believes in purely authoritarian motivations tends to come up with motivations that evoke authoritarian instead of loving attitudes in other family members.

Using the concept of protection still allows symptoms to be viewed as incongruities in family hierarchy (Madanes, 1981). The symptomatic person is simultaneously taking a superior and an inferior position. For example, parents are in a hierarchical class above a child, but "the child is in a superior position to the parents by protecting them through symptomatic behavior" (Madanes, 1981, p. 99).

UNIT The unit of three, the triangle, is the basic unit of construct in strategic therapy. The triad is a large enough unit to allow for the description of coalition and other complex interaction (Haley, 1980). Yet it is sufficiently simple to be practical for a therapist to use. A therapist may have 20 clients in her office involved with a presenting problem, but she will try to view their relationships to the presenting problem as being a matter of triangulation of groups and individuals.

A unit of three has been maintained as the appropriate one for a therapist because thinking in groups larger than three is too difficult. Observe the number of directions of interaction involved in the following example. If one observes a group of three people saying hello to each other, one will hear six greetings. If the members of a group of five people say hello to each other, there will be twenty greetings. The geometric progression of complexity makes trying to use large units almost impossible for the practical clinician.

There are two important advantages of triangles over dyads. First, a triangle allows for coalition theory, and a dyad does not (a coalition is a minimum of two joining against a minimum of one). Second, a triangle allows for simultaneous coalition and hierarchy within a social group.

SEQUENCE Sequence refers to the sequential ordering of interactions involved in the presenting problem. Sequences in strategic therapy may be described in linear or circular orders. The goal of strategic therapy is to replace the maladaptive sequences of behavior with healthier ones (Haley, 1976). The new sequences should lead to an elimination of the presenting problem and healthier hierarchy. The tendency is that successful therapy replaces escalating sequences between loved ones with soothing sequences (Keim, 1993b). The sequence should also be appropriate for the clients' stage of their family life cycle. The goal of therapy with a failing 25-year-old still living at home will probably be not only to get the young adult more rewardingly involved in life; sensitivity to the family life cycle would suggest that happiness will come in part from the young adult's becoming happily motivated to move out on his own, as this would be life-cycle appropriate.

HIERARCHY Hierarchy is a generationally sensitive delineation of the expression of love and authority within a social system. It can also be thought of as the degree of fit between role and function within a family. The Washington School does not address whether hierarchy changes cause problems; it is interested in how understanding or changing hierarchy can facilitate change.

Understanding hierarchy includes the need for a therapist to understand how authority can be distributed in different ways in different cultures. If we use the example of an acting out adolescent, for example, not inviting the adolescent's mother's brother to an interview could sabotage the therapy in some cultural contexts. In other cultural contexts, a grandparent can typically be more effective than a parent in influencing a child (Yeo, 1993). In doing therapy with a Japanese family facing the deteriorating health of an elderly neighbor, it would be important to understand the hierarchical differences between the various adult children of the elder whose health is of concern.

Attempting to change hierarchy is one of the most commonly used interventions in the Washington School. Marital difficulties are often mapped as having power imbalances in the marital hierarchy, for example, and a client goal of refinding a benevolent balance of influence would be conceived by the therapist as equalizing the hierarchy.

In therapy with children and adolescents, using the map of hierarchy can be especially empowering. Sometimes the therapy attempts to help children and parents by helping each better function in their preferred roles. The chart below depicts some issues that play a strong part in determining who is functioning as an adult in a social system. To the degree that children are assuming the roles described below, they tend to claim the authority of adults. To the degree to which adults carry out the interpersonal tasks below in a benevolent fashion, and to the degree to which there is a balance between the "hard" and "soft" sides of hierarchy, adults tend to increase their benevolent ability to guide and protect children.

THE HARD SIDE OF HIERARCHY

who makes the rules
who defines the punishments
who carries out punishments
who tells whom what to do
who has final responsibility for
  making major decisions
who is responsible for making others
  feel safe and provided for

THE SOFT SIDE OF HIERARCHY

who soothes whom
who provides reassurance to whom
who protects whom
who has responsibility for expressing
  love, affection, and empathy
who is the provider of good things
  and good times
who usually determines the mood
  of situations
who has the responsibility to listen
  to whom

When it is the perception of a child that his or her parents or equivalent authority and care figures are not fulfilling their responsibilities as described above, the youth will tend to respond by assuming these responsibilities and by farming out his or her needs to others, especially peers. In order for a youth to assume an age-appropriate behavior, the hard and soft sides of hierarchy need to be created by what is perceived of as an adult generation.

The Washington School also pays special attention to cross-generational coalitions. Coalitions between members of the same level of hierarchy are expected (Minuchin, 1974). Coalitions that cross generations can handicap positive change and may serve as warning that the social context has greater potential for violence. Examples of cross-generational coalitions are one between a child and grandparent against the parent or a coalition between a father and son against the child's mother. Haley has suggested that situations are pathogenic in direct proportion to the number of cross-generational coalitions (Haley, 1976).

THE MAP: FACE

FACE addresses the cooperative requirements of a directive therapy:

*F*amiliarity with problem and family context

*A*ppreciation

*C*ompetence

*E*mpathy

Each of these contributes to a cooperative relationship between therapist and clients. To the degree that any of these criteria have not been met, the therapy is much more difficult and less likely to be successful.

FAMILIARITY WITH PROBLEM AND CONTEXT This attribute describes the state in which the therapist and the clients feel that the therapist knows the facts of the problem and social context.

APPRECIATION This is the measure of the importance of the clients' believing that the therapist likes them. In strategic therapy, the therapists make it their own responsibility to like their clients. A therapist has a duty to organize an interview in a way that makes clients interesting and likeable. Often this involves discovering common interests. From another perspective, if a therapist does not like a client, it is possible that the clinician's judgment can be impaired. Disliking one's clients does not mean, however, that therapy cannot be successful; it will, however, be much more difficult.

COMPETENCE Competence describes the need for both the therapist and the clients to believe that the therapist knows what she or he is doing. Therapists must conduct themselves in ways that inspire such confidence. Particular attention is paid, to paraphrase Oscar Wilde, to avoid insulting clients unintentionally. As an example, with a very traditional Chinese family from Taiwan, if the therapist asks questions in a way that does not respect the parents' hierarchical position, cooperation may be lost.

EMPATHY This is the point reached in the therapeutic relationship at which the client feels that the therapist knows what it feels like to be in the client's predicament. Empathy is not to be confused with pity. Empathy, as one client noted, is a compassionate state; pity is a state of condescension. Whereas strategic therapists do not believe that the clinician's expression of empathy creates change (Haley, 1963, 1976), empathy is viewed as the most important requirement in the development of the cooperative relationship.

The primary reason for therapists' failure is the inability to build a cooperative relationship based on these criteria. Haley emphasizes that a trusting relationship is essential in this approach (1973).

ETHICAL BEHAVIOR

Strategic therapists adhere to a core of beliefs about the ethical practice of family therapy, including:

1.   The first rule of strategic therapy is an adoption of the age-old medical maxim, "do no harm." Simply stated, therapy should not hurt the clients, society, or therapists. One guideline recommended by Haley is that a therapist should use only those therapeutic procedures that the therapist is willing to experience or have his or her children experience. No therapist may ask a client to undertake any harmful, immoral, or illegal action, even as a paradoxical intervention (Haley, 1989). Part of not doing harm is the responsibility to avoid giving damaging diagnostic labels.

2.   The therapist must practice in a competent manner and must accept responsibility for creating change in therapy. Not accepting responsibility for change results in blaming clients for failure in therapy. Blaming the clients results in patronizing their treatment, decreased effort on the part of the therapist, and perpetuation of blame cycles that are part of the pathology of the client's social context.

3.   Therapists must assume that they wield tremendous influence. Clients are safest when therapists assume they yield too much rather than too little influence. Therapists must take responsibility for the intended and unintended effects of their direct and indirect influence on clients and the clients' social system. A therapist is not the same as a classroom lecturer whose audience is relatively free to accept or reject his or her teachings. A client in therapy should be considered to be in an extraordinarily vulnerable position, much like that of a hypnotic subject in a trance, and should not be taken advantage of.

4.   Therapy must be respectful of the clients. Because of their influence, therapists are in a uniquely powerful position to denigrate clients, and therefore must be all the more sensitive. Live supervision is especially helpful in training therapists to notice their inadvertent insults.

5.   Therapists should have a minimalist view of changing clients' world views; this ensures maximum respect of the world view of the client. It is a given that, in successful therapy, the therapist instigates a change in the clients' world views. However, attempts to change a client's world view should be limited to the presenting problem that the therapist has contracted to change. Consciousness-raising, here defined as influencing a client for a purpose not directly related to solving the presenting problem, must not be confused with therapy. For example, the Nazi ideology of a Mr. Smith would have to be addressed when the presenting problem is the violence of the son. However, the Nazi ideology would not necessarily be addressed if Mr. Smith came to therapy for help in dealing with the death of his 80-year-old mother.

A minimalist view of changing clients is a consequence of recognizing that the therapist's construction of reality is not in general more valid than that of the client's (Haley, 1973; Watzlawick, 1984). For example, it is helpful for a therapist to view problems in terms of hierarchy and sequence; however, it could be a terrible idea for clients to view problems in these terms. Different constructs of reality can be simultaneously valid depending on the different roles of the parties involved (Watzlawick, 1984).

6.   Therapists must maintain an awareness of the advantages and disadvantages of the use of overt versus indirect directives. The following discussion compares skillfully given overt and indirect directives. With an overt directive, the therapist's influence is open and clearly identifiable to clients. Dependence on the therapist is more likely to occur with the use of overt directives because sometimes

clients credit the therapist instead of themselves as being responsible for change. However, the intent and influence of overt directives is open to review by the clients and is thus less likely to lead to abuse. With an indirect directive, the therapist's influence is not clearly identifiable and may even be invisible to the client. The client receiving the indirect directive is more vulnerable to bad interventions because the directive is not as easily reviewed. The advantage of indirect directives is that clients' feelings of self-determination and self-confidence tend to be increased more by indirect than by overt directives. Clients internalize more quickly and take more credit for change resulting from indirect than from overt directives. Thus, both overt and indirect directives have their advantages and disadvantages that must be monitored in each case. In general, indirect interventions require more clinical skill.

7.   Common sense is as important as theory when determining what might harm clients. Therapists should trust their gut feelings about appropriateness of interventions and discuss uneasiness with a supervisor before proceeding.

8.   The therapist is responsible for using the most dignified, least intrusive intervention that will work within a reasonable time frame.

9.   Therapy must not be oriented toward blame, nor should it collude in irresponsible or dangerous behavior or in the forfeiture of individual responsibility.

APPLICATIONS AND TECHNIQUES

TRAINING

One of the most precious values is the belief in direct, interpersonal, and thorough training. Training is direct when the supervisor is basing perceptions on actual viewing of clinical work through live supervision or video representation. Training is interpersonal when there is a relationship and a two-way conversation between the supervisor and trainee. Training is thorough when it is frequent enough to guide a therapist through a diverse range of crises within individual cases and lengthy enough to guide the trainee through a diverse range of clients, cultures, and presenting problems. Trainees learn not only a large number of interventions but, more challengingly, how to really listen to clients and how to maintain a good relationship with them through the change process.

Beyond improving clinical skill, year-long intensive training programs create supportive professional and personal relationships that enrich the quality of life of participants. In this sense, the training tradition meets part of the expanded view of what a model should offer: personal enrichment.

THE THERAPY

There is often a playful nature to the therapy, and humor is used frequently. The therapist is expected to work within the clients' own world views whenever possible. Because all cultures are believed to have the necessary vocabulary to describe problems, relationships, and change, it is sometimes seen as disrespectful to introduce "new" vocabulary or concepts instead of using the clients' own. Therapy starts with the view that clients are competent or are capable of being competent if the social context will allow. Although training and consultation make use of one-way mirrors, the therapist is trained to work unaided during the interview. Flexibility is a hallmark of this model, and different approaches are needed for the variety of presenting problems, as well as cultural, ethnic, and social contexts brought to therapy. The primary skill of the strategic therapist is not the ability to think of brilliant new interventions; it is the ability to develop a cooperative relationship with clients and to use common sense while experimenting in pursuit of the desired change.

The tone of Washington School therapy is warm, inquisitive, and respectful. The single most important clinical moment is the making of the therapy contract. The contract guides the therapy, and problems that are not contracted for are not worked on. A therapist may strongly recommend working on a problem outside the contract, but, unless the problem threatens severe harm, the therapist will not work on it without permission.

When mapping out presenting problems in their own minds and notes, Washington School therapists pay special attention to constructs such as interactional sequences, hierarchy, triangles, and protection. By training, they are especially sensitive to maintaining a cooperative relationship with clients and to listening very carefully to direct and indirect messages in client communication.

THE FIRST INTERVIEW

The first interview is a microcosm of the overall therapy process. The stages of the complete therapy differ according to problem, clients, and context, but, for the sake of explanation, a generic description is offered below. In *Problem-Solving Therapy*, Haley described a generic first interview in five stages: a social stage, a problem-exploration stage, an interactional stage, a goal-setting stage, and a task-setting stage (1976). During the social stage, the therapist begins to create a cooperative relationship characterized by warmth and respect. In the problem-exploration stage, the therapist asks clients and significant others about the presenting problem. The interactional stage involves having the clients then discuss these views with each other; the emphasis here is on having the clients interact with each other, not with the therapist. At this stage, the therapist may ask the clients to demonstrate the symptomatic behavior and the consequent reactions. In studying clients, greater import is given to actions than to words. The fourth stage, goal setting, involves the creation of a therapeutic contract. The presenting problems and goals of therapy are defined in practical, workable terms. The contributions that each party will make to the therapy are made clear. In the fifth and last stage, task setting, directives are given to families that in various ways address the presenting problem. Part of the task-setting stage is ending the session in such a way that the clients feel comfortable with the therapist and capable of and committed to solving the presenting problems.

THE PROGRESSION OF THERAPY

Strategic therapy requires flexibility, and each case tends to follow a unique course. A generic description of the typical progression of therapy is offered. The average strategic therapy lasts eight to ten sessions (in a minority of cases, such as the therapy of severe psychosis or sexual abuse, treatments usually do not end in less than a year). The first two-thirds of the average therapy tend to be directed at solving the presenting problem, and the last third tends to be oriented toward maintenance of change, orientation of the clients toward the future, and termination.

STAGE ONE: PREPARATION AND COOPERATION This description relates to cases that are not crisis interventions and which involve clients who are not highly motivated. With crisis situations and highly motivated clients, passage through stage one to stage two occurs very quickly in the first interview. With other, less motivated clients, the goal of the therapy at this first stage is to prepare the therapy context and the clients' social context for change. During stage one, the therapist develops a cooperative relationship with clients (described later in more detail). Preparing the clients for change involves two steps. First, clients must view themselves as being able and, at least with the therapist's help, competent enough to solve the problem. This is usually achieved through assurances from the therapist and may also involve small homework assignments whose main goal is to provide small, confidence-boosting successes. Second, relationships between important persons must become cooperative and loving enough to carry out the therapist's directive. An example would be a case in which a couple needs to pull together in order to deal with their adolescent child in a firm, united, and loving way. If the relationship between the parents is disunited or cold, the therapist may work first or simultaneously on the marital relationship. When the parents can be appropriate with each other, it will be much easier for them to be appropriate with a difficult adolescent child.

The preparation/cooperation stage is characterized by the emphasis on preparatory interventions. A preparatory intervention is one that is primarily meant to prepare the social context for change, as opposed to directly addressing the presenting problem (Keim, 1993b). The act of defining a problem in workable form is one of the more common interventions employed at this stage. Another example of therapy at the preparation/cooperation stage comes from Erickson. Surprised clients were asked by Erickson to climb a small mountain as a way of positively changing their contexts. Although the presenting problem would not be cured, the clients would return with a new confidence and a more positive perspective; this new change in social perspective made easier the solving of the presenting problem. In another therapist's case, a couple who were involved with their teenage daughters to the exclusion of their romantic relationship came for marital therapy. The therapist asked the husband to buy his wife a tasteful piece of lingerie and to present it in a wrapped box not in front of but within eyesight of their children. The wife was instructed to receive the gift with a sexy gaze and to give her husband a kiss. The wife was instructed to answer any questions her daughters might ask with the phrase, "you'll understand when you are married." This directive was meant to playfully create more appropriate distance between the couple and their children; following completion of this task, the couple's social context was much more receptive to more energetic efforts to improve the marriage.

The preparation and cooperation stage is characterized by contracting, by an emphasis on preparation of the social context for change and on gaining client co-operation rather than on directly solving the presenting problem. However, maintaining preparation and cooperation is a continual challenge for the therapist throughout the therapy.

PROBLEM-SOLVING STAGE The shift from primarily preparing the context for change to focusing on changing the presenting problem itself marks entry into the problem-solving stage. Quite often, three or four different combinations of tasks are attempted before the presenting problem is solved. Different combinations of tasks are also used because the very first attempt to directly solve the presenting problem often does not work. As a matter of fact, it is the difficulties encountered during the first attempts to solve the problem that tend to give the therapist the final insights required for success. A therapeutic style that encourages patience and does not create unrealistic expectation of immediate change is most common. It should be noted, however, that in a minority of cases, such as crisis interventions, an aggressive attempt to end the presenting problem begins during the first session and continues until the problem is solved. Examples of the problem-solving phase of therapy are addressed in the section of this chapter entitled "Directives."

TERMINATION When the presenting problem has been solved, the termination stage begins. While training therapists, Haley points out that success in changing the presenting problem is often disorienting for novice therapists. This is because the novice clinician can become so focused on the presenting problem that the larger context of therapy is forgotten.

Success requires consolidation. The therapist and clients often jointly develop an explanation as to why they have solved the presenting problem. The explanation for success is very important, as it defines the way clients will approach problems in the future. It is usually described in terms of having successfully adjusted to a new stage of life. The description is one that empowers clients; the goal is for clients to be able to handle problems on their own. The description is also made in the clients' own language, with the belief that knowledge encoded in organic terms is more easily accessed than knowledge encoded in a foreign terminology (Keim, 1993b).

After the presenting problem has been solved, the therapist may predict a relapse. Predicting a relapse has several benefits. If unprepared, clients often lose complete confidence in themselves when there is a relapse. Planning for the occasion thus prevents this loss. Predicting a relapse also gives clients a chance to plan how such a problem may be handled, further increasing the clients' confidence. Furthermore, clients sometimes resist such a prediction by stubbornly refusing to relapse, thus paradoxically maintaining positive change.

Therapy tends to begin with the therapist's taking an expert role and end with the therapist's taking a more egalitarian approach. Ending in this fashion encourages clients to think of themselves as having regained competence to the extent that they no longer need the therapist.

The current practice of strategic therapy also employs periodic check-ups for clients. After the initial therapy is over, clients are asked to come back periodically for "check-up" sessions. These follow-up sessions are thought to help maintain the influence of the therapy and make it easier for clients to come back should problems arise. Periodic interviews also give the clinician a chance to gather outcome information from clients.

The following section of applications and techniques moves from describing the stages of therapy to describing techniques and interventions used with the approach.

UNDERSTANDING THE METAPHOR

Erickson stressed the need to understand not only communication in metaphor but also the metaphorical nature of symptoms (Haley, 1973). In *Strategic Family Therapy*, Madanes describes how a symptom may be viewed as a metaphor for an internal state of an individual, as a metaphor for another person's internal state, as a metaphor for an interactional sequence the identified patient is involved in, or as a metaphor for an interactional sequence another group of persons is in (1981). In planning interventions, understanding the metaphorical nature of a symptom is essential. For example, a case was referred to the Family Therapy Institute involving a 10-year-old girl who made a suicide gesture. The referring therapist viewed the gesture only as being a statement about how sad the child was. The strategic therapist viewed the symptom not only as a statement of the child's internal state but also as a metaphor for another person or relationship in the child's social context. The strategic therapist suspected that another family member was feeling suicidal, and, in fact, the child's mother had been contemplating taking her life, although the woman had not told anybody. Treatment for this family addressed not only the child's unhappiness but the mother's as well. Experiencing improvement in her mother was the major intervention that allowed the daughter to return to being a happy child.

DIRECTIVES

The Washington School is known for its creative and novel use of directives. A directive in the context of therapy is defined as an overt or covert message from the therapist to clients to take an action or make a change of some sort in relation to the presenting problem. The goal of directives is to get clients to experience and adapt new ways of interacting (Haley, 1976). In the modern practice of the Washington School, directives are usually "open," which means that their purpose and methods of helpfulness are explained to clients.

The Washington School approach to directives was influenced by Erickson and by Buddhist teaching stories (Haley, 1993). Therapeutic directives rarely in and of themselves solve problems; instead, it is best to view directives as catalyzing change rather than as being the change themselves. For example, Mr. Jones was referred for treatment of what his physician referred to as "severe Type II personality stress." Mr. Jones had had a heart attack at the age of 40 and had high blood pressure that was only partially responding to medication. As part of the treatment, Mr. Jones was given the directive that he should go to the supermarket, purchase a single item, and choose the longest, most irritating line in the store to wait in. Furthermore, on the trip home, Mr. Jones was to drive safely behind the slowest, little old car he could find. "Oh my God," Mr. Jones exclaimed, "I don't know if I can stand this, but I don't want to leave my kids without a father, so I'm committed to giving it a try." The therapist explained to Mr. Jones how and why the directives work to help Type II personality excesses. Rather than solving the problem, Mr. Jones was told, these sorts of directives force a person to come up with coping strategies to deal with such extreme stress. People learn to somehow accept that the situation is out of their control and then take the step of relaxing themselves. The same strategies that one develops to deal with the driving and supermarket line experiences will inform the handling of stress in other situations.

Mr. Jones responded to the stress of the supermarket line by picking up a book and reading it. He responded to the stress of driving by doing relaxation exercises and also by listening to books on tape. He began to always carry a book with him and even began to hope for delays that would create additional reading time. Much to the shock of his physician, Mr. Jones began to take longer routes by car that allowed him more time to listen to his books on tape. The Washington School directives served in the case of Mr. Jones not to solve a presenting problem (inadequate stress-reduction strategies) but, rather, motivated the development and use of solutions by Mr. Jones.

SOME COMMON MISTAKES USING DIRECTIVES One of the most common mistakes that new therapists make with Washington School directives is trying to use them to solve rather than motivate the solution of problems. In the case of Mr. Jones, the directive motivated his finding successful strategies rather than providing them directly.

Another common mistake in giving directives is insensitivity to client motivation. For a directive to be helpful, the clients must want the directive. They need to feel that the directive is a great way to address the presenting problem for which they are seeking therapy. And the clients need to feel that the directive is within their resources. The directive must therefore be customized to each client or group of clients; differences in what motivates people and in what clients are willing to do to solve problems mean that the same presenting problem will be approached in very different ways from case to case.

Another common mistake relates to failing to create a strong enough therapeutic relationship with clients. Clients will tend not to accept advice that comes from a clinician who does not yet seem to have a grasp of the problem or of the pain that the problem creates.

DELIVERY OF DIRECTIVES Delivery of directives must take into consideration the cultures and personalities of the clients. Some people want to be given advice in a straightforward, open manner that makes the opinion of the therapist clear. At the other extreme are individuals who are very conflict avoidant, who do not want to be put into a position of ever having to say to a therapist "that doesn't sound like a good idea," and who would prefer that any advice be given in a form that does not place pressure on the receiver to comply. Therapy must be customized to the degree of directiveness or nondirectiveness preferred by the clients.

The delivery of directives must also take into consideration the interactive context of the cultures of the clients and therapist. Historically marginalized populations frequently are "pushed around" by the dominant cultures, and a mix of clients from a marginalized group and a therapist from a dominant group requires the therapist to differentiate between giving requested advice and "pushing" clients around.

DIRECT OR INDIRECT DIRECTIVES As previously discussed, directives may be described as being straightforward (direct) or indirect (Haley, 1976). A straightforward directive is one in which a therapist openly and directly asks clients to take specific actions. The therapist's influence is overt and clearly identifiable to the clients (Haley, 1976, p. 59). In my personal experience, clients tend to remember actions they take in response to straightforward directives as being made in response to the therapist's suggestions (Keim, 1993b). Examples of straightforward directives are:

- A female therapist suggests to a man that he apologize to his wife in an effort to repair the spousal relationship. When the therapist asked the husband later in therapy why he apologized, the husband stated that it was mainly because he was wrong and had hurt his wife, but added that the therapist had influenced him to do so in order to help his marriage. In this case, the therapist's influence was overt and its goal was clear to the client.

- A therapist recommends to a parent that he punish a teenager for violating an important house rule.

An indirect directive is used when a therapist wants clients to take action and influences them to do so without openly and directly asking for action (Haley, 1976). For the client, the indirect directive is not clearly identifiable nor is its immediate goal clear. In my personal experience, clients tend to remember actions made in response to a therapist's indirect directive as being their own rather than the therapist's ideas (Keim, 1993b).

Another, separate reason for indirect directives is that they do not put as much pressure on the client to follow through. A therapist may wish for a client to consider an idea without feeling that rejection of the idea would hurt the therapist's feelings.

Examples of indirect directives are:

- In a hypnotic demonstration, a professor hypnotizes a subject and gives the directive that, upon awakening and retaking his seat, the subject shall put on his coat and not remember what he was asked to do. The subject is awakened from the trance, takes his seat, and puts on his coat. When asked by the professor why he put on his coat, the subject answers that he was worried that the coat would fall on the floor if just placed on the back of his chair. The subject does not consciously recognize that he responded to an external directive as opposed to a purely internal one. Interestingly, the subject usually believes his own excuse to be a true and complete explanation.

- A therapist is seeing a family that follows through energetically with even the slightest of recommendations. The therapist wants the family to consider taking a vacation but does not want to exert much pressure on them to do so. In an offhand way that appears to be a digression, the therapist tells the family a story about a friend of hers who went on vacation to escape from stress. The clients come in the following week refreshed from a short vacation, but they did not identify the implied directive.

• A client named Joe seeks therapy for a drug problem, and tells his therapist, Mary, that he wants suggestions but has such bad associations with advice. Experience shows that Joe responds very poorly to direct advice. During an interview, Joe tells Mary that a friend of his from the past, a drug dealer, is in town and has left a message requesting that he and Joe get together. Joe asks what Mary thinks he should do. The average therapeutic response to this situation is for the clinician to say that she doesn't recommend that someone fighting to stay off drugs socialize with a drug dealer. However, because Joe does not respond well to direct advice of this sort, what the therapist does instead is tell an amusing story of a cousin whom she likes but had to stop socializing with for a while in college because the cousin constantly got Mary into trouble. Joe laughs at the story, receives the message recommending against socializing with the drug dealer, and is not made to feel overpressured.

THE FUNCTIONS OF A DIRECTIVE Directives may be described as primary, preparatory, and terminal (Keim, 1993b). A primary directive directly addresses and attempts to inspire a solution to the presenting problem (Keim, 1993b). For example, in the case of Mr. Jones, the presenting problem was that he needed to improve his handling of stress. In this case, the intervention directly addressed the presenting problem and thus is considered to be a primary directive.

As previously discussed, a preparatory directive (Keim, 1993b) creates the context necessary for solving the presenting problem but does not address it. The preparatory directive prepares the way for the primary directive that will solve the presenting problem. An example is a reframing that empowers clients to change without giving specific direction to that change. Another example would be suggesting that parents with a problem adolescent take a romantic weekend alone. While not directly addressing the problem of the adolescent, the romantic weekend could significantly improve the ability of the parents to communicate and work together and thus make the next step, addressing the adolescent's problem, much easier. Sometimes a preparatory directive is given that, to the surprise of the therapist, solves the presenting problem. Once family members are able to cooperate better, on occasion they need no specific help from the therapist to solve the problem.

A terminal directive (Keim, 1993b) helps end the therapy after the presenting problem has been solved. Predicting a relapse at some point in the future is an example of a terminal directive, for it gives permission to end treatment now with the understanding the family may return for further assistance at a later time.

PARADOX

The use of paradox is one of the most often misunderstood aspects of strategic therapy. For a period in the 1970s and 1980s, the concept of paradox was misused and misapplied to such extremes that the term came close to losing any functional meaning. Although important, paradoxical directives are not as commonly used as many other types of interventions.

Using the analytic tools applied to the double bind, Haley and Weakland in the 1950s began to direct much attention to Erickson's therapeutic use of paradox.

In his book *Problem-Solving Therapy* (1976), Haley proposed that all therapy involves paradox, although this is sometimes not the intent of the practitioner. A paradoxical directive, however, is deliberately given. A paradoxical intervention is one in which "one directive is qualified by another, at a different level of abstraction, in a conflictual way" (Madanes, 1981, p. 7). Strategic therapists use three types of paradoxical directives: Two come from Erickson—prescribing the symptom (Haley, 1973) and restraint from improvement (Haley, 1976). The third, pretending, was developed by Madanes (1981).

Prescribing the symptom is the asking of clients to continue to have the symptom that they have contracted with the therapist to change. Restraint is the asking of clients to refrain from changing. "These tasks," wrote Haley, "may seem paradoxical to family members because the therapist has told them he wants to help them change but at the same time he is asking them not to change" (Haley, 1976, p. 77). In response to the therapist's request not to change, clients resist by changing in a way that solves the presenting problem.

Pretending is a paradoxical directive that requires compliance, not resistance, of clients to the therapist's directive (Madanes, 1981). The therapist asks clients to playfully pretend to have symptoms. This is essentially a request that the clients control behavior that is simultaneously defined as uncontrollable. It is the playful, nonconfrontational nature of this type of paradox that truly differentiates it from other types—such as Palazzoli's prescribing the rules of the system (Palazzoli et al., 1978). Pretending directives have wide applications and are especially useful in treating problems with children that are metaphors for problems of or between adults (Madanes, 1981). An example is having a parent request of a child that the child pretend to help the parent (Madanes, 1981). This is a directive that would be given when a therapist is trying to change a child's efforts to protect parents by exhibiting symptomatic behavior. The therapist is asking the parents to overtly take an inferior position to the child, and "both parents and child will resist the inappropriateness of this hierarchical organization, and the family will reorganize so that the parents regain a superior position" (p. 77).

Paradoxical interventions are to be used only by experienced therapists or by those under direct supervision of an experienced clinician. Paradox must not be used with people who have difficulties understanding motivations of others or who have thought disturbances. It should be employed only in the context of a strong therapeutic relationship in which the benevolent intentions of the therapist are beyond question.

CHOOSING INTERVENTIONS

In *Sex, Love, and Violence*, Madanes (1990) offers an important framework to help clinicians find appropriate interventions. Human dilemmas brought to therapy are viewed as being a struggle between love and violence. In delineating this struggle, four dimensions of metaphorical family interaction become clear: domination and control, the desire to be loved, love and protection, and repentance and forgiveness.

The dimension of domination and control is characterized by the clients' struggles to dominate and control one another, often through intimidation and exploitation. Examples of cases often associated with this dimension are problems of delinquency, some substance abuse, and bizarre behavior. The orientation of the therapy tends to veer toward the redistribution of power among family members "so that, instead of punitiveness, protection and caring prevail" (Madanes, 1990, p. 17).

In the second dimension, the desire to be loved is the metaphor of the problem. Characteristic issues are eating disorders, some psychosomatic symptoms, phobias, some types of depression, and anxiety. The interactions of the family often involve excessive demands, rivalry, discrimination, and criticism. Communication is full of expressions of pain, internal strife, and emptiness, and it is characteristic that when one member is upset, another member becomes sick. The orientation of the therapy tends to involve the overt expression of the symptoms between family members and the metaphorical change of the function of symptoms.

Love and protection, the third dimension, is characterized by the centrality of the attempt to love and protect significant others. Problems brought to therapy often involve intrusiveness, possessiveness, some types of domination, and some acts of violence. A common justification given for this category of behavior is that it was an act of love or jealousy. Characteristic of this stage are problems of obsessiveness, suicidal tendencies, abuse, and neglect. Sometimes there is a vying for roles of "most guilty" and "most worthy of love" (Madanes, 1990, p. 33). Intervention usually involves reversing exclusion, changing which members are being helpful to one another and how they are being helpful, and the introduction of metaphors of love.

The fourth dimension is repentance and forgiveness, the central issue between family members. Therapy addressing sexual abuse and sadistic acts often works at this dimension. The families involved are often characterized by secretiveness and extremes in interpersonal fusion and distance. These families often exhibit inappropriate expression of empathy and conscience. Interventions emphasize personal responsibility, reality, the replacement of secrecy and inappropriate coalitions, and movement to higher levels of compassion and spirituality.

The interventions are grouped below in relation to the four dimensions of the love–violence continuum. Their grouping suggests only a tendency for these to be the central focus of the intervention. Certain strategies, such as correcting the hierarchy, are to some degree involved in all interventions but are grouped in one category because of the emphasis the dimension places on this type of intervention. A fifth category below, "generally applied," includes interventions that are too general to categorize.

I. Domination and Control
    1. Correcting the hierarchy (Minuchin, 1974; Haley, 1976; Madanes, 1981)
    2. Negotiations and contracts (Minuchin, 1974; Haley, 1976; Madanes, 1981)
    3. Changing benefits (Madanes, 1981, 1984)
    4. Rituals (Haley, 1973; Madanes, 1981; Haley, 1984)
    5. Ordeals (Haley, 1973, 1984)
    6. Paradoxical restraint from improvement (Haley, 1973, 1976)
    7. Paradoxical contracts (Haley, 1973; Madanes, 1981)
    8. Prescribing the presenting problem with a small modification in context (Haley, 1973; Madanes, 1981, 1984)

II. The Desire to be Loved
    9. Changing a parent's involvement (Minuchin, 1974; Haley, 1976, 1980)

    10. Changing memories (Haley, 1973; Madanes, 1984, 1990)
    11. Prescribing the symptom (Haley, 1973, 1976, 1980)
    12. Prescribing the pretending of the symptom (Madanes, 1981)
    13. Prescribing a symbolic act (Madanes, 1981)
    14. Asking parents to prescribe the presenting problem or the symbolic representation of the presenting problem (Madanes, 1981)
    15. Prescribing the pretending of the function of the symptom (Madanes, 1981)
    16. Strengthening or weakening relationships (Minuchin, 1974; Haley, 1976; Madanes, 1981)
    17. The illusion of being alone in the world (Madanes, 1984)

III. Love and Protection
    18. Reuniting family members (Minuchin, 1974; Haley, 1976; Madanes, 1981)
    19. Changing who is helpful to whom (Madanes, 1981)
    20. Empowering children to be appropriately helpful (Madanes, 1981)
    21. Orienting or projection into the future (Haley, 1973, 1976; Madanes, 1981)
    22. Prescribing a reversal in the family hierarchy (Madanes, 1981, 1984)
    23. Prescribing who will have the presenting problem (Madanes, 1984)

IV. Repentance and Forgiveness
    24. Repentance and reparation (Madanes, 1990)
    25. Reframing (Haley, 1973, 1976; Madanes, 1981)
    26. Creating a positive framework (Madanes, 1981, 1984)
    27. Finding protectors (Madanes, 1990)
    28. Eliciting compassion (Madanes, 1990)

V. Generally Applied
    29. The illusion of no alternatives (Haley, 1973; Madanes, 1981, 1984)
    30. Asking the client to come up with a solution (Haley, 1973, 1976)
    31. Repetition of clients' own previously successful strategies (Haley, 1973, 1976)

CASE EXAMPLE

A single parent, Debbie Smith, came alone to my office for a consultation regarding her daughter Natalie, aged 14. Ms. Smith, a 30-year-old Caucasian woman, had grown up in a small town in Wyoming. She had become pregnant by a friend when she was in her late teens and did not marry the father. The child was given to Debbie's mother to raise while Debbie worked and attended community college in Denver.

Debbie became a successful office manager and purchased her own home. When Natalie was 12, her mother brought her to Denver to live. After a short honeymoon period, Debbie began to have trouble with her daughter. Natalie started to question her mother's authority and disobey rules. Debbie worked from 7 a.m. to 7 p.m. each day, and it was hard for her to supervise her daughter during the week. Debbie's fears increased greatly when her daughter became friends with and started to date a number of African American teenagers. When

Natalie was 14, she had a pregnancy scare that turned out to be false, and this made the mother even more anxious. Their fighting increased, and Natalie ran away to her grandmother's in Wyoming. While Natalie was there, her grandmother overheard a telephone conversation in which Natalie claimed to have been sexually abused by one of her mother's boyfriends. After hearing about the possible sexual abuse, Debbie came alone for a consultation with me.

The first interview was with the mother alone. I succeeded in gaining the strong trust of the mother and reviewed the history of the family and difficulties. The contract stated that the therapist was being hired to help the mother break a communication block that seemed to prevent her and her daughter from discussing anything important and to help address the possibility of sexual abuse. A plan was made to bring Natalie to the next session for an extremely gentle and respectful conversation on the possibility of sexual abuse. The following week, I consulted with Clinic Director Haley on the case. Haley agreed to supervise the next interview from behind a one-way mirror.

Debbie and her daughter showed up late for their session and marched angrily into the office. The previous week's plans for an extraordinarily gentle and empathic session dissolved with the first words spoken by the mother; another issue had appeared in the intervening days.

J = Jim Keim

N = Natalie

D = Debbie, Natalie's mom

> D: I understand she thinks she's pregnant AGAIN. I will not have a half-breed in my family. I will not be considered that...
>
> (Therapist babbles incoherently in surprise and shock at the turn of events.)
>
> D: She doesn't care because she knows that, if and when she is, she's out of my house, she's out of my life. I am not having a black, half-black kid in my family.
>
> J: Well, let's discuss some of the specific issues involved and I understand how...
>
> D: Well, I was getting at...
>
> J: When it's your own daughter and you're thinking of her as a child, to think of your child having a child gives you a very negative first reaction. But we'll talk some more about this in a bit but... (Speaking now to Natalie) when did you find out?
>
> D: A week ago (not allowing Natalie to answer for herself).
>
> J: Ahh.
>
> D: But there's two black families up here that are willing to take her in, which are broken families, which one of 'em the dad's in and out constantly. I mean...she just doesn't care about me because these people are gonna take care of her.
>
> (It has become clear to me that Debbie is momentarily too upset to be engaging in a conversation with her daughter. I asked Debbie in the kindest of tones to step out into the waiting room so that I might chat alone with Natalie.)
>
> J: I'll tell you what, you know, if I might, I'd like just to talk to your daughter alone for just a minute. Natalie, if you wouldn't mind coming over here (Gesturing to a nearby chair).

(Mother goes to waiting room.)

J: Boy this must have been a rough week in your house…

(Natalie nods emotionally.)

J: Gosh. Well…um…who else have you told about this?

N: Just my friends.

J: Yeah, who are your best friends?

N: This girl Taneesha is one of the girls she [Debbie] don't want me hanging with and…um…Jenny and this other girl named Lana, but we're like good friends.

J: Now they live near you?

N: Well Taneesha does; Jenny lives like over by the Mile-High Mall.

J: Have they been pretty nice to you through all this? Have any of them been through a similar kind of scare?

N: Well, yeah.

J: You don't need to say who.

N: One of 'em's pregnant now.

J: One of them's pregnant now, gosh. And…um…ah…your mom, when she found out, did she throw a big fit right there or did she just…

N: She don't know if it's true or not; she just overheard it.

J: So she never really asked you about it.

(The conversation revealed that Natalie's friends are trying to get pregnant at the same time and have plans to move in together. Natalie states that she does not know if she is pregnant or not. I am struck by the lack of anxiety that Natalie exhibits at the idea of being pregnant.)

J: Where did your mom get the idea that there are these two families that want to take you in?

N: Because…I don't know, they…they know how my mom is…

J: OK.

N: They just said that they'd take me in if my mom ever kicked me out. I could, you know, come stay with them.

J: Well…

N: I told my mom that one time, and she got all mad. I don't know why.

J: Well, you know it's the normal reaction of a parent when their child is…maybe pregnant that they get very pissed off and say all sorts of things they don't mean. But I've talked with your mom a lot. You know that what you need to worry about is her hanging on to you, you know, forever. I don't think it's gonna be a situation where you're gonna get kicked out.…She's gonna pull back on the reins even harder.…It wouldn't surprise me if after you turned 18 she tried to keep you home and so…

N: She'll try to keep me home.

(I know the mother well enough from the previous interview to believe that she would not, in a calm moment, put a pregnant daughter on the streets. I find it more empowering at this moment to focus Natalie not on the rejection threats from her mom but rather on the mother's overprotectiveness. The overprotectiveness of Debbie, though less vivid than the mother's racist threats of expulsion, are a more dominant and long-term theme in the mother–daughter relationship. Helping the daughter deal with the mother's overprotectiveness becomes the therapeutic contract between Natalie and me.)

J: You need to have a normal social life. You need to have fun. You need to be with your friends. Yet the kind of course that things are headed on means your mom's gonna be restricting you.

(Time lapse)

J: Your mother...why does she not like your boyfriends?

N: Well, she...I guess most of 'em are black, but I don't see nothing wrong with it but she does.

J: And, um, in other words you're saying she's prejudiced. Do you think that she, you know, that she can overcome that?

N: I think if she would just meet my boyfriends or whatever she would just get to know them.

J: I'm a little bit familiar with the town your mom is from, and it's very common [there for people to have] a reaction...that's a little bit prejudiced...But it's just possible that if your mom gets to know your friends a little better that she might be, you know, a bit easier but you know your mom's very protective of you.

N: She's TOO protective.

(Time lapse)

J: Yeah, well if we can find some sort of meeting ground, you know, maybe there are some things that she'll let you do. This whole situation will be happier because you need a good social life. OK, let me chat with your mom for a minute now.

(Natalie leaves, and Debbie enters.)

D: Is she going to talk?

J: Yes...she was very nice. Gosh, so for the last week, you've been worried about her being pregnant?

D: Mm hmm.

J: That must have been terrible

D: My mom overheard her on the phone talking.

J: Oh your mom overheard her...

D: Talking to a girlfriend. That's the first time she heard me say it.

J: Mmm...

D: Again I didn't think it's true [that she's pregnant]. I think she just likes to talk because I know her monthly cycle and I know she had it last month. So why she's already saying it, it's pretty wild I tell you...because that first time [that Natalie had a pregnancy scare some months before] I did take her for a pregnancy test and I thought I was gonna have a nervous breakdown.

J: I don't blame you.

D: Sitting there in the waiting room [of the doctors' office waiting to find out the pregnancy results]…

J: I don't blame you, gosh.

D: But anyway…

J: It's what a worry…

D: At 14…

J: Well listen, what you really need to do and what you really need to have is some authority with her.

D: Mm hmm, yeah, I've lost that!

(In saying that the mother needs to regain her authority, I am repeating back to the mother a phrase that she used frequently in the first interview. The mother shakes her head in strong agreement and appears to feel understood, at ease, and supported by me.)

J: Because the things that you care about, that you want her to do, are not just for the sake of worry but mostly for her own protection.

D: Not only that, it's her education.

J: …and her education, that's right.

D: I keep telling her [that in] ninth grade you've got to crack down. You're in high school now starting the way of your life right now. You've got to get your education. You can't loaf through school. I don't want to see her do what I had to do, have a baby and try to go to school. Because, I mean, that was hard, and I think that's probably my mistake too that I haven't been around her that much 'cause I was going to school and working at nights. You know it's been hard, and I don't want her to do that, but I don't want her to ruin her life either.

J: And you know she's too young to know better and she needs your guidance and she needs your influence.

D: I know.

(Time lapse)

J: Well, let's talk about a couple of steps you can take.

D: OK.

J: I've been doing this for a long time so I know these things are gonna help you a lot.

D: OK.

J: First you have to watch out for ways of tempting you to meet her worst expectations. She's always kind of tempting you to threaten to kick her out. And she does it pretty powerfully…I mean, for goodness sake, pregnancy?

(Debbie laughs.)

J: So you and I know it's really gonna take some superhuman effort on your part to handle the situation. Believe me, I would not want to be in your shoes having to put up with all of these…ways of tempting you…to see if you'll confirm her worst fears. Given her age and so on, probably her worst fear is rejection from you.

D: OK.

J: And so she's gonna tempt you to reject her.

D: Is this why she makes me so angry?

J: That's one of the reasons.

(Time lapse)

J: But she's testing you…it's for a good reason, in her soul she wants to for you to prove your love. And this is what's so crazy about teenagers because there are easier ways [to find out how much one is loved].

D: Yeah I heard her make the comment the other night to her friends she said I never tell her I love her…but of course she keeps me so angry.

J: That's what doesn't make sense about teenagers.

(The discussion between the mother and me moves to the issue of how to react to the possibility of pregnancy. I recommend that the mother speak more honestly about what might happen if Natalie is pregnant. Rather than make empty threats of expulsion, the mother is encouraged to allow her protectiveness to be expressed. This requires that the mom drop the threat of expulsion based on racism.)

J: [You need to say] black or white or whatever, I'm not gonna let you [leave home] until I feel you're ready.

(Mom laughs and looks at the therapist with relief.)

J: Honestly…it's the truth, it's the truth, you want her to be launched well. You want her to be a success in life. You want her to avoid a lot of the difficulties you've had.

(I am again repeating back to the mother what she had said in the first session. These recommendations are only effective because they represent the stronger instincts and feelings she has for her daughter. The mother is struggling with two different narratives. One is a racist narrative that evokes rejecting and threatening behavior from the mom [for example, saying that if her daughter has a baby by a black father then she will be out of my house…out of my life]. The other narrative is that of a single parent who has struggled to give her daughter a better life. In this second narrative, the mother fears that her efforts have failed, as she now finds her daughter making the same great mistakes that she did by becoming an unwed adolescent mother. I had guided the mother toward the second, more loving, more powerful narrative. I recommend that reality, rather than threats, be the basis of the upcoming conversation with Natalie. The mother and I plan on how to make it clear that having a child is not a way of escaping one's mother; in fact, it ties a teenager down. Natalie is brought back into the room with her mother and me.)

J: OK, now that we're all relaxed I'd like to have a very frank discussion.

(Mom laughs with embarrassment at the reference to her opening tirade.)

D: Well, Natalie, I guess if you want to have a baby, and you think you're going to, I guess I'll have to accept it, BUT it's gonna be a big responsibility on you. You're the only one that's gonna have to take care of it but of course that means you're stuck with me longer cause you really can't leave my house until I'm sure that you're old enough to be out on your own.

(Natalie stares up at the ceiling in shock.)

J: And that your grandchild is going to be OK...

D: That's true. Nowadays, the housing thing up here is [impossible]. I'm not all that familiar with it but it takes you forever to get it. I know that you have to be homeless to get it so, you know, if you're gonna have a baby now, you're just gonna be stuck with me for the next eight years. So that's your choice. But if that's what you want to do...

J: Tell her that, black or white, it doesn't matter. This is your grandchild and your daughter that we're talking about.

D: Well that's hard to say but I guess I'll have to accept it.

(The mother's honest statement that she would have to accept a mixed-race grandchild, although not happily, is emotional enough to convince the daughter of its authenticity. A look of happy amazement comes over Natalie's face.)

J: It's difficult to imagine your daughter having a baby, but...you accept it and you have to do all the more parenting not for your grandchild but for your daughter. Because your daughter will actually need you all the more if she has a baby.

D: Yeah, 'cause you see how hard it is for Sarah [a relative who is a single parent].

(As the interview continues, the warmth and power of the mother shines through. She sits next to her daughter and hugs her. Natalie, previously so out of touch with her emotions during the session, begins to cry. Given the warmth and supportive nature of the moment, I decide to bring up the issue of possible sexual abuse.)

J: OK, and there's one final issue that that we don't have time to talk about and I'd like to talk about next time...if you want why don't you just go ahead and bring it up?

D: I would like to know in the past year if somebody had touched you...

J: And that's something that we'll discuss later...but very specifically are you worried about a certain individual?

D: Was it Nad?

(Natalie shakes her head in the negative.)

D: Was there somebody?

(Natalie shakes her head in the affirmative. In shock, Debbie looks away from her daughter's face and physically begins to lean away. Despite the previous session's planning, the revelation of abuse shocks the mother. Concerned that Natalie will interpret the mom's movement as rejection, I speak up.)

J: Now put your arm around her.

(Debbie hugs Natalie.)

D: Come here…so you want to talk about it?

N: (Crying) No.

(Sensing that the mother is beginning to drift again, I do more coaching, to which the mom responds.)

D: I am your mother, Natalie, and I always want to protect you and I'm always here, OK? I love you.

J: You're always going to be responsible for her, her whole life.

D: I'll always be responsible for you all right?

J: And if you've failed her at some time, at some point say that you're sorry and we'll talk about it more.

D: If I have failed you I am sorry but we'll talk about it…OK? OK? But I am sorry for it.

(The mother's statement that "I'm always here" is not historically accurate, but I did not feel it was appropriate to ask the mother to specifically correct those words at that moment. Rather, I asked the mother to open the discussion to the ways of the mom's shortcomings; this was achieved by having her note that she would take responsibility for her failings, and that this would be discussed at an appropriate time [when the emphasis no longer needed to be the soothing of Natalie]. The mother's mentioning the possibility of her own failings as a parent made for a more honest, open, and thus safer atmosphere for Natalie. She continued to cry, but I had the sense that the mother and daughter had resumed a helpful state of interaction. I, therefore—as is often the practice after there has been a need for strong coaching—left the two alone. After heavy coaching by a therapist of a conversation, leaving the clients alone gives them a chance to interact without help. The clients can be even more sure that the feelings and words are legitimate and not the influence of the therapist. After I had left the room, the conversation between mother and daughter continued.)

D: Why didn't you tell me what had happened?

N: I didn't know.

D: (Gently) What do you mean you didn't know?

N: I didn't know what he was doing (Starts crying again and reaches for mother).

(In tears, Debbie draws Natalie to her and the daughter accepts the embrace.)

D: Don't worry, it's not your fault. It's not your fault. I love you. I love you.

N: I love you too.

D: I'm sorry.

(They continue to embrace in silence. It was agreed that the mother and daughter would return the following week together with Debbie's mother who had raised Natalie for much of the girl's life.)

Natalie did turn out to be pregnant by her boyfriend, and the grandmother, mother, and Natalie decided together that it would be best for the teenager to return to Wyoming to live with the grandmother. The family was referred to a therapist in Wyoming. Natalie had the baby and gave it up for adoption; she continued to live with the grandmother.

CASE DISCUSSION

PROTECTION Protection is a helpful construct in part because it helps the therapist think in terms of positive motivations. Outside of abuse situations, problems between family members are initially viewed as being "love gone wrong." This is a similar concept to that of Weakland, Fisch, and Watzlawick's that presenting problems can be viewed as unfortunate efforts at creating solutions (Weakland, Fisch, Watzlawick, & Bodin, 1974). In the experience of the Washington School, therapists who perceive some positive motivation among clients are kinder, gentler, and more likely to evoke love and caring in the therapy session.

The construct of protection inspired the following "spin" on the presenting problem. The therapist viewed this case as in part involving a mother who wanted to better protect and love her child but was having difficulty doing so. The daughter was viewed as desiring to have a better connection and more love from the mother, and her behavior was viewed as being in part an attempt to provoke demonstrations of love and support from the mother.

UNIT The concept of unit refers to the conscious consideration of the triangles involved in a case. The search for triangles is a structured reminder to view the problem interactionally and to search for coalitions among those present and those not present in the therapy session. Triangles are not viewed as being either healthy or unhealthy; they are constructs of observation that move the clinician past habitually narrow points of observation.

Important triangles include the mother, daughter, grandmother grouping. The grandmother raised Natalie for most of the child's life and is an important figure in any solution and in the therapy process. Her presence was requested for the next interview. The grandmother–mother–daughter triangle in cases where a child has been raised by both adults at different times is very complicated, especially when parental responsibilities are shifted from the grandmother to the mother.

Other triangles worthy of consideration are those involving peers and other families. Natalie was part of a peer group whose members were getting pregnant and hoped to get Section 8 housing together (these youths were not aware of the difficulties involved in getting housing). The mother also brought up at the beginning of the interview the issue that two families in the neighborhood had volunteered to take Natalie in should she kick the daughter out.

SEQUENCE The problem sequence appeared to be one in which the daughter, feeling distant and insufficiently loved, began to triangulate with competing third parties (boyfriends and "other families that would take her in"). The mother responded to these cries for attention not by becoming more parental but rather by becoming distant and threatening. The more distant the mother became, the more the daughter triangulated with others who could in any way meet her needs.

The sequence that the mother wanted was not the problem sequence but rather one in which she could respond to the daughter's difficulties by being able to help her make good decisions. The mother's definition of the preferred sequence creates the goal of therapy, and we see this goal verbalized below.

J: …What you really need to have is some authority with her.

D: Mm hmm, yeah, I've lost that!

J: Because the things that you care about, that you want her to do, are not just for the sake of worry but mostly for her own protection.

D: Not only that, it's her education.

J: …and her education, that's right.

D: I keep telling her [that in] ninth grade you've got to crack down. You're in high school now starting the way of your life right now. You've got to get your education. You can't loaf through school. I don't want to see her do what I had to do, have a baby and try to go to school. Because, I mean, that was hard, and I think that's probably my mistake too that I haven't been around her that much either 'cause I was going to school and working at nights. You know it's been hard, and I don't want her to do that, but I don't want her to ruin her life either.

HIERARCHY I viewed this as a situation in which the parent's ability to benevolently guide and help her daughter was severely compromised. Using the map of hierarchy, I thought that the mother would be better positioned to help her daughter if the mother could more effectively fulfill the soft side of hierarchical expectations. The soft-side behaviors that would empower the mother within the hierarchy were empathy, soothing, and protectiveness.

When the mother soothed her daughter and demonstrated the ability to handle hot topics (for example, a mixed-race baby) in an empathic manner, Debbie resumed a level of parental authority missing earlier in the therapy. Natalie responded by developing a fuller emotional range and an expanded ability to discuss issues with her mother. These changes are consistent with Washington School expectations from hierarchical interventions; when there is better fit between role and function—when parents act and feel like parents and their children feel unburdened by adult responsibilities—there is often an increased ability within the system to solve problems.

The hierarchy of the system also includes the grandmother, who was not present in the system. It seems probable that if Natalie had stayed with her mother, Debbie's hierarchical position would have to be affirmed by the grandmother.

DEFINING THE PROBLEM IN AN EMPOWERING WAY

A therapist-initiated change in the client's construction of a problem is known as a reframing. In the Washington School, reframing is not viewed as usually solving the presenting problem. Reframing is usually part of the process of creating a definition of the problem that is empowering to both therapist and client. The central reframing in this case was revisioning of authority as the ability to soothe and benevolently guide the daughter.

With Debbie, the concept of authority was expanded to one that better fits the situation. The mom had previously tried to exert authority through threats of expulsion; in this construct, authority is obedience sought through threats and punitive behavior. During the therapy, authority takes on an expanded definition; it becomes the ability to influence the daughter to make healthier and safer decisions.

With Natalie, the problem was defined as finding a way to have more freedom in the context of a relationship with a mother who was headed in the direction of greater control. Dealing with their parents' efforts at control is one of the most common motivations for adolescents to voluntarily participate in therapy.

I was faced with two vivid narratives, one marked by racism, disconnection, and expulsion ("you're out of my house...out of my life") and the other involving a desire to love, protect, and guide. The Washington School therapist would not believe that one was "true" and the other "false," but rather would view one narrative as more deserving of therapeutic emphasis because it is more likely to solve the presenting problem. At times, therapy helps by making a more helpful narrative the dominant one in the system (Minuchin & Fishman, 1981; Keim et al., 1988; Madanes, 1990). The narrative characterized by racism and disconnection left the mother and daughter unable to resolve difficulties or even talk. When the alternative narrative became dominant (that of the loving, protective mother who has made mistakes and wants to help her daughter avoid those same mistakes), the goals for which the therapist was hired—to help the mother and daughter improve their relationship and to address the issue of sexual abuse—could gradually be addressed.

THE TREATMENT OF SEXUAL ABUSE

A concern presented in the case study was the issue of sexual abuse. Addressing physical, sexual, and substance abuse is one of the great challenges faced by therapists. In the 1980s, Madanes developed a specialized, 16-step approach to sexual offenses. The treatment is a family approach to helping the offenders take responsibility and show sorrow and repentance for their actions. Described in *Sex, Love, and Violence* (Madanes, 1990), the approach simultaneously treats offenders and victims. Research conducted in part by the Maryland Department of Juvenile Services showed a startling five-year success rate (defined by no new sexual offenses) average of over 95%. This research appears in the book *The Violence of Men* (Madanes, Keim, & Smelser, 1995). This approach is especially impressive not only because of the outcome but also because, as stated above, it allows simultaneous treatment of victim and offender (when they are in the family) by a single therapist. Using just one therapist greatly reduces the complexity and expense involved in treating this population of victims and offenders. Madanes's approach further reduces the need for institutionalization and for the breaking up of families where abuse has occurred.

EVALUATION

The Washington School does not separate training from technique; in other words, the measure of an intervention is its use in the hands of a thoroughly trained clinician. This approach trains clinicians to develop mature joining, listening, and diplomatic skills, and most of its interventions are meant to be practiced by those with such abilities.

Prominent figures in strategic therapy—and specifically the Washington School—have been associated with hundreds of research publications, but most have employed qualitative or case study design. Outcome studies are unfortunately less common. Following are descriptions of three areas that have been addressed by outcome studies.

THE CARLSSON STUDY OF STRATEGIC THERAPY OF EATING DISORDERS (CARLSSON, 1998)

This program applied a strategic approach to eating disorders that combines inpatient and outpatient treatment. Of 33 patients who completed a five-year follow-up, 82% (27) did not meet the criteria for an eating disorder. Several patients (4) met the criteria for anorexia, and 2 met the criteria for nonspecific eating disorders. Of 218 patients who ended therapy and received a six-month follow-up, 76% (163) no longer met the criteria for an eating disorder.

THE TREATMENT OF ADOLESCENT SEX OFFENDERS (MADANES, KEIM, & SMELSER, 1995)

In a study conducted by The State of Maryland Department of Juvenile Services and by the Family Therapy Institute of Washington, D.C., 72 juvenile sex offenders were followed. They received treatment at the Juvenile Sex Offender Program at the Family Therapy Institute, which was directed by Haley and Madanes.

Six of the offenders had been referred to long-term institutionalization after court-ordered evaluations found the youths to be inappropriate for outpatient treatment; however, lack of funding prevented these six from being placed in institutions, and they were instead referred to the Institute for outpatient treatment. At two-year follow-up after the end of therapy, there were only three repeat sexual offenses as determined by case notes, therapist interview, and State of Maryland review of legal files—which note charges and convictions.

SUBSTANCE ABUSE

Lewis and colleagues noted that Stanton and Todd's research on structural-strategic therapy for heroin use (for which Haley was a consultant) had been identified as "one of the best controlled studies in family therapy.... Specifically, they found a significant decrease in adult heroin usage" (p. 31, 1991). Not only did the therapy significantly impact heroin use, but it also significantly lowered mortality rates of participants (Stanton, Todd, & Associates, 1982). Szapocnik and Kurtines also published significant research (1989) showing that strategic therapy significantly decreased adolescent drug abuse.

SUMMARY

The Washington School of strategic therapy remains dedicated to the premise that therapists should practice in a flexible, humanistic, and skillful fashion. The model does not describe the universe of human behavior. Strategic therapy is specifically designed to guide clinicians in the context of psychotherapy.

The Washington School has always found it somewhat challenging to describe the tremendous range and variation of practice. Each therapy is tailored to the requests and needs of each group of clients. This means that one client may receive only the mildest of directives in the form of carefully timed smiles and reassurances, of which Carl Rogers was a master, while the next client might receive directives to undertake exotic and fun adventures in search of solutions. Yet the next clients may receive only "traffic cop" services that allow a family to have a relatively uninterrupted conversation. For the Washington School, the different approaches to the interviews are determined not by the preferences of the therapist but rather by the requests and needs of the client. The true challenge of the clinician is therefore to train in a wide variety of directive styles and techniques to help a wide variety of client situations and cultures. Training must also teach the sensitivity and diplomacy necessary to understand what the clients desire and to maintain their cooperation through the therapy.

Maintaining a tradition from its Philadelphia influence, the Washington School has taken a special interest in working with violence and with problems related to the poor. Structural and strategic therapy have trained more clinicians than any other approach in family therapy, and it is a matter of the greatest pride that these approaches have taken their greatest hold in social service institutions where pragmatism is the ruling philosophy. The challenge for the new generation of Washington School clinicians will be to continue to evolve the model to meet the needs of a changing world.

A CRISIS IN TRAINING

One of the challenges that the Washington School faces is maintaining both growth and coherence at a time when live supervision, the traditional training method of the Washington School, is becoming increasingly unavailable outside university settings. The vast majority of family therapy institutes that opened in the 1980s closed under the financial pressures of the managed-care era. Although a new and spirited generation of Washington School clinicians is publishing books and giving workshops around the world and at major association conferences, there is not as much opportunity to do the characteristic high-quality training with direct supervision.

One response to the training crisis is that Washington School and structural family therapists have started to collaborate on creating a guided peer supervision program. This multimedia project is creating a study guide of psychotherapy cases that groups of clinicians can use as a basis for peer training and supervision. Such a program will not be dependent upon the financially restrictive requirement of having an experienced supervisor. Jay Lappin, Montalvo, Keim, and other trainers from the Washington and structural schools are working on this project.

A second response to the training crisis is increased reliance on university-based live supervision programs. Adding to this pressure is the "ready to work" trend, a movement dedicated to producing graduates who are ready to work instead of merely ready to train. It is especially the case that social service agencies do not have the time and money to train clinicians; this results in high rates of resignation in many protective service agencies because of the increased professional demands of workers being trained as they work.

Greatly increasing the availability of university-based intensive training, however, is partly dependent upon overcoming an old prejudice in the university system; professorships and prestige are granted in many university departments mainly in relation to research and grant acquisition, and clinical work is often viewed as a second-rate activity. Too often, supervision is done by professors hired on the basis of their research and publication skills. Too often, psychotherapy-related courses are taught by faculty who have not proved competence in clinical practice. It is the belief of this author that only when skill in clinical supervision is given equal value to academic scholarship in the hiring and promotion of professors will universities as a general trend improve in training clinicians.

There will always, however, be a minority of graduate departments that overcome this tendency and create splendid clinical programs. Such programs tend to carefully scrutinize the clinical and supervisory skills of professors as part of the hiring interviews. Such departments also seem to be aware that they are mainly producing clinicians, not academicians, and they tend to accord tremendous respect to training faculty.

ANNOTATED SUGGESTED READINGS

The first two books recommended for the study of the Washington School are Jay Haley's *Problem-Solving Therapy: New Strategies for Effective Family Therapy* (1976) and Cloe Madanes's *Strategic Family Therapy* (1981). Haley's work *Learning and Teaching Therapy* (1996) is quickly becoming a standard graduate text for the Washington School and a source of general ideas about systems therapy. Haley's book *Uncommon Therapy: The Psychiatric Techniques of Milton Erickson, M.D.* (1973) continues to be a best-selling guide to the work of Milton Erickson and is an easy introduction to strategic therapy. Cloe Madanes's book *Sex, Love, and Violence: Strategies for Transformation* (1990) is a crucial primer for those interested in the strategic approach to violence and sex offenses.

"Next generation" authors include David Grove, coauthor with Haley of *Conversations on Therapy* (1993); James Keim, coauthor with Dinah Smelser and Cloe Madanes of *The Violence of Men: New Techniques for Working with Abusive Families: A Therapy of Social Action* (1995); Jerry Price, author of *Power and Compassion: Working with Difficult Adolescents and Abused Parents* (1996); Marilyn Wedge, author of *In the Therapist's Mirror: Reality in the Making* (1996); Richard Whiteside, author of *The Art of Using and Losing Control* (1998) and coauthor with Frances Steinberg of *Whispers from the East* (1999); and Anthony Yeo, author of *Counseling: A Problem-Solving Approach* (1993). Wes Crenshaw is expected to publish an important book on the Washington School in 1999.

Michael Fox, M.D., is a prominent strategic clinician and has published some of the first articles representing the more collaborative trend in the Washington School, including "Strategic Inpatient Family Therapy with Adolescent Substance Abusers," in T. Todd and M. Selekman (Eds.), *Family Therapy Approaches with Adolescent Substance*

Abusers (1991). He is perhaps the pioneering clinician of the next generation of the Washington School.

Other significant figures such as Richard Belson, Neil Schiff, Marcha Ortiz, David Eddy, Judith Mazza, Lyn Stycinski, Leonard Greenberg, and Dennis Schwartz have contributed to the Washington School literature and deserve greater mention than space allows.

Washington School clinical training includes required familiarity with the works of Milton Erickson, Don Jackson, Salvador Minuchin, Braulio Montalvo, H. Charles Fishman, Duke Stanton, Tom Todd, Gerald Patterson, James Alexander, MRI (Weakland, Fisch, and Watzlawick), John Gottman, Margaret Singer, Jeff Zeig, Scott Miller, Barry Duncan, Mark Hubble, Steve de Shazer, Anne Rambo, Joe Eron, Tom Lund, and Ron Taffel.

REFERENCES

Bateson, G. (1972). *Steps toward an ecology of mind*. New York: Ballantine Books.

Bateson, G. (1979). *Mind and nature*. New York: E. P. Dutton.

Bateson, G., & Bateson, M. C. (1972). *Angels fear*. New York: Macmillan Publishing Company.

Bateson, G., & Jackson, D. D. (1968). Some varieties of pathogenic organization. In D. D. Jackson (Ed.), *Communication, family, and marriage*. Palo Alto, CA: Science and Behavior Books.

Bateson, G., Jackson, D. D., Haley, J., & Weakland, J. (1956). Toward a theory of schizophrenia. *Behavioral Science, 1*, 251–264.

Carlsson, G. (1998). Strategic therapy and hypnosis in eating disorders. In *The Milton H. Erickson Foundation Newsletter, 18*, No. 3, Fall.

Grove, D., & Haley, J. (1993). *Conversations on therapy*. New York: Norton.

Haley, J. (1963). *Strategies of psychotherapy*. New York: Harcourt Brace Jovanovich, Inc.

Haley, J. (1973). *Uncommon therapy: The psychiatric techniques of Milton Erickson, M.D.* New York: Norton

Haley, J. (1976). *Problem-solving therapy: New strategies for effective family therapy*. San Francisco: Jossey-Bass.

Haley, J. (1980). *Leaving home: The therapy of disturbed young people*. New York: McGraw-Hill.

Haley, J. (1984). *Ordeal therapy*. San Francisco: Jossey-Bass.

Haley, J. (1989). *Fifth profession ethics*. Unpublished manuscript.

Haley, J. (1993). *Jay Haley on Milton Erickson*. New York: Brunner/Mazel.

Keim, I., Lentine, G., Keim, J., & Madanes, C. (1988). Strategies for changing the past. *Journal of Strategic and Systemic Therapies, 6*(3), 2–17.

Keim, J. (1993b). Triangulation and the art of negotiation. *Journal of Systemic Therapies, 12*, 76–87.

Kesey, K. (1962). *One flew over the cuckoo's nest*. New York: Viking Press.

Lewis, D., Sypher, H. E., & Bukoski, W. J. (Eds.). (1991). *Persuasive communication and drug abuse prevention*. Hillside, NJ: L. Erlbaum Associates.

Madanes, C. (1981). *Strategic family therapy*. San Francisco: Jossey-Bass.

Madanes, C. (1984). *Behind the one-way mirror*. San Francisco: Jossey-Bass.

Madanes, C. (1990). *Sex, love, and violence: Strategies for transformation.* New York: Norton.

Madanes, C., Keim, J. P., & Smelser, D. (1995). *The violence of men: New techniques for working with abusive families: A therapy of social action.* San Francisco: Jossey-Bass.

Minuchin, S. (1974). *Families and family therapy.* Cambridge, MA: Harvard University Press.

Minuchin, S., & Fishman, H. D. (1981). *Family therapy techniques.* Cambridge, MA: Harvard University Press.

Nichols, M. P., & Schwartz, R. C. (1998). *Family therapy: Concepts and methods* (4th ed.). Boston: Allyn & Bacon.

Palazzoli, M. S., Boscolo, L., Cecchin, G., & Prata, G. (1978). *Paradox and counterparadox.* New York: Jason Erinson, Inc.

Price, J. (1996). *Power and compassion: Working with difficult adolescents and abused parents.* New York: Guilford Press.

Price, J., & Keim, J. (1993). Introduction to special edition on strategic humanism. *Journal of Systemic Therapies* (pp. 1a–1b). Winter.

Stanton, D., Todd, T., & Associates. (1982). *The family therapy of drug abuse and addiction.* New York: Guilford Press.

Steinberg, F., & Whiteside, R. (1999). *Whispers from the East.* Phoenix, AZ: Zeig, Tucker, & Co.

Szapocnik, J., & Kurtines, W. M. (1989). *Breakthroughs in family therapy with drug abusing and problem youth.* New York: Guilford Press.

Watzlawick, P. (Ed). (1984) *The invented reality.* New York: Norton.

Weakland, J. (1960). The double-bind hypothesis of schizophrenia and three-party interaction. In D. D. Jackson (Ed.), *The Etiology of schizophrenia.* New York: Basic Books.

Weakland, J. (1995). [Letter to the editor] *Family Therapy Networker, 19*(5), 16.

Wedge, M. (1996). *In the therapist's mirror: Reality in the making.* New York: Norton.

Whiteside, R. (1998). *The art of using and losing control.* New York: Brunner/Mazel.

Yeo, A. (1993). *Counseling: A problem-solving approach.* Singapore: Armour Publishing Pte., Ltd.

CHAPTER 8

Taking a Narrative Turn

Social Constructionism and Family Therapy

STEVEN M. KOGAN AND JERRY E. GALE

Social reality is not external to she who experiences, makes, or observes it. Conceive of it this way: people bring into being for one another a "structure" (I use the term metaphorically here) which they inhabit temporarily and which drops away behind them; of course it is not made any way we want; what we put together in the past shapes the direction and framework of the future; what we build interlocks with what others build; we build what we know how to build with the materials that come to hand. None the less we move into the future as into a building, the walls, floors, and roof of which we put together with one another as we go into it. It is an ongoing creation of and in *action*.

– Dorothy Smith (1990, p. 53)

INTRODUCTION

Bert: I've been hearing a lot about narrative therapy—I read an article where the therapist externalized a problem, then wrote the clients a letter about their session. She also talked about reauthoring stories, collaboration, dominant "discourses," postmodern philosophy…I'm not really sure how it all fits together. How does externalizing a problem fit in with postmodernism and writing letters? Why do narrative therapists always seem to talk funny about things, and how do they think up those really wild questions?

Ernie: Those are really good questions, I find it all pretty hard to piece together too. It is also hard for me to give you an exact description or prescription of what narrative therapy is, and even if I could, that would really only be my current version of what I think it is. I would like to hear more about your experience of things, though. So let me ask you a question. What is it about narrative therapy (NT) that attracts you?

Bert: Well, some colleagues of mine who use NT say they don't use diagnoses…they talk about stories, multiple selves, and how interesting their clients are. My clients are interesting too, but sometimes I get frustrated and don't know how to help them change. I was hoping that NT may be a way that will help me to be more effective in helping people and maybe have more enjoyment and excitement doing therapy.

Ernie: There are a lot of things you have brought up here: diagnoses, stories, being frustrated in trying to help people change. Where should we begin? All of these are really important issues, but a lot to unpack. Could we start with the idea of people and change? How do you understand how change works?

Bert: Well, people come to me in distress, and I believe I have to help them find some way to feel better and to behave differently. In my family therapy training we really emphasized that change has to be concrete. You need to get people to do something *different*.

Ernie: Are there times when you feel more pressed to get people to change or frustrated with it than other times?

Bert: Well, I think I struggle with families who are resistant to change, you know, they don't want to seem to try anything new, or talk about the really important things.

Ernie: Do you have a sense of when ideas of resistance intrude into your relationship with families? Or perhaps how it sneaks in to how you view clients?

Bert: That's a funny way of putting it. What I think it really comes down to is when everything I try is rejected or not even considered, I start to separate from them. I just don't understand where they're coming from, and I start to think that maybe they really are weird or kind of crazy. I begin to feel incompetent, and I don't like feeling that way. It's very frustrating for me.

Ernie: That does sound like quite a struggle for you. I wonder at these times how the family understands these struggles.

Bert: Huh? What do you mean?

Ernie: Well I wonder if perhaps they don't understand why you won't talk about the really important things. Are they perhaps wondering why they can't get through to you as well?

Bert: You really ask tough questions. I wasn't really thinking about how they were seeing me. I suppose they see me as pretty strange too, but they're the ones coming to me for help.

Ernie: Sure. I wonder about what sort of things might be keeping them from connecting to you, and you to them so that they can be helped.

Bert: What do you mean?

Ernie: There could be a lot of things—disconnecting practices might come from the expectations of your agency, cultural differences between you and your clients that are hard to talk about, even ideas about resistance or the role of the therapist that we are taught in counseling school. There are many hidden stories that may shed light on how people are making sense of things.

Bert: Well sure, if I knew all that stuff that would be great, but that's the problem! How do we get there?

Ernie: Hmm, maybe we should take a look at what sort of practices of connection and disconnection are at play...but since this conversation may take a while let's go ahead and start the chapter, I think it might help, and we can talk some more later.

Bert: OK by me.

DEFINITION: ON LOCATING A "NARRATIVE" THERAPY

When we first heard the term "narrative" applied to psychology and psychotherapy we thought of stories and literature; something to do with plots—with narrators, storytellers, authorship and audiences, perhaps with writing in general. It seemed odd to be talking about "narrative" and social science or therapy. Our first exposure to narrative in family therapy was through the work of Michael White, a therapist from Australia, and his colleague David Epston, who was trained as an anthropologist. Their book, *Narrative Means to Therapeutic Ends* (White & Epston, 1990), outlined their narrative approach to therapy. They asked a range of circular questions in therapy that seemed to reshape the possibilities for meaning in clients' ideas about problems, about each other, and about themselves (White, 1988, Winter). They "externalized" problems, conceptualizing the family's life as a territory under the influence of the problem, and talked about how to resist that influence. They did not seem to be intent on correcting family hierarchies, as would structural or strategic therapists, though often the outcome would be parents or a "sole" parent functioning with greater authority. At first we thought this was "narrative" therapy, because at the end of the session they would write a letter to the clients, and these letters would artfully document the session with rich metaphors, new possibilities, novel links, and stimulating questions regarding the future.

We now understand narrative to be a "new" lens for understanding the social world, one that has had effects on many social science disciplines. Where the idea of a narrative, or a story, has had the connotation of being something less than true, or something made up, narrative theorists posit that all knowing—even "scientific" knowing—is a form of story. We can approach the social world like a literary critic approaching a work of fiction. The critic might read a book naively—just jumping into the world that the text is constructing. The story being told is accepted as an "objective" account of events. In therapy this might be like treating the family's accounts of their problems as being literal, and if people's stories conflicted, we would need to get to the *real* story somehow. In a more thoughtful mood, a critic might read the story for underlying themes, or hidden meanings. In therapy, this would be akin to listening for the underlying dynamics that the family's talk is representing. Another literary approach might entail examining the story's structure for how it relates to meaning, and the literary or rhetorical devices the author used to construct a reality in the story that pushes and pulls on the reader. How does this story work? How is languaging being used to create a sense of what is real, and what things are like? In therapy we might examine how the family is constructing a meaningful sense of their reality and how we as therapists are participating in that process.

If we just jump into the story and accept it, we are treating language as *transparent*, that language is representing some reality outside of the words themselves. The story is then a more or less realistic account of something. If we look for themes, we still see language as representing something, or as metaphorical, only now that "something" is hidden in the story (like Freud interpreting the real meaning of a dream or fantasy). When we begin examining how words and language are being used to construct a sense of reality, we may say that language is *functional* or *constitutive*. Language is not a mirror of the world, but an action, whose usage creates, shapes, and evolves our sense of living in a "real" and stable world. Meaning is not merely there, but must be performed through language. While narrative theory has encompassed all these different levels of the consideration of language use, it is this last emphasis that has had such a profound and controversial effect on the social sciences. When Bert asked Ernie about narrative therapy, Ernie did not give Bert a realist, descriptive account of what it *is*. Nor did he provide an interpretation of the underlying meaning of narrative therapy. He engaged Bert in a conversation whereby they would talk the "what is" of narrative therapy into being anew. Ernie believed (we know what Ernie was thinking because we made him up!) that reality was something we did together through talk and communication in the present. Thus he attended to his talk and interaction with Bert as an opportunity to produce meaning together.

We hope in this chapter to introduce narrative as a subtle and complex world view, and to discuss how that world view is related to family therapy. It is often easy for people, on the one hand, to reject it out of hand as unscientific or relativistic, or to enthusiastically accept the idea without considering how this might effect one's practices as a clinician. Sometimes clinicians take to these ideas too quickly, in the attempt to help clients have a different story or construction of their problem. While narrative theory examines how we make sense of the world and create social realities, it is important to understand that this process occurs in *communities* of interaction that are located within particular cultures and historical eras. We are not free to have any story about things that we want, and all meanings are not of equal value or consequence.

Narrative therapy focuses on the construction of reality in both the spaces "between" as well as "within" people (Sawicki, 1991). A story is not just in our minds but is lived through the ways we act in the world with others, and how they interact with us. Thus a story is not an innocent verbal event, but is always linked to bodies acting upon bodies based on meaningful events. Stories and storytelling can be used to account for and perpetuate oppression, to attempt to liberate oneself, to create and fit into a social order, to argue for or against a truth, or to represent a therapy theory. What stories emerge in talk are influenced and restrained (though not completely determined) by cultural stories or norms. What stories or systems of meaning that prevail in an interaction also reflect social hierarchies. These may be based on institutional status (the therapist's story of events tends to have more credibility then a client's story in this culture) or based on cultural identity factors such as gender, race, ethnicity, sexual orientation, class, disability, and age (consider how many women's stories of health problems have been dismissed by a male-dominated medical establishment).

Narrative family therapy has some similarities with other models of family therapy. Like the cybernetic and systemic theories that have undergirded much practice, narrative therapy focuses on interaction. It is a "between" people therapy. However, rather than a dysfunctional system that we as therapists diagnose as *causing* the presenting problems (the view that language represents an underlying dynamic), narrative therapists might view problems as generating systems (Anderson & Goolishian, 1988). Instead of our family structure encouraging us to react in particular ways, we are active creators and producers of what our family is like. Problems may be understood as fluid, part of a local process of constructing meanings. With this subtle though crucial shift, it has become increasingly important to understand how individuals and families make sense of the world and their experience of things.

This shift entails putting the therapist into the interactive equation in a new way. Cybernetic theories focused primarily on interactional process. Through tracking sequences of behavior we could hypothesize patterns, then structures, and then rules or myths (Watzlawick, Jackson, & Beavin, 1967). By changing or influencing sequences, patterns, rules, and the like, the system would shift and members would have access to different experience. The therapist is outside, observing the family's process and not really a participant in how the problem was conceived. In narrative therapy, the therapist is always a full participant in how reality is being constructed. We are never outside the conversations that are creating our world. We create, shape, and maintain social realities through continual conversation with others. Narrative therapists attempt to cocreate with clients a new, more expansive story, that informs both how to view the world and self, and how to act in it. This includes "subvert[ing] taken-for-granted realities and practices" that currently restrain clients' lives and experience (White & Epston, 1990, p. 27).

White and Epston (1990) discussed narrative therapy as a means to coconstruct or liberate an untold or "subjugated" story. The new story then has symbolic, behavioral, and political effects on lives. In this chapter, we will explore the historical development of this narrative turn in the social sciences and in family therapy. We will examine how some of these ideas have come to influence family therapists and how they premise their understanding of therapy with narrative ideas. While we wish to emphasize that narrative is a means to understand, to pluralize, and to politicize the social world—and not an approach with particular steps, phases, or interventions—we will nonetheless strive to offer some maps in the "doing" of "a" narrative therapy. We will offer some therapy stories as a means to locate oneself in a narrative epistemology. Finally, we will explore how narrative has functioned as a research tool, as well as provide some critical perspective on the narrative turn.

Rejoinder:

Bert: OK, OK, I think I'm starting to get the picture. You're just saying that there is no absolute truth, that everything is relative and we create our own realities. It's kind of like reframing, where you try and change the meaning of a situation. I've used reframing before.

Ernie: Well, I understand that there is some similarity, but I do still see it kind of differently. I'm not so sure that everything is that relative really, and I hope I'm not being that instrumental, that strategic.

Bert: Well, if there is no one reality, then we can make up all kinds of things to explain problems, and people will think differently if they buy it or if it fits.

Ernie: I think that maybe an important difference may be our sense of where the location of "reality" is.

Bert: Huh?

Ernie: Well, if reality is performed between and among people as well as within people, it's not just a matter of changing one's mind. We live in communities of discourse that shape us and that we use to shape others.

Bert: Well, what if I see a violent man who batters his partner? Should I just go and deeply value his story and go with him where he wants to go? His story could be that "she deserved it" or "she likes to be dominated."

Ernie: I think that is exactly what might happen if narrative were really about relativism. I think it is more about *how* situations, beliefs, and ideologies and their associated actions get constructed. I don't believe all constructions or stories are equal because some individuals construct situations of domination, pain, and horror. But I think being able to help people deconstruct these situations is crucial for being able to coconstruct a different situation.

Bert: So you would deconstruct the violent man's story? How would you do that?

Ernie: I don't have a set strategy for how to do that; I hope I would be listening carefully and responding to the man. I do really like some orienting questions that Michael White (1993) talked about with violence. He begins by considering the question, if a man wanted to dominate a female partner, what actions and ideas would best entrap her? How does the man talk to the woman, to himself, and to the therapist in ways that keep the abuse alive? Does he justify or minimize it? Does he blame her? These are meaning constructions that do not usually lead to alternative stories of accountability and responsibility. By examining with the man the ideas and practices that construct the situation, there emerge possibilities to challenge and make visible important issues, possibilities to resist ideas and practices of abuse, and the space to consider alternative ways of constructing one's life. Also there are many stories regarding male dominance in this culture the man may tap into to use to support and continue his violence. We may need to look at how stories of what a man and a woman are "like" in this culture operate in everyday lives.

HISTORICAL DEVELOPMENT

Narrative has been a part of human communication since the dawn of history. According to many evolutionary biologists, psychologists, linguists, and others, it is language that makes us distinctly human. The structure of story and talk, through everyday communication, through ritual, through drama, through all forms of written, drawn, or oral discourse is the most encompassing context of our humanity (Bruner, 1990). Since the rise of Enlightenment science in the seventeenth and eighteenth centuries, the notion of narrative, as a means of representing the world, has been associated with ambiguity, particularism, and idiosyncracy (Ewick & Silbey, 1995). Narrative, as a construct of knowing or telling, was relegated to fiction or folk theory (Bruner, 1990). Scientific or rational discourse was considered a privileged form. Psychologist Jerome Bruner (1986) described two paradigms of knowledge: the logico-scientific and the narrative. Logico-scientific discourse makes propositions that aim for a transcendent truth or logic, one that is true for all situations. Scientists sought TRUTH, in the form of universal principles and laws that underline the multiplicity of forms and ideas that we apprehend.

Narrative knowing, in contrast, accepts and celebrates the multiplicity and contradiction of the lived world as is. To capture the social world we need not reduce it to universal principles, or totalizing theoretical frameworks; we can describe the many differences of thought and experience, and accept these differences as "true" (small "t") for people experiencing their lives. According to Bruner, all experience is storied through narrative forms. To make sense of the world, we cast our experience into linear forms with plots, protagonists, tragic flaws, climaxes, rising and falling action, and so forth. The term "narrative" has also come to be associated with the "interpretive turn" in the social sciences that is challenging realist methods of contemporary scientific discourse (Denzin & Lincoln, 1994). This interpretive turn has been linked to a number of contemporary figures including Clifford Geertz in anthropology, Roland Barthes in literary criticism, Mikhail Bakhtin in speech communication, Michel Foucault and Jacques Derrida in philosophy, among others (Riessman, 1993).

An important context to the development of narrative theory is related to postmodern (or post-structural) critiques of knowledge and Enlightenment humanism. Enlightenment thinkers, drawing inspiration from classical Greece, sought to resist the power structure of the Church and the deity-centered metanarrative that premised the Middle Ages. In the Middle Ages, God was the epistemological center of life. According to the new story of Enlightenment humanism, "man" became the center from which the world might be known. By employing scientific method, reason and observation would lead to a progressive unraveling of nature's mysteries. Humanism is thus a term that may be best understood as a centering of man, rather than God or the Church, as the starting point for understanding the world. Many feminists note that the Enlightenment was a centering of "man"-kind, inasmuch as this story of scientific progress toward truth has been perpetuated, enforced, and proliferated within a historical context of the subjugation of both women's stories and experience, as well as those of people of color. One effect of this metanarrative is the formation of a hierarchy where "rational" Western culture is viewed as the center of things and the birthplace of the predominant modes to truth. Another effect is the notion of progress.

Accordingly, as a culture, we are marching toward some horizon of knowledge where things are more clear, more true, and more just. In this myth of progress, the nearer we get to this horizon, the better our lives become, and our lives always seem increasingly "advanced" compared to those before.

Jean Lyotard (1979), among others, critiqued the totalizing and imperial nature of this Enlightenment foundation to our sense of what is real knowledge and how we conceptualize individual identity. He coined the term "postmodern" to refer to that challenge and a time in history where the grand narratives of the Enlightenment have begun to lose sway over conceptions of knowledge and the self. Accordingly, we are entering an era where multiplicity and contradiction are a new norm, where the idea of a single shared reality is being replaced by "multiple realities" and partial knowledges. French post-structuralist philosophers challenged the notion that there is any essence or structure to social facts or that reality itself is determinate (Sarup, 1993). Foucault and Derrida described methods whereby they would interrogate any object of knowledge or social fact that presumed to have a precultural status, an obvious or natural essence (Foucault, 1972; 1980b; Shumway, 1989; Spivak, 1976). For instance, Foucault (1965) challenged the notion that we have become more humane in our treatment of "madness," or that any notion of historical progress at all could be taken for granted. He noted how we have created different forms for enslaving those who do not fit into a social order, while celebrating our own humanitarianism. Derrida (1976) challenged the notion that great philosophical works had any singular underlying meaning. He deconstructed philosophical texts, providing interpretations that were opposite to the traditionally accepted understandings. These notions are not just a part of French philosophy; ideas of multiplism have influenced the heart of traditional social science methodology in the form of critical multiplism (Cook, 1985).

In some spheres of social science, these critiques have engendered a crisis of representation and a crisis of legitimation (Denzin & Lincoln, 1994). The fundamental questions of whether the world is knowable and what will count as valid knowledge are deeply contested. Previous notions of creating representations of the world with more or less accuracy can no longer be taken for granted. We cannot be sure that, when we make a representation (e.g., by giving a case history or creating a model of how behavior works), we are depicting something about the world "out there" rather than our own immediate situation. Many scholars are arguing that the world is characterized by a multiplicity of valid perspectives, by contingency, change, and political struggle. Accordingly, we have entered an era in which very little seems certain or stable. For some this is a cause of concern and fear, while for others (narrative therapists!?) it is an opportunity for liberation.

NARRATIVE IN FAMILY THERAPY HISTORY

As we have noted, the narrative metaphor began influencing family therapy in the late 1980s and throughout the 1990s. Often considered as part of a larger social constructionist view, narrative has been called a third wave within the family therapy field (O'Hanlon, 1994). The first wave, developing in the 1950s, highlighted a cybernetic, systems metaphor, which was a paradigmatic change for the psychotherapy field. The implications of cybernetic theory included a shift from linear to circular causality, a focus on feedback relationships between people, and therapists taking a more active role in therapy (Hoffman, 1981). The therapist's role was analogous to a systems analyst or a communication expert who could diagnose and intervene in troubled systems (Haley, 1976).

In the early and mid-1980s the influence of cognitive science, evolutionary biology, and Gregory Bateson's later ideas characterized a second wave in the field that Lynn Hoffman (1985) chronicled as "second-order"cybernetics. From this perspective, the notion of an independent observer outside of the family system was disputed. The therapist's views and actions impacted both what she or he observed as well as the interactive process itself. Reality, rather than an external phenomenon, was a complex and relative construct influenced by the nature of interacting systems, perceptional apparatuses, boundary distinctions, and the organizational properties of organisms (Keeney, 1983; Maturana & Varela, 1987; Watzlawick, 1984). The role of the therapist as systems analyst was critiqued (Golann, 1988; Goolishian & Anderson, 1992) and this second-order perspective introduced to family therapy constructivism, which was popularized in the work of Brad Keeney (1983), Paul Watzlawick (1984), and others.

Around the late 1980s and early 1990s, social constructionism, a third paradigmatic shift, emerged in the family therapy field. Building on the work of Bruner and social psychologist Ken Gergen (1985), social constructionism offered a different philosophical framework than constructivism. While maintaining a nonobjectivist stance (there is no single knowable or objective reality), social constructionism highlighted the social matrix within which reality construction occurs (Hoffman, 1992). These two positions—constructivism and social constructionism—are at times confused with each other. Constructivism however, focuses more on an individual's personal construction of reality through the interfacing of senses with the environment. Constructivism accepts the individual psyche as a given, and examines the perceptual mechanisms and properties of the psyche as a reality-constructing instrument. Social constructionism sees the production of reality not only as an individual phenomenon but as a social one. It focuses more on language use and interaction, and tends to be critical of cognitive science. To social constructionists, theories of how the mind operates are viewed as constructions or stories related to the ways a culture conceives of the mind. In this third wave, social discourse and language metaphors such as story, text, myth, discourse, and narrative are utilized to describe human interaction. An ethnographic approach to understanding families evolved that highlighted social embeddedness and personal experience. These ideas could be found in the work of Anderson and Goolishian (1988), at the Galveston Family Institute, and in the work of White and Epston (1990).

Harlene Anderson and Harry Goolishian (1988) articulated a vision of therapy based on problems determining systems, rather than systems functioning to maintain problems. They described this as a shift away from the "cognitive and constructivist models that define humans as simple *information-processing machines* as opposed to *meaning-generating beings*" (Anderson & Goolishian, 1992, p. 26, italics in the original). Their "collaborative language approach" endorsed a *dialogic* mode of therapy. Understanding and meaning are achieved in the moment-to-moment context of interaction. They maintained the notion of "systems," but saw human communities as "collaborative language systems." The goal of therapy was to "dissolve" the system of languaged interaction that had coalesced around the problem issue. They emphasized conversational questioning and a "not-knowing" stance by the therapist, an appreciation of the client as expert, and assisting the therapeutic conversation to express the "not-yet-said" (Anderson & Goolishian, 1992).

The version of narrative therapy that impacts this chapter most significantly is from Michael White's Dulwiche Centre group and other narrative therapists from Australia and New Zealand. Drawing on narrative premises from Bruner and Geertz, and the post-structural philosophy of Foucault, White articulated an approach that highlights constructing new client stories while maintaining an awareness of dominant social discourses or norms. This therapy is highly political, incorporating an awareness of both the micro- and macro-level politics at play in any therapeutic encounter. Narrative therapists from "down under" have also offered examples of narrative work with violent males (Jenkins, 1990), sexual abuse (Durrant & White, 1990), perspectives on prisons (Denborough, 1996), and a range of various problems and issues.

Rejoinder:

Bert: Wow, that was a heady section; you started talking like a textbook.

Ernie: Sorry about that, but the editor wanted us to cover these things. We're going to try and be a little less narratively distant from here on out.

Bert: I was wondering why you didn't mention solution-focused therapy. Where does it fit in with all of this?

Ernie: Ooh, boy, that's a good question. There's been a quite a bit of debate about the two approaches. Wetchler (1996) considered solution-focused therapy as one of the social constructionist therapies. Zimmerman and Dickerson (1996) felt there were major differences in the approaches. Solution-focused (SF) therapy tends to be more minimalist than narrative in regard to examining meanings and behaviors. The focus is on exceptions to the problem and preferred change. For example, an SF therapist might approach a problem by trying to find times when the problem does not occur or the client overcomes it. SF therapists try to avoid talking about problems in general, focusing on "solution talk." They are not as interested in locating stories and ideas in social contexts and interactions. Narrative therapy à la White and Epston brings in a lot more information regarding the context and the meaning systems around the problem. A narrative therapist would likely be less minimalist, would be interested in how the problem got talked into being, and how it might be related to cultural stories.

"TENETS" OF THE MODEL

There is an Indian story—at least I heard it as an Indian story—about an Englishman who, having been told that the world rested on a platform which rested on the back of an elephant which rested in turn on the back of a turtle, asked (perhaps he was an ethnographer; it is the way they behave), what did the turtle rest on? Another turtle. And that turtle? "Ah Sahib, after that it is turtles all the way down." (Geertz, 1973, pp. 28–29)

Like all other accounts about what something is, or what something means, there is no grand consensus regarding the truth or the substance of narrative theory and therapy. Even between the authors of this chapter, we have no absolute consensus on what narrative is, or how to recognize or prescribe it in practice (nor do we especially feel it is necessary to "forge" a specific meaning). The structuring of a "tenets" section then is problematic—in narrative, all is story and constructed, leading many authors to refer to these ideas as post-foundational. After we have let go of notions of foundation, essence, and deep structure, we can recognize how through the medium of language we produce the social world and are produced as knowing selves. In narrative theory there is a pervasive and insistent questioning or deconstruction of any object of knowledge. This includes questioning notions of truth, of the self, of the family, of marriage, and so on. Narrative theorists and therapists examine ideas and concepts via questions such as How is this notion produced? What social practices and behaviors are involved in that production? What are the conditions necessary for this kind of idea to come about? And, what does this idea as practiced exclude (Butler, 1992)? With these cautions in mind we will discuss what we see as some key ideas and concepts in narrative therapy: locality, discourse, knowledge/power, reflexivity, and deconstruction.

LOCALITY

One theme that we found useful in understanding narrative involves the local production of knowledge, or what we call *locality*. By local, we mean right here, right now, proximate, grassroots, person to person. So much of our talking about therapy and the social world involves constructs that supposedly explain what is going on (Gubrium, 1992; Gubrium & Holstein, 1990). When a child acts out, someone will say "it's the family," or "its a need for attention." "Stress" makes things happen. He acts that way because he is "all boy." We constantly tend to hypothesize social forces or explanations that are shaping or driving human behavior from the outside. These are examples of top-down thinking, that humans are shaped or driven by conceptual abstractions such as social factors or internal drives. This view represents abstract ideas as really "out there" doing something to people, or really "inside there" compelling certain actions. From a narrative perspective, meaning is not already present awaiting discovery; rather it is performed.

Karl Tomm provided a wonderful example of the local production of reality from his series of articles about interviewing (Tomm, 1987). Tomm discussed, in therapy with a family who had a somewhat tyrannical father, his efforts to lessen the tension in the session with questions such as "What if Mother became ill and Father had to do all the caretaking?" While the children at first claimed it would be awful, as they storied around the possibility of Dad's doing the details of child care their sense of him became quite different. They envisioned Dad cooking and helping with their homework and their personal problems, and needing him more than before. Coming from a Milan-style approach at the time, Tomm thought of the "intervention" as being the prescription or reframe at the end of the session. He positively connoted the father's harshness and prescribed a ritual around it. By this time, however, the children objected that father wasn't harsh—that the prescription and connotation made no sense and were not "true." The meaning of Dad—his identity—had changed from the conversation! This example acknowledges the local production of *what* a person is. Tomm illustrated how the therapy interview itself was not merely diagnostic of a system, but that talk in interaction *is* intervention. How we are talking, how we are practicing meaning with others through language is always creating (and delimiting) the *what* of the situation and the meaning of people's actions and identities.

DISCOURSE

A useful idea in understanding *how* we construct meaning in interaction involves the idea of referencing *discourse*. A discourse in this sense refers to a system of related statements about the world that specify not only particular meanings but courses of action and behavior (Bové, 1990). In some ways discourse seems like beliefs about the social world that are "at large" in a culture (Gubrium & Holstein, 1993). People draw on these systems of statements to give meaning to their experience of unfolding events in order to moderate their own behavior in regard to the events. Discourse does not actually exist "out there," outside of people referencing it.

When creating meaning, people draw upon multiple discourses to give sense and shape to experience. Many are linked and mutually reinforcing, while others seem contradictory. Also, discourses are not totally discrete "things" with specific boundaries. As situations change, public stocks of knowledge—the "available ideas" about the world—change and transform. Discourses shape our ability to make sense of the world whether we are aware of them or not. As Kathy Weingarten (1995) noted:

> A discourse may be so familiar to us that we cannot distinguish the messages that we are getting. Whether we are aware of a discourse or not, it can powerfully shape the stories we can tell and the stories we can hear. This discourse of sexual abuse provides a clear example of this for clinicians. Up until twenty years ago, therapists operated within a discursive community that made it very difficult to "hear" stories of sexual abuse. Instead, therapists often "heard" stories of hysteria. Today, it is hard to imagine a therapist who wouldn't recognize and acknowledge a sexual abuse narrative told by a distraught client. (p. 11)

Referencing discourse to make sense of the world is a pervasive human practice. Recall that in narrative theory we spoke of language as being *functional* or *constitutive;* that is, through language and discourse we construct the world, and it has no inherent meaning outside of our systems of language. At times we refer to the *discursive context* of something, which for us is a shorthand way of talking about the discourses at play in a particular situation. Taking a narrative view, the "system" we are interested in is not specifically tied to the members of a particular family or a particular person. We are working with the language systems by which people are making sense of, and thereby shaping, the world.

Psychological discourses prompt attention to feeling and proliferate concepts of emotional hygiene such as proper grieving, catharsis, the need for psychotherapy, and so forth (Parker et al., 1995). Family therapy has constructed discourses around healthy relationships, utilizing systems of statements that include the dysfunctional family, enmeshment, the rubber fence, triangles, and so forth. These are all ideas, or theories if you will, that are available to someone try-ing to define or make sense of what an interaction is. Depending on how we de-fine the situation, and what is available to us for making definitions, different actions and social practices are called for.

An important system of discourses that has been examined by the feminist critique is mother blaming (Bograd, 1988). Accordingly, in our culture we have constructed appropriate motherhood as always being there for children and family, and being responsible for the domestic sphere. When things go wrong, be it wife abuse, child sexual abuse, or child behavior problems, many therapists construct explanations that implicate Mom as the problem. In this fashion, ther-apy also reproduces the kind of discursive context in which women will refer-ence that idea to their lives—feeling guilty, feeling at fault, and never being a good enough mother in the social gaze of therapists, friends, family, and so forth. Discourses that support mother blaming may include gender role discourses, hysteria and female weakness discourses, as well as discourses that protect fa-thers from responsibility, such as "boys will be boys" (and thus can't be responsi-ble for important things) (see also Hare-Mustin, 1994; Weingarten, 1995). Perhaps the most overt example was the notion that men sexually abused their children because their wives were not satisfying them sexually.

From available discourses we construct with others personal identities that re-strain our sense of ourselves and how we will act toward others. How we conceive of identity has many social consequences. If we draw on a resource that a person in a wheelchair is crippled, this suggests a limited and limiting representation of that person's identity. The discursive context of a gay/lesbian or bisexual person is informed by discourses of compulsory heterosexuality (Rich, 1993). For ex-ample, less than 30 years ago, a gay man in therapy would experience a situation in which his sexuality was defined as a pathology. He was behaving shamefully and it was widely accepted that he was a form of moral or psychological degenerate. Nancy Boyd-Franklin (1989) has spoken eloquently of the effects of discourses that are drawn upon to define or understand African American men. She noted how people tend to interpret African American men as dangerous, as potential criminals, or as shifty and lazy. At times men may internalize these ideas: That is, they form self-stories or personal autobiographies based on the discourses avail-able in the dominant culture.

KNOWLEDGE/POWER

While meaning in one sense is fundamentally *indeterminate*—there is not fixed meaning to anything—the production of meaning is tied to systems of power. Any story cannot be told at any time. Some discourses are dominant and others are marginalized. Thus we are not completely free to make any meaning, or con-struct any identity that we wish. Cultural norms and social positions all con-tribute to what meanings seem enduring or appropriate. According to Foucault (1980a; 1980b), all social interaction is a "contested site," a situation in which multiple ideas and discourses conflict and evolve. Some social stories are ren-dered more legitimate and, since identity and self are storied forms, people are also rendered more or less legitimate. I (Steve) can recall working in a mental hospital as an eager young family systems therapist. Working within that system, one that focused on psychopathology, I was acutely aware of the political nature of meaning making. Where in the comfort of a marriage and family therapy clinic with one-way mirrors we might hypothesize, reflect, adjust, and explore our own and the family's creativity, systems ideas were not welcome at the hospital. Being unable (or unwilling) to fit in the discursive premises of an institution often leads to *marginalization* (in my case, I got fired!). One's effectiveness, one's goodness, and what is "really" going on are determined by evaluation and comparison to a normative cultural *center*. The cultural center in that hospital adjudged certain stories and related procedures about mental health and people as more viable and realistic, and within that context "obvious."

Conforming to a local institution's culture or predominant discourses does not guarantee that one will or will not be seen as effective, appropriate, or the like. Discourses around gender, race, ethnicity, class, ability status, age, and so forth also affect the meaning and the politics of the situation. There are always complex rules (both covert and overt) for governing who has the right to speak, when one has the right to speak, and what is appropriate for the context (Ewick & Silbey, 1995). Complex networks of power relationships exist, and our access to *voice* or authorship is different from context to context. Defining what is appropriate to say has to do with beliefs about status in the culture. While it is easy to acknowledge the differential in social power based on institutional statuses such as occupation (doctor/nurse; therapist/client), issues of race, gender, ethnicity, and so forth tend to be much more difficult to acknowledge. These cultural markers influence what kinds of context will be constructed.

REFLEXIVITY

As cocreators of context with the families with whom we visit, therapists can no longer be viewed as neutral or objective observers. The stories told in therapy and the new stories that unfold are intimately related to the person of the therapist (Hoffman, 1990). After all, we must perform, ourselves, as therapists as our families perform, themselves, as clients. What stories get told then will have just as much to do with us (our thoughts, feelings, gender, family of origin, race, class, and so forth) as they have to do with the other (clients, families). Acknowledging this, many narrative therapists theorize a clinical posture of *reflexivity*. That is, we must look carefully and critically toward ourselves as people, as therapists, and as a part of a particular institution, not just as experts applying objective or neutral techniques.

Let's look at this in action in a case story told by Hoffman, in which she was working with an estranged mother and daughter who were trying to mend their relationship:

> After several sessions of failing to reconcile them, I asked myself whether I really understood their conflict. So I told these two women that I thought I'd been going in the wrong direction. My trying to push them together could have been the worst thing in the world for them…I also said that I might not be the right therapist for them because my own grown daughters had become estranged from me. I said for that reason, I might be trying too hard to push them back together again. I had been feeling more and more indignant with the mother because she was so angry, but when I said that,

I felt my own anger fall away. The first thing the mother said to me was, "Then why are we paying you for therapy?" A little later, out of the blue she turned to her daughter and said, "I want you to know that I don't hold you responsible for my depression after Nana's death." After that, mother and daughter had their first positive exchange in three years. (in Simon, 1992, p. 161)

In this story, Hoffman acts out of her recognition that what is going on "out there" in the therapy is intimately intertwined with her own life.

Rejoinder:

Ernie: Wait a minute there, this is getting a little beyond what I'm comfortable with here. You are not proposing that we tell all our thoughts and feelings to our clients are you?

Bert: No, I don't think that's necessarily what reflexivity would entail.

Ernie: I could see some therapists really getting involved with their own personal stuff, I mean isn't keeping your own personal issues out of therapy and trying to be neutral or objective the most important part of being able to help somebody?

Ernie: Well, I agree that Lynn Hoffman's self-disclosure could be pretty controversial. We really don't know the whole context of the moment in which she made her comment. It also doesn't seem like the clients felt that Hoffman was asking them to take care of her. Perhaps there is a difference between trying to be honest and accountable for the ways you, as therapist, are participating in how the dialogue unfolds, and exploiting clients for one's own needs. What I liked about that little vignette is the way it demonstrated how the therapist's thoughts and feelings are almost always a part of the way the problem is unfolding in the conversation. I also don't believe we are ever objective or neutral. We are always making subtle judgements about what to attend to, how to phrase our questions. Our perceptions of things are always colored by our gender, our cultural background, our personal and family-of-origin experiences, and so forth.

Bert: How would you tell the difference between self-disclosing to be accountable and self-disclosing that is irresponsible?

Ernie: Hey you're starting to sound like a narrative therapist! That's a wonderful question! I do believe this approach invites continuous ethical self-questioning. I always try and think about what are the effects of my actions. Am I opening up space for difficult conversations that are useful and new? Am I attending carefully to the family and their reactions? I also try to establish an atmosphere in which clients can feel OK about challenging my "authority" as therapist. I try to share decision-making power, and have a balance of following the clients and moving the discourse. If I am still unsure, I talk with colleagues and supervisors. I try to seek out accountability as part of my development as a therapist and as part of my life. Reflexivity is also connected with other issues. I'm going to send you back to the narrator voice now to hear more....

Reflexivity also refers to a critique of the institutional mask of the therapist that operates according to the objectifying discourses of mental health treatment. By objectifying discourses, we are simply referring to the ways that typical practices of mental health—for example, case notes, case conferences where clients are not present, diagnoses, assessment procedures that classify people, and so forth—tend to cast the client as a thing rather than a person. In discussing ways to counter this objectification, Melissa Griffith and James Griffith (1992) noted that:

> An emotional posture inviting curiosity, openness, and respect is facilitated by careful attention to how a therapist talks with him/herself. When a therapist talks about the family and its problem in her/his own inner dialogues, with colleagues, or in written chart notes, the therapist should strive to find language that describes everything witnessed in the therapy session, yet is also language that the family members would find affiliative if they were to hear it or read it....The therapist's private dialogues strongly shape the emotional posture the therapist brings to the family. (pp. 8–9)

Narrative therapy promotes a sense of respect for the right of others to be the authors of their lives and to determine their own personal truths. This is in contrast to the truth of the therapist or the truth of institutions such as psychology or family therapy. Rather than families being an object of the mental health professional who must fix, enlighten, or restructure them, therapy promotes the client or family's status as subject, as the protagonist of their stories. Reflexivity in practice represents talking to clients the same way we talk about them to our colleagues and acknowledging that our institutional position is just part of another construction process.

Another important reflexive practice involves using a reflecting team. This term was first coined by Tom Andersen (1991) and his associates in Norway. They began feeling uncomfortable with the hierarchical nature of the typical strategic model of therapy in which a team watched the family interacting with the therapist and contrived rituals and prescriptions to disrupt family patterns. Instead, Andersen decided to actually switch rooms with the family and ask the family to watch (and then comment upon) the team discussing the problem in the open. The family was able to see the team process about the problem, and it created a very creative and empowering situation. Family members seemed to appreciate the openness, and team members felt that they were participating less in a mysterious, powerful, and strategic intervention, and more as collaborators and consultants. Solutions were cocreated with the family members, and family members were able to hear multiple ideas and opinions regarding their situation.

DECONSTRUCTION

By viewing knowledges as locally produced and related to networks of power, we are in essence *deconstructing* ideas, concepts, and interactions. We are "troubling" the familiar ideas of "what" something is or what it means. Rather than someone being deficient, we can break down the notion of pathology or deficiency into what discourses are at play and how this particular problem identity or situation was *constructed*. From this view, identity—or self—is fluid, always in process. This extends to a family's shared sense of identity. All meaning is in process and related to interaction. When certain ideas and behaviors seem to be fixed or stable, a deconstructive reading of the situation would highlight how that stability has been produced.

By specifying how an identity gets fixed, a person can immediately experience a new sense of freedom. Discursive ideas and practices link and reinforce one another to create a sense of reality. Susan Bordo (1989) used these ideas in her discussion of anorexia. Rather than seeing anorexia as a mental disease or a psychological affliction, she noted how anorexia is an interlocking system of behaviors, ideas, and practices, embedded within a particular social context:

> Through the pursuit of an ever-changing homogenizing, elusive ideal of femininity—a pursuit without terminus, a resting point, requiring that women constantly attend to minute and often whimsical changes in fashion—female bodies become what Foucault called "docile bodies"—bodies whose forces and energies are habituated to external regulation, subjection, transformation, "improvement." Through the exacting and normalizing disciplines of diet, make-up, and dress— central organizing principles of time and space in the days of many women—we are rendered less socially oriented and more centripetally focused on self-modification. Through these disciplines, we continue to memorize on our bodies the feel and conviction of lack, insufficiency, of never being good enough. At the farthest extremes, the practices of femininity may lead us to utter demoralization, debilitation, and death. (Bordo, 1989, p. 14)

By identifying these networks and their operations, a therapist may help people separate from and resist stories and practices that specify experience in painful or dispreferred ways. Clients (and therapists too) can never be "outside" of discourse and the power/knowledge regimes they constitute. However, we don't always have to cooperate with the dominant stories that through their meeting apparatus direct us to think, believe, and behave in specific ways (Foucault, 1980a; White, 1993). The goal, however, is not finding one preferred way to think or act but to increase the possibilities for different self-definitions and subsequent lifestyles.

A THERAPY STORY ILLUSTRATING THE "TENETS"

I (Steve) remember a quite powerful example for me of both finding my own theory and the ways that power and knowledge are related. I had been seeing Jan, a white woman in her mid-40s, in individual therapy for several months. We had talked about her struggles with an abusive ex-husband, and the extraordinary experience of waking up from a car accident several years ago feeling cognitively different. At the time, neurologists had no understanding of the effects of some head injuries that did not show up on their tests. Jan knew something was wrong. She struggled against short-term memory problems, confusion, and difficulty organizing simple tasks. And yet she was told that her struggles were emotional or psychological. She experienced a growing difficulty connecting with people, which encouraged her to accept "self-distrust" in her life. I thought to myself of the long history of mental health discourses that propagated in so many women a sense of being crazy, that they didn't see things as they were—in true (male?) reality.

Jan was remarried while this confusion still had a strong hold of her, to a man she would soon come to fear. He seemed to have a ready technology to create and then exploit the self-doubt that had invaded Jan's thinking about herself.[1] They had a child, and the husband became increasingly emotionally and physically abusive. Gathering her courage, Jan escaped with her daughter to start a new life two thousand miles away. In her story, I felt how powerfully what we recognize and how we label things affect our lived experience and the practices or behaviors with which we then engage the world.

Power and knowledge were not, however, only an object of a past story, but a part of our interactions as well. After we had been meeting for about seven months, I knew I was going to leave my position at the clinic. I began wondering about issues of dependency. Had therapy become Jan's significant system, and was that restraining her from establishing other relationships (a "homeostasis" explanation)? The theories and models I had been taught about brief systemic therapy seeped into our conversations. Rather than honor her desire to continue in therapy, to have support and "a sounding board," I deconstructed the idea of needing to continue. I was constituted in or recruited by discourses that "told me" that discontinuing therapy was the most "appropriate" thing for Jan's well-being. Self-doubt caused me to use my training and Jan's trust in me to convince her and myself that we didn't know what was in her own best interest. Should she trust herself? Maybe Steve was *right* and she should be more independent? The discourse of dependence began to affect the therapy and impact the meanings we both attributed to the situation. Issues of autonomy, differentiation, and instrumentality were discourses being used to ascribe meaning to the situation, and these implied particular versions of reality and of behavior that were limiting Jan's voice.

I was very grateful that, in spite of the hierarchies implicit in a therapist/client relationship, Jan resisted this discourse. At some point (I'm not sure how) I realized there was no compelling reason to push this issue, and I wondered how the idea got so compelling, that I would ignore a clear and very reasonable request by someone who was working to take charge of her life. I, too, had been constituted and constructed within the discourses of my training and my gender. I thought about the discourses of brief therapy, and how our success as therapists often gets measured by being able to describe discrete changes and discrete endings.

APPLICATIONS AND TECHNIQUES

Narrative therapy proposes that stories shape lives and provide structure of meaning; however, they can never express the full complexity and richness of lived experiences (Bruner, 1986; White & Epston, 1990). The role of therapy "is to bring these alternative stories out of the shadows and to elevate them so that they play a far more central role in the shaping of people's lives" (White, cited

---

[1]*Bert:* There is one those narrative words again, "technology." Does this mean that he had devised a scheme or some sort of science to be mean to Jan? It was that intentional and conscious?

Ernie: I think "technology" here refers to the ways abuse relies on a whole system of intersecting ideas and practices for its sustenance. Many believe that much of what is typical of male socialization in our culture teaches boys to treat women as objects, to justify acting on impulse ("boys will be boys"), and to dodge responsibility. There are many ways an abusive man may foster and feed ideas of self-doubt and worthlessness in his partner. Examined in this light, these practices of abuse and irresponsibility seem like a technology, a science of maintaining abuse.

in Nicholson, 1995, p. 23). This process is intimately connected to the relationship with the people in the room. It is important to be attending and responding to the client's and one's own moment-to-moment experiences and sense of meaning. In addition to the relationship, the cornerstone of narrative therapy involves both asking questions that help people deconstruct the current dominant story of the problem and asking other questions that help reconstruct a preferred narrative.

One means to do this is the use of *externalization*. By externalizing the problem, the social matrix that sustains and generates the current story can become available (White, 1988a). This involves a simple reversal of positing that instead of the person (or family) having the problem, the problem "has" or manages the person (or family). The following questions are examples of how to bring out this distinction:

> When did tempers begin to push you around? How does depression get you to think about yourself? When did "conflict" begin to take over your relationship? How does "conflict" enlist you to react to your family? How does anorexia want you to view your body?

The "problem" that gets externalized is negotiated, and can change as different understandings of the problem evolve. In the earlier stages of therapy, this type of conversation can also provide a means for exploring elements in the social context that contributed to the production of the current story. Nicholson (1995) noted that White's questions can relate across the dimensions of time (past, present, and future) and perspective (self, family, culture). These domains can be used as a guideline to "fill in" stories and get more vivid descriptions. For example, here are externalizing questions across different domains:

PAST/SELF	When did depression begin to convince you that you were nobody?
PAST/FAMILY	How did depression try and separate you from your wife?
PAST/CULTURE	How does depression use messages about financial success to strengthen its hold on you?
PRESENT/SELF	How has anger affected the way you see your self?
PRESENT/FAMILY	How has your anger affected your partner's life?
PRESENT/CULTURE	What messages about men or masculinity from friends and coworkers tend to convince you that to be a man you have to be "top dog?"
FUTURE/SELF	What will your life look like in 10 years if anxiety keeps pushing you around?
FUTURE/FAMILY	How will anxiety affect your relationship with your parents?
FUTURE/CULTURE	What ideas about mental health will seem to capture you in 10 years?

The process of externalizing the problem, of separating the person and the problem, leads to what White calls "relative influence questioning." These type of questions examine the extent to which the person feels that his or her life, behaviors, and meanings have become saturated or managed by the problem. Again, notice that questions can be formed in different domains of the social context:

> To what extent is anger dominating your relationships? How much of what you think you are like has been determined by depression? If I asked your Aunt Rose, how much would she say fear has taken over your life?

A natural progression then would be to explore the client/family's resistance to the problem-saturated lifestyle or events that already contradict the problem narrative. These stages are not discrete however. Often clients in the externalizing conversation will begin identifying "unique outcomes" that the problem did not dominate. In earlier work, White (1986) discussed a phase of therapy in which the future with the problem was explored in great detail. Then a challenge or choice point would be discussed: "Is this lifestyle tolerable and, if not, how might we perform our resistance to it?" Later works by White tend to have more of an organic flow, and not to be dependent upon a specific progression of types of conversation. Again, a wide range of questions can be used to investigate "unique outcomes," and how to produce them:

> What steps might you take to begin to show tempers that they're not your boss? When have you noticed Johnny fighting off the tempers instead of letting them push him into trouble? Who will be the most surprised that you decided to resist the influence of laziness? What will be the first thing they notice about you when you meet? How have you managed to keep anorexia from taking over 20% of your life?

Part of exploring the family's resistance to the problem involves the search for "unique outcomes." These are "previously neglected but vital aspects of lived experience—aspects that could not have been predicted from a reading of the dominant story" (White & Epston, 1990, p. 41). The dominant story of the problem overrides many aspects of experience that do not fit into the problem narrative. As people separate and deconstruct these problem stories, alternative versions of their lives are evident. These include times when a person may have resisted the influence of the problem, or resisted a problem lifestyle in some way. Unique outcomes provide valuable places to expand the newer story:

> What did you say to yourself before you stood up to tempers, and didn't let them convince you to throw a tantrum? Do you think tempers felt like they had more or less of a hold on your life that day? How might discovering that you can fight back against fears affect your relationship with your mom? How do you think Dad will see you differently since he's learned about this new discovery?

Another distinction or domain of questioning that White (borrowing from Bruner, 1986) refers to is the landscape of consciousness and the landscape of experience. These refer to the domain of actions and events on one hand—the episode that can be narrated according to a plot line—and the domain of meanings and interpretations of the story on the other. Thus, landscape of experience questions will refer to public events in the world:

> How have fears recruited your parents to treat you differently? How can you tell when fears have convinced them you can't take care of yourself?

Landscape of consciousness questions refer to meanings and ideas:

> What kind of person does anger want to convince you that you are? How has failure tried to get you to see yourself?

A final category of questions of interest involves restorying the past. From a narrative perspective, the past is a fluid set of ideas usually referenced according to present circumstances. When we are depressed we tend to select events from the past that accord with our present feelings and as such construct a problem-saturated story that extends into the past. This same type of process can also be used to help solidify preferred narratives:

> Who in your past would have predicted these victories over sadness? What did that person see in you that you forgot?

Our friends Bert and Ernie:

> *Bert:* Wow! Those are great ideas, I can't wait to try out some of these questions. I think I can do this now. First I externalize the problem, flesh out the influence of the problem, then look for exceptions. Why didn't you just tell me that and skip all that philosophy?
>
> *Ernie:* Well, because I never could get the formula to work for me.
>
> *Bert:* But you're supposed to be so into narrative—isn't it what you do?
>
> *Ernie:* Oh, I tried the formula. I used to think about questions all day. I even wrote down questions I wanted to try and ask families before we met. I figured if I could just ask the right questions, then it would work just like in the books.
>
> *Bert:* Well didn't it?
>
> *Ernie:* Nope. It wasn't a magic technique that I could just do at will and have miraculous results. The questions I had in my mind never exactly fit the moment I was having with real people in the room. And my timing really stunk. I would be thinking about whether or not I should switch to relative influence questioning or exploring unique outcomes, or did I do enough consciousness questions or enough cultural questions. At times I felt really down because I thought that in comparison to the narrative therapy books I had read, I was very clumsy. My questions never seemed elegant enough and I felt I wasn't living up to the promises that books and articles made for what this therapy could do.
>
> *Bert:* So do you still do narrative? What happened?
>
> *Ernie:* Well I think I do. I realized that trying to live up to some imaginary standard that I perceived from books, and that trying to be a perfect narrative therapist, was a practice of disconnection in therapy, and one of misery in general! Now I try to follow more, to stay closer in touch with people, and I ask questions about what I am genuinely curious about. I wonder how did these problems get constructed and what social discourses are at play. It was hard for me to let go of the pressure to try and change people and work on understanding and cocreating with people. But I feel that I have become not only more respectful as a therapist, but generally more useful to my clients.
>
> *Bert:* Well if it's not the questions that "do" it, then why isn't this just good relationship therapy like Carl Rogers or some object–relations approaches?
>
> *Ernie:* Maybe it is. I really don't mind the idea that maybe its just the empowering relationship that is at play. I guess we can account for what causes change in all sort of ways. I do believe that narrative is a bit more than that

because we consider the social context and the politics of interaction. I think narrative therapy does have in common with those approaches a focus on experience and relationship.

Following are some ideas and activities for practicing a narrative therapy.

1. Many narrative-oriented therapists find letter writing valuable and even use letters in place of case notes. This practice encourages using collaborative language. Rather than the typical therapist story one finds in case notes where objectified "patients" are treated by the clinician (who is the narrating protagonist), there is a mutual story of discovery and change. After each session, try writing a letter to your clients. Think about the major themes of the session, the dilemmas, and how you were affected by their struggles. Note changes the clients have made and ideas for further change that were discussed.

2. Many feel that externalizing conversations is the hallmark of narrative therapy. Sally Roth and David Epston (1996) discussed an exercise for developing externalizing conversations. Working in small groups with colleagues, they had group members choose a familiar problem and had people familiar with that problem play it as a role. The rest of the group would interview the "problem" regarding how it took over people's lives. Group members are able to practice constructing questions for investigating the tricks that this problem might ply to gain more control or management over people's lives. Another group member then is selected to play the problem, and the interviewers explore the problem's weaknesses and possibilities for its defeat.

3. We believe thinking hard about gender, race/ethnicity, class, sexual orientation, physical ability, status, and age can transform and deeply unsettle clinical practice. If you were to think about how this problem may be the result of our culture's prescriptions for behavior based on culturally marked "difference" instead of a "family" problem, how would your thinking change? What issues might arise? Do you believe everyone in our culture has equal access to power and privilege?

4. We find it useful to treat ideas as actions. This could include labels, personality attributions, beliefs, and attitudes. For example, if someone says he believes his partner is "crazy," we might explore how the idea that the partner is crazy functions in their interaction. How does this idea change the way they act with one another? What practices does this label justify? How would a different interpretation affect the way people interacted with one another?

5. One useful image that Goolishian and Anderson (1992) often spoke of is that of the ethnographer. It can be useful to imagine you are from another country, trying to understand a new culture, and realizing that you may have to suspend your first ideas and favorite theories about how things work. You may want to experiment with multiple theories and multiple frameworks for understanding a family.

6. The image of a historian of ideas and beliefs is a valuable one we have found often in feminist scholarship. A longer view of time seems to make apparent that our present truths are quite temporary. Consider examining the history of important ideas and how meanings evolved. How did a particular notion come to influence the family? Who was influenced first? In what ways was this idea or belief present in families of origin? And to what effect?

7. I (Steve) remember one of my supervisors talking about being a "weaver" of themes and ideas. I like to experiment with new connections and different implications for issues that the family discusses. I try to apply words and ideas the family discusses in different contexts:

- You spoke of your father as very traditional. Which of your family's traditions do you like and which might you wish to change? What new traditions do you want to establish in your own family? What traditions do you think your partner wishes to maintain or to resist? How do you think these traditions may influence your daughter when she starts a family?

- I was thinking about your comment last week that your son is "all boy." What would it mean if he was part girl? How much boy and girl seems like a good mix? What characteristics seems to be boy or girl ones? Are there times when the same characteristic seems to be boy, then seems to be girl?

8. Sometimes in considering the creative aspects of meaning making it is easy to forget that constructing the world is a political act. Any idea, theory, or belief about what people or situations are like means that some other ideas are being marginalized. It is important to consider what are the politics of making sense of the world in the family and the therapy system. Who seems to have more say about what reality is like or should be? Might this be related to issues of gender? Whose ideas and perspectives don't seem to count, and how is this marginalization maintained?

9. I (Jerry) have heard many new therapists struggle with their concern for not being oppressive to their clients—to the point of feeling paralyzed. I don't believe that being open to multiple perspectives means that you have to follow the family's reality anywhere and try to make yourself invisible. I think therapists can have perspectives too. The question is how to democratize perspectives and open those that are being marginalized. Consider the following therapist statements that have clear agendas but show an openness to negotiation:

- I was wondering if we might spend a few minutes talking about how your experience of abuse has affected you as a parent. I'll understand if its too painful, though, and you'd rather not.

- (opening statement of a session) I've been thinking about you over the past week and have some things I'm curious about, though first I would like to hear about your thoughts for today's agenda. What will be most important for you to talk about or accomplish today?

10. Some critics have raised concerns about narrative therapy with abusive people. If they become "people under the influence of abuse," can't they use that to avoid responsibility? We believe narrative therapy is an invitation to respect and accountability, not to irresponsibility. We have a responsibility to address violence and abuse, and to expose the discourses and systems of practices that enable them to capture people. However it is important to maintain a sense of reflexivity and carry these responsibilities out while maintaining a collaborative position: Alan Jenkins's book *Invitation to Responsibility* is recommended for learning about

a narrative approach to violence and abuse. (See the Annotated Suggested Readings at the end of the chapter.)

- I realize this is painful and frightening but we will have to report this to the Department of Child and Family Services. Do you have ideas about how we should handle the call? Are there ways I can help during this process? I realize this may make you feel angry with me and I understand if you decide to get another therapist. I want you to know, though, that I am still committed to helping you end abuse in your lives.

- I am uncomfortable with talking about communication problems when there is the threat of violence toward your partner. I'm afraid for her safety. I feel that if we focus only on communication issues I may be helping keep violence going instead of addressing it.

11. Could your weekly staffing or case consultation become a reflecting team? I (Steve) like to ask permission from clients for discussing their lives in consultation if we can't do a "live" reflecting team. I then try and report back the conversation. Consultation sessions can even be videotaped, and then clients can view your discussion and reflect on it.

12. White and Epston (1990) discussed how particular stories are maintained by social networks. They at times recommended letter-writing campaigns publicizing someone's intent to struggle against a problem, seeking help from friends, relatives, school teachers, and so forth. They also created various clubs of people who defeated problems and would later become consultants. For example, they created a "fear tamers" league with children whom they had assisted in escaping the influence of fear. Stephen Madigan (1994) in Canada organized an "anti-anorexia league" in which participants would eventually create helpful videos and write recommendations for other women battling the influence of anorexia.

13. A powerful use of community resources is described by the Just Therapy Group in New Zealand (Waldegrave, 1990). This group is passionately committed to social justice (hence "just" therapy), and in order to bring out the hidden power dynamics within many therapeutic encounters, they invite cultural consultants to view the therapy and counsel the therapist. For example, if a pakeha (a white New Zealander) therapist is meeting with a Maori family, that therapist would be accountable to a Maori cultural consultant. This consultant might be a respected elder who would be in a position to assist the therapist in being accountable to the specific needs of the Maori family. This process would also occur if a male therapist was seeing a female survivor of sexual abuse. The therapist would be accountable to a female consultant.

14. Explore "unique outcomes" and "sparkling facts" about your own career as a counselor. Michael White (1989) and John Neal (1996) discussed ways to reauthor one's own story as a therapist. They asked trainees to consider the unique outcomes that led to their participation in the training or their interest in narrative. They also focused on sparkling facts, times when therapy felt productive and transformative:

- How did your decision to become therapist come about? What did it represent to you? What influences helped you to make this decision? How are these influences useful to you now as you practice?

- How did you help Al turn his anger into a chance to think about the future? What events in your life have led you to this place where you were capable of such insight/empathy with this family? Who in your life inspired you to learn and practice patience?

CASE EXAMPLE

Karen and Jim were a young white heterosexual couple who had been married for three years. During our first meeting they identified their major conflict—Karen's love of animals. She had brought many animals into their house, always adopting pets, and their household lives now required a lot of adaptation to this very large family. I (Steve) recall how when we first met, this interest had become a producer of many ideas and stories about Karen and the couple's health. One story included the idea that Karen had an emotional problem, likely from her past, that caused her to want to "rescue" animals to fulfill some need. This story, which had been somewhat capturing of Karen and Jim, and Karen's previous therapist, specified a range of things. One unfortunate result was that it encouraged Karen to wonder if she was perhaps emotionally impaired, and this idea at times also seemed to capture Jim. The emotional problem story led Karen into questioning her own thoughts and ideas and feelings. This resulted in a personal sense of diminished legitimacy relative to her compassion for animals.

The "emotional problem" discourse intertwined with a "fear or irrationality" discourse that seemed to have captured Jim. Growing up, Jim's mom had been mentally ill, and though his personal memory of her was of a free spirit whom he enjoyed immensely, as a child with his father and brother this sense of freedom was anathema. Ideas of "seriousness" and fears of "spontaneity" circulated in their lives. Jim had made many decisions in his past based on resisting the forms of lifestyle specified by "rationality," though many of these decisions had receded into the background of late. These discourses had clear gender articulations as well. Women's actions are often constructed as being irrational or motivated from emotional problems, and men have much experience and support in patrolling the boundaries of rationality. This consists of judging and supervising, and contesting versions of reality that seem emotional or crazy.

In our talks together we examined how these discourses were constitutive of Karen and Jim in their relationship. Wanting to resist the dominant characterizations, I explored Karen's sense of caring for animals and came to wonder if perhaps she was a "gardener of animals." This rang true for Karen. Even though they as a couple would need to negotiate the care of their family, she began to feel within those negotiations that she was "OK" for loving her pets and free of the narrative that would describe her as being controlled by her love for animals. We talked about possibilities for resisting the sometimes rigid requirements of rationalism in Jim's—and through him, the couple's—life. We explored the costs and consequences of a purely "rational" lifestyle and envisioned where reason could be a useful ally rather than a dictator. We noted "unique outcomes" in Jim's life in which he resisted the fears and supervisions of a rigidly rational lifestyle, and he reconnected with stories of his softness and his spontaneity.

EVALUATION OF THE THEORY

Narrative therapy per se has not been studied as a therapeutic model with traditional outcome studies. No quantitative data of outcome or process information are available that we know of. There have been critical evaluations of narrative therapy. These derive from two camps—one "external" to social constructionist ideas, and one internal, or sympathetic to constructionist thinking. Barbara Held (1995) critiqued the narrative/social constructionist movement in therapy. She raised a number of concerns that echo a post-positivist view of knowledge. In post-positivism, the world is considered ultimately unknowable, but we may get useful information utilizing a modest realism. From this position, social constructionism is considered "antirealist." Held contended that narrative therapy is rife with contradictions in that it elevates the experiences and narratives people use to talk about life while claiming not to believe in any fundamental reality. Why then elevate experience? Does this then mean that narrative is the way to do therapy with everyone, and isn't that foundational? Held argued that to have a therapy that is both systematic and individualized we need to examine how many forms of therapy models operate. From a post-positivist framework in general, narrative therapy is simply too unsystematic and unspecific. It promotes relativism and doesn't provide reliable standards for assessment of its outcomes and its truth claims.

Vincent Fish (1993) also critiqued the narrative conversationalist movement and its use of postmodern philosophers. Fish is sympathetic to a constructionist viewpoint; however, he believed that therapists were borrowing ideas that were most similar to the constructivist ideas of Bateson. Batesonian ideas were roundly critiqued by feminist family therapists for denying the social and material context of therapy and clients' lives. Fish was concerned that the misuse of postmodern ideas would deny power imbalances in family therapy, and fail to critique the field as an institution, a use that Fish would see as more appropriate to a postmodern stance. Hare-Mustin (1994) brought up similar concerns. She also felt that a constructivist therapy that does not consider how power relationships are constructed differently will reproduce injustice under a narrative banner. Thus both post-positivist and feminist postmodern critiques are concerned with the difference between what might be considered constructivist aspects of these new therapies. In common, both critiques are concerned with relativism, that narrative means that anything goes, and that they will uncritically privilege experience. Held contended that highlighting of the particular comes at the cost of being unsystemic and neglects the commonalities in people's experiences.

We feel these are important and useful critiques. We agree that many clinicians seem to be entranced by narrative ideas in a way that neglects that the social construction of reality is not always a peaceful negotiation but may be a political battlefield. In response to Held's concerns, however, we wonder about the innocence of traditional social science methods, and what might be hidden assumptions within a modest realism. The problem of a modest realism is that it will inevitably serve to marginalize some ideas and privilege others. This returns to the notion, discussed earlier, that knowledge and power are inseparable. How can we know what effects our modest realism may have on those who do not submit or are not favored by the current ideology in vogue? Is this modest reality going to be agreed on by everyone as legitimate and sufficiently realistic? Or are some people going to find it untenable or unrelated to their experience?

We are all aware that beliefs about marriage and relationships, raising children, psychological health, and so on have changed drastically from decade to decade. Each generation has its "experts" and its breakthroughs, which are in turn critiqued and "improved upon." Rather than viewing research as leading to a better, more systematic and reliable therapy, we tend to see these endeavors as producing meaning rather "discovering" it. Modest or not, we are skeptical of all claims to truth, and tend to want to investigate the claim for its effects and the history of its construction.

NARRATIVE EVALUATION OF THE THEORY AS A FORM OF INQUIRY

Many researchers have found narrative ideas useful in investigating novel questions from a constructionist perspective. Discourse analysis (DA) is a form of research that considers social situations as texts, investigating how language is being used. Forms of DA may be found in social psychology (Potter & Wetherell, 1987), sociology (Gubrium & Holstein, 1993; Heritage, 1984), legal studies (Ewick & Silbey, 1995), and more. Analysts study a variety of situations, including transcriptions of interviews, scientist's behavior, courtrooms, psychology texts, and recordings of therapy sessions (Potter & Wetherell, 1987). The results are not definitive theories about the world, but descriptions of how discourse has been deployed, and how the active operations of language in our lives become invisible. This type of work can be useful for critiquing cherished theories and ideas, as well as for challenging scientific methods that support a political status quo.

In our interest in narrative and postmodernism in therapy we have used DA in studying therapy process (Gale & Newfield, 1992; Kogan & Gale, 1997). We would like to show some examples of the kind of information these methods might yield. In a sense, we are applying narrative ideas as a research tool by examining the practices that are being employed in a therapy session to construct meaning. We feel this is a very similar mind-set to what we do in therapy, and it has been of great value to us to practice deconstruction on transcribed therapy tapes. One project (Kogan & Gale, 1997) involved an analysis of a session by a prominent narrative therapist. The following examples come from a transcribed demonstration session recorded at a family counseling conference (see Table 8.1 for a transcription guide).

This first section illustrates how a narrative therapist might deconstruct ideas and beliefs that may have problematic effects in people's lives. The therapist is talking with a married couple, Tom and Jane, about their conception of past problems.

EXEMPLAR 1

Tom: ...I want to try and again maybe bring you up to speed here (yeh) real quick because one of the problems that I had (.) and I think one of the big

TABLE 8.1 | TRANSCRIPTION NOTATION

(.)	A pause that is noticeable but too short to measure.
(.5)	A pause timed in tenths of a second.
=	There is no discernible pause between the end of a speaker's utterance and the start of the next utterance.
:	One or more colons indicate an extension of the preceding vowel sound.
Under	Underlining indicates words that were uttered with added emphasis.
CAPITAL	Words in capital are uttered louder than surrounding talk.
(.hhh)	Exhale of breath, number of h's indicates length.
(hhh)	Inhale of breath, number of h's indicates length.
( )	Indicates a back channel comment or sound from previous speaker that does not interrupt the present turn.
[	Overlap of talk
(( ))	Double parentheses indicate clarificatory information, e.g., ((laughter)).
?	Indicates rising inflection.
!	Indicates animated tone.
.	Indicates a stopping fall in tone.

Adapted from Sacks, Schegloff, & Jefferson (1974).

trouble's with our relationship was and this is what we're working on now (yeh) coming from a failed relationship (.) I was terribly afraid that the *second* relationship was going to fail and I was terribly worried that if I argued with Jane in any way whatsoever or disagreed with her and she got angry with me (4.0) ((strangled sound)) in a threatening way this relationship would fail and we would have arguments from time to time about things and she would get angry with me (.) I would back off what I've learned recently is that it is OK for me to get angry with Jane and to tell her how I feel about things…

Jane: and I have to say that um (.) that I would always I had to um be in control of everything, I had to be in control of (.) him (yeh) of our relationship I thought I I thought if I could keep it all under control (.) um for some reason I would be a hap happier and my contribution is to let go and to own up and to take his advice.

Therapist: (hh) When you say in control you mean like sort of take responsibility for (1.0) for most things o::r or feel that you are responsible for lots of things is that what you mean by in control o::r do you mean something else?

Jane: (3.0) um yeh I probably had to take responsibility (.) (yeh) for everything (.) (yeh) mhm (yeh).

Tom and Jane provide an explanation of the problem where by Jane is constructed as powerful and dominant. Tom was "fearful" or arguing with her. Jane accepts this definition, accounting for herself as being controlling. The therapist's responses address a possible subjugated story within the couple's description of a typical "pursuer–distancer" cycle. Rather than Jane being domineering or "controlling" (with its negative connotations in our culture), the therapist explores the possibility that an untold story may involve feeling "responsible." If Jane feels or defines the problem as being controlling, she must respond by letting someone else be in control. In the control formulation of the problem, Jane's personal agency and the struggles that make sense of her life are neglected. Also, by being couched as the "active" one in the relationship, there is the implication that her actions led to the marital problems. Jane also seemed in this session to accept a definition of herself as told through the experience of Tom. The therapist provided an opening for Jane to have a more personal definition of the situation, with different implications. It is quite a different situation to believe that one has been controlling versus that one has been responsible! It is also interesting how the therapist offers this suggestion to Jane in that he provides ample opportunity for Jane to correct or contest this definition.

In the next example, the therapist uses deconstruction to illustrate how Tom's talk is contributing to objectifying Jane. He reverses the perspective of reality construction from Tom's centered position assessing Jane, to the story as it might be seen from Jane's perspective:

EXEMPLAR 2

Tom: (hh) I have noticed this is a new a new area for us this is good ((chuckles)) I have noticed I guess in the last six six years four to six years with all the problems I have felt that Jane has not (1.5) dressed for me that she's not (.) she she used to, I thought (.) dress for me you know how it is when you date and the woman kind of dresses for the guy a little bit and tries to make things kind of ((chuckling)) interesting=

Therapist: would you do the same the other way around does that (inaudible)

                                                                    [   ]

                 [   ]
Tom: I may have lost that also, yes I would yes you bet=

Therapist: =you would=

Tom: =sure=

Therapist: So you would be dressing for each other=

Tom: (hh) (2.0) I don't know (right) I don't know if the point is being (inaudible) or not

[   ]

[   ]

Therapist: yeh yeh sure ((looking at Jane)) so is it also important uh for Tom to dress for you is that also important?

Jane: yes it is

             [   ]

             [   ]

Therapist: It was important

Recall that the legitimacy or truth of a story depends upon the perspective one is taking and how one is located within different contexts. It is, in this culture, quite common for women to be viewed as objects for men to gaze upon. This is supported by the media, patriarchal value systems, and beliefs about what is beautiful or sexy. The therapist resists this dominant discourse, and provides a space for a "subjugated story"—the perspective of Jane as subject rather than object. Also note how the therapist then asks Jane for her perspective rather than commenting on it for her. The therapist brings in Jane's voice rather than assuming an element of her experience.

DISCOURSE ANALYSIS EXERCISE

The sensibilities of discourse analysis can be used to examine any form of communication: texts in a book, stories about a problem, art work, poetry, and so forth. We can also use discourse analysis to deconstruct ideas about situations. Below is a section of talk by a man accounting for his violence toward his partner (borrowed from a discourse analytic research project by Hyden & McCarthy, 1994). We would like you to consider this section of text according to the kind of analyses we have discussed. Recall that rather than jumping into the story and accepting it, or looking for an underlying meaning, we are interested in how the use of language is compelling a certain perspective. Consider the following questions:

- How are people portrayed?
- Of what is the narrator trying to convince you?
- How does the narrator try to convince you of things?
- What alternative stories can you think of that would explain the situation just as well?
- What do you think is the narrator's investment in *not telling* these different stories?
- How does this story specify the shape, meaning, and quality of people's lives? What are the effects of telling this story in this particular way?

Here is a short section from a series of interviews analyzed by Hyden and McCarthy (1994):

> ...we have fights, sure. When she starts harping about something and doesn't stop, one really gets down. Then we have an argument...First comes the screaming, back and forth, then maybe some flowers go flying...but don't call this assault. There was no hitting with fists or in the face...It was more like this (acts out slaps and shoves). It was just a reaction...you start shoving...react like a human being....Maybe sometimes you spit in her face. (p. 553)

The storyteller appears to us to be working quite hard to dismiss responsibility for himself. To accomplish this, he uses several strategies—a discursive technology—that include stressing reciprocity, providing a building sequence for explanation, defining the parameters of violence, and justifying his actions. Notice how this narrator uses "we" throughout the account, assigning responsibility to the couple rather than himself. He provides a building action from verbal arguments to slaps and shoves that is linked to action by the couple rather than himself ("back and forth," "we have an argument," "some flowers go flying"). In his account, the narrator defines what will be counted as abuse—there were no fists to the face—and slaps, shoves, and spitting are not to count. Finally he links this whole "logical" sequence with how "human being[s]" react, placing all his actions in a morally benign and universal category.

By examining how this type of account is produced, we may gain insight into the types of conversations and discourses at play that are sustaining abuse. These include emphasizing reciprocity in interactions and minimizing or ignoring the victim's experience. These discourses are "available" to the man to sustain his violent behavior. In fact, the discourse of mutuality and equality in interactions was supported for a long time by family systems therapists (Avis, 1992). This formulation of things, however, neglected the power differential in violent relationships between men and women. It also led to explanations implying that, since women were participating in interactions that led to abuse, at some level they must be bringing it on themselves or wanting to be abused. In this way, discourses of mutuality or reciprocity are intimately connected to discourses of victim blaming.

A Final Rejoinder:

Bert: Well Ernie, I have to tell you, that this was all interesting, but I'm still not quite sure what I can do with it all. I am really fascinated by a lot of these ideas. Are there other books to read? Is there anyone who can teach me more about it?

Ernie: Sure, there's been a lot of interest in narrative approaches and there are several training centers in North America.[2] Following is a list of recommended reading. I realize a lot of the language can be overwhelming, but I'm glad you're interested in learning more. I hope you have many more puzzling, fascinating, and fun conversations with people about this stuff.

ANNOTATED SUGGESTED READINGS

Anderson, H., & Goolishian, H. (1988). Human systems as linguistic systems: Preliminary and evolving ideas about the implication for clinical theory. *Family Process, 27,* 371–393.
> A classic paper outlining the premises of a "collaborative language" approach. One of the earliest and most influential works on social constructionism in the field. This is at times a difficult read, but well worth the effort.

Durrant, M. & White, C. (Eds.). (1992). *Ideas for therapy with sexual abuse.* Adelaide, Australia: Dulwiche Centre Publications.
> A collection of essays dealing with a narrative approach to sexual abuse. Demonstrates how narrative might be used with survivors of sexual abuse, with families at the time of disclosure, and with sexual offenders. Highlights the importance of the offender being accountable and responsible and explores the way the culture may support the offender's irresponsibility.

Freedman, J., & Combs, G. (1996). *Narrative therapy: The social construction of preferred realities.* New York: Norton.
> This is a well-written and clearly explicated book on NT. Freedman and Comb's writing always embodies a great deal of respect for the process of therapy, as well as

---

[2] In addition to the Dulwiche Centre in Adelaide, Australia, there are a number of training centers that work from a narrative epistemology (e.g., Jill Freedman and Gene Combs in Chicago, Kathy Weingarten and Sally Ann Roth in Cambridge, Massachusetts, Jeffery Zimmerman and Victoria Dickerson in San Francisco, and Steven Madigan in Vancouver and Toronto).

their personal delight in being therapists. A bit easier to follow then White and Epston's work if you are new to the subject.

Griffith, J., & Griffith, M. (1992). Owning one's epistemological stance in therapy. *Dulwiche Centre Newsletter, 1*, 5–11.

> A wonderful article that talks about the difference between narrative as a technique and embodying narrative ideas in practice.

Hare-Mustin, R. (1994). Discourses in the mirrored room: A postmodern analysis of therapy. *Family Process, 33*, 19–36.

> Discusses the dangers of not considering dominant social discourses in the construction of therapy and presenting problems.

Jenkins, A. (1990). *Invitation to responsibility.* Adelaide, Australia: Dulwiche Centre Publications.

> How to do narrative therapy with violent and sexually abusive men. Provides a map for a therapy that holds offenders accountable while maintaining a collaborative and respectful stance. This book provides a startling counterpoint to many confrontational therapies while focusing on holding violent and abusive men accountable and not blaming victims.

McNamee, S., & Gergen, K. J. (1992). Introduction. In S. McNamee & K. J. Gergen (Eds.), *Therapy as social construction.* London: Sage.

> A collection of case stories and theoretical essays by famous constructionist therapists and social scientists including Lynn Hoffman, Ken Gergen, David Epston, Karl Tomm, and others. An excellent introduction to social constructionism.

Weingarten, K. (Ed.). (1995). *Cultural resistance: Challenging beliefs about men, women, and therapy.* New York: Harrington Park Press.

> Originally published as two issues of the *Journal of Feminist Family Therapy*, these essays discuss therapy as a form of cultural resistance to dominant discourse

White, M. (1993). Deconstruction and therapy. In S. Gilligan & R. Price (Eds.), *Therapeutic conversations* (pp. 22–61). New York:. Norton.

> White discusses the latest evolution of his model. This includes a more postmodern and culturally aware position than his 1990 book. He provides two case examples and discusses the landscape of consciousness and experience.

White, M., & Epston, D. (1990). *Narrative means to therapeutic ends.* New York: Norton.

> Now authors of a classic, White and Epston provide a thorough theoretical grounding in the first chapter that can be daunting. In contrast, the rest of the book makes the approach seem deceptively simple. White and Epston share a variety of case examples in letters they have written to clients and families during the process of therapy.

Zimmerman, J. L., & Dickerson, V. C. (1996). *If problems talked: Narrative therapy in action.* New York: Guilford Press.

> An interactive text written to give the reader a feeling for narrative while engaging the book. By writing the whole book through dialogues, many difficult ideas are brought to life. Often humorous and creative, this is a very useful book for gaining more insight into a narrative approach.

REFERENCES

Andersen, T. (1991). *The reflecting team: Dialogues and dialogues about the dialogues.* New York: Norton.

Anderson, H., & Goolishian, H. (1988). Human systems as linguistic systems: Preliminary and evolving ideas about the implications for clinical theory. *Family Process, 27*, 371–393.

Anderson, H., & Goolishian, H. (1992). The client is the expert: A not-knowing approach to therapy. In S. McNamee & K. J. Gergen (Eds.), *Therapy as social construction* (pp. 25–39). London: Sage.

Avis, J. M. (1992). Where are all the family therapists? Abuse and violence within families and family therapy's response. *Journal of Marital and Family Therapy, 18*(3), 225–232.

Bograd, M. (1988). Scapegoating mothers in family therapy: Re-exploring enmeshment. In M. Mirkin (Ed.), *The social and political contexts of family therapy.* New York: Gardner Press.

Bordo, S. R. (1989). The body and the reproduction of femininity: A feminist appropriation of Foucault. In A. M. Jaggar and S. R. Bordo (Eds.), *Gender/Body/Knowledge: Feminist reconstructions of being and knowing* (pp. 13–33). New Brunswick, NJ: Rutgers University Press.

Bové, P. A. (1990). Discourse. In F. Lentricchia & T. McLaughlin (Eds.), *Critical terms for literary study* (pp. 50–65). Chicago: University of Chicago Press.

Boyd-Franklin, N. (1989). *Black families in therapy: A multisystem approach.* New York: Guilford.

Bruner, J. (1986). *Actual minds: Possible worlds.* Cambridge, MA: Harvard University Press.

Bruner, J. (1990). *Acts of meaning.* Cambridge, MA: Harvard University Press.

Butler, J. (1992). Contingent foundations: Feminism and the question of postmodernism. In J. Butler & J. W. Scott (Eds.), *Feminists theorize the political* (pp. 3–21). New York: Routledge.

Cook, T. D. (1985). Postpositivist critical multiplism. In R. L. Shotland & M. M. Mark (Eds.), *Social science and social policy* (pp. 21–62). Thousand Oaks, CA: Sage.

Denborough, D. (1996). *Beyond the prison: Gathering dreams of freedom.* Adelaide, Australia: Dulwiche Centre Publications.

Denzin, N. K., & Lincoln, Y. S. (1994). Entering the field of qualitative research. In N. K. Denzin & Y. S. Lincoln (Eds.), *The handbook of qualitative research* (pp. 1–17). Thousand Oaks, CA: Sage.

Derrida, J. (1976). *Of grammatology* (Gayatri Chakravorty Spivak, Trans.). Baltimore, MD: Johns Hopkins University Press.

Durrant, M., & White, C. (Eds.). (1990). *Ideas for therapy with sexual abuse.* Adelaide, Australia: Dulwiche Centre Publications.

Ewick, P., & Silbey, S. S. (1995). Subversive stories and hegemonic tales: Toward a sociology of narrative. *Law and Society Review, 29*(2), 197–226.

Fish, V. (1993). Poststructuralism in family therapy: Interrogating the narrative/conversational mode. *Journal of Marital and Family Therapy, 19,* 223–234.

Foucault, M. (1965). *Madness and civilization: A history of insanity in the age of reason.* New York: Random House.

Foucault M. (1972). *The archaeology of knowledge and the discourse on language* (A. M. Sheridan-Smith, Trans.). New York: Pantheon Books.

Foucault, M. (1980a). *The history of sexuality, Vol. 1: An introduction* (R. Hurley, Trans.). New York: Vintage/Random House.

Foucault, M. (1980b). *Power/Knowledge: Selected interviews and other writings 1972–1977* (C. Gordon, L. Marshall, J. Meppham, K. Soper, Trans.). New York: Pantheon.

Freedman, J., & Combs, G. (1996). *Narrative therapy: The social construction of preferred realities.* New York: Norton.

Gale, J. E., & Newfield, N. (1992). A conversation analysis of a solution-focused marital therapy session. *Journal of Marital and Family Therapy, 18*(2), 153–166.

Geertz, C. (1973). *The interpretation of cultures: Selected essays.* New York: HarperCollins.

Gergen, K. (1985). The social contructionist movement in modern psychology. *American Psychologist, 40,* 266–275.

Golann, S. (1988). On second-order family therapy. *Family Process, 27,* 51–65.

Goolishian, H. A., & Anderson, H. (1992). Strategy and intervention versus nonintervention: A matter of theory. *Journal of Marital and Family Therapy, 18*(1), 5–16.

Griffith, J., & Griffith, M. (1992). Owning one's epistemological stance in therapy. *Dulwiche Centre Newsletter, 1,* 5–11.

Gubrium, J. F. (1992). *Out of control: Family therapy and domestic order.* Thousand Oaks, CA: Sage.

Gubrium, J. F., & Holstein, J. A. (1990). *What is family?* Mountain View, CA: Mayfield Publishing Co.

Gubrium, J. F., & Holstein, J. A. (1993). Phenomenology, ethnomethodology, and family discourse. In P. G. Boss, W. J. Doherty, R. LaRossa, W. R. Schumm, & S. K. Steinmetz (Eds.), *Sourcebook of family theories and methods: A contextual approach* (pp. 651–672). New York: Plenum.

Haley, J. (1976). *Problem solving therapy: New strategies for effective family therapy.* San Francisco: Jossey-Bass.

Hare-Mustin, R. T. (1994). Discourses in the mirrored room: A postmodern analysis of therapy. *Family Process, 33*(1), 19–35.

Held, B. S. (1995). *Back to reality: A critique of postmodern theory in psychotherapy.* New York: Norton.

Heritage, J. (1984). *Garfinkel and ethnomethodology.* Cambridge, England: Polity.

Hoffman, L. (1981). *The foundations of family therapy.* New York: Basic Books.

Hoffman, L. (1985). Beyond power and control: Toward a "second order" family systems therapy. *Family Systems Medicine, 3*(4), 381–396.

Hoffman, L. (1990). Constructing realities: An art of lenses. *Family Process, 29,* 1–12.

Hoffman, L. (1992). A reflexive stance for family therapy. In S. McNamee & K. J. Gergen (Eds.), *Therapy as social construction* (pp. 7–24). London: Sage.

Hyden, M., & McCarthy, I. C. (1994). Women battering and father-daughter incest disclosure: Discourses of denial and acknowledgement. *Dicourse and Society, 5*(4), 543–565.

Jenkins, A. (1990). *Invitations to responsibility.* Adelaide, Australia: Dulwiche Centre Publications.

Keeney, B. (1983). *Aesthetics of change.* New York: Guilford Press.

Kogan, S. M., & Gale, J. E. (1997). Decentering therapy: A textual analysis of a narrative therapy session. *Family Process, 36,* 101–126.

Lyotard, J. F. (1979). *The postmodern condition: A report on knowledge* (G. Bennington, B. Massumi, Trans.). Minneapolis: University of Minnesota Press.

Madigan, S. (1994). Body politics. *Family Therapy Networker, 18*(6), 27.

Maturana, H. R., & Varela, F. J. (1987). *The tree of knowledge: The biological roots of human understanding.* Boston: Shambhala.

Neal, J. H. (1996). Narrative therapy training and supervision. *Journal of Systemic Therapies, 15*(1), 63–77.

Nicholson, S. (1995). The narrative dance: A practice map for White's therapy. *Australian and New Zealand Journal of Family Therapy, 16*(1), 23–28.

O'Hanlon, B. (1994). The third wave. *The Family Therapy Networker, 18,* 18–26, 28–29.

Parker, I., Georgaca, E., Harper, D., McLaughlin, T., & Stowell-Smith, M. (1995). *Deconstructing psychopathology*. London: Sage.

Potter, J., & Wetherell, M. (1987). *Discourse and social psychology: Beyond attitudes and behavior*. London: Sage.

Rich, A. (1993). Compulsory heterosexuality and lesbian existence. In H. Abelove, M. A. Barale, & D. M. Halperin (Eds.), *The lesbian and gay studies reader* (pp. 274–293). New York: Routledge.

Riessman, C. K. (1993). *Narrative analysis* (Vol. 30). Thousand Oaks, CA: Sage.

Roth, S., & Epston, D. (1996). Developing externalizing conversations: An exercise. *Journal of Systemic Therapies, 15*, 5–12.

Sacks, H., Schegloff, E. A., & Jefferson, G. (1974). A simplist systematics for the organization of turn-taking for conversation. *Language, 50*, 696–735.

Sarup, M. (1993). *An Introductory guide to post-structuralism and postmodernism*. Athens: University of Georgia Press.

Sawicki, J. (1991). *Disciplining Foucault: Feminism, power, and the body*. New York: Routledge.

Shumway, D. R. (1989). *Michel Foucault*. Boston: Twayne Publishers.

Simon, R. (1992). *One on one: Conversations with the shapers of family therapy*. New York: Guilford Press.

Spivak, G. C. (1976). Translator's Preface. In Derrida, J. (Ed.), *Of grammatology* (pp. ix–lxxxix). Baltimore, MD: Johns Hopkins University Press.

Tomm, K. (1987). Interventive interviewing: Part I. Strategizing as a fourth guideline for the therapist. *Family Process, 26*, 3–13.

Waldegrave, C. (1990). Just therapy. *Dulwiche Centre Newsletter, 1*, 6–46.

Watzlawick, P. (Ed.). (1984). *The invented reality: How do we know what we believe we know? Contributions to constructivism*. New York: Norton.

Watzlawick, P., Jackson, D., & Beavin, J. (1967). *The pragmatics of human communication*. New York: Norton.

Weingarten, K. (1995). Radical listening: Challenging cultural beliefs for and about mothers. *Journal of Feminist Family Therapy, 7*(1/2), 7–22.

Wetchler, J. L. (1996) Social constructionist therapies. In F. P. Piercy, D. H. Sprenkle, J. L. Wetchler, & Associates (Eds.), *Family therapy sourcebook, 2nd ed.* (pp. 129–154). New York: Guilford Press.

White, M. (1986). Negative explanation, restraint and double description: A template for family therapy. *Family Process, 25*, 169–184.

White, M. (1988, Winter). The process of questioning: A therapy of literary merit? *Dulwiche Centre Newsletter*, 8–14.

White, M. (1989, Summer). Family therapy training and supervision in a world of experience and narrative. *Dulwiche Centre Newsletter*, 27–38.

White, M. (1993). Deconstruction and therapy. In S. Gilligan & R. Price (Eds.), *Therapeutic conversations* (pp. 22–61). New York: Norton.

White, M., & Epston, D. (1990). *Narrative means to therapeutic ends*. New York: Norton.

Zimmerman, J. L., Dickerson, V. D. (1996). *If problems talked: Narrative therapy in action*. New York: Guilford Press.

CHAPTER 9

Brief Family Therapy

**ALICIA M. HOMRICH AND
ARTHUR M. HORNE**

DEFINITION

Brief family therapy typically emphasizes the strengths and resiliencies inherent in the family system, which are then used to facilitate positive change. Generally, brief family therapy approaches include a problem-solving, solution-focused emphasis structured around the presenting complaint of the client. Brief family therapists may work with the family, couple, or individual. The temporal orientation is on the present and the future. Future-oriented goals that are based on the client's description of the desired outcomes for functioning are carefully constructed with the family and guide the focus of treatment. Through the deliberate use of language, conveying to the client that successful goal attainment is expected, the emphasis of therapy is placed on attaining goals rather than exploring the origin of the problem. Through cognitive and behavioral interventions, this approach is designed to assist families and couples in reconceptualizing their world, moving from self-limiting and/or ineffective ways of being to more desirable and effective functioning. Brief family therapy helps clients diversify their problem-solving skills by drawing on their own positive experiences and their vision of future successful functioning as resources to create desired changes.

Change is an important concept in brief family therapy. Brief family therapists assume that families are constantly changing and utilize this belief as a cornerstone in the therapeutic process. It is assumed that if people, families, and couples are constantly changing, they and their situations can change positively as easily as they can negatively, thus creating a sense of hopefulness and the expectation for success. This philosophical perspective is based on the belief that resiliency, flexibility, and the unique abilities of the individual are valuable resources. The therapist gathers evidence based on previous successful functioning, described as exceptions to the problems, that endorses the individual's or family's potential for change. The idea that even a small change is important is based on the systemic notion that a shift in any part of the system is evidence that change is possible, which will then create a ripple effect expanding to create greater transformation as momentum increases. This future-oriented change perspective offers a context of hope for the therapy and for the family.

Often simplistic sounding initially, brief therapy is a very deliberate treatment approach aimed at assisting clients to achieve very specific behavioral goals. Generally, the therapeutic process begins with the client family defining their goal or goals for therapy. The therapist's role is to assist the family in attaining their goals by skillfully using language to create the expectation for success, crafting opportunities for the clients to recognize and/or experience change, and helping the family to generalize their positive ability to change to other areas of their lives. Initial assessment of the presenting situation is important for successful problem resolution and includes ascertaining a clear definition of the desired outcome as well as the resources the clients possess that may help achieve their goal. The therapist's role in accurately assessing the family's strengths and resources is critical. In the brief therapy perspective, people are viewed as creative, functioning, resourceful individuals capable of effecting change in their lives.

Goals play a very important role in brief therapy. The therapist is expected to assist in the development of well-defined goals, described in brief therapy as "desired outcomes" or a description of what the clients would be doing differently if the problem did not occur. The desired outcomes are based on the vision of the family members, not the expertise or recommendations of the therapist. In the case of family and couples therapy, the construction of shared, mutually agreed upon goals is particularly important and sometimes challenging to negotiate among or between the individuals.

The skillful use of language is another aspect critical to successful brief therapy. Language is an important tool that is used to create the expectation for success, identify and amplify expectations to the presenting problem, imply the assumption of continuous change, and instill the sense of hopefulness and belief that the client is capable of resolving problems with minimal therapist input. For example, a therapist would reflect these assumptions with phrasing such as: "In the future, *when* you are getting along better, what *will* you notice first about your interactions?" Working from the brief therapy perspective, the therapist also uses communication to encourage the family to generalize successful changes to other areas of their lives.

The structure of brief therapy sessions is important in creating an environment of encouragement and change. In order to assist the change process, the brief therapist creates learning opportunities for the clients to recognize and/or experience their own skills and abilities. Sessions are usually quite structured, questions and observations are carefully constructed, and homework assignments are collaboratively detailed with the intention of achieving the clients' goals through experiential learning. For example, a therapist might elicit a very detailed description or picture of the family's vision for future positive functioning through detailed questioning and then work with the clients to select one small aspect of that picture that can be behaviorally implemented before the next family meeting.

Even though brief family therapy is often conceptualized as "a-theoretical" because interventions are not directly tied to a theory of functioning or personality development, brief therapy is not a single method or technique that can be applied to any situation. It is a custom-created, innovative intervention that is designed to achieve a specific, predetermined goal identified by the family. The brief approach presumes that change is inevitable, and it requires a high level of therapist activity and involvement in the therapeutic process while honoring the clients as experts of their own process and direction.

COMPARISON TO OTHER APPROACHES

The brief approach takes a different perspective from the many traditional systemic, analytical, or intrapsychic approaches to therapy. Long-term therapies generally focus more on hypotheses making and interpretation of behavior. This may include theorizing about the cause of a problem or the ideological conceptualizations of the "why" of a presenting issue in an effort to help people better understand their actions. In contrast, brief therapy is a focused discussion about a specific outcome that is desired by the family seeking treatment. Many therapeutic approaches from different theoretical orientations have recently self-defined or redefined themselves as "brief" based on reducing the number of sessions. Even psychodynamic approaches, historically known for their depth and duration of treatment, have developed contemporary versions described as time-limited. However, many models that call themselves "brief" delve into family-of-origin issues or the history of the presenting problem. The brief therapy perspective entertains the retracing of problematic history only to the extent to which exceptions to the presenting problem can be identified for the purpose of encouraging future change potential. In other words, the brief therapist gathers history in order to identify times when the problem did not exist or to ascertain when creative solutions to the problem occurred, not to analyze the long-term impact on functioning. Based on this definition, models of therapy using the current terminology that includes "short-term," "time-limited," "solution-focused," and "solution-oriented" in their titles are not necessarily all variations of brief family therapy. The most important aspect of brief therapy is not whether it meets some arbitrary criteria for being "brief" or a limited number of sessions, but whether its focus is on successful outcomes. Identifying and establishing clear, positive goals, and focusing on clients to broaden their view of their functioning and resulting behaviors in order to creatively achieve these goals, are considered the measures of effective treatment.

HISTORICAL DEVELOPMENT

Many of the contemporary models of brief therapy originated within the early family therapy movement, primarily from the strategic approaches that were developed in the late 1950s and early 1960s. Many of the current practitioners of brief family therapy credit Milton Erickson, a leading practitioner of medical hypnosis, with introducing important concepts that ultimately influenced the development of the brief approach. Erickson's conceptualizations included valuing the uniqueness of the individual, identifying the individual as the source of solution, and restricting the focus of therapy to finding a solution for the presenting complaint using the individual's capabilities as the primary resource. Erickson's masterful approach to therapy was "predicated upon the assumption that there is a strong tendency for the personality to adjust if given the opportunity" (Haley, 1967, p. 417). Erickson's world view of utilizing the client's own cognitive processes and applying them to problematic situations in ways that changed behaviors inspired the development of new approaches to human problems (Cade & O'Hanlon, 1993).

Erickson's approach has been called "a-theoretical," as he did not work from a comprehensive theory or model of therapy. Instead, his therapeutic interventions were unique for each individual and problem he encountered, for it was his belief that entering and using the client's world and behaviors created the opportunity for change. Erickson also based his "utilization" approach on a future orientation and employed symbolic and metaphorical communication in his therapy—important tenets of current practitioners of brief therapy.

Erickson influenced the development of brief therapy by sharing his ideas with an eclectic group of theorists/therapists interested in systems communication models and the cybernetics of human functioning. This group of theorists, led by Gregory Bateson, eventually evolved into the Mental Research Institute (MRI) in Palo Alto, California, founded in 1959 by Don Jackson. The MRI family therapy model was a blend of Erickson's approach with the early theories developed by Bateson, John Weakland, Jay Haley, Virginia Satir, Don Jackson, and William Fry—several of whom went on to become theorists in their own right within the family therapy movement. As it evolved, the MRI approach was termed the "brief problem-focused therapy" model and operated from a pragmatic approach to human problem solving.

The MRI approach is very goal directed and involves the idea of inducing doubt about the problematic situation by reframing the problem from a negative to a positive perspective in some way. The family's goal is achieved by redirecting the behavior within the new framework. The problem is described as the result of the mishandling of everyday events, which are continued by the very efforts the family makes to resolve the problem. The actions meant to relieve or help with the problem result in exacerbating it. Brief therapy, according to the MRI approach, is then designed to define the problem, interrupt the pattern, and substitute a new pattern of behavior. Many of the most innovative techniques used in therapy today originated in the early works of the MRI practitioners. The MRI continues to develop its version of brief therapy by refining techniques and approaches to help families become more functional.

Another brief family therapy approach that paralleled the work of the MRI theorists developed in Milan, Italy, in the early 1970s. The Milan group, led by Mara Selvini Palazzoli, Luigi Boscolo, Gianfranco Cecchin, and Guiliana Prata, incorporated the concept of "positive connotation," which suggested that the symptoms and patterns of the problem were good or positive and served to maintain homeostasis in the family system. From this perspective, the group worked with the family to create new strategies for maintaining family balance, while at the same time making changes for more satisfactory functioning. As with the

MRI, the approach of the Milan Associates developed into a separate school within the family therapy movement. The concepts of the MRI, the Milan group, and Haley's theory of strategic family therapy are described in greater detail in other chapters in this book; however, they all influenced the early development of the brief therapy approach to working with families.

The Brief Family Therapy Center (BFTC) in Milwaukee, Wisconsin, founded by Steve de Shazer in the late 1970s, incorporated aspects of the MRI model along with the influences of the Ericksonian perspective. Beginning in the early 1980s, a model emerged focusing on solution development (de Shazer, 1985, 1990), which is currently known as solution-focused therapy. Based on this approach, the family's presenting problem was not examined as much as the exceptions to the problem, or the times the problem did not occur. This approach induces doubt about the extent of the problem and introduces the possibility that problem-free times can be expanded. The task of therapy is designed to focus on solutions by using identified exceptions to help the family reach their goal, a very significant shift in the previous brief therapy approaches that focused on problem development. The Brief Family Therapy Center continues to be a source of new techniques and interventions vital to the tenets of the brief solution-focused approach. Other significant founders and contributors to this model include Insoo Kim Berg, de Shazer's wife and colleague, and Eve Lipchik. These theorists have refined their work to the extent that it appears almost minimalist in nature. However, the simplicity of the brief approach does not undermine its profound effectiveness, as demonstrated by therapists at the Brief Family Therapy Center.

Variations in the approaches developed by the Brief Family Therapy Center took place in the late 1980s and early 1990s under the leadership of several individuals. Lipchik was joined by Anthony Kubicki to develop specific aspects and applications of solution-focused brief therapy, especially as it relates to work within the field of domestic violence. Lipchik's affiliation with the Brief Family Therapy Center laid the groundwork for their innovative work on this issue. Michele Weiner-Davis, also a former affiliate of the Brief Family Therapy Center, has developed a specialized application of the solution-oriented approach targeted at assisting couples with directing their thoughts and actions toward the desired direction of their relationship. Her work combines a self-help approach with solution-focused techniques to assist couples in reestablishing their relationship to a more optimistic and encouraging position. William Hudson O'Hanlon, a practitioner in Omaha, Nebraska, has expanded the brief approach with his own version of solution-oriented therapy termed "possibility therapy." His innovative work, influenced by his early career affiliation with Erickson, combines components of several contemporary theoretical orientations, including the narrative perspective. He has designed an inclusive model of therapeutic work that is focused on expanding the clients' perspective of the possibilities in order to effect change. Some of his early work focuses on assisting adult survivors of sexual abuse in expanding their perceived possibilities for functioning by utilizing their own strengths and inner resources. O'Hanlon has also combined efforts with therapist Patricia Hudson to develop a body of work addressing couple relationships from a self-help perspective. Lipchik, O'Hanlon, and Weiner-Davis have all, individually, expanded upon the influence of Erickson and the solution-focused approach of the brief family therapy model developed by de Shazer at the Brief Family Therapy Cente in Milwaukee.

TENETS OF THE MODEL

Brief family therapy (BFT) emphasizes the attainment of clearly described future-oriented goals or desired outcomes as defined by the family, the couple, or the individual seeking therapy. The process of brief family therapy includes cognitive, behavioral, and constructivist components. The skillful use of language that presupposes successful outcomes and taps into the strengths and resiliency resources of clients is an important tool for the brief therapist. Careful attention is given to the meaning and perceptions embedded in language and guides many of the techniques and approaches utilized by brief family therapists.

ASSUMPTIONS ABOUT FAMILY FUNCTIONING

The brief approaches based in Ericksonian tradition are often considered a-theoretical, as they focus more on the uniqueness of the individual than on generalized assumptions about human behavior. The belief in the flexibility and creativity of the family or individual client is highly valued. Brief therapists don't approach the case from the standpoint of a theoretical framework or with preconceived ideas about family functioning but view their role as helping the family initiate change while assuming that they have the capability and resources to change themselves.

Within the BFT model, based on the constructivist view, there is no standard for normal family functioning. Brief family therapists, especially from the solution-oriented school, believe that family functioning is in the eye of the beholder—in this case, the clients'. The approach is based not on a deficit model of functioning, but rather on the acknowledgement that families form habits making it difficult for them to believe they can change in a positive direction. Therefore, psychopathology, theories of dysfunction, and diagnostic formulations are avoided in the brief solution-oriented approach because they are viewed as imposing and limiting. Solution-oriented practitioners deviate from the "traditional" systemic models in that they do not approach therapy from the perspective that family problems serve ulterior functions for individuals and the family as a whole. They operate from the position that people really do want to change and improve their marriage and/or family environment. The perspective of solution-oriented brief therapists is that the family or couple do the best they can in their situations. They do not view behavior as maintained deliberately or for unconscious gain. Clients may lack the skills for changing their outcomes, but more likely they lack an awareness of the skills they do possess or can utilize to obtain their desired solutions. In other words, clients have abilities to solve problems but come to therapy stuck in a rut not knowing how to get out. The process of change in BFT involves assisting clients in identifying their inner strengths and resources—keys for solutions—that they possess and can use to bring about a new and more satisfying outcome in their lives.

An assumption of the brief therapeutic approach is that positive functioning in the world is more important than being in therapy. Therefore, the brief approach focuses on present-centered problems and ongoing life situations instead of an understanding of the origin of the problem. For this reason, brief approaches to family therapy include both perceptual and experiential components that interact to create new and more satisfying outcomes for family functioning in the present, with the expectation that these learnings can be applied in the future to other problematic situations that may be experienced in the normal course of living.

Brief family therapy is goal directed. It focuses on a desired outcome that usually involves a constructive change in how the family members feel, think, or relate to each other. From a systemic perspective, brief therapy is based on an interactional view of human problems. This interactional perspective creates a natural context for couple and family therapy. This approach often includes relatives and others significant to the client(s) in the treatment process in order to document past exceptions to the problem and/or help generate potential solutions to obtain positive outcomes. By its nature, brief therapy is viewed as a resource for families to be used throughout the life cycle, most often during stressful periods that may occur during the normal developmental crisis points encountered on an ongoing basis.

EMPHASIS OF THERAPY

The basic emphasis of therapy is on helping the family modify their belief framework about the presenting problem by utilizing information—such as evidence from past problem-free experiences or descriptions of envisioned functioning—that introduces the idea that the problem does not always occur and viable solutions exist and become more real to the family. Another perspective on this idea is that the family is not the problem, the problem is the problem. The goal of the therapeutic process is to identify problem-free occasions and generalize them to future problem-free functioning. This is done by (1) identifying times when the family has handled the problem successfully in the past, (2) structuring opportunities to view the problem in different ways that bring about change, and/or (3) creating experiences in which the problematic situation is experienced differently. In other words, the therapist helps to modify the repetitive sequences that surround the problem and to incur a hopeful perspective about change.

For example, a mother and teen-age daughter who have come to therapy due to frequent fights about a variety of issues are asked to consider times when they get along well or have interactions free of conflict. After much deliberation, the mother observes that on the days that she does not wake her daughter before the daughter's alarm clock goes off, their interactions begin more positively and remain better throughout the day. This seemingly small observation can then be expanded upon as the family reaches an agreement that the mother will refrain from waking her daughter early, thus changing a sequence of interactions that will be expected to lead to an increase in the number of days of positive relations.

PROCESS OF THE BRIEF THERAPY APPROACH

O'Hanlon (1990) believes that brief therapists have two important goals or tasks: to "change the viewing" of the problem and "change the doing" of the problem. The focus and deliberate activity of the brief therapeutic process centers around the attempt to accomplish both these tasks. In "changing the viewing," the therapist assists the family in reframing from the stance of a problematic situation to a challenge or opportunity for growth. For example, a problem can be viewed as creating an opportunity to find a new way of relating, of caring, of interacting. This involves cognitive restructuring and reframing. Changing the viewing of a problem suggests altering the family's perception or frame of reference of the complaint. In "changing the doing," solution-focused therapists attempt to motivate families to change their behavioral actions and interactions. This takes place through structured activities, including homework, that invite the family members to experience problematic situations in new—and hopefully, more satisfying—ways.

Brief therapists must stay focused on the clues that are signs of successful goal attainment. De Shazer (1988) defines three dictums that underlie the philosophy of the brief therapy approach and help the therapist focus on successful goal-attainment: (1) "If it ain't broke, don't fix it" suggests that therapists not delve into problems or issues of the family that aren't presented by the family, no matter how obvious the problem may be to the therapist; (2) "Once you know what works, do more of it," which applies especially to "prescribing" behaviors that have been identified as exceptions to the problem or engaging in more newly discovered successful behaviors or perspectives; and (3) "If it doesn't work, don't do it again. Do something different," which means that the therapist, along with the family, should use unsuccessful outcomes as examples of what doesn't work in order to avoid repeating frustrating pitfalls and continue the search for solutions elsewhere (pp. 93–94).

CLIENTS' WORLD VIEW

In addition to cognitive and behavioral approaches to therapy, solution-oriented brief family therapy requires a constructivist approach to the concept of reality. Solution-oriented brief therapy acknowledges that there is no singular fixed truth, only individual perspectives forming multiple views. The approach to therapy in the brief context is driven by the family's perspective, not the therapist's. This stance applies to the description of the problem, the goals, and the desired outcomes of the therapeutic process. As mentioned previously, the clients are viewed as their own experts in the therapeutic process. The problem is identified and constructed from the family's perspective, and it is the role of the therapist to understand it from their perspective. This avoids what O'Hanlon (1990) describes as "delusions of uncertainty," when self-perceived experts are convinced that the observations they make while assessing a family are "real" and objective. The therapist's role is not to define reality but to ascertain the clients' view of their own problems and their needs and to help them achieve their goals. Of course, the therapist is the "expert" when it comes to helping the family, as the therapist knows how to skillfully facilitate the therapeutic process, moving from a problem-focused to a solution-focused perspective, and to effectively use tools and techniques to guide the clients to a successful outcome. Often therapists who attempt to eclectically combine theories find it impossible to integrate this approach with others, as most other forms of therapy are driven by predetermined explanations for client functioning instead of respecting the family's description of themselves, the problem, and the desired outcome.

THE PERSPECTIVE OF TIME

The temporal orientation of brief family therapy is based on the present description of the problem and the desired future envisioned by the clients. For this reason, the history of the problem or family functioning is not explored in great detail, except to identify times when the problem did not exist, was less of a concern, or was successfully addressed. These "exceptions" to the problem story, as presented by the family, are very important pieces of information that can be culled from an account of the problem history by an astute therapist; however, the etiology of the complaint is not the focus of treatment or attention in brief therapy. This is not to imply that the solution-focused, brief family therapist does not respect the clients' need to tell the story or be heard. Nor does it preclude the expression of emotions necessary for a family to move to the process of change. It is expected that clients will have a need to describe their problem, which should be met with the universally important empathic stance of therapy. The skillful use of language is very important in this initial aspect of therapeutic intervention, as it is a tool for differentiating and reinforcing the history of successes experienced by the clients versus reifying the hopelessness of the situation. The solution-focused brief therapist will also be listening for information on the times the problem did not exist as well as assessing the clients' readiness for change, instead of theorizing about the problem causation or becoming caught in the family's view of themselves as dysfunctional, problematic, or hopeless.

THE IMPACT OF CHANGE

An important tenet of the brief approach to therapy is that change is inevitable and stability is an illusion. Brief solution-oriented therapy capitalizes on this construct as a resource in family therapy to instill hope for the opportunity for positive change. In the case of family therapy, a caveat must be offered that change *will* occur, and that clients can influence what will emerge in place of the problem. This is especially important if only some members of the family or one spouse is attending therapy. The entire balance of the relationship(s) may be changed, and it is expected that individuals will begin relating differently. This perspective of change is a powerful one and is amplified through the use of strategic language.

Another important concept in the perspective of change in brief therapy, which is common to most approaches to family therapy, is the idea that even small change is encouraging. Once people effectively utilize their resources to bring about change in the way they think about and enact the problem, they can then positively generalize these changes to other aspects of their functioning. In other words, change can generate greater change through the ripple effect as past successes initiate the expectation for future successes.

READINESS FOR CHANGE

An important component of the solution-focused approach to brief family therapy is the assessment of the clients' readiness for change. As most clinicians have experienced, some families or couples come to therapy motivated for change and ready to participate in treatment. De Shazer (1988) refers to these clients as "customers for change." Others come to therapy because they are mandated, coerced, or just want someone to talk with; they are termed "visitors" or "window shoppers," as they don't have an identifiable problem or a willingness to change.

Finally, couples or families who only want to offer complaints and are unable to describe desired outcomes are considered "complainants."

Visitors, window shoppers, and complainants, until they become customers for change, will certainly impact the outcome of therapy in that they are not invested in participating in the change process by altering behaviors or views. An effective brief therapist is able to assess the clients' interest in change and will proceed with successful treatment when customers are identified. An example of such a situation would be a family who has a member with a substance abuse problem. The nonabusing family members are experiencing the most difficulty with the problem and may be coming to therapy as "complainants," while the alcoholic may not believe that he or she has a problem at all and is attending therapy as a coerced "visitor." A brief family therapist would note the presenting roles and, in an attempt to recruit customers for change, may approach the situation by complimenting the family's coping abilities, or noticing strengths, or asking questions from a "Columbo-esque" stance of confusion about their presence in therapy and avoiding confrontation. Interacting with visitors or window shoppers might include complimenting them and prescribing that they restrain from doing anything that might create a change in their situation in an effort to assess the seriousness of their intentions to change. It is important to ascertain what type of client you are treating, listening especially to the complaint and for indications of the motivation for change. Generally, brief family therapists work with the family members who are motivated to change and demonstrate their investment by attending sessions and completing between-session tasks, because they believe that even a small change in one person will bring about changes in the other members of the family.

The concept of "resistance" is often discussed with regard to "noncompliant" families. De Shazer (1989) believes that it is the responsibility of the therapist to find the keys to the family's presenting problem or puzzle. He believes that resistance, or an unwillingness to fully participate in therapy, rests not with the family but with the methodology of the therapy, as well as with the skill and personal qualities of the therapist. He believes that when clients are determined to be uncooperative, it is their way of informing the therapist that he or she has not found the appropriate way to interact with the family and their problem. It is the therapist's responsibility to employ new approaches and to develop innovative resources by which to address a client who is a customer for change.

THE IMPORTANCE OF LANGUAGE

The skillful use of language is very important in the brief therapy model, especially as it pertains to a solution-focused perspective of treatment. Words (descriptions of events) are usually thought of as representing an experience; however, language in this treatment approach is considered to be creational rather than representative. The treatment is based on the premise that our assumptions create, rather that reflect, reality. As Watzlawick (1990) suggests, therapy is what we say it is, the names we operate with, the explanatory principles we use, and the reality we thereby create. Words are very powerful tools that can create experiences of good, bad, healthy, unhealthy, acceptable, unacceptable, and so on. Whereas language does not represent the actual experience, it is inseparable from it. This observation is tantamount to reversing the cause and effect, or coming to the realization that language and experience are simultaneous creations that influence each other profoundly. Language can reify points of view and thus influence perceptions of reality. Words can create a different frame on a story or perception about one's self or family. The brief therapist is very aware of this dynamic and uses language as a tool to expand possibilities and instill the hopefulness of change (O'Hanlon & Weiner-Davis, 1989).

The influence of a stated expectation is an important consideration of this therapeutic approach. Consider the use of words such as "short term," "brief," and "solution-focused." They are words of impact that set up expectations within the clients, the therapist, and others connected to the family system. Language creates not simply assumptions, or even expectations, but realities from which to proceed. One might suggest that this is the "placebo effect" in action. A more hopeful reframe in the assumption of brief therapy is that problems can be handled with the resources already inherent in the individuals in a relatively short period of time, making them normal dilemmas of living. Reification, or the process of constructing pseudorealities, can be used to the advantage of a positive outcome in brief therapy.

The inability to achieve a solution results from a family's belief that the problem or complaint always *happens*. Families typically come to therapy perceiving themselves not as *having* a problem, but *being* a problem. By the time a client or clients (couple or family) present to therapy, they have used specific language to describe themselves so often that they have convinced themselves that they "are" something that will never change. A common perception with families is the self-assigned label of "dysfunctional." Often this perspective on a problem is accompanied by the attitude that the situation is hopeless and unsolvable. This rigid self-definition supplants resiliency, hopefulness, and the realization that change is inevitable. It is the therapist's task to listen carefully to the family's language to find the exceptions to the rule, or belief, that the problem or complaint "always" occurs, and then use language to amplify this discovery. This search for solutions or exceptions is an essential component of brief therapy, and once it is touched upon, avenues of hopefulness are opened as the clients' rigid views are softened. In most brief therapy this vital step is attained without a discussion of the problem or its etiology. There is no litany of the pattern, nor is there theorizing of the causal factors. The therapeutic context is used to discuss the occasions when the problem does not occur and to reconstruct the view, through language, that positive change is expected.

GOAL DIRECTED

According to the cliché, "one cannot hit a target without a target." In order for brief therapy to be effective (and short term), it is important for all those involved to clearly understand the desired outcome. This requires that the clients construct a clear and congruent understanding of what they want to be and how they will know when they have achieved the goal. Well-defined, measurable, attainable goals that are framed in a positive or proactive manner are the cornerstone of brief therapy. Goals should derive primarily from the family's vision of what constitutes success. A clear, vivid description of what life would look like after successful therapy (versus lofty, vague outcomes) is one way to ascertain the clients' behavioral goals. For example, O'Hanlon (1990) uses the term "video talk" and encourages the couple or family to describe in pictorial terms what they would be doing—as if watching a video of how the individuals would be acting if the situation were ideal, or at least improved. This might include the clients' description of what they would be doing if they were "happy" or a couple's depiction of what would happen if they were "not fighting all the time." This line of discussion can also open the opportunity to identify past exceptions to the "always" perception of the problem.

As with any therapy or life setting, small, achievable, concrete goals are easier to achieve and to measure. This is often difficult for families who have been entrenched in a problem over a period of time, making it a greater challenge to construct a vision of life without the problem. It is very important that the therapist assist the family in constructing a detailed description of what life would be like after successful therapy in order to provide a guide for the work to be accomplished.

The measurement of success should come from the family's reports of change in the problematic situation. If the family says that the initial problem or complaint is no longer a problem, or has been eliminated, then therapy can be considered effective. This approach hinges not on insight, or the opinion of an expert, but on self-reported satisfaction based on self-observed change.

CONCLUSION OF THERAPY

The course of therapy is focused on the presenting problem as clarified by the goals constructed during the initial sessions. Further sessions center on the effect of the intervention given in the previous session as well as any change or exceptions that occur in the time between sessions. When the family or couple reports that they are experiencing behaviors that are more congruent with their goals, the therapist helps clarify and amplify the appreciated changes. After this progress is clear to all family members, the therapist's role is to focus on maintaining and expanding these desired outcomes in the future, as well as encouraging the generalization of the family's success to all other situations. At this point, therapy is concluded and the family is expected to function in more positive ways that reflect the realizations of their own strengths, resiliency, and ability to solve problems.

LENGTH OF THERAPY

How brief is brief therapy? According to research, most clients expect therapy to be a brief experience, and more than 70% begin therapy expecting to accomplish their treatment goals in 10 or fewer sessions (McKeel, 1996). Furthermore, studies on the duration of therapy, brief or traditional, reveal that the average length of treatment is four to eight sessions (Koss & Shiang, 1994). Family therapy may be even more complicated, as it takes quite a bit more effort to get two or several people to a therapy session than just one individual. In addition, participants may not all have the same level of commitment. The pressure exists for quick results, or couples and families will self-terminate therapy that they perceive as ineffective. In other words, most family therapy is short-term anyway. In addition, managed health care often dictates the length of treatment contractually or sets financial limitations.

Regardless of this reality, the duration of time-limited, brief, or short-term therapy lies quite often in the theoretical approach of the therapist and the specific model. Therapy defined as brief or short-term can range from a single session to 50 sessions; the median is around 20, depending on the source. Some theorists believe that any number of sessions exceeding 15 is no longer considered short-term therapy. Finally, the perspective of brief family therapists is usually on the effectiveness of the therapy rather than on a predetermined formula for the number of sessions. How long should brief therapy be? As long as it takes!

APPLICATIONS AND TECHNIQUES

Although the focus of this section will be on applications and techniques, their importance is secondary to the development of a positive working relationship with the family, couple, or individual who is presenting for therapy. Even though the therapeutic relationship may be time-limited, the basis of brief therapy requires that an atmosphere of trust, positive regard, and hopefulness for change be created. Research on solution-focused family therapy has found that being supported and validated was the most frequently mentioned helpful element of the therapeutic process (Lee, 1997). As mentioned in the previous section, the therapist creates a solution-focused atmosphere with the use of language. At the same time, genuine human interaction is also required to create a context in which positive change can occur.

Brief family therapy, from both the strategic and solution-focused models, is known by some of the therapeutic "tasks" that are routinely included in these approaches. These tasks sometimes appear to those outside the field as "gimmicky" or simplistic tricks; however, these techniques are well-thought-out interactions that are both congruent with the philosophy of the therapy and designed to create the opportunity for perceptual and behavioral shifts necessary for change to occur. Many of these techniques are also assessment devices that generate extremely important information about the individuals with regard to their desired direction, their motivation, and their progress toward their goal—all critical components of the ongoing assessment process in brief therapy.

THERAPEUTIC TASKS

CHANGING THE PATTERN OF THE PROBLEM As mentioned previously, changing the "doing" of a situation from a negative pattern to a positive pattern is a desired outcome in brief therapy. "Doing something different" is an intervention that can change the clients' frame of reference about the problem, which may then evoke the clients' use of personal strengths and resources. This directive is especially useful when families complain about repeated sequences of problematic interactions, such as fights or temper tantrums, to which family members historically react in the same ineffective manner. The therapist may ask the family: "Is what you are doing working?" If the answer is "yes" then the family can be encouraged to continue with the behavior. If the answer is "no" the therapist can then suggest that the family try something different. Changing the "doing" of the complaint or problem behavior involves giving assignments to the family or couple that include some change in the pattern. Such an intervention might direct the family to change (1) the frequency or rate of the problematic activity (agree to remind the children to do their homework only once each day instead of repeatedly), (2) the timing of the problem pattern (agree to postpone all arguments until the period between 5:00 p.m. and 6:00 p.m., (3) the duration of the problematic behavior (agree to set a timer for a specific amount of time of avoiding chores), (4) the location at which the problem activity takes place (agree to argue only in the bathroom), or (5) the sequence of the elements or events in the problematic behavior (agree to eat a forbidden snack only after walking around the block one time). Other ways to shift the problem pattern are to suggest or prescribe the addition of new elements to the pattern, break the pattern into smaller elements, or associate the pattern with some other burdensome activity. O'Hanlon and Weiner-Davis (1989) offer excellent examples for each of these pattern interventions that serve to bring the presenting problem into a new light or "view" for the clients, which can then create a context for changing the situation.

FORMULA TASKS Used by both the Milan team and the therapists at the Brief Family Therapy Center, formula tasks are designed to impact the process of the family's problem rather than address the content of the problem, which is considered less important in the application of formula tasks. Formula tasks interrupt the complaint sequence pattern, as described in the previous section, and build on preexisting solutions and strengths, which may then prompt new perceptions and behaviors. Formula tasks are assignments that are often universally effective regardless of the presenting problem. In fact, some theorists suggest that brief therapy can be conducted without even knowing the problem situation, and, rather, limiting intervention to addressing the process of the problem.

The most common of these approaches is the "first-session formula task." This directive, as described by de Shazer, is often given at the end of the first therapy session:

> Between now and the next time we meet, we [I] want you to observe, so that you can describe to us [me] next time, what happens in your [life, marriage, family, or relationship] that you want to continue to have happen. (de Shazer, 1984, p. 298)

This intervention establishes the expectation of the therapist that something worthwhile is routinely happening and also serves to place the clients' focus on the positive things they are already doing, which is often a significant change in perspective for the family or couple who are used to noticing only their negative functioning. This intervention may also facilitate an immediate change in the pattern of behavior despite the fact that the clients were not asked to behave any differently. Thus, any shift in behavior at this point in the therapy is client directed and is a more effective initiation of positive change. Client-initiated change is also a direct reflection of their own unique strengths and their abilities to find solutions within themselves—empowering information for any family, couple, or individual. The therapy session following the first-session formula task focuses on exploring the continuation of the more desirable behavior.

Another formula task prescribes a "surprise" factor designed to disrupt the typical behavior pattern. The surprise is subsequently used to show the family that they can change. Utilized quite often with couple and parent–child relationships, this task invites the opportunity for creative thinking, fun, caring, and other positive, desirable behaviors. Prescribed between sessions, it can be presented something like this:

> Do at least one or two things that will surprise your [parents, spouse, partner].
>
> Don't tell them what it is. Parents [partner], your job is to see if you can tell what it is that she [he] is doing. Don't compare notes; we will do that in the next session. (O'Hanlon & Weiner-Davis, 1989, p. 137)

Again, this task allows the family to shift their focus from old, problematic complaints to creating and looking for new patterns of behavior. It also introduces the opportunity for fun and a new way of interacting with each other. During the follow-up session, the person who was the intended recipient of the changed behavior is asked if he or she had noticed any unexpected changes since the last meeting. The recipient often attributes unintentionally caused positive behaviors to the other family member, along with the planned surprises. This task serves to reverse the chronic cycle of negative observation of the problem or situation to a solution-focused perspective that is encouraging to both the giver and recipient of the new behavior. Family members begin catching each other doing things right instead of searching for hurtful interactions, which creates a new view or "story" about their relationship.

ASSESSING PRE-SESSION CHANGE Once a family has taken the initiative to place a telephone call to set an appointment with a therapist, they are usually aware of their problem and desire some sort of relief. The intention to change can be amplified by both observation and the use of questions. In addition to asking the family or couple the usual "Why now?" questions about coming to therapy, brief family therapists often inquire about any pre-session change that has occurred. This question asks the family if they have noticed any change in their complaint between the time of placing the telephone call and the first therapy session. As clients have come to therapy with a problem, it is easy to focus on it solely and lose sight of the likelihood that the family has already done things to decrease the problem. The observation, during the first session, that change has already occurred can encourage the family to continue to effect positive change. Even small changes provide the therapist with the opportunity to support, enhance, and amplify the change process. Weiner-Davis, de Shazer, and Gingerich (1987) reported that in at least two-thirds of the cases they researched, clients reported some pre-session change, even if the time between the phone call and the first session was as little as 24 hours.

QUESTIONS OF CHANGE

Most family therapists are very aware of the power of questions. Brief family therapists, especially those who are solution focused, view questions as a strategic intervention that sets the expectation of success. Not only are questions used to elicit a thorough understanding of the problematic behavior, they are also important to facilitate the development of cogent goals and ascertain the family's desired outcomes. The utilization of specific language, in the form of questions, is considered a major therapeutic intervention. When done well, the question/response process connects therapists and clients and creates cognitive, behavioral, and emotional change.

Insoo Kim Berg (1994), for example, discusses the importance of language during the initial interviewing. She provides multiple examples of constructing questions that broaden the context of the clients' view of themselves and their situation. Her most well-known inquiry is "How did you do it [that]?" which, accompanied by the appropriate intonation and expression, is, in her view, the most empowering question that can be asked of a client (Berg, 1994, p. 115). This question allows the family to reflect upon and call into consciousness their own abilities, strengths, and personal resources for success. It also further encourages the solution-focused dialogue vital to brief family therapy by emphasizing the exceptions to the problem instead of the problem.

Other examples of intervention questions that imply the expectation for success include: "Who do you think will notice first when you begin to feel better?" "What do you suggest you do when you are feeling this way?" "And when you start acting differently, how do you usually feel?" "When you are more loving toward your partner, how does she or he treat you differently?" "How do you feel differently since you and your partner began fighting less?" "What are you likely to be doing together the next time you all find yourselves laughing?" and "Who worries about your daughter the least, you or your partner?" These examples encompass many of the basic tenets of family therapy from a solution-oriented perspective. They can be crafted to fit any unique situation, or used generically to set the expectation for change.

EXCEPTION QUESTIONS Exception questions, such as the ones given in the previous examples, help the therapist and the clients understand times when the problem did not or does not occur. With this information, the therapist can utilize the exception to the problem by prescribing more of what works. Exceptions are times when the problem/complaint does not occur, or occurs with less frequency or less intensity. The solution-focused model suggests that it is often more productive to increase existing successes than to attempt to eliminate the problem directly through problem solving. Asking exception questions also helps interrupt the family's or couple's focus on the negative situation by implying that there are times when the problem does not always occur. The emphasis is shifted to the times and circumstances when alternative, more satisfying experiences take place.

By focusing on previous positive outcomes or better times, the therapist can also reduce the defensiveness and blaming that may be present in an initial session. Specifically, in reviewing the clients' history, inquiries are made about past behavior that, by the family's standards, is considered functional or desirable. Inquiries that follow may include "What were you doing right at that time?" "How did you manage to do that?!" "How did you keep pushing through that difficult time?" or other questions that elicit information about past strengths and weaknesses and exceptions to the problem scenario.

SCALING QUESTIONS These questions are assessment inquiries that provide the therapist with critical information about client progress. They also create the opportunity for the client to self-observe that change is occurring. Scaling questions are especially helpful in describing problems that have abstract components or are not as clearly defined, such as depression, unhappiness, communication, and pain. A scaling question defines the problem in terms of gradients, and gauges its intensity in degrees, percentages, or other units of measurement. An example of a scaling question is:

> On a scale from zero to ten where zero represents things at their worst, and ten represents how things will be when these problems are resolved, where would you place yourself today? (Cade & O'Hanlon, 1993, p. 105)

The answer to this question offers an indication of progress between sessions. It also sets the stage for a solution-focused discussion of what created a positive movement, or what was different at times when a desired outcome was achieved.

The use of scaling questions also implies a more realistic range of perspectives about the problem versus a dichotomous view of successful problem resolution as an all or nothing proposition (e.g., happy or unhappy). Scaling also introduces the opportunity to suggest a coping stance for unsolvable problems such as managing a difficult but permanent family situation (e.g., a scale that measures the level of comfort with or tolerance of a situation such as pain). The utilization of scaling questions can set the stage for follow-up dialogues about smaller, more feasible steps toward positive change as gradients of the scale are broken down further. For example, the therapist might ask "What might you do to move up one point (or a half a point) on the scale between now and the next time we meet?" This idea can help the family or couple consider more manageable steps toward change that will perpetuate positive movement. These coconstructed actions can become between-session tasks or homework assignments.

THE MIRACLE QUESTION Possibly the most well known question in brief therapy, the "miracle question," characterizes a simple method used to ascertain the clients' desired outcome for their own functioning. Originally developed by Alfred Adler to ascertain whether the true source of a somatic complaint was a psychological or an organic condition (Dreikurs, 1958), this question can also serve to uncover clients' goals in concrete, behavioral terms. The miracle question also is useful in sidestepping causal assumptions about the problem that often take the form of complaints and blaming that lead to further disagreement within a family. It is congruent with the goal of brief solution-focused family therapy, which is to move away from the problem and toward a desired outcome or state of being. De Shazer's version of this question is:

> Suppose that one night, while you were sleeping, there was a miracle and the problem was solved. How would you know? What would you be doing the next day that would tell you there had been a miracle? How would other people know without your having told them? (de Shazer, 1990, p. 97)

The response not only provides insight for a differential diagnosis, it also offers clues to the real problem and can provide a behavioral description of what life would be like if the presenting complaint were no longer present. The family's answer also keeps the therapeutic focus solution-oriented, reinforcing the positive picture instead of reifying the negative, problematic situation.

TECHNIQUES

REFRAMING Brief therapists, as with many other family therapy approaches, often use reframing to change the context provided by the current arrangement of the problem information by offering alternate meanings to problematic behavior. This technique helps clients change their own frame on the problem by a therapist-initiated observation. It is intended to serve as encouragement for the development of new or alternative approaches to situations. Reframing may be considered the most basic and necessary operation in the process of change. According to Cade and O'Hanlon (1993), "everything else is subordinate and either aids or, alternatively, impedes this process" (p. 113).

ANALOGY AND METAPHOR Anecdotes, parables, stories, jokes, and metaphors are used by many brief therapists. These approaches can be powerful tools to help teach, redirect, encourage critical or creative thinking, challenge, and even baffle families into discovering information that may be useful and applicable to their situation. They can also be used to explain a task, amplify a point, relieve tension, normalize situations of concern, and empower relationships. Like children's fairy tales, stories can be the source of solutions that are applicable to current life situations. They can be presented, indirectly or directly, to highlight an important point in therapy or in the progress of the clients. Erickson was a master of the use of metaphors, and practitioners of brief therapy often study his writings to gain a better understanding of this approach.

Some of the simplest and most useful applications of analogy are cross-references from one of the senses to another. Cade and O'Hanlon (1993) offer "a warm smile," "my heart is heavy," "a stony silence," or "his mood was black" as examples (p. 137). A discussion on this level, in this metaphorical language, can introduce a view of the problem from new or different representational systems that can then be used in therapeutic intervention such as reframing or describing a desired outcome using new words. Families also bring metaphorical descriptions of their situation to therapy. These indirect "descriptions" of the problem can be utilized by the therapist to create a dialogue using the clients' language as well as a stepping-off point for such activities as goal setting, redefinition, and reframing.

Metaphorical tasks are also used in brief family therapy. Some brief strategic therapists prescribe metaphorical tasks for their clients that, at times, may appear senseless and silly. These tasks serve to interrupt the problematic pattern, especially if they are judged by the family as ridiculous and are rejected along with the problem behavior. These types of task assignments are often enactments of problematic family dynamics in creative ways that amplify the situation and create an opportunity for change. De Shazer (1980) discusses the serious assignment of a water pistol fight in which family members were given very specific tasks to be conducted in a ritualistic manner. The absurdity of this metaphorical task brought the family together in a playful way that was different than their usual combative mode of relating, shifting the context in which they viewed themselves.

Metaphor enables family therapists to address many different dimensions of the family system, thereby opening up the possibilities for change that may be outside the family's current awareness. Not only does it make therapy more interesting, it can also allow clients the opportunity to respond in new ways to current problematic situations. On a larger scale, metaphorical stories can be used to suggest alternative courses of action for families. There are many current references on the use of metaphor in therapy, including books containing therapeutic stories designed for a counseling context.

It is important to note that all of these tasks must be carefully designed to parallel the presenting problem or family pattern, and to fit within the family's unique manner of interacting. "Any sign from the family that they are rejecting the assignment means that the therapist has not found the family's way of co-operating, and therefore he should abort the planned intervention" (de Shazer, 1980, p. 475).

CHEERLEADING Used to facilitate the continuation of change, cheerleading provides positive encouragement and support that is intended to boost the confidence the clients have in their ability to change a situation and create the desired outcome. As with any behavioral approach, reinforcement of desired behavior encourages the repetition of the behavior. An enthusiastic therapist who responds positively to change not only helps family members notice the significance of their successes, but teaches them to celebrate and enjoy their progress, as well as creating the likelihood of additional positive interactions. In addition, cheerleading can help shift the ownership of change from the therapist to the family.

BETTING This technique is often used with children or couples who are experiencing difficulty and, as with other techniques, places the focus on positive outcomes. It is especially useful in competitive situations and with individuals who respond to external challenges. Once a desired behavior or pattern is identified, the therapist offers a challenge concerning the continuation of the change in the form of a bet. It is important that the behavior be described in very concrete terms so that determining the winner of the bet will be clear, thereby avoiding further conflict. It is important that the bet be a worthy challenge that is, at the same time, attainable. A third party may be invited to moderate the terms of the bet, or place the bet, so the therapist and the identified individual can create an alliance. For example, the therapist can join a husband in betting the wife that his new, positive behavior will continue. As with all bets, contingencies and the actual reward should be clearly defined at the outset.

PREDICTING Prediction tasks are used to amplify inadvertent or chance behaviors that happen to be useful and consistent with the family's goals. "Catching" a positive behavior, deliberate or otherwise, and predicting that it will continue encourages the family members to behave in similar ways again on a less random basis. The prediction technique is usually implemented when the clients have identified a random exception to the complaint pattern. This is especially effective with clients who are willing to cooperate with homework assignments. The family or couple is asked to predict whether the following day is going to be a good day or a bad day. When the prediction is consistent with the results, inquiries are made about what the clients did to bring about such an outcome. If the prediction is not consistent with the results, the clients are asked to account for the inconsistency. This technique invites a dialogue about the impact that specific behaviors have on reaching the desired outcomes. It also helps family members act more purposefully and with a sense of efficacy versus operating on the basis of being a victim to randomness.

FLAGGING THE MINEFIELD This simple technique, which also includes a predictive quality, is used to identify pitfalls that can then be consciously avoided by the family. To "flag the minefield," clients are asked to identify factors that could result in relapse to an old pattern or problematic situation. This approach not only implies that the family has overcome the problematic behavior but empowers them by assuming they have a control over their old problem behaviors. This technique can be accompanied with a prediction for relapse that can serve to normalize the fluidity of family functioning and avoid the pitfall of discouragement should a recurrence of the problem appear. According to Kral and Kowalski (1989), this approach helps the family identify potential problems in advance and predetermines useful responses so the family or couple will be in a better position to avoid a recurrence of the problematic issue.

HOMEWORK Between-session assignments are a cornerstone of brief therapy. Therapeutic change takes place between sessions, and homework provides the opportunity to change the "viewing" and the "doing" of the problem behavior along with information about the challenges of change. Several of the techniques previously described could be used as homework tasks. The therapist might prescribe specific tasks that require "doing more of the same" once a positive sequence has been enacted by the family or couple. An assignment that might be especially useful toward the end of therapy involves asking the family members to write a letter to the therapist about the changes they have made since beginning therapy. This type of task not only clarifies that change occurred, but breaks it down into specifics that can be generalized to remedy future problems. The therapist might also wish to ask for a letter describing what was helpful to the clients, such as a description of the best or most memorable session, as well as the worst or least helpful situation or session. Again, this empowers the family to identify their role in the change process.

CASE EXAMPLE

BRIEF, SOLUTION-ORIENTED THERAPY WITH A COUPLE IN DISTRESS

REFERRAL This couple was referred to the marriage and family therapy clinic by a psychologist at a university health center. The psychologist had administered a battery of tests to each spouse, met with the wife twice due to her symptoms of depression, and then met with both spouses to provide feedback on their psychological evaluations.

INITIAL SESSION The couple presented to the first session describing their relationship as in great distress, and both spouses stated that they were "real scared." They reported that they could not hold a conversation, that they were frustrated, and that they "couldn't take much more." They desperately wanted help for their marriage and were very afraid that help could not be found and/or would not have an impact. This couple were very direct in their expression of hopelessness, especially since they had received discouraging indications from the referring psychologist, who had indicated that, based on the husband's test results and a tentative diagnosis of a personality disorder, he may be unable to communicate in a way conducive to a satisfactory marital relationship.

Going into greater detail, Jeff and Diane reported a decline in their five-year marital relationship over the last year. Diane stated that she was very unhappy with the relationship and didn't want to lose it, but couldn't continue in the same way. She reported that Jeff had not followed through with school or financial responsibilities and that she found herself having to check on him, follow up on his activities, nag him, and be responsible for him. She could no longer trust his word about taking care of tasks. She was also in the process of trying to disengage from the vigilant stance she had developed over Jeff's behavior. She stated that she felt both "guilty and very angry." During the session, her manner was controlled but she also appeared to be very emotional—expressing a combination of anger, fear, hurt, and hopelessness. When reflecting on this observation, Diane responded that: "I am looking for someone, anyone, to tell me to stay in the marriage and that it is salvageable, but I haven't gotten that from anyone yet." She also stated that she was scared of being alone and losing the relationship.

Jeff acknowledged that his communication skills were lacking. He stated that it was difficult for him to relate to his wife and to others. Jeff justified each of his actions with regard to his lack of follow-through on school and financial commitments. He stated that he had just "hit a slump" and believed he was capable of being responsible. During the interview Jeff showed very little emotion, and usually responded only when asked. However, he seemed to "tear up" when asked about the marriage.

When asked about pre-session change (what had changed between the time they made the appointment one month prior and today), Diane stated that the situation had become hopeless. Jeff, however, said that he was committed to making the marriage work and had attempted to be more communicative since the couple decided to come to therapy.

The couple were then asked about the satisfaction of their marriage:

Therapist: On a scale of one to ten, with ten being the most satisfying your relationship has ever been, or could ever be, and one being the worst your relationship has ever been, or could ever be, what rating would you give your relationship right now? Where would you place your satisfaction level on that scale from one to ten?

Diane: (To Jeff) You go first.

Jeff: I guess, well, I guess I would put is somewhere around a three or a four.

Diane: I would put it at a three.

The initial observations and information briefly described above indicated that Diane was experiencing, among other emotions, a strong sense of discouragement, anger, and fear. Jeff, despite his flat affect, was also scared and confused about what to do to change the situation. The couple believed that they were "stuck" and were sinking with the realization that they could not become unstuck without help. Diane and Jeff needed hope and a sense that things could change before they left the session.

In order to ascertain exceptions to the current problem pattern and to obtain concrete information about what had worked for them before, Diane and Jeff were asked to talk about how they met and what had attracted them to each other initially. They were directed to detail their responses into specific behaviors and observations. For example, when Diane reported that Jeff "showed affection," she was questioned further to elicit behavioral examples. Her more specific responses included that "he held my hand" and "he rubbed my shoulders." This initial investigation seemed to lighten the mood, bring out a few smiles, and relax the couple. They started looking at each other as they spoke about memories of their first dating experiences. The discussion was then directed to a recounting of the positive, successful, and/or satisfying events in their relationship in recent months in an effort to obtain more recent exceptions to the problem behavior.

Goals for therapy were initiated by a series of presuppositional questions such as "When you reach the point that your marriage is satisfactory to you, say an eight or nine, what will you be doing?" or "What would someone see who was watching a videotape of you interacting when you have reached your goals for satisfaction?" A conversation followed about how each spouse would ideally want the marriage to be like, described in as behavioral terms as possible. At the conclusion of the session, Diane and Jeff were given a homework task:

> *Therapist:* Between now and the next time we meet I would like you to notice the things that happen that are what you are hoping for in the relationship, the actions that would tell you that things are going well. Please keep a list of every big and little thing that happens over the next few weeks that was successful and satisfying to each of you.

This couple came to therapy with the hope to retrieve their marriage. Their desire to improve their relationship and find new, more satisfying ways of relating, although not obvious in their initial words, was inherent in their presence and their stated fear of loss of the marriage. Jeff and Diane reported a previous history of a positive, successful relationship and were searching for new ways in which to redefine and enrich not only their marriage but their individual needs for growth and development.

TREATMENT PLAN The solution-oriented treatment plan conceptualized for Jeff and Diane was based on the assumption that they had the ability to recreate the relationship they had somehow lost. The role of the therapist was to listen to this couple very carefully and facilitate hopefulness by reflecting on their past evidence of success and formulating a clear, attainable description of a new, desirable relationship in the future (whatever that meant to them). The therapist was also charged with creating the conditions wherein this couple realized that they had the strengths and capabilities to achieve their vision. The initial treatment plan was to help Diane and Jeff recognize what they were doing currently that was working and then to do more of it. In other words, they were to identify the exceptions to the "problem story" they presented during the initial session and construct a new "solution story." In doing this, they would, hopefully, refocus their attention from deficits and problems to strengths and possibilities.

SECOND SESSION At each session, the couple was asked to report on their homework assignment since the last session. They were asked what they had observed in their interactions that were examples of what they desired in their relationship. What had worked? What happened that fit their picture of a satisfying marriage? Their assessment of their own situation was the important aspect at this stage of therapy. During the second session, Jeff and Diane reported that many things had happened and their marriage was "changing." They stated that they had become more affectionate and had adopted dating behaviors. When asked about these behaviors, Diane stated that they were communicating much more directly. She said she was stating her needs more clearly. Jeff reported that they were holding hands and had taken some walks. Some of these activities were the same ones revealed in the "exception" conversation conducted during the first session, when the couple identified past behaviors that were mutually satisfying and created closeness. Jeff and Diane were also asked the scaling question again.

> *Therapist:* Think back to the last session. I asked you a question about your marriage using a scale of one to ten, with ten being the most satisfying. Where on that scale would you place your satisfaction level today?
>
> *Jeff:* Well, I guess I would put it at about an eight or nine.
>
> *Diane:* I would say a nine. Things are going pretty good. If things stayed like they are, I would be happy.
>
> *Therapist:* Wow! How did you do that? How did you move from a three or four to an eight or nine in one week? How did you make that happen?

Interestingly, both partners recalled that their initial scaling report was four to five and were surprised that they had reported it to be three. A conversation followed about the changes they made, with particular emphasis on their ability to create change and including a review of their strengths such as their commitment to the marriage, their apparent caring for each other, their ability to have fun together, and their willingness to take responsibility for their own actions. In addition to the affection behaviors they reported, Jeff and Diane also stated that they were being more responsible for their own activities. Specifically, Diane was entrusting Jeff with agreed-upon responsibilities, and he was following through with a renewed enthusiasm.

THIRD SESSION The marriage and family therapy clinic where this case was seen provided the opportunity for a reflecting team. The couple agreed to conduct the session in front of the team as a source of feedback. After a review of the week's progress and continued activity in the direction of marital satisfaction (including maintenance at the same level on the scaling question), the therapist and couple traded places with a reflecting team (the individuals who had been observing the therapy interaction) halfway through the session. Diane, Jeff, and the therapist watched a discussion between two therapists about the session they had just observed. The team spoke to each other about the hopefulness of the situation based on the couple's own reports of their progress. They also discussed specific strengths they had observed in Diane and Jeff. Of particular significance was their acknowledgment that, in spite of her concerns, Diane had really let go of monitoring Jeff's actions and was being more responsible for her own needs. The team observed that this change was probably difficult, and framed it as an act of love to trust Jeff in ways that may seem counterintuitive. The team also predicted that the level of satisfaction would most likely not stay as high as it was currently and wondered out loud how Diane and Jeff had prepared to handle the normal ups and downs of marriage. They suggested that this couple had the strength to endure hard times and might consider planning for unsatisfactory events based on their current insight into their capabilities.

As the team spoke to each other, the couple watched them intently. At times Jeff and Diane sweetly touched each other, looked each other in the eyes, and nodded their heads at what they heard. There were even a few tears as they listened to the affirming observations of their progress in such a short time. When they returned to the therapy room with their therapist, Diane and Jeff said that the team's observation that "less is more" in detaching from each other certainly applied to them. The reaction to the reflection team was most empowering and insightful for the couple as well as the therapist.

FOURTH SESSION During the fourth session, the couple continued to report positive change. Jeff stated that their marriage was "almost like a whole new relationship" and upgraded his view of the marriage to a nine or ten. Diane evaluated it as a nine and said "I know it's getting there." The couple had become more comfortable with problems they encountered and reported a recent incident that could have led to a big fight and feelings of discouragement. However, Diane stated that she removed herself from the situation until she could gather her thoughts and address Jeff more directly instead of escalating the disagreements. Jeff stated that he did not follow his past tendency to withdraw into himself and "shut down" after the incident, but trusted that they would come to a resolution after they had some individual time to think about their own needs. Later that day they had a positive discussion instead of a fight.

Jeff and Diane, almost three months after the first session, were asked to review the course of therapy. They described their relationship as "liberating" and appeared very enthusiastic about their new connection. The therapist made the observation that Jeff's affect had changed significantly since the first session. He was much more talkative and participatory in conversations, often taking the initiative in answering questions and offering his viewpoints—and Diane gave him the space to do so (which was also applauded by the therapist). The last session provided an opportunity for reflexive questioning in which the couple reflected on their views of each other in light of their new-found changes in individual functioning.

> *Therapist:* I am wondering what you think your spouse has noticed that is different about you over the past two months? What do you think that your partner would say about you if I asked how you had changed?
>
> *Jeff:* Well, I think Diane would say that I am following through on school and work. She would have noticed that I am being more responsible about the finances. I think she would say these things about me.
>
> *Diane:* That I wasn't in his business. Jeff would say that he has noticed that I have let go of making sure he does things. I don't check on his school assignments anymore, because I know he will do them, and if he doesn't then he is the one who is responsible for that. He would also notice that I am doing more things for myself, like I am starting a new job that I had wanted to go for, and I am just focusing more on my own things instead of his.

According to the couple, their successes have also had an impact on their individual functioning outside the relationship. Both have quit their part-time jobs at a department store and are now doing work that they are much more excited about (totally separate from each other). Jeff had contracted for an extracurricular opportunity over the school break that would help him gain more experience in his field of study. Also, Jeff and Diane had visited their families while on vacation and discovered that they acted and reacted differently in those situations than during previous visits. They both reported that they felt more united as a couple and more supportive of each other when visiting their families, and they experienced much more satisfying outcomes during these recent visits.

Toward the end of the fourth session the couple was asked to provide feedback about the therapeutic process to help the therapist understand what was helpful, or not helpful, for information to be used in helping other couples. They both stated that the hopefulness that was encouraged in the first session by the dialogue reflecting back on the happier times in their relationship had been very helpful. Diane reported that the conversation between the therapist and Jeff in the initial session, in which he was provided with the opportunity to speak about the pain he was experiencing accompanied by the reflection of his struggle, had been most useful to her as it had cast Jeff in a different light. She realized from that interaction that Jeff really cared about her and that in her distress she had lost sight of this.

When asked about their readiness to conclude therapy, the couple stated that they believed they weren't quite ready to end therapy and asked for a monthly check-in for the next couple of months, at which time they expect to conclude counseling. Interestingly, when called for the check-in, they reported that they did not need to make a follow-up appointment. They reported, with pride, that they were doing very well and expected to continue to do so.

EVALUATION OF THE THEORY

Brief family therapy has been in practice since the early 1960s. The development of this approach has progressed through several models and is currently practiced in several modes, including solution-oriented and strategic treatments. Other philosophies have adjusted their traditional long-term approaches to therapy by developing time-limited or briefer versions to meet the current market demands of health management organizations. These changes have been controversial and have obscured the tenets of the original brief therapy approaches. This has resulted in complex evaluation of brief therapy on a generic level; however, brief family therapy from a strategic or solution-focused perspective has a history of effectiveness that can be addressed.

Outcome studies on solution-focused brief therapy have evaluated its effectiveness. Research has found that brief therapy can be effective for many clinical issues, including severe and chronic presentations (McKeel, 1996). In addition, brief therapeutic approaches have been found to be as effective as long-term psychotherapies in assisting clients in meeting their treatment goals (Koss & Shiang, 1994). As discussed in a previous section, therapy is often brief by default, not by design, as clients self-terminate treatment earlier than may be anticipated by a therapeutic or theoretical model. Brief family therapy is intended to be short in duration by design. Outcome research, although limited, indicates that it is highly effective as well. Research findings of clients from the Brief

Family Therapy Center indicated that there was an 80.4% success rate, with 65.6% of the individuals accomplishing their treatment goals and another 14.7% making significant improvement during therapy (Kiser, 1988; Kiser & Nunnally, 1990). This success rate increased to 86% based on the report of an 18-month follow-up. Another follow-up study on clients at the Mental Research Institute found a 72% success rate with an average of seven sessions (Weakland, Fisch, Watzlawick, & Bodin, 1974). Lee (1997) found a 64.9% success rate for an average of 5.5 therapy sessions over an average of 3.9 months of solution-focused brief family therapy. In addition to outcome results, McKeel (1996) reviews the findings of the effectiveness of specific process components of solution-oriented brief therapy including formula tasks, solution-oriented language, and presuppositional questions, finding these interventions effective aspects of the brief therapy process.

Some critics of brief therapy have suggested that it is not appropriate for a wide variety of problems and oversimplifies severe pathology. Such a specific problem is paranoia, although organic disorders, severe acute trauma and sexual abuse, and end-stage addictions are considered problems that brief therapy is limited in addressing (Greenfield, 1995). Proponents of the model disagree with this assessment and cite high levels of success rates with a wide range of problems (De Jong & Hopwood, 1996; de Shazer, 1991). According to Cooper (1995), existing concerns about exclusionary criteria for brief therapies are primarily associated with psychodynamic perspectives and are based on theory rather than empirical data.

Brief family therapy has demonstrated effectiveness in helping individuals, couples, and families with a wide range of presenting problems. This approach emphasizes a philosophical perspective about the process of change and potential opportunities for—and process of—therapeutic helping. From a cross-cultural or feminist perspective, the therapy may be evaluated in a positive light. Research findings suggest that the solution-oriented brief therapy approach may be equally effective with families with boys and girls from different age groups who live in diverse family constellations and different socioeconomic backgrounds (Lee, 1997). Consistent with the cross-cultural and feminist perspectives, the brief therapy approach is based on the clients' view of reality, whatever that may be, as well as his or her own view of the desired behavior. It is not based on the therapist's perspective of "truth" or "reality" or "rightness." In this approach, the therapist is not the expert; the client is the expert about his or her own world. Respect for the variability of individuals and events in their lives is emphasized by allowing the clients to construct their own description of desired outcomes. In addition, the brief approach does not attempt to interpret the cause or unconscious motives behind a person's or a family's behavior.

The brief therapist assists the clients with getting to where they want to go, not observing or pontificating about the family's intentions—an often intrusive and autocratic imposition. The possibility that the therapist's dictums, in other therapies, can victimize a client as easily as they can help is sidestepped considerably by this approach. It is unreasonable to suggest that the therapist has no influence on this change process. His or her own values and biases are essentially present; however, the brief approach assumes that not only does the client have a vision for a more satisfactory way of functioning, but also that he or she has the resources to achieve such. This may vary in the orientation of the brief therapist. Therapists from some schools of thought often design interventions or paradoxical situations that are considered, by some, as either manipulative or intrusive.

SUMMARY

Brief family therapy emanates from two schools of thought: the solution-oriented approach of the Brief Family Therapy Center in Milwaukee, Wisconsin, and the strategic-oriented approach developed by family therapists at the Mental Research Institute in Palo Alto, California. The models are similar in that they both maintain a specific focus during the course of therapy and assist families, couples, and individuals in changing their present situation to attain a more desirable level of functioning.

The brief therapy models emphasize the ability of families to creatively use their unique strengths to alter their presenting problems. The level of intervention in brief therapy is the cognitions and behaviors of the family; however, affective components are addressed by some practitioners and certainly play an important role in building rapport and joining together to form an essential, therapeutic working alliance. Strategies and techniques in brief family therapy focus on changing the way the problem is viewed and enacted. This is accomplished through the use of language, task assignments, and therapeutic interventions that alter problematic pattern in favor of more satisfactory behaviors.

The MRI approach is based on inducing doubt about the problem by reframing it in a different context that calls for different behavior, prompting goal achievement. This approach utilizes strategic interventions that recast the problem in a new light. The Brief Family Therapy Center approach is based on inducing doubt about the problem by identifying exceptions to the problem situation and amplifying those exceptions as unique strengths of the client that can be expanded upon to achieve the desired goals or outcomes. In this later model the problem is bypassed completely in favor of identifying problem-free times.

Brief family therapists are expected to be active, attentive, selectively focused, intuitive, and willing to take risks. Their role in the therapy is more interactive than in many other therapies. They are responsible for focusing in on and carefully assessing the presenting problem, using presuppositional language that creates the expectation for change, assisting clients in establishing clear and achievable goals, scouting out exceptions to the presenting complaint and/or creating scenarios in which exceptions can be experienced, changing the family's view of their own functioning, and concluding therapy once the goals have been accomplished. Brief therapists use techniques such as reframing, analogy and metaphor, strategic use of questions, and assignment of homework tasks as important aspects of treatment.

Brief therapy is an approach to working with families that is based not in a theory of personality, but rather, in a theory of change. It effectively assists clients in meeting their goals in fewer sessions than traditional long-term therapies. In addition, the duration of brief family therapies is congruent with clients' expectations of treatment.

ANNOTATED SUGGESTED READINGS

Berg, I. K. (1994). *Family based services: A solution-focused approach.* New York: Norton.
This book is written for professionals who work in the field of family and social services. It provides step-by-step guidelines for applying the principles of solution-focused, brief family therapy directly to clientele as well as within the agency setting.

Budman, S. H., & Gurman, A. S. (1988). *Theory and practice of brief therapy.* New York: Guilford Press.
A comprehensive handbook of brief therapies, conveying many aspects of this approach across theoretical orientations.

Cade, B., & O'Hanlon, W. H. (1993). *A brief guide to brief therapy.* New York: Norton.
This book contains the historical and theoretical tenets of the brief therapy model based on Ericksonian theory. An array of techniques, accompanied by case examples, is also presented.

Cooper, J. F. (1995). *A primer of brief therapy.* New York: Norton.
A very user-friendly guide to implementing brief therapy in a clinical context.

de Shazer, S. (1988). *Clues: Investigating solutions in brief therapy.* New York: Norton.
This book is one of the early comprehensive presentations of the construction of the theory as developed by the Brief Family Therapy Center. Nineteen case examples are also presented and discussed.

de Shazer, S. (1991). *Putting difference to work.* New York: Norton.
In addition to historical information and comparisons to other contemporary theories, this book offers detailed application of the theory to case examples.

O'Hanlon, W. H., & Weiner-Davis, M. (1989). *In search of solutions.* New York: Norton.
Another "early" presentation of theory and application, this book takes a broader view of the solution-oriented approach, presenting it in a form that may be easier for clinicians to understand and apply.

Quick, E. K. (1996). *Doing what works in brief therapy: A strategic solution focused approach.* New York: Academic Press.
This work incorporates the tenets of brief and strategic therapies into a succinct presentation.

Walter, J. L., & Peller, J. E. (1992). *Becoming solution-focused in brief therapy.* New York: Brunner/Mazel.
This is a comprehensive guide to the theory and practice of brief, solution-focused therapy. It includes an easy-to-read, but comprehensive review of the model, clinical techniques, and application of the model to a variety of presenting problems and settings.

Weiner-Davis, M. (1992). *Divorce busting.* New York: Simon & Schuster.
A relationship focused, self-help book, this work is a very useful guide for couples as well as clinicians who wish to implement relationship-saving techniques.

REFERENCES

Berg, I. K. (1994). *Family based services: A solution-focused approach.* New York: Norton.

Cade, B., & O'Hanlon, W. H. (1993). *A brief guide to brief therapy.* New York: Norton.

Cooper, J. F. (1995). *A primer of brief therapy.* New York: Norton.

De Jong, P., & Hopwood, L. E. (1996). Outcome research on treatment conducted at the Brief Family Therapy Center, 1992–1993. In S. D. Miller, M. A. Hubble, & B. L. Duncan (Eds.), *Handbook of solution-focused brief therapy* (pp. 272–298). San Francisco: Jossey-Bass.

de Shazer, S. (1980) Brief family therapy: A metaphorical task. *Journal of Marital and Family Therapy, 10,* 471–476.

de Shazer, S. (1984). Four useful interventions in brief family therapy. *Journal of Marital and Family Therapy, 10,* 297–304.

de Shazer, S. (1985). *Keys to solution in brief therapy.* New York: Norton.

de Shazer, S. (1988). *Clues: Investigating solutions in brief therapy.* New York: Norton.

de Shazer, S. (1989). Resistance revisited. *Contemporary Family Therapy, 11,* pp. 227–233.

de Shazer, S. 1990). What is it about brief therapy that works? In J. K. Zeig & S. L. Gilligan (Eds.), *Brief therapy: Myths, methods, and metaphors* (pp. 90–99). New York: Brunner/Mazel.

de Shazer, S. (1991). *Putting difference to work.* New York: Norton.

Dreikurs, R. (1958). A reliable differential diagnosis of psychological or somatic disturbance. *International Record of Medicine, 171,* 238–242.

Greenfield, D. N. (1995, August). *Solution-focused approaches to psychotherapy: Utilizing therapeutic challenges.* Paper presented at the meeting of the American Psychological Association, New York.

Haley, J. (1967). Advanced techniques of hypnosis and therapy: Selected papers of Milton H. Erickson, MD. New York: Grune & Stratton.

Kiser, D. (1988). *A follow-up study conducted at the Brief Family Therapy Center.* Unpublished manuscript.

Kiser, D., & Nunnally, E. (1990) *The relationship between treatment length and goal achievement in solution-focused therapy.* Unpublished manuscript.

Koss, M. P., & Shiang. J. (1994). Research on brief psychotherapy. In S. L. Garfield & A. E. Bergin (Eds.), *Handbook of psychotherapy and behavior change* (4th ed., pp. 664–700). New York: Wiley.

Kral, R., & Kowalski, K. (1989). After the miracle: The second stage in solution-focused brief therapy. *Journal of Strategic and Systemic Therapies, 8,* 73–76.

Lee, M. Y. (1997). A study of solution-focused brief family therapy: Outcomes and issues. *The American Journal of Family Therapy, 25,* 3–17.

McKeel, A. J. (1996). A clinician's guide to research on solution-focused brief therapy. In S. D. Miller, M. A. Hubble, & B. L. Duncan (Eds.), *Handbook of solution-focused brief therapy* (pp. 251–271). San Francisco: Jossey-Bass.

O'Hanlon, W. H. (1990). A grand unified theory for brief therapy: Putting problems in context. In J. K. Zeig & S. L. Gilligan (Eds.), *Brief therapy: Myths, methods, and metaphors* (pp. 78–89). New York: Brunner/Mazel.

O'Hanlon, W. H., & Weiner-Davis, M. (1989). *In search of solutions.* New York: Norton.

Watzlawick, P. (1990). Therapy is what you say it is. In J. K. Zeig & S. L. Gilligan (Eds.), *Brief therapy: Myths, methods, and metaphors* (pp. 55–61). New York: Brunner/Mazel.

Weakland, J. H., Fisch, R., Watzlawick, P., & Bodin, A., (1974). *Change.* New York: Norton.

Weiner-Davis, M., de Shazer, S., & Gingerich, W. (1987). Building on pretreatment change to construct the therapeutic solution: An exploratory study. *Journal of Marital and Family Therapy, 13,* 359–365.

CHAPTER 10

The Bowen Theory

"Science of Human Behavior"

Natural System Theory

DANIEL V. PAPERO

INTRODUCTION

Human, feeling-based subjectivity manufactures innumerable explanations for why the human behaves in a particular manner at a particular time. Subjective explanations remain generally unsatisfying, and some people have sought a different, scientific understanding of human behavior to balance such subjectivity. As the twentieth century turned, it seemed that a science of the human was within reach. Like a great *tsunami*, Darwin's ideas surged against and eroded the island of human uniqueness as people discovered and reluctantly acknowledged an ancient lineage. If evolution could become accepted as scientific fact, a foundation could be laid for a new human science. Freud's discoveries closely followed those of Darwin. Freud saw a new aspect of the person, and he worked toward a new theory. The secrets of human nature seemed about to open to scientific inquiry.

As the century nears its end, that early promise remains unfulfilled. A science of human behavior has not yet been achieved. The Bowen theory, however, is the product of one person's lifelong interest in such a science. While acknowledging that human behavior is not yet scientific, Murray Bowen wrote recently, "My life work has been based on an opposing viewpoint (to that which doubts the possibility of a human science). It says merely that the physical structure of the human is scientific, that the human brain *functions* to create feelings and subjective states, and that the brain is capable of separating structure from function. My premise merely states that the human is a passenger on

planet Earth and that sometime in the future the human can clarify the difference between *what the human is from what the human feels, imagines, and says*"
(Kerr & Bowen, 1988, pp. 354–355).

HISTORICAL DEVELOPMENT

Bowen's lifelong journey toward a science of human behavior has been well chronicled elsewhere (Bowen, 1978; Kerr & Bowen, 1988). He reports a childhood interest and ability in science and in solving difficult puzzles. As a young physician,
he explored many medical specialties. He had decided upon a residence in surgery
when he entered military service presumably for one year in 1941. He remained
for the duration of World War II. During the war years, he heard of a "new psychiatry" based on Freud that was reported to be scientific. He decided to forgo the
residency in surgery in favor of psychiatry. In 1946, he entered residency training
at the Menninger Foundation, a center for the new ideas, in Topeka, Kansas.

Bowen refers to the times in Topeka (1946–1954) as "the most important period
in the development of a different theory" (Kerr & Bowen, 1988, p. 347). It became apparent to him that in spite of its many contributions, the body of ideas referred to as
Freud's theory could not gain acceptance as a science. The major problem concerned
the subjectivity introduced when Freud selected terms to describe his thinking. His
use of literary concepts moved him away from scientific facts that could be validated.
No matter how valuable Freud's insights were for therapy, there was no way to bring
his theoretical thinking in line with the accepted sciences.

Bowen completed the basic thinking for the new theory while at the Menninger Foundation. He refers to his movement toward a new theory as an
"odyssey" and breaks it down into three phases (Kerr & Bowen, 1988). The first,
where theory has lost science, involved much reading and working to understand
recognized science's objections to Freud. The second phase, *clinical experience*,
involved comparing the various concepts from literature with the actual clinical
situation. During the third phase, *steps toward science*, he read extensively in all
the professional disciplines concerned with humans. His goal was to understand
the basic thought of each discipline and how these disciplines had managed to
separate scientific fact from feeling.

A new theory emerged from this effort, that is, "a natural systems theory,
designed to fit precisely with the principles of evolution and the human as an
evolutionary being" (Kerr & Bowen, 1988, p. 360). He was ready to develop the
new ideas in a planned manner and sought a research institution where this could
be carried out. In 1954, he moved to the National Institute of Mental Health
(NIMH) in Bethesda, Maryland.

Bowen spent approximately five years at the clinical center of the NIMH
(1954–1959). He was able to bring entire families onto his research ward, which
he directed in accordance with the principles of the new theory. He reports that
the theoretical concepts of the emotional system and differentiation of self allowed him to predict in detail the sorts of abnormal behavior that might occur and
to specify the required corrective action.

In essence, Bowen created a master theory that was always subject to revision
when its predictions were inaccurate. When such inaccuracy occurred, either the

theory had not been comprehensive enough or there had been an error on the part of the staff. When theory turned out to be incomplete, it was extended or modified. In this manner, the master theory developed continuously and spelled out actions to be taken. The staff's tendency to make decisions and change behavior in response to feeling could be avoided.

The new theory led to a host of new observations and findings. Concepts were developed for inclusion in the theory alongside the emotional system and differentiation of self, among them triangles, the nuclear family emotional system, fusion, cutoff, the family diagram, projection to children, and overadequate-inadequate reciprocity. A derivative of the research was a method of family therapy based on the premise that "if the family is cause of the problem, the therapy should be directed to the family" (Kerr & Bowen, 1988, p. 361).

Recognizing that new theories and new ideas were slow to be accepted, Bowen attempted to use simple descriptive terms, where possible, and to avoid creating new words. Terms were borrowed from biology and used in a manner that closely approximated usage there. He kept his focus more on theory than on therapy, although the professions quickly made family therapy a major endeavor. The goal was to move toward science and to speak to researchers and basic scientists a century or two in the future, when a science of human behavior might be at hand.

Although the families involved in the NIMH research included a person called schizophrenic, Bowen's interest was in theory rather than in schizophrenia as a phenomenon (Kerr & Bowen, 1988). By 1957, Bowen was satisfied that the relationship patterns found in the research families could be seen in all families. Schizophrenia could be conceptualized, therefore, as one small piece of a broader process involving even people considered normal. The various clinical entities, each bearing a diagnosis, were part of a single continuum. As Bowen puts it, "the only difference between schizophrenia and the milder states was in duration and fixedness of the process of differentiation of self" (Kerr & Bowen, 1988, p. 367).

In 1959, Bowen moved from the NIMH to the school of medicine at Georgetown University. With this decision he remained within the framework of medicine, a step he considered important for the further development of theory and the efforts to move toward the natural sciences. At Georgetown, he continued to expand on the developments at the NIMH. He extended theoretical development beyond the family to work and social systems, and even beyond to the larger systems of society.

Many of the theoretical concepts, initially defined separately, were integrated in the mid-1960s. This period of great effort and productivity resulted in a paper, "The Use of Family Theory in Clinical Practice" (Bowen, 1966), which Bowen notes as a milestone in his odyssey. The effort culminated in a visit to his own family (described in a well-known paper presented in 1967 to a national meeting of family therapists and published in 1972 with the authorship listed as anonymous), during which he knew he had found his way through the family emotional system. Bowen's report set off a national trend about therapists' own families. In the rush to incorporate the extended family into the process of therapy, the professions tended to lose sight of the theoretical premises that guided the effort.

In 1968, the family faculty was formed at Georgetown. The faculty members were selected on the basis of their efforts in family research, and they volunteered their time. The first postgraduate training program began at this time, although the family faculty had no fixed location and conducted their activities in borrowed space at the medical center. In 1975, the faculty occupied the Georgetown University Family Center in office space located off campus but near the medical school.

During the 1970s, Bowen used the term the *Bowen theory* to refer to this work in place of the term *family systems theory*, because the latter had come to be widely used to convey ideas that were not a part of his theoretical framework. In 1973, an additional concept concerning society was introduced to the Bowen theory. Society could be seen to go through cycles of better and poorer functioning, much as a family.

DEFINITION

A central piece of the foundation to the Bowen theory is the concept of the *emotional system*. Bowen explains what he means: "It [the emotional system] includes the forces that biology defines as instinct, reproduction, the automatic activity controlled by the autonomic nervous system, subjective emotional and feeling states, and the forces that govern relationship systems.... In broad terms, the emotional system governs the 'dance of life' in all living things" (Bowen, 1975, p. 380). The emotional system is thought of as a guidance system, a product of a long evolutionary history, that forms the basis of behavior for all living things. The emotional system governs a creature's ability to exploit opportunities and to adjust to changes in its environment. While all organisms have such a guidance system, emotional systems differ among species and even among individuals.

A sunflower can model the operation of an emotional system. The sunflower's head follows the course of the sun across the sky; such behavior is governed by the emotional system of the species. Nevertheless, individual sunflowers may vary slightly in their ability to track the sun. Such slight variations, on a genetic level, form the basis of evolution. Living things reproduce themselves almost exactly, but the "almost" contains within it a wide range of variation when geological time and environmental factors are considered.

While genes are certainly considered a part of the organism's emotional system, that system is not seen simply as the inflexible development of a genetic code. The experience of individuals, those products of the organism's interaction with its environment that are retained, must also be included. To borrow an analogy from the world of computers, the emotional system includes both the operating system and the application programs that govern the behavior of the organism.

The emotional system of a species can work against the survival of individuals under certain circumstances. John B. Calhoun of the NIMH studies extensively the effects of population density on colonies of small mammals. From Calhoun's viewpoint, pathology can be defined as the inability to adjust to changing conditions. Any set of circumstances producing conditions with which the individual is unable to cope can be called an *ecological trap*.

As an example, Calhoun cites the lemming (Calhoun, 1967). The population of lemmings in arctic regions becomes extremely dense at regular intervals, but large numbers of these small mammals frequently die off, thereby solving the dilemma. Under some circumstances, however, the animals migrate en masse. These migrations generally serve simply to disperse the animals and relieve the population crisis. In Scandinavia, however, the tundra is marked by long valleys extending to the sea. The pressure for the lemmings to disperse (a function of their emotional systems) triggers the movement. The long valleys do not allow the animals to spread out, maintaining the pressure, with the result that the lemmings swim out to sea until they drown.

The physiological foundations of emotional systems vary considerably from early to more recently evolved forms. In single-cell organisms, chemical processes may well suffice to guide the creature through its world. With the addition of nerve tracts and a central junction (spinal column and ultimately brain), other sorts of capacities and complexities are added to the emotional system.

An obvious manifestation of the emotional system is the reactivity of the individual to its environment. It is likely that reactivity is rooted in physiology, in the cells and organ systems of the body and not just in the central nervous system. For the human, the tight stomach, sweating palms, pounding heart, and other characteristic signs of physiological reactivity frequently precede the psychological indicators of reactivity. Basic reactivity leads to reactive behavior with sufficient intensity. The organism acts automatically in a recognizable and often predictable manner. Such automatic or reflexive behavior impacts on other individuals who may react in turn. The result is a pattern of behavior for the group or unit as a whole.

Examples of human reactivity range from the subtle to the overt. A speaker's palms become damp as she hears her introduction to the podium. A mother scans her surroundings when she hears the cry of her child. A little boy cringes involuntarily when he hears his father angrily reprimanding a sibling. The muscles of a veteran tighten and his breathing becomes more rapid when he remembers a combat experience. In the middle of a difficult exam, a student begins to lose himself in sexual fantasies, and so forth.

The evolutionary course toward the family was set when sexual reproduction evolved. Mammals developed further the connection between the parent and offspring. It is characteristic for the human to form a mating pair and to live in a group comprised of the mating pair and offspring, the nuclear family. The tendency to form a family group is an aspect of the human emotional system.

Bowen observed that people vary greatly in their ability to manage reactivity. Some people seem to be continually reactive. For them, life tends to become primarily a matter of feeling well or feeling poorly. Minor changes in environment tend to produce intensely reactive postures. On the other hand, some people appear to have greater control of their reactive responses. While they react emotionally at times, they can make important decisions with careful thought and little reactivity. Such people have a choice. They can respond to a situation emotionally or in a less reactive, more thoughtful manner.

TENETS OF THE MODEL

With this discussion of the emotional system, reactivity, and individual variation, we now approach the concept of differentiation of self. The basic idea is that different individuals have different capacities to adjust to changing conditions. Some have no choice but to yield to the environment. Others have some ability to compel the environment to adjust to them. Such a difference is a product of heredity and history. Following are discussions of the eight tenets of the Bowen theory.

DIFFERENTIATION OF SELF

Bowen took the term *differentiation* from biology. From essentially the same material, cells develop, or *differentiate*, to perform separate yet related functions in the organism. In terms of the Bowen theory, differentiation of self refers to the degree to which an individual manages across a lifetime to separate emotional and thinking systems and therefore to retain some choice between behavior governed by thinking and by emotional reactivity.

One could attempt to present the distinction between the emotional system and the intellectual system in terms of objectivity and subjectivity. With the human brain dependent on a host of relays to convey information to it, complete objectivity is impossible. Nevertheless, one can distinguish between a subjective focus and a broader, objective view. Subjectivity defines self as the center of the universe, and all events and phenomena are interpreted in terms of the impact on self. The objective viewpoint sees the self as a responding part of a larger whole.

The distinction between emotional reactivity and thinking is often subtle and elusive. Some sorts of cerebration are clearly related to intense automatic processes. Easily recognized examples include the mental processes commonly called paranoia, the fantasies and mental events connected with falling in love, and those associated with intense anxiety and panic. A few characteristics of emotionally based mental processes include a narrowing perspective frequently marked by polarization (an either-or dichotomy), ambivalence, confusion, and a tendency to rely on what "feels right" and on whatever relieves discomfort. A kind of clear thought is also available to the human, at least under some circumstances. A broad perspective with an appreciation of complexity is the hallmark of such thinking. Fact and knowledge are important ingredients. Feeling is recognized and respected but does not dominate the mental activity.

The basic level of differentiation of self is manifested in the degree to which an individual manages across a lifetime to keep thinking and emotional systems separate and to retain choice between thoughtful behavior and reactivity. The Bowen theory postulates that the *basic level* of differentiation of self for any person develops and becomes relatively fixed early in life. For a particular individual, that level is roughly similar to that of the parents or primary caretakers. In a group of siblings, one child may be a little more differentiated than the parents, and another a little less.

While the basic level is established early in life, it can be expanded in later life through disciplined effort. This is the basis of family systems therapy. The basic level of differentiation is solid and not negotiable in the relationship system. In contrast, the *functional level* of differentiation changes in response to relationship variables. For example, one can appear principled and thoughtful with the support of a group, but when the group's approval shifts, so does the posture of the individual. With effort, one can always influence one's functional level of differentiation.

Among mammals, a clearly visible movement toward group functioning can be noted, particularly in the presence of perceived threat, whether real or imagined. It is also evident in mating behaviors of a wide range of species. Bowen called this tendency in the human a *togetherness force*. Among humans, the togetherness force tends to heighten emotional functioning at the expense of intellectual functioning. The togetherness force can so intensify emotional system functioning that it overrides intellectual functioning altogether.

To value the intellectual system over the emotional misses the point, however. The human emotional system is as old as evolution itself. It incorporates within it the gigantic step that separated mammals from reptiles. Organisms need an internal guidance system operating beyond conscious awareness. Mating and attachment are as much emotional system functions as hostility and aggression. Togetherness, or the functioning of individuals as a unit, may be necessary under some circumstances for the maintenance of life itself. The blending of emotional functioning in a group, or the joining of one emotional system to another, may lie at the core of the concept of support for much of life.

Yet too much togetherness can create problems both for the individual and for the group. Individuals can become too reactive to one another. The group can so influence individual behavior that a life course becomes altered or impaired. Individuals can reach a point at which they cannot function without one another, a fairly simple definition of *symbiosis*. Togetherness pressures can sweep people in directions they would not have chosen on their own and that may not be in their best interest.

Anxiety, the perception of real or imagined threat, is a critical variable affecting the balance of togetherness and individuation. Anxiety often triggers and intensifies the togetherness pressures, and the advantages of the group may not always relieve the anxiety. Differentiation has to do with the ability of the individual to maintain a degree of thoughtful autonomy in spite of the anxious pressures for togetherness. Differentiation does not deny the connectedness of people, but the well-differentiated person understands the advantages of both togetherness and individuation.

While the concept of differentiation of self occupies the center of the Bowen theory, the remaining seven concepts are closely associated with it. Each of the remaining seven concepts will be presented briefly in relationship to the concept of differentiation. Serious students of the Bowen theory will require a more thorough discussion and may consult Bowen (1978) and Kerr and Bowen (1988).

TRIANGLES

The level of differentiation of any person governs his or her sensitivity to others, the intensity of the feeling states and responses that accompany such sensitivity, and the degree to which automatic or instinctive processes override or decrease that person's ability to guide behavior with careful reflection. The less well differentiated a person, the more his or her life decisions are rooted in the sensitivity and response to important others. The more such sensitivity governs the behavior of each party to a relationship, the more the pair acts as a unit rather than as separate individuals. When sufficient anxiety is present, such a unit behaves in a characteristic and predictable manner. The concept of the triangle describes this process.

A two-person relationship is essentially unstable. When sufficiently anxious, one of the two will automatically involve a significant third. This movement is predictable and can be known in detail. The effect of involving a third person in a tense two-person relationship can reduce anxiety. When anxiety is high, however, the basic triangle cannot contain and dissolve the tension, which results in further triangling and the activation of a web of interlocking triangles.

A clear example of the triangle exists in the affair. A spouse in a tense marriage can be involved in an affair of mild to moderate intensity that appears to have a calming effect on the marriage. The other spouse is generally not aware of the existence of a rival. Should the same affair become more intense, however, the uninvolved spouse becomes aware of it quickly and reacts by drawing others into the situation.

In a triangle, there are characteristically two relatively calm relationships and one anxious one. The intense relationship may shift around the three pairs of the triangle or may become fixed in a particular twosome. When free of anxiety, the participants may appear relatively autonomous and not intensely involved with one another. In the presence of anxiety, however, the characteristic interactions emerge predictably.

The system of interlocking triangles comes into play when anxiety can no longer be contained within a single triangle. The system of interlocking triangles in a particular network can be mapped out with precision. When a fourth person is brought in, the original third is discarded only temporarily and can be reinvolved again. In this fashion, important others become involved in the process. Depending upon the level of anxiety in the network or family, various additional triangles are stirred up and become dormant in a regular pattern.

NUCLEAR FAMILY EMOTIONAL PROCESS

When two or more people function as an emotional unit, the greater is the potential loss of autonomy for each. Pressures come into play for greater closeness and for greater distance, particularly when people are anxious. Bowen called the joining of two or more selves into a single self *fusion*. The greater the fusion of a unit, the more natural mechanisms are employed to manage the discomfort and anxiety produced by the togetherness. The greater the undifferentiation in the individuals, the greater the vulnerability of each to loss of autonomy to others.

Four such mechanisms or processes can be observed in the nuclear family. Generally, they involve the marital pair, with others being drawn in as anxiety increases. Each of these mechanisms will be discussed briefly in the following paragraphs.

EMOTIONAL DISTANCE People often react to the intensity of emotional contact by pulling away. Emotional intensity, whether tinged positively or negatively, frequently produces distance, as if people were withdrawing from a hot stove. The distance can be actual, or it can be the result of a series of internal operations that effectively shield a person from contact with another. Where the distance is external, one may find a way to spend much time away from the other. He or she may seek employment that requires lengthy separations, but long work hours or great community involvement can produce the same result.

In essence, opportunities for intense contact are reduced or avoided altogether. The internal processes leading to distances are often more subtle and difficult to see. Chronic irritability, involvement in an activity to the exclusion of all else, or simply "tuning out" another person all can manifest an internal shutting down of emotional contact.

Distancing occurs automatically and generally without the involved persons being acutely aware of it initially. As time passes, it comes to be an accepted way of living, so long as nothing increases the intensity of anxiety that the mechanism defuses. Efforts that one or the other makes to reduce the distance often increase it. Although distancing is a sort of safety valve built into the relationship system, it usually produces more distance than people want. What people actually seem to be avoiding is their own discomfort and reactivity to one another.

MARITAL CONFLICT Marital conflict is generally recognized as a symptom of tension in a family, but its function as a mechanism to regulate anxiety and maintain equilibrium in a family is less well understood. Conflict can range from mild to severe. The critical variables are the degree of fusion in the relationship and the intensity of anxiety that propels the process.

Partners in conflict have high emotional reactivity to one another. Each tends to ruminate a great deal about the other, generally about the other's obstinacy and lack of caring. Conflict can flare up with little apparent provocation and escalate quickly in intensity. If the conflict exceeds the capacity of the relationship to manage it, others are brought in. In extreme examples, outside agencies (e.g., police or crisis intervention services) are attracted to the relationship and actively intervene. A familiar cycle involves conflict and ensuing distance. Conflictual episodes are followed by periods of warm togetherness. A subsequent increase in tension seems inevitable, and the closeness yields to distance and ultimately conflict once again.

One often hears concern expressed about children raised in a family with intense marital conflict. Yet from a theoretical perspective, the more anxiety that can be contained within the marital unit, the less likely it is to affect a child. Clinical observation suggests that children run a greater risk when a parent becomes anxious about the effects of marital interaction on the child. Such anxiety frequently leads to a parental effort to compensate the child in some manner. Such compensatory effort is based more in parental anxiety than in the child's need. The anxious involvement of the child with the parent is the basis for the third major mechanism of nuclear family emotional process.

TRANSMISSION OF THE PROBLEM TO A CHILD All children become involved to a degree in the emotional process of their parents. An entire concept in the Bowen theory, the concept of the multigenerational transmission process, is based on that premise. In some families, however, the process is so intense and major that the child's functioning in life is impaired.

The process is relatively easy to describe. Anxiety in the primary caretaker is expressed in sensitivity and reactivity to a child. In effect, anxiety about the child affects the caretaker's ability to provide basic care. The caretaker's involvement may appear as positive, loving involvement or as nagging worry and frustration. In the former, the caretaker has difficulty realistically assessing the child's behavior and development. Nothing is too good for the child, who can do no wrong in the eyes of the parent. In the latter version, the caretaker focuses on a real or supposed problem in the child. The caretaker, while wanting the child to be autonomous, appears afraid to allow the child to move beyond his or her range of guidance and control. The child comes quickly to behave as if she or he cannot function appropriately without such guidance.

To speak simply of caretaker and child is accurate but narrow. The primary caretaker is frequently one member of a breeding pair, usually the mother. Anxiety in the relationship between the parents directly relates to the involvement of the child. Lack of differentiation in the relationship directly impacts on each parent's ability to view self and the child objectively. Heightened emotionality between the parents often tends to result in the greater involvement of the caretaker and child.

To isolate the phenomenon in a particular generation of caretaker and child is misleading. That framework too easily allows the assignment of blame to the parent–caretaker and the status of victim to the child. The phenomenon sweeps across generations in a family, with each generation having some version of the relationship. Such a viewpoint also inadequately addresses the automatic, even physiological, proportions of the relationship between the caretaker and child. In intense forms, the union approaches symbiosis in the biological sense of the term. Each appears to have lost the ability to function and even to survive independently in the world.

DYSFUNCTION IN A SPOUSE In many, perhaps all, marriages there are repeated compromises in which one spouse yields to the other to avoid conflict. This pattern is highly functional and is effective to a point in containing anxiety and preserving harmony. Often such adaptivity is two-sided, with each yielding to the other in different situations. In some marriages, however, the process becomes intense and relatively fixed. The result is increasing dysfunction in one partner and an apparent overfunctioning in the other. Bowen described the pattern in an early paper. "One denies the immaturity and functions with a facade of adequacy. The other accentuates the immaturity and functions with a facade of inadequacy. Neither can function in the midground between overadequacy and inadequacy" (Bowen, 1978, p. 19). In a sense, this arrangement is functional. Without someone taking charge, such families might never reach decisions. The price, however, is high.

Both people contribute to this outcome. The overfunctioning one may have been trained to decide for others in the family from which he or she came. The underfunctioning one may have been programmed to go along with the decisions of others. These postures are based in the relationship and not in particular personality flaws in one or both people. When the relationship changes, the pattern disappears. For example, when illness or injury incapacitates the overfunctioning one, the other will often display a dramatic improvement in functioning that is maintained until the original relationship is reestablished.

When anxiety is low, the relationship pattern may not be evident. Under conditions of sustained chronic anxiety, the low-functioning individual may develop a physical, emotional, or social dysfunction. The course of the symptom may ebb and flow in response to levels of anxiety. The presence of such a symptom, however, across time can lead to new roles or postures for other family members in response to the dysfunctional one. Nursing and caretaker roles may

ease interpersonal anxiety, but they also tend to make the symptom more intractable within the family system.

FAMILY PROJECTION PROCESS

In a family, the primary caretaker's (generally the mother's) degree of emotional
involvement varies among her children. Characteristically, the caretaker's sensitivity and response are greater to one child than to the others. Anxiety increases
the caretaker's reactivity toward the child. The caretaker responds as if his or her
anxiety were a problem in the child rather than in the caretaker. The involvement
can begin even before the birth of the child. The caretaker's feelings can be intense and range from an overpositive, protective posture to revulsion. The child
becomes sensitive to the anxiety in the caretaker and responds in ways that appear
to justify his or her anxious concern.

Often the anxiety driving the process in a given generation rests between
the parents. Each is sensitive and reactive to the other, but the basic problem between them is submerged in a concern about the child. The dysfunction of the
parents as a unit leads to the inclusion of the child in the emotional process between them. When other mechanisms to regulate anxiety are effectively employed, a child may be only occasionally involved with little resulting impairment.

The process is marked initially by emotional shifts within the parental unit
that are expressed in the mother's response to the child. If positive, she may over-
value, overprotect, and in general behave in ways that foster immaturity in the
child. If negative, she may be overly harsh and restrictive. It is important to remember that the process appears to originate in the parent. The child quickly
comes to play a role in triggering the caretaker's reactivity. While the emotional
involvement is generally most observable between the mother and child, the father is equally involved in the process. The level of his own anxiety and mechanisms he employs to preserve his own functioning have great impact on the
mother and the child. If he withdraws, the intensity between the mother and
child increases. If he supports the mother's concern, the problem tends to become more firmly fixed in the child.

Where the process involves only one child, other children remain relatively
free from involvement. If anxiety is intense and prolonged, other siblings may become involved. The functioning of such compromised children is labile, tending to
improve or deteriorate in response to anxiety in important relationships. Neither
parent nor child is at fault in this process. Parents themselves have been involved
with their parents to some degree, and their parents with their parents across the
generations. The parents may have some awareness of the intensity of the relationships but find themselves unable to act differently. In short, the process in one
generation represents the cumulative effects of what has happened in preceding
generations. This is the basis for the fifth concept of the Bowen theory.

THE MULTIGENERATIONAL TRANSMISSION PROCESS

The family projection process, operating across the generations, results in
branches of families that move toward greater and lesser levels of differentiation.

People tend to pick as a mate a person of about the same level of differentiation of self. If a person, as a consequence of the family projection process, grows up with a lower level of differentiation than the parents and marries someone with a similar level, that next generation will emerge with a lower level of differentiation than that of the original parents. In this manner, across time, sections of families move toward greater and lesser levels of differentiation.

The most involved child is thought to have a slightly lower level of differentiation than that of the parents. The less involved children develop similar or slightly higher levels than their parents. This variation has important theoretical implications for life course. The higher the level of differentiation, the less vulnerable the person is to the effects of prolonged anxiety and reactivity.

As previously stated, the Bowen theory also presumes that people marry partners with a level of differentiation similar to their own. Over the generations, therefore, the invested children of each generation marry partners with like levels of differentiation and operate with greater emotional intensity than did their parents. Their siblings create families with emotional levels as, or less intense than, those of the original family. From this perspective, in any family there are lines moving through time toward greater and lesser levels of differentiation. Events in any generation can slow the process down. Similarly, unfavorable circumstances can speed it up. The ability of other mechanisms than the projection process to absorb anxiety is an important variable.

SIBLING POSITION

In 1961, Walter Toman published *Family Constellation: A Psychological Game*. Drawing from studies of several hundred families, Toman presents a series of profiles of behavioral characteristics of individuals occupying specific sibling positions in a family. The work consolidates and clarifies an entire area of Bowen's thinking. The information about sibling position, along with the knowledge of triangles, makes it possible to see the mechanisms of the nuclear family clearly. It also makes it possible to work backward to reconstruct presumable relationship patterns in prior generations.

Toman's work involves "normal families," and it does not address the processes by which a child becomes involved in parental undifferentiation. Anxiety also plays a role in the expression of sibling-position characteristics in a family. An anxious older brother can become more dogmatic and authoritarian than is the case when he is calmer. The youngest sister of several brothers may appear more helpless and needy when anxious than when not. In clinical practice, the knowledge of sibling-position characteristics may provide a person a first glimpse of his or her own reactive behavior and its impact on another.

EMOTIONAL CUTOFF

A basic element in the concept of differentiation of self is the notion of unresolved emotional attachment to one's parents. To manage the loss of autonomy in the relationship to the parents (and to other important figures in one's life), the person maintains a certain distance. The distance can be intrapsychic or actual. While the distance may insulate one from some of the discomfort of the attachment, he or she remains vulnerable to loss of autonomy in other important relationships.

The emotional cutoff is a natural process. On a simple level, people speak of the need for personal space or sometimes even freedom as a means of explaining their avoidance of others. Distance seems to be the safety valve of the emotional system. Yet distance also leaves people primed for, but reactive to, closeness. In extreme examples, people search continually for closeness but react intensely when it is at hand. Although the cutoff appears to handle the relationship to parents, the individual remains vulnerable to other intense relationships. In a marriage, a pattern and level of intensity can develop that is similar to that from which one was cut off in the original family.

EMOTIONAL PROCESS IN SOCIETY

This eighth concept in the Bowen theory extends thinking to societal behavior. Bowen became interested in the way anxious, poorly differentiated parents deal with teenage behavior problems and in the way society, through its representatives, deals with the same phenomenon. The pressures for togetherness and individuation operate in society as in the family. The greater the level of socieal anxiety at any point in time, the more togetherness erodes individuation. The primary generators of societal anxiety appear to be a burgeoning human population, dwindling resources, and humankind's propensity to defile its habitat.

Societal projection processes intensify in an anxious climate. Two groups join together and enhance their own functioning at the expense of the third. This is similar to the family projection process. The twosome can force the outsider into submission, the outsider can force the other two to treat him or her as impaired, or each can match the expectation of the other. It is difficult if not impossible to reduce the intensity of societal processes without first decreasing the anxiety that propels it.

The emotional climate and processes of society represent yet another element in the emotional climate of the family. The anxious society, like the anxious family, has difficulty resolving its problems without polarization, cutoff, reciprocal overfunctioning and underfunctioning, and so forth. The result is a series of crises, generally resolved on the basis of restoring comfort rather than with a thoughtful approach based upon principle, knowledge, and a degree of respect for differing viewpoints.

APPLICATION

The appearance of a symptom in an individual or in a relationship signals that anxiety within the emotional system in which the individual or relationship is embedded has exceeded the level that the natural mechanisms of that system can handle without difficulty. When anxiety can be reduced, the symptom will abate and even disappear. Whether the symptom disappears for good depends on whether the level of anxiety again reaches symptomatic range and whether more fundamental changes in the unit that reduce vulnerability have taken place.

Anxiety can be defined as the fear of real or imagined threat. More specifically, one can think of anxiety as the arousal of the organism preparatory to action to preserve the safety of the individual. Anxiety is also infectious. It spreads quickly among people, as the well-known injunction against crying "fire" in a crowded theater readily illustrates. The more anxious people are, the greater the tendency is for them to act automatically, based on instinct and feeling. Any sort of clinical effort, therefore, must somehow initially assist the individual and the unit to reduce anxiety.

The methodology of family systems therapy is relatively simple. It is determined by theoretical considerations as much as possible. The most important goal or outcome of such therapy is improved differentiation of self (Bowen, 1974). Differentiation of self addresses the basic vulnerability of the individual and the unit to anxiety. Better differentiated people can tolerate greater levels of anxiety without losing the ability to think their way through situations. As you will recall, differentiation of self involves the ability of the individual to maintain separation of emotional and intellectual functioning, to preserve the ability to choose between reaction and intellectually directed action.

Family systems therapy attempts to assist each person to think and to gain some control of his or her reactivity. Often when people can begin to think about a situation, their anxiety decreases correspondingly. To the best of his or her abilities, the clinician attempts to relate calmly and neutrally to the family. There is no active attempt to make the family different. Interventions, or planned moves by the therapist to pressure the family to change, play little if any role. The clinician attempts to gather information, to maintain a thoughtful and broad perspective, to remain emotionally neutral, and to preserve an attitude of interested inquiry as much as possible.

The effort of the clinician to maintain an investigative or inquiring attitude is important and easily overlooked in efforts to apply the Bowen theory in clinical practice. The facts of the family are important. The facts lead to innumerable questions about the processes of the family. Real questions—that is, questions aimed only at acquiring information—assist the clinician to know more about the family and the family to know more about itself. No single piece of information is particularly important, but each fact leads to further inquiry and a clearer view of how the emotional system of the individual and of the family operates to create the mosaic of life.

Family systems therapy does not require the presence of all family members. Often the two spouses, considered the responsible architects of the family, are seen together in clinical practice. This general guideline is not hard and fast, however. Other members of the family may be seen at different times as motivation shifts among family members and the clinician attempts to learn more about the group. In the late 1960s, Bowen's theoretical work led to an approach that included only one member of the family in the session. This development will be discussed later.

Bowen (1971) lists four main functions for the therapist in dealing with the spouses: (1) defining and clarifying the relationship between spouses, (2) keeping self detriangled from the family emotional system, (3) demonstrating differentiation by managing self during the course of therapy, and (4) teaching the functioning of emotional systems. Each function is rooted in theory and will be discussed more fully in the following paragraphs.

DEFINING AND CLARIFYING THE EMOTIONAL PROCESS BETWEEN SPOUSES

In a family, people become sensitive and reactive to one another. Spouses recognize each other's emotional sensitivities and reactivity quite well, knowing how to stir up the other's reactivity as well as how to calm the other down. Over time, the sensitive areas between people tend to be avoided in conversation and general interaction. When such areas are entered, an emotional chain reaction tends to occur, with each reacting to the other in an increasing crescendo. The chain reaction can be loud or quiet, but it tends to hamper substantially the individuals' efforts to resolve differences and address problems.

The format of therapy aids the therapist in controlling the interchange between spouses. The clinician talks directly to one, often employing low-key questions, while the other listens. The questions and comments are directed to the thinking rather than the feelings of each person. They elicit observations about reactivity, both in self and in other. Often such a dialogue between clinician and spouse allows the listening partner to hear the other's views and thoughts about matters important to both. It is not unusual for one or the other to comment that his or her partner's views are particularly interesting and unexpected. Spouses sometimes come to look forward to the sessions as an opportunity to learn more about one another.

When it becomes clear that feelings and reactivity are being stirred up, the clinician may increase the tempo of the questions, asking people to talk about the feelings rather than expressing them directly at the other person. For example, when tears come into the eyes of one, the clinician may ask the other if he or she noticed the tears and what kinds of thoughts the tears produced. When anger threatens to lead to direct conflict, the therapist can step up the pace and accentuate the low-key nature of the questions. What are the triggers that set off the chain reaction? What is there about self that makes the other so mad? What sort of formula has the couple worked out to slow the chain reaction when it threatens to run away with them? An important goal is to touch upon emotionally important issues and elicit thoughtful, calm responses (Bowen, 1971).

KEEPING SELF DETRIANGLED FROM THE FAMILY EMOTIONAL PROCESS

The emotional process between two people reaches out frequently to involve an important other. This is the process of the triangle described previously. When that third can remain in active contact with each of the others while remaining outside the emotional field between them, the emotional reactivity in the original twosome can resolve itself (Bowen, 1966, 1971). This is the theoretical basis for the task of maintaining emotional neutrality.

There are innumerable ways in which a clinician can take sides in the emotional process between the spouses. This can occur as easily when the clinician is quiet as when active. This is not much different from the manner in which he or she took sides in the process between his or her own parents. When one takes sides, one has joined the emotional process in the family. The effort to remain emotionally neutral is a central challenging task for the clinician in any clinical session. The effort to detriangle oneself from the family emotional process is the same as the effort to remain neutral.

When the clinician becomes absorbed in the content issues of the family, neutrality is easily compromised. A family can produce issues without end. When one such issue is apparently resolved, the family can produce another. The original issue can appear again at a later time as if it were a new topic. General themes of content include sex, money, and children and tend to revolve around the emotional themes of right and wrong, fairness, and rights.

When the therapist can find a relatively objective, neutral position from which to relate to the family, the flow of emotion between people and patterns of reactivity become apparent. Bowen (1971) comments on a position that is neither too close to nor too distant from the emotional process of the family. From that point, he is able to watch the emotional flow and view the process without becoming entangled. He is able to comment either seriously or with humor.

Such flexibility is the hallmark of the clinician who understands the nature of triangles and manages self well within them. It is not so much what the therapist says but his or her emotional position that is important. When caught in the family emotional process, almost anything he or she says produces reactivity in the family. When the clinician is neutral, almost anything he or she says aids thought and eases anxiety. Moreover, to be neutral is more than being humorous. Often light humor can dissolve the tension of an overly serious presentation of content. But the pursuit of humor can mark the therapist's own reactivity to the family. The idea is to relate to the emotionally difficult areas for the family without becoming a part of its emotional system.

DEMONSTRATING DIFFERENTIATION BY MANAGING SELF DURING THERAPY

The pressures toward togetherness operate between the clinician and family members just as within the family itself. When a person can state his or her convictions and principles clearly and then act in accordance with such beliefs, it is possible for the togetherness pressures to abate. In defining and acting on such a position, the clinician does not criticize the family or become involved in a feeling-laden debate. Bowen referred to this firm position for self as an *I-position*.

The I-position is more than a simple technique. It requires that the clinician have a clear grasp of his or her responsibility, particularly at times when the family emotional system is pressing him or her toward irresponsibility. The I-position is a movement to define and preserve self in the face of pressures to make all the same. With experience, a clinician can become familiar with routine sorts of situations that require a clear definition of self to a family. Nevertheless, anxious families can present unique situations without clear precedents, testing to the limits of the clinician's differentiation of self.

The I-position can be a simple statement of disagreement: "I'm listening to your words, but I don't agree with what you're saying." More complex and intense situations involve pressures for or against hospitalization, suicidal threats and gestures, pressures from the community, and a host of other efforts to press the clinician to behave in a manner contrary to his or her principles and responsibilities.

TEACHING THE FUNCTIONING OF EMOTIONAL SYSTEMS

Teaching about emotional systems is a natural part of assisting people to think about their situation and to work at managing their reactivity. Timing plays an important role in teaching. Early in the course of therapy and when anxiety is high, the clinician teaches by example. I-positions are part of the effort, and stories can help make a point that could not be heard if stated directly. When anxiety is low, ideas and comments can be presented more directly without problem. At such times, family members can hear ideas and consider them thoughtfully.

While the effort with two spouses remains an effective method of family therapy, it is not the only method derived from the Bowen theory. In the late 1960s, Bowen presented an account of his efforts to manage himself in his own family, to a conference of well-known family therapists. The ideas presented there began to enter his teaching efforts at Georgetown. He soon observed that the students were applying these ideas in their own families and were making faster progress in their nuclear families and in clinical work than others, including those in weekly family therapy. They were automatically transferring what they learned in their efforts with their families into their nuclear families and into their clinical work.

From such observations arose a new method of therapy called *coaching*. In this technique, the clinician functions more as a consultant and teacher than as a traditional therapist. Often coaching takes place with only one member of the family, although others may be seen as well. Sessions are often infrequent, with people seen generally once a month or at even less frequent intervals. The focus is on differentiation of self, with the coach assisting the direction of the effort. Progress comes from the person's own efforts at differentiation in the family and in other important relationships.

The following general guidelines help structure the process of coaching. The person works (1) to become a more accurate observer of self and the family, (2) to develop person-to-person relationships with each member of the family, (3) to increase the ability to control emotional reactivity to the family, and (4) to remain neutral or detriangled while relating to the emotional issues of the family.

BECOMING AN ACCURATE OBSERVER AND MANAGING REACTIVITY

Recognition and regulation of one's own emotional reactivity are central to the effort to becoming a more accurate observer of self and family. The better control one has over reactivity, the more detached one can be from emotional process and, consequently, one can be a more accurate observer. And the effort to observe more carefully, of course, leads to greater detachment and regulation of reactivity.

Any increase in objectivity about self and family that results from the effort to observe more accurately is of great benefit. One can see the interplay of people in the creation and maintenance of a problem. Taking sides becomes more difficult, and it becomes possible to understand emotionally that no one person is to blame for what happens in a family. When one understands that everyone plays a part, including oneself, it is difficult to be angry at anyone.

DEVELOPING PERSON-TO-PERSON RELATIONSHIPS

"In broad terms, a person-to-person relationship is one in which two people can relate personally to each other about each other, without talking about others (triangling), and without talking about impersonal things" (Bowen, 1974, p. 79). What is so simply described appears difficult for people to attain. In general, conversations can stay on this personal level only for a few seconds before the discomfort in one or both parties shifts the content to other people or events.

INCREASING THE ABILITY TO CONTROL EMOTIONAL REACTIVITY

The long-term effort to establish a person-to-person relationship to all living members of one's family is a significant challenge. Essentially an exercise in developing maturity and perspective, it requires that a person recognize and increasingly master the feelings and reactive behaviors that work against relating to another on a personal level. The specific behaviors and feelings are not the same for each person. For me, the effort highlights the mechanisms used to insulate self from others. One's own bluster and retreat cannot be overlooked as important factors in the inability to relate to another. Other people learn about physical responses to important others or about mental patterns that occur repeatedly, and so forth. The learning from such an effort is primarily for self, but the relationship system may benefit as well from the effort.

A variation of the effort to relate personally to each member of the family is to develop a person-to-person relationship with each parent. People often fail to see the point of such an effort. It is, indeed, very difficult. Relating tends to occur in well-established patterns of interaction. The parent tends to fall into parentlike behavior and the child into childlike postures and responses. Many people structure the relationship to parents to preserve a calm congeniality that blocks the person-to-person effort as effectively as conflictual distance. To relate personally to one's parents is a difficult place to begin to work on differentiation, and a coach may often suggest that a person begin with a more peripheral set of relationships surrounding the parents. A coach can be invaluable in embarking on and sustaining such an effort, particularly when the inevitable obstacles and diversions materialize.

REMAINING NEUTRAL

The effort to remain neutral in an emotional field is fundamentally the same as remaining detriangled, discussed earlier. Attention must be paid to interlocking triangles that constantly accompany the effort. One can seem to be progressing in a given triangle only to lose ground when an emotional onslaught comes from an unexpected direction. Allies are as much a problem as those who are antagonistic. The effort toward increased differentiation of self is by self, for self. It cannot be a joint project with another.

Frequent contact with family members, particularly when emotional reactivity is high, is important in the effort to remain neutral and ultimately to increase differentiation. Face-to-face contact is desirable, particularly during periods of anxiety. Generally, one is better off going alone to see family, at least when neutrality and differentiation are the goal. Spouses and children are obviously important people, but their presence can complicate the effort considerably. Bowen (1974) cautions that one cannot tell the family what one is trying to do and still make it work. Helpers and opponents can each stall a person's effort, and natural forces and processes can build into an insurmountable roadblock. A person who has some control of emotional reactivity and some ability to relate personally becomes important to everyone in the family.

Efforts with one's family should be undertaken with a great deal of thought and planning. Families are not all alike, and no general prescription can be given that will apply to all. Sometimes the effort to relate to one's family can lead to great personal reactivity. The coach needs to be aware of such possibilities and assist the person to think clearly about self, the family, and what can be accomplished. The effort to increase differentiation of self takes place minute by minute and day by day. When one can locate the effort in one's family, it is a plus. But it is not the only arena where the effort takes place.

Family systems therapy begins with a survey of the family emotional field or system. Much of the information is collected during the initial sessions, and the family and the clinician attempt to define the problem. The clinician gathers factual information producing a picture of how the family has functioned over time. Each nuclear family incorporates within themselves the processes characterizing the families of previous generations. The survey of the family emotional field serves as a road map or blueprint that the clinician can read and at times teach to the motivated family member.

As the information is collected, it is entered on the family diagram (see Figure 10.1). A few general conventions guide the construction of a family diagram, making the information it contains accessible to a knowledgeable reader. Males are represented by small squares and females by circles. The husband and wife of a nuclear family are depicted with the male on the left and the female on the right. A solid line (three sides of a rectangle in shape with the male on the upper left corner and the female on the upper right) connects them. Each of the children produced by the breeding paid is connected to the marital unit by a straight line. The birth order of the children is represented by placing the oldest on the left, and each succeeding sibling is placed to the right of the older sibling preceding it. In this manner each successive generation is represented, with the most recent generation on the bottom of the diagram.

FIGURE 10.1 | **THE W FAMILY'S FAMILY DIAGRAM**

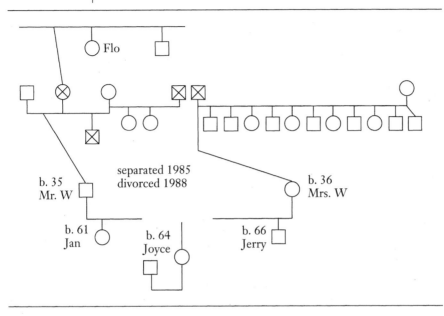

Basic information about each person is added to the diagram as it is collect-ed. Where possible, the date and place of birth; date, place, and cause of death (where applicable); level of education completed; brief employment history; and a brief summary of the individual's health, including all major health problems and those of a chronic nature, should be included for each person represented on the diagram. Dates are important and should be noted for all events listed. Employ-ment histories should include dates of job change, stated reasons for the change, and notable periods of unemployment. If health problems have been cited, the date of onset, the length and course of treatment, and the outcome should be added. A composite picture of the functioning of each family member is collect-ed in this manner.

In addition to information about each person, the clinician gathers data about the functioning of nuclear and extended family systems. Each spouse has a per-spective on the nuclear family. Their history has been marked by good and bad times, periods of tranquility and great upset. How does the family perceive the differences and account for the changes? Specific dates and events are always im-portant. Separations and divorces are significant events in the history of a family. How does each person view such an event? What changes accompanied it, and how does each person explain the change? Did people seem to function better or worse after the event? The composition of the household can change from time to time. Children grow up and leave home. Older family members come to live with younger ones. Births and deaths occur. How have such changes impacted on the family, and what does each person think about the changes?

In addition to information about a nuclear family, the extended family is also important. The clinician collects much the same information for the extended family. Furthermore, the frequency and the nature of contact between members of the nuclear and extended families is of interest. How does such contact influence the nuclear and extended family? Dates and accurate information about the nature of events in the extended family are important. Gradually the facts of a family across several generations can be collected, and a relatively accurate picture of its emotional functioning is produced.

The information of the family diagram need not be completed by the end of the first session. There are many ways to collect family information. Much of it is volunteered by informants in response to other questions asked by the clinician. The therapist begins simply by asking what has brought them to the point of involving a stranger in their family. What is the problem, what has been done to this point, and what have been the results? How do people think about what is happening and what has occurred? People will frequently have different points of view about the problem and how it works. As people begin to describe the problem and their thoughts about it, the clinician can gather basic information rather easily.

For the thoughtful clinician, the family diagram is never completed. No problem or event is ever understood fully. As *nodal events* (events subsequent to which the functioning of the family has shifted) become clear, more questions are available about the nature of the event and its impact. It is always important to separate fact from opinion, although both are important. Family members have opinions and assumptions that govern their behavior, but the framework of fact can tell a different, sometimes conflicting story. The squares, circles, and lines of a family diagram are unimportant in themselves. The information is only useful alongside the theoretical thinking of the clinician. It is part of the overall attitude of inquiry that the clinician seeks to maintain at all times. When linked to theory, the family diagram illustrates and illuminates the processes that have shaped a family's history and its present.

CASE EXAMPLE

The format of this volume requires that a case example is provided to illustrate the methodology of each therapy. While such a report can be valuable to a serious student, the reader tends to focus on what the clinician does to change the family, to make a difference. The thoughtful reader will have already garnered the point of the preceding paragraphs. From the point of view of the Bowen theory, the clinician works mostly to manage self, not to change the family. While the general guidelines of such an effort can be described, it is not possible to illustrate with dialogue excerpts the processes within the clinician.

This point is worth discussing in some detail. There is a great deal of interest in the therapy community in changing the client or the family. This is generally expressed in terms of an intervention that the therapist and/or others plan and then implement. There are numerous techniques accompanying such an effort. Some involve how the therapist speaks to the person or family; others focus on what the therapist does (e.g., where he or she sits, how the therapist positions others in the room, etc.). Yet other technical applications involve who attends the clinical session and how it is structured.

The point to be made, however, is that a clinician following the guidelines of the Bowen theory does not think in terms of changing the family directly. Consequently, there is no preparation of an intervention and no active effort to make the family different. How the clinician thinks is extremely important from this point of view, as is how he or she uses thinking to manage self. The clinician does not know what is best for a family, at least from this perspective. It is each person's task to think for self and to determine what action incorporates his or her own best interest and fulfills his or her responsibility to others.

It would be inaccurate, however, to suggest that the clinician attempting to practice with the Bowen theory as a guide eschews technique altogether. Clearly, each clinician maintains an armamentarium of techniques that are employed under certain conditions to produce certain results. The clinician applies the technical side of his or her effort mainly to self, however, and not to the family. For example, I have a number of self-regulatory techniques learned from many sources to recognize and manage my own reactivity. I draw on these at any time to help manage self in the presence of others. For the clinician, the overriding goal is the maintenance of emotional neutrality and differentiation of self, and each approaches this in different ways based on his or her own level of anxiety and differentiation of self.

The following case summary will attempt to describe the clinical effort with one family over a three-and-a-half-year period. During that time, only one person in the family was seen in 149 hour-long sessions. You may want to refer to the family diagram for orientation (Figure 10.1). Because of space limitations, nonessential information will be omitted, and additional important basic information will not be placed on the family diagram but will be given in the text. Three generations are represented. The Ws' three children, Jan, Joyce, and Jerry, represent the youngest generation. Mr. W's aunt (Flo) and Mrs. W's mother represent the oldest generation.

Mrs. W contacted the clinician in early 1986, about a year after she had left her husband of 30 years. The formal divorce negotiations had gotten underway poorly, and the tension level in the W family was very high. Mrs. W was extremely concerned about her children and their reactions to the separation and impending divorce. At that time, Jan, the oldest, was living with her father and was estranged from Mrs. W. Jan avoided all contact with her mother. Joyce, the middle child, was equally distant from her father. Joyce had married and was a strong advocate for her mother's position. Jerry, the youngest, was a college student. When at home, he lived in his father's house and was the only child to have contact with both parents.

The Ws had met and married as young adults. Mrs. W reported devoting herself in the early years of the marriage to helping her husband progress through the ranks of a large national corporation. Marital conflict arose relatively early, roughly coinciding with the first pregnancy. From that point on, the Ws' marriage was generally tense and rocky. Mrs. W generally saw Mr. W's behavior as the problem. She believed him to be critical of her and unpredictable. During this same period, Mrs. W began what became a long series of visits to mental health professionals and clergy, seeking help with the problem. Mr. W, in turn, found Mrs. W's behavior incomprehensible. Occasionally, he attended mental health consultations, but little relief was gained for either him or his wife in the process. Mrs. W did find it useful to talk to someone when tension levels in the family increased dramatically. A few years before reaching the decision to leave her husband, Mrs. W launched a small business that gave her purpose and some independent income. With her youngest child in college, Mrs. W decided the time had come to take action in the marital stalemate.

From the clinician's point of view, the W family was in a state of heightened anxiety manifested in intense emotional reactivity. The interlocking triangles of the W family operated in such a way that the anxiety came to be located primarily between the spouses and secondarily between Jan and Mrs. W and between Joyce and Mr. W. Mrs. W was a central figure in the family drama. The clinician believed that if he could understand the role of his own anxiety and reactivity in the family and if he could do something about his part of the problem, he would function differently in the family, and the family in turn could respond differently to him. Therefore, the initial task for the clinician was to manage himself in a way that was emotionally neutral while staying in contact with the emotional issues of the family as played out through Mrs. W.

The central reactive issues that Mrs. W presented during the first year and a half of consultation centered on her views of Mr. W's behavior, the difficulty of the divorce process, and the welfare of the oldest child, Jan, whom Mrs. W believed to be overly influenced by Mr. W. Mrs. W's frequent question was, "Will he [or she depending on the person referred to] ever see [Mrs. W's point of view and the reasons for her decisions]?" In short, her primary focus was to change the others, particularly Mr. W and Jan.

The clinician worked to maintain a position from which he could say whatever he thought to Mrs. W in a manner that minimized her tendency to overreact to him. He worked to communicate to Mrs. W that she had a choice in the reactive process between herself and her husband. She could act and react to him in a manner that stirred up the conflict, or she could work to manage herself in a more grown-up manner. The latter was the more difficult course initially, but it had within it the potential for a better resolution of the family problem. The choice was hers. She could remain mired in bitterness and anger; however, if she chose to pursue a different course, the clinician would do what he could to help her out. Mrs. W focused initially on revenge and "making him pay" for the problems in the marriage. The more she sought vengeance, the more Mr. W reacted, the more upset the children became, and the more complicated and stalled the divorce process became. Gradually, she understood the clinician's point, and despite many relapses she set out to manage herself less reactively to her husband.

In a similar vein, the clinician suggested to Mrs. W that she could view Jan as a helpless infant who needed her protection, or she could recognize that Jan was making important decisions and permit her the opportunity to bear the consequences of those decisions. On a practical level, that meant stopping the flood of anxiety directed at Jan in the form of pleas for togetherness, love, understanding, and closeness while simultaneously leaving the door open for Jan to approach if or when she chose. After considerable thought, Mrs. W began to challenge her own emotional view of her daughter.

Mrs. W slowly began to gain some control of her anxiety and reactivity. As she became less anxious, the clinician could act more as a coach and make further suggestions to her. One involved her own family. Mrs. W is the oldest of 12 children. Her parents had been relatively childlike people who assumed helpless postures toward the world. As the oldest, Mrs. W had stepped in to make the family function in the best way she knew how. She begged and borrowed food when the pantry was bare. She taught younger brothers and sisters, looked after their health, and did everything she knew to provide them with essential support.

Mrs. W's father died a few years prior to her separation, but her mother was still living. Mrs. W was highly reactive to her mother, frequently seeing her as deceptive, critical, and unpredictable. She never seemed to be able to please her mother. Although Mrs. W had remained involved with her family, generally as a figure of authority to be reckoned with, she had tended to avoid personal interactions with her mother. The clinician suggested that Mrs. W was fortunate to have two relationships of central importance in which she could practice managing her reactivity. Whenever Mr. W got the better of her, she could practice with her mother, and vice versa. Mrs. W slowly began to resume contact with her mother. As she learned more about managing her reactivity with her mother, Mrs. W appeared to translate what she had learned into her relationship with Mr. W. In fits and starts, the divorce negotiations began to progress.

A second suggestion concerned Mr. W's family, many of whom Mrs. W had known personally during the years of marriage. These people were unaware of the Ws' separation and impending divorce. The clinician suggested that Mrs. W might find it useful to resume her contacts with people in that family who had been important to her. The goal would not be to embarrass anyone or to reveal any secrets but to keep important people in contact with one another and to allow what resources the family could bring to bear on the situation to have full play. In early 1987, when a death occurred in the family, Mrs. W attended the funeral. She was well received by the family and reestablished contact with Mr. W's aunt, Flo. This became an important contact.

About a month after this event, a major shift took place in the divorce negotiations. Mrs. W dropped her notions of revenge and thought out a clear proposal for a settlement that met her needs and that allowed Mr. W room for negotiation. She presented her proposal to him immediately. Although negotiations continued with progress and regression, this proposal was essentially accepted and became the basis of the divorce decree a few months later. Various family members pressured Mrs. W to change her mind. Some argued she was being too harsh and others too lenient. Mrs. W thought her position was equitable and said so. Because she had developed her position carefully and clearly, she was able to maintain it under pressure, providing the stability for the divorce decree, which was arrived at without trial by mutual agreement.

Mrs. W had been plagued continually by an intense fear that she would "lose her children to her husband." This meant for her that her children would abandon her, accept her husband's viewpoint that she was the cause of the problem, blame her for the disruption of the family, and be unduly influenced by him in ways she considered unsound. Although she had begun to work on this anxiety with regard to Jan, it persisted after the divorce. In later summer 1988, following the divorce, Mrs. W traveled to spend a few days with Flo. She returned with a new sense of stability and perspective on the family and its problems. Shortly thereafter, Flo began to correspond with Jan and the other children. She had tended to function like a grandmother to the W children, who had not known why contact had decreased in recent years. Jan responded to Flo, and Mrs. W's anxieties about Jan decreased, even though Jan remained out of contact with her mother. Later that fall, Flo came for a visit. She made contact directly with Mr. W and with Jan. The Ws appeared to relax.

Early the following year, as part of the final settlement of the divorce, the Ws were to exchange family mementos. Mrs. W had many from their wedding, and Mr. W had a collection of their children's items. The mementos were an emotional issue for Mrs. W, and the exchange became bogged down. Mrs. W became upset and threatened legal action. The clinician simply pointed out to Mrs. W that she had an interesting opportunity to approach the problem of her anxiety about the children. Over a period of several days, Mrs. W wrote Mr. W a detailed personal letter reciting her memories of the children. She realized, in fact, that she had the mementos in her memory. She reported to Mr. W that she had laughed and cried as she remembered the various objects and the episodes they represented. She knew he had always tried to be a good and responsible father, and she would leave the mementos with him because he would undoubtedly enjoy them. She took the letter and her own items to Mr. W at his house, gave them to him, and they talked for a few minutes on the porch. Afterward she reported a great sense of relief and the complete disappearance of the anxiety about the children. From that point on, she and Mr. W were able to establish basic communication with one another, particularly in matters concerning the welfare of the children. This has resulted over time in a gradual lessening of the estrangement between Joyce and her father, who now have created a shaky but nonetheless working relationship with one another.

Within a month or two of these events with Mr. W, Mrs. W had an opportunity to manage her own reactivity differently with her family of origin. Her youngest brother had always been a focus of her mother's concern. This brother, Jay, had been married and divorced and was at the time living in a trailer on the farm, not far from his mother, who occupied the farmhouse. Jay's life course had been difficult, and his functioning appeared marginal. His mother began to express indirectly her wish that the family farm be left to Jay when she died. This created a furor among the 12 siblings. The farm represented many emotional things to different members of the family. Those opposed to their mother's idea turned to Mrs. W to lead the fight. She had always been a proponent of "fairness" in the family, and she had always occupied an influential position within the family emotional network. Those favoring Jay's inheritance began to sound her out as well, trying to determine her position and how best to contend with her opposition.

Mrs. W initially reacted with anger at her mother's wish. As she thought about the situation, however, she began to recognize more clearly her emotional position in the family. She described that position as one of overresponsibility and "knowing what's best" for everyone. She thought through more carefully her own idea of responsibility for herself and to the family. She composed a personal letter to her mother, going over past emotional events and commenting on her changing understanding of her mother's position and the factors with which she had to contend. She concluded by communicating to her mother her own position on the matter of the inheritance, namely that it was her mother's responsibility to distribute her property as she saw the need and Mrs. W would support her wishes. She worked to retain a relatively neutral stance to her siblings. She did not tell them of her communication to her mother but encouraged each to think his or her position through independently and communicate it to their mother.

Events came to a head at a family reunion held at the farm. Mrs. W attended and worked to have personal contact with all of her siblings. She spent time alone with her mother on a more personal basis than she had for many years previously. Her oldest brother, the second child in the family, asked to see her. They met in the barn, where he demanded to know what she wanted and how she intended to influence the inheritance. Mrs. W was able to stay relatively calm. She told him she had communicated her views to their mother and that "fair was fair." Her brother remained angry, and Mrs. W disengaged herself from the conflict without attacking her brother in retaliation. From this point on, Mrs. W began to have more contact with this brother. Their old childhood rivalries surfaced in ways that Mrs. W could recognize more clearly than ever before. She was able to manage herself differently with him. Along with the more childish interactions, a different level of communication also occurred, one more mature and interesting to both. This brother also had more interaction with their mother.

Following this series of exchanges, Mrs. W began a project of thinking through her relationship to each of her brothers and sisters and, as she called it, "letting them go." She spent much time thinking about herself and each of them. She wrote personal letters to each, outlining her thinking about them and herself. As she progressed, she would report being increasingly calm. She reported a greater sense of aloneness, which she carefully distinguished from loneliness. The aloneness was at times uncomfortable, but it also made clear to her that she now had the responsibility only for herself and not for the others.

She also began to be interested in past generations of her family. She began a project to learn more about her grandparents and their lives. This led her to contact older members of the family, distant relatives with whom she had little or no contact for years. She was generally well received, and she found the visits interesting and satisfying. In the process, she began to examine her own relationship to her paternal grandmother, an important figure in her early years whom she tended to idolize. As she became more objective about her grandmother, recognizing her weaknesses as well as her strengths, she also began to see her own mother from a somewhat different viewpoint. This led to a further series of interactions with her mother. She was able to visit her grandmother's grave, which she had never done, and she reported a brief period of mourning that she had not experienced at the time of her grandmother's death.

Mrs. W continues her efforts with her family. Jan remains essentially out of contact, although she has seen her mother on two family occasions. These meetings did not result in conflict. Mrs. W is able to have contact with Mr. W when needed, and they can communicate about events in the family important to each other. Mrs. W is in ever-increasing and widening contact with her family. As she learns more about herself and her past, she behaves with less anxiety and reactivity. She describes her family as calmer than ever before.

Mrs. W reports that she is functioning better than she has ever previously. She is active, employed, and in contact with a great number of people. Her family comments on the difference in her but appear baffled by it. Some inquire if she is ill; others seem delighted. For the past two years, the role of the coach has been minimal. Mrs. W has developed a motivation and plan of her own, which she implements in her own way. Members of her family, with responsibility for themselves squarely on their own shoulders, appear to be functioning with greater stability than previously.

EVALUATION

A working theory is not static. As more thinking occurs and attempts are made to expand both theory and application, changes occur. The Bowen theory of 1990 is not the same theory as that of 1966, even though the major concepts remain the same. At any given moment in time, staff members are engaged in a variety of projects in theory development and application. The list of interesting areas is long, including a major area applying theory to chronic illness. Currently various staff members of the Family Center use the Bowen theory to guide their work with AIDS, cancer, and other difficult disease presentations. The use of various biofeedback devices is often a part of the effort, as staff work to understand more fully the operation of the human emotional system and reactivity.

A second area of interest applies the Bowen theory to processes in society. This interest appears particularly relevant, as conditions in the world are expected to change over the next century faster than at any previous time in the history of life on Earth. The pace of change will require living things to adjust at an apparently unprecedented rate. No one knows for sure what the outcome will be, but theory can help us predict how humans will adjust and how the anxiety generated by changing conditions may be manifested.

Any theory that aims toward a linkage with science must be consistent with the natural world. It must fit with what is known and developing as scientific fact. Consequently, there is a great deal of interest in the natural sciences, with various individuals pursuing avenues for contacting and connecting with researchers and thinkers outside the traditional disciplines of mental health. Often such people are invited to address Family Center meetings and to participate less formally in other activities. The list of distinguished guest lecturers at the annual Georgetown Symposium reflects this interest: J. T. Bonner, E. O. Wilson, Verner Suomi, Stephen Suomi, Melvin Konner, and Roger Payne, among others.

The potential for the applications of a natural systems theory is vast. The descriptions given here are just a few of the various subjects and projects that surface at the Family Center. The results of such efforts are presented each year at various symposia sponsored by the Family Center and other organizations. Occasionally, the papers from such symposia are published as a group; but the effort is time-consuming and expensive, and many of these presentations never reach publication. Various individuals on the faculty and staff of the Family Center contribute sections to various anthologies of the family therapy literature and write more substantial pieces on theory.

The Family Center itself does not conduct formal research on the efficacy of psychotherapy. With limited time and resources available, individuals have directed their energies more toward the advancement, refinement, and extension of theory to new areas. Each investigator presents his or her findings at various discussion meetings, and each develops ways for checking up on self. From time to time, staff agree to participate in various studies conducted by people outside the Family Center. Generally, the results turn up in someone's doctoral dissertation and are never published. In the late 1970s and early 1980s, however, faculty and staff participated in a therapy outcome research project sponsored by the court system of a large state. This research was designed and conducted by an outside organization and involved other clinical groups in addition to the Family Center. The results of this study have not yet been published by the responsible organization but should be in the near future.

ANNOTATED SUGGESTED READINGS

Bowen, M. (1978). *Family therapy in clinical practice*. Northvale, NJ: Jason Aronson.
     The development of Bowen's ideas and the Bowen theory are traced through this collection of his published papers, arranged chronologically. The primary source for the Bowen theory.

Kerr, M. E., & Bowen, M. (1988). *Family evaluation: An approach based on Bowen theory*. New York: Norton.
     A detailed discussion of the Bowen theory, culminating in a chapter on the clinical aspects of family evaluation. Bowen details the development of his ideas and his commitment to theory in an epilogue.

Papero, D. V. (1990). *Bowen family systems theory*. Boston: Allyn & Bacon.
     This slim volume provides a basic introduction to the Bowen theory.

REFERENCES

Bowen, M. (1966). The use of family theory in clinical practice. *Comprehensive Psychiatry*, 7, 345–374.

Bowen, M. (1971). Family therapy and family group therapy. In H. Kaplan & B. Saddock (Eds.), *Comprehensive group psychotherapy*. Baltimore: Williams & Wilkins.

Bowen, M. (1974). Toward the differentiation of self in one's own family of origin. In P. Lorio & R. Andres (Eds.), *Georgetown family symposia: Volume L*. Washington, DC: Department of Psychiatry, Georgetown Medical Center.

Bowen, M. (1975). Family therapy after twenty years. In S. Arieti (Ed.), *American handbook of psychiatry*. New York: Basic Books.

Bowen, M. (1978). *Family therapy in clinical practice*. New York: Jason Aronson.

Calhoun, J. B. (1967). Ecological factors in the development of behavioral anomalies. In *Comparative psychiatry*. New York: Grune & Stratton.

Kerr, M. E., & M. Bowen. (1988). *Family evaluation: An approach based on Bowen theory*. New York: Norton.

Toman, W. (1961). *Family constellation: A psychological game*. New York: Springer.

CHAPTER 11

Object Relations Family Therapy

ALLIE C. KILPATRICK,
EBB G. KILPATRICK, JR., AND
JANICE T. CALLAWAY

DEFINITION

A relatively new model of family treatment—object relations theory—is considered to be the bridge between psychoanalysis, the study of individuals, and family theory, the study of social relationships. It may be defined as

> ...the psychoanalytic study of the origin and nature of interpersonal relationships, and of the intrapsychic structures which grew out of past relationships and remain to influence present interpersonal relations. The emphasis is on those mental structures that preserve early interpersonal experiences in the form of *self and object-images*. (Nichols, 1984, p. 183)

Object relations theory is an existing general framework in psychoanalysis and psychiatry that provides the means for understanding the earliest developmental phases of childhood. It studies the attachment and differentiation from others—a process that is of much importance not only for the personality functioning of the individual, but also for families and social adaptation. The lack of differentiation of family members has become one of the cornerstones of Bowen's work (1978) in understanding distressed families, as well as Stierlin's work (1976) in studying larger social group functioning (Slipp, 1984).

Object relations family therapy (ORFT) is derived from the application of object relations theory to family development and treatment. Object relations theory and its therapeutic approach regard the individual's inner world and external family as components of an open system. It can be used to develop typologies of family interaction and treatment that take into consideration the intrapsychic influences on family patterns, which in turn affect the client's personality. As Slipp (1984) has stated, psychoanalysis and family therapy can complement each other in a number of ways to enhance the theoretical understanding in both fields and to foster a treatment approach that is dependent not on the theoretical orientation of the therapist but rather on the needs of the client couple and the significant others surrounding the couple.

Object relations theories have not been well integrated. Finkelstein (1987) describes them as generally the result of various individuals writing alone or as parts of different "schools," using different terms and confronting different aspects of relationships with others. Therefore, each writer presents a somewhat different picture of human development and interpersonal relationships. Object relations theories are based primarily on the two sources: (1) the psychoanalysis of individual adults and (2) the direct observation of infants and children and their parents. The observation of adult couples has not played a part in the development of psychoanalytic object relations theories although practitioners have applied object relations theory in marital therapy.

HISTORICAL DEVELOPMENT

While there is no integrated object relations theory, many theorists have developed their own idiosyncratic object relations perspective that roughly fits Freud's root theory. These theorists have developed new concepts and constructs that build on those of Freud, yet also add to his theories. For example, Ackerman, Boszormenyi-Nagy, Bowen, Jackson, Lidz, Minuchin, Satir, Whitaker, and other pioneers of the family therapy movement had their training in psychoanalytic theory. Most have retained at least some of these concepts in the development of their own models of family theory. Although they abandoned the depth psychology of individuals and the focus on unconscious vicissitudes of instinctual drives, the early family therapists studied the realities of family and social interactions and built constructs of relationships.

Freud is undisputedly considered the father of psychoanalysis. Psychoanalysis is historically a conservative discipline and, as described by Nichols (1984), its followers choose to modify and refine its basic concepts rather than replace them with new ones. Therefore, it seems appropriate to begin by acknowledging Freud's contribution to the psychoanalytic study of family life and its foundation for object relations family therapy.

FREUD

Freud's (1905, 1940) psychology was a study of instinctual drives, which he labels the id. He sees the family as the social context in which the child develops through the oral, anal, phallic, genital, and later stages and learns to control and channel impulses in socially acceptable ways through the ego and the superego (Brill,

1938). Since most of this learning occurs very early in life, and since sexual frustration is highly charged with anxiety, many of these crucial interactions are repressed and unconscious. Freud declares that a cure for emotional problems is based on making the unconscious conscious (Breuer & Freud, 1895). He first postulated that the basic drives were sexual and self-preservative. He later dropped the self-preservative drive in favor of the erotic or sexual drive as the major instinctual life force (libido), but then even later he added the aggressive drive as the destructive life force element.

Freud, in his first major presentation of his ideas to his psychiatric colleagues, set forth his seduction theory as the cause of hysterical neurosis. This early theory states that, as a result of an actual traumatic event—the seduction by an adult or older sibling—the child developed hysterical or obsessional symptoms (Freud, 1940). Freud later abandoned this theory and turned away from traumatic events in the family—actual interaction—to focus on unconscious fantasy and instinctual drives. Slipp (1984) and others believe that family therapy as a field would likely have been established sooner had Freud not abandoned his initial formulation of the seduction theory, as this was the first psychiatric theory that involved family dynamics and emphasized the pathological influence of one person on another. Freud studied the developmental psychology of children, but he was more concerned with the influence of the family on individual personality development than with family dynamics.

Freud's view was really, as Dicks (1967) suggests, a physiological psychology of impulse gratifications sufficient to account for the physical base of sexual attraction, perhaps, but short of the human's search for relationships. It should be pointed out, in fairness to Freud, that he does associate the libido concept with object seeking. *Object* in psychoanalytic literature refers to persons or things that are significant in one's psychic life. The phrase *object relations* refers to the individual's attitude and behavior toward such objects. The infant's first contacts with its significant objects, for example, the mother's breast, are exclusively self-centered and concerned simply with the gratification the objects afford. When the infant begins to experience need satisfaction through the object, then the object is "cathected," or psychic energy is expended toward the object or the mental representations of the object. Psychoanalysts assume that a continuing relationship with an object develops only gradually to the point at which, even in the absence of the object, the child maintains an interest in the object. One of the important characteristics of the experience of early object relations is a high degree of ambivalence. Feelings of love alternate with feelings of hate, the hate resulting from frustrating experiences when gratifications are not experienced. As the child grows, the conscious feelings toward the object tend to be loving, whereas the unconscious bears more of the hateful feelings (Barnard & Corrales, 1979; Brenner, 1973).

Freud influenced many theorists who modified his work. Those who have had a part historically in the early development of object relations theory and therapy have included Ferenczi, Klein, Fairbairn, and others. Historians give varying degrees of credit to various of these contributors for the extent and influence of their contributions, some of which are briefly presented here as they developed historically.

FERENCZI

One of the most gifted of Freud's pupils, Ferenczi is generally considered to be the father of object relations theory. He maintains that Freud's original seduction theory was correct and should never have been abandoned. It is not the distortions of reality caused by the client's fantasies and instincts that cause psychiatric illness, but actual parental neglect and trauma. Ferenczi's "active" approach to treatment attempts to re-create the early parent–child interaction so the client can relive and master the parental deprivations (Ferenczi, 1920). The therapist's empathic responsiveness during this regressive reenactment of the parental relationship encourages resumption of the client's growth and development. Ferenczi believes that a passive and abstinent approach with sicker clients only recapitulated and reinforced the client's experience of parental neglect and emotional abandonment. He differs from Freud also in his awareness of the interpersonal relationship of the therapist and client, and his approach avoids a negative transference and a resultant poor therapeutic outcome. Ferenczi thinks that with sicker clients there are always countertransference feelings that cannot and should not be avoided. Emotional interaction between the client and the analyst does occur and has to be worked with in a controlled fashion. Therapy, therefore, becomes a dyadic system rather than one in which the therapist is a detached, objective observer. Ferenczi was the first to report that clients projected their internal fantasies onto the analyst and others in an attempt to use these persons to fulfill their needs. Such reports were precursors of the concept of projective identification. Ferenczi was also the first to note that a child could act out the unconscious conflicts of a parent (Slipp, 1984).

KLEIN

Klein (1948), one of Ferenczi's analysts, brings together many of his insights into a systematic theory. In studying her adult and child clients, she focuses on the earliest years of life and has contributed significantly to our awareness of infant–mother interaction. Klein sees the infant as object-oriented from birth. Object relations theory has Klein's work as its basic foundation, especially the subjective dialogue between the self and the projected or introjected object. Through the interplay of projection and introjection, the infant attempts to relate to the mother, who is seen as good and bad, as a part, and later as a whole object.

According to Slipp (1984), Klein's major contribution to the understanding of infantile development is the role played by fantasy. For her, object relations derive from fantasies. Fantasy is the method the infant uses to regulate itself and to become attached to objects. The infant employs fantasy to explore its world and to communicate with the mother. It uses fantasy as the basis for the primitive mental mechanisms known as splitting, projective identification, and introjection. *Splitting* is the fantasy that the ego can split itself off from an unwanted aspect of itself as pain, hunger, and so forth, or can split an object into two or more objects as good and bad, pain and comfort, and pleasure and displeasure. *Projective identification* is the result of the projection of parts of the self into an object. It can be viewed as the infant's attempt to control or return to the mother's body. *Introjection* occurs when the object is incorporated into the ego, which then identifies with some or all of the object's characteristics (Segal, 1973). Klein postulates that in the first six months of life, the infant organizes experiences by primitive mental processes of splitting, projection, and introjection. At about eight months, the infant begins to recognize its mother as a whole person about whom ambivalence is felt. As an object, she need no longer be split into separate part-objects.

FAIRBAIRN

Fairbairn (1954) goes much further than Klein toward object relations and away from instinctual drive psychology. He elaborates upon the concepts of Freud and Klein and is said to have evolved the purest, clearest object relations theory. His view provides a viable bridge between intrapsychic dynamics and the interpersonal or systems level. Fairbairn believes that libido is object-seeking— not pleasure-seeking, as Freud had postulated. Pleasure thus is not a goal in itself but a means of forming an attachment. To Fairbairn the most basic motive of life is a person's need for a satisfying object relationship. He saw the individual's need for others and the desire to feel needed by them as the foundation for social life. Instinct is merely a function of the ego, and aggression is a response to frustration of a person's efforts to find affirmation and satisfaction from the object sought.

The process of interacting with one's significant others is seen by Fairbairn as a mixture of satisfying and frustrating experiences, love and hate, acceptance and rejection. If, however, the family system is such that the child can test the reality of the parents' responses and can recognize the real person of the mother, father, and siblings, the child can learn a basic sense of trust in self and in one's significant others. He or she can thus develop a tolerance for ambivalent aspects of his or her relationships. Fairbairn equates maturity with the capacity for closeness and intimacy. While he recognizes the importance of individuation, he stresses the importance of tolerance or regression in adult relationships. He also provides a model of the personality in which regression and the gratification of childish needs are part of a healthy and intimate marriage. Finkelstein (1987) believes that the power of Fairbairn's analysis is that he has evolved an object relations theory that is in total harmony with the marital vows. Applying his theories, marriage appears to be based on one's most basic and lifelong need for attachment.

BALINT

Balint (1968) notes that some clients must face the awfulness of there being nothing but an emptiness, something missing in their personality. He realizes that this is an early, fundamental flaw that influences the way the ego related to objects thereafter. He calls it "the basic fault," and suggests that it arose from a failure of fit between mother and baby and led to insecurity in future object relations. For Balint, the basis for personality development rests upon satisfactory object relations. Therefore, therapists would need to offer themselves as objects with whom the client dares to relate again in order to repair the fault and recover human relatedness (Balint, 1968; Scharff & Scharff, 1987).

WINNICOTT

Winnicott (1965) has noted a split in the personality resulting from difficulties in early mother–baby interactions. He believes that unempathic mothering can cause the baby to try to mold itself to its mother's needs when its mother cannot respond in a flexible way to her baby. This leads to the baby's suppression of its "true self" and to the development of a "false self," which is typically compliant while the true self diminishes or is nourished secretly inside the self. Winnicott thinks that mothering does not have to be perfect but "good enough" that the infant can feel loved and cared for by the mother and valued for himself or herself. In this situation of trust and good-enough mothering, the infant's true self will develop without distortion. Winnicott's major contribution to understanding self and otherness is in his concept of *transitional objects*. If the early relationship with its mother is secure and loving, the infant will gradually be able to give her up, meanwhile retaining her loving support in the form of a good internal object. In the process, most little children adopt a transitional object to ease the loss—a stuffed animal or blanket that the child clings to during the time when he or she starts to realize that the mother is a separate object and can go out of sight (Winnicott, 1965).

GUNTRIP

Guntrip (1961) adds to Fairbairn's view the hypothesis that in severely regressed schizoid states, the libidinal system is further subdivided when part of it is split off as a withdrawn, regressed unconscious self that has no object to which to relate. This withdrawal from reality into the self may become the major part of the psyche in severely pathological states, or it may be a heavily defended, secret part of the self that is not readily discovered. Guntrip sees this need for withdrawal as proof of terrifying anxiety about losing the self and disappearing into the void (Guntrip, 1961; Scharff & Scharff, 1987).

DICKS

Dicks (1967) applies object relations theory to couples dynamics in a pioneering psychodynamic method of marital therapy. During selection of a marriage partner, the ego chooses on the basis of finding an ideal object in the spouse. Because the marital relationship is similar to the early mothering experience, offering a permanent attachment to a caring figure, it brings out feelings from the infantile experience. In the perceived safety of the marital relationship, the repressed object relationships of the original parenting experiences return to seek expression, both good and bad. Each spouse now sees the other as partly ideal and partly exciting and rejecting of need, as were former objects. In an open, healthy relationship, this offers an opportunity to reintegrate the repressed systems and expand the ego. However, in a closed, rigid system, the repressed relationships are repeated and further repressed to preserve the marriage despite impoverishing it. The ego, instead of confirming the separate identity of the object or spouse, then expects the spouse to conform to fit this inner picture. This mutual collusion to repress the troublesome object relationships causes problems for the couple. The tendency is to preserve the marital relationship by projecting the objects or ego onto the children. The children are then seen as a hated part of the self or spouse and bear a resemblance to a hated part of the grandparents. Any one child may be more or less predisposed by birth order, sex, physical likeness, constitution, or circumstance to carry any one projection.

BION

Bion (1961) applies the projection hypothesis to the functioning of groups. He views the work group as one beset by behaviors that relate to defenses against anxiety, not to work. Certain members of the group deal with their confusion and helplessness by projecting parts of themselves into other group members who, for their own reasons, become like the projections. Multiple processes of this projective identification cluster around subgroups within the group that express basic defenses against the anxiety of the whole group in relation to the group leader. This group theory proved to be applicable to families, which can be seen as small, parent-led groups trying to do their work of raising the next generation (Scharff & Scharff, 1987).

KERNBERG

Kernberg (1975, 1976) has made a crucial contribution to integrating psychoanalytic theory and practice into a unified approach by bringing together object relations theory, drive theory, structural theory, and ego psychology. He considers biologic and social forces as interactive, not distinct dichotomies; uses general systems theories; and traces the process through developmental stages. His contributions are further elaborated later in this chapter.

CURRENT STATUS

As stated earlier, object relations family therapy has no overall integrated theory. Various theorists have developed their own perspectives over the years, and others have made attempts at integration. In 1974, Foley made the point that the major issue in family therapy at that time seemed to be the relationship of an intrapsychic viewpoint to a systems concept. His question was, "Is it possible to reconcile the two, or is there any value in doing this?" (p. 167). He then pointed to Framo and Boszormenyi-Nagy—two theorists who would bring the intrapsychic and the systems concepts together by attempting to relate ideas derived mainly from psychoanalysis, such as transference and introjects, to systems theory.

Framo (1972) calls his approach a transactional one that leans heavily on the notion of projective identification as applied to a family system and that presents a new way of viewing transference. He builds on Fairbairn's notion of the fundamental need for a satisfying object-relationship. He feels that when a child interprets the parents' behavior as rejection or desertion and cannot give up the external object, it internalizes this loved but hated parent in the inner world of self as an introject or psychological representation. In the course of time, these split-off object relations become important as the person begins to force close relationships into fitting this internal role model. Framo goes beyond Dicks in that he attempts to widen the dyadic, marital field by including several generations of the family. He sees the introject of the parent as a critical issue in family therapy and one that is much neglected. Framo is trying to combine a basically intrapshychic concept, introjects, with a systems concept. In doing so, he draws out the implications in Bowen's formulation of family theory for object relations theory.

Boszormenyi-Nagy and Spark (1973) maintain that parents who have been deprived of their own parents through death or separation often see their child as a parental substitute. This is similar to Bowen's concepts of triangulation and the need for a three-generational viewpoint. Unlike Bowen, Boszormenyi-Nagy and Spark are concerned about introjects and object relations. They see family functioning as a specialized multiperson organization of shared fantasies and complementary need gratification patterns that are maintained for the purpose of handling past object loss experience.

Foley (1974) also interviewed Jay Haley, who stated that no compromise is possible between intrapsychic and systems concepts since the frames of reference are totally different. Haley sees the introduction of object relations into family therapy as an attempt to placate the psychoanalytic community since the concept belongs to an intrapsychic approach. However, placating or not, therapists and theorists are currently achieving just this integration. Monumental groundbreaking work in this area has been done by Scharff and Scharff (1982, 1987) and Scharff (1989) who coined the term *object relations family therapy*, and Slipp (1984, 1988).

For Scharff (1987), object relations family therapy derives from psychoanalytic principles of "listening, responding to unconscious material, interpreting, developing insight, and working in the transference and countertransference toward understanding and growth" (p. 3). The family, however, is not related to as a set of individuals but is viewed as a system comprising sets of relationships that function in ways unique to that family. The immediate goal is not symptom resolution, but progression through the current developmental phase of family life, with improved ability to work as a unit and to differentiate among and meet the individual members' needs.

Slipp (1984, 1988) differs from the main thrust of object relations theory—the psychoanalytic study and treatment of borderline and narcissistic personality disorders. His work broadened the focus to include other client populations and applied its concepts to family studies in order to search for defeating patterns in the family influencing the identified patient. He studied diverse client populations and their families to explore the interaction and interdependence of individual dynamics and family system functioning. His ultimate goal is to apply an integrated understanding to family treatment.

Some of the major contributions of Scharff and Scharff, Slipp, and others are explicated in the following section on the tenets of the object relations model of family therapy. Current therapists have made great strides toward providing an integrated theory and model for object relations family therapy.

TENETS OF THE MODEL

A fundamental tenet of object relations family therapy is that treatment of the individual and treatment of the family are theoretically and therapeutically consistent with each other and are both parts of an open system. Both intrapersonal and interpersonal components have a constantly dynamic relationship with each other. An assumption is that resolving problems in relationships in the client's current family necessitates intrapsychic exploration and resolution of those unconscious object relationships internalized from early parent–child relationships. A further assumption is that these influences affect and explain the nature of present interpersonal problems.

The basic tenets of object relations family therapy, though based upon psychoanalysis, continue to be modified and refined. Specific tenets and concepts currently used in assessment and intervention are presented for further understanding.

SPLITTING

Freud (1940) originally mentions *splitting* as a defense mechanism of the ego and defines it as a lifelong coexistence of two contradictory dispositions that do not influence each other. Kernberg (1972) traces the process of splitting through developmental stages. The first stage, from birth to two months, is undifferentiated. The second stage, from two to eight months, involves splitting of the "all good" (organized around pleasurable mother–child interactions) and "all bad" (derived from painful and frustrating interactions) self-images, object-images, and their affective links. The third stage, from 8 to 36 months, involves the separation of the self from object-representations. Splitting into good and bad persists, and this is seen as the fixation point for clients with borderline characteristics. The fourth stage consists of integrating these opposing good and bad emotional images so that the separate self and object representations are each both good and bad. It is at this point that the ego, superego, and id become firmly established as intrapsychic structures, and the defenses of splitting are replaced by repression. Slipp (1984) sees this stage as the fixation point for neurotic dysfunction. In the last stage, internalized object representations are reshaped through actual current experiences with real people. A goal of object relations family therapy is to assist in the development of this integration and reshaping.

INTROJECTION

Introjection is a crude and global form of taking in, as if those fragments of self-other interactions were swallowed whole. It is the earliest and most primitive form of the internalization of object relations, starting on a relatively crude level and becoming more sophisticated as the child develops (Nichols, 1984). The child reproduces and fixates its interactions with significant others by organizing memory traces that include images of the object, the self interacting with the object, and the associated affect. Good and bad internal objects are included, each with images of the object and self. For example, if the mother or mothering parent yells, images of a bad parent and an unworthy self are stored.

The infant's first internalized objects are fragmented or experienced as part objects, and as either "good" or "bad." Klein (1946) developed two developmental positions that depend on the role of object relations, replacing Freud's instinctual maturational phases of oral, anal, phallic, and genital. Introjection of bad objects, like an empty breast or angry face, generates fear and anxiety, leading the baby into a paranoid position. Around the time of weaning, the infant begins to experience the mother as one person, with both good and bad qualities. The infant also discovers that he or she has the capacity to hurt loved ones. This leads to a depressive position where the baby is ambivalent toward the mother and feels guilty about inflicting pain on her. This position is instrumental in the development of oedipal conflict beginning in the second year of life (Nichols, 1984). The paranoid and depressive positions play crucial roles in the understanding of dynamics and formulation of treatment in object relations family therapy.

PROJECTIVE IDENTIFICATION

Identification is a more complex level of internalization involving the internalization of a role. Objects and self-images are clearly differentiated. The result of identification is the child's taking on certain roles and behaviors of the parents. A child of two can be observed imitating parents in many ways. On the other hand, *projective identification* is a defense mechanism that operates unconsciously whereby unwanted aspects of the self are attributed to another person and that person is induced to behave in accordance with these projected attitudes and feelings (Nichols, 1984). Unlike projection, it is truly an interactional process. The concepts of transference (Freud, 1905), scapegoating (Vogel & Bell, 1960), trading of dissociations (Wynne, 1965), merging (Boszormenyi-Nagy, 1967), irrational role assignments (Framo, 1970), symbiosis (Mahler, 1952), and family projective process (Bowen, 1965) are all variants of Klein's (1946) concept of projective identification.

COLLUSION

An integral part of projective identification is the concept of *collusion*, by which the recipient of the split-off part of the partner does not disown the projection but acts on the conscious or unconscious message (Stewart, Peters, Marsh, & Peters, 1975). Simply stated, a need for a "strong" man to gratify a "weak" woman requires that both partners agree to the assigned roles. Such collusion is often obvious and circumscribed and may not be problematic for the couple or family. When the assigned roles are challenged, the couple experiences discomfort or symptom formation. Each partner's ego identity (which includes both good and bad objects) is preserved by having one or more bad objects split off onto his or her partner. Thus each partner disowns bad-object introjects, and needs the other to accept the projection of these introjects. Each begins to subtly conform to the inner role model of the other in a collusive manner (Piercy et al., 1986). Dicks (1963) believes that this collusive process continues because both partners hope for integration of lost introjects by finding them in each other.

Difficulty within the therapeutic context arises when there are a denial of collusion, an exaggeration of differences, and attempts to obscure clarification of the process. Therapists using object relations theory attempt in various ways to help couples own their introjects and begin seeing their partners as actual individuals, and not projected parts of themselves. Collusion, shared fantasy, and projective identification are not limited to the marital dyad but may be seen in all of an individual's significant relationships, including the one with the therapist.

EGO IDENTITY

Erikson (1956, 1963) theorizes that introjections and identifications form the basis of ego identity, representing the most sophisticated level of the internalization process. Ego identity is the overall organization of synthesized identifications and introjections. It provides a coherent, continuous self-concept and a consolidated world of object representations and fantasies. The internal world of object relations never exactly corresponds to the actual world of real people. It is an approximation that is strongly influenced by the earliest object images, introjections, and identifications.

This phenomenon corresponds to the concept of *contructivism*, which posits that an organism is never able to recognize, depict, or mirror reality and can only construct a model that fits. These theories are highly relevant in family therapy, not only for the world views or realities that various families construct but also for the picture the therapist forms of a particular family (Simon, Stierlin, & Wynne, 1985).

As the inner world gradually matures and develops, it becomes closer to what is seen as reality. Kernberg (1976) further describes ego identity at its highest level of development and maturity:

> A harmonious world of internalized object-representations, including not only significant others from the family and immediate friends but also a social group and a cultural identity, constitutes an ever growing internal world providing love, reconfirmation, support, and guidance within the object relations system of the ego. Such an internal world, in turn, gives depth to the present interaction with others. In periods of crisis, such as loss, abandonment, separation, failure, and loneliness, the individual can temporarily fall back on his internal world: in this way, the intrapsycic and the interpersonal worlds relate to and reinforce each other. (p. 73)

THE HOLDING ENVIRONMENT

Winnicott (1958) relates his notion of "good-enough mothering" to the idea of a "holding environment." The "good-enough mother" or primary nurturing person provides a "holding environment" that is safe, secure, responsive, nurturing, nonretaliating, and supportive of the separation–individuation process. The child can then achieve a firmer sense of identity and a lifelong capacity for developing nonsymbiotic object relations.

Scharff and Scharff (1987) develop Winnicott's concept further in their thoughts on centered relating, centered holding, and contextual holding. *Centered relating* is facilitated by a mirroring function in which the mother or mothering object reflects back to the baby its moods and its effects on the mother while baby reflects back to mother its experience of her mothering. Through this experience of relating to each other centrally, at the very core of their selves, the nucleus of the infant's internal object relations is built and the mother's internal object relations are fundamentally altered as the baby attributes the experience that gives her identity as a mother. *Centered holding* is the mother's ability to provide the space and material for centered relating through her physical handling of and mental preoccupation with her baby. The space in which this centered relating takes place is the distance at which the mother can still feel in communication with her baby. For working mothers, this may extend to their offices and require that they hand over the "centered holding" to a trusted substitute for a period of time. Yet it is still the mother who provides the "envelope." Scharff and Scharff call this the *mother's contextual holding*.

The father (or secondary nurturing partner) also has a role in providing holding for the baby. Traditionally, the father's direct exchanges with his infant are different and less central than the ongoing exchanges between the mother and baby. In fact, the father's exchanges with the baby have the purpose of pulling the infant out of the mother's influence for increasing periods of time, supporting later separation and individuation of the infant from the mother. Therefore, part of the father's role is to interrupt the mother's centered and contextual holding. Primarily, however, he supports the holding physically, financially, and emotionally. In other words, the partner holds the mother as she holds the baby. Scharff and Scharff call this the *father's contextual holding*. This contextual holding provides an environmental extension of the mother's presence, which later extends outward to grandparents and family, neighbors, and others.

Centered and contextual holding also apply to object relations family therapy. The therapist offers both aspects in the therapeutic engagement with the family. The contextual holding is provided through the handling of arrangements, competence in interviewing, concern for the family, and seeing the entire family. Centered holding is provided by engaging with the central issues of the family and being centrally caring, interactive, and understanding.

Feminist object relations family therapists have a somewhat different view. Luepnitz (1988) states:

> What feminist object-relations theory has to teach therapists who treat families is the overarching importance of creating a new father, a man who will not be the tired nightly visitor, who will be more than a therapist-appointed expert, more than a coach to his irresolute wife, more than her back-up, more than the separator of mothers and children, but an authentic presence, a tender and engaged parent, a knower of children in the way that mothers have been knowers of children. (p. 183)

The father, in this context, has a more central role with his children. This is considered critical because, among other reasons, "Many men without loving fathers grow up expecting women to give them all the warmth and limit setting they were denied—and then hating women for not succeeding in what is, after all, an impossible task" (Luepnitz, 1988, p. 183).

Feminist-informed object relations theory additionally considers the influence of gender on the holding environment. Sex role differentiation and shifting sex role mores are considered to affect the holding environment that is created within the couple, marital, and family settings (Joslyn, 1982; Juni, 1992; Juni & Grimm, 1994). Traditional concepts of masculine and feminine roles are challenged with the emergence of new realities that defy gender specification. A holding environment that typifies excessive power imbalances between couples may be understood within the context of early object relations (Silverstein, 1994). The role of dominance and power, particularly in the area of sexual arousal and pleasure, has been suggested to evolve from excessive control/coercion by a powerful parental object during early psychosexual development.

TRANSFERENCE AND COUNTERTRANSFERENCE

The psychoanalytic term *transference* is defined as distorted emotional reactions to present relationships (primarily to the analyst) based on unresolved, early family relations (Nicols, 1984). Scharff and Scharff (1987) extended the concept to include the repetition in the therapeutic relationship (transfamilial) of early relationships and even earlier part-object relationships. Transference is regarded as the living history of ways of relating, influenced by the vicissitudes of infantile dependence and by primitive emotions of a sexual and aggressive nature that arise in pursuit of attachment. Transference is considered a universal mental function that may well be the basis for all human relationships. Going further, Scharff and Scharff suggest that transference operates between family members (intrafamilial) whereby any present relationship is influenced by relationships experienced at earlier developmental stages. These are usually transgenerational and could be from parent to child or child to parent. Transferences in individuals operate as valences or magnets in engagements with others who have similar or complementary tendencies to relate in certain characteristic ways.

Countertransference is the emotional reaction, usually unconscious and often distorted, on the part of the therapist to a patient or member of a family in treatment (Nichols, 1984). Part of this countertransference is the development of a personal quality of "negative capability." This is a capacity to tolerate "not knowing," and to suspend the need to know for long enough to let the meaning of an experience emerge from inside the experience itself. Scharff and Scharff (1987) suggest that when we are able to do this successfully, the countertransference experience tells us, eventually, everything we need to know about our relationship with our clients and with a depth we cannot have if we impose only theory as a way of understanding. They see "negative capability" as exemplifying object relations as being a way of working rather than as a theory.

In family treatment, where the relationships are seen firsthand and can be worked with directly, the need for developing individual transferences with the therapist is lessened as the intrafamilial transference processes tend to give the most information. Countertransference gains an expanded significance and can now be applied to a therapist's attitudes, perceptions, and "blind spots" that hinder attempts to maintain a fair and evenly empathic attitude toward the whole family. As a rule, the countertransference problems that therapists have will often be bound with experiences and unresolved conflicts within their own family of origin (Simon et al., 1985).

ISOMORPHISMS

This is a precise mathematical term borrowed by systems theorists utilizing object relations concepts. Hofstadter (1979) notes that *isomorphism:*

> ...applies when two complex structures can be mapped onto each other in such a way that to each part of the structure there is a corresponding part in the other structure, where "corresponding" means that the two play similar roles in their respective structures. (p. 49)

The copy preserves all the information in the original theme, in the sense that the theme is fully recovered from any of the copies. Isomorphism, therefore, is an "information-preserving transformation" (Hofstadter, 1979, p. 9). This concept is most helpful to object relations family therapists when looking for similar structures and connections on various levels stemming from splitting, projective identification, collusion, or transference processes. Given that the essential task of family therapists is to understand and influence structures and patterns, therapists must decide to what extent patterns of behavior and communication are isomorphic in a family unit, the parents' families of origin, the therapeutic system (family, therapists, supervisors), the treatment team, and the therapists' families of origin (Simon et al., 1985).

CONCEPTS FOR MARITAL THERAPY

Some theorists have focused specifically on the application of object relations theory to the practice of marital therapy. Meissner (1978) states that the capacity to successfully function as a partner is largely a consequence of one's childhood relationships with and to one's own parents. He further states that:

> ...the relative success that the marital partners experience and the manner in which these developmental tasks are approached and accomplished are determined to a large extent by the residues of internalized objects and the organization of introjects which form the core of the sense of self and contribute in significant ways to the integration of their respective identities. The extent to which spouses are unsuccessful in merging these individual identities into a constructive and productive shared marital experience is contaminated by pathogenic introjects they each may bring to it, rather than being organized in terms of a successful differentiated and individuated sense of self and identity. (p. 27)

Finkelstein (1987) utilizes the work of Fairbairn (1954), Kohut (1984), Gilligan (1982), and others to formulate a summary of certain object relations assumptions that have specific applicability to the understanding of marital relationships and couples therapy. This summary (Table 11.1) serves to pull together many of the concepts previously discussed in this chapter, as well as to point out their particular relevance to marriages and couples.

These object relations concepts relate to attachment, connectedness, bonding, caring, love, and responsibility. They serve to provide an understanding of the deeper reasons for the three most common complaints in marriage and committed relationships (lack of communication, constant arguments, and unmet emotional needs). Such complaints can be seen as the results of the failure of relatedness, of deficiencies in self-object functioning, and of conflicts between relationship goals and individual goals (Finkelstein, 1987).

TABLE 11.1 | **OBJECT RELATIONS CONCEPTS APPLICABLE TO MARITAL RELATIONSHIPS**

- Object-seeking and attachment to others can be viewed as a primary motivational force in human beings.
- Object-seeking is lifelong, and attachments can be a source of fulfillment and gratification.
- Maturity can be measured not only in terms of the development of autonomy but also in terms of the capacity for intimate, mutually interdependent, satisfying relationships, which allow for appropriate regression without loss of respect.
- Mutually enhancing and satisfying marital relations are based on mutual self-object functioning.
- Aggression can be seen as due to the failure of each partner to provide for the other's dependent or self-object needs; that is, aggression can be seen as frustration aggression. Alternately, aggression results from a break in one's connection to one's spouse.
- Sexual problems in marriage reflect relational problems as well as individual inhibitions and anxieties.
- Conflicts resulting from each marital spouse's striving for individuation and separation, as well as his or her striving for attachment and commitment, are an ongoing source of tension and conflict in marriage.

Source: Finkelstein (1987, pp. 296–297).

APPLICATION

DIVERSE POPULATIONS

Object relations family therapy deals with shared, unconscious, internalized object relations. According to Slipp (1988) it looks for the primitive defenses of splitting and projective identification as the link between intrapsychic and family dynamics. As a result of these defenses and their associated effects, an unconscious collusive system between family members develops, fostering certain behaviors and symptomatology. Therefore, object relations theory can be utilized in order to understand a vast array of behaviors, problem areas, and symptomatology.

The judgment as to whether object relations family therapy is an effective approach to use in a given situation can be informed by previous studies and experiences. For those cases in which family relationships appear to reinforce unproductive behaviors and symptomatology as previously discussed, a family therapy approach does seem indicated. The family unit dynamics may aggravate or perpetuate problem areas associated with family differentiation, autonomy, projective identification, splitting, self-concept, and identity. Slipp (1988) states that, although ORFT is appropriate for those families who desire and can tolerate intensity and closeness, it is certainly not restricted to those families already tolerant of closeness. As families develop trust, openness, and closeness with the therapist, therapy itself can serve as a model for more open and intimate relationships among family members.

Slipp feels strongly that perhaps the most significant variable in deciding which type of family therapy is most suitable in a particular instance is the socioeconomic level of the family. Slipp's (1988) study showed that the ORFT approach is particularly suited for and effective with middle-class families. He also found that it is effective with a blue collar population. On the basis of his study findings, ORFT is least effective with lower socioeconomic families and is not recommended. Clients with overriding poverty and social problems may require help that is more immediate and less abstract.

Scharff and Scharff (1987), however, caution therapists that it should not be assumed that the poor, or culturally or intellectually disadvantaged, cannot benefit from ORFT. Psychological maturity is not necessarily related to intelligence, education, or socioeconomic status. Some families may fit cultural stereotypes of concrete thinking and dependency on directives and immediate gratification, whereas others may use a more reflective approach. Therefore, it can be said that ORFT may not be for all families, but it is effective for those that demonstrate an interest in understanding, not just in symptom relief.

Is sexual orientation or ethnicity a factor as to whether ORFT is indicated? Therapists generally use the same treatment methods with both traditional and same-sex couples (Parker, 1996). One must remember, however, that lack of societal supports and resources, as well as societal sanctions imposed by the dominant culture, must be addressed within the therapeutic dialogue. Slipp (1988) observes that in his experience ethnic differences alone need not dictate the choice of treatment. Although there are differences at the beginning of treatment between ethnic groups, if the therapist is sensitive to these differences and has skill as a clinician, these differences can be utilized as strengths within treatment. Applegate (1990) has explored aspects of object relations theory within the sociocultural context of family constellations, child-rearing practices, race, and ethnicity. The interrelationship of the internal world of object relations and the external world of multiculturalism is offered as a clinically useful way of examining issues arising from ethnic differences.

Considering individual and family life-cycle development, object relations theory offers a linkage for understanding interactions, roles, and developmental status (Blanck & Blanck, 1987; Freed, 1985; Nicholson, 1988). Within residential treatment centers, the emotional, physical, and psychological separation of adolescents from their families can be understood through the merging of family systems and object relation theories (Jones, 1985). Quasi-parental/quasi-marital adolescent relationships may be formed to compensate for inadequate access to parents during the adolescent development period for the family (Rosenberger, 1990). Object relations theory can be considered for assessment and treatment strategies when responding to the developmental needs accompanying an adolescent's transition to adulthood. Families with bulimic members can be understood within intergenerational and transgenerational contexts that propose that all family members have experienced inadequacies with early parental holding environments (Humphrey & Stern, 1988). Adaptations to these deficits determine the level and quality of later intrapsychic and interpersonal experiences. Additionally, Juni (1992) has studied marital couples with adult children, examining the basic additional mechanisms and generalized object relations styles within the family. Consistent similarities were found across families between object relations style and adaptational mechanisms, particularly between husband–wife, father–son, and mother–daughter dyads.

GOALS OF THE THERAPEUTIC PROCESS

The immediate goal of ORFT is not symptom resolution. Progression through the current developmental phase of family life, improved ability for work as a unit, and improved ability to differentiate and to meet the needs of both the family unit and individual members are key elements of goal attainment (Scharff & Scharff, 1987). More specifically, the general goals are included in Table 11.2.

As Guntrip (1961) put it, the goal is the "reintegration of the split ego, the restoration of lost wholeness" (p. 94). Concepts such as splitting, projective identification, collusion, and shared fantasy provide an emphasis on the existing need for other family members. However, family members have a need to establish individual ego boundaries and a sense of personal identity. Additionally, the ability to tolerate their own ambivalence and conflict (all aspects of personality) are parts of the treatment goal (Stewart et al., 1975). Overall goals are as open-ended as the treatment itself because goals change as growth occurs, leading to an expanded vision of future possibilities.

THERAPIST'S ROLE AND FUNCTION

THERAPEUTIC ENVIRONMENT The therapeutic environment is established by the therapist's encouragement of open dialogue, respecting confidentiality and setting up the mechanics of treatment (i.e., whom to include, time, place, fee, length of time, etc.) in an atmosphere of safety and mutual helpfulness in resolving problems. The therapist must be aware of the theoretical orientation framing the sessions. Respect for family and individual members' autonomy is held. The therapist avoids assuming a directive approach by not giving advice, reassurance, or instruction, but attends to the interactions within relationships in the session as described by Slipp (1988). The past is linked to the present through increasing awareness of the transferences, particularly the ways they are acted out interpersonally

---

TABLE 11.2 | **GOALS OF OBJECT RELATIONS FAMILY THERAPY**

- Recognizing and reworking the defensive projective identifications that have previously been required in the family.
- Treating the family's capacity to provide contextual holding for its members so that their needs for attachment and conditions for growth can be met.
- Reinstating or constructing the series of centered holding relationships between each of its members to support their needs for attachment, individuation, and growth sufficient to allow each individual to "take it from there."
- Returning the family to the overall developmental level appropriate to its tasks as set by its own preferences and by the needs of the family members.
- Clarifying the remaining individual needs in family members so that they can get them met with as much support as they need from the family. By this, we specifically include individual needs for psychotherapy, as well as more general needs for other growth endeavors.

Source: Scharff & Scharff (1987, p. 448).

in present, ongoing family relationships. In order to facilitate this awareness, the therapist empathically engages the family and creates a safe and secure holding environment where space for understanding is provided. Creating such a safe holding environment was found to be the most crucial element for change and growth in the psychotherapy research of Sampson and Weiss (1977).

There are also two other essential elements that ORFT introduces into the process (Slipp, 1988): (1) how the therapist parcels out internalized object relations through projective identification onto family members, and (2) how the family similarly evacuates internalized object relations onto the therapist. Therapists use their own empathy as a form of vicarious introspection in order to enter the subjective inner world of the family members. In addition, therapists allow their own inner worlds to be entered by the family through their use of projective identification. Therapists then attempt to monitor their own counter-transference responses that are influenced by, and that in turn influence, the family. The therapist's stance with the family is one that reflects an awareness that he or she affects and is affected by the family.

Slipp (1988) has described the therapist–family relationship as follows:

> Object relations family therapy allows for the greatest degree of closeness between the family and the therapist. The therapist, while maintaining autonomy, is able to empathically experience and understand each of the family members. Thus, at a concrete level, object relations family therapy serves as a model to unlearn old, distant and controlling interaction, and to learn how to be both an authentic individual as well as an integrated member of the family group. It provides a framework within which individual boundaries and autonomy are respected and confirmed, along with sensitivity to one another in the family. An extreme of either one of these positions leads to either narcissistic distancing or overly close symbiotic relatedness. Object relations family therapy fosters the kind of meaningful shared intimacy with respect for one another's individuality that the philosopher Martin Buber (1958) so aptly described as the "I-Thou Relationship." (p. 24)

ASSESSMENT Assessment is a vital part of the therapist's role and function. Schaff and Scharff (1987) cite six major tasks in assessment: (1) the provision of therapeutic space; (2) assessment of developmental phase and level; (3) demonstration of defensive functioning; (4) exploration of unconscious assumptions and underlying anxiety; (5) testing of the response to interpretation and assessment format; and (6) making an assessment formulation, recommendation, and treatment plan. A summary of Slipp's (1984, pp. 204–205) review of the steps in the assessment process is provided in Table 11.3. In addition to the ethnic differences or conflicts noted by Slipp, attention must also be given to other sociocultural–environmental factors that influence and impact the family unit.

PRIMARY TREATMENT TECHNIQUES

There are some specific techniques that ORFT uses in the beginning, middle, and last phases of treatment. Slipp (1988, pp. 199–200) has developed such a formulation in outline form that can be used as a guide for therapists (Table 11.4).

All these techniques are discussed in detail by Slipp (1988) as they are used in the appropriate phase of treatment. As the reader can readily recognize, most of

TABLE 11.3 | **ASSESSMENT PROCESS IN OBJECT RELATIONS FAMILY THERAPY**

- *Explore the presenting problem* of patient and its background.
  1. Does it seem related to overall family functioning, and/or to stress from a family life-cycle stage?
  2. What has been done so far to remedy the problem?

- *Establish an individual diagnosis* for each family member including a judgement concerning the level of differentiation, and the use of primitive or mature defenses.
  1. Gather data on the client and family development.
  2. Note any ethnic differences or conflicts.

- *Evaluate family constancy* to determine if parents can maintain their own narcissistic equilibrium, or if patient is needed to sustain their self-esteem and survival.
  1. Does a rigid homeostasis or defensive equilibrium exist that binds and prevents the patient from individuating and separating?
  2. Is there pressure for personality compliance within the family, or social achievement outside the family?
  3. What affiliative, oppositional, and alienated attitudes exist?

- *Explore precipitating stress* and its relation to a loss or other traumatic event (negative or positive) or a transitional point in the family life cycle that has disrupted homeostasis.

- *Define individual boundaries* for members. These may be rigidly too open (a symbiotically close relationship) or too closed (an emotionally divorced and distant relationship).
  1. Are generational boundaries intact, or are there parent–child coalitions?
  2. Are the parental coalition, the subsystems, and authority hierarchy intact?

- *Define the family boundary* to see if it is too open (symbiotic relations persist with family of origin) or too closed (family is isolated from community without social support system).

- *Determine the ability to negotiate differences and problem-solve* through verbal dialogue involving respect for one's own and others' views, opinions, and motivations versus an egocentric controlling viewpoint resulting in coercion and manipulation.

- *Observe* communication patterns and kinesic regulation for evidence of spontaneous versus rigid stereotyping, distancing, or obfuscating; level of initiative versus passivity; rigidity of family rules; and the power-role structure.

- *Evaluate the loving and caring feelings* among members that allow for separateness (rather than acceptance only by conformity) and provide warmth, support, and comfort.

- *Define the treatment goals* in terms of difficulties that have been uncovered, and present the frame or boundaries of the treatment process.

Source: Slipp (1984, pp. 204–205).

TABLE 11.4 | **PHASES OF TREATMENT IN OBJECT RELATIONS FAMILY THERAPY**

- During the beginning phase of treatment the techniques are to:

  1. Develop a safe holding environment through empathy, evenhandedness, and containment; an environment that facilitates trust, lowers defensiveness, and allows aggression to be worked with constructively.

  2. Interpret the circular positive or negative systemic interaction in a sequential nonblaming manner by:

     a defining its origin
     b. defining what was hoped to be gained
     c. describing its effects

- During the middle phase of treatment, the techniques are to:

  1. Interpret projective identification by:

     a. reframing its purpose to give it a positive aim
     b. linking it with a generic reconstruction
     c. clarifying why an aspect of the self needed to be disowned and projected

     This process diminishes defensiveness, enhances the therapeutic alliance, and facilitates continued work with the reowned projective identification.

  2. Use the objective countertransference as a tool to understand the transferences and to provide material for interpreting projective identification.

- During the last phase of treatment, the techniques are to:

  1. Work through individual conflicts and developmental arrests in the intrapsychic sphere. This process is gradual and may continue in individual therapy after the family treatment terminates.

  2. Terminate treatment.

Source: Slipp (1988, pp. 199–200).

the concepts contained in the outline have been previously discussed in this chapter. However, the added dimensions of when they are to be used in the treatment process and how they fit together are important.

Specific treatment techniques that differentiate the object relations approach from other approaches can be identified. These serve to highlight overall techniques used in ORFT as well as to discriminate this approach further. Table 11.5 outlines the six areas of differentiation as described by Stewart et al. (1975, pp. 176–177).

CASE EXAMPLE

This is a case with which the authors were involved intensively for six months and then periodically over a period of about seven years. The setting was a private practice office.

TABLE 11.5	**OBJECT RELATIONS THERAPY APPROACH DIFFERENTIATED FROM OTHER MARITAL/FAMILY APPROACHES**

- While many marital partners may seem quite different, it soon becomes apparent that their psychic structures are very similar. Although they may behaviorally manifest these intrapsychic processes differently through collusion, projective identification, shared fantasy, etc., the similarities should be discusses and made explicit to the couple.

- The ORFT approach goes beyond countertransference usage in allowing the partner to "put into" the therapist disowned or split-off parts of herself or himself. The more classical analytic approach considers the therapist's reactions as irrational countertransference phenomena. The ORFT approach regards such material as a valid, legitimate statement of issues with which the patient is struggling.

- When therapists split up a couple to see each of them individually, the emotional exchanges between the therapists will be similar to and/or mirror the affective transactions between the partners in the marital dyad.

- This ORFT approach provides a way of understanding family problems when a child is presented as the identified patient. The child becomes a carrier or container of the split-off, unacceptable impulses of the parent. The child may be idealized just as he or she may be denigrated.

- The more classical approach focuses on interpreting the patient's perception in terms of internal processes based on early experiences. This system considers the perception to be based on a need to solve an internal conflict through the use of external objects as carriers. There is an active invitation to other people to fulfill these roles.

- In classical analytical theory, the focus is upon individual psychotherapy and pathological involvement. Behaviorally oriented approaches also emphasize individual functioning. In contrast, object relations theory offers a perspective of the individual as a unit in which even the more pathological traits have a healthy reparative aspect. Consequently, the marital dyad continues to function in defiance of apparent breakdown and irreconcilable differences and conflicts. Awareness of the reciprocal, pathological, and subtle attempts to carry out ego repair generates a greater understanding in the therapist of the durability and maintenance of the marital dyad.

Source: Stewart et al. (1975, pp. 176–177).

PRESENTING PROBLEM

Sam and Sally came into treatment with the presenting problem as Sam's anger. He had lost control of his anger and physically assaulted his wife. After a disagreement that escalated, Sally made a remark that activated intense anger and rage in Sam. Before he knew what was really happening he had lunged across the room, physically grabbed his wife, and slammed her against the wall. Sally's head hit the wall, temporarily dazing her; she sank to the floor, stunned and bewildered. At first Sam did not realize how hard he had thrown her or that she was semiconscious. He continued to verbally abuse her. When she failed to respond and when tears came to her eyes, he began to realize how deeply he had hurt her—physically and emotionally. He immediately began to apologize, assuring her that he did not mean to hurt her and that he was really sorry for what had happened.

This incident was the straw that broke the camel's back. Many of the other problems that had surfaced over the first 11 years of Sam and Sally's marriage had still not been addressed. This last frightening incident plus the other unresolved problems motivated them to conclude, for the first time, that they needed help. Sam kept wondering where his intense feelings came from and how they could be controlled. Particular transition stress from a life-cycle stage perspective was not apparent at intake.

ASSESSMENT

Sam and Sally perceived themselves, as the community did, as the typical family. Sam had participated in high school football, track, basketball, and baseball. Sally had excelled academically and graduated at the top of her class. They had met and fallen in love while in college. Sam was three years older than Sally. At the time they were first seen for therapy they had been married 11 years and their children were eight and six years of age.

Sam and Sally were asked to relate their childhood experiences with their parents. Sam said he was born prematurely and there was some concern on the part of the doctors as to whether he would survive. His impressions were that from his mother's perspective, the pregnancy was somewhat ill timed. His premature birth and stay in the incubator had likely created a considerable amount of anxiety in his mother, possibly causing her at times to be overly indulgent and at other times to be somewhat cold and indifferent to him. Sam felt that she continued to communicate her ambivalence toward him in various ways throughout his childhood.

This experience with his mother had a profound impact upon the formulation of Sam's personality. He felt extremely close and loving to his mother at some times; at other times, he felt quite angry with her and had difficulty controlling his rage. This experience of closeness to and distance from his mother was certainly perpetuated in his marriage inasmuch as he had no other role model and knew no other way to relate to females. Either the marriage was extremely good with a tremendous amount of closeness, love, and sexual compatibility, or it was characterized by anger, distance, coldness, aloofness, and instances of outright punitiveness on his part toward his wife. Sally had a great deal of difficulty handling these unpredictable mood swings.

Sally grew up in somewhat different circumstances. While Sam was the older of two sons in his family, Sally was the fourth of five children. Being so far down the line of siblings, she spent a great deal of time and energy trying to get her parents' attention, especially her father's. She did this by excelling at school, in sports, and at work on the farm, in some ways filling the role of a son. She idolized her father greatly and tried both consciously and unconsciously to win his affirmation and approval.

Sam and Sally were attracted to each other in several areas. Sam came from a family that expressed a wide range of emotions, especially intense anger and negative feelings, while Sally came from a family that did not express strong feelings. Sally was an achiever, especially academically, while Sam was more easygoing and relaxed. They shared a strong sense of humor and a love for sports. No ethnic or cultural conflicts were evidenced.

In this intake material, it can be seen what each individual contributed to the marital relationship. Both brought the patterns and processes from their families of origin plus unresolved issues. These unresolved issues obviously began to surface in the marital relationship and ultimately led to a considerable amount of pain, turmoil, and conflict. Some personalities are more integrated and differentiated than others; the more integrated and differentiated, the less family-of-origin material needs to be worked through in the marital relationship. Each individual then can pursue his or her own professions or interests, and less psychic energy is needed in working on the marital relationship. Consequently, treatment is designed to help sort out many of the issues that each individual brings to the marriage. In this case the underlying processes of splitting, introjection, projective identification, and collusion as they are manifested in Sam and Sally's relationship needed to be addressed within the context of a therapeutic, centered holding environment.

PROCESS OF TREATMENT

The first agenda was to assure a safe holding environment for Sally. Sam assured Sally that physical abuse would never happen again. A contract was drawn up and signed to this effect, and instructions were given to Sally entailing what actions would be taken in the event that it did happen. The next agenda was to assist the couple to recognize the circular systemic interactions of the cycle of violence. A primary issue that needed to be resolved was Sam's handling his anger effectively. Sam always said that it was his wife who activated his anger; however, it was actually the unresolved issues of early deprivation and his resulting rage toward his mother that were manifested through the splitting of the good-mother/bad-mother introject. The bad-mother image was projected onto Sally. Her collusion was shown through her withdrawal when he became angry, thus becoming "the depriving mother," and through her constant search for ways not to activate his anger, thus assuming all the responsibility for his wrath. The working-through process was considerably time-consuming and painful as Sam began to relive many of the negative aspects of his relationship with his mother. He felt caught in a terrible bind. On one hand he loved his mother deeply; on the other, he was extremely angry with her. He hated many aspects of his mother's personality and the way she had dealt with him.

In reviewing these experiences, one becomes quite aware of the multigenerational transmission process. Sam's mother acted out many of the issues that she brought from her own family of origin and projected them onto Sam. Sam in turn carried on the same process in his relationship with his wife. Our challenge was to help him work through that anger and to intervene so that the process would not be projected onto the next generation.

The following incident illustrates the typical splitting, projection, and collusion process in Sam and Sally's relationship: Sally was going to town to buy groceries. On her way out Sam requested that she pick up some birdseed, which he usually purchased from a particular store. It was during the Christmas holidays, and Sally was falling behind in her schedule. Therefore, rather than taking an extra 10 or 15 minutes to go to this particular store, she saw birdseed at a good price in the store where she was shopping, so bought a bag there. When she gave the birdseed to Sam, he immediately saw that it was not the brand he usually bought. He accused her of purposely buying seed that he did not like in order to upset him; he examined the bag and found many things about the birdseed that he felt were unacceptable. This triggered anger in Sally, in order to preserve peace in the family, she got back in the car and returned to the store to buy the other birdseed, which required an additional 30 minutes of her time. When this issue was shared in therapy in an effort to try to understand the dynamics, the projection process was apparent. Sam was dealing with his feelings of being betrayed and deprived by his mother, who he felt deliberately went out of her way to do things that hurt him. The other dynamic was that Sally fell into the trap of the projection process in which she fulfilled the role of his expectations. He really did not believe she would do what he asked her to anyway. This deprivation–betrayal scenario was obviously played out in many forms. Basically, Sam was working out his relationship and unfinished business with his mother through his wife, who unwittingly colluded and fulfilled the role of his punitive mother.

During the therapeutic process, Sam was encouraged to obtain more information regarding his family of origin. It seemed appropriate that he spend time with his parents, inquiring about some of the issues of his parents' relationship and perhaps what went on between his parents and their parents. Sam tried to obtain information from his mother, but she was never very enthusiastic about sharing information regarding her own family of origin. She would only allude to growing up in a very fine family where there was little conflict. Sam turned to his father to ask if he knew very much about his mother's family. His father told him that after dating for approximately one year, he had asked his prospective wife to marry him. She had been ambivalent regarding marrying him and a few days later sent his father a letter in which she shared some very important and pertinent information—namely, that her father had at one time become involved in bootlegging and been arrested, tried, convicted, and sentenced to the state prison. Sam's mother had never visited her father in prison, although her mother had continued to be very devoted to him. It was so embarrassing to Sam's mother that she never even talked about it. To Sam's knowledge it was never mentioned again during the whole 50 years of his parent's marriage.

When Sam learned of this, he immediately began to connect childhood incidents when his mother became extremely angry about the resistance he had toward her instructions. When this resistance was acted out, she accused him of being a criminal and predicted that his life would end in the penal system. She would specifically say, "You're going to end up in the chain-gang." Therefore, we can see some of the splitting in her own struggles, in which she projected the negative images of her father onto Sam and the positive images onto Sam's brother. This whole splitting issue could be traced easily through the multigenerational process where good and bad were divided and in many instances never integrated. The unwitting victim of the projective identification process is either all good or all bad, with very little room for anything in between.

Over a period of six months, Sam's anger level diminished. He was able to articulate more accurately his anger toward his wife without acting it out. He became much more aware that many of the issues he struggled with were really issues between him and his mother. As Sally became more aware of her extreme need to have Sam's approval, much as she had needed her father's approval, she gradually became less dependent on Sam for validation. She also learned to be less reactive to Sam's anger, to detach from the projective process, and to take responsibility only for her own reactions and behaviors. She concluded that Sam's anger was not related to what she did or did not do but might be imposed on any situation.

Sam seemed to have focused more of his anger on his wife and less on his children. This had not been true with his mother, who had focused considerable anger on her children and less on her husband—which was done in order to maintain the marriage. Sam and Sally's two children were brought into the sessions periodically. They continued to perform well in school and evidenced no problems.

The reliving and working through of such painful material would not have taken place outside the safe, caring, holding environment created in session with the therapists. By utilizing transference and countertransference processes, the therapists linked the past with the present, particularly the ways the past was being acted out interpersonally in ongoing family relationships. After staying in treatment for an intense period of six months and then periodically over the next seven years, Sam and Sally had come to understand their underlying dynamics, had developed some controls for Sam's anger (triggered by feelings of deprivation and betrayal), were continuing to monitor their own projection and collusion processes, and were working through individual conflicts and developmental arrests.

EVALUATION

Object relations family therapists generally rely on subjective assessment by therapists and clients of the effectiveness of the treatment. Because symptom reduction is not the goal of this model, it cannot serve as the primary measure of effectiveness. The presence or absence of unconscious conflict, since it is not apparent to family members or outside observers, is difficult to measure. Therefore, assessment of effectiveness depends upon the subjective clinical judgment of the therapist, the family's reactions, and their perceptions.

But are these measures sufficient for this generation's focus on scientific evidence and cost-effectiveness? Previous psychoanalytic therapists have answered yes. Clinicians consider the therapist's observations to be entirely valid as a means of evaluating theory and treatment. Blanck and Blanck (1972), in regard to Margaret Mailer's methods and model, state, "Clinicians who employ her theories technically question neither the methodology nor the findings, for they can confirm them clinically, a form of validation that meets as closely as possible the experimentalist's insistence upon replication as criterion of the scientific method" (p. 675). Along the same lines, Langs (1982) states that the ultimate test of a therapist's formulation is in his or her use of these impressions as a basis for intervention. He further states that the client's reactions, conscious and unconscious, constitute the ultimate litmus test of these interventions, and that true validation involves both cognitive and interpersonal responses from the client.

Eminent object relations family therapists hold similar views. Slipp (1988) states that meeting the goals of treatment is the criterion that both the family and therapist use to consider ending treatment. Theses general goals, as previously discusses, do not lend themselves to empirical measurement, but to subjective assessment by therapists and families. Scharff and Scharff (1987) state that at termination, the family can provide the contextual and centered holding for its members that is so necessary for attachment and growth. The family is able to return to or reach an appropriate development level, so that they fit with the individuals' developmental needs for intimacy and autonomy. Slipp (1988) further describes the end result as the restructuring of the internal world of object relations with resultant modification of the family's interpersonal relations. The self is experienced as separate and less dependent on external objects to sustain self-esteem and identity, and the family will be able to function as a group in a more intimate and adaptive fashion that meets each member's needs.

Typically, outcome reports are primarily uncontrolled case studies. However, Dicks (1967) reported on a survey of the outcome of couples therapy at the Tavistock Clinic. He rated 72.8% of a random sample of cases as having been successfully treated. Others have investigated specific tenets of the ORFT theory. For example, Slipp (1984) conducted a controlled clinical research study of some of the factors involved in the intergenerational transmission of psychopathology. Using nine children of Nazi Holocaust survivors as subjects, he employed questionnaires, scales, and other standardized inventories plus a structured clinical interview. His findings provide further empirical evidence of the attempt to validate the existence of a double bind on achievement in the families of depressed members.

SUMMARY

Object relations family therapy bridges the gap between the psychoanalytic study, treatment of individuals, and system understanding of family development, interactions, and family therapy. Most of the pioneers of the family therapy movement had training in psychoanalytic theory and have retained at least some of these concepts in the development of their models (Sussal, 1992). While object relations family therapy has had no overall integrated theory, much work has been done by Scharff and Scharff, Slipp, Stewart et al., Finkelstein, and others toward integration.

Major concepts used in object relations family therapy include splitting, introjection, projective identification, collusion, ego identity, the holding environment, transference and countertransference, and isomorphisms. This model of working with families has been found to be effective with the blue collar as well as for middle-class families and others who are interested in understanding and not simply resolving symptoms. It is not recommended for low-socioeconomic class families with problems requiring more immediate help and concrete services.

Object relations family therapy fosters meaningful shared intimacy that respects one another's individuality. The therapist creates a therapeutic holding environment within which change may take place. He or she works with projective identification among family members, on a multigenerational level, and within the transference and countertransference phenomena. Goals and readiness for termination as well as effectiveness of outcome are generally determined subjectively by the therapist and family.

ANNOTATED SUGGESTED READINGS

Dicks, H. V. (1963). Object relations theory and marital status. *British Journal of Medical Psychology, 36,* 125–129.

> A classic article that extends the object relations theory of Klein, Fairbairn, and Guntrip to the study of marital relationships. Dicks discusses marriage as a mutual process of attribution or projection, with each spouse seen to a degree as an internal object.

Dicks, H. V. (1967). *Marital tensions.* New York: Basic Books.

> Dicks applies Fairbairn's object relations concepts to the understanding and treatment of marital dysfunction in this important volume.

Fairbairn, W. R. D. (1952). *An object-relations theory of the personality.* New York: Basic Books.

> A seminal work in object relations theory that has had a significant influence on the later work of Dicks, Bowen, Framo, and others. Required reading for those interested in the role of object relations in psychopathology.

Finkelstein, L. (1987). Toward an object-relations approach in psychoanalytic marital therapy. *Journal of Marital and Family Therapy, 13*(3), 287–298.

> Describes the features that distinguish psychoanalytic marital therapy from other forms of marital therapy, states how object relations theories can be applied to psychoanalytic marital therapy, and indicates certain directions for further study.

Scharff, D. E., & Scharff, J. S. (1987). *Object relations family therapy.* Northvale, NJ: Jason Aronson.

> Represents the Scharff's efforts to develop a psychoanalytic object relations approach to families and family therapy. The Scharffs demonstrate that object relations theory provides the theoretical framework for understanding and the language for working with the dynamics of both the individual and the family system.

Slipp, S. (1988). *The technique and practice of object relations family therapy.* Northvale, NJ: Jason Aronson.

> This book extends the clinical application of object relations family therapy that Slipp began earlier. He further develops the application of his family typology to the treatment process, with specific attention to techniques and process.

REFERENCES

Applegate, J. S. (1990). Theory, culture, and behavior: Objective relations in context. *Child and Adolescent Social Work Journal, 7*(2), 85–100.

Balint, M. (1968). *The basic fault: Therapeutic aspects of regression.* London: Tavistock.

Barnard, C. P., & Corrales, R. B. (1979). *The theory and technique of family therapy.* Springfield, IL: Charles C. Thomas.

Bion, W. R. (1961). *Experience in groups and other papers.* London: Tavistock.

Blanck, G., & Blanck, R. (1972). Toward a psychoanalytic developmental psychology. *Journal of the American Psychoanalytic Association, 20,* 668–710.

Blanck, G. & Blanck, R. (1987). Developmental object relations theory. *Clinical Social Work Journal, 15,* 318–327.

Boszormenyi-Nagy, I. (1967). Relational modes and meaning. In G. H. Zuk & I. Boszormenyi-Nagy (Eds.), *Family therapy and disturbed families.* Palo Alto: Science and Behavior Books.

Boszormenyi-Nagy, I., & Spark, G. (1973). *Invisible loyalties.* New York: Harper and Row.

Bowen, M. (1965). Family psychotherapy with schizophrenia in the hospital and in private practice. *Comprehensive Psychiatry, 7,* 345–374.

Bowen, M. (1978). *Family theory in clinical practice*. New York: Jason Aronson.

Brenner, C. (1973). *An elementary textbook of psychoanalysis*. New York: International Universities Press.

Breuer, J., & Freud, S. (1895). Studies on hysteria. In *The standard edition of the complete psychological works of Sigmund Freud* (Vol. 2, pp. 1–307). London: Hogarth Press [1955].

Brill, A. A. (1938). *The basic writings of Sigmund Freud*. New York: The Modern Library.

Dicks, H. V. (1963). Object relations theory and marital studies. *British Journal of Medical Psychology, 36*, 125–129.

Dicks, H. V. (1967). *Marital tensions*. New York: Basic Books.

Erikson, E. H. (1956). The problem of ego identity. *Journal of the American Psychoanalytic Association, 4*, 56–121.

Erikson, E. H. (1963). *Childhood and society*. New York: Norton.

Fairbairn, W. R. D. (1954). *An object-relations theory of personality*. New York: Basic Books.

Ferenczi, S. (1920). The further development of an active therapy in psychoanalysis. In *Further contributions to the theory and technique of psychoanalysis* (J. Rickman, Trans.). London: Hogarth Press

Finkelstein, L. (1987). Toward an object-relations approach in psychoanalytic marital therapy. *Journal of Marital and Family Therapy, 13*(3), 287–298.

Foley, V. D. (1974). *An introduction to family therapy*. New York: Grune & Stratton.

Framo, J. L. (1970). Symptoms from a family transactional viewpoint. In N.W. Ackerman, N. Lielg, & J. Pearce (Eds.), *Family therapy in transition*. Boston: Little, Brown.

Freed, A. D. (1985). Linking developmental, family, and life cycle theories. *Smith College Studies in Social Work, 55*, 169–182.

Freud, S. (1905). Fragment of an analysis of a case of hysteria. *Collected papers*. New York: Basic Books.

Freud, S. (1940). *An outline of psychoanalysis*. Standard Edition, *23*, 139–171.

Gilligan, C. (1982). *In a different voice*. Cambridge, MA: Harvard University Press.

Guntrip, H. (1961). *Personality structure and human interaction: The developing synthesis of psychodynamic theory*. London: Hogarth Press and the Institute of Psychoanalysis.

Hofstadter, D. R. (1979). *Godel, Escher, Bach: An eternal golden braid*. New York: Basic Books.

Humphrey, L. L., & Stern, S. (1988). Object relations and the family system in bulimia: A theoretical integration. *Journal of Marital and Family Therapy, 14*, 337–350.

Jones, J. M. (1985). Stages of family involvement in the residential treatment of adolescents. *Journal of Marital and Family Therapy, 14*, 337–350.

Joslyn, B. E. (1982). Shifting sex roles: The silence of family therapy literature. *Clinical Social Work Journal, 10*, 39–51.

Juni, S. (1992). Familial dyadic patterns in defenses and object relations. *Contemporary Family Therapy, 14*, 259–268.

Juni, S., & Grimm, D. W. (1994). Sex roles as factors in defense mechanisms and object relations. *Journal of Genetic Psychology, 155*, 99–106.

Kernberg, O. F. (1972). Early ego integration and object relations. *Annals of the New York Academy of Science, 193*, 233–247.

Kernberg, O. F. (1975). *Borderline conditions and pathological narcissism*. New York: Jason Aronson.

Kernberg, O. F. (1976). *Object relations theory and clinical psychoanalysis*. New York: Jason Aronson.

Klein, M. (1946). Notes on some schizoid mechanisms. *International Journal of Psychoanalysis, 27*, 99–110.

Klein, M. (1948). *Contributions to psychoanalysis, 1921–1945.* London: Hogarth Press and the Institute of Psychoanalysis.

Kohut, H. (1984). *How does analysis cure?* Chicago: University of Chicago Press.

Langs, R. (1982). *Psychotherpy: A basic text.* New York: Jason Aronson.

Luepnitz, D. A. (1988). *The family interpreted: Feminist theory in clinical practice.* New York: Basic Books.

Mahler, M. S. (1952). On child psychosis and schizophrenia: Autistic and symbiotic infantile psychoses. In *Psychoanalytic study of the child* (Vol. 7, pp. 286–305). New Haven, CT: Yale University Press.

Meissner, W. W. (1978). The conceptualization of marriage and family dynamics from a psychoanalytic perspective. In T. J. Paolino & B. S. McCrady, *Marriage and marital therapy.* New York: Brunner/Mazel.

Nichols, M. (1984). *Family therapy: Concepts and methods.* New York: Gardner Press.

Nicholson, B. (1988). Object relations theory revisited: Integrating essential concepts with developmental phase theory. *Journal of Independent Social Work, 2*(3), 25–38.

Parker, G. (December 12, 1996). Personal communication with A. Kilpatrick.

Piercy, F. P., Sprenkle, D. H., et al. (1986). *Family therapy sourcebook.* New York: Guilford Press.

Rosenberger, J. B. (1990). Transitional relationships: Clinical observations on a form of peer parenting. *Clinical Social Work Journal, 18*, 155–165.

Sampson, H., & Weiss, J. (1977). Research on the psychoanalytic process: An overview. *The Psychotherapy Research Group*, Bulletin No. 2 (March), Department of Psychiatry, Mt. Zion Hospital and Medical Center.

Scharff, D. E. (1982). *The sexual relationship: An object relations view of sex and the family.* Boston: Routledge & Kegan Paul.

Scharff, D. E., & Scharff, J. S. (1987). *Object relations family therapy.* Northvale, NJ: Jason Aronson.

Scharff, J. S. (Ed.). (1989). *Foundations of object relations family therapy.* Northvale, NJ: Jason Aronson.

Segal, H. (1973). *Introduction to the work of Melanie Klein.* New enlarged edition. London: Hogarth Press.

Silverstein, J. L. (1994). Power and sexuality: Influence of early object relations. *Psychoanalytic Psychology, 11*, 33–46.

Simon, F. B., Stierlin, H., & Wynne, L. C. (1985). *The language of family therapy: A systemic vocabulary and source book.* New York: Family Process Press.

Slipp, S. (1984). *Object relations: A dynamic bridge between individual and family treatment.* Northvale, NJ: Jason Aronson.

Slipp, S. (1988). *The technique and practice of object relations family therapy.* Northvale, NJ: Jason Aronson.

Stewart, R. H., Peters, T. C., Marsh, S., & Peters, M. J. (1975). An object-relations approach to psychotherapy with marital couples, families and children. *Family Process. 14*(2) (June), 161–178.

Stierlin, H. (1976). The dynamics of owning and disowning: Psychoanalytic and family perspectives. *Family Process, 15*(3), 277–288.

Sussal, C. M. (1992). Object relations family therapy as a model for practice. *Clinical Social Work Journal, 20,* 313–321.

Vogel, E. F., & Bell, N. W. (1960). The emotionally disturbed as the family scapegoat. In N. W. Bell & E. F. Vogel (Eds.), *The family.* Glencoe, IL: Free Press.

Winnicott, D. W. (1965). *The maturational processes and the facilitation of environment.* London: Hogarth Press.

Wynne, L. C. (1965). Some indications and contraindications for exploratory family therapy. In I. Boszormenyi-Nagy & J. L. Franco (Eds.), *Intensive family therapy.* New York: Hoeber.

CHAPTER 12

Toward a Person-Centered Approach to Family Therapy

LOUIS THAYER

DEFINITION

The founder and the key developer of the person-centered approach to family therapy was Carl R. Rogers (1902–1987). The formal beginnings of the approach started with the publication of *Counseling and Psychotherapy* by Rogers in 1942. Since that time, the movement has had a number of name changes. The labels have changed from nondirective counseling in the 1940s, to client-centered therapy in the 1950s and 1960s, to the person-centered approach in the mid-1970s, 1980s, and 1990s. The most recent label for the movement characterizes its expanded application into new areas of human behavior. Labels have also been attached to specific areas within the movement to indicate particular themes—student-centered teaching, group-centered leadership, and, more recently, family-centered therapy. This chapter is also applicable to therapy with couples.

What is the primary focus? One key emphasis in this approach is on individuals' tremendous potential for growth and change. There is an inherent tendency in persons to actualize their full capacities for maintenance and enhancement of the self. This basic respect for the dignity and integrity of persons and their forward momentum is based on research and much clinical experience in therapy. A second key building block of this approach is the formative tendency, a universal trend in all things toward increased order and interrelated complexity.

What are the conditions for change? When a therapist is genuine and integrated in the therapy situation, holds a positive regard for persons that is without conditions, and seeks to experience an empathic understanding of the persons' realities, then a relationship can develop in which the persons can discover within themselves the capacities to use the relationship for growth and change. The facilitative climate tends to help release the potentials within individuals and families for self-awareness, self-worth, and self-direction in resolving concerns. People have a basically positive directional process. Based on research and experiences in therapy, the movement is away from the "oughts" and "shoulds" dictated by elements outside the self and family toward a direction based more on persons' and families' inner awareness and potentials and their own phenomenological views of the world.

Person-centered therapy continues to be one of the most human approaches. It has an openness to change and is continually taking root in new areas such as couple and family therapy. The person-centered philosophy is becoming a way of living for many persons who started exploring concepts in helping.

HISTORICAL DEVELOPMENT

PRECURSORS

Rogers first formulated his views from his experiences in clinical work and subsequent research. Later, he confirmed his ideas and writings and compared them to the ideas of significant historical thinkers as the writings of these people came to his attention.

The concepts of the person-centered approach can be linked to Eastern writings such as the *Lao Tzu/Tao Teh Ching* (Wu & Sih, 1961). There are many passages in the *Tao* that speak of the quiet, persistent, inward journey made by a person who becomes at peace with human nature, living creatures, and life. Rogers (1961a, p. 26) said that he, too, had learned that "what is most personal is most general."

In interviews (Thayer, 1987, 1989), Rogers was asked about his response to a passage from the *Lao Tzu/Tao Teh Ching* (Wu & Sih, 1961, pp. 81–83). Rogers indicated that the passage held a great deal of meaning for him. He offered the following excerpt from a different translation of the *Tao Teh Ching*, adding that this passage, his talisman, was the only thing of this nature that he carried in his wallet.

A leader is best

when people barely know he exists.

Not so good

when people obey and acclaim him,

worse when they despise him...

But of a good leader, who talks little,

When his work is done, his aim fulfilled,

They will say, "We did this ourselves."

–(Bynner, 1962, pp. 34–35)

Rogers (1980b) enjoyed the teachings of Lao Tzu and learned some Taoist principles. Lao Tzu's *Tao Te Ching* has been adapted for the leader of a group and may be especially helpful to the family therapist (Heider, 1985). Thayer and Harrigan (1990) have compared and contrasted key principles of the person-centered approach with basic principles of Taoist thinking and the physical representation of Taoism in Tai Chi Ch'uan.

Rogers found many of his person-centered ideas confirmed in the existential thought of Søren Kierkegaard and Martin Buber, and he was especially fond of Ralph Waldo Emerson's views. Like Rogers, these philosophers seem to have valued and trusted that which was within themselves as a guide to their lives and creativeness.

Sufi teaching stories (Shah, 1972) have been used to help individuals gain a more holistic view of consciousness (Ornstein, 1986) by developing the "right brain" potentials. And Joseph Campbell (1988) aided us in understanding our commonalties and our more universal experiences as he looked at myth and its power. Rogers's approach in therapy aids people in discovering the more mysterious, intuitive parts of themselves and in trusting these elements of their personality. Rogers (1961a, p. 22) comments that his "total organismic sensing of a situation" is more trustworthy than his intellect.

Not surprisingly, person-centered theory has had its formative stage here in the United States. Our system of democracy and its valuing of the person have fostered individualism, self-reliance, and personal creativeness, and the fundamentals of democracy in action have offered the rich soil for the development of a whole theory of the person. The openness of the system and its acceptance of individual creativity have facilitated Rogers's work in really understanding how people develop their inner selves and trust their own experiences. Rogers's criticisms of institutions and organizations are an effort to maintain and enhance the openness and acceptance of individuals in the system in order to allow them to develop their full capacities in humanness and creativity.

Rogers and his colleagues set a path for themselves. The path is one that has "heart," one in which they looked to their experiences and to themselves for key questions and tentative directional conclusions. Their experiences in therapeutic sessions helped them formulate the questions that would set a process in motion that continues to evolve as a major theoretical approach to helping, humanness, and living.

The person-centered approach offers the basis for a *wave of the future*—an existential view of ways for people "being" together in all forms of relationships in life. These relationships range from love, work, play, and friends to families, organizations, educational institutions, religious groups, and nations. Glimpses of this *wave* appear in persons, families, organizations, political and governmental groups, and directions of a nation that are "emerging" with new ways of relating and being in this complex world (Lietaer, Rombauts, & Van Balen, 1990; Patterson, 1985; Rogers, 1977; Suhd, 1995).

BEGINNINGS

Rogers carried the main responsibility for the theoretical formulations of the person-centered theory. He grew up in a highly conservative Protestant family that valued hard work. When he was 12, his family moved to a farm. Rogers's reading and work with feeds and feeding, soils, animal husbandry, and the farm activities instilled in him a respect for the scientific method for solving problems.

As Rogers moved away from his family's view of religion, he chose to spend two years at Union Theological Seminary, which was committed to freedom of philosophical thought—regardless of whether the thought led to or away from religion. Because of his changing views on religion, he moved to Teachers College, Columbia University, from 1924 to 1928, where he received a thorough exposure to statistics and objectivity. It was at Teachers College that Rogers was thoroughly exposed to the writings of John Dewey through the teachings of William H. Kilpatrick. Rogers, like Dewey, came to hold his own "experience" as the highest authority (Rogers, 1961a, p. 23). The major contrast with the Teachers College view came in 1927–28, when Rogers spent a year of internship at the Institute of Child Guidance. The Institute was strictly psychoanalytic. The first step in working with a child was to take a long case history from all members of the family. Then a case conference was held to determine what the treatment should be. The psychiatrist conducted treatment interviews with the child, the psychologist did tutoring or other needed activities, and the social worker dealt with the parents. Rogers subscribed to the analytic way of thinking for a time, because he distinctly remembered Alfred Adler's saying that some conclusions could be drawn from talking with the child.

Next, Rogers went to Rochester, New York, for 12 years where he worked first in a Child Study Department of the Society for Prevention of Cruelty to Children and then served as director for the Rochester Guidance Center. The staff took a case history from the parents and from the child, administered multiple tests, interviewed the child, and then held a case conference to decide on the treatment of the child. Rogers felt that these conferences were the best in the country. The staff worked with the teacher, the parents, the social agency involved, the school social worker, the court (probation officer), or any agency that was concerned with the situation. Together, they decided on a plan of treatment for the child. And they saw to it that the plan was put into effect. The staff had a lot of power over the child, and they used it.

Rogers said that he began to change during those years in Rochester, primarily because of his listening experiences. He told a story about his learning to listen:

> One of our staff members was working with a child in play therapy—a very cantankerous, difficult boy. I was seeing the mother to help in the treatment process. In those days, we called them treatment interviews, not therapy, not counseling. And as I worked with the mother, we had already decided in case conference that the basic problem was the mother's rejection of the boy. So, I endeavored to very gently and persuasively get that across to her, that she was really the problem and that it was her attitude that was causing the difficulties with the boy. I look back on that now with

a certain amount of horror, but anyway that was what I was doing. Strangely enough, she did not seem to accept what I was saying. We worked very hard on this. I was very conscientious. After a number of interviews, I realized that we were not getting anywhere. I thought we should probably call it quits. She agreed that she didn't think it was helping either. So, she got up to leave the office. As she got to the door, she turned around and said, "Do you ever take adults for counseling here?" And I said, "Yes." So, she came back to the same chair that she left and began to pour out her own problems as she saw them from her point of view. And it was so different from the nice orderly case history that we had gotten that I couldn't believe that this was the same woman talking. As she poured out her own problems with her husband and so on, very little about the boy, it began to be what I would now say was a real therapy relationship. I didn't know what to do. I was quite nonplussed by this whole situation, so I primarily listened. We worked together then for quite a number of interviews. Her marital situation improved. The boy's behavior changed. And I realized that possibly if I wanted to be the real expert, I would go about it in the same way that I always had. If I wanted to be of help to people, possibly it was better to listen. I began to pay much more attention to focusing on the person who came in rather than on my thoughts about that person. (Rogers, 1980a)

Then Rogers came into brief contact with Otto Rank and some of Rank's social work students and psychiatrists from the Philadelphia School of Social Work. Rogers liked Rank's (1936) ideas on "will" therapy with the client taking responsibility. These ideas began to influence Rogers's thinking. Later, a social worker, Elizabeth Davis, who had studied with Rank came to work at the Clinic. Rogers learned a great deal from her about paying attention to the feelings behind words and responding to those feelings rather than to the content of the words. Rogers suspects that the idea of "reflecting feelings" in the therapy interview is something that he picked up from her.

Another influence about that time was Jessie Taft's book *The Dynamics of Therapy* (1933). The book contained a story of therapy with a child. It was clear that the relationship was what counted with the therapist, who depended on the child to take positive steps. The book had a great impact on Rogers. Rogers realized that his views were changing from his making an expert's diagnosis to one of relying on the initiative and self-directive authority of the client.

As a result of his experience at Rochester, Rogers wrote *The Clinical Treatment of the Problem Child* (1939). In 1940, Rogers moved to Ohio State University. He found that his new methods for helping others were different from the approaches used by other therapists. In 1942, his classic, *Counseling and Psychotherapy*, was published, and it began to lay the foundation of his new approach. Rogers and Wallen (1946) also wrote *Counseling with Returned Servicemen*, which contained a short chapter on marital and family counseling.

The five years at Ohio State University and the subsequent 12 years at the Counseling Center of the University of Chicago put Rogers in touch with open-minded graduate students who were creative, eager to experience new methods, and willing to contribute to theory, research, and knowledge in this new approach. During the 1940s, the "nondirective" counseling-therapy label was attached to Rogers's approach because the direction for the process came from the person, not the therapist. But, in the early 1950s, the name of the approach was changed to "client-centered therapy." This name fit better because it indicated where the keys to the potential for therapeutic movement rested—within the client.

Client-Centered Therapy, published by Rogers in 1951, opened the way for major advances in theory and research during the 1950s. *Psychotherapy and Personality Change* with Dymond (1954) presented studies of change factors in therapy. Also, four remarkable papers were published by Rogers that had much impact on training programs, research, and education: "The Necessary and Sufficient Conditions for Therapeutic Personality Change" (1957a), "Personal Thoughts on Teaching and Learning" (1957b), "A Theory of Therapy, Personality, and Interpersonal Relationships, As Developed in the Client-Centered Framework" (1959), and "A Process Conception of Psychotherapy" (1961b). The third paper stands as a major statement of the theory.

From 1928 to 1958, Rogers spent 15 to 20 hours a week, except on vacations, working therapeutically with individuals. From these helping experiences, he gained many of his insights into therapy and questions for research. Rogers moved to the University of Wisconsin in 1957 to teach and do research. In 1961, the classic, *On Becoming a Person*, was published, and it serves today as an inspiration to those in the helping professions. After a one-year stay at the Center for Advanced Study in the Behavioral Sciences in Stanford, California (1962–63), Rogers left the University of Wisconsin and in 1964 went to work at the Western Behavioral Sciences Institute (WBSI) in La Jolla, California. In 1968, after several years of writing and research there, Rogers and several colleagues severed their relationship with WBSI and created The Center for Studies of the Person (CSP) in La Jolla—a nonprofit, "non-organization" organization. Rogers also completed work on several other books: *The Therapeutic Relationship and Its Impact: A Study of Psychotherapy with Schizophrenics* with E.T. Gendlin, P. J. Kiesler, and C. Truax (1967), *Person to Person: The Problem of Being Human* with B. Stevens (1967), and *Man and The Science of Man* with W. Coulson (1968).

CURRENT STATUS

From about 1964, Rogers had been spending increasing amounts of time in small encounter groups and larger community learning groups, as well as continuing to write and to give presentations. The groundwork for the expansion of his theoretical formulations outside the therapeutic interview (Rogers, 1959) had been laid, as described in the following books: *Freedom to Learn: A View of What Education Might Become* (1969), *Carl Rogers on Encounter Groups* (1970), and *On Becoming Partners: Marriage and Its Alternatives* (1972). In the late 1960s, the 17-day La Jolla Program (a CSP project), directed by W. Coulson, D. Land, and B. Meador, was established. It received attention for its creation of a healthy and supportive psychological climate (Coulson, Land, & Meador, 1977). Rogers, a consultant to the project, contributed with his philosophy on how persons grow.

As Rogers began to examine the incredible learning that took place in the small groups and in the larger community, a renewed optimism, potential, and energy in his approach surfaced. In 1974, he and several colleagues experimented with two three-week workshops on community building and his approach. As the approach moved from the realm of the therapeutic milieu, the term "person" seemed more fitting with the focus: the person and his or her inner potential. The term "person-centered approach" was adopted for the 1975 workshop.

In 1977 *Carl Rogers on Personal Power* was published, which focused on the politics of a person-centered approach and development of the power of the person. Rogers was writing about his new experiences in large groups that were developing a sense of community and of related social and political implications. Rogers continued to spend time in large-group workshops and seminars and had speaking engagements throughout the world.

Rogers's book *A Way of Being* (1980b) provides additional insights into his approach. It also offers an opportunity to examine some of his thinking as he grew older and yet remained a learner. In 1983, he published *Freedom to Learn for the 80's*.

In 1981, David J. Cain founded the Association for the Development of the Person-Centered Approach (ADPCA). The Association has a newsletter, *Renaissance*, and Cain served as editor of ADPCA's journal, *Person-Centered Review*. The first issue of *Person-Centered Review* was published in February, 1986, and it continued for five years. A new publication, the *Person-Centered Journal*, was published in October, 1992, by coeditors Jerold D. Bozarth and Fred M. Zimring. This journal continues under the editorship of Jeanne P. Stubbs.

As Rogers continued his professional journey, his efforts turned toward peace (Rogers, 1986a, 1986b, 1987), and he worked to help factions within countries and between countries try to resolve conflicts. A special issue of *Counseling and Values* (1987) was guest-edited by John Whiteley and focused on Rogers's person-centered approach to peace. In interviews, Rogers also spoke of his efforts to seek peaceful solutions to human conflict and the use of person-centered principles to foster peace (Thayer, 1987, 1989).

Since his death, a number of books have focused on the person-centered approach: *Person-Centered Counselling in Action* (Mearns & Thorne, 1988), *The Carl Rogers Reader* (Kirschenbaum & Henderson, 1989b), *Carl Rogers: Dialogues* (Kirschenbaum & Henderson, 1989a), *Experiences of Counselling in Action* (Mearns & Dryden, 1990), *Client-Centered and Experiential Psychotherapy in the Nineties* (Lietaer, Rombauts, & Van Balen, 1990), *Gentle Roads to Survival: Making Self-Healing Choices in Difficult Circumstances* (Auw, 1991), *Carl Rogers* (Thorne, 1992), *Beyond Carl Rogers* (Brazier, 1993), *The Creative Connection: Expressive Arts as Healing* (Rogers, 1993), *Developing Person-Centered Counselling* (Mearns, 1994), *Freedom to Learn* (Rogers & Frieberg, 1994), *Positive Regard: Carl Rogers and Other Notables He Influenced* (Suhd, 1995), *Child-Centered Counseling and Psychotherapy* (Boy & Pine, 1995), and a special issue of the *Journal of Humanistic Psychology* (1995) entitled "Carl Rogers—The Man and His Ideas."

TENETS OF THE MODEL

The tenets on which the person-centered model are based have come from the work of several people. Forty of the tenets are discussed in Rogers's (1959, pp. 194–212) chapter on "Therapy, Personality, and Interpersonal Relationships." The chapter offers an extended discussion of these constructs. Brief definitions of 25 key constructs are provided here.

1. *Actualizing Tendency.* "This is the inherent tendency of the organism to develop all its capacities in ways which serve to maintain or enhance the organism." The movement is toward more autonomy and away from control by others.

2. *Tendency Toward Self-Actualization.* "Following the development of the self-structure, this general tendency toward actualization expresses itself also in the actualization of that portion of the experience of the organism which is symbolized in the self."

3. *Experience* (noun). This concept includes "all that is going on within the envelope of the organism at any given moment which is potentially available to awareness."

4. *Experience* (verb). "To experience means simply to receive in the organism the impact of the sensory or physiological events which are happening at the moment..."

5. *Feeling, Experiencing a Feeling.* This concept means "an emotionally tinged experience, together with its personal meaning." "Experiencing a feeling fully" is denoted when the individual is "congruent in his (her) experience (of the feeling), his (her) awareness (of it), and his (her) expression (of it)."

6. *Awareness, Symbolization, Consciousness.* The three synonymous terms are seen as "the symbolic representation (not necessarily in verbal terms) of some portion of our experience."

7. *Perceive, Perception.* Perception and awareness are synonymous terms; however, perception emphasizes the stimulus in the process, while awareness is the "symbolizations and meanings which arise from such purely internal stimuli as memory traces, visceral changes, and the like, as well as from external stimuli."

8. *Self, Concept of Self, Self-Structure.* "These terms refer to the organized, consistent conceptual gestalt composed of perceptions of the characteristics of the 'I' or 'me' to others and to various aspects of life, together with the values attached to these perceptions."

9. *Ideal Self.* This is "the self-concept which the individual would most like to possess, upon which he (she) places the highest value for himself (herself)."

10. *Incongruence Between Self and Experience.* Here "a discrepancy frequently develops between the self as perceived, and the actual experience of the organism."

11. *Vulnerability.* This term refers to the "state of incongruence between self and experience, when it is desired to emphasize the potentialities of this state for creating psychological disorganization. When incongruence exists, and the individual is unaware of it, then he (she) is potentially vulnerable to anxiety, threat, and disorganization."

12. *Anxiety.* "Anxiety is phenomenologically a state of uneasiness or tension whose cause is unknown."

13. *Threat.* "Threat is the state which exists when an experience is perceived or anticipated (subceived) as incongruent with the structure of the self."

14. *Psychological Maladjustment.* "Psychological maladjustment exists when the organism denies to awareness, or distorts in awareness, significant experiences,

which consequently are not accurately symbolized and organized into the gestalt of the self-structure, thus creating an incongruence between self and experience."

15. *Defense, Defensiveness.* "Defense is the behavioral response of the organism to threat, the goal of which is the maintenance of the current structure of the self."

16. *Congruence, Congruence of Self and Experience.* Here "the individual appears to be revising his (her) concept of self to bring it into congruence with his (her) experience, accurately symbolized." Synonymous terms are integrated, whole, genuine.

17. *Openness to Experience.* "When the individual is in no way threatened, then he (she) is open to his (her) experience."

18. *Psychological Adjustment.* "Optimal psychological adjustment is thus synonymous with complete congruence of self and experience, or complete openness to experience."

19. *Mature, Maturity.* "The individual exhibits mature behavior when he (she) perceives realistically and in an extensional manner, is not defensive, accepts the responsibility of being different from others, accepts responsibility for his (her) own behavior, evaluates experience in terms of the evidence coming from his (her) own senses, changes his (her) evaluation of experience only on the basis of new evidence, accepts others as unique individuals different from himself (herself), prizes himself (herself), and prizes others."

The following constructs (20 through 24) have been developed by Standal (1954) to replace less rigorously defined ones.

20. *Contact.* "Two persons are in psychological contact, or have the minimum essential of a relationship, when each makes a perceived or subceived difference in the experiential field of the other."

21. *Unconditional Positive Regard.* This is a key construct in the theory. "If the self-experiences of another are perceived by me in such a way that no self-experience can be discriminated as more or less worthy of positive regard than any other, then I am experiencing unconditional positive regard for this individual." Rogers likes John Dewey's term of "prize" to express this caring for another. It means "to value a person, irrespective of the differential values which one might place on his (her) specific behaviors." Another term used is acceptance.

22. *Locus of Evaluation.* "The internal locus of evaluation, within the individual himself (herself), means that he (she) is the center of the valuing process, the evidence being supplied by his (her) own senses. When the locus of evaluation resides in others, their judgment as to the value of an object or experience becomes the criterion of value for the individual."

23. *Organismic Valuing Process.* "This concept describes an ongoing process in which values are never fixed or rigid, but experiences are being accurately symbolized and continually and freshly valued in terms of the satisfactions organismically experienced; the organism experiences satisfaction of those stimuli or behaviors which maintain and enhance the organism and the self, both in the immediate present and in the long range."

24. *Empathy*. This is "to perceive the internal frame of reference of another with accuracy, and with the emotional components and meanings which pertain thereto, as if one were the other person, but without ever losing the 'as if' condition....If this 'as if' quality is lost, then the state is one of identification."

A more recent theoretical construct that, along with the actualizing tendency, serves as a foundation block of the person-centered approach is the *formative tendency*. This construct, broader and more universal in nature, is the opposite of entropy. It represents the creative, building energy present in the universe rather than the deterioration process. Rogers's hypothesis is stated this way:

25. There is a formative directional tendency in the universe, which can be traced and observed in stellar space, in crystals, in micro-organisms, in more complex organic life, and in human beings. This is an evolutionary tendency toward greater order, greater complexity, greater interrelatedness. In humankind, this tendency exhibits itself as the individual moves from a single-cell origin to complex functioning, to knowing and sensing below the level of consciousness, to a conscious awareness of the organism and the external world, to a transcendent awareness of the harmony and unity of the cosmic system, including humankind. (Rogers, 1980b, p. 133)

OTHER SYSTEMS: THERAPIST-CENTERED OR FAMILY-CENTERED?

Perhaps a way to approach a discussion about other systems is to formulate a set of questions that may be used in reviewing theories in family therapy. In a sense, the divergences and convergences in family therapy may be placed on a continuum, with the therapist as director–expert on one end and the family members as the directors–experts on the other end.

What are the key values inherent in the person-centered approach (PCA) to family therapy, and where do the differences exist with other approaches? To what extent do family therapists foster independence and responsibility or do they, through their expertise and articulateness, subtly reinforce dependence on themselves and their prescriptive directions? Of high value in the PCA is the person and a respect for the integrity and dignity of each person in the family, regardless of age or role. The family's potential is exemplified and extolled in each individual member. The PCA recognizes the rights of family members to express their feelings and participate in an open, free, and increasingly family-directed process.

What are the therapists' views about the nature of the person? Do therapists generally perceive people as rational or irrational, as innately bad (must be socialized by and for society) or innately good (having a positive direction in growth), or not viewed on a good/bad dimension at all? What fosters healthy development of children and enhances the continuing mature growth of adults? To what extent are therapists helping each family member develop and reach for a healthy personality and a healthy family? Normative behavior may not be healthy for each individual (Jourard, 1959). The PCA views people in a positive way: If the right psychological conditions are offered, then persons and families will develop their potentials as well as maintain and enhance themselves.

How does the behavior develop in the context of a family? Is a conditioning process present where a child or person "operates on" an environment and, subsequently, behaviors are extinguished or reinforced by external events? Or is there an inner actualizing tendency in the organism that motivates the person to maintain and enhance the self? As the person symbolizes experiences in awareness, the person perceives what is experienced, desired, or rejected. Therapists' views about how behavior and/or attitudes develop will most certainly affect their methods of helping families with issues.

What is the therapist's role in helping others to grow and change? Is the therapist the expert on families who understands most nuances of family development and individual psychological development? To what extent does the expert family therapist determine who will be seen in therapy, diagnose the family problems, probe for causes of problems, prescribe remedial family actions, reinforce and challenge selected behaviors of family members to bring about resolutions to conflict, and generally direct the total therapy process? The PCA strives to understand the inner worlds of the family members, with all their feelings, and to help the family move in a direction that they choose. O'Leary (1989) suggests that person-centered family therapists need to address the objective reality of the family as well as respond to the personal meanings of the individual.

What are the psychological conditions of therapy that are necessary for therapeutic changes in families? Is it enough to say that a positive therapeutic relationship between a therapist and a family is a crucial factor in family change? What are the key ingredients of a facilitative therapeutic climate? The PCA seeks to establish facilitative conditions for a family developmental process. If the core conditions are present to a certain minimal degree, then a relationship and a forward-moving process with exploration, growth, and change takes place. A therapist focuses on the conditions and the process because the results are inherent in the process. A family will move in positive, healthy psychological directions and seek resolutions to concerns consistent with the family dynamics. When trusted, a family will do what is best for itself; the family *can* be trusted.

How does the family therapy process unfold? To what extent does the focus center on the past (there and then), the present (here and now), or the future? If the climate and a trusting relationship are present for the family, will the process inevitably occur? Does the therapist use a previously developed psychological model to diagnose the family problems and then prescribe directions/procedures in therapy? Or to what extent do the family members, under positive therapeutic conditions, serve as the key diagnosticians and determine the therapeutic directions based on their own views?

What are the differences and similarities in the techniques that help the process evolve? To what extent does the therapist analyze and interpret the meanings of the family's communications or does the therapist help the family discover the meanings of their own experiences? To what extent does the therapist manipulate and frustrate the family members into discovery of their main problems? What meanings do transference and countertransference hold in the therapy process? The PCA sees the therapist's helping behaviors as reflections of inner attitudes toward the family. The PCA is not a bagful of tricks and techniques. The PCA therapist does not interpret the meanings of family experiences to the family. The PCA attempts to help clients explore feelings and express inner thoughts as well as discover the meanings of their feelings and thoughts and how these motivate the daily, interactional living behaviors of family members.

What are the most visible outcomes in different approaches? Is the goal of therapy to change behavior or to change self-concept and family esteem? To what extent is the goal to change specific situational behavior or to recognize inner potentials for dealing effectively with situational events? Is the therapeutic movement away from "non-response-ability" toward "response-ability" in handling life situations, away from a more behavioral view of events toward construing events in a more phenomenological-perceptual view? Is the new locus of evaluation resting within the family or with significant other persons? Is the direction of change toward more self-responsibility and self-direction by the family? As Barrett-Lennard (1984) discusses a person-centered systems view of family relationships, his key point is that "the membership structure of a family has direct and profound bearing on the relationships that are possible and likely to be experienced and, therefore, on the learning developmental potentialities of each member" (p. 222). Individual family members are also viewed in diverse and multiple family interactions and relationships. Levant (1984) compares a psychodynamic perspective of the family as a system and the basic assumptions underlying client-centered family therapy.

APPLICATION

FAMILY ISSUES FOR WHICH THE PERSON-CENTERED APPROACH ARE APPLICABLE

Because of the evolving nature of the person-centered approach through practice and research, it has special meaning for most family issues that involve interpersonal relationships (Rogers, 1959). The family group is probably the closest of all interpersonal circles and has high emotional intensity.

Issues vary and families are different. That is why the therapist may work with many different family configurations in therapy situations. The family members in attendance may vary depending on who in the family will make a commitment to the therapy process.

The following family issues are not in any way intended to cause a therapist to develop preconceived notions about what to look for in a family therapy situation. Rather, they are ones that have often surfaced in therapy situations. Following are six general family issues for which the person-centered approach can be of particular help.

1. REALNESS IN FAMILY RELATIONSHIPS Clients often believe that they become more vulnerable in the family when they express their true thoughts, feelings, and views about family dynamics. In a sense, there is a fear of loss—loss of love or place in the family.

There is the question of trusting family members: "Can I trust other members with my real self?" "Can I bring my thoughts and feelings out in the open?"

In essence, the family situation cannot be lived on a real basis because the clients perceive the need to be defensive and shield their inner selves. When defensiveness is present, there is an incongruence "within" some individual members that is reflected "between" members of the family in interpersonal relationships.

2. THE EXPRESSION OF FEELINGS IN THE FAMILY The expression of innermost feelings is essentially part of being genuine in family relationships. How can family members learn to accept their own feelings as well as accept the feelings of their family members if there is the constant question of whether other family members will accept the persons and their feelings? Expressing positive feelings of love and affection can be just as much of a problem as expressing negative feelings. When feelings are suppressed, family members may decrease their trust in their own experiencing. Often, family members have denied their feelings for so long that they are not fully aware of their feelings toward people and events in the family. Family members may live family relationships according to what someone else believes is right rather than what they believe is right. If members pay attention, the nonverbal communication of family members carries a heavy load of feelings being expressed.

3. FAMILY MEMBERS AS INDIVIDUALS At times, family members believe that they are not viewed as unique, with their own ideas and potential. Consequently, they are not perceived so much as individuals as they are perceived to be a family group. The notion that each individual has a set of potentials and abilities to give direction to his or her life is subsumed under the family plan for the future. There is "a" prescribed reality for the family, and each member is not viewed as having his or her own separate reality (Rogers, 1978). Therefore, forced identification with family doctrines may hurt individuals, and the inner realities of each individual member may affect the family.

Family expectations of its members can be an issue for members—wives, husbands, children, and others. The roles and role expectations of the family are often not the same expectations as those of the individual. Occasionally, parents and close relatives try to mold the children and others with their expectations, goals, enthusiasms, unfulfilled wishes, and unexplored dreams. Ellinwood (1989) stresses that children in the family therapy process need to be heard and understood. The children as well as the adults need to be offered the conditions of empathic understanding, unconditional positive regard, and genuineness.

The perceived lack of support by members is another aspect of this issue. Many family members seek to identify with the family, a tight-knit support group, and still maintain individuality and separateness.

4. LISTENING AND TWO-WAY COMMUNICATION When there is a breakdown in communication, members perceive that they are not listened to and certainly not understood. They believe that other members do not understand their experiences in the family and in the world. The process of communication may be only a one-way avenue with one family member giving out orders, decisions, values to follow, and guidelines for living. Power over others is used to resolve conflicts. Some individuals may not be allowed to maintain such personal power in the family. Since there is little mutual listening, there is less acceptance of the views of others. Members' views are not respected, and authority may reside in one person.

Lack of communication and understanding can put undue pressures on the family group. If members are not communicating, they may be working at cross-purposes and not be mutually consulted and involved. They lack each other's support and resources.

Communication issues have another effect that devastates a family. The real expression of affection between family members is decreased proportionately to the lack of communication. Love, caring, and acceptance within a family are crucial to the survival of its members and the family group. There is a breakdown in the process of relating to each other when there is a lack of communication.

5. A PROCESS FOR FAMILY DEVELOPMENT AND PROBLEM SOLVING

Another cause of family problems stems from the lack of a method or process through which the family can resolve issues and problems as they arise. Too often, no process for handling developmental issues and problem solving exists, and problems are either left to one person to solve or are ignored as if they never existed. Without a process to handle family problems and issues, both change and positive, healthy family development are hindered. Families often have no mechanism to deal with crisis situations such as death, grief from loss or separation, accidents, or other traumatic events.

Each adult partner in a family brings with him or her a definition or concept of "family" (van der Veen & Olson, 1983). This definition may include rules for living, roles to be assumed by various family members, and expectations for various roles. Sometimes these deep inner views are not communicated until one partner violates the unwritten rules or there are children in the family. This whole definitional or conceptual set may not even be in the partners' awareness and yet it certainly affects the family dynamics, development, and new developing family concept. Family therapy offers partners an opportunity to clarify these definitions, synthesize them with their partners, and establish new avenues of communications for the family.

There may be no process for discussing values, decision making, and living. How does a family member gain values and a sense of clarity about these values? The individual may feel like a receptacle for the values of others and see no opportunity for a search and clarification of personal values.

6. CLARITY OF SOCIETAL EFFECTS ON THE FAMILY GROUP

The family competes with many societal influences for the attention and development of its members. The demands of careers, education, peers, television, wars, and world events may sap the very energies of the family. Does the family become the first priority or do external interests take over? Is there a family process for "thinking the priorities?" Does the family serve as a support group as its members become accountable in the world outside the family? Can a family set its own pace of life and not let the pace be set by society?

GOALS FOR THE COUNSELING PROCESS

First, the therapist enters therapy without a preconceived model of how families interact and how problems are generated by specific interactions in components of that model. The therapist begins therapy without a model of exactly how a family should believe, change, and live or whether it is always in the members' best interest to remain together as a family. Patterson (1968) says that the therapy process is not one of "influencing attitudes, beliefs, or behavior or means of persuading, leading, or convincing no matter how indirectly, subtly, or painlessly. It is not the process of getting someone to think or behave in ways in which we want him (her) to think or behave, or in ways we think best for him (her)" (p. 1).

The therapist does not begin therapy with a preconceived idea of who might be seen in counseling. The therapist does not perceive that he or she will be the expert, skilled diagnostician who, single-handedly, pinpoints the family's problems and prescribes a treatment plan. Heider (1985) offers a passage saying that "the wise leader does not impose a personal agenda or value system on the group." The family therapist would be open and attentive to whatever emerges. Heider says that "openness is simply more potent than any system of judgments ever devised" (p. 97).

Each family is viewed as a group of unique individuals with unique interactional patterns and issues. The members are also seen as possessing many potentials of their own for maintaining and enhancing themselves, as well as the family. They are capable of shaping their own growth both as individuals and as a family group. The therapist shows a tremendous respect for the family's potential to be actualizing and self-determining. The therapist recognizes that the family or some part of the family seeks therapy because of their own state of incongruence or conflict in the family group or with one or more members of the family. Although there may be similarities among families, the therapist remains open to the specialness and the nuances of each and every family and its members.

The therapist strives to establish a healthy psychological climate (Rogers, 1957a, 1970, Ch. 3) which the family members can use to establish realness in family relationships, express true feelings, remain separate and yet identify with the family, develop effective two-way communication, start a healthy process for family development and problem solving, and clarify societal effects on the family as well as clarify conflicts, seek solutions, explore values, make decisions, experiment with new behaviors, and develop a family model/direction unique to its needs and wants. The family experiences a climate in which they are not judged or evaluated. They have the opportunity to explore their difficulties in a nonthreatening environment when they are with the therapist. The members experience a sense of caring, honesty, and understanding from the therapist. A mutual, close, trusting relationship often develops between the therapist and family members.

The six conditions that Rogers (1957a) postulates from the individual therapeutic process are as follows.

1. Two persons are in psychological contact.
2. The first, whom we shall term the client, is in a state of incongruence, being vulnerable or anxious.
3. The second person, whom we shall term the therapist, is congruent or integrated in the relationship.
4. The therapist experiences unconditional positive regard for the client.
5. The therapist experiences an empathic understanding of the client's frame of reference and endeavors to communicate this experience to the client.

6. The communication to the client of the therapist's empathic understanding and unconditional positive regard is to a minimal degree achieved. (p. 96)

These conditions are necessary and sufficient for a process of constructive personality change to occur. Gaylin (1989) has reviewed the six conditions as they address the family therapeutic process and has found them "to be a good foundation for the refining and clarifying occurring within the family therapy hour" (p. 275). He elaborates on these conditions for family therapy and how they are viewed in the context of family helping. He indicates that family therapists need a basic knowledge of child development. In their article on person-centered family therapy with couples, Bozarth and Shanks (1989) support the actualizing process in the family as well as the formative tendency in the family as an organismic unit that moves toward health and wellness.

What are the components of this healthy psychological climate? The first component is that of the therapist's genuineness with the family members. *Genuineness or congruence* involves an attempt to be real with them as family members and as persons. What a therapist experiences inside is present in his or her awareness and is part of his or her communication. The therapist who is genuine strives to be whole and fully present in the therapy situation. Such a therapist shows his or her true inner feelings—irritation as well as enjoyment—and seeks to be congruent and to avoid presenting a facade or being phony. He or she is open and expresses feelings and thoughts as they arise in the "here and now" family therapy session. Although therapist's responsibilities may differ somewhat from those of the family members, he or she is, like each of them, a person with feelings, thoughts, and ideas. The effective family therapist has a clear sense of being.

When family members perceive a realness on the therapist's part, they become more genuine and honest in their interactions—not only with the therapist, but also with the other members. More openness exists in the members' expressions when every one is more open to events in terms of the "here and now" family therapy process. The members strive to be more in touch with their own thoughts and feelings as these emerge into awareness and become present in members' communications. When the therapist places more trust in the members, they come to trust themselves more and to feel themselves worthy of trust. As the therapist is more genuine in the relationship, the family members also become more honest and real in the therapy process, in the family interaction, and outside the therapy setting.

A second component is that of the therapist's ability to care for the members and to prize them. The therapist experiences an *unconditional positive regard* for the members and for the family as a group. The members are accepted as persons, even though all behaviors of the members may not be likable. The dignity and integrity of each person in the family is respected as well as the "whole" family group. If the family members perceive that the therapist prizes them and cares about them, they will come to prize themselves more. They will believe in themselves and see themselves as more worthwhile. In other words, their self-concepts will begin to change and affect family relationships and their view or concept of the family. Perhaps there is no other place where the potential for unconditional positive regard is greater than in the family. Heider (1985) proposes that the wise leader (family therapist) is like water—"water cleanses and refreshes all creatures without distinction and without judgment; water freely and fearlessly goes beneath the surface of things; water is fluid and responsive..." (p. 5).

A third component is the therapist's willingness to listen carefully with *empathic understanding* to what family members have to share. An effective therapist hears and understands family members' needs, wants, conflicts, fears, joys, loves, goals, values, hates, disappointments, dreams, sorrows, and their worlds or realities. Family members' realities are often described from their vivid imagery with rich metaphors and stories that, when understood, can add significantly to the therapy process. The therapist also senses how metaphors and stories are used to teach children lessons on life and living. Members are encouraged and helped to explore, clarify, and understand their own meanings and how these relate to the family milieu. The therapist tries to understand each family member's view of the family problem(s) as well as the family themes that may emerge. Then the therapist's understanding is communicated to the family members. This communication helps the therapist stay in touch with the direction taken by the members in the counseling process. Heider (1985) says "to know what is happening, push less, open out and be aware. See without staring. Listen quietly rather than listening hard. Use intuition and reflection rather than trying to figure things out" (p. 27).

If members find that the therapist listens and attempts to understand their issues, feelings, and hopes, they will work toward understanding themselves better and, in turn, will work at understanding other family members in the family as a group. They will work at not making assumptions about what other members mean to communicate. The members tend to develop an ability to be empathic with each other. When members perceive that they are understood by the therapist and other family members, they feel a part of the process and the family problem-solving group. They see themselves as needed resources within the group. Members identify with the family, and *family esteem* begins to change in positive directions.

The three components are essential to an effective counseling process. When the therapist attempts to experience unconditional positive regard for family members, to be integrated and genuine in the therapy situation, and to show empathic understanding by listening to members, the members also demonstrate these qualities with other family members as well as with the therapist. *They learn what they are experiencing.* If the conditions of empathic understanding and unconditional positive regard are perceived to a minimal degree by the family, they begin to work together to create and define their separate and shared visions of the family; a trusting relationship develops (psychological contact) and a creative process unfolds. When family members also learn helping skills and become facilitative in the process, this speeds up the process of therapy. Some family members pick up very fast on how the therapist is facilitating in the situation (Ohlsen, 1979). At this point in the therapy process, constructive and positive conditions for a healthy psychological environment have emerged within the family group. Then family members can proceed to tackle family problems in a caring environment characterized by a growing mutual trust between members, a lack of threat, more risk-taking by members, feedback between members, real behaviors, and family members' growth. The therapist's commitment to the process also includes an *intent* to be fully present by focusing on the family's potentials and growth resources. The family and its members remain the focus, the center of the process. The task of the therapist is to facilitate each member's discovery of the inherent potentials of the family members to solve their own problems and to be more the persons that they wish to be as individuals and as a family. The therapist must be constantly aware of the therapy process and of the members' thoughts, feelings, fears, and hopes. Finally, the family learns a process for family development and problem solving. The family therapy situation may be one place where family members can experience support, acceptance, and encouragement to develop their potentials as separate individuals and as family members.

PRIMARY RESPONSIBILITIES OF FAMILY MEMBERS IN THERAPY

The responsibilities taken by the family members have an emergent quality about them. The members accept more responsibility for the process and their part in it as therapy progresses. Often, in the beginning, the members look to the therapist for direction and advice on problem solutions, and when they do not receive advice and solutions to their problems, the members can become dismayed. Occasionally, family members have not liked this responsibility. They have wanted the therapist, as an expert, to tell them what to do and to take responsibility for the outcome. Yet the therapist seeks to help them reach solutions by listening, caring, and being real in the therapeutic relationship. If the therapist is able to offer a facilitative climate, then a therapeutic process of growth and change will "inevitably" occur. The therapist believes in the members and respects their own strengths, abilities, and potentials to use the therapy process, to clarify issues, and to resolve problems, regardless of the members' ages. Family members can accept the responsibility for actions and consequences. They are the agents of change. Ultimately, the locus of evaluation for family actions and results resides in the family members as a group.

The movement in therapy is from dependence and lack of "response-ability" on the part of the family toward more independence and use of their abilities to be responsive to family problems. The movement is toward responsibility, direction, determination, decision making, and assessment by family members.

The readiness and commitment to the therapy process are up to the family members. They have the freedom to choose who will participate in therapy, the extent of the participation, and the pattern of participation. The process is open, and all members may be encouraged to participate.

As well as determining who will participate, the members participate fully in the exploration part of the process and identification of the problem on which therapy is to be focused. In this sense, the members are very much a part of diagnosing what the problem is, what appear to be the current determinants of the problem, and what steps should be taken inside and outside of therapy. In the therapy process, the family group weighs its members' values and often comes in touch with a *family-valuing* approach. This weighing of values is closely followed by a *family decision-making* segment with all members in the therapy group taking part in the decision. With the therapist's help, the family members contribute significantly to the counseling/treatment plans as well as in the assessment of the effectiveness of those plans for the family group. As a result of assessment, new directions and plans are determined by the members.

All of these responsibilities are assumed by the family members over the course of therapy. Complete ownership and acceptance of the problem is a major task for the family group. The risks for change belong to the family members, and so do the consequences, satisfactions, and disappointments. It is the family members' responsibility to explore the meanings of their actions and the family therapy experience, to initiate actions for change, and to terminate the sessions when all members perceive it to be appropriate to do so.

FUNCTIONS OF A THERAPIST

As the family therapist begins to enter a counseling relationship, several questions may serve as helpful checks. These come from a passage (Heider, 1985) on unbiased leadership: "Can you mediate emotional issues without taking sides or picking favorites? Can you breathe freely and remain relaxed even in the presence of passionate fears and desires? Are your own conflicts clarified? Is your own house clean? Can you be gentle with all factions and lead the group without dominating? Can you remain open and receptive, no matter what issues arise? Can you know what is emerging, yet keep your peace while others discover for themselves?..." (p. 19). Combs (1989) views the therapist's self as a most crucial instrument in the therapy process.

In helping family members move toward responsibility and independence in problem solving, the therapist attempts to offer the conditions that create a positive climate for therapy. These human qualities of the therapist were described earlier: a willingness to understand the perceptions and realities of family members (empathic understanding), a desire to be genuine in the therapy situation (congruence), and a prizing of the family members as persons (unconditional positive regard). *These human qualities, the more significant aspects of therapy, are reflected in the therapist's helping behavior.* In this chapter, *these reflections will be called skills.* The importance of reflecting these qualities cannot be stressed too much because of the numerous person-to-person interactions in family therapy situations. Therapist–family interactions call for much communicative skill in understanding the wants, needs, thoughts, and feelings of family members. The therapist must be aware of the surface meaning and the strategic meaning and have empathy for the emotional reality underlying the interaction. Guerney and Guerney (1989) and Gaylin (1989) believe strongly that, at times, the family therapist needs to offer educational guidance and teaching of selected parenting/relationship skills. The family members also learn the skills of helping by watching and experiencing the therapist. Thayer (1977) has described an experiential approach to learning helping skills.

The following skills are some of the basic ones that contribute to the expression of the therapist's human qualities (Thayer, 1981). These skills do not represent all of the "particulars" of helping family members.

BEING ATTENTIVE Attentiveness communicates a readiness on the therapist's part to focus on the members and what they are thinking and feeling. The therapist's physical posture is turned toward the person who is speaking to show interest in what is being communicated. Communication is facilitated by helping the members talk about the subjects that they have chosen. Rather than directing the discussion, the therapist follows the member's expressions of thoughts, feelings, and meanings regarding the family situation.

BEING RELAXED To aid in attentiveness to the members and to the process, the therapist is comfortable in the situation and comfortable with families. The muscles of the therapist's body are relaxed. In contrast, tenseness suggests that other conditions or events, such as uneasiness about the current situation or personal concerns, are distracting the therapist and might impair the therapy process.

SENSING AND COMMUNICATING AN UNDERSTANDING OF THOUGHTS (VERBAL MESSAGES) The therapist is able to hear the members' messages and state in his or her own words what the members are saying. Such statements communicate to the family what is heard and allow for an accuracy check by the members. The therapist's communication helps to assure the group members that someone is really trying to understand their ways of viewing life in the family situation. The *intent* is to follow the members' leads in order to understand the members and then, in turn, to communicate this understanding to the group. Questions are used infrequently since they often represent the therapist's curiosity and desire to direct the process. Instead, the therapist encourages the members to direct the flow of communication because they know what the concerns are.

SENSING AND COMMUNICATING AN UNDERSTANDING OF FEELINGS AND MEANINGS The therapist listens carefully for "feeling" words and observes the simultaneous nonverbal messages in the family's voices and physical expressions. Responding to feelings and meanings is a key skill that can communicate to the family members the therapist's understanding of their worlds. The therapist must be particularly sensitive to the nonverbal messages of family members, because these messages are not always the same as the verbal messages. As much as 65% of the feelings and meanings of messages are communicated nonverbally; thus, it is important for the therapist to be aware of facial expressions, voice tones, eye contact, hand gestures, body movements, and other nonverbal components. A difference between verbal and nonverbal messages may signal that members are not completely aware of their own experiencing. The member(s) may be in a state of incongruence.

BEING AWARE OF PERSONAL EXPERIENCING AND EXPRESSING THE RELATED THOUGHTS AND FEELINGS The therapist tries to pay attention to his or her own inner self and internal dialogue. He or she focuses inward to be aware of feelings and thoughts and then expresses these feelings and thoughts appropriately in "I" messages. Using "I" indicates that the therapist owns these messages and is responsible for them. Expressing inner feelings and thoughts helps the therapist become more honest and direct in interactions with the family, more integrated as a person in the therapeutic relationship.

EXPERIENCING POSITIVE REGARD AND APPRECIATION FOR FAMILY MEMBERS AS PERSONS AND SHOWING RESPECT FOR THEM AND FOR ONESELF The therapist reflects a caring attitude, taking time to consider the feelings and thoughts of the family members as well as his or her own rights as a person in the therapy situation. In essence, the therapist tries to demonstrate to the members "I prize you as persons and as members of this family."

TRUSTING AND EXPRESSING INTUITIVE HUNCHES Often, instincts are more valuable to the therapy process than logic and intellect. The therapist who remains open with all senses will, at some points, experience a real "gut," visceral sensation about family members, the therapy process, and what the members are experiencing. This hunch, often perceived only minimally by the therapist, can become a very accurate indicative perception and a useful tool in the therapy process. A therapist needs to test out the accuracy of these hunches in safe situations outside of therapy, learn to trust their usefulness, and then incorporate them into his or her helping style.

Three additional skills are noted for use by the family therapist (Thayer, 1984).

RECOGNIZING AND RESPONDING TO THAT PERSONAL MATERIAL THAT IS MOST CONSPICUOUS BY ITS ABSENCE Occasionally, family members will communicate information that reveals some component of feelings, thoughts, or information that is conspicuously absent. With sensitivity, the therapist may choose to respond, depending on what the missing component might be. Take, for example, a teenager who talked of sports, school, his mother, siblings, grades, and teachers. The component that seemed obviously missing was talk of his father. Responding to the absent information, the therapist learned that the boy's father had died several months earlier and that it was difficult for the boy to accept his father's death. In this case, the situation was sensitive. The therapist had to respond with care. But much can be learned by understanding what family members or a family group are speaking about and what is conspicuously absent in the themes of communication.

PAYING ATTENTION TO PERSONAL (THERAPIST) MENTAL IMAGES Images based on stimulus statements and communication from the family provide a rich source of data for understanding the world of the family members. At times, concurrent feelings and thoughts will be generated in the therapist that bring him or her closer to the visual/perceptual world of a family member or family. Trying to visualize what the family member is describing can make for greater empathic understanding and personal relevancy of therapy.

RECOGNIZING POLARITIES AND HELPING FAMILY MEMBERS BALANCE THESE APPARENT DIFFERENCES Frequently in family situations, polar differences are dealt with separately when they might be seen as part of the same unit. Too often, family members have been caused to deny feelings and their relationship to the total process of family. The therapist has an exciting adventure ahead if he or she can help members recognize and understand the polarities that exist, balance the different aspects of family, stop denying the affective part, and recognize that the result will be a whole, fuller process of therapy, greater than the sum of the two parts.

THE PROCESS OF FAMILY THERAPY

The focus in this section is on what is occurring "within" the individuals and "between" family members in the process of family therapy.

Rogers (1961b) has a view of how the process of therapy affects personality change. Rogers has taken a more "naturalist's observational, descriptive approach" (p. 128) to the events in therapy. From these observations, he has made "low-level inferences" about the most basic events in the process. Although the process to be discussed describes the individual in therapy, the stages are also indicative of what happens "within" individuals in family therapy. The potential for the family's being a healthy, creative, complex whole lies "within" each family member.

Heider (1985) reminds the therapist that "you are facilitating another person's process. It is not your process. Do not intrude. Do not control. Do not force your own needs and insights into the foreground. If you do not trust a person's process, that person will not trust you" (p. 33). In many ways, this statement applies to the therapy process for family members and the family.

Of special note in Rogers's study of the therapeutic process is the importance of feelings, coming closer to experiencing the feelings of the moment, accurately symbolizing this experiencing of feelings for better communication and "moments of movement" in therapy. Anderson (1989b) believes that the therapist's empathic responses to the personal and subjective narrative self-stories of the individuals can be expanded or shifted to include and have relevance to shared, collective experiences of the family.

If the optimal conditions described earlier are present and perceived by the individual family members, then a therapeutic process emerges. Rogers's view of an emerging continuum is "from fixity to changingness, from rigid structure to flow, from stasis to process" (Rogers, 1961b, p. 131). But the process is "not forced." Given the appropriate conditions, the therapy process will flow. The family sets a pace. The clients' expressions would be indicators of where they stood on this process continuum.

Although seven stages are noted in the process conception, Rogers maintains that the process is a continuum. The clients would most likely be at approximately one stage in their development and would not necessarily show characteristics of several other stages. The stages of the process follow (Rogers, 1961b, pp. 132–154):

[Stage One] Communication is only about externals....Feelings and personal meanings are neither recognized nor owned. No problems are recognized or perceived at this stage. There is no desire to change.

[Stage Two] Expression begins to flow in regard to non-self topics....There is no sense of personal responsibility in problems....Feelings may be exhibited, but are not recognized as such or owned....

[Stage Three] There is much expression about or description of feelings and personal meanings not now present....There is very little acceptance of feelings. For the most part, feelings are revealed as something shameful, bad, or abnormal, or unacceptable in other ways. Feelings are exhibited, and then sometimes recognized as feelings. Experiencing is described as in the past, or as somewhat remote from self....Personal choices are often seen as ineffective.

[Stage Four] There is a tendency toward experiencing feelings in the immediate present, and there is distrust and fear of this possibility....There is little open acceptance of feelings, though some acceptance is exhibited....There is a realization of concern about contradictions and incongruences between experience and self....There are feelings of self-responsibility in problems, though such feelings vacillate. Though a close relationship still seems dangerous, the client risks himself (herself), relating to some small extent on a feeling basis.

[Stage Five] Feelings are expressed freely as in the present. Feelings are very close to being fully experienced....There is an increasing ownership of self feelings, and a desire to be these, to be the "real me"....There is an increasing quality of acceptance of self-responsibility for the problems being faced, and a concern as to how he (she) has contributed.

[Stage Six] A present feeling is directly experienced with immediacy and richness. This immediacy of experiencing, and the feeling which constitutes its contents, are accepted....In this stage, internal communication is free and relatively unblocked....The incongruence between experience and awareness is vividly experienced as it disappears into congruence....In this stage, there are no longer "problems," external or internal. The client is living, subjectively, a phase of his (her) problem.

[Stage Seven] New feelings are experienced with immediacy and richness of detail, both in the therapeutic relationship and outside....There is a growing and continuing sense of acceptant ownership of these changing feelings, a basic trust in his (her) own process....Internal communication is clear, with feelings and symbols well matched, and fresh terms for new feelings. There is the experiencing of effective choice of new ways of being.

This process is one that is set in motion when clients are fully accepted. Cognitive components are part of this process at every point. Generally, "the process moves from a point of fixity, where all the elements and threads described above are separately discernible and separately understandable, to the flowing peak moments of therapy in which all these threads become inseparably woven together" (Rogers, 1961b, p. 158).

Family therapy process emphasizes not only what happens "within" individual members but also what occurs "between" family members in their interpersonal relationships. The challenge for the family therapist is to be congruent in the relationship, to prize the family, and to understand empathically each member's subjective meaning while understanding and responding to the interpersonal, intersubjective meaning in the context of the family (Anderson, 1989a). This distinguishes family therapy from individual therapy. The therapy situation offers the family an opportunity to interact in an increasingly nonthreatening environment where they are respected as individuals and not labeled in any way by the therapist. Since the members often hold deep, intense emotions about family events, another aspect of family therapy appears very much like the process in an encounter group experience. Again, Rogers (1970, Ch. 2) has described the observable events in encounter groups, and these are similar to the events that have been observed in family therapy; yet more study needs to be conducted on person-centered family therapy. A key difference in family therapy and encounter groups is that after a family leaves a therapy session, they may go home together or see each other a great deal before the subsequent session. The family staying together has its advantages and certainly adds to the complexities of therapy. Family members may be encouraged to practice their new communication skills at home.

Families do not always start in the first stage of a therapy process, because some parts of a helping process may have already been worked through. Here is a brief overview of the stages based on work with encounter groups (Rogers, 1970, Ch. 2).

1. *Milling around.* Family members are uncertain what their responsibilities will be in setting the structure of therapy. The members will attempt to answer "What is our purpose for being here?"

2. *Resistance to personal expression or exploration.* Members may tend not to reveal their thoughts and feelings about family events or about themselves. There is often a subtle testing of the therapist and other family members. "How safe is it to express views here?" Members may fear revealing themselves and may lack a trust in the family group.

3. *Description of past feelings.* The expression of feelings consumes more of the therapy time, but the feelings are about past events or ones external to the therapy situation.

4. *Expression of negative feelings.* A hint that the first real "here and now" feelings are negative in nature. They may be directed at other members, the therapist, or the therapy situation in general. These negative feelings may be a way to test the trustworthiness of the members and the freedom of the therapy situation. "Is this a place where individuals can truly be themselves, regardless of the nature of their feelings and thoughts?"

5. *Expression and exploration of personally meaningful material.* A member of the family may take the risk of revealing himself or herself to the other family members. Although there is a risk in expressing oneself, a climate of trust is building.

6. *The expression of immediate interpersonal feelings in the group.* Members are beginning to express their moment-to-moment feelings toward one another. These feelings may be positive or negative. The members may begin to understand intuitively that something in the family is changing.

7. *The development of a healing capacity in the group.* Some family members can intuitively sense what others are experiencing and, in a climate of trust and freedom, can respond with acceptance and understanding. Individual members are helped to be aware of and deal with their present experiencing.

8. *Self-acceptance and the beginning of change.* As family members come to accept themselves as they are, this acceptance of self signals the starting of change. Resistance to change subsides as members begin to accept themselves as they are in the family. This acceptance generates more self-exploration and initial acceptance of others. More genuineness is evident from members. The acceptance of one's own experiencing is a significant event.

9. *The cracking of facades.* As the process continues, family members are less patient with defenses. Members demand realness of others in terms of current feelings and thoughts. This component can be hurtful, at times, but the other members respond with sensitivity and caring for the family member and help to heal the hurting person.

10. *The individual receives feedback.* Individual members receive data on how they appear to others in the family. With caring and openness, feedback is often quite constructive, regardless of its positive or negative tone. The feedback can trigger more self-exploration and sharing between family members. Members are learning to request, accept, and use feedback (Ohlsen, Horne, & Lawe, 1988).

11. *Confrontation.* Constructive feedback is occasionally too mild a word to describe the intense interaction between family members. Confrontation can be positive but is often decidedly negative.

12. *The helping relationship outside the group sessions.* Family members take advantage of the numerous opportunities outside of therapy to offer support and

understanding to other individual members. This is one of the significant signs of changes occurring in the interpersonal relationships between family members. They are exhibiting their abilities to be accepting, caring, supportive, and helping.

13. *The basic encounter.* As the trusting climate has developed, family members are coming closer and in more direct contact than is customary. The intense experiencing appears to release the potentials of the members to be genuine in the family and to work together to solve issues confronting the family. A change in one member affects all other events and members in the family dynamics.

14. *The expression of positive feelings and closeness.* As sessions proceed, an increasing amount of feelings of warmth, family spirit, and trust is developed. There is significant realness in the family's interpersonal relationships. Members can work toward the resolution of issues because there is a feeling of acceptance among members and a feeling of worthwhileness by individuals. There is a sharing and acceptance of responsibility for resolving family problems.

15. *Behavior changes in the family group.* Family members listen to each other with more understanding, and two-way communication is better. The family members have proceeded in learning a process in which they can continue to explore and clarify values, examine and make decisions, and challenge the issues that may come before the family.

When they are at home, there is a need for family members to maintain the level of openness that they reached in therapy. They need to continue the work of providing support for members, making acceptance of each other "real" in the interpersonal relationships. There also may be times when a member of a family will need to continue in therapy alone because of additional need for support. The family can be a support system for this person.

While there continually seems to be an emergent, fluid quality in the family therapy process, several family directions seem to stand out. The family seems to move *away from* facades and *toward* genuineness and increased openness in family interpersonal relationships. They move away from meeting the "oughts" and expectations of others toward greater self-direction as a family. And as the family experiences more prizing, accepting of its members, and listening more carefully to its own members' feelings, thoughts, and meanings, then the family moves toward greater acceptance of the family as a group and understanding of the dynamic, changing, actualizing, forming group (Rogers, 1961c). The self-esteem of individual members as well as the general esteem of the family as a group are enhanced. The family recognizes its own tremendous potential for development and positive, healthy psychological change.

THE DEVELOPMENT OF FAMILY MEETINGS

The person-centered view may be applied in families who are not in therapy. Rogers (1977, pp. 34–37) tells of Ben and Claire and their unique situation as they searched for new ways of living in family relationships.

What happens when parents regard their children as unique persons in an ever-changing communicative relationship? The story of Ben and Claire illustrates the dynamics of this process. Claire had raised her children along authoritarian lines until her divorce and remarriage to a man who was committed to the person-centered approach. Each partner brought to this marriage children by previous marriages, and there were many new relationships with varying degrees of trust and communication. Claire found herself changing.

In trying to resolve some of the new issues, Ben and Claire decided to have meetings in which every member of the family, no matter how young or old, was free to express his (or her) feelings—the complaints, satisfactions, or reactions—to the others.

The father of Walter, Claire's oldest son, had disappeared from Walter's life with little warning. Otherwise Claire's statement is self-explanatory. I simply asked her how their family group meetings had started.

Claire: We scheduled them. We picked a time. It turned out that it was every Tuesday. And nothing interfered with Tuesday—not a business meeting or a movie or entertaining, or if somebody came over we had to ask them to leave and come over another day. The children learned to count on that. There were a lot of adjustments to be made between me and Ben, between Ben and my children, and me and his children. And Ben had been involved in group work before and wanted this kind of experience—the closeness and sharing and expression of feelings—to be a natural part of the family unit. He called a meeting following dinner. We all stayed at the table—the children wondering what was going to happen. He started it by trying to teach them how to express feelings and get away from accusations, you know— "You are a bully," or "You pick on me." I was picked to be the first one to start going around the circle. There were eight of us at the table and I had seven people to cover and to tell them how I felt about them, each one. And not only the positive but some of the negative things, some of my concerns and worries that were very different with each child. And it was really the first time I had talked about negative things in a constructive way in front of everybody else. That usually is a private thing. I could say to one of the boys how proud I felt of his scholastic accomplishments but at the same time how worried I was about what I perceived as selfishness—that I didn't really understand where it came from and I wanted to talk to him more about it so that we could resolve it or I could understand it better. It was the first time I hadn't just shouted at him and said, "Share this with your sister, what's the matter with you?" And he could *hear* me. The children were restless and embarrassed at first. And then Ben, my husband, was next and he was a lot more skilled than I and topped off what I had said from his point of view. By that time the children had settled down and one of them was first and went around the circle—they really did a darned good job. I was surprised and very pleased. And they were proud and surprised and pleased with themselves.

And then an important thing happened. My oldest son, Walter, had had the hardest time with my divorce. He was the one who was chewing his fingernails and having nightmares. And not doing very well in school. He adored Ben. He was so happy to have Ben for his father—his stepfather. When he went around in the circle he said a lot of things about all of us, but when he got to Ben he just said, "And of course I love you," and passed right on. And we were all aware of something missing there. But as soon as Walter finished, Ben was the first one to say, "Gee, Walter, I feel cheated. Everyone seemed to get so much more from you, and I love hearing that you love me but there must be more and I really want some of that." And Walter in kind of a cool way said, "Well, ah ... I don't want to give you any more. I don't want to love you too much or get too close to you because I am afraid you are going to leave me." Wow! Tears started all around the table. We never would have heard that coming from Walter, would never even have known that was a part of him if we hadn't had this kind of structured scene to get in touch with this sort of thing. It gave

Ben an opportunity to let Walter know he understood him, like, I know how you loved your father and trusted him to be with you always and he left you and then your mother has had two other men she was seriously interested in who claimed to love you and they left. And now here I am and I claim to love you and you don't have any guarantees about me. And then he said, "But I'll tell you something: I want you to know that I am going to love you just as long as I live and you can trust me to be available to you and never leave you for as long as you want me." And Walter looked at him and started to cry and got up and walked around the table and just threw himself in Ben's arms and they sobbed. And everybody did. And the children at the table...got up and touched Walter. It was just a natural thing for them to do. At any rate, you can imagine it was something.

Rogers (1977) discusses what he sees as some of the significant contrasts with the traditional family relationship—a family that is communicating as psychological equals:

1) The focus on the relationships between the members of the family had higher priority than any other engagement of any kind. 2) The effort was made to focus on owned feelings, not accusations or judgments of another. 3) This shift was fully as hard for the parents as for the children. For Claire to change from "Share that with your sister!" to "I don't understand your selfishness" (as it appears to me) is an enormous change. 4) The new approach is not initially trusted. Everyone is uneasy, a bit suspicious, except possibly Ben. 5) The respect for the children is highly rewarded, because they turn out to be worthy of respect. 6) The openness which develops leads to a totally unexpected self-revelation and a deep communication. 7) The relationship between all members of the family as separate but independent persons is much strengthened. (p. 37)

PERSONALIZING THE TEACHING/LEARNING PROCESS FOR PROSPECTIVE COUNSELORS

Thayer (1981, 1997) has written about an assignment in the education of prospective counselors that involves the learners in planning, experiencing, and assessing a self-life experience. It is called an "experience module." The process goal is to help learners personalize the outside-of-class experience by asking them to design a project based on their wants and needs in relation to the topical subject. The learner determines the goals, the nature of the process, the level of risk, any necessary materials and resources, the location or setting, the people to be involved, the time commitment, how the experience will be reported, and how the affective and cognitive learning outcomes will be assessed—however significant or insignificant. The professor serves as a resource person, not one with veto power, to assist in helping ways—listening, brainstorming for ideas, exploring possible risks and consequences, facilitating decision making, securing materials, providing information and feedback, and the like.

Experience modules may take many forms and may be personally or topically directed. When learners' involvement is greater in the learning process, they share more in the joys and responsibilities of learning as well as the disappointments. Several examples of experience modules from graduate courses are provided below. Some of these have been completed in a couple and family counseling course.

1. Reestablish "feeling level" communication with my husband in order to enhance our relationship.
2. Resolve a conflict situation with my sister.
3. Plan and spend an enjoyable day with my father with whom I've recently spent so little time.
4. Locate and establish a relationship with my biological mother while maintaining a relationship with my adoptive parents.
5. Write a children's book with my own two children in order to help them accept and understand the changes in our lives that have occurred as a result of divorce, remarriage, and becoming a step-family (Schulz, 1992).
6. Develop "memories" of my father, who died in the Korean War, by learning more about his life and involvement in the war and by making contact with those who knew him at the time.
7. Learn more about the roots of my family by talking to my parents about their emigration from the "old country" (Italy).
8. Write a last will and testament outlining the nonmaterial possessions (values/qualities) that I wish to leave each of my five children and identifying the strengths that I see in each of them.
9. Research the genealogy of my family of origin and create a family tree to share with my mother, brother, and sister.
10. Travel to my grandmother's hometown, look at her birthplace and family gravesite, and review birth and death records.
11. Work on and reassess the nature of my relationship with my spouse, improve the intimacy and romance in our life since these have been affected by jobs and schooling as well as the transition of boys going to college and leaving home, and improve our ability to resolve conflicts.

Learners may find unique ways in which to process and report their feelings, thoughts, perceptions, and results of the experience module. Assessments vary from student journals/diaries to short books, poems, booklets including pictures, audio-taped presentations with music, videos, special skits, and written reports. Learners expend much energy on the modules. Results are usually positive and very meaningful. (And occasionally, the results are not predictable.) The modules can be used to complement classroom work and personalize aspects of the learning process.

EVALUATION

Cain (1989) poses a number of questions about the adequacy of a therapy model based on work with individuals rather than with families. He supports the need for more research and dialogue on family therapy practices and theory. Formulations of family therapy need to be made so that specific hypotheses can be tested to determine the effects and effectiveness of the person-centered approach. Rogers and his colleagues have undertaken research and have opened up therapy sessions for examination with the use of recording equipment. Studies by Aspy and Roebuck, 1974; Barrett-Lennard, 1962; Meador, 1971; Raskin, 1952, Ch. 6;

Rogers and Dymond, 1954; Rogers et al., 1967b; Shlien and Zimring, 1970; Standal, 1954; Stephenson, 1953; Tomlinson and Hart, 1962; and Walker, Rablen, and Rogers, 1960, have evaluated the therapeutic conditions, process, and other aspects of person-centered theory. These results suggest that the core conditions of congruence, empathic understanding, and unconditional positive regard are effective in facilitating learning, development, and positive therapeutic change. The results are supportive of the person-centered theory and its effectiveness.

In terms of family therapy, an additional construct has been formulated. The construct, *family concept*, is the family member's view of his or her family (van der Veen, Heubner, Jorgens, & Neja, Jr., 1964). "The *family concept* consists essentially of the feelings, attitudes, and expectations each of us has regarding his or her family life…. The family concept is assumed to have several characteristics: It influences behavior; it can be referred to and talked about by the individual; and it can change as a result of new experience and understanding" (Raskin & van der Veen, 1970, p. 389).

An instrument called the *Family Concept Q Sort* has been developed by van der Veen to measure change in the family concept associated with family therapy. The *Q Sort* contains 80 family items that relate to psychological functioning and to clinical interaction. "The items concern the entire family unit, not individual relationships within the family. Thus, the test provides a description of the most salient aspects of a person's family experience, regardless of the specific relationships involved" (Raskin & van der Veen, 1970, pp. 400–401).

Other professionals have also adapted the person-centered approach to family-related training seminars and experiments. Gordon (1970a, 1970b) has developed a person-centered training program for parents called *PET—Parent Effectiveness Training*. This program highlights may person-centered principles as a means of preparing parents for healthier interpersonal relationships with their children. More recently, Gordon has developed a program similar to *PET* for young people, *Youth Effectiveness*. The new *YET* program provides young people with interpersonal relationship skills and helps build their self-esteem. Guerney and Guerney (1989) have developed child relationship enhancement (CRE) family therapy to teach parents the skills and behaviors of the child-centered play therapist and the Parent Skills Training Program (PSTP) to teach parents to use empathy in daily interactions with their children. Snyder (1989) describes the relationship enhancement approach that was designed by Guerney (1977). She shows how he has brought together Rogers's philosophy and the family systems views of Gregory Bateson. Coulson (1978) tells his story in *Banding*, as his family had a jazz band that had a tremendous effect on their family togetherness and priorities. Thayer (1994) indicates that there is much "potential for offering more experiences and education for 'being a family.' Learning experiences could be offered on family valuing, family decision making, family spending, family meetings, family-centered activities, family work issues, or 'on becoming a healthy, fully functioning family.'"

SUMMARY

The proponents of the person-centered approach believe that families have much potential to resolve many of their own problems. Given the optimal psychological conditions, energies and inner potentials of family members will be released to solve family issues.

If family members perceive these optimal conditions of congruence in the relationship on the part of the therapist, an unconditional prizing of the family members by the therapist, and an accurate empathic understanding of the members' worlds by the therapist, they will experience a process of family therapy with a forward direction.

When these psychological conditions exist, the family's forward directions reflect certain characteristics:

1. Family members become more in touch with their own experiencing of the family. There is a greater genuineness *within* individual members and more honesty *between* family members.

2. Each family member is viewed as a unique and separate person who is to be encouraged in his or her development as a person.

3. Members work at trying to hear and understand what other family members are communicating while also having the opportunity to have their own views heard. Communication and understanding aid tremendously in the process of solving family problems.

4. As a result of experiencing person-centered therapy, a family also learns a process of sharing and experiencing that can be continued at home for the purpose of solving problems, clarifying values, and making decisions.

5. The therapy process aids the family in helping it to establish priorities related to the external community and demands of the larger society. The process facilitates the family's accountability and response to the world outside the home. Healthy individual and family actualizing processes unfold.

When all members of the family cooperate, they tend to reorganize it into a new form—more coherent, more ordered, more complex, more psychologically healthy, and moving in the direction of wellness. The family has the option of creating harmony in a person-centered climate. Together, they build new interpersonal relationships.

The person-centered approach is a wave of the future that is applicable outside of therapy situations as well as in therapeutic settings. It can already be seen in the movement of some families toward a more democratic process involving all family members—the emerging family. The new emerging family will not have its power concentrated in one authority figure, but will have a family process with far greater resources and power to heal, to resolve family issues, and to provide positive experiences for growth and recreation. The new family is truly a support group for the person as he or she seeks a path with "heart" for living.

ANNOTATED SUGGESTED READINGS

The Association for the Development of the Person-Centered Approach (ADPCA).
ADPCA was founded in 1981 by David J. Cain. For additional information on the Association, the newsletter, the journal, the annual conference, and the group's purposes, please write to Ms. Julie Rabin, ADPCA, P.O. Box 396, Orange, MA 01364 USA. The journal, edited by Jeanne P. Stubbs, State University of West Georgia, Carrollton, carries information on person-centered activities, workshops, and learning programs (e.g.,

The Carl Rogers Institute for Psychotherapy, Training, and Supervision, directed by Norman Chambers, La Jolla, CA; Center for Interpersonal Growth, directed by Peggy Natiello and Curtis Graf, Port Jefferson, New York; Training in Focusing, directed by Eugene Gendlin, Chicago; Living Now Institute, directed by Gay Swenson of Mt. View, Hawaii; La Jolla Program, directed by Bruce Meador, La Jolla, CA; Person-Centered Expressive Therapy Institute, directed by Natalie Rogers, Santa Rosa, CA; The International Forums for the Person-Centered Approach; and The Carl Rogers Memorial Library established by Nel Kandel and the learning activities of the Center for Studies of the Person, 1125 Torrey Pines Road, La Jolla, CA 92037).

Counseling and Values, 1987, *32*(1).
The journal of the Association for Spiritual, Ethical, and Religious Values Issues in Counseling provided a special issue on Carl R. Rogers and The Person-Centered Approach to Peace. John M. Whitely served as guest editor of this excellent issue. Many of the articles are by Rogers. They focus on his experiences in South Africa and the Soviet Union as well as his views on tension reduction and the underlying theory in working toward peaceful solutions to human conflict.

Gordan, T., & Adams, L. (1997). *Family Effectiveness Training*. Solana Beach, CA: Gordon Training International.
Family Effectiveness Training is a video-guided home study program for building strong and loving relationships between family members. The new program teaches skills for use in resolving family conflicts, setting guidelines for family members, influencing others to respect your needs, handling value differences, reducing resentments, and other skills. The materials include a videotape, a resource book for adults, an audiotape, and a resource book for young adults (age 12+) that may be used in the suggested six-week schedule.

Journal of Humanistic Psychology, 1995, *35*(4).
This journal provided an excellent special issue on "Carl Rogers—The Man and His Ideas." The issue carries a previously unpublished manuscript by Rogers on "what understanding and acceptance mean to me." Additional articles by other scholars look at religious dimensions, Rogers as scientist and mystic, the influence of Otto Rank, Rogers's emphasis on his direct experience, and others. Single copies may be purchased for $15.00 from Sage Publications, Inc., 2455 Teller road, Thousand Oaks, CA 91320.

Kirschenbaum, H. (1979). *On becoming Carl Rogers*. New York: Delacorte Press.
This biography is a good resource book for information and insights on Rogers's personal and professional life. The reader will also learn more about Helen Rogers, a caring person who had a key role in Carl Rogers's life.

Levant, R. F., & Shlien, J. M. (Eds.). (1984). *Client-centered therapy and the person-centered approach: New directions in theory, research, and practice*. New York: Praeger.
This book is an excellent resource for examining the continuing evolution of client-centered therapy and the person-centered approach. Sections focus on the facilitative conditions, focusing, self-concept, individual psychotherapy, family therapy and enhancement, clinical supervision, large groups, and other applications of this theoretical view.

Person-Centered Review, 1989, *4*(3).
This issue of the journal of the Association for the Development of the Person-Centered Approach focuses on "Person-Centered Approaches with Families." David J. Cain, editor, and two editorial board members, Wayne Anderson and Charlotte Ellinwood, collaborated on this issue. Topics focus on various components of person-centered family theory and practice with young children, couples, families, and other theoretical aspects of Rogers's concepts as related to family work.

Rogers, C. R. (1959). A theory of therapy, personality, and interpersonal relationships, as developed in the client-centered framework. In S. Koch (Ed.), *Psychology: A study of a science. Vol. III. Formulations of the person and the social context* (pp. 184–256). New York: McGraw-Hill.

> This 1959 chapter is rich in ideas for research and clinical practice. It lays the theoretical framework for the person-centered approach. The chapter makes a systematic presentation of the person-centered theory and shows how the theory, which was developed from experiences in therapy and research, has application in other fields in human experience that involve interpersonal relationships and personality/behavior change. It has a small theoretical section on family life.

Rogers, C. R. (1961). *On becoming a person.* Boston: Houghton Mifflin.

> This is a very special book about how individuals grow. It has touched many people and aided them in developing their own inner potentials. Three chapters are related to family therapy—the characteristics of a helping relationship, a process conception of psychotherapy, and the implications of client-centered therapy for family life. This book provides a personal, yet professional, statement on the philosophy of a person-centered approach.

Rogers, C. R. (1970). *Carl Rogers on encounter groups.* New York: Harper and Row.

> Family therapy groups often have a flavor of encounter groups. This book provides a good discussion of the process of encounter groups and what it takes to be facilitative in an encounter group. It is excellent reading for therapists working with groups.

Rogers, C. R. (1972). *On becoming partners: Marriage and its alternatives.* New York: Delacorte Press.

> This book presents an inner view of several intimate man–woman relationships with all their complexities and growth-producing events. Good-bad judgments are not made about the relationships. It is an excellent book to provoke thoughts and feelings about one's own values and behavior in man–woman relationships.

Rogers, C. R. (1977). *Carl Rogers on personal power: Inner strength and its revolutionary impact.* New York: Delacorte Press.

> Empowering the person and the impact of the person-centered approach are major themes of this book. Three chapters are especially related to family therapy. These chapters focus on the new family, on a person-centered community-building workshop, and on the emerging person. The book has far-reaching implications for the person-centered approach in many aspects of living: marriage and partnerships, education, administration, intercultural tensions, and the political base of the person-centered approach. It is a book about power.

Rogers, C. R. (1980). *A way of being.* Boston: Houghton Mifflin.

> This book represents Rogers's thinking in the 1970s. It presents his changing views of the person-centered approach and its relationship to living—"a way of being." Of special interest are the chapters on the changes during the last 46 years of his life.

REFERENCES

Anderson, W. J. (1989a). Client/person-centered approaches to couple and family therapy: Expanding theory and practice. *Person-Centered Review, 4*(3), 245–247.

Anderson, W. J. (1989b). Family therapy in the client-centered tradition: A legacy in the narrative mode. *Person-Centered Review, 4*(3), 295–307.

Aspy, D. N., & Roebuck, F. M. (1974). From humane ideas to human technology and back again many times. *Education, 95*(2), 163–171.

Auw, A. (1991). *Gentle roads to survival: Making self-healing choices in difficult circumstances.* Lower Lake, CA: Aslan Publishing.

Barrett-Lennard, G. T. (1962). Dimensions of therapist response as causal factors in therapeutic change. *Psychological Monographs, 76,* Whole No. 562.

Barrett-Lennard, G. T. (1984). The world of family relationships: A person-centered systems view. In R. F. Levant & J. M. Shlien (Eds.), *Client-centered therapy and the person-centered approach: New directions in theory, research, and practice* (pp. 222–242). New York: Praeger Publishers.

Boy, A. V., & Pine, G. J. (1995). *Child-centered counseling and psychotherapy.* Springfield, IL: Charles C. Thomas.

Bozarth, J. D., & Shanks, A. (1989). Person-centered family therapy with couples. *Person-Centered Review, 4*(3), 280–294.

Brazier, D. (Ed.). (1993). *Beyond Carl Rogers.* London: Constable & Company Limited.

Bynner, W. (Tr.). (1962). *The way of life according to Lao Tzu.* New York: Capricorn Books (Putnam).

Cain, D. J. (1989). From the individual to the family. *Person-Centered Review, 4*(3), 248–255.

Campbell, J., with B. Moyers. (1988). *The power of myth.* New York: Doubleday.

Combs, A. W. (1989). *A theory of therapy: Guidelines for counseling practice.* Newbury Park, CA: Sage.

Coulson, W. R. (1978). *Banding: The psychology of family success.* La Jolla, CA: Helicon House.

Coulson, W. R., Land, D., & Meador, B. (1977). *The La Jolla experiment: Eight personal views.* La Jolla, CA: The La Jolla Program, Center for Studies of the Person.

Coulson, W. R., & Rogers, C. R. (1968). *Man and the science of man.* Columbus, OH: Charles E. Merrill.

Ellinwood, C. (1989). The young child in person-centered family therapy. *Person-Centered Review, 4*(3), 256–262.

Gaylin, N. L. (1989). The necessary and sufficient conditions for change: Individual versus family therapy. *Person-Centered Review, 4*(3), 263–279.

Gordon, T. (1970a). A theory of healthy relationships and a program of parent effectiveness training. In J.T. Hart & T. M. Tomlinson (Eds.), *New directions in client-centered therapy.* Boston: Houghton Mifflin.

Gordon, T. (1970b). *Parent effectiveness training: The "no-lose" program for raising responsible children.* New York: Peter H. Wyden.

Guerney, B. G., Jr. (1977). *Relationship enhancement: Skill-training programs for therapy, problem prevention, and enrichment.* San Francisco: Jossey-Bass.

Guerney, L., & Guerney, B. G., Jr. (1989). Child relationship enhancement: Family therapy and parent education. *Person-Centered Review, 4*(3), 344–357.

Heider, J. (1985). *The Tao of leadership: Lao Tzu's Tao Teh Ching adapted for a new age.* Atlanta, GA: Humanics Limited.

Jourard, S. M. (1959). Healthy personality and self-disclosure. *Mental Hygiene, 43,* 499–507.

Kirschenbaum, H., & Henderson, V. L. (Eds.) (1989a). *Carl Rogers dialogues: Conversations with Martin Buber, Paul Tillich, B. F. Skinner, Gregory Bateson, Michael Polanyi, Rollo May, and others.* Boston: Houghton Mifflin.

Kirschenbaum, H., & Henderson, V. L. (Eds.) (1989b). *The Carl Rogers reader.* Boston: Houghton Mifflin.

Levant, R. F. (1984). *Family therapy: A comprehensive overview.* Englewood Cliffs, NJ: Prentice-Hall.

Lietaer, G., Rombauts, J., & Van Balen, R. (Eds.). (1990). *Client-centered and experiential psychotherapy in the nineties.* Leuven/Louvain, Belgium: Leuven University Press.

Meador, B. D. (1971). Individual process in a basic encounter group. *Journal of Counseling Psychology, 18,* 70–76.

Mearns, D. (1994). *Developing person-centered counselling.* Thousand Oaks, CA: Sage.

Mearns, D., & Dryden, W. (Eds.). (1990). *Experience of counselling in action.* Thousand Oaks, CA: Sage.

Mearns, D., & Thorne, B. (1988). *Person-centered counselling in action.* Thousand Oaks, CA: Sage.

Ohlsen, M. M. (1979). *Marriage counseling in groups.* Champaign, IL: Research Press.

Ohlsen, M. M., Horne, A. M., & Lawe, C. F. (1988). *Group counselling* (3rd ed.). New York: Holt, Rinehart and Winston.

O'Leary, C. J. (1989). The person-centered approach and family therapy: A dialogue between two traditions. *Person-Centered Review, 4*(3), 308–323.

Ornstein, R. (1986). *The psychology of consciousness* (Rev. ed.). New York: Penguin Books.

Patterson, C. H. (1968). The nature of counselling: Some basic principles. *Michigan College Personnel Association Journal, 5,* 1–11.

Patterson, C. H. (1985). *The therapeutic relationship: Foundations for an eclectic psychotherapy.* Monterey, CA: Brooks/Cole.

Rank, O. (1936). *Will therapy.* New York: Alfred A. Knopf.

Raskin, N. J. (1952). An objective study of the locus-of-evaluation factor in psychotherapy. In W. Wolff and J. A. Precker (Eds.), *Success in psychotherapy.* New York: Grune & Stratton.

Raskin, N. J., & van der Veen, F. (1970). Client-centered family therapy: Some clinical and research perspectives. In J.T. Hart & T. M. Tomlinson (Eds.), *New directions in client-centered therapy.* Boston: Houghton Mifflin.

Rogers, C. R. (1939). *The clinical treatment of the problem child.* Boston: Houghton Mifflin.

Rogers, C. R. (1942). *Counseling and psychotherapy.* Boston: Houghton Mifflin.

Rogers, C. R. (1951). *Client-centered therapy.* Boston: Houghton Mifflin.

Rogers, C. R. (1957a). The necessary and sufficient conditions of therapeutic personality change. *Journal of Counseling Psychology, 21*(2), 95–103.

Rogers, C. R. (1957b). Personal thoughts on teaching and learning. *Merrill-Palmer Quarterly,* Summer, *3,* 241–243.

Rogers, C. R. (1959). A theory of therapy, personality, and interpersonal relationships, as developed in the client-centered framework. In S. Koch (Ed.), *Psychology: A study of a science, Vol. III. Formulations of the person and the social context.* New York: McGraw-Hill.

Rogers, C. R. (1961a). *On becoming a person.* Boston: Houghton Mifflin.

Rogers, C. R. (1961b). A process conception of psychotherapy. In C. R. Rogers, *On becoming a person* (pp. 125–159). Boston: Houghton Mifflin.

Rogers, C. R. (1961c). To be that self which one truly is: A therapist's view of personal goals. In C. R. Rogers, *On becoming a person* (pp. 163–182). Boston: Houghton Mifflin.

Rogers, C. R.(1969). *Freedom to learn: A view of what education might become.* Columbus, OH: Charles E. Merrill.

Rogers, C. R. (1970). *Carl Rogers on encounter groups.* New York: Harper and Row.

Rogers, C. R. (1972). *On becoming partners: Marriage and its alternatives.* New York: Dell Publishing.

Rogers, C. R. (1977). *Carl Rogers on personal power: Inner strength and its revolutionary impact.* New York: Delacorte Press.

Rogers, C. R. (1978). Do we need "a" reality? *Dawnpoint*, Second Issue, Winter, 6–9.

Rogers, C. R. (1980a). A presentation by C. Rogers on the development of PCA. Presented at The Person-Centered Two-Week Workshop, San Diego, August.

Rogers, C. R. (1980b). *A way of being.* Boston: Houghton Mifflin.

Rogers, C. R. (1983). *Freedom to learn for the 80's.* Columbus, OH: Charles E. Merrill.

Rogers, C. R. (1986a). The dilemmas of a South African white. *Person-Centered Review*, *1*(1), 15–35.

Rogers, C. R. (1986b). The Rust workshop: A personal overview. *Journal of Humanistic Psychology*, *26*, 23–45.

Rogers, C. R. (1987). Inside the world of the Soviet professional. *Counseling and Values*, *32*(1), 47–66.

Rogers, C. R., & Dymond, R. F. (Eds.). (1954). *Psychotherapy and personality change.* Chicago: University of Chicago Press.

Rogers, C. R., & Freiberg, H. J. (1994). *Freedom to learn* (3rd ed.). New York: Merrill, Macmillan College Publishing Company.

Rogers, C. R., Gendlin, E. T., Kiesler, D. J., & Truax, C. (Eds.). (1967). *The therapeutic relationship and its impact: A study of psychotherapy with schizophrenics.* Madison: University of Wisconsin Press.

Rogers, C. R. & Wallen, J. L. (1946). *Counseling with returned servicemen.* New York: McGraw-Hill.

Rogers, N. (1993). *The creative connection: Expressive arts as healing.* Palo Alto, CA: Science and Behavior Books.

Schulz, L. (1992). *I have two dads.* Omaha, NE. Centering Corporation.

Shah, I. (1972). *The exploits of the incomparable Mulla Nasrudin.* New York: E. Dutton.

Shlien, J. M., & Zimring, F. M. (1970). Research directives and methods in client-centered therapy. In J. T. Hart & T. M. Tomlinson (Eds.), *New directions in client-centered therapy.* Boston: Houghton Mifflin.

Snyder, M. (1989). The Relationship Enhancement model of couple therapy: An integration of Rogers and Bateson. *Person-Centered Review*, *4*(3), 358–383.

Standal, S. (1954). The need for positive regard: A contribution to client-centered theory. Doctoral dissertation, University of Chicago.

Stephenson, W. (1953). *The study of behavior: Q-techniques and its methodology.* Chicago: University of Chicago Press.

Suhd, M. M. (Ed.) (1995). *Positive regard: Carl Rogers & other notables he influenced.* Palo Alto, CA: Science and Behavior Books.

Taft, J. (1933). *The dynamics of therapy.* New York: Macmillan.

Thayer, L. (1977). An experiential approach to learning skills. *The Humanist Educator*, *15*(3), 132–139.

Thayer, L. (1981). Toward experiential learning with a person-centered approach. In L. Thayer (Ed.), *50 strategies for experiential learning: Book two.* Saline, MI: LT Resources.

Thayer, L. (1984). On person-centered experiential learning and affective development. In G. L. Jennings (Ed.), *Affective learning in industrial arts*, The American Council on Industrial Arts Teacher Education Yearbook (33rd ed., pp. 52–103). Bloomington, IL: McKnight Publishers.

Thayer, L. (1987). An interview with Carl R. Rogers: Toward peaceful solutions to human conflict—Part I. *Michigan Journal of Counseling and Development, 19*(2), 2–7. (Available from LT, 8594 Sleepy Hollow Drive, Saline, MI 48176.)

Thayer, L. (1989). An interview with Carl R. Rogers: Toward peaceful solutions to human conflict—Part II. *Michigan Journal of Counseling and Development, 19*(2), 2–7. (Available from LT, 8594 Sleepy Hollow Drive, Saline, MI 48176.)

Thayer, L. (1994). A matter of choice: Families in the '90s. *Journal of Humanistic Education and Development, 33*(1), 43–46.

Thayer, L. (1997). The experience module: Personalizing the learning process. Unpublished paper, Ypsilanti, MI: Eastern Michigan University.

Thayer, L., & Harrigan, S. (1990). PCA and Taoism: Comparing facets from each. A presentation at the Annual Convention of the American Association for Counseling and Development (AACD), Cincinnati, OH, March 17.

Thorne, B. (1992). *Carl Rogers.* Thousand Oaks, CA: Sage.

Tomlinson, T. M., & Hart, J. T., Jr. (1962). A validation study of the process scale. *Journal of Consulting Psychology, 26,* 74–78.

van der Veen, F., Heubner, B., Jorgens, B., & Neja, P., Jr. (1964). Relationships between the parent's concept of the family and family adjustment. *American Journal of Orthopsychiatry, 34,* 45–55.

van der Veen, F., & Olson, R. E. (1983). *Manual and handbook for the family assessment method.* Encinitas, CA: F. van der Veen.

Walker, A. M., Rablen, R. A., & Rogers, C. R. (1960). Development of a scale to measure process changes in psychotherapy. *Journal of Clinical Psychology, 16,* 79–85.

Whiteley, J. M. (1987). *Counseling and values, 32*(1), Whole Issue.

Wu, J. C. H. (Tr.), & Sih, P. K. T. (Ed.) (1961). *Lao Tzu/Tao Teh Ching.* New York: St. John's University Press.

CHAPTER 13

Adlerian Family Therapy

JOHN C. DAGLEY

INTRODUCTION

Adlerian family therapy is a contemporary approach with a rich heritage and a comprehensive theoretical foundation in Alfred Adler's *Individual Psychology*. By way of introduction, the Adlerian approach can be characterized concisely (meaning accurately but inadequately) as holistic, subjectivistic, social, goal-directed, and cognitive. This is an interpersonal therapy, in terms of both its conceptual framework as well as its intervention practices. Human behavior, whether that of an individual or of a family, is understood in its broader social context and purpose. No person or system is isolated. "Each individual is socially embedded in an interacting social system. This embeddedness and the interactions within these systems influence each person's behavior. Any movement in the individual, the family, or the environment (the larger ecosystems), and the cosmos instantly creates movement in all the other components" (Sherman & Dinkmeyer, 1987, p. 5).

THE UNIT OF FOCUS

In Adlerian family therapy the unit of focus is the family, as well as its individual members. Because of the holistic-systemic constructs that comprise the basic theory of personality development and change, Adlerian therapists easily go from working with the whole family at one setting, including extended and multigenerational family members or extrafamilial members, to working with couples alone, with children alone, or with any individual family member. Change, of either an individual nature or systemic, can start with an individual member or the small group as a whole. Of course, today the word *family* is an ambiguous term that no longer can be assumed to refer to a traditional nuclear family consisting of two parents and children (Carlson & Lewis, 1991). In fact, nontraditional families may be more the norm than traditional ones.

THE PROCESS OF CHANGE

Change requires courage. Moreover, it most likely requires increased understanding of each family member as well as the family as a whole by each member, improved skills (particularly communication skills and problem-solving skills), and enhanced social interest (a commitment to act cooperatively and constructively toward the common good of the family, its members, and humanity). Adlerians believe that change can take place best within each individual, even if the focus and goal is systemic change; it is easier and more effective to help each individual in the family take personal responsibility for making a positive change. It is harder to help family members stop expecting the other(s) to change first.

ROLES OF INSIGHT, AFFECT, AND BEHAVIOR

Although nothing significant happens without accompanying or preemptive cognitive insight, ultimate change is measured by new and different actions. In this approach, emotions are seen as less significant than insight, in that emotions are perceived as either products of thought or action-energizers produced by thought. Emotions serve a functional purpose, often to justify our attitudes and actions (Adler, 1929/1969). Further, emotions provide the steam with which we empower ourselves to move in the directions we want to go (Dreikurs, 1971). We use emotions in purposive ways. It is our style of life that determines our feelings and emotions, not vice versa.

Three Adlerian constructs deserve a few more introductory words and much more detailed attention later because of their signal importance in defining the approach: social interest, life style, and goal-directedness.

DEFINITION

SOCIAL INTEREST

One of the unique features of Adlerian family therapy, both in terms of conceptualization as well as therapeutic intervention, is the construct of "social interest." Adlerians believe that a basic motivating force in life is the desire to belong to the broader community of humanity by making positive and useful contributions. It is this desire to develop oneself into the kind of person who can contribute to others, and to become interested in the interests of others to the point of taking action in the direction of cooperating with others for the common good that Adlerians refer to as social interest. Within the family it means helping individuals develop their abilities to act in ways that enhance other family members' lives and contribute to the family's forward movement.

Social interest is a sign of a family's mental health, as well as that of its members. While each individual is born with this innate tendency to strive to overcome self-perceived personal inferiorities and limitations in order to behave in ways to enable the individual to feel as if he or she belongs to the family and to the larger group of society, the feelings have to be evoked, nurtured, and developed. The family, as the individual's first social group, plays a critical role in nurturing or neglecting social interest.

LIFE STYLE

A neophyte in family therapy may be misled to conclude that the Adlerian approach is a one-on-one therapy model disguised as a family intervention approach because of the presence of the word "individual" in the title of the basic theory—*Individual Psychology*. In actuality, the title refers not to a preferred modality nor to a therapeutic alliance, but to a belief that a person or a social system is best understood in its wholeness, its individuality. Some of today's family theorists have used "nonsummativity" to refer to a related belief that a family is more than just the sum of its members. For Adler, "individual" meant much more.

What's in a name, anyway? What's the importance? Why introduce a family therapy system by focusing on the name of its undergirding personality theory? Largely, because there can be symbolic or literal significance to a name, as most family therapists know who have experienced especially meaningful discussions about the significance clients often attach to family names and surnames. Adler and his colleagues selected the name, Individual Psychology, in 1912 to make a positive and strong statement in support of recognizing the indivisibility of the person. The significance of their decision is particularly noteworthy because of the timing. The relatively young field of psychology was still dominated at the time by a mechanistic and reductionistic mind–body dualism of opposing forces, instincts, and intrapsychic conscious and unconscious parts. While the name individual psychology often has been misunderstood, even from the beginning, the word "individual," taken from the Latin word *individuum* was selected as the term to highlight Adler's proposed doctrine of the unity and self-consistency of personality.

Apparently, some attention had been given to using "personality psychology" as a name for the group because of a central working hypothesis that a person's actions could be understood only in connection with the "whole" of the individual's psychic picture (Furtmüller, 1946/1979, p. 364). There was a concern over the possibility that if the word "individual" were selected it might imply that their focus would be on an isolated individual, rather than on that individual in the context of the social groups in which the individual lived. In the end, Adler chose individual psychology as more specifically reflective of the desired holistic perspective, referring to a renowned medical researcher by the name of Virchow, who had offered the view in 1859 that "the individual is a unified community in which all parts work together for a common purpose" (Ansbacher, 1974, p. 44).

"The whole tells much more than the analysis of the parts. Also, nothing new can emerge through synthesis if one simply puts the parts together" (Adler, 1933/1979d, p. 30). He also liked the contribution of psychology—commonly defined as a "science of the soul" (Adler, 1935/1996a). Together, the two words implied a sense of an entity beyond that which is easily seen or felt but which is nonetheless personal, unique, and unifying.

Thus, individual psychology was selected as having unique value in the emphasis it placed on the irreducible integrity of the person, and on the person's own subjective role in creating his or her own individuality. An individual is an undivided unit, more than a mere collection of feelings, cognitions, isolated physical characteristics, and known or unknown forces. In this position, Adler seemed to have been influenced by his former medical school professor, internist Herman Nothnagel, who had told his students that physicians "must always look at the patient as a whole, not as an isolated organ or an isolated ailment" (Manaster, Painter, Deutsch, & Overholt, 1977, p. 10). Interestingly, it was also Nothnagel who had advised his students that "to be a good doctor, you have to be a kind person" (Manaster et al., 1977, p. 10), or from another translation or time, "Only a good man can be a great physician" (Hoffman, 1994, p. 21). Adler seemed to take both advisements to heart, for each became an important element in his social psychiatry.

Actually, it would have seemed more accurate to refer to the approach as "contextual psychology" (Ansbacher & Ansbacher, 1956, p. 3), or as "social psychology" (p. 157), or even "systems psychology" (Nicoll, 1989) because of Adler's deep and overarching commitment to contextual, social, and systemic thinking. Dreikurs speculated that if Adler had given a name to his own group later he probably would have called it "holistic psychology" (Dreikurs & Allen, 1971, p. 49). Holistic thinking has become a common staple in the more popular approaches to family therapy today. Clearly, families are conceptualized as more than a collection of individual members. The family is seen as an entity itself, a unit inside many other social systems, both small and large. Family therapists will recognize the holistic perspective, as outlined by Adler, in the principle of "synergy" outlined in general systems theory some years later (Bertalanffy, 1968).

Holism takes shape in the form of decisions individuals make as they grow up. Adler believed in the creative power of the individual; he saw each person as building his or her own personality from the meanings constructed of personal experiences. In fact, the patterns and themes that emerge in a person's style of living become a guiding plan or a direction for the individual. Unfortunately, we tend to develop these styles fairly early in life and then just reaffirm them rather than reevaluate them in the light of a maturing perspective. Thus, life styles often lead to misperceptions and mistaken attitudes about life.

GOAL-DIRECTEDNESS

Adlerian psychology is teleogical in that it stresses the motivational force of goals. It is more instructive to know a person's pulls than imagined pushes, purposes rather than causes, and a person's uses of hereditary endowments and environmental opportunities rather than possessions. "Without the sense of a goal individual activity would cease to have any meaning" (Adler, 1929/1969, p. 2). The power of one's own creative goal orientation repudiates, for Adlerians, determinism and causality as explanatory principles for understanding human behavior. "No experience is a cause of success or failure. We do not suffer from the shock of our experiences—the so-called trauma—but we make out of them just what suits our purposes. We are self-determined by the meaning we give to our experiences. Meanings are not determined by the situations, but we determine ourselves by the meanings we give to situations" (Adler, 1931/1980, p. 14). As his son, Kurt Adler, a psychiatrist in New York for most of his career, later said, "Adler believed all thinking, feeling, willing, and acting were directed toward a goal, a goal that the person had constructed himself as the ideal of what he should be, what people should be, and what his or her relations with people should be" (1994, p. 134).

Every individual wants to belong. And each wants to belong in a socially useful way. "Every human being strives for significance; but people always make mistakes if they do not see that their whole significance must consist in their contribution to the lives of others" (Adler, 1931/1980, p. 8). Discouraged individuals, however, eventually strive to belong in socially useless or even destructive ways.

From infancy and early childhood, children strive to overcome real and imagined personal perceptions of inferiority. Adler described this striving as a fictional pursuit of perfection or superiority, not in the sense of mastery over people, as much as a desired superiority over imagined or perceived positions of inferiority as encountered in the primary life tasks of love, work, and friendship. Every person's line of movement goes from a felt minus position in life to a plus. No one wants to be inferior, or to be perceived as less than another. No individuals want to consider themselves or be considered by others to be inadequate or unequal in any way. They respond by compensating and sometimes even overcompensating for assignments or assumptions of such minus positions. It was this movement in patients who made efforts to compensate for an inferior physical organ and to overcome a perceived inferior position in life that Adler first began to notice in his early medical practice, and that consequently led him to use a law of overcoming as a major building block in his conceptual schema and therapeutic approach. "The fundamental law of overcoming recognized the inherent capacity within each individual to feel inferior. These feelings are part of the human heritage and relate to inadequacies growing out of biological weakness and cosmic smallness" (Lowe, 1982, p. 331).

AN INTRODUCTORY FRAME

The family therapy profession as a discipline has matured over the past few decades to its present point at which it spends less time stressing its systemic perspective as a sole "raison d'être," and more time on developing a deeper theoretical base with increasingly sophisticated applied research and innovative intervention tools. Adlerians have helped enlarge the therapeutic circle to include a wider range of systems in family therapy, such as schools and a variety of community agencies (Sherman, Shumsky, & Rountree, 1994). There is still a need to deepen the commitment of psychologists to systemic thinking, just as there is a continuing need for family therapists to value a focus on "systemic" work with whomever is present rather than insisting on the presence of all extended family members. Today, family therapy seems more open to Adlerians who value working with individuals as well as whole families, without a discomforting certainty that one would be labeled, à la Defraia (1984, cited in Hirschorn, 1987), a "systems thought criminal" or a "closet individual psychotherapist" (p. 32).

Unfortunately, beginning therapists often feel that they "belong" only after they declare allegiance to a theory. While it is truly necessary to devote a great deal of time and energy to fully learn an approach to family therapy, one does not have to become an unquestioning disciple. There is an inherent danger in labels, not only for patients but also for therapists. We are not equivalent to our labels (Stewart, 1997). Family therapists need to remain alert to what Korzybski (1941) referred to as the E Prime factor in general semantics theory, wherein the various forms of the verb "to be" become restrictive factors in identity. The only paradoxical caveat to add to this point is that there is also a danger in the other direction, namely, succumbing to the seductive allure of eclecticism, where an insufficiently trained therapist picks and chooses freely from many theories, even those in contradiction or opposition. Adler (1977, p. 121) referred to this tendency as an attempt to please everyone and to offend no one.

Parsimony is considered a fundamental characteristic of a good theory. However, in a summary of a family therapy approach with nearly a century of history, parsimony is a large order. By now, four different generations have built upon Adler's original formulations. Contrary to the evolution of other approaches of a similar vintage—Freud's psychoanalysis for example—the changes that have come about in the conceptualization or practice of individual psychology have been complementary or have taken the form of natural extensions and additions, rather than contradictions or competing constructs and techniques (Manaster & Corsini, 1982). Nonetheless, much has taken place in Adlerian psychology to sharpen, extend, and update the approach. After all, it's not like founders of schools of psychological thought have "said all there is to say" (Ellis, 1987, p. 279). If so, then we would be involved in battlegrounds over contrasting dogmas rather than informing science with the results of our research and practice (Dreikurs, 1960; Ellis, 1987).

HISTORICAL DEVELOPMENT

PERSONAL BACKGROUND

Adler took pride in his ability to relate to the common people with whom he lived and worked. He seemed to thrive on interactions with others, as was obvious in the untold number of hours he spent in collegial conversation with friends in his much-loved Vienna coffeehouses. He was indeed a social person. It is not surprising that his approach was interpersonal as well. Indeed, individual psychology is a positive, respectful, collegial, interpersonal approach to therapy.

Biographical reviews (Bottome, 1939; Furtmüller, 1946/1979; Hoffman, 1994; Manaster et al., 1977) yield images of a man who loved the simple and natural experiences of life like walking, talking, laughing, and singing. Born second in a family of seven children (five boys and two girls), Adler spent much of his childhood and adolescence in the outskirts of Vienna, Austria.

EARLY MEMORIES

Adler's recollections of his youth seemed to revolve around sickness and medical intervention (Hoffman, 1994). One of his most vivid memories was of a time, around the age of two, when he was sitting on a park bench recuperating from a disabling bout of rickets, wistfully watching his older brother run freely and happily around him. Another recollection, again a very vivid one for Adler, was when he awakened one morning around the age of four to find that his younger brother Rudolf had died (of diphtheria) next to him in bed. And possibly the most impactful recollection was of a personal life-threatening experience with pneumonia around the age of five. Apparently, after being examined by a doctor, Adler heard the physician say to Adler's father, "Give yourself no more trouble, the boy is lost" (Hoffman, 1994, p. 8). However, after being treated by a second doctor, Adler recovered. The experience led him to decide then to become a doctor, to overcome death and its fears.

EARLY MEDICAL PRACTICE

Adler set up a clinical practice in Leopoldstadt near the Prater, an amusement park. With his practice located in this lower middle-class Vienna neighborhood, Adler treated a wide range of patients from successful attorneys and merchants to governesses and cooks. His most unusual patients, however, were the special employees of the amusement park itself, including the circus-act trapeze acrobats, the variously talented unique artists of one sort or another, and the athletic strongmen. He observed a phenomenon that he called "organ inferiority," wherein these entertainers often had "compensated" for a congenital weakness early in life by striving to overcome it through a compensatory prowess. Later, he developed this thesis into a book entitled *The Study of Organ Inferiority*.

Adler's first publication, though, was a relatively brief booklet he wrote in 1898 entitled *Health Book for the Tailor Trade*. In it he outlined the terrible economic conditions of the trade and the connected diseases of its workers. Adler believed that the logical and noble challenge of the science of medicine was not to treat and cure sick people but to protect healthy people from sickness (Ansbacher, 1992). From his first years in practice to the end of his career, he retained a deep belief in preventive medicine and the importance of promoting public health through education (Manaster et al., 1977, p. 13). In fact, the four articles he wrote after his first piece were on topics related to public health. In 1904, he published "The Physician as Educator," an article he considered his first psychological paper and the beginning of individual psychology (Ansbacher, 1992).

PHILOSOPHICAL ROOTS

An eminent physiologist of the nineteenth century and founder of cellular pathology, Rudolf Virchow seems to have had a large impact on Adler.

> In "Atoms and Individuals," a popular lecture from which Adler (1912a) had quoted, Virchow (1859) attributed to the individual, in contrast to the atom, purposiveness, unity, uniqueness, self-determination, and community orientation. These humanistic concepts became basic in Adler's individual psychology, as did Virchow's optimistic outlook. (Ansbacher, 1992, p. 9)

Although his medical training had emphasized the importance of diagnostic exactitude over patient care and treatment (Hoffman, 1994), Adler always seemed to be more interested in viewing and treating the patient as a whole. Adler held a deep belief in the creative power of the individual in constructing personal meanings of life's events. Linden (1984) makes a solid case for tracing the roots of certain Adlerian ideas to such early philosophers as Epictetus, Spinoza, and Kant. It was Epictetus who observed as far back as 100 A.D. that "What disturbs men's minds is not events but their judgments of events" (cited in Linden, 1984). There are other connections to earlier philosophers; for example, Adler often referred to Nietsche and Kant in his descriptions of the important role that fictions play in a person's creative use of goals.

RELATIONSHIP WITH FREUD

It is unclear how the relationship between Adler and Sigmund Freud actually started, though it's quite clear how and why it ended so acrimoniously. Objectivity is oftentimes an elusive goal for biographers, so the complete truth may never be known about how Freud became aware of Adler, and then felt impressed enough to invite him, along with three other young Viennese physicians, to join a group at his house to discuss psychology and neurology. Freud's account in his monograph on the history of psychoanalysis was that a group of young admirers had sought him out to teach them psychoanalysis, and that he consented to do so (Hoffman, 1994). Bottome (1939), Adler's biographer, presented a different picture, one that allegedly started with Adler writing a defense of Freud's *Interpretation of Dreams* after it had been mocked in the press. Neither of these accounts is true, however, according to the most recent Adler biographer, Edward Hoffman (1994). No evidence can be found of a published letter or paper of defense by Adler, so Bottome's account is somewhat suspect. Likewise, Freud's account is untrue and is easily refutable by Adler's possession of a postcard from Freud inviting him to join with Rudolf Reitler, Max Kahane, William Stekel, and himself at the first meeting (Hoffman, 1994, p. 42). In actuality, the encouragement to form a small discussion group apparently came from Stekel, whom Freud had successfully treated for impotence. Kurt Adler, in a 1977 symposium at the University of Oregon on his father's works, reported that Adler had been called in as practicing physician to help with Freud's step-brother who was sick with pneumonia and for whom there was little hope of survival. At the time, Adler had developed a reputation as an excellent diagnostician. "He saved the step-brother's life. Of this he never told except in camaraderie…Freud invited him because he had talked with him about it" (K. A. Adler, 1977, p. 99). Regardless of the exact details of how the relationship started, it is clear from the various accounts that it did start in 1902 and that there was a good deal of exciting dialogue and stimulation for several years in The Wednesday Psychological Society, as they called themselves. Discussions among the small group were free and mutually enjoyable, by all accounts. At first informal, and led by Freud, the group eventually became more formal, named Adler as president, and became known as the Vienna Psychoanalytic Society. Otto Rank served as the first paid secretary.

Apparently, as the size of the group grew, though, so too did its formality and fractious combativeness, as well as its desire to promote a single way of thought. At the second International Psychoanalytic Convention, held in Nürnberg, Germany, in 1910, the internal conflicts came to a head when Freud transferred the power of the movement from Vienna to Switzerland, and to Carl Jung specifically, whom he wanted to serve as a censor for all psychoanalytical publications. Soon thereafter, upon Adler's publication of an article that reemphasized his belief in the importance of the construct of inferiority as the basis for neurosis, the break became inevitable, The major shift to a subjective psychology, as expressed in different ways by Adler, is truly what led to Freud's increasing concern that Adler was going in directions incompatible with his own views of psychoanalysis. It was increasingly clear that Adler did not believe in the primacy of the libido. "Many psychologists believe that the development of sexuality is the basis for the development of the whole mind and psyche, as well as for all the physical movements. In the view of the present writer, this is not true. Rather, the entire form and development of sexuality depend on the personality—the style of life and the prototype" (Adler, 1978, p. 82). In other words, according to Adler, it is not sex that determines the personality, but the personality that determines one's approach to sex.

From an early interest in a possible "aggression drive," Adler later shifted to believing that there is a democracy of drives, with no drive deserving any supremacy. Thus, even from the beginning he had not agreed with Freud's emphasis on the sex drive or sexual instinct as the prime motivator for human behavior. Later, as Adler's core psychological beliefs began to take shape, and as he moved from a physiological (objective) psychology to a cultural (subjective) psychology, he no longer ascribed importance to a will to power but to a principle of overcoming, a desire to move from a felt minus position to a felt plus. The evolution of this principle in Adler's thinking is reflected in the terminology he used at various stages to refer to it: aggression drive, masculine protest, will to power, striving for superiority, striving to overcome, striving for significance, striving to belong, striving to contribute. Later, he restricted and refined the meaning of the term masculine protest, but he first used the term to refer to the desire to be strong and powerful as a compensatory move to feeling weak, inferior, and unmanly.

In addition to the substantive differences, significant personal differences also contributed to the break in the relationship between Freud and Adler. Freud was more private, cerebral, reclusive, formal, and even aristocratic, whereas Adler was public, informal, social, fun, and in many ways typical of the Austrian peasant. Yet another difference was the way they approached medicine; Freud preferred the role of a researcher, and Adler a clinician. Freud was an introvert and Adler was an extrovert (Dolliver, 1994); while Freud preferred controlled interactions with others, Adler enjoyed open interactions. Whereas Freud preferred to speak in small, intimate circles of friends and avoided public appearances where he may have been questioned, Adler loved the interaction with audiences in his many public lectures and demonstrations, even if he was presenting in a foreign language. Freud preferred writing, Adler speaking.

Moreover, "while Freud maintained an exclusiveness among his followers, and imposed a formality upon his patients, who were bound to lie down and have their therapist be a silent and invisible presence behind them, ...Adler, in his professional encounters with patients sat facing them, the two in comfortable chairs so that the treatment had an almost social ambiance" (Manaster et al., 1977, p. 12). "Adler treated his patients on a footing of absolute equality...there they sat, Adler and his patient, hobnobbing knee to knee and often smoking like chimneys while they talked" (Bottome, 1939, p. 59).

Unfortunately, the acrimony between Freud and Adler grew unabated throughout their lives—even beyond, with their followers. Nonetheless, their early relationship in The Wednesday Psychological Society seemed to be mutually satisfying and synergistic.

STAGES OF DEVELOPMENT

There were four distinguishable periods in Adler's development, roughly equivalent to decades beginning in 1898: Social and Clinical Medicine; Initial Development of Individual Psychology; Maturation, Integration, and Synthesis of Theoretical Constructs; and Dissemination Efforts. Ansbacher (1978b) described the same periods with similar terms: Prior to Explicit Concept of Man; Prior to Social Interest; Social Interest—Phase I: Counterforce; and Social Interest—Phase II: Cognitive Function.

Regardless of how one might characterize these distinct yet overlapping periods, it is apparent that Adler and his colleagues—and later his students—continued to refine the basic constructs of the approach. From his focus on social medicine and on socialism of his first decade's professional experience in clinical medicine, he moved into his social psychiatry decade, during which time he formulated the essential elements of his approach to psychotherapy and education. Upon returning from his war experience as a military physician, he enriched many of the basic constructs of the theory. So the third decade was one of refinement and maturity, where "social interest" and "life style" were first fully developed, and where specificity and direction were added to the construct of "masculine protest." But more than anything else, his time and energies in the third decade were devoted to his work in education through the schools as well as the many child and family guidance centers that he and his colleagues established in Vienna. Finally, his fourth decade saw him devote his time to dissemination of individual psychology through teaching and lecturing in America and in Europe.

CHILD AND FAMILY GUIDANCE CENTERS

After World War I, Adler devoted much of his attention to education. While psychotherapy always remained a very strong interest, working with teachers and parents became a very close second, if not primary, interest; some say that "the education of children had become the thing nearest and dearest to his heart" (Manaster et al., 1977). Before the war, he and his close friend Carl Furt-müller had edited a book entitled *To Heal and to Educate*. Even prior to that, both had presented papers to The Wednesday Psychological Society on educa-tion. In Furtmüller's "Fatalism or Education?" he had presciently argued that economic changes had increasingly separated children from the lives of their parents, leaving educators with a greater responsibility for helping young peo-ple develop social skills (Hoffman, 1994). In Adler's paper on "The Child's Need for Affection," he had recommended that parents and teachers needed to focus on facilitating the child's development of courage and self-confidence (Ansbacher & Ansbacher, 1956), but he worried about teachers' relative ab-sence of knowledge about the psychic development of the child (Hoffman, 1994). He believed very strongly that punishment had no place in a school or in the family, for he believed that we needed to put our efforts into winning the children's cooperation, not in discouraging them or threatening them. Of all the mistakes in education and child-rearing, however, the one that bothered Adler the most was to lose faith in the child, or to believe in hereditary limits (Adler, 1931/1980, p. 167).

Given the opportunity by Viennese educational officials to develop special preparation programs for teachers, the University of Vienna refused, so the local Vienna school system set up the Pedagogical Institute, and asked Adler to serve as a professor. Having already served for several years as a lecturer at The Volk-sheim Institute (a community/continuing education institute), Adler accepted and became a very popular lecturer. One of the teachers involved in the work later said, "A teacher who has once worked on Adler's theories will never work on any others. They could not do so if they wanted to—because he taught us to un-derstand children, and no good teacher would ever give that up, for his own sake as well as the child's" (Bottome, 1939, p. 122).

The popular child and family guidance centers eventually numbered over 30 before they were closed in the pre-Hitler days before World War II. "Treatment teams" worked with families in front of an audience of other parents and teachers. First, the team would see the parents or the children as a subgroup, and then see the other generational subgroup, before gathering and seeing all of them together. The focus was an educational one, wherein parents, children, and teachers were each helped to learn concepts and intervention techniques relating to children and their ef-forts to learn, and their efforts to try to belong usefully at home and in the school.

There is little doubt that individual psychology was the first school of psy-chology to focus on child guidance and family counseling (Dinkmeyer & Dinkmeyer, 1991; Lowe, 1982; Sherman & Dinkmeyer, 1987). Similarly, it was the first approach to add significantly to what is known about childhood, adoles-cence, democratic parenting, and teaching. Adler also was the first to regard the father–child bond as extremely significant, in contrast to other approaches of his day (Hoffman, 1994, p. 219). The Adlerian approach certainly was the first to work with a whole family, recognizing that oftentimes it is the significant adults in a discouraged child's life who may need to change to bring about a lasting change in the child. "The approach to Adlerian family counseling is essentially fa-cilitative in that it seeks to assist parents and teachers, in a group setting, learn to manage themselves when the potential for conflict with children is present" (Lowe, 1982, p. 342).

The public forum type of family counseling service was extended throughout Europe and America as Adlerians established centers in such places as Germany, The Netherlands, Canada (Toronto), and America (Chicago, Portland, San Francisco, New York) to name a few. In Chicago alone, there were nine such centers opened after Dreikurs opened the first one in 1939 at the Abraham Lincoln Center (Lowe, 1982).

DIVERSITY

Interestingly, in terms of today's newly energized efforts of the therapeutic community to become multicultural in both theory and practice, Dreikurs started his work at the neighborhood house referred to as the Lincoln Center by working with 40 families, 23 of whom were black—the same proportion as the population at the time (Sherman & Dinkmeyer, 1987, p. 288). With social equality as a fundamental principle of the Adlerian approach, the theory is truly multicultural. "Of all the various counseling theories, Adlerian psychology seems to come closest to providing a belief system plus a rationale for behavior that encompasses the sociocultural factors necessary to understand minority families" (Newlon & Arciniega, 1991, p. 198). Nonetheless, as Sicher (Davidson, 1991) reminds us, in a comment on the American Declaration of Independence, true multiculturalism can only come from interdependence: "the trinity of word, meaning, and deed condenses itself to a unity representing the ideal goal of mankind's future: oneness in interdependence. And then, perhaps, the truth would become evident, even self-evident: that all men are created equal" (p. 16).

Diversity takes the form of differences other than race. One such difference that shaped the early medical work and theory development of Adler was the working-class background of most of his early patients. Adler enjoyed working with the common man. According to a comparative study by Wasserman (1958, cited in Furtmüller, 1946/1979) of Adler's reported cases and Freud's reported cases, Adler's patients were considerably less wealthy than Freud's: Adler—35% lower class, 40% middle class, and 25% from upper class; Freud—3% lower class, 23% middle class, and 74% upper class.

COUPLES COUNSELING AND FAMILY COUNSELING

While Adler advocated premarital counseling and even proposed marital advisory councils as early as 1926, he did not report any actual marriage counseling cases. It was his colleagues and students who expanded the approach into that modality and actually conducted marriage counseling. In fact, one of Adler's associates, Sofie Lazarsfeld, opened a marriage counseling and sex counseling center in 1926 (Ansbacher, 1978a). She is also credited with the first Adlerian book in English on sexuality addressed to women, entitled *Rhythm of Life: A Guide to Sexual Harmony for Women* (1931). "Sexuality is not an autonomous area, separate from the rest of psychological life, but influences the entire behavior of a person as the latter influences the sexuality" (Lazarsfeld, 1931, cited in Ansbacher, 1978a, p. 337). An advocate of equality of the sexes, Lazarsfeld reported an active caseload of approximately 300 in 1929–30, of which 168 showed the following complaints:

29% general extramarital affairs; 24% marital difficulties; 18% loneliness; and 29% sexual matters (cited in Ansbacher, 1978a, p. 337). A second Adlerian book on sex and marriage, entitled *The Art of Being a Woman*, was written by Olga Knopf in 1932. Dreikurs followed later with his book entitled *The Challenge of Marriage* (1946). Danica Deutsch was also an early Adlerian marital counselor. She worked in The Alfred Adler Hygiene Clinic in New York, where she instituted group therapy with married couples (Deutsch, 1956, 1967a, 1967b).

EVOLUTION INTO ADLERIAN FAMILY THERAPY

From the early years of individual psychology's traditional psychotherapeutic focus on one-on-one therapy, the Adlerian approach was expanded, as described above, into working with parents and teachers in the child and family guidance centers. From there, Adlerians opened marriage counseling and sex counseling centers, where in some they began to extend the approach into group work. Next, Adlerians began to focus on family education and family enrichment. Generations of Adlerians across the world have now developed and used materials to improve parenting, teaching, and marital satisfaction. Dinkmeyer, a student of Dreikurs in Chicago, has been the person most responsible in the current generation for developing, with several colleagues, a wide range of popular Adlerian programs: the DUSO Program (Developing an Understanding of Self and Others) (Dinkmeyer & Dinkmeyer, 1982), a primary school guidance curriculum program; the series of programs referred to as STEP (Systematic Training for Effective Parenting—STEP, Early Childhood STEP, STEP Teen) (Dinkmeyer & McKay, 1976); STET (Systematic Training for Effective Teaching); and *TIME* (Training in Marriage Enrichment) (Dinkmeyer & Carlson, 1984). Each of these is set up in a structured group training format.

Adlerian family counseling took the shape of open forums in which families were invited to attend large group sessions where it was expected that they could learn vicariously, before it was their turn to participate more actively as the family with whom the counselors would work in front of the group. The process typically involved a counseling session with parents while children were seen in a playroom, then followed by a session with the children, and then the whole family is brought together, or just the parents again (Christensen & Marchant, 1993; Dreikurs, Corsini, Lowe, & Sonstegard, 1959).

These evolutionary steps have collectively served as a precursor to Adlerian family therapy. Few approaches have as distinguished a history. Clearly, the rarest contribution that Adler's individual psychology has made to family therapy is its depth and breadth of knowledge and techniques in working with children as equal members of families. The Adlerian approach is a systematic approach with substance, not just gimmicky atheoretical interventions. It is a consistent, comprehensive system of systemic constructs for understanding people in relationship with one another in ever increasing sizes of systems from the family to the school, the community, and on through humanity and the planet's inhabitants.

CURRENT STATUS OF ADLERIAN PSYCHOLOGY

The Adlerian approach continues to gain in popularity and use, albeit more slowly than its adherents would desire. The membership in the North American Society for Adlerian Psychology is modest, but strong and stable, as with its various international counterparts. There are a large number of Adlerian training institutes throughout the world, including perhaps the largest one in Chicago, which is now called the Adlerian School for Professional Psychology, and an even larger number of courses in colleges, universities, hospitals, and schools. The number of parenting programs is virtually incalculable. The national and international journals thrive, printing largely theoretical, practice, and application articles, but also a growing number of research articles. In addition, there are several very solid textbooks in use. By now there have been several generations of Adlerians who have used and added to the approach—too many to even mention or highlight by name or region.

RELATIONSHIP TO OTHER APPROACHES

Undoubtedly, there is no other approach from which so much has been taken, with credit or without, than Adler's individual psychology. As Albert Ellis (1987) has said, "so what?": Such use or usurpment merely provides a presumptive validation, or at least it enables many clients to benefit from better therapy (p. 277). Or perhaps it is as once conjectured by psychiatrist Joseph Wilder (cited in Ansbacher, 1979, p. 13) when he said, "The proper question is not whether one is Adlerian but how much of an Adlerian one is."

Adler emphasized simplicity and common sense in his approach. One time, in fact, when he was criticized by a questioner for being too simplistic, he replied, "I would perhaps say that all neurosis was vanity, but that might be too simple to be understood" (Manaster et al., 1977, p. 54). At times, however, it may have been the simplicity and common sense that precluded Adler from the credit he deserved for leaving such an influential legacy.

Many of Adler's concepts have become so much a part of the substance and style of therapists from a wide range of schools that the original source simply has been forgotten. Or perhaps, like Heine, "whose little masterpiece, *The Lorelei*, attained such prompt popularity that when he himself asked a group of people singing it for the name of the author, he was told, 'Why nobody wrote it—it's a folk song'" (Munroe, 1955, p. 335). The thousands of articles in the professional literature as well as in the popular press on the topics of birth order and family constellation provide concrete evidence of the value of the constructs. The topics have become part of our culture, but not necessarily a part of a legacy attributed to Adler. The same can be said of his life style construct, a term that has been so used and abused over the decades that it has lost its original meaning, and is now used in current advertising slang more than it is in the helping professions. The misattributions go so far at times that reference to an Adlerian construct is wrongly credited to Freud or Jung, as Toman does in his book *Family Constellation: Theory and Practice of a Psychological Game* (1961). "Theorists for the last 20 years have been writing books re-expressing many of Adler's concepts without reference to Adler, although sometimes twisting and turning considerably in order to prove that these ideas were accepted by Freud" (Rotter, 1960, p. 383).

Essentially, that is the case with the neo-Freudians or neoanalysts. Shifts in psychoanalysis by such neo-Freudians as Karen Horney, Harry Stack Sullivan, and

Erich Fromm make them at least as neo-Adlerian as neo-Freudian, if not more. Several noted theorists from various disciplines and schools of thought have pointed to the often unrecognized contributions of Adler, particularly when viewed in the context of the Freudian approach:

> It is incredible that human behavior can be discussed from a psychoanalytic point of view without mentioning Adler's name. Or that some so-called "neo-Freudians" can deliver "fresh" ideas with an air of discovery, when many of these ideas were adumbrated by Adler over a half-century ago. (Becker, 1962)

> The influence of Adler...seems in retrospect to have been scarcely less extensive than that of Freud....The lonely course Adler embarked upon in 1911 has either anticipated or encouraged such vigorous developments as neo-Freudianism (or neo-Adlerianism), psychoanalytic ego psychology, client-centered therapy, existential psychology and contemporary personality theory. From the perspective of our own day, it might even be argued (with conscious heresy) that it was the turn first taken by Adler some fifty years ago which has come to be the "mainstream" of the psychoanalytic movement—and that taken by Freud which has been in fact the "deviation." (Matson, 1964)

> It has to be said that Adler's influence is much greater then is usually admitted. The entire neo-psychoanalytic school, including Horney, Fromm, and Sullivan, is no less neo-Adlerian than it is neo-Freudian. (Wolman, 1960, p. 298)

> It is an interesting fact...that the essential ideas of Adlerian psychology crop up again and again in the writings of other psychologists, often persons who begin with a Freudian psychoanalytic orientation. (Sundberg & Tyler, 1962, p. 394)

> In certain respects it is legitimate to say that Freudian psychology is in the process of catching up with Adler...the first pioneering steps toward an ego psychology within psychoanalysis were taken by Alfred Adler. (White, 1957)

> It would not be easy to find another author from whom so much has been borrowed from all sides without acknowledgment than Alfred Adler. (Ellenburger, 1970, p. 645)

Even Freud borrowed some of Adler's ideas early in the meetings of The Wednesday Psychological Society; but, to be fair, that's what the meetings were about in the first place—exchanging ideas stimulated by Freud's original ideas about analysis. Adler was the one who first identified the ways in which a person uses "safeguarding tendencies" to protect self-esteem, a construct that Freud later termed defense mechanisms. And even though Freud at first criticized Adler for his suggestion that the aggression drive was a force in behavior, he later incorporated it into his psychoanalysis and renamed it Thanatos.

By way of balance, it is important to note that Adler has been acknowledged forthrightly by many schools of thought as a major influence on their work. Maslow (1954), for example, identified Adler as the first among those who made up the third force, a humanistic approach that served as a counterweight to the prior two movements of behaviorism and psychoanalysis. Adler has also been acknowledged as the first social psychologist, the first field theorist, and, as previously mentioned, the first ego psychologist. In addition, Adler was essentially the first in psychotherapy to stress the organism as an important intervening variable in the stimulus–response paradigm, and therefore is acknowledged as the first cognitive therapist. His influence can be noted in the following shifts over the past few decades in psychology and psychotherapy:

- Denial of instincts as key motive for human behavior
- Shift from objective psychology to subjective

- De-emphasis of deterministic, reductionistic framework
- Importance of holism and self construction in meaning-making
- Increased attention to ego needs and defenses
- Denial of primacy of sexual drive
- Increased importance of social context and systemic thinking
- Increased understanding of women's striving for equality
- Acknowledge role of ethics and values in therapy

Hall and Lindzey, the authors of the most popular personality theory text over the past four decades, added yet another point of Adlerian influence: "Adler fashioned a humanistic theory of personality which was the antithesis of Freud's conception of man. By endowing man with altruism, humanitarianism, cooperation, creativity, uniqueness and awareness, he restored to man a sense of dignity and worth that psychoanalysis had pretty largely destroyed" (1957, p. 125).

Interestingly, however, few modern family therapy schools acknowledge Adler, much less as a pioneer, even though comparative studies have shown that Adlerian family therapy has the most potential for serving as an integrative framework for family work. In a set of earlier studies comparing personality theories, Adler's theory came out consistently as the theory with the most similarity to other major theories. Taft (1958) subjected Hall and Lindzey's (1957) ratings of theorists on 18 different dimensions to a cluster analysis, and found that Adlerian theory came out with the most similarity to the other 16 theories. From that, Taft concluded that Adlerian theory was either very eclectic or that it had had a major influence on the other theories. Farberow and Shneidman (1961) reached a similar conclusion after soliciting blind case analyses of therapists from six different schools, and found through a factor analysis of the Q-Sort technique that Adlerian theory yielded the greatest communality.

It seems possible to conclude that Adlerian theory contains a core that is common to other approaches or at least better represents a consensus perspective (Ansbacher, 1979). Sherman and Dinkmeyer (1987) reached a similar conclusion after their more recent comparison of six different approaches to family therapy. As did Hall and Lindzey earlier, they compared the six theories on many different dimensions (66 items in three general areas) and found Adlerian theory to be in general agreement with the other theories in over 74% of the items, a higher percentage than any other theory. "Adler's concerns, ideas, and methods cut across what today are called structural, strategic, communications, experiential, behavioral, cognitive, multigenerational, and ego psychology approaches to the family" (Sherman & Dinkmeyer, 1987, p. xi).

TENETS OF THE MODEL

Several fundamental principles guide the work of Adlerian family therapists. Together, the tenets of individual psychology form a consistent and comprehensive perspective of human behavior. While the basic principles of the theory can be presented separately to enhance clarity, in practice, there is unity of function just as there is within each human and within each family. Each tenet makes more sense in relation to the whole. Three sets of basic Adlerian principles are presented here: tenets related to individual family members, tenets that pertain specifically to the family as a whole, and finally, tenets related to children as a family subset.

PRINCIPLES FOR UNDERSTANDING INDIVIDUAL FAMILY MEMBERS

SOCIAL CONTEXT The Adlerian approach offers a social paradigm as a context for understanding family life, in that all behavior is seen as having social meaning—not only within the rules, roles, and dynamics of living in the small group known as the family, but also as having contextual meaning in larger groups within society and the world. From birth, humans are social beings. We begin life dependent on others for nurturance and sustenance. Then, as we go through life we spend much of our time in some kind of interaction with others. In fact, social interaction is not an option, but a requirement of life (Sherman & Dinkmeyer, 1987).

Social embeddedness is an important construct in the Adlerian approach. Adler described this principle in several ways:

> Individual Psychology regards and examines the individual as socially embedded. We refuse to recognize and examine an isolated human being. (Ansbacher & Ansbacher, 1956, p. 2)
>
> Self-boundedness is an artifact. (Ansbacher & Ansbacher, 1956, p. 138)
>
> Before the individual life of man there was the community. (Ansbacher & Ansbacher, 1956, p. 128)

Human beings tend to seek personal significance through belonging in social systems. The same is true in families. Yet, it is fairly common in families who come to therapy for one or more members to lack a sense of belonging. In fact, some report feeling unaccepted, and others rejected or alienated (Sherman & Dinkmeyer, 1987). Adlerians seek solutions to such problems not by going "deeper" into the unconscious of the individual, but by placing the problem into its larger social context (Ansbacher, 1978a). In this case, the family represents the most important larger context. Thus, the Adlerian approach is naturally systemic, always looking at context, from the small group of the family to the limitless number of groups that combine to form the community of humanity. In this sense, then, the social context becomes a rich resource for understanding the individual as well as the family (Dinkmeyer & Dinkmeyer, 1991).

Our species has apparently lived in families and groups of one type or another as long as recorded history. In a Darwinian sense, the species has undoubtedly found strength in numbers. Humans are inherently social. By this, we do not mean that we love to talk, or that we are all extroverts. Rather, social embeddedness refers to the context in which we make decisions. Our family of origin provides us with our first context. It is through our interactions with our primary caregivers that we begin to form our individual approaches to life. It is in this first small group where we begin trying to make sense out of our subjective perceptions. As we do so, we begin to think, feel, and act in self-consistent ways. Adler referred to this self-consistency as one's style of living.

LIFE STYLE Adler first used the term *life style* in 1926 to refer to the holistic unity of the individual. He had previously referred to the construct with terms such as guiding image, life form, life plan, life line, personality, whole individual, and line of movement (Ansbacher, 1978b). Apparently, the term life style had originally been used by the German sociologist Max Weber to refer to the differing ways people lead their lives in various subcultures (Hoffman, 1994). For Adler, it meant much more: It was the creative power of the individual that he emphasized in his use of the term "life style." He believed that the individual crafted his or her own way of going about life.

> Do not forget the most important fact that not heredity and not environment are determining factors. Both are giving only the frame and the influences which are answered by the individual in regard to his styled creative power. (Adler, cited in Ansbacher & Ansbacher, 1956, pp. xxiv)

Given whatever genetic parameters or environmental opportunities, it was the use an individual made of one's potentialities that counted (Adler, 1935/1996a, p. 353). Individual psychology is one of use, not possession (Adler, 1932/1979e, p. 194). It matters less what you have than what you do with what you have.

A person makes decisions about life's challenges and acts according to those decisions. Over time, these decisions begin to form characteristic patterns, oftentimes outside our awareness, but nonetheless in recurring, predictable directions. We develop convictions about ourselves, about others, and about the world that guide our behaviors. Unfortunately, this process of generalizing from imagined or real experiences begins at birth, and comes together as a pattern by five or six years of age. At such a young age it is easy to misperceive or overgeneralize. "Although children are excellent observers and have extraordinarily sharp perception, they lack the experience and maturity necessary to evaluate their observations adequately" (Dinkmeyer, Dinkmeyer, & Sperry, 1987, p. 34). For example, it is easy to conclude that "I'm stupid," or "People love only winners," "You gotta look out for number one," or "I'm OK, as long as I do everything they want." If a child begins to internalize such thoughts and then begins to act on premature judgments without testing external reality or the degree to which others share those beliefs, then the *private logic* that is developed may guide him or her away from common logic, or "common sense." Adler referred often to the problems associated with private mental attitudes (1929/1969, p. 8). Later, Dreikurs (1973b) identified three psychological processes that comprise the private logic: long-term goals of the life style, the immediate goals of responding to a specific situation, and the hidden reasons a person uses to justify his or her behavior.

The most basic problem with private self-statements is that they can remain hidden and go untested if never spoken aloud or shared. They can begin to take on a life of their own, regardless of their degree of veracity or usefulness.

The life style is an attitude about life. It is a basic orientation to life that is more noticeable to others than to one's self. The life style is like a mosaic. A life style is more apparent from a reasonable distance than up close. The difference in perspective is like that of seeing a train from atop a cliff at a thousand yards versus a perspective of the train from a distance of a car length, as at a crossing.

Life styles, for both individuals and families, are unique. Yet, there are some similarities, enough even to permit a few basic summary typologies: The ruling type, the getting type, the avoiding type, and the socially useful type (Adler, 1935/1979c, p. 68); or the martyrs, the getters, the drivers, the pleasers, the victims, and the controllers (Dreikurs, 1973b; Mosak, 1971, 1973). While these and other types have been identified and fully described over the years, the principal value in typologies is merely to provide prototypes that may serve to alert and inform therapists as to the forms life styles can take.

SUBJECTIVE PERCEPTION Adlerian family therapists believe in the active decision-making abilities of each family member. This belief comes from a conviction that each person is responsible for his or her own subjective view of life. Individuals are not just reactors, but creative actors who perceive in accordance with their own life style. Reality is in the subjective perception of each human being. It is not likely that any two family members will perceive the same situation or action in the same exact way because of their own creative contributions to perception itself. Adler applied this same subjectivity to meaning:

> We experience reality always through the meaning we give it. (Adler, 1931/1980, p. 3)

> There is no general meaning in life; the meaning of life is that which you give to your own life. (Manaster et al., 1977, p. 73)

> There are as many meanings given to life as there are human beings. (Adler, 1931/1980, p. 4)

> People give all of their experiences meaning. (Sherman & Dinkmeyer, 1987, p. 8)

> What is the meaning of life?...is a question humans ask only when they have suffered a defeat. (Adler, 1931/1980, p. 3)

In seeking a place in the family of origin, a child develops a phenomenological field of perception that is biased by basic convictions. Once developed, the biased apperception forms a field of vision and a lens for viewing the world. In actuality, we see what we want to see. "We tend to behave according to how things appear to us, and, when our perception changes, our behavior changes accordingly. Perception thus determines behavior perhaps more than 'reality' does" (Dinkmeyer, Dinkmeyer, & Sperry, 1987, p. 18). Family members' perceptions of family interactions can often be conflicting, and subsequently can become target points for intervention in family therapy. Communication skills training can help family members learn how to check their own biased apperceptions adeptly and the ways in which they may contribute to miscommunication.

UNIQUENESS OF THE INDIVIDUAL The complexity of human life requires a phenomenological perspective that is built on an understanding of the individual's role in creating his or her own approach to life. We are solely products neither of our heredity nor our environment, but we build upon the contributions or limitations of each. Humans are not easy to understand, at least at the level of depth required in therapy that actually has a chance to result in real behavioral change. "There is no 'Aha' psychology," cautioned Lydia Sicher, one of Adler's closest Vienna colleagues and, in fact, the person to whom he entrusted the leadership of his clinics in Vienna when he emigrated to America (cited in Davidson, 1991, p. 169). Just because we learn one fact about a person, such as his or her ordinal birth position, shouldn't lead us to declare "Aha," now I've got it.

Aldlerians believe in the indivisible unity of the individual. There is a natural nonsummativity in viewing human beings as whole persons, rather than as a set of complexes, opposing forces, or isolated human beings. Just as it is important to see a person holistically, it is also imperative to see each as unique, regardless of how many characteristics may be shared with all others, or with some others. Adler believed deeply in the uniqueness of each individual, and the importance of avoiding rigid rules that did not allow for "thousands of variations" (Ansbacher & Ansbacher, 1979, p. 66) in the individual case.

> I believe that I am not bound by any strict rule or prejudice but prefer to subscribe to the principle "Everything can also be different" (Alles kann auch anders sein). The uniqueness of the individual cannot be expressed in a short formula, and general rules—even those laid down by individual psychology, by my own creation—should be regarded as nothing more than an aid to a preliminary illumination of the field of view in which the single individual can be found—or missed. (Adler, cited in Ansbacher & Ansbacher, 1956, p. 194)

BEHAVIOR IS PURPOSIVE "A basic tenet of Adlerian psychology is the purposiveness of all human behavior. Behavior is goal directed. It is teleological movement toward a goal" (Sherman & Dinkmeyer, 1987, p. 5). Adler first came to his belief in a teleological life force in his early medical training, probably from the influence of Virchow, the noted pathologist, who had earlier described an individual as a unified community of cells working together to achieve a common purpose (cited in Ansbacher, 1974, p. 44). "We cannot think, feel, will or act without the perception of some goal" (Adler, 1925/1973, p. 3). The significance of this viewpoint is that it took psychology in a totally different direction from the determinism of the Freudian analytical approach that focused so heavily on the past and on the identification of causal events in personality development. In Adler's view, the motivating power that explains behavior is in the pull of anticipated goals, not the push of past causal events. Behavior is best understood in terms of its goal-directedness. Therefore the task of the Adlerian therapist is to identify and understand goals that are not usually in the client's awareness.

Adler described three primary life tasks that individuals face: love, work, and friendship. On occasion, Adler made reference to these tasks as ties to the community, as problems, as challenges, and even as a collective reality. Also, he used referents such as "sexual," "occupational," and "social" as interchangeable terms. Regardless of terminology, he placed a great deal of emphasis on the importance of these tasks in each person's life. "These three ties, therefore, set three problems: how to find an occupation, which will enable us to survive under the limitations set by the nature of the earth; how to find a position among our fellows, so that we may cooperate and share the benefits of cooperation; how to accommodate ourselves to the fact that we live in two sexes and that the continuance and furtherance of mankind depends upon our love-life" (Adler, 1931/1980, p. 7). The quality of one's life is to a large extent a product of the degree to which the individual finds a decent balance in accomplishing these basic life tasks. It is clear that an individual with superior achievement in a single area, perhaps work, or even in two areas, has difficulty compensating for the loss of satisfaction in the other area. Quality emanates from balance.

SOCIAL INTEREST The heart and soul of Adler's individual psychology lies in the construct of *Gemeinschaftsgefühl*, or social interest, as it has been most commonly translated. While the difficulty of the translation of the word has contributed to some of the confusion regarding the exact meaning of the term, there has been little disagreement among Adlerians as to its primary meaning or its significance. It is more than the meaning of the words, individually or collectively, in that social interest means more than being social or being interested in society. Basically, the construct refers to a community feeling, or a sense of "feeling a part of the community of man" (K. A. Adler, 1994, p. 131). There is an action element in the term; it is not just a Pollyanna-like fuzzy feeling of being a do-gooder. Social interest requires contact—a doing—that is with others, not for others. It is a manifestation of an ability to contact, to join, to cooperate, and to contribute meaningfully to the common good of all who share the crust of the planet without thought of reward or status. It implies the feeling of belonging, not just through membership, but through effort and useful action. Social interest reflects a capacity to give and take, not necessarily to a present-day real group in the community or society, nor to a political or religious group, but more to the betterment of all. It is a matter of contributing. It is a matter of making contact and of cooperating. Though innate, social interest requires evocation, nurturance, and development.

Other theorists and therapists of note have attempted to help clarify the definition of social interest. "This word, invented by Alfred Adler, is the only one available that describes well the flavor of the feelings for mankind expressed by self-actualizing subjects. They have for human beings in general a deep feeling of identification, sympathy, and affection....They have a genuine desire to help the human race. It is as if they were all members of a single family" (Maslow, 1954, 217). O'Connell (1991) preferred identification (humanistic) as a wider referent than social. Bitter (1996), like William James's biographer, Ralph Barton Perry (cited in Ansbacher, 1991), suggested that defining the construct in terms of "an interest in the interest of others" would preclude other negative connotations possibly associated with the word "social." Further, Lydia Sicher (Davidson, 1991) preferred social consciousness, social awareness, or communal feeling. Sicher went on to offer that social interest "is far more difficult to understand than any other term because you can understand every other term logically. But this is something you have to experience within yourself, it is an awareness, not a knowing about" (Sicher, 1991).

Social interest as evidenced in a community feeling wherein one feels a natural part of life as a valued being enables one to empathize with others and to make a lasting contribution to others (Bitter, 1996, p. 312). Social interest does not mean merely that a person must have a passive interest in others, nor does it mean that one must do good to or for another, but rather it does mean "that individuals have to have an interest in developing themselves so that the rest of the human race has the advantage of these constructive contributions" (Sicher, 1991).

Social interest "is a major component of family loyalty and cohesiveness, and the family's participation in the larger community" (Sherman & Dinkmeyer, 1987, p. 12). It is important for family therapists to uncover the degree to which families exhibit a willingness to commit time and energy to each other and to the family as a whole, even if it means giving up their individual personal preferences. Obviously, families with higher levels of social interest have a greater chance of successfully meeting life's challenges.

SOCIAL EQUALITY Another key construct of individual psychology that is somewhat difficult to define with precision is social equality. For Adler, it simply made sense to look at people as social equals. While human history is obviously replete with caste and class systems, Adler felt that people would be free to contribute and to cooperate only if they lived in a society where individuals enjoyed the same social status and where people treated each other with mutual respect. Unfortunately, the construct is often compared to the doctrine of equal opportunity, though the two are actually oppositional (Dreikurs, 1971, p. 187). Equality of opportunity is to social equality as competition is to cooperation; it merely defends the equal right to become unequal through competition. "Adler recognized equality as a fundamental prerequisite for the logic of social living; without it, there can be no stability or social harmony" (Dreikurs, 1971, p. x). Whenever any class or group sets itself up as superior or dominant, it creates instability because no person and no group wants to exist in a one-down or inferior position. Social inequality is seen as antithetical to social interest in that, in such conditions, individuals do not feel that they belong or that they can contribute. Thus, efforts become directed toward self-elevation, rather than toward the common good. Inequality inevitably leads to feelings of inferiority, and concomitantly superiority. While general feelings of physiological or cosmic inferiority serve to unite humans in cooperative endeavors, social inferiority stimulates compensatory efforts toward superiority and power (Lowe, 1982, p. 332).

From the French, American, and Russian revolutions onward, democratic equality has been slowly and inexorably moving forward. Dreikurs (1971) pointed to the evolution of democracy in America as possibly the greatest opportunity to date for achieving social equality. "Our present predicament arises from the fact that while we all have legally become equals, we do not know how to deal with each other as equals" (Dreikurs, 1971, p. 189). Further, legal equality seems to have simply intensified the conflicts between previously dominant and submissive groups. Nonetheless, the rules have changed, and for the better. Vestiges of violence in the workplace, government, and at home mark the struggles of learning how to shift from dominance and authoritarianism to equality, but nonetheless the struggle to participate as equals continues unabated. The challenge is to move from living on a vertical plane, where one has to step over or knock off those who are above or on top, to a *horizontal plane*, where all can move along side by side to contribute in accordance with their own unique qualities and efforts (Sicher, 1991).

"Equality is the most pressing problem of our times....The world is a battlefield where two forces meet: the most powerful seeking to retain their power and the weaker seeking to gain influence" (Dreikurs, 1946, p. 251). Equal relationships cannot be based on superior-inferior positions. Essentially, social equality in the form of racial equality became public policy when Kenneth B. Clark used the theoretical construct to support his brief submitted to the U.S. Supreme Court in the most important civil rights case decided in the country's history, *Brown v. Board of Education*, in 1954. "I do not believe it is an unpardonable exaggeration to assert that this finding reflects a major contribution of Alfred Adler to man's endless struggle for justice and dignity" (Clark, cited in Terner & Pew, 1978, p. 316).

Beyond race, the move toward equality is no more evident, nor more troublesome, than in the home. Children and adolescents are finding, often painfully, new ways of belonging; so too are couples. Yet, we continue to struggle with efforts to live as equals.

MASCULINE PROTEST Privileged masculinity has for centuries dominated the social structure of human life, based on a myth that women were naturally inferior to men. Adler believed that such a myth was damaging for both women and men, and subsequently for marital relationships. From the beginning of individual psychology, Adler championed the protest of such superiority–inferiority positions of the sexes. Certain of no biological basis for such a position, he believed that women rightly resented their assigned inferior position. "No one can be content with a subordinate position" (Adler, 1931/1980, p. 122).

Contrary to Freud, Adler believed that it was not penis envy that women experienced, but rather an envy of masculine power and privilege. Since every person is measured by the ideal of privileged masculinity, it is little wonder that men feel a constant pressure and a duty to measure up, and women a resentment for not being allowed full participation. Adler encouraged young girls and women to pursue self-development and full participation in society, pointing to a study that provided supporting evidence that girls whose mothers' worked in independent occupations scored higher on aptitude testing than other boys or girls. He speculated that their performance simply indicated that they didn't buy the myth that women were less capable (Adler, 1978, p. 13).

Adler postulated that the inferiority myth, and the restrictions it spawned, not only created difficulties for men and women in their personal relationships, but also "prevented humanity from using half of its powers" (Terner & Pew, 1978, p. 43). Predating the relatively recent move toward removing sexist language from the public vocabulary, Adler, in 1936, called for the removal of the cultural bias against women in language (cited in Ansbacher, 1978a, p. 259). As a small indication of that sensitivity to language, Adler never referred to the sexes as opposite, but rather chose to refer to the "other" sex, because he felt that we shared too much in common to be called opposite.

"It is not easy in our culture for a girl to have self-confidence and courage" (Adler, 1978, p. 13). This same message, unfortunately, continues to be heard too much today, as in the powerful writings of a best-selling therapist, Mary Pipher (1995, 1996), who writes insightfully and dramatically about her work with young girls. Courage can be evoked and nurtured, and will be in a society where we go further than just say we are created equal. "The full emancipation of women is necessary for the development of equal human rights" (Dreikurs, 1946, p. 258).

STRIVING FOR SIGNIFICANCE As infants, humans are totally dependent upon others for basic survival. Even later, the growing child is still quite dependent, especially for sustenance and nurturance. Thus, it is easy to develop a sense of smallness and inferiority. Then later, as we grow into adulthood and realize the incredible enormity of the universe, while at the same time we begin to become more and more aware of our very real limits, the inferiority feelings form a master motive for our behavior—to overcome our relative insignificance and to prepare ourselves to master life's challenges. Every person to some degree has inferiority feelings, which are not in themselves abnormal or bad. In fact, they may be considered the cause of all improvements in the human condition

(Adler, 1931/1980, p. 55). We compensate for these inferiority feelings by cooperating with others. We want to make contact with others. We want to belong. We want to fit in with the group. We want to contribute to the common good. We continuously strive to grow and to develop, and to move from a felt minus position to a felt plus.

Adler referred to this desire as a striving for perfection, and claimed that it is as innate as life itself. "To live is to develop....[T]he striving for perfection is innate as something which belongs to life, as thriving, an urge, a developing, a something without which one could not even conceive of life" (Adler, 1979d, p. 31). Individuals with courage and a sense of adequacy will approach such a striving with the courage to be imperfect, because they know that perfection and faultlessness are not within the human experience (Lazarsfeld, 1991, p. 95). Others, however, can reach the conclusion that they are significant only if they are perfect. Perfectionism becomes a way of life for such people. When a physician suggests taking up gardening for relaxation, the perfectionist will attack the task with a characteristic approach to life and seek to plow the perfectly straight row, and cultivate the ultimate tomato. "Individuals can only do their best. To be the best is not possible because it is an unreachable goal" (Sicher, 1991).

The striving for significance can sometimes become derailed into a striving for superiority. In such situations, we are not just compensating, but overcompensating, like the leaders who wish to act as equals only after they've established superiority, as in the acquisition of military weaponry. "The more intense the inferiority, the more violent the superiority" (Adler, 1969, p. 320). The greater challenge for humans is to learn how to cooperate with each other to achieve mastery over real difficulties and challenges in life, without resorting to the adoption of a passive approach marked by a desire to feel superior but lacking the effort to become stronger, more competent, and more adequate to life's tasks. Cooperation requires everyone's competence and best effort.

PRINCIPLES FOR UNDERSTANDING FAMILY RELATIONSHIPS

FAMILY ATMOSPHERE Two of the most significant forces that contribute to a child's life style development process are the family atmosphere and the family constellation. The former refers to the child's perception of the climate or environment in which the family lives, and the latter to the system of relationships that make up one's family of origin.

The family atmosphere is composed of sets of rules that serve the family as guidelines for acceptable behavior. In some ways the atmosphere is most evident in the expectations and roles assigned and assumed by its members. The family atmosphere is shaped by dominant (or shared) family values. Shared values are those that both parents hold in high regard. These values and beliefs often find their expression in expectations. For example, if the parents hold excessively high standards of performance, then the family atmosphere is likely to be one dominated by various shades of achievement orientation; likewise, if the atmosphere is marked by independence, then self-sufficiency expectations can develop and dominate. There is not a one-to-one causal relationship between family atmosphere and life style development because the child plays a very active role in deciding upon the degree to which he or she will adopt, adapt, oppose, or ignore the family's shared values. Nonetheless, the atmosphere creates the background for the child's development of an approach to life.

As one might expect, there are some general atmospheres that can be recognized. One, for example, is the family atmosphere in which it is apparent immediately that children occupy the center of the family's attention. Often, such an atmosphere takes one of two forms: Either the parents place excessive expectations on the children and overdemand, or they pamper the children to the point of doing everything for them. Likewise, some parents simply ignore the children, who then learn at an early age that it really doesn't much matter what they do, as long as they stay out of the way of the rest of the family. Such an atmosphere often influences children to feel neglected and ignored, or devalued. Another atmosphere that is increasingly evident is an environment in which one of the adults is abusive, either physically, sexually, or verbally, leading children often to conclude that they must "control" all aspects of their environment to ensure their own safety.

There is a multigenerational component to family atmosphere, in that a family develops its own characteristic way of handling life, including the assumptive values and the unfinished business of previous generations of the two families now combined into one. In fact, new couples often discover in therapy that the source of some difficulties is often found in issues not of their own making, but of parents, in-laws, or even previous generations. Today, these conflicts often take the form of squabbles over career commitments and child-rearing practices.

FAMILY CONSTELLATION Adler used this construct to refer to the composition of the family. Who comprises the family? What is the birth order of the children? What is each child's psychological position in the family, or in other words, what is each child's creative response to his or her ordinal position? What are the dominant family goals and values? Who lives in the family home, including nonrelatives?

"The family constellation position is influenced by factors such as emotional ties between family members, age differences, sex of siblings, size of the family, characteristics of each sibling, alliances with parents, the relationship between parents, and the absence of a parent" (Sherman & Dinkmeyer, 1987, p. 10). In spite of how it might seem, children do not grow up in the same family or in the same environment, because the family is so dynamic and changing. "No two children grow up under exactly the same conditions" (Adler, 1930/1970, p. 140). Birth order may seem to be a static influence on a child's life, but, instead, even birth order is a dynamic construct. It is not the actual ordinal position that is so influential. Rather, it is the child's interpretation or use of the position. Thus, psychological position is far more important that mere ordinal position. In addition, the oldest position in one family may be something very different than the oldest in another.

Nowhere is it more enticing for therapists to fall into the "Aha" trap than in the area of birth order. It is a lot like typologies. Sometimes, helpers forget that positions and typologies are only models. Individuals in the same ordinal position as others may share some characteristics, yet be very different as related to others. Undoubtedly, no other Adlerian construct has become more commonplace in our culture than birth order. Literally thousands of articles have been published, mostly in lay magazines, but also in the professional literature (Stewart & Stewart, 1995).

It is not difficult to imagine how children who are firstborns develop a feeling of special privilege and entitlement. The first baby, particularly if it's the first to arrive in a new generation of the extended family, typically gets an incredible amount of attention. Even family pets give the firstborn child in their owner's family an inordinate amount of attention. Anxious to please and to do things right, firstborns tend to become quite responsible and rules-oriented. They become naturally oriented to power and authority because of their unique position of being first and more powerful. Being the center of attention can be quite fulfilling; such a position may make it relatively easy to feel like one belongs. In some societies throughout history, various forms of entitlement accompanied firstborn status, particularly for the oldest male. Nonetheless, it can be a tough position because of all the expectations and responsibilities. Moreover, many oldest children have to learn how to deal with one of the toughest emotional upheavals of all, an experience that Adler referred as "dethronement" (Ansbacher & Ansbacher, 1956, p. 377). It is the sense of losing one's throne, or special position, that can accompany the sudden arrival of another baby, particularly if the baby comes before the oldest child has reached three years of age or so. No other child experiences such an event.

Middle children, according to Adler, often experience the world as though they are in a race, always trying to catch up to the oldest who had a head start. If the firstborn dreams of "falling," as though from an exalted place or from being on top, the middle child probably dreams of "running," to catch up with the more privileged (Adler, cited in Ansbacher & Ansbacher, 1956, p. 379). For some, the race seems so impossible that they choose to go in far different directions than the oldest, and make a place for themselves by not competing. Also, such a position may give the middle child opportunities, early and often, to learn how to cooperate because there is someone on each side. The running may also be required to stay ahead of the next child in line. One of the unique experiences that can accompany the middle position is that he or she can begin to feel "squeezed" between the oldest and the youngest.

The youngest has a unique position in that he or she never has to share or change position. If a child is the last born of a family, he or she never has to deal with dethronement. And the youngest can benefit from the stimulation and standards set by siblings. At the same time, a youngest can look around and conclude that everyone is older, stronger, and more capable, and become discouraged. "He has no followers but many pacemakers" (Adler, cited in Ansbacher & Ansbacher, 1956, p. 380). Youngest children often become achievement-oriented, to the extent that they want to excel in everything. But the toughest part of growing up healthy as the "baby" in the family is to appropriately handle the pampering and spoiling that often comes with the territory. Pampered children often grow up with a lot of assumptions about being served. "A spoiled child can never be independent" (Adler, 1931/1980, p. 151). For such children, no demand is unreasonable, no limitation or restriction is acceptable, no rule is unbreakable, and no expectation is too outrageous (Lowe, 1982, p. 335).

"Only" children often conclude that being the center of attention is their birthright. Perhaps more than children in other positions, only children tend to become adult-oriented, and are impacted more by their perceptions of how they are measuring up to "ideals." Children without siblings are also influenced a bit more by extended family members, for example cousins, or even nonfamily members, such as neighbors and close friends. Only children naturally have fewer opportunities for learning how to cooperate and to share, but that doesn't automatically mean that they become uncooperative or selfish. Much depends on the family values and expectations.

All positions in the family, like personality characteristics, have their pluses and minuses. There is no perfect or best psychological position, nor likewise, is there a worst position. The critical psychological ingredient is in how the child interprets and assigns meaning to his or her position and situation. Gender expectations certainly impact the family constellation, as do other variables such as the original ordinal/psychological position of each of the parents. The number of years between children also plays a role, as does the gender distribution.

Today's families are comprised of many combinations of parents (biological, step, adoptive, single, homosexual, grandparent) and children (biological, adoptive, blended, mixed, multicultural, multigenerational). While combinations of parents and their children can make family constellations quite complicated, and even dramatic, children still try to learn how to fit in the group. It is the task of the family therapist to use family constellation characteristics to understand the family dynamics. In doing so, it is critically important to bear in mind the richness of the family constellation construct, and to avoid the "Aha" pressure. It is not a psychological game, as Toman (1961) has suggested, but more a framework for building enriched understandings of what it's like for each child in his or her own unique family situation.

SYSTEMIC DYNAMICS Adlerian family therapists view family relationships as consisting of three interactive sets of reciprocal systems: the family as a whole; parents as a couple; and the children as a subset. In line with Adler's systemic focus in general, family therapists with Adlerian perspectives see families as developing consistent patterns of interactions and expectations.

Groups of individuals living together as families develop *family life styles*, just as individuals do. The family life style is a unique individualized creation of its members in the context of larger social groups in the broader society, and in the context of multigenerational and sociological influences as well. Patterns of interactional relationships within the systems and among the systems are routinely examined by Adlerian family therapists. In fact, it is important to assess the manner in which individual family members' life styles mesh with the other members of the family and with the family's collective life style (Sherman & Dinkmeyer, 1987). Adlerian therapists focus on helping the family as a whole develop a better understanding of its own internal unity in the form of its style of living. Then, the therapist provides the kind of support and challenge that facilitates the constructive changes the family may decide to make either in their individual and collective goals, or in their ways of going about achieving their goals.

What constitutes the healthy family? It is popular today in family therapy circles to say that the nature of the family has changed so dramatically that there is no such thing as a normal family. It is true that family composition has indeed changed to the point that we now have families in increasingly equal percentages who are comprised of all kinds of combinations of biological and nonbiological parents and children. Therefore, it is inappropriate to conceptualize typical family life as consisting of two biological parents and their offspring living together. Nonetheless, although family composition has shifted, and thereby changed what is considered normal in terms of who lives together, what remains clear is what constitutes healthy family life.

Adlerian family therapists believe it is essential that family members develop and demonstrate an interest in other members (Adler, 1931/1980, p. 252). The deeper the commitment to the family as a whole, the healthier the family. Social interest makes for healthy family living. The basic task in living as a family is to focus less on self and more on others—but not to the degree that one essentially becomes self-indulgent by giving service or by becoming a martyr. The challenge is to find ways to join, to cooperate, and to contribute to the common good of the family.

Like other small groups, families share common interactional dynamics. Families are built on shared goals, go through developmental stages, share varying degrees of cohesiveness and trust, and operate under norms and functional rules. Thus, families function within the parameters of small-group dynamics to some extent. For example, it is common in family therapy for leaders to help members avoid scapegoating or identifying one member as the wearer of the family symptoms. Also, as in group work, family therapists work a great deal on goal alignment and cohesion building. Family therapy, again like group work, requires leadership that is focused on both task and maintenance functions, and leaders who facilitate moderate risk-taking behavior of family members as well as of the family as a whole to move the group toward change and growth. Finally, as do group workers, family therapists try to instill a sense of hope and encouragement that the family is in this together as a group, and together can make interactions and communications go more effectively.

Some systemic therapists view the individual family member as powerless, and focus only on the family system as a whole. Moreover, when family members are perceived as being mere artifacts of the system as a whole, individuals are disempowered and portrayed as helpless (McKelvie, 1987, p. 169). Adlerian family therapists feel, on the other hand, that individuals can make a difference in a dysfunctional system. In fact, change is seen as more efficient and effective when it begins at the individual level. An empowered partner, for example, would decide to change his or her own behavior in the system, rather than wait on the other to change (Huber, 1991; McKelvie, 1987). Therapists who prefer to strategically manipulate the system rather than relate to the individuals who comprise the system can lead members to a dependent, powerless position and end up shifting the attention of therapy to their own actions and interventions at the expense of the family.

Adlerians search out power dimensions of family relationships, and then direct the family's attention to the task of developing more egalitarian interactions. Inferiority–superiority relationships are not helpful in families, nor, for that matter, between therapists and families. True, generational boundaries in families are important, but not in the form of rigid authoritarian rule. In democratic families, members work out differences in family meetings, and establish rules and consequences together. Coalitions and triangulations are to be expected but not supported. Conflict in families is usually between two people; a third person, in the form of a referee, judge, or an ally only complicates the problem-solving process. As Dreikurs and Soltz said (1964, p. 224), "individual relationships between two people belong to the two involved." That is, unless the conflict involves a power differential where one member deserves and requires protection.

Families function more effectively with consistent, clear roles and rules. Everyone needs to contribute by helping the system as a whole function smoothly. Routine is good, unless a family gets bogged down in a quagmire of routine and is unable to do anything spontaneously or different. Families, in an Adlerian perspective, function most effectively when they share goals, identify ways in which each member can responsibly participate according to strengths and preferences, hold each other accountable for carrying out agreed-upon responsibilities, and participate in democratically led family meetings.

PARENTAL RELATIONSHIP DYNAMICS Parents are leaders of the family, and as such serve as role models for family interaction, intentionally or not. Therefore, it is helpful to understand the basic characteristics and actions of the couple toward and with each other. Beginning even before they have met, couples tend to develop expectations of partners, marriage, and family life. Most of the time individuals are only marginally aware of these expectations and anticipations. But we do tend to develop attachment relationships and intimate partnerships on the basis of complementarities or similarities. Some would say we tend to move from the former in younger relationships toward the latter in later relationships. At any rate, we do tend to make decisions in terms of our own preferences. Four priorities that seem to influence our ways of going about life, as well as ways of going about coupling, include those identified as superiority, pleasing, control, and comfort (Kefir & Corsini, 1974). If we are anxious to please others, it makes sense that we're likely to couple up with someone who wants to be pleased or served. In other words, we seek relationships that help us pursue our favorite ways of fitting in and belonging, and simultaneously help us avoid what we consider our worst sources of stress in life: *superiority/meaninglessness*—if we want to avoid a life of meaninglessness, we strive to achieve; *pleasing/rejection*—if rejection is our worst nightmare, then we diligently find ways to serve others; *control/humiliation*—if we want to avoid humiliation, we work hard to keep everything and everyone in control; *comfort/tension*—if the absence of stress is critically important to a sense of well-being, then we seek comfort.

PRINCIPLES FOR UNDERSTANDING CHILDREN

Adler's contributions to child psychology and to family guidance were remarkable in their breadth and depth, particularly for his time. Adler understood children, and committed a great deal of his energy to working with children in the 31 child and family guidance centers he and his colleagues established in Vienna after World War I. His most prominent student, Dreikurs, went even further in defining and describing what is known about childhood and adolescence. Together, the two of them made a tremendous difference, not only in the professions of psychology and family guidance, but even more so in education and in parenting circles. One can hardly pick up a book on children, parenting, or family life written in the twentieth century that does not discuss children and parenting in ways reflective of Adlerian teachings. Of course, many of his ideas regarding child-rearing, teaching, and parenting have become so accepted that neither parents nor professionals think the methods are anything but "common sense." For example, the lead article in a recent issue (October, 1977) of *Parenting*, a popular monthly magazine, is all about Dreikurs's goals of misbehavior. Of course, neither Dreikurs nor Adler was credited with the content, but nonetheless, the entire article discusses children in the context of Adler's original constructs and Dreikurs's "goals of misbehavior."

Virtually no other approach in family therapy discusses children, except as artifacts of the family system. Satir included children in therapy and worked well with them, but her focus was largely on the adult relationships (Bitter, 1987), whereas Adlerians tend to place more emphasis on the children. Adlerians are the only family therapists to focus a good deal of attention on the whole family in therapy. Most family therapists merely give lip service to children, and focus most of their attention on the adults in the family, or the grown children. In effect, such treatment neglects and negates young children as important family members.

GOALS OF MISBEHAVIOR Children act with a purpose. Each action is intended to aid in movement toward a goal. For most, the goal is to belong to the group, to fit in with others in the family by making useful contributions. While children may not always be fully conscious of their goals, they are consistent and persistent in their efforts to find a way to belong. When discouraged with the results of unsuccessful constructive efforts to find a place, children typically find more destructive ways to be a part of the group. Discouraged children misbehave; even a misbehaving child, however, is still trying to feel important and significant, if not in the family, then in his or her own part of the world.

Dreikurs (1968b, pp. 27–32) described four common goals of a child's misbehavior. A child may choose to find assurance of fitting in through *attention-getting* behavior, marked by efforts to get family members' attention, recognition, or service. By doing so the child chooses an approach that is destined to failure. Eventually, others grow annoyed or frustrated with constant demands for undue attention. On the receiving end of such behaviors, it feels as though you can never pour enough attention into the leaky bucket. Other children choose to pursue feelings of belonging by involving others in *power* struggles. These kinds of behaviors are particularly noticeable in adolescents who, as a group, seem to be continually striving to prove to themselves and to the world that they're no longer children. They are experts at getting others into power conflicts. Still others choose to engage in acts of *revenge* to get even with others. Reflecting a high level of discouragement, revengeful children show the pain they feel when they choose to hurt others. Finally, the most discouraged children are the ones who choose to *display inadequacy* to keep others from expecting anything of them. Paradoxically, some of these children possess the greatest amount of ambition. They want to be able to do it all very well, they get discouraged when they can't, and they then try to protect their own image of themselves by doing nothing, and by working hard to convince others that they are hopeless. It is relatively easy for a parent or a family therapist to recognize specific goals by identifying their own emotional response. For example, it is common to feel annoyed when confronted with an attention-seeking child, and to feel angry with a child who is into power struggles. Further, it is common to feel hurt by revengeful behavior, and to feel pity for those who present themselves as inadequate. Walton (1980) and others (Walton & Powers, 1974) identified an additional goal of misbehavior that is particularly noticeable in teenagers: *excitement*. Often, teenagers misbehave merely to create action. To understand teenagers, it is also important to remember that the group to which they want to belong has shifted from family to peers. Therefore, their behavior always makes more sense in the context of peers.

Children's misbehavior can be understood in two additional dimensions: active-passive and constructive-destructive (Dreikurs, 1968b, p. 30; Dreikurs, Grunewald, & Pepper, 1971; Pepper, 1980, p. 37). Children with less courage pursue passive and destructive behaviors that result in useless contributions, aimed usually at reinforcing their own sense of social status or beliefs that they belong. Whereas children with courage will tend to act more assertively and actively, and at first constructively.

Growing up in a democratic family, where family meetings are common, and interlocking responsibilities are shared, children develop a natural sense of cooperation. On the other hand, if children grow up in an atmosphere that emphasizes competition, they develop sibling rivalries in which actions are aimed at creating winners and losers.

Adolescence is a stage of human development contrived by adults in modern society to facilitate what was once more natural and also more brief—namely, that of moving from childhood to adulthood. Lowe (1993) believes the construct of adolescence serves no one well, in that the special term serves to inhibit natural motivation for growth on the part of the "adolescents," and serves to reduce the naturally positive attitudes of adults. "For almost every child, adolescence means one thing above all else: he must prove that he is no longer a child" (Adler, 1931/1980, p. 182). Nonetheless, amidst all the dangers of this age period, adolescence does not change character. Adolescence may disguise character, but it won't necessarily change it. In fact, in a healthy environment, we become more and more like ourselves throughout life (Carlson & Fullmer, 1991).

APPLICATIONS AND TECHNIQUES

There is little room for uncertainty and circularity in today's managed care environment where increasingly strident voices call for therapists to precisely define diagnoses and then to apply strategically selected, time-limited, outcome-related techniques as a carefully orchestrated treatment plan. Unfortunately, the true process of family therapy doesn't follow such a linear path. Each family therapist would like to think that the profession's prescriptive technology is sufficiently sophisticated to enable such cause-effect therapy, but veteran therapists know better. Family therapy is simply more circular and more complex.

Nowhere is the "shortsightedness of linearity" (Mozdzierz & Greenblatt, 1994, p. 233) more apparent than in the wholesale use of techniques—out of context—that seems so omnipresent in family therapy. Techniques cannot be applied in a simple linear fashion as though the unique context of each family is of no importance. In so doing, therapists succeed only in making discrete, concrete "things" out of "processes" (Mozdzierz & Greenblatt, 1994, p. 241). Once techniques become things, beginning therapists tend to become preoccupied with themselves and the task of mastering a "bag of tricks." Such an overemphasis on the therapist and a misunderstanding of the potential role of theory-based applications results in a focus on techniques as the producers of family change, rather than on the family itself. Paradoxically, the more the therapist focuses on strategic interventions, the less they develop the empathic understanding of what it is like for that family at that time to live as they do; surely, such an understanding should be considered a basic prerequisite for the use of a "technique" or strategic intervention. In the long run, it is the creative capacity of the family to change, as well as their concomitant commitment to change, that determines real change. Artful applications of strategic interventions simply facilitate the family's efforts. "Adler (Ansbacher & Ansbacher, 1956) long advocated that the locus of therapeutic change was neither the technique nor the theory. Rather, the power to change lies in the creative capacity of the individual patient/client" (Mozdzierz & Greenblatt, 1994, p. 234).

One of the unfortunate by-products of an overemphasis on techniques is that a neophyte therapist can feel less than adequate without mastery of such techniques. Such inferiority feelings are unnecessary because most schools of thought in therapy believe more in the power of the therapeutic relationship than in the use of techniques. Therapists who are overly concerned about their inabilities to use techniques become discouraged. In turn, the discouragement and worry about making mistakes or not "doing" the right technique (or the technique right) get in their way of creating effective therapeutic relationships. Adler, on the other hand, encouraged his students to trust the process. "Do not let your vanity get in your way; do your best and let the chips fall where they may" (Manaster et al., 1977, p. 62). After all, effectiveness in family therapy is less a function of technique mastery than it is a function of the degree to which therapists believe in (1) the family's ability to change, (2) their own capacity to facilitate a meaningful therapeutic relationship, and (3) themselves as a therapeutic agent.

It is important to note that theory-based techniques can be very helpful in family therapy when used properly and skillfully. To live up to their promise, techniques must be applied "in the greater perspective and appropriate context of good judgment and therapeutic caring" (Mozdzierz & Greenblatt, 1994, p. 246). Techniques in themselves are not panaceas, but they can function as timely interventions that can make a positive difference in family therapy. What is a technique? What techniques are considered uniquely Adlerian, or applied in unique ways by Adlerian family therapists? What techniques characterize the Adlerian approach to family therapy? Simple questions, but unfortunately, the answers are not so simple. For example, should empathy be considered a technique? In many ways it seems as though empathy is not solely a technique, but more a way of being (Rogers, 1975). Nonetheless, if the application of empathy is of significance in Adlerian family therapy, as it is, should empathy be considered Adlerian?

Empathy is most closely associated with Carl Rogers and his client-centered therapy (1951), but several philosophers, psychologists, and theorists, including Adler, had previously described the construct of empathy and the role it can play in therapy. Adler's unique contribution to the construct was in describing empathy in terms of social feeling (1928/1979b). In an early description of empathy, Adler made reference to an unnamed English author: "To see with the eyes of another, to hear with the ears of another, and to feel with the heart of another" (Adler, 1928/1979b, p. 42). For Adler, empathy meant to feel a part of a larger whole, to identify with, and to feel harmonious with others. Thus, he related empathy to identification and social interest. "The ability to identify must be trained. This can be done only if a person grows up in a connection with others and feels himself a part of the whole" (p. 43). Adlerian family therapists do emphasize the importance of empathy, not only as a technique, but more so as a way of being, in therapy and outside as well. One can not play at empathy, or "do" empathy. Too often, beginning therapists seem to focus solely on the cognitive part of identification, or empathic "insight." Empathic understanding is more than intellectual insight; it is about developing a genuine interest in others (Adler, 1931/1980, p. 72). Moreover, empathy is about relationships, about connectedness and interpersonal belonging. Empathy provides a starting point for treatment in that it provides a solid foundation for the development of an effective therapeutic relationship (Mozdzierz, 1996, p. 347).

THE PROCESS OF ADLERIAN FAMILY THERAPY

Where does one start in family therapy? Adler suggested that therapists could start anywhere because everything is in anything. By that he meant that the unity and consistency of the personality is such that we are always ourselves. "First, we can begin wherever we choose: Every expression will lead us in the same direction—towards the one motive, the one melody, around which the personality is built. Secondly, we are provided with a vast store of material. Every word, thought, feeling or gesture contributes to our understanding" (Adler, 1931/1980, p. 71). "With every sentence, with every word,…I consider: What is the real meaning of what she is saying?" (Adler, 1929, cited in Hoffman, 1994, p. 214). Therefore, as a natural extension from individual psychotherapy, it stands to reason that a family therapist could start wherever the family as a whole wants, or for that matter where any single family member wants to start. The family life style, with its inherent strengths and weaknesses, will emerge from a start at any point.

With whom does a therapist start in family therapy? Contrary to prevailing approaches of the time, Adler, and later Dreikurs, believed in the importance of working with families as a whole. "As all problems are interpersonal problems, we prefer to work with all parties involved simultaneously" (Dreikurs, 1949/1973a, p. 257). Instead of seeing family members individually as though the problems were independent and intrapsychic in nature, Dreikurs saw the disturbed interpersonal relationship as the common link shared by all family members, and "what they should change together" (p. 257). However, Adlerian family therapists will work with any family members present, regardless of who's unavailable.

What is the basic process of Adlerian family therapy? While the therapeutic process naturally differs with each family, there are recognizable developmental stages. In fact, the stages reflected in the process of working with a family throughout the course of therapy are also noticeable in each session. As in group therapy, there is a beginning stage, an ending, and two or three working stages in between. Dreikurs (1949/1973a) identified four basic stages of counseling: relationship establishment; understanding; enhancement of client's understanding; and reorientation. Others have added a stage or two and have changed the titles of one or two of the phases (e.g., Dinkmeyer, Dinkmeyer, & Sperry, 1987: relationship, analysis and assessment, formulation of life style, insight, and reorientation), but the process remains fairly uniform in Adlerian family therapy.

ADLERIAN TECHNIQUES AND STRATEGIES

The Adlerian approach can be characterized as consisting of a process with four fairly predictable stages, each with its own target outcome: engagement (relationship establishment); exploration and assessment (empathic understanding); insight (consensual commitment); and change (follow-through and follow-up actions). Adlerians begin building relationships from the first family contact. Consistent with the theoretical tenet of social equality, Adlerian family therapists build relationships on the basis of mutual respect and caring.

ENGAGEMENT

HORIZONTAL RELATIONSHIPS From the beginning, it is important to relate to family members from a horizontal position, rather than vertical. The focus is on building a team mentality where the therapist can be experienced as a person with special leadership and communication competencies who is committed to helping the family develop a greater understanding of their strengths and challenges, and to contributing some intervention ideas for making a positive difference in the ways in which the family solves its normal problems.

The first challenge for a family therapist is to "win them over" to a cooperative approach to problem solving (Walton, 1980; Walton & Powers, 1974). "Treatment itself is an exercise in cooperation and a test of cooperation" (Adler, 1931/1980, p. 72). A therapist cannot force cooperation, nor require respect. Each has to be earned, and one can earn such only by giving cooperation and respect from a position of equality.

Adler believed there was great value in bringing humor into therapy. While he did not harbor the kind of jokes that were denigrating to anyone or to any group, he did believe in the power of funny stories and incidents. Humor can serve to win patients over in cases where nothing else seems to work.

LAW OF MOVEMENT Families often come into therapy wanting to "feel" different more than they want to "be" different. Adler referred to this phenomenon as a false goal. Instead of working to develop new skills to handle family conflict, family members often put their energies into more passionately defending individual positions and into deluding themselves into "feeling" that they are "superior" to the difficulty; "it is someone else's problem." Referring to an individual in such a situation of false movement, Adler described the situation thusly: "If he feels weak, he moves into circumstances where he can feel strong. He does not train to be stronger, to be more adequate; he trains to *appear* stronger in his own eyes" (Adler, 1931/1980, p. 51). Family therapists often see this kind of false movement in families with adolescents who work diligently to appear strong. To be different, to truly change familial ways of interacting requires real action. Adlerian family therapists trust only movement, not words. One of the most important skills an Adlerian family therapist uses early in the process is to focus on the family's real movement, and to avoid being misled by the family's words. The task is to focus on what the family members "do," and what the family as a whole "does," not necessarily what they say. "Behavior never lies, though talk and verbalization may be misleading" (Sherman & Dinkmeyer, 1987, p. 12).

MODELING COMMUNICATION SKILLS Effective family therapists demonstrate routinely high levels of communication skills, particularly an ability to listen. However, just as empathic understanding is more than a cognitive exercise, communication is more than listening. Effective therapists employ a concrete, descriptive, and wide-ranging verbal and nonverbal language to communicate their understanding of family dynamics. Communicating in a language that is easily understood by each family member can be quite a challenge on a number of levels. Teens, in particular, often hear "differently" than parents. Adlerians work diligently to learn how each family member communicates. In fact, much of the early attention in family therapy is on ferreting out communication difficulties. Passive and blaming language patterns tend to dominate early sessions. Adler (1931/1980) also warned of the deleterious effects of "water power"—tears—in preventing communication. Therapy is a good place to help families continue their communication through the tears instead of being stopped by the tears, regardless of their origin.

GOAL ALIGNMENT A critically important task to accomplish in the beginning phase of family therapy is to align family goals and those of the therapist. Without consensual goals, neither the therapist nor the family will know when they get to where they want to be. Goals should be specific, meaningful, time-appropriate, achievable, and measurable. Beyond the standard therapeutic goals of generating understanding and stimulating change, therapy is about identifying specific movement and change. Typically, the changes will take place in one or more of several basic dimensions of family dynamics: "power and decision-making, boundaries and intimacy, coalitions, roles, rules, similarities, complementarities and differences, myths, and patterns and styles of communication" (Sherman & Dinkmeyer, 1987, p. 28). Psychological goals, whether individual or family goals, are usually subjective and outside of awareness. Therefore Adlerian therapists strive to influence subjective goals and mistaken perceptions of each family member and the family as a unit by bringing goals to awareness (Sherman & Dinkmeyer, 1987, p. 6). Once the goals are in the open, families can choose to redecide, and make changes in their perceptions, beliefs, and actions. Goals are most evident in their results, particularly in the emotional tone of interactions. For example, families engaged in power struggles create an angry environment; families overwhelmed with their problems or with an identified patient among their members often create an atmosphere of despair and doom. Sensitive therapists can feel these emotional tones in the sessions.

THERAPEUTIC QUESTIONING Most Adlerian therapists start by asking each member to talk about what he or she considers the outstanding reasons the family is in therapy (i.e., What brings you here?). From that basic question, the therapist can get some idea as to what each person thinks is happening in the family, and what each may want to happen. It is important to include all family members in the initial inquiry; in fact, it is a good idea to include the youngest family member present fairly early in the sequence, in the first meeting if possible. Presenting problems deserve attention, particularly if the therapy is likely to be brief in duration. Presenting problems are like windows into the soul of the family providing glimpses of where the family life style is no longer working effectively. The task is to see what life is like for the family, what it was like for the family when things were going better, and to identify new behaviors and approaches that may have more potential for success and mutual satisfaction.

Questions that can guide early efforts to identify therapy goals include those that arise from basic Adlerian constructs.

- *Family Atmosphere.* How does the family function? What is the degree of acceptance and nurturance in the family? What are the basic rules of the family? Is the family atmosphere democratic? What boundaries exist, and to what degree of exclusivity? What are the primary partnerships/coalitions? How tolerant and flexible is the family?

- *Family Life Style.* What are the strengths and assets of the family? What characterizes family life? What are the dominant assumptive values and guiding principles that govern family life? What is life like for each member of the family? What level of interaction represents typical daily life? What is each member's level of self-esteem?

- *Family Constellation.* How does each member belong? What are the basic roles assumed by each member and the roles assigned by the others for each? What does it feel like to be a member of this family? What does each think of each other member of the family? Who does what with whom?

- *Social Interest.* What is the level of togetherness, cohesiveness, and community in the family? Is there a sense of family unity? To what degree do members demonstrate an active interest in other family members, and in the family as a whole? How accepted does each feel by the others? Is there a sense of interdependence in the family? What is the individual and collective "courage to be imperfect?" How does the family feel connected with the community, and the broader society? How does the family "belong" in the community and to humanity?

- *Equality and Mutual Respect.* Does the family show an active regard for individual differences within and outside the family? Does each family member show respect in interpersonal communication? How individuated and differentiated are family members?

EXPLORATION AND ASSESSMENT

THE QUESTION The exploration and assessment phase of Adlerian family therapy starts with what Adlerians refer to as "The Question." Adler pointed out the importance of distinguishing between presenting problems and underlying life style issues. He believed people presented complaints that masked more direct problems with daily living. "If we were to put the question to the patient, 'What would you do if you were quite well?' he would almost certainly name the particular demand of society that it might be assumed he was trying to evade" (Adler, 1925/1973, p. 201). Or put another way, "What do you expect will come out of our work together?" (Powers & Griffith, 1987, p. 55). Adlerians working with individuals often use this technique as a shortcut approach to distinguishing between organic and functional etiologies of complaints. For example, if the presenting complaint is the mother's trouble at work because of recurring physical maladies, such as headaches, the question may be asked something like, "How might things be different if you didn't have these headaches?" If the answer is a variation of "I would be free of this pain," the recommendation may be to pursue a medical check-up. However, if the response is something like, "I would probably get that promotion," or "I would be better able to handle my coworkers," then a different direction might be taken in therapy. Family therapists use The Question to identify possible ways in which the identified patient carries the family symptoms to deflect attention from the family's principal life task difficulties.

TYPICAL DAY REVIEW To obtain perspective of the context within which the presenting problems exist, Adlerian family therapists often ask the family to describe the details of a typical day of life in the family. Such a discussion often reveals many aspects of the family's life style, including roles, rules, rituals, traditions, expectations, and holiday celebrations.

TRACKING Verbal following is a communication skill that beginning therapists work diligently to master. It is a particularly important skill for family therapists because its use enables the therapist and the family members to follow the course of a symptom or behavior pattern throughout the family. Essentially the therapist employs the technique of tracking to ascertain, in turn, what each family member does in exhibiting and responding to symptomatic behavior. Use of the technique often results in increasing the family's awareness of the extent to which they "are in this together." Tracking can help the family come to terms with the ways in which even the most severe pathology may be seen as interdependent and reflective of a family system rather than just the single symptom bearer. An Adlerian perspective of anorexia nervosa, for example, would propose that the individual is in control of the disorder, particularly during the early stages of the disorder, instead of being controlled by it, and that the behavior often is a choice made by adolescents who live in families with blurred boundaries, commitment to denying problems, and a seeming inability to resolve conflict (Keen, 1996). Tracking typically reveals efforts of at least one parent to overcontrol, overprotect, and overindulge daughters struggling for independence (Keen, 1996, p. 389). The value of tracking aloud is to increase each member's understanding of what the others are doing and feeling. Tracking also enables the therapist to model effective communication skills, and to teach the family members how to ensure that each member is heard.

LIFE STYLE ANALYSIS A fundamental set of theoretical applications involves the use of a variety of techniques to develop a sense of the family's life style, and that of each member. Clearly, the challenge is to develop the understanding without making the information-acquisition process the focus. In other words, a life style analysis is the most efficient and effective method for exploring life style patterns and issues. However, it makes little sense to take the kind of time that would be required to do a life style analysis on each individual in the family. It is more important to keep the focus on the current situation and the therapeutic goals developed from the presenting problems; in counseling, reference to the life style should be indirect or omitted (Dreikurs, 1949/1973a, p. 258). It is typically a matter of using the psychological constructs of the life style as a contextual frame or as a conceptual referent for understanding the content and feeling of a family session. Yet, on occasion it is helpful to conduct the rather structured informal interview directly. Couples, for example, often need to learn more about themselves and each other. Similarly, children can often benefit from a more direct interview to learn more about their basic approaches to life. So, life style information can be obtained directly or indirectly. As mentioned before, the constructs also apply, albeit a little bit differently, to families as a whole. Establishing the life style of children in newly blended families has special potential for the remarried parents, in that they obtain a greater understanding of the complexities of children's efforts to belong to a new group and yet maintain membership in an old group. Uniquely Adlerian, the life style analysis takes a somewhat different shape with each Adlerian therapist. Nonetheless, there are common features. Basically, the life style analysis is a structured interview designed to gain information about important formative experiences that may have influenced the individual's or the family's approach to life. The aim is to help identify a person's primary life goal, the kinds of obstacles that may tend to attach to one's basic priority, and the successful and unsuccessful strategies the individual uses to overcome barriers and obstacles. Similar goals provide the rationale for using the life style assessment interview in family therapy.

Several versions of a structured interview guide are available in Adler's early writings (Adler, 1930/1970, p. 251), but the one that seemed to serve as a stimulus for later students was the one developed in 1933 by the International Society for Individual Psychology (Ansbacher & Ansbacher, 1956, p. 404). Other life style analysis guides are available, including Dreikurs's original "psychological interview in medicine" (Dreikurs, 1954; Eckstein, Baruth, & Mahrer, 1975; Mosak, Schneider, & Mosak, 1980; Mosak & Shulman, 1971).

EARLY RECOLLECTIONS Next, it is important to obtain early recollections. While it is possible to acquire these early memories at any time in the interview or for that matter at any time in therapy, there is special value in getting them early to avoid contamination or confusion of other information likely to be shared in the interview. "Early recollections have special significance. To begin with, they show the style of life in its origins and in its simplest expressions" (Adler, 1931/1980, p. 74). Of all the events and experiences in life, whether real or imagined—accurately or inaccurately recalled, the individual chooses to remember only those that have personal meaning. "There are no chance memories" (p. 73). As with emotions, we use our memories, consistent with our life style; in fact, "memories can never run counter to the life style" (p. 75). Just as the first memory shows the individual's fundamental view of life (p. 75), couples' first memories of each other may have metaphorical relevance for the main themes of their current relationship (Belove, 1980, p. 191). Experience helps the therapist build the competencies required to elicit and understand early recollections. At first, it is difficult for the therapist to differentiate between early recollections and general family stories. While the latter may have value, it is the more personal and more exact recollection that has special therapeutic value. Recollections are obtained by inviting one of the family members to think back to his or her very early childhood and recall the earliest specific event or incident.

Follow-up questions help pinpoint the details of the day, event, persons involved, the feelings and the results. It is the quality of the follow-up that sets apart the masters of this projective technique from the beginners. Recollections may be targeted or directed to specific areas. For example, in family therapy it is common to ask a member to recall a first incident with a grandparent, or with a newly arrived sibling.

USE OF STRUCTURED TECHNIQUES Because of a strong belief in the influence of group context, Adlerian family therapists also make use of several other structured techniques to help provide sociological and psychological perspectives (see Sherman & Fredman, 1986, for an excellent collection of structured techniques such as sociograms and ecograms). It is particularly important to help families understand their own sociological heritage, particularly in terms of family role expectations. The need is especially great if the presenting problems involve tension between teens in the family and the parents. It is common in Adlerian family therapy to use various structured techniques, including family sculpting, sociodrama, and psychodrama to help the family physically depict the content and feelings of special events or incidents (Starr, 1973). It can be dramatically informative (especially for the children in the family) for parents to capture and present what life was like for their parents and grandparents at their present age, focusing specifically on age-related and gender-related role expectations. McKelvie's (1987) "kinetic family sculpting," for example, provides all family members opportunities for collective insight on what it may have been like at various stages of family life from courtship, through the birth of children, schooling, work, aging parents, and so forth.

The structured technique, other than a life style analysis, that Adlerians probably use more extensively than others is the traditional genogram (McGoldrick & Gerson, 1985). While it is not necessarily Adlerian in origin, Adlerian theory gives the genogram a more compatible home and a more comprehensive base. Unfortunately, most family therapists use the technique atheoretically, as though family dynamics need no explanatory principles. To be helpful, a therapist needs to go beyond simply noting dysfunctional patterns in relationships. There is a natural limit to how much it helps a family to simply discover a history of abusive relationships. As Adler advised, it is never helpful to simply tell a patient what he or she is suffering from; it is more important to encourage the patient at the very point where discouragement led to the suffering (1931/1980, p. 49). Encouragement requires an accurate empathic understanding that goes beyond the typical genogram exercises in family therapy. It is akin to the Adlerian adage that "a tactless truth can never be the whole truth; it shows that our understanding was not sufficient" (p. 72).

EXAMINATION OF MARITAL RELATIONSHIP In the assessment phase of family therapy, Adlerians also spend some time examining the nature of the parental/spousal relationship. Significant relationships of single parents are examined as well, not only present relationships but also those of relevance in the past. Spouses serve as a subunit within the family, and thereby significantly influence the family dynamics. On occasion, family therapists will decide, on the basis of their examination of the marital relationship, to see couples apart from the rest of the family, particularly if the marital relationship seems deeply strained or dysfunctional.

Adlerian therapists focus on several dimensions of marital relations: cooperation, equality, social interest, commitment, and courage. The degree of cooperation in the couple's relationship is an indicator of their preparation for marriage. Adler liked to refer to the old custom in a certain district in Germany where premarital couples were given a two-handed saw with which to cut a tree. Without cooperative trust, they simply pull against each other and accomplish nothing. "These German villagers have recognized that cooperation is the chief prerequisite for marriage" (Adler, 1931/1980, p. 263). Marriage is a partnership of two equals who work at their life tasks and their relationship simultaneously. In a letter to his oldest daughter (Vali) on her marriage, Adler suggested that she should not "forget that married life is a task at which both must work, with joy....Don't allow either of you to become subordinate to the other...or allow anyone else to gain influence over the shaping of your marriage relation" (cited in Ansbacher, 1978a, pp. 340–341). Adler believed successful marriages were built on a love of equals: "Don't look up to your mate, and don't look down: Approach love as an equal" (p. 324). "Since marriage is a partnership, no one member should be supreme....In the whole conduct of family life there is no call for the use of authority; and it is unfortunate if one member is especially prominent or considered more than the others" (Adler, 1931/1980, p. 133). Adlerians try to sniff out feelings of inferiority and superiority in marital relations because such feelings usually predict inequalities and resentments, which typically result in uncooperative acts of self-defense and self-promotion, at the expense of cooperation.

The Adlerian construct of social interest finds no more fitting home than in love and marriage. While it is common to assume that love is a passive emotion that "happens" to us, Dreikurs (1946) articulately described many ways in which we use the emotion of love purposively, just as we do other emotions. Love, as an active expression of social interest, can be the ultimate contribution a person can make to another, and represents the prototypical expression of one's desire to belong (Dreikurs, 1946, p. 15). Adler encouraged couples to avoid the pitfalls of a self-centered, expecting, getting approach to marital relations, and instead asked them to commit themselves "to a more task-centered, self-transcending, contributing, mature, cooperative outlook informed by social interest" (1978, p. 336). It takes courage to achieve a vulnerability of trust that is a natural part of committing one's self fully and monogamously to another. Such a depth of courage is fed by a faith that one is up to the challenges life may present. Optimism, a sense of self-adequacy, the courage to commit one's self to a cooperative venture with another, and the willingness to contribute to another selflessly are all important ingredients of a successful marriage. Adlerian family therapists encourage self-esteem and social interest in marital couples as a primary strategy toward improving family life. Rather than focusing on marital pathology and dysfunction, the Adlerian approach is characterized by a primary focus on education, a correction of faulty assumptions and mistaken expectations, adjustments of attitudinal expressions, and on increasing one's interest in the interests of the other (Nicoll, 1989).

APPRAISAL INSTRUMENTS The exploration and assessment phase typically has no real ending, in that information about the family is always sought for achieving new understandings. Nonetheless, near the end of this phase, the therapist may ask family members to complete any one of several appraisal instruments. One of the more promising clinical instruments is *The BASIS-A* (Kern, Wheeler, & Curlette, 1993). Its predecessor, *The Lifestyle Scale* (Kern, 1982) is also a useful instrument. Both provide perspectives on the individual's basic life style and personal priorities. In addition, Dinkmeyer and Dinkmeyer (1983) have developed the useful *Marital Inventory* for couples. Stiles and Wilborn (1992) have developed a life style scale for children. Several instruments that measure social interest have been developed as well: Crandall (1975) developed the *Social Interest Scale*; Sulliman (1973) created the *Sulliman Social Interest Scale*; Greever, Tseng, and Friedland built the *Social Interest Index* (1973); and Zarski, Bubenzer, and West (1986) constructed the *Tasks of Life Survey* on the basis of earlier work on the *Social Interest Index*.

INSIGHT

EDUCATED GUESSING The enhancement of the family's insight into their own behavior comprises the bulk of the third phase of Adlerian family therapy. Understanding increases the power to choose alternative methods for achieving constructive life goals. It is not enough in family therapy for only the therapist to understand what's going on with the family. Insight on the part of the therapist is far less important than new insight and understanding on the part of individual family members and the family as a whole. Adlerians use a method commonly referred to as educated guessing to give continuous feedback to family members about what the therapist is perceiving, thinking, and feeling. Almost line by line and moment by moment, Adlerian therapists focus on the verbal and nonverbal input of family members, and then share tentative hypotheses as to what might be going on in the family and in the therapy. Using minimal encouragers and such simple questions as "Could it be...?" or "Is it possible...?" to frame interpretive responses and questions, Adlerian therapists try to keep the focus on the purposes of behavior.

Most Adlerians automatically stay alert to a reaction that Dreikurs (1953) termed a "recognition reflex," an involuntary affirmative response like a sudden smile or nervous chuckle, when the therapist has shared feedback in the form of an interpretation that seems particularly on target. "You can tell if a person has really understood what you've told him. He will always laugh" (Adler, cited in Manaster et al., 1977, p. 49). This stochastic method of questioning offers family members the chance to learn along with and from the therapist. Insight is thus enhanced as the therapy progresses. For Adler, guessing was a preferred term to what is commonly described as "intuition." Rather than reserved for only the gifted, guessing is used continuously by everyone, particularly effectively by those with a high degree of social contact and interest (Ansbacher & Ansbacher, 1956, p. 329). The task of the therapist is to use both common knowledge as well as professional training to improve the quality of the "educated" guessing. The degree of insight achieved by the family and its members is largely a product of the quality of the educated guessing. By understanding the whole person, Adlerian therapists can jump to conclusions and provide additive feedback regarding the patterns of one's life (Dreikurs, 1970, p. viii). If the "premature" conclusions are slightly off base or simply wrong, then therapists should look for other ways in—much like a burglar who goes to the second floor windows after finding the first floor windows and doors locked (Nicoll, 1990).

CONFRONTATION The Adlerian spin on the common therapeutic technique of confrontation is what Adler referred to as "spitting in the soup." Referring to the old boarding-house approach to getting someone else's soup by spitting it, Adler suggested that the therapist ought to bring to the open a patient's goals and true intentions in such a way that the person engages his or her conscience but still feels a sense of freedom to continue the behavior. The therapist simply addresses comments to a member of the family or to the family as a whole that acknowledges aloud a possible goal of a particular behavior in such a way that the person may continue the behavior, but it will not "taste" as good, or be as effective. By bringing a purpose to awareness, it loses some of its mystique and power, primarily because a person's conscience plays a role in modifying the behavior. Adler also called the approach "besmirching a clean conscience." Confrontation can allow the person to choose an alternative, more constructive, route to a goal.

The skill in using confrontation effectively with a family is composed of three key elements. First, the therapist needs both a strong level of confidence in the empathic understanding of the family, and at the same time a willingness to be imperfect if he or she is wrong or not fully accurate in interpretation of family actions. Secondly, there is a special decision-making ability that is required in choosing to intervene confrontationally when there is a noticeable discrepancy between the family's actions and goals, or when what they say seems to be in conflict with what they feel. Adlerian confrontation reflects an attempt to invite immediate change in perception, feeling, or action (Dinkmeyer, Dinkmeyer, & Sperry, 1987, p. 101), as well as an immediate response. Third, the therapist must deliver the confrontation in such a way that the family or family member feels as though the therapist is offering support and caring, along with a challenge to review goals and behaviors. A confronted family ought to feel sufficiently supported to actually use their resources to consider the content of the challenge, rather than simply choose a defensive mode. Effectively delivered confrontation has the potential for revealing hidden reasons for behavior, or mistaken beliefs and perceptions. The task is to be both challenging and supportive. "Without encouragement neither insight nor change is possible" (Dreikurs, 1967, p. 13).

Insight can come from many sources. The easiest and sometimes most effective technique for sharing insight is to simply reframe the family's perceived minuses to pluses. What at first may look like a game, reframing negatives to positives is a first order of change. For example, instead of a family focusing solely on the negatives of a member's "stubbornness," the therapist could help the family consider the possible strengths and contributions the individual may be making by being a person who can be counted on to hold strong convictions, and also by demonstrating the courage to share them openly. While, at times, stubborn behaviors and strategies may seem nothing but distracters and negative forces, families who seem to lack courage of conviction to the point that they are willing to think or do anything to please others might even benefit from a person with strong opinions. The omnipresent task is to see how a specific disturbance of the family's equilibrium serves constructively, or fails to serve, to help the family achieve their goals.

IN-SESSION TASKS Insight is more powerful when it's earned, rather than given. Self-understanding is always more impactful and durable than externally derived knowledge. Therefore, Adlerian family therapists use action in therapy, in the form of in-session structured activities, to facilitate self-enhanced insight of family members. Psychodrama, life style analyses, sociodrama, role reversals, role rehearsals, encouragement workshop exercises, communication change practice sessions, and in-session family meetings represent some of the structured techniques used. While these techniques are common to several approaches, Adlerian family therapy adds unique substance to such interventions with its comprehensive theoretical tenets. Even so, insight doesn't become a natural part of life before a sufficient amount of practice enables the family to actually act differently. The art of therapy is involved in the therapist's ability to stimulate change, to facilitate new understandings that will create internal energy and commitment to change, and to provide sufficient psychological support to firm up initial efforts to try new behaviors, thoughts, and feelings. Eventually, the changes themselves provide the fuel for long-term change and improvement.

THE LANGUAGE OF CHANGE Insight naturally leads family members to changes in language and communication styles. Family members find value in improving their ability to own their messages, and to exchange their passive, blaming language patterns for more active, accepting styles of communicating. Adlerian therapists spend time training family members how to accept responsibility for their own behavior, how to send I-messages in their communications, and how to make changes in their own behaviors and thoughts, rather than expecting others to change first. Further, the therapist takes every opportunity to facilitate intrafamilial communication, urging each member to talk directly to each other rather than indirectly or through others.

CHANGE

CONFLICT RESOLUTION The fourth and final phase of Adlerian family therapy focuses on change. Adlerians commonly refer to this stage as reorientation. One of the most common areas of change worked on in this phase is in learning how to resolve conflict successfully as equals, rather than relying on the temporary answer of authority-based solutions. "Whenever any conflict arises, the first decision both parties make—definitely, although unconsciously—is whether to use these incidents as an occasion to fight, for hurting and being hurt, or whether to try sincerely to solve the problem" (Dreikurs, 1946, p. 109). Fighting requires cooperation between the two fighters, as does problem solving. Once the decision is reached to move toward solution, then it is possible to resolve conflict. Dreikurs (1972) outlined four steps in teaching conflict-resolution skills to help fighters move toward solutions rather than continue to fight: show mutual respect, pinpoint the real issue, seek mutual agreement, and share decision-making responsibility. Dreikurs's initial admonition is to neither fight nor give in because the former denigrates the other, and giving in violates respect for one's self. Resolution starts with an awareness that there are two sides to the issue, and that each person is worthy of respect for his or her convictions. Secondly, it is important to identify the real issue that underlies the conflict. Typically the factual situation is not the real issue, but a convenient carrier or repository—such as sex or money in marital squabbles. "The real issue at stake usually centers on feelings of resentment, humiliation, hurt, or defeat. Put another way, the issue revolves around 'Who is right?' or 'Who has the power to decide?' or 'Who counts?'" (Terner & Pew, 1978, p. 362). Next, those in conflict need to be helped to find some mutually acceptable middle ground or acceptable alternative. In the long run, each person only has control over the self, so movement must occur in one's own behavior rather than to demand change in another. From a systemic perspective, a change in one person's behavior causes a ripple effect in the system, and changes it. Therefore, it is more effective to start change with one's self. Finally, each person in conflict needs to be taught how to share responsibility for making decisions. Democratic leadership and full participation in family decisions prevent conflicts, but in the event that conflicts do arise, each member helps resolve those that do develop. Conflicts become "our" problems, rather than "your" problems. "Change does not occur through wishful thinking, only through new behavior" (Sherman, 1983a, p. 23). It takes time and courage to learn how to behave differently.

PARADOXICAL INTERVENTIONS Adler was the first to suggest that therapists should "prescribe the symptoms" as a strategic intervention. It was his contention that the best way to strengthen a symptom was to fight it, so instead of feeding the problem, he preferred to acquiesce to the patients' wishes, join them in a cooperative experiment, and simply ask them to expand or increase their symptoms. For example, instead of adding to worry about insomnia, he would suggest that the person try to stay awake that night, and take advantage of the newly available time to jot down all of his or her thoughts and bring them back to therapy to work on them. Paradox accomplishes two things: First, it enables the therapist to engage the client in a spirit of cooperation, doing what he or she is already doing, rather than fighting it and engaging the family in competition; and secondly, paradox provides an opportunity for the family member to learn just how much control exists over a symptom that before seemed out of their control. If one can increase an action, one can surely decrease an action.

ENCOURAGEMENT No one likes to feel less than another person or less than capable of handling a task. Each of us would like to feel as though we are equal to the tasks with which life confronts us, and equal to any person. Yet, life's challenges can loom rather large when one feels burdened by imperfections and inferiorities, or when one feels alone. Unfortunately, in today's mistake-conscious society, our "red-penciled" mentality often produces feelings of inadequacy and discouragement. We seem to find it easy to lose confidence. Our mastery of the put-down message, directed toward ourselves as well as others, has simply deepened our discouragement, to the point that some don't even try to live useful lives, but instead opt for a false sense of belonging by leading "useless" lives.

Life can become overwhelming and discouraging. Such is the case for most families who come into therapy. It is not so much that families are "dysfunctional," to use the common label of today, but rather that families are discouraged. They simply feel incapable of handling the difficulties of life. The more discouraged the family, the more they turn inward and become a collection of self-oriented individuals rather than a family filled with social interest and committed to the betterment of each others' lives. They have reached their level of "psychological tolerance" (Ansbacher & Ansbacher, 1956, p. 243), at which they no longer have the courage to contribute usefully to family life. Families with greater social interest have higher thresholds of psychological tolerance.

Encouragement is fundamental to the task of helping families develop the courage to try new behaviors when current behaviors no longer work (Carlson &

Fullmer, 1991). In some ways it could be considered that the most important task of Adlerian family therapists is to encourage families. In the midst of all the "dysfunction," Adlerian therapists look for the family's assets and strengths. Like a miner digging for precious stones, Adlerians search for family resources that can be tapped to help them regain their courage to handle problems as a family. Diagnoses or labels do little for discouraged families. Insight is helpful, but it is not the only therapeutic agent, or even the most effective. The therapist works to build a restoration of faith in the family's sense of adequacy. At the same time, efforts are directed at helping facilitate a renewal of their courage to stay with daily challenges until they can find workable solutions. The problem is that courage is not easily built; it cannot be given externally. Courage requires a new foundation of self-affirming constructs to replace the self-defeating thoughts; it also requires carefully planned practice strategies. "Encouragement is more than a kind word and a pat on the back; it is a complex process" (Dreikurs, 1973a, p. 62). It is a process of providing the family both challenge and support. Family change does not typically come in big chunks: An encouraging therapist focuses on minimal movement, and affirms effort. Because problems brought to family therapy often reflect alienation of one or more members from the others or a member's sense of not being appreciated or accepted by the others (Dinkmeyer & Dinkmeyer, 1991), therapists often focus the encouragement process on positive interaction and mutual support. Adlerian therapists believe in the process of family therapy, and in the ability of families to learn to behave more cooperatively and constructively.

FAMILY MEETINGS One of the most common strategies employed in Adlerian family therapy is to teach families how to hold family meetings or family councils. While individual therapists differ on how they go about this process, most try to persuade families to participate in democratic meetings of all members. In such meetings, it is vital that each person is respected as an equal participant, regardless of age or position, and to recognize that each deserves to be fully heard. Beyond that, family members need to commit themselves to view their lives together as a whole. The regular meetings should aid the group in making decisions together, in sharing work responsibilities, in encouraging and supporting each other, and in planning proactive positive outings.

Family meetings are an excellent place for children and adults to learn from the logical consequences of their behavior. Logical consequences are different from the "natural" consequences of behavior, in that with the latter the correction is a part of the action itself (e.g., the individual overextends self physically and experiences soreness and fatigue). The consequences for missing mealtime are the "logical" result of having to cook for one's self and clean up. In this case, the consequence is not natural, but is created because more than one person is involved. Natural and logical consequences replace the superiority-inferiority relationships of authoritarian power structures.

OBSTACLES/STRATEGIES One of the final tasks in Adlerian family therapy is to help the family discuss openly their family life style, particularly in terms of the favorite strategies that they have used in the past as a family to handle internal conflicts and life's common tasks and challenges. It is important for each family member to know how each contributes to the family style. Part of the process is to help the family predict how their strategies may actually prevent their achieving the goals for change they've set as new priorities. The focus can be on what kinds of obstacles might get in their way, and how they might plan proactively to tackle those challenges. Finally, it is important to build in encouragement sessions along the way. Every relationship in the family, including the family as a whole, deserves regular nurturance and support. Some may choose to hold brief encouragement sessions for dyads and the group on a fairly regular basis.

SUMMARY

Adlerian family therapy follows a four-phase process with specific developmental tasks: engagement (relationship establishment); exploration and assessment (empathic understanding of family dynamics and family life style); insight (analysis, intervention, resolution, and consensus); and change (encouragement, follow-through and follow-up). Of all of the applications typically employed by Adlerian family therapists, encouragement is the most difficult and the most vital. The family's ability to build their social interest will determine in large part their success as a unit.

EVALUATION OF THE THEORY

Process-outcome studies of family therapy have not been overly impressive in quantity or quality. Family therapists are known for their clinical expertise much more than for their research acumen and devotion. Nonetheless, evidence is accruing that family therapy is effective. Adlerian family therapy shares a similar past and present. From the time of the University of Vienna's rejection of Adler's original application for a position equivalent to today's adjunct professorship because his approach was more philosophical than scientific (Bottome, 1939, p. 96), to the present, critics of the Adlerian approach have called for greater empirical evidence to support claims and to document the therapeutic effectiveness of individual psychology (Rotter, 1962; Schooler, 1972; Sundberg, 1963). Of course, part of the problem has been the nature of research itself. Zealous researchers eager to find exact cause and effect relationships often operate from a paradigm that is too reductionistic, deterministic, and simple for today (Allred, 1987). "Adlerian approaches are based upon ideographic, goal directed, holistic and indeterministic thinking and where does one find an experimental model that lends itself readily to researching these kinds of thinking?" (Lowe, 1982, p. 356). Family therapists, like their one-on-one clinical colleagues of the past, have been practice-oriented and have written extensively about individual family cases and therapeutic techniques. Research has come along lately, however, as qualitative methodology in particular has become sufficiently sophisticated "to catch up with Adlerian theory" (Shulman, 1975, p. x).

While it is true that Adlerian family therapy has not yet received its due research attention, Adlerian theory in general has stimulated much thought in the professional literature over the past several decades (Powers, 1975). Mosak and Mosak (1975) listed nearly 10,000 entries in a bibliography dedicated to Adlerian psychology and comprised largely of works by Adlerians or of direct relevance to Adlerians. Later, Manaster and Corsini (1982) estimated that only about 250 of the 10,000 qualified as nomothetic empirical research studies. However, Watkins (1983, 1986, 1992) has documented a trend of increasing numbers of research studies published in the '70s and '80s. Focusing solely on articles appearing in the *Journal of Individual Psychology*, Watkins (1983) identified 75 research studies published over a twelve-year period (1970–81), and 103 studies over the following nine years from 1982–90 (Watkins, 1992). While there were some subtle shifts in focus over the time periods, the research was largely directed at explorations of four major Adlerian constructs: birth order, social interest, early recollections, and life style analysis. Birth order, by a very large margin, is the favorite topic, whether the treatment is research or theory. Stewart and Stewart (1995) identified more than 1,000 publications on birth order from 1976 to 1993, of which, incidentally, less than 1% focused on birth order and therapy. Research on early recollections has apparently increased quite significantly (Reichlin & Niederehe, 1980; Watkins, 1992). More recently, the research focus has shifted to instrument development as detailed in the applications section of this chapter. Kern (1997) reports a dramatic increase in the number of research studies conducted recently on the BASIS-A alone (40).

The need remains great for solid research on the effectiveness of Adlerian family therapy. While there is some good evidence of the Adlerian approach's potential for serving family therapy as an integrative model (Sherman & Dinkmeyer, 1987), there is still a pressing need for systematic research to determine the unique effectiveness of Adlerian family therapy. It would be interesting, for example, to see results of a study designed to test the long-term changes in social interest of family members as a result of Adlerian family therapy. Similarly, a six-month follow-up study designed to assess the degree to which families interact more democratically would add important data to an Adlerian research agenda. The Adlerian approach has a rich uniqueness in its direct and obvious relationship to diversity issues and concerns that deserves research exploration and confirmation. Clearly, the focus of any future research agenda, as in therapy itself, needs to shift from techniques to outcome. Nonetheless, Lowe (1993, p. 121) best summarizes the state of Adlerian family therapy evaluation: "At the present time our beliefs are stronger than our knowledge."

SUMMARY

In reality, the task of fully describing a comprehensive theoretical approach to family therapy in a single chapter is quite formidable. Regardless of the effort, it always seems as if there ought to be more said to do the theory justice. It's somewhat like the situation Adler described in response to the inquiry by the hostess of his desire for dessert after a multicourse meal. "In Austria it would be announced that on a certain day the emperor would leave the castle in his carriage. For many hours before the appointed time, people would crowd into the square which the castle faced until there was not room, it would seem, for anyone to even raise his arms. Then, all of a sudden, they would hear the cry 'make room for the emperor,' and as if by magic, a pathway opened up. That's exactly what's happening to me—yes, thank you, I'll have dessert" (cited in Manaster et al., 1977, p. 36). Even though much has been said, perhaps a few summary comments would serve well.

Adlerian family therapy is an approach to working with families that emphasizes cooperation and social interest. Families are viewed as natural systems always growing and moving, not so much back to a homeostatic state as much as toward goals. Families in conflict or disarray are seen as discouraged families rather than dysfunctional. Encouraged families are better able to understand their mutual interdependence and develop constructive interest in each other and the family as a whole. Family therapy is seen as a learning process wherein family members are provided opportunities in a structured, supportive atmosphere to practice democratic living. "Therapeutic change takes place in the system as a result of developing new subjective perceptions, goals, information, skills, improved communication, and the reorganization of places and roles in the system" (Dinkmeyer & Dinkmeyer, 1991, p. 390).

Adler's greatest contribution to family therapy is his deep understanding of children. Unfortunately, most family therapists and their supporting theories still view children as minor players in the family system. For Adler, all members of the family are equally important. After all, it is in the family of origin where a child first learns how to belong, constructively or destructively. It is the family of origin that evokes and nurtures the child's social interest and striving for significance, or adds to feelings of inferiority and inadequacy. "Life will correct it if children get too big-headed. But it doesn't do the reverse if they get discouraged. There was an old saying in the Viennese Circus....'It's not terribly difficult to tame a lion, but is there anyone who has learned to make the lamb roar?'" (cited in Hoffman, 1994, pp. 243–244). Children and all other family members deserve a level of understanding and support that will naturally build their courage to face whatever tasks and challenges life presents them. The principal task of the Adlerian family therapist is to help families build the kind of courage that finds its strength in a foundation of mutual interdependence and cooperation.

ANNOTATED SUGGESTED READINGS

Adler, A. (1969). *The science of living* (H. L. Ansbacher, Ed.). Garden City, NY: Doubleday. (Original work published in 1929)
> Of the many books authored by Alfred Adler, this is one of his most readable.

Adler, A. (1980). *What life should mean to you* (A. Porter, Trans. & Ed.). New York: Putman. (Original work published in 1931)
> In spite of the marketing-driven title, this is an excellent book, and another one of Adler's most readable.

Ansbacher, H. L., & Ansbacher, R. R. (1956). *The individual psychology of Alfred Adler*. New York: Harper and Row.
> This book remains the single best reference for presentation, interpretation, and analysis of Adler's original writings.

Dinkmeyer, D. C., Dinkmeyer, D. C., Jr., & Sperry, L. (1987). *Adlerian counseling and psychotherapy* (2nd ed.). Columbus, OH: Merrill Publishing.
> A very readable and useful general text that serves as an excellent overview of the Adlerian approach.

Dreikurs. R., & Soltz, V. (1964). *Children: The challenge*. New York: Hawthorn Books.
> While dated, this book still stimulates the reader to consider superb child-rearing principles and suggestions.

Sherman, R., & Dinkmeyer, D. C. (1987). *Systems of family therapy: An Adlerian integration.* New York: Brunner/Mazel.

> Robert Sherman is one of today's most articulate Adlerian family therapists, and Don Dinkmeyer has developed some of the most creative and powerful Adlerian educational tools in use today. Therefore, it should be no surprise that their text is easily the most definitive statement of Adlerian family therapy in print. Each has coauthored several other important texts, many of which are listed in the references.

Terner, J., & Pew, W. L. (1978). *The courage to be imperfect: The life and work of Rudolf Dreikurs.* New York: Hawthorn Books.

> A comprehensive biography of Dreikurs and his work.

REFERENCES

Adler, A. (1969). *The science of living* (H. L. Ansbacher, Ed.). Garden City, NY: Doubleday. (Original work published in 1929)

Adler, A. (1970). *The education of children* (E. Jensen & F. Jensen, Trans.). Chicago: Henry Regnery Company. (Original work published in 1930)

Adler, A. (1973). *The practice and theory of Individual Psychology* (P. Radin, Trans.). Totowa, NJ: Littlefield, Adams & Company. (Original work published in 1925)

Adler, A. (1977). A fable on the inferiority complex. In G. J. Manaster, G. Painter, D. Deutsch, & B. J. Overholt (Eds.), *Alfred Adler: As we remember him* (pp. 115–122). Chicago: North American Society of Adlerian Psychology.

Adler, A. (1978). *Cooperation between the sexes: Writings on women, love, and marriage, sexuality and its disorders* (H. L. Ansbacher & R. R. Ansbacher, Trans. & Eds.). Garden City, NY: Anchor Books.

Adler, A. (1979c). Typology of meeting life's problems. In H. L. Ansbacher & R. R. Ansbacher (Eds.), *Superiority and social interest* (pp. 66–70). New York: Norton. (Original work published in 1935)

Adler, A. (1979d). On the origin of the striving for superiority and of social interest. In H. L. Ansbacher & R. R. Ansbacher (Eds.), *Superiority and social interest* (pp. 29–40). New York: Norton. (Original work published in 1933)

Adler, A. (1979e). Technique of treatment. In H. L. Ansbacher & R. R. Ansbacher (Eds.), *Superiority and social interest* (pp. 191–201). New York: Norton. (Original work published in 1932)

Adler, A. (1980). *What life should mean to you* (A. Porter, Trans. & Ed.). New York: Putnam. (Original work published in 1931)

Adler, A. (1996a). The structure of neurosis. *Individual Psychology, 52,* 4, 351–362. (Original work published in 1935)

Adler, K. A. (1977). Personal comments from audience during an interview with Heinz and Rowena Ansbacher (conducted by L. Tyler). In *proceedings of the symposium on the individual psychology of Alfred Adler* (p. 99). Eugene, OR: The University of Oregon.

Adler, K. A. (1994). Socialist influence on Adlerian psychology. *Individual Psychology, 50,* 2, June, 131–141.

Allred, G. H. (1987). Beyond numbers: The human element in research. *Individual Psychology, 43,* 3, 329–338.

Ansbacher, H. L. (1969). Introduction. In A. Adler, *The science of living* (H. L. Ansbacher, Ed.) (pp. vii–xxii). Garden City, NY: Doubleday. (Original work published in 1929)

Ansbacher, H. L. (1974). Adler and Virchow: New light on the name "individual psychology." *Journal of Individual Psychology, 30,* 1, 43–52.

Ansbacher, H. L. (1978a). Essay: Adler's sex theories. In A. Adler, *Cooperation between the sexes: Writings on women, love and marriage, sexuality and its disorders* (H. L. Ansbacher & R. R. Ansbacher, Trans. & Eds.) (pp. 248–412). Garden City, NY: Anchor Books.

Ansbacher, H. L. (1978b). The development of Adler's concept of social interest: A cultural study. *Journal of Individual Psychology, 34*, 2, 118–152.

Ansbacher, H. L. (1979). The recognition of Adler. In A. Adler, *Superiority and social interest: A collection of later writings* (3rd Rev. ed.) (H. L. Ansbacher & R. R. Ansbacher, Eds.) (pp. 3–20). New York: Norton.

Ansbacher, H. L. (1992). Alfred Adler, pioneer in prevention of mental disorders. *Individual Psychology, 48*, 1, March 3–34.

Ansbacher, H. L., & Ansbacher, R. R. (1956). *The individual psychology of Alfred Adler.* New York: Harper and Row.

Ansbacher, H. L., & Ansbacher, R. R. (Eds.). (1979). *Alfred Adler: Superiority and social interest—A collection of later writings* (3rd Rev. ed.). New York: Norton.

Becker, E. (1962). *The birth and death of meaning: A perspective in psychiatry and anthropology.* New York: Free Press of Glencoe.

Belove, L. (1980). First encounters of the close kind (FECK): The use of the story of the first interaction as an early recollection of a marriage. *Journal of Individual Psychology, 36*, 2, 191–208.

Bitter, J. R. (1987). Communication and meaning: Satir in Adlerian context. In R. Sherman & D. Dinkmeyer, *Systems of family therapy: An Adlerian integration* (pp. 109–142). New York: Brunner/Mazel.

Bitter, J. R. (1996). On neurosis: An introduction to Adler's concepts and approach. *Individual Psychology, 52*, 4, 310–317.

Bottome, P. (1939). *Alfred Adler: A biography.* New York: Putman.

Carlson, J., & Faiber, B. R. (1991). Parenting. In J. Carlson & J. Lewis (Eds.), *Family Counseling: Strategies and Issues* (pp. 131–152). Denver: Love Publishing Co.

Carlson, J., & Fullmer, D. (1991). Family counseling: Principles for growth. In J. Carlson & J. Lewis (Eds.), *Family Counseling: Strategies and Issues* (pp. 57–78). Denver: Love Publishing Co.

Carlson, J., & Lewis, J. (1991). An introduction to family counseling. In J. Carlson & J. Lewis (Eds.), *Family Counseling: Strategies and Issues.* (pp. 3–11). Denver: Love Publishing Co.

Christensen, O. C., & Marchant, W. C. (1993). The family counseling process. In O. C. Christensen (Ed.), *Adlerian family counseling* (Rev. ed.). Minneapolis: Educational Media Corporation.

Crandall, J.E. (1975). A scale for social interest. *Journal of Individual Psychology, 31*, 187–195.

Davidson, A. K. (Ed.). (1991). *The collected works of Lydia Sicher: An Adlerian perspective.* Ft. Bragg, CA: QED Press.

Defraia, G. (1984). *The Family Networker, 8*, 4, 29–32.

Deutsch. D. (1956). A step toward success. *American Journal of Individual Psychology, 12*, 78–83.

Deutsch, D. (1967a). Family therapy and family lifestyle. *Journal of Individual Psychology, 23*, 2, 217–223.

Deutsch D. (1967b). Group therapy with married couples: The pangs of a new family life style in marriage. *Individual Psychologist, 4*, 56–62.

Dinkmeyer, D. C., & Carlson, J. (1984). *Time for a better marriage.* Circle Pines, MN: American Guidance Services.

Dinkmeyer, D. C., & Dinkmeyer, D. C., Jr. (1982). *Developing understanding of self and others, Revised*. Circle Pines, MN: American Guidance Services.

Dinkmeyer, D. C., Jr., & Dinkmeyer, D. C. (1991). Adlerian family therapy. In A. M. Horne & J. L. Passmore (Eds.), *Family counseling and therapy* (2nd ed., pp. 383–401). Itasca, IL: F. E. Peacock.

Dinkmeyer, D. C., & Dinkmeyer, J. (1983). *Marital inventory*. Coral Springs, FL: CMTI Press.

Dinkmeyer, D. C., Dinkmeyer, D. C., Jr., & Sperry, L. (1987). *Adlerian counseling and psychotherapy* (2nd ed.). Columbus, OH: Merrill.

Dinkmeyer, D. C., & McKay, D. (1976). *Systematic training for effective parenting*. Circle Pines, MN: American Guidance Services.

Dolliver, R. H. (1994). Classifying the personality theories and personalities of Adler, Freud, and Jung with introversion/extraversion. *Individual Psychology, 50, 2*, 192–202.

Dreikurs, R. (1946). *The challenge of marriage*. New York: Hawthorn/Dutton.

Dreikurs, R. (1954). The psychological interview in medicine. *American Journal of Individual Psychology, 10*, 99–122.

Dreikurs, R. (1960). Are psychological schools of thought outdated? *Journal of Individual Psychology, 16*, 3–10.

Dreikurs, R. (1967). *Psychodynamics, psychotherapy and counseling*. Chicago: Alfred Adler Institute.

Dreikurs, R. (1968b). *Psychology in the classroom* (2nd ed.). New York: Harper and Row.

Dreikurs, R. (1970). Introduction. In *Alfred Adler: The education of children* (E. Jensen & F. Jensen, Trans.) (p. viii). Chicago: Henry Regnery Company.

Dreikurs, R. (1971). *Social equality: The challenge of today*. Chicago: Henry Regnery Company.

Dreikurs, R. (1972). Technology of conflict resolution. *Journal of Individual Psychology, 28*, 203–206.

Dreikurs, R. (1973a). Counseling for family adjustment. In R. Dreikurs, *Psychodynamics, psychotherapy, and counseling* (Rev. ed.). Chicago: Alfred Adler Institute. (Original work published in 1949)

Dreikurs, R. (1973b). The private logic. In H. H. Mosak (Ed.), *Alfred Adler: His influence on psychology today* (pp. 19–32). Park Ridge, NJ: Noyes Press.

Dreikurs, R., & Allen, T. (1971). An interview with Rudolf Dreikurs. *The Counseling Psychologist, 3, 1*, 49–54.

Dreikurs, R., Corsini, R., Lowe, R., & Sonstegard, M. (Eds.), (1959). *Adlerian family counseling: A manual for counseling centers*. Eugene, OR: The University of Oregon Press.

Dreikurs, R., Grunewald, B., & Pepper, F. C. (1971). *Maintaining sanity in the classroom*. New York: Harper and Row.

Dreikurs, R., & Soltz, V. (1964). *Children: The challenge*. New York: Hawthorn Books.

Eckstein, D., Baruth, L., & Mahrer, D. (1975). *An introduction to life style assessment*. Dubuque, IA: Kendall-Hunt Publishing.

Ellenberger, H. F. (1970). *The discovery of the unconscious: The history and evolution of dynamic psychiatry*. New York: Basic Books.

Ellis, A. (1987). Comments on editor's comments on individual psychology. *Individual Psychology, 43, 3*, 277–279.

Farberow, N. L., & Shneidman, E. S. (Eds.). (1961). *The cry for help*. New York: McGraw-Hill.

Furtmüller, C. (1979). Alfred Adler: A biographical essay. In Alfred Adler, *Superiority and social interest* (H. L. Ansbacher & R. R. Ansbacher, Trans. & Eds.). New York: Norton. (Original work written in 1946)

Greever, K. B., Tseng, M. S., & Friedland, B. U. (1973). Development of the Social Interest Index. *Journal of Consulting and Clinical Psychology, 41*, 454–458.

Hall, C. S., & Lindzey, G. (1957). *Theories of personality*. New York: John Wiley.

Hirschorn, S. (1987). Structural therapy and Adlerian family therapy: A comparison. In R. Sherman & D. Dinkmeyer, *Systems of family therapy: An Adlerian integration* (pp. 199–231). New York: Brunner/Mazel.

Hoffman, E. (1994). *The drive for self: Alfred Adler and the founding of individual psychology*. New York: Addison-Wesley.

Huber, C. H. (1991). Marital counseling. In J. Carlson & J. Lewis (Eds.), *Family counseling: Strategies and issues* (pp. 79–100). Denver: Love Publishing Co.

Keen, D. R. (1996). Anorexia nervosa: An Adlerian perspective on etiology and treatment. *Individual Psychology, 52*, 4, 386–405.

Kefir, N., & Corsini, R. J. (1974). Dispositional sets: A contribution to typology. *Journal of Individual Psychology, 30*, 163–178.

Kern, R. M. (1982). *Lifestyle scale*. Coral Springs, FL: CMTI Press.

Kern, R. M. (1997). Interpretation and use of the BASIS-A. Presentation at the University of Georgia, Athens (July).

Kern, R. M., Wheeler, M. S., & Curlette, W. L. (1993). *BASIS-A Inventory Interpretive Manual: A psychological theory*. Highlands, NC: TRT.

Knopf, O. (1932). *The art of being a woman*. Boston: Little, Brown.

Korzybski, A. (1941). *Science and sanity: An introduction to non-Aristotelian systems and general semantics* (2nd ed.). New York: Science Press.

Lazarsfeld, S. (1991). The courage for imperfection. *Individual Psychology, 47*, 1, 93–100. (Original work published in 1966)

Linden, G. W. (1984). Some philosophical roots of Adlerian psychology. *Individual Psychology, 40*, 3, 254–269.

Lowe, R. N. (1982). Adlerian/Dreikursian family counseling. In A. M. Horne & M. M. Ohlsen (Eds.), *Family counseling and therapy*. Itasca, IL: F. E. Peacock.

Lowe, R. N. (1993). Adolescents and their families in counseling. In O. C. Christensen (Ed.), *Adlerian family counseling* (Rev. ed.) (pp. 91–124). Minneapolis: Educational Media Corporation.

Manaster, G. J., & Corsini, R. J. (1982). *Individual psychology: Theory and practice*. Itasca, IL: F. E. Peacock.

Manaster, G. J., Painter, G., Deutsch, D., Overholt, B. J. (Eds.). (1977). *Alfred Adler: As we remember him*. Chicago: North American Society of Adlerian Psychology.

Maslow, A. H. (1954). *Motivation and personality*. New York: Harper and Row.

Matson, F. W. (1964). *The broken image*. Garden City, NY: Anchor Books.

McGoldrick, M., & Gerson, R. (1985). *Genograms in family assessment*. New York: Norton.

McKelvie, W. H. (1987). Kinetic family sculpture: Experiencing family change through time. *Individual Psychology, 43*, 2, 160–173.

Mosak, H. H. (1971). Life style. In A. G. Nikelly (Ed.), *Techniques for behavior change*. Springfield, IL: Charles C. Thomas.

Mosak, H. H. (1973). The controller: A social interpretation of the anal character. In H. H. Mosak (Ed.), *Alfred Adler: His influence on psychology today*. Park Ridge, NJ: Noyes Press.

Mosak, H. H., & Mosak, B. (1975). *A bibliography for Adlerian psychology*. Washington, DC: Hemisphere Publishing Company.

Mosak, H. H., & Schneider, S., & Mosak, L. E. (1980). *A lifestyle: A workbook*. Chicago: Alfred Adler Institute.

Mosak, H. H., & Shulman, B. H. (1971). *The life style inventory*. Chicago: Alfred Adler Institute.

Mozdzierz, G. J. (1996). Adler's "What is neurosis?": Clinical and predictive revelations from the past. *Individual Psychology, 52*, 4, 342–350.

Mozdzierz, G. J., & Greenblatt, R. L. (1994). Technique in psychotherapy: Cautions and concerns. *Individual Psychology, 50*, 2, June, 232–249.

Munroe, R. L. (1955). *Schools of psychoanalytic thought*. New York: Dryden.

Newlon, B. J., & Arciniega, M. (1991). Counseling minority families: An Adlerian perspective. In J. Carlson & J. Lewis (Eds.), *Family counseling: Strategies and issues* (pp. 189–208). Denver: Love Publishing Co.

Nicoll, W. G. (1989). Adlerian marital therapy: History, theory and process. In R. M. Kern, E. C. Hawes, & O. C. Christensen (Eds.), *Couples therapy: An Adlerian perspective* (pp. 1–28). Minneapolis: Educational Media Corporation.

Nicoll, W. G. (1990). Strategies and techniques in counseling: Integrating Adlerian and systems approaches. Presentation at North American Society of Adlerian Psychology, Region III Conference, Orlando, Florida, February 25.

O'Connell, W. E. (1991). Humanistic identification: A new translation for *Gemeinschaftsgefühl*. *Individual Psychology, 47*, 1, 26–27.

Pepper, F. C. (1980). Why children misbehave. *Individual Psychology, 17*, 19–37.

Pipher, M. (1995). *Reviving Ophelia: Saving the selves of adolescent girls*. New York: Ballantine Books.

Pipher, M. (1996). *The shelter of each other*. New York: Putnam.

Powers, R. L. (1975). Foreword. In H. H. Mosak & B. Mosak, *A bibliography for Adlerian psychology* (p. ix). Washington, DC: Hemisphere Publishing Corporation.

Powers, R. L., & Griffith, J. (1987). *Understanding life-style: The psycho-clarity process*. Chicago: The Americas Institute of Adlerian Studies, LTD., Publishers.

Reichlin, R. E., & Niederehe, G. (1980). Early memories: A comprehensive bibliography. *Journal of Individual Psychology, 36*, 2, 209–218.

Rogers, C. R. (1951). *Client-centered therapy*. Boston: Houghton Mifflin.

Rogers, C. R. (1975). Empathic: An unappreciated way of being. *The Counseling Psychologist, 5*, 2–10.

Rotter, J. B. (1960). Psychotherapy. *Annual Review of Psychology*, 11, 381–414.

Rotter, J. B. (1962). An analysis of Adlerian psychology from a research orientation. *Journal of Individual Psychology, 18*, 3–11.

Schooler, C. (1972). Birth order effects: Not here, not now! *Psychological Bulletin, 78*, 161–175.

Sherman, R. (1983a). Counseling the urban economically disadvantaged family. *American Journal of Family Therapy, 11*, 1, 22–30.

Sherman, R., & Dinkmeyer, D. (1987). *Systems of family therapy: An Adlerian integration*. New York: Brunner/Mazel.

Sherman, R., & Fredman, N. (1986). *Handbook of structured techniques in marriage and family therapy*. New York: Brunner/Mazel.

Sherman, R., Oresky, P., & Rountree, Y. B. (1994). *Solving problems in couples and family therapy*. New York: Brunner/Mazel.

Sherman, R., Shumsky, A., & Rountree, Y. B. (1994). *Enlarging the therapeutic circle*. New York: Brunner/Mazel.

Shulman, B. H. (1975). Foreword. In H. H. Mosak & B. Mosak, *A bibliography for Adlerian psychology* (p. x). Washington, DC: Hemisphere Publishing Corporation.

Sicher, L. (1991). A declaration of interdependence. *Individual Psychology, 47*, 1, 10–16.

Starr, A. (1973). Sociometry of the family. In H. H. Mosak (Ed.), *Alfred Adler: His influence on psychology today*. Park Ridge, NJ: Noyes Press.

Stewart, A. E. (1997). E-prime and multivalued logic: The role of general semantics in understanding and facilitating the career development process. Athens, GA: The University of Georgia, Unpublished manuscript.

Stewart, A. E., & Stewart, E. A. (1995). Trends in birth-order research: 1976–1993. *Individual Psychology, 51*, 1, 21–36.

Stiles, K., & Wilborn, B. (1992). A life-style instrument for children. *Individual Psychology, 48*, 1, 96–106.

Sulliman, J. R. (1973). The development of a scale for the measurement of social interest. *Dissertation Abstracts International, 34*, 2914-B.

Sundberg, N. D. (1963). Adler's technique with children: A special review. *Journal of Individual Psychology, 19*, 2, 226–231.

Sundberg, N. D., & Tyler, L. E. (1962). *Clinical psychology: An introduction to research and practice*. New York: Appleton-Century-Crofts.

Taft, R. (1958). A cluster analysis for Hall and Lindzey. *Contemporary Psychology, 3*, 143–144.

Terner, J., & Pew, W. L. (1978). *The courage to be imperfect: The life and work of Rudolf Dreikurs*. New York: Hawthorn Books.

Toman, W. (1961). *Family constellation: Theory and practice of a psychological game*. New York: Springer.

von Bertalanffy, L. (1968). *General systems theory: Foundations, development, application*. New York: Braziller.

Walton, F. X. (1980). *Winning teenagers over in home and school*. Columbia, SC: Adlerian Child Care Books.

Walton, F. X., & Powers, R. L. (1974). *Winning children over: A manual for teachers, counselors, principals, and parents*. Chicago: Practical Psychology Associates.

Wasserman, I. (1958). Letter to the editor. *American Journal of Psychotherapy, 12*, 623–627.

Watkins, C. E., Jr. (1983). Some characteristics of research on Adlerian psychological theory, 1970–1981. *Individual Psychology, 39*, 99–110.

Watkins, C. E., Jr. (1986). A research bibliography on Adlerian psychological theory. *Individual Psychology, 42*, 1, 123–132.

Watkins, C. E., Jr. (1992). Research activity with Adler's theory. *Individual Psychology, 48*, 1, March, 107–108.

White, R. W. (1957). Adler and the future of ego psychology. *Journal of Individual Psychology, 13*, 112–124.

Wolman, B. B. (1960). *Contemporary theories and systems in psychology*. New York: Harper and Row.

Zarski, J. J., Bubenzer, D. L., & West, J. D. (1986). Social interest, stress, and the prediction of health status. *Journal of Counseling and Development, 64*, 386–389.

CHAPTER 14

Reality Therapy

ROBERT E. WUBBOLDING

DEFINITION

Since the first major publication, *Reality Therapy*, by William Glasser, M.D., in 1965, there has been a steady increase in interest and application of the principles of reality therapy. It is now used by counselors, therapists, teachers, nurses, youth workers, geriatric workers, clergy, lawyers, supervisors, forepersons, and company managers—as well as parents. Although mastering the skills requires study, practice, and supervision, the techniques can be used even after brief exposure to them. For example, many parents use the suggestions with their children after hearing about some aspects of the system. The principles of reality therapy are sometimes described as "down-to-earth," "easy to understand," and "jargon-free." The user of the ideas takes a positive approach, stresses present and future behavior, and refrains from blaming or criticizing. Nevertheless, to become proficient in learning and practicing the principles requires the development of detailed skills. The theory and method are easy to understand; but, like the rules of a sport that are easy to understand, the implementation of the method, like playing the sport, is more difficult.

The theory underlying reality therapy and the method itself have evolved significantly over the years and have developed far beyond the original publication by Glasser. Reality therapy has become more simplified in some ways and far more detailed and complicated in others. Nevertheless, throughout its history, those formulating the principles of reality therapy have sought to use language that can be clearly understood by most people. An explicit effort has been made to avoid a unique vocabulary. Thus, words such as *belonging, power, needs, wants, plans,* and *consequences*—words easily understood by most people—are used to explain the concepts.

There is often discussion at training workshops about where reality therapy fits among the various schools of thought: behavioral, humanistic, cognitive. Some have mistakenly stated that reality therapy is a system of behavior modification. In my opinion, the system belongs in the cognitive school of thought, for it is based on a theory of brain functioning that was formerly named "control system theory" or "control theory." In 1996 Glasser changed the name to "choice theory" because of the emphasis on the fact that human beings choose their own behavior. While the method of reality therapy contains action plans as a significant component, they are preceded by evaluation of one's life direction, specific behaviors, and attainability of goals. In short, a considerable amount of cognitive change is included in changing a behavior.

Finally, Wubbolding (1996d) provides a summary definition of reality therapy:

> It is a method of helping people take better control of their lives. It helps people to identify and to clarify what they want and what they need and then to evaluate whether they can realistically attain what they want. It helps them to examine their own behaviors and to evaluate them with clear criteria. This is followed by positive planning, a strategy designed to help people control their own lives as well as to fulfill their realistic wants and their needs. The result is added strength, more self-confidence, better human relations, and a personal plan for a more effective life. Thus, reality therapy provides people with a self-help tool to use daily to cope with adversity, to grow personally, to gain more effective control of their lives, and to make more effective choices.
>
> Reality therapy is based on several principles, such as:
>
> 1. People—not society, not heredity, not past history—are responsible for their own behavior.
>
> 2. People can change and live more effective lives.
>
> 3. People behave for a purpose—to mold their environment as a sculptor molds clay, to match their own inner *quality world* pictures of what they want.
>
> The intended results described are achievable through continuous effort and hard work. (p. 42)

HISTORICAL DEVELOPMENT

> Reality Therapy is one of the newest of man's formal attempts to explain mankind, to set rules for behavior, and to map out how one person can help another to achieve happiness and success; but at the same time, paradoxically, it represents one of the oldest sets of maxims referring to human conduct. (Glasser & Zunin, 1973, p. 287)

The contribution of reality therapy is that it has enshrined in the practice of counseling and psychotherapy some of the most fundamental, multicultural, and philosophical principles of human conduct that are universally accepted and lived by millions of people. Central to these underlying principles is that human beings are responsible for their behavior. They cannot blame past history, environment, or their unconscious drives. Rather, they choose their behavior with, of course, varying degrees of freedom.

PRECURSORS

The principles of personal responsibility for our behavior were not discovered in the nineteenth or twentieth centuries. In the second century A.D., Marcus Aurelius wrote, "If anything is within the powers and province of man, believe that it is within your own compass also" and "Men's actions cannot agitate us, but our own views regarding them." Similarly, "The agitations that beset you are superfluous and depend wholly on judgments that are your own" (Antoninus, 1944, p. 21).

Glasser and Zunin (1973) cite Paul Dubois, a Swiss physician, as a direct spiritual ancestor. Dubois helped his patients substitute healthful thoughts for disease-laden thoughts. The assumption is that the patients can have at least some control and choice regarding health matters. William James is often quoted as saying that one of the greatest discoveries in history is that we can alter the circumstances of our lives by altering our attitudes. He stated, "We do not sing because we are happy. We are happy because we sing."

A more direct influence in the development of reality therapy was Helmuth Kaiser. Kaiser was a training analyst at the Menninger Foundation, where G. L. Harrington—later to be Glasser's teacher—worked for 10 years. Though Kaiser stated that it is the responsibility of the analyst to cure the patient (a principle not incorporated into reality therapy), he stated that "it is the analyst's task to make the patient feel responsible for his own words and his own actions..." (Kaiser, 1955, p. 4).

Kaiser also influenced Harrington to approach the therapeutic relationship from a more egalitarian perspective and to view labeling the relationship "patient–therapist" as less than crucial. Glasser and Zunin (1973) add, "He also, and perhaps inadvertently, illustrated that a basic assumption for therapy is that the therapist be healthier than the patient and that, if he is not, he must at least be healthier in the area of the patient's illness" (p. 289).

The most important precursor to the development of reality therapy as it is known today was Harrington himself. It was due to his influence and inspiration that Glasser began and continued to develop the principles of reality therapy.

BEGINNINGS

Reality therapy began when Glasser became dissatisfied with the Freudian methodology that he learned during his residency at the UCLA Medical Center. Harrington, whom Glasser still calls "my teacher," provided a sympathetic ear because of his own similar beliefs. Ford (1982) states, "This encouragement from his supervisor plus his own determination to seek a more practical way of helping people gave Glasser the impetus to develop his ideas further" (p. 389). Within a few years Glasser and Harrington introduced the seminal notions of reality therapy to the most disturbed patients at the Veterans Administration Hospital in Los Angeles. Prior to their innovation, there seemed to be a tacit acceptance among hospital personnel of the fact that the patients were there to stay and that they should remain "peacefully psychotic." As Glasser and Zunin (1973) state, "Harrington began to shatter this contract when he took over the ward" (p. 289).

The new program had astonishing results. In a unit of 210 patients whose average stay had been 17 years, 90 left the hospital in three years, 85 left in two years, and 45 left the hospital in one year (Glasser and Zunin, 1973).

In our society, we separate people from the mainstream who break either the written laws or the unwritten laws. When the patients described above could abide by the unwritten laws, (i.e., could act normal and sane), they were returned to society. There is no written law that says a person should not hear voices. But there seems to be an unwritten law that states that no one should allow imaginary voices to interfere with work or family life. When such interference is judged excessive, the person in question is taken to the mental hospital. On the other hand, there are written laws that we are required to respect. When people break these laws, they are ushered off to jail.

Glasser further developed the background ideas in a correctional institution, the Ventura School, for delinquent girls near Los Angeles, where he served as a consultant in the late 1950s. He laid the groundwork for his yet to be named theory in a book, *Mental Health or Mental Illness?* (Glasser, 1961). When his work at the Ventura School became successful, he labeled his method "reality psychiatry," and presented it to the 1962 meeting of the National Association of Youth Training Schools. He said that the response was "phenomenal" adding, "Evidently many people doubted the effectiveness of any therapy that did not ask people to accept responsibility for what they chose to do with their lives" (Glasser, 1984, p. 327).

The term reality therapy was initially used in the book by the same name that was first published in 1965. In this landmark work, Glasser speaks of his practice in mental health and in corrections. He also began to develop the basic theory, especially the importance of human needs as motivators of behavior, love, and self-worth. He stressed the importance of responsibility, which he defined as "the ability to fulfill one's needs, and to do so in a way that does not deprive others of their ability to fulfill their needs" (Glasser, 1965, p. xi).

While acceptance of the concepts was less than universal among therapists, the principles elucidated in reality therapy struck a responsive chord among educators. Since the institution in which people break both the written and unwritten laws early in life is the school, it seemed only logical to apply the same successful principles to schools. Thus, out of his experience in the schools of Palo Alto and in the Los Angeles area, Glasser wrote *Schools Without Failure* (1968), which described a program designed to eliminate failure from schools. Concerning the application to schools, O'Donnell (1987) says, "Glasser's book *Schools Without Failure*, published in 1968, turned out to be one of the biggest sellers in education since the John Dewey books" (p. 4). When counselors, teachers, and correctional workers used reality therapy, they found that it was effective for building inner responsibility in students and clients who had little experience with such a notion.

Still, it was not clear as to why it was effective. Then when Glasser happened to read a statement from Marshall McLuhan that students are searching for a role, not a goal (Glasser, 1972), it became clear that reality therapy helped people to find out who they were by providing them with tools to fulfill their psychological needs. It seemed that, as Ford (1982) said, people were becoming more interested in their identity needs, "sociability and personal worth, and less concerned with...survival and security" (p. 390). Glasser pointed out that in the 1960s American society witnessed not just rebellion, but a cultural revolution. He observed that people became interested in identity needs for three reasons: increased affluence because of which the survival needs of most people were insured, laws that ensured equality among groups of people, and increased communication because of the efficiency of the instant media. Even if affluence and equality were not experienced by large segments of our society, still they realized that it was possible to achieve them and in fact became more frustrated at not being able to fulfill their psychological needs as fully as others could.

Another significant thread in the development of reality therapy was the idea that there could be a short cut from a failure identity to a success identity. This could be achieved not in an *easy* way but rather through the performance of effortful behaviors that would be carried out for 6 to 12 months for relatively brief daily time intervals. These activities do not engage the person's concentration but rather allow the mind "to float" and to wander in a productive and positive manner. *Positive Addiction* (Glasser, 1976) reflected this idea and provided another tool for the reality therapist to use in helping clients gain a success identity, added inner responsibility, increased self-esteem, and more effective control over their lives.

It is at this point that yet another thread of history becomes evident. As with many therapies, reality therapy as a method developed first, followed by a formulation of the theory. The sociological theory had been sculpted in *Identity Society* (Glasser, 1972), but a psychological theory of brain functioning was lacking. This was formulated by Glasser in *Stations of the Mind* (1981), in which he explained the principles of control system theory or control theory in the context of psychotherapy. Describing the human brain as a psychosocial, biological negative feedback input control system is not new with reality therapy. Wiener (1948) described the human brain as a cybernetic loop that seeks input from the world around it. He spoke of the role of feedback in engineering and in biology. He later warned of possible excesses in the use of feedback machines (Wiener, 1950).

The immediate predecessor of Glasser's contribution to control theory is the work of William Powers, *Behavior: The Control of Perception* (1973). As in other works by control theorists, Powers states that the brain seeks input from the world around it. Human beings are driven by forces inside them, not merely conditioned by external stimuli, as the behaviorists teach. Glasser (1981) has applied and extended control theory by incorporating the human needs belonging, power, fun, and freedom as the genetic instructions or forces that drive human beings.

The fact that human output (behavior) has a purpose and is a choice is emphasized in Glasser's most significant work, *Control Theory* (1985). That we choose our behavior is a central element in that control theory as taught by Glasser (1986). Because of this added emphasis on the role of choice, Glasser has changed the name of the theory to "choice theory" (1996, 1998).

And so reality therapy, along with its companion and theoretical base, choice theory, should be seen as ideas that have evolved over many years. Their current status consists of applications to nearly every type of personal and professional interaction (Glasser & Wubbolding, 1995).

CURRENT STATUS

The William Glasser Institute has developed an 18-month training program for people seeking certification in the practice of reality therapy. It begins with attendance at a Basic Intensive Week. During this four-day program, the participants learn both the theory and methodology, as well as have the opportunity to practice specific skills in small groups under the supervision of an approved instructor. This is followed by a practicum period of at least six months, during which the candidate takes a practicum with an approved supervisor. The next step in training is an Advanced Intensive Week and an advanced practicum. These are at least as long as the Basic Week and practicum. However, a higher level of skill is required at this stage of the training. The final phase of the certification process is a five-day session in which the candidates prove to a faculty member that they have adequate knowledge and are skilled in reality therapy.

The philosophy underlying this program is that of inclusion. Every effort is made to spread the concepts of reality therapy rather than restrict them to a few professionals. The program is designed to appeal to people who have full-time employment and cannot leave work to do lengthy and costly internships. The Center for Reality Therapy in Cincinnati, Ohio, in conjunction with the Institute conducts such workshops Saturday through Tuesday so that participants will miss only two or three days of work instead of four. Since the inception of the certification process in 1975, over 4500 people have been certified by the Institute. At present, over 200 therapists are certified each year.

Currently, reality therapy is widely used in drug and alcohol programs, with over 90% of 200 drug and alcohol programs for the U.S. military using reality therapy as their preferred modality for treatment (Glasser, 1984). Moreover, thousands of teachers have been trained to use the Schools Without Failure (SWF) program, the heart of which is class meetings.

The applications of reality therapy to schools include not only the SWF program but also substance abuse education. The CHOICE Program (Glasser, 1988) is a drug prevention program that emphasizes the application of choice theory to grades seven through nine. It can be incorporated into the school curriculum through the use of lesson plans and includes a major component involving parents. Advancement in the application to schools consists of the mingling of Glasserian thought with that of Deming (1982) within the school context. Through the application of reality therapy in the "Quality School," students are led to higher achievement and better relationships without coercion and with involvement (Glasser, 1990, 1992).

The application of reality therapy in counseling and psychotherapy continues to be further delineated and extended. Reality therapy has also been used successfully in group homes, marriage relationships, suicide prevention, psychosis, adolescent counseling, geriatrics, and other contexts (N. Glasser, 1980, 1989). Elija Mickel has applied control (choice) theory to family mediation as well as in multicultural settings (1994, 1995). In his book *Using Reality Therapy*, Wubbolding (1988) describes a reality therapy model of counseling applied to marriage and family. He also has incorporated paradoxical techniques as ways to deal with resistance, and his application of reality therapy as a "cycle of counseling" (Wubbolding, 1996a) will be explained later. These ideas have been further developed with emphasis on self-evaluation (Wubbolding, 1996c).

Relationship counseling within the context of reality therapy has been developed by Ford, who stressed the importance of common need-fulfilling behaviors, time spent together, and changing perceptions toward the other person (Ford, 1974, 1983; Ford & Englund, 1979). The parent–child relationship has received special attention by reality therapists. Ford (1977) described effective ways to show love, build discipline, and assist children in developing an abiding faith or belief in something outside themselves. Similarly, Bluestein and Collins (1985) describe ways for parents to fulfill their needs, as well as how to negotiate and how to use consequences. Glasser, himself, has developed a needs profile and a system for strengthening relationships (1995).

In the world of work, the principles of reality therapy were called "reality management" or "reality performance management." The current description is "lead management." The goal of these applications is to train supervisors and managers to create an environment that is need-fulfilling for workers as well as to help them develop coaching skills that they can use to help employees increase responsible behavior (Glasser, 1980; Wubbolding, 1985b, 1990a, 1996b).

The principles of reality therapy have been applied to nearly every genus of human interaction, and the field of self-help has not been neglected. Since the ideas can be expressed in language understandable to most people, clients are often asked to be on a reading program so that they can take better control of their lives. They are asked to spend time writing about goals, plans, and perceptions (Wubbolding, 1990b). They can be encouraged to examine their behaviors relative to their needs and to take direct action on their own regarding their problems. Specific applications to problems for which many people seek help are categorized as burnout. Reality therapy offers a rationale for this phenomenon as well as specific ways to address such upsetting feelings (Edelwich, 1980; Wubbolding, 1979).

The phrase "reality therapy" was coined because the world in which we live is organized on certain principles: People decide what they want, evaluate their behavior, and plan to achieve it. In the conduct of daily life, individuals do not routinely examine unconscious and unresolved conflicts. The principles of reality therapy have universal application because they have been derived from common-sense observation of how healthy people live their lives.

TENETS OF THE MODEL

In order to grasp the principles of reality therapy, it is first necessary to understand choice theory as developed and applied by William Glasser (1981, 1985, 1998). According to reality theory, each individual has a control system by which he or she perceives the world. A control system acts on its environment so that it can get the input it has sought by its behavior. Wubbolding (1991) described a sculptor molding and shaping clay so that it matches his image of how he wants it to appear. We are all sculptors who mold the world around us to make it congruent with our perceptions of what we want.

The human brain as a control (choice) system is best understood through the analogy of a thermostat. This mechanism is designed to control its environment, to get a "perception" of its own impact on the world around it. If the control on the thermostat is set at 72°, the thermostat sends a signal to the furnace or air conditioner to generate specific and purposeful actions. These actions are designed to fulfill a "desire" within the mechanism—to keep the room at the level of 72°. The thermostat "perceives" the effectiveness of its behaviors through its thermometer. In other words, the thermometer tells the control how it is doing, or whether its behavior is effective.

An interesting and important sidelight is that the system can be fooled. If a match is held under the thermometer, it will read and report the room temperature inaccurately. All the control can know is what it perceives. Through its "perceptual system" (the thermometer), it believes the room is much hotter than it really is. As a consequence, it relentlessly drives the air conditioner harder and harder. It will continue to drive the machinery until it receives another perception (temperature reading) or until the air conditioner ceases to function.

So, too, it is with the human brain. It seeks to get what it wants from the world around it. Through its perceptual system, it gets feedback on how effective its behavioral choices have been. But the feedback can be very misleading. Alcohol and drugs, for example, provide the illusion that behavior is more effective than it really is. Family members who are drug-free perceive the alcoholic's behavior quite differently. They see the chemically dependent person's behavior as very destructive.

Reality therapy recognizes four components to the human control system: needs, behaviors, perceptions, and the outside world. Each influences the interpretations that the individual makes about the situation, which, in turn, influence the choices that he or she makes in acting. These four components are explored separately in the following sections.

HUMAN NEEDS

Unlike a thermostat, the human control (choice) system—the brain—is driven by what Glasser has termed "genetic instructions." These are human needs or internal forces that are the root causes of all human behavior. Throughout our entire lives we seek, by means of our behaviors, to meet one or more of the innate needs. Sometimes the behavior is effective, sometimes not effective, and sometimes, even, counterproductive. But whether it is effective or not, all human endeavor is purposeful. It is an attempt to gain survival, belonging or involvement with people, power or achievement, enjoyment or fun, and freedom or independence.

SURVIVAL We all have a need to live, to maintain health, to breathe air. In fact, when our survival is threatened, we frequently take radical action to preserve it.

BELONGING All human beings are born with a need to relate to others. In family counseling this need is of paramount importance, because the family is the natural environment in which belonging is met. Family members are taught that demeaning each other within the counseling or at home is always harmful. Ventilating anger at each other is discouraged. The person releasing a pent-up feeling might feel better for the moment, but a sense of belonging is not enhanced. To counteract this, members of the family are encouraged to spend time together so that pleasant perceptions of each other as need fulfilling can be increased and stored for further use at a later time. These positive memories, valuable in themselves, also serve as a foundation for future plan making and compromise. This concept of "quality time" will be explained in detail later.

POWER, ACHIEVEMENT The word *power* has come to imply dominance, exploitation, and even ruthlessness. Here it is used to denote the meaning from the French *pouvoir* and the Spanish *poder*—"to be capable," "to be able." It is a broad concept and a strong need that is paramount for many people. In the initial stages of relationships, the need for belonging is more pronounced. After the heat and enthusiasm of the initial stages of a relationship have cooled, there often emerges a struggle related to power. The new baby fulfills a yearning for more belonging from the parents. Yet, before long, the baby seeks constant attention (power) at all hours, sometimes resulting in parental frustration at having to give so much attention to the new family member. When children grow to the teen years, they seek ways to fulfill power that often conflict with the need fulfillment of the parents and other family members. Such struggles surround the use of a car, homework, grades, sexual behavior, and a myriad of other family problems.

Another aspect of the need for personal power is that we all seek a sense of competence and adequacy. Parents want to see themselves as having done a good, if not superior, job of parenting. Children seek the same fulfillment at their level. When members feel inadequate in the family, they often resort to illusory ways to gain a sense of importance—through drugs, antisocial behavior, withdrawing, getting depressed, or even by becoming psychotic. These negative symptoms are often signs of inadequate power-need fulfillment.

ENJOYMENT, FUN Aristotle said that people are human because we are "risible"; that is, we can laugh. A fundamental human desire is to escape boredom and at least maintain a sense of interest in our world, our behavior. A quality separating us from the animal kingdom is our ability to see humor and play. Playing seems natural to children, and through it they grow intellectually and fulfill their needs. Often, when a family seeks counseling, the enjoyment they experience is sought outside family relationships. In other families, members' experience of fun is the result of behaviors that are hurtful to the other members of the family. A prank becomes teasing; teasing becomes vicious; viciousness becomes violence. Sometimes such families voluntarily seek or are court-ordered to attend family counseling sessions. The counselor's goal is to help the family learn enjoyment-directed behaviors that lead to more intimate relationships and closeness within the family.

FREEDOM, INDEPENDENCE This need is sometimes seen as similar to power. It means that we all need to have choices and to stand on our own. We wish to make our own schedules, live in places we opt for, have friends we select for ourselves, and act in many other autonomous ways.

In families, a choice of one member often interferes with the choice of another family member. The range of choices surrounding chemical dependency, for instance, often infringes on the choices of the other family members. When the failure to adequately fulfill this need is linked to out-of-control behaviors, there is often a clash of choices related to all four needs.

It should be understood that these needs are general. They can be likened to empty bowls that we seek to fill by means of a variety of behaviors. They are not specific. We have a need for belonging, but we have a specific want for relationships with specific people. These particular wants are related to each need and are changeable. We can change what we want, but we cannot change what we need. Likewise, these needs are universal. Everyone has them. They seem to be present in people from all cultures.

It is a basic tenet of reality therapy that human needs are truly multicultural. Persons attending training workshops in the United States represent the diverse cultures and ideologies of North America—African American, Native American, Hispanic, Asian American, and others. Donnie Branch, from the Nicholas Treatment Center in Dayton, Ohio, having investigated many theories, is convinced that reality therapy is eminently suited to the African American family. Used properly, it is active, it is directive, and it is respectful. In addition, I have personally taught reality therapy to enthusiastic groups in Korea, Japan, Hong Kong, India, Taiwan, and Singapore, as well as Europe and the Middle East. Others have also taught reality therapy internationally and multiculturally in these same regions and elsewhere.

The needs described earlier are seen as universal and can serve as a binding force for all cultures, for they are the human motivators from which specific and diverse wants and behaviors originate. On the other hand, the specific wants and behaviors described below are unique to each individual but can be circumscribed by cultural experiences. Thus, family conflict is universal, but the ways it is expressed are unique to individual families within a particular cultural heritage.

HUMAN WANTS While the needs are the fundamental driving forces of human behavior, the specific wants are the most proximate energizers for what we do, think, and feel. It is useful to think of the spectrum of wants as analogous to a picture album. Glasser (1990) has also referred to the picture album as the "quality world," with each picture in the album or quality world representing a want. We have pictures or wants related to each need. Some are more important than others. Some are better defined than others. The counselor using reality therapy explores this picture album with the family members by asking them what they want from the family relative to each member's need. Family members are asked to define what they want that they are not getting from the family members, their friends, their jobs, their schools, and even the counselor. It is clear that a person's experience influences his or her wants. A minority person who has not had many opportunities would have a series of wants quite diverse from someone with no minority experience.

In exploring the wants of the family members, it is crucial to help them determine their level of commitment. Wubbolding (1988) has described five levels of commitment that clients exhibit:

1. "We don't want to be here. You can't help us." This is the lowest level of commitment and must change if amelioration of family problems is to occur. Families coerced into counseling frequently display this level in the beginning sessions. By utilizing the principles described as "environment" and "procedures," the reality therapist can help the client move to a higher level of commitment.

2. "We'd like the pleasure of the outcome but not the effort required to achieve it." Such a level is seen in the family that has some desire to change and work out problems. They know they are troubled and even desire a better life for themselves, but they have not yet made the commitment to take action, to do anything differently, or to change their direction.

3. "We'll try; we might; we could." This level of commitment is higher than the first two. Here the family is motivated to change. They feel the pain of not getting what they want from their family life, but they are not yet to the point at which they are totally committed to changing behaviors. An escape hatch to failure has been preserved. They subsequently can say, "We *tried*, but we simply couldn't work out the family problems."

4. "We'll do our best." This level represents a very high level of commitment to work toward harmony. Family members are willing to evaluate their behavior, to make plans, to follow through if they don't have to "change too much." The counselor builds on this level and helps them to attain an even higher level of commitment.

5. "We'll do whatever it takes." The highest level of commitment is expressed by this statement. The family is willing to put 100% effort into the achievement of the counseling goals.

It is important to help the family members to individually commit themselves to work toward the resolution of problems. They can be asked about their level of commitment occasionally when resistance is encountered (i.e., a low level can evolve to a higher one). In fact, a major task of the reality therapist in the first several sessions is to help members increase their commitment to a more effective level.

BEHAVIOR

Another component of the human control system is behavior. It is given a slightly different definition than in other systems of therapy. Behavior is here seen as having four components: (1) acting or doing, (2) thinking or cognition, (3) feeling or emotion, and (4) physiology. All behavior contains these four elements. The "acting" component receives most, but by no means all, of the emphasis in the counseling sessions for two reasons. First, human beings have more control over the doing or acting aspect of their behavior. A mother, father, or child can rarely change his or her feelings of anger or resentment by a simple fiat. They can, however, change more easily what they say to each other. They can *choose* to spend time together. They can choose to remain silent, though often with much difficulty, when they *feel* like exploding in anger or resentment. Second, human beings are less aware of their "acting" than they are of their thoughts, feelings, and physiology. People are generally aware of how they feel at a given moment: awake, tired, hungry, upset, angry, guilty, and so forth.

Though people are often unable to attach a clinical label to their feelings, they generally know if they feel good or bad. But it takes reflection to attend to the acting. While I write these words I am aware of thirst, hunger, feeling good about what is written, but I am less aware of how I'm sitting: arm on table, feet on floor or on rung of chair. In families, the members are aware of their upset feelings, but less aware of how they spend their time, what they say to each other, and how they treat the other family members.

Thus, in reality therapy the counselor pays attention to the feelings, talks about them, and allows the family to acknowledge and discuss them. The therapist, however, makes a concerted effort to connect the feelings with the doing because feelings are like the warning lights on the dashboard of the automobile. When they light up, the driver knows when something is wrong, as well as when something is right. Then, action is planned and taken to resolve the problem.

PERCEPTION

The next component of the human control system is how the person views the world. Perception functions through two filters, high and low. Through the high filter the person puts a value on incoming perceptions and images. For example, when parents see a child hitting another family member, they disapprove, or see the behavior from a high negative level. If the child hits a punching bag in order to stay in good physical condition, the parents might see this behavior from a high positive level, thereby giving approval. Seeing one's circumstances from a low level of perception means simply recognizing the environment without making a judgment. Most events in families are seen from a low level of perception. For example, when people walk into a room, they observe the room without explicitly approving or disapproving of the furniture, the carpeting, or the atmosphere. They often relate later that they don't even remember the physical setting they were in. They have no strong pleasant or unpleasant memories of it because they saw the circumstances from a low level of perception.

Cultural differences manifest themselves in this perceptual component more than in any other part of the choice system. For some people, assertiveness is a sign of mental health, indeed almost a virtue, but in some cultures it is regarded as impolite, brash, and even aggressive. Communication is often indirect in some families. If a child wants to communicate a painful idea to the father, it may be necessary to use the mother as intermediary. The skilled reality therapist respects these cultural boundaries.

THE OUTSIDE WORLD

The last element is not a part of the human choice system, but it requires explanation relative to the choice system. The world outside us impinges on us in many ways, and through our behavior we seek to change it to match what we want. In a family, the individual members often want the "world"—the other family members—to change. Consider a couple, each hoping that the other person will change. If this were to occur, they insist, the world would be a better place for each of them. Yet it is difficult, indeed impossible, to change another person directly. What can be hoped for and held out to the family is that if each one can commit to even a slight change, the others might also choose to change.

In summary, the person is seen as a choice system that seeks to get what it wants from a world around it. It generates behaviors designed to mold the world as a sculptor molds clay. In families, the sculptors often conflict with each other. Their choices are to change what they want, to vary their behavior, or to alter their perceptions. These three elements are interconnected, so that a change in one results in a change in the other two. The most easily changed part of the system is the "doing" component of the behavioral system.

APPLICATION

CLIENTS FOR WHOM REALITY FAMILY THERAPY IS EFFECTIVE

Reality therapy was first developed in two institutions in which mildly, moderately, and severely disturbed people were treated: a mental hospital and a correctional school for young women. It has since been applied to virtually every kind of client. It is used with families who have major or minor problems, including those that are verbal or nonverbal, from upper or lower socioeconomic levels, and from a wide spectrum of cultures including many Asian groups. It has been used to remediate severe family problems such as alcoholism and abuse, as well as to develop family growth and closeness. The application to problems has been more widespread because families more often seek counseling to solve problems than to enhance family growth or closeness.

GOALS OF THE THERAPEUTIC PROCESS

The general aim of reality family therapy is to help the family gain a sense of inner control that is the result of choices. When a family enters counseling, members often feel even more out of control than before they made the decision to seek help. They believe that not only do they have a problem, but now it has reached a level so serious that they must involve an "outsider" in their personal family business. This is especially true in some minority cultures where the tendency is to "keep the problem in the house." Thus, it is important that the family gain a sense of relief or inner control in order to establish the validity of the intervention for the family. More specific goals include the following:

GAIN AT LEAST A MODICUM OF NEED FULFILLMENT Each person must feel some sense of belonging or involvement with the family, or at least with one other member. If the counseling is to be successful, each family member must feel some degree of power. If they are at least listened to and appreciated during the session, some feeling of power and competence is felt by the family members. This is especially true in families who honor the authority figure. Also, all members need to feel enjoyment or fun. The counseling sessions themselves should occasionally contain *some* fun. Even if this is not possible at every meeting, the counselor helps the family to have fun together outside the sessions. The final psychological need, freedom, is experienced when all family members make individual choices as well as choices to spend time together or to relinquish ineffective behaviors (Glasser, 1995).

CHANGE LEVELS OF PERCEPTION The members of the family are also assisted in altering their levels of perception toward the problems and toward each other. For example, if they see each other's behavior from a high emotional level of disapproval, they are taught to lower their perceptions so that their behavior is less impassioned. On the other hand, if a perception of the family or family member is low, the counselor might help them raise it. Thus, when the chemically dependent member or perpetrator of abuse does not perceive such behavior as a problem, the counselor assists the family member(s) to raise the level of perception so that judgments are made regarding such behavior. It has been said that this specific skill is "comforting the afflicted" and "afflicting the comfortable."

CREATE QUALITY TIME One of the most important outcomes of reality family therapy is increased quality time. This is the foundation of any change. It includes time spent together in a noncritical manner, and it will be explained later as one of the cornerstones of reality family therapy as well as a prerequisite for fulfillment of the following goal.

CHANGE BEHAVIOR A more measurable and tangible goal of counseling is to help the family to change behavior—more specifically, to change how they act toward one another. This means changing how they talk to each other in and out of the sessions as well as how they treat each other. If they are able to spend time together and build up a bank of positive memories about each other, they will be more likely to be able to communicate in a mutually need-fulfilling manner, as well as to negotiate effective compromises.

CLIENTS' PRIMARY RESPONSIBILITIES

Reality therapy is based on the beliefs that people are accountable for their behaviors and can choose more effective actions. Every choice is generated with the aim of shaping the external world in a way that matches internal wants (Wubbolding, 1988). It is the clients' responsibility to realize that changes come from within. Behavior is *chosen* and not caused by outside forces. This is in contrast to the conventional wisdom that external stimuli—or the environment—are responsible for our behavior. Indications of this kind of thinking among family members include statements such as, "You *make* me angry"; "You *cause* me such great pain"; "I had an anxiety *attack*"; "A fit of depression *came over* me." Others see their *locus of control* as existing somewhere in their past history. Their own childhood abuse or parents' chemical dependence is perceived as the cause for their present abuse of their children or their alcoholism. Therefore, in reality therapy, the client is called upon to take responsibility for his or her own, chosen behaviors.

Another client responsibility is to want to *do* something to change. There is a major distinction between wanting *a* change and wanting *to* change. When the family members want *a* change in the family, they at least have some motivation for improvement. They are probably at the second level of commitment: "We'd like the pleasure of the outcome but not the effort required to achieve it." However, better control and more effective need fulfillment require a higher level of commitment—at least "We'll try."

Beyond the verbal commitment to change is the willingness to follow through on action plans. This is demonstrated when families make plans to incorporate quality time, to negotiate family boundaries, to communicate in more emphatic ways, and so forth. Reality therapy requires that family members be willing to try new behaviors, that they rearrange priorities, that they examine and evaluate their expectations of themselves and each other. Family members must develop trust in the therapist because, especially in the early sessions, they will be required to follow suggestions and prescriptions of the therapist.

It is important to note that these family responsibilities cannot be separated from the responsibilities of the counselor. Though therapists cannot *force* the family to accept these responsibilities, they can set an atmosphere and utilize procedures that make it possible and need fulfilling for the family members to make more responsible choices and to accept these responsibilities.

THERAPIST'S ROLE AND FUNCTION

The general work of the therapist is to create an atmosphere conducive to change. Glasser (1996) stated that counselors should attempt to create supportive environments within which clients can begin to make changes in their lives. Wubbolding (1988, 1996c) has described in detail how a reality therapist sets an environment for change. Positive suggestions include assuming an attitude that "we will work things out." This is in no way a guarantee, but it is an attempt to communicate a feeling of hope to the family. Reframing is a paradoxical technique that is used extensively and can be employed in the very beginning of the counseling relationship in order to have clients do the unexpected. The suggestion of Weeks and L'Abate (1982) is quite helpful: When family members first arrive for counseling, they are congratulated for having taken a first step to improve. They have already begun to take action. This is an effort to help them abandon their feeling of weakness and powerlessness and to recognize that they have begun the healing process. This statement is especially engaging for families whose cultural values have prevented them from seeking outside help.

Like any therapist, the reality family therapist utilizes good listening and empathy skills. Especially useful is the ability to hear and use metaphors spoken by the family members and to provide added ones. When the mother of a family said, "I feel like we're in a plane that's on automatic pilot, and I don't know if we're headed up or down," the counselor helped the family members to define their own roles on the plane (copilot, navigator, passenger, or terrorist), as well as to explore how they could get better control of the aircraft by working together. When the family members describe their perceptions of family life, the counselor encourages them to focus on themselves rather than on the others. They are gently encouraged to describe "WDEP" as it applies to them. "WDEP" stands for each member's *Wants*, what members *Do*, the *Evaluations* of their own behavior, and their own *Plans*. The skilled reality therapist combines directness, empathy, and confrontation in a manner that allows openness, frankness, and responsible communication by the family members.

As a result of practicing the above skills, the reality therapist avoids several negative situations. For instance, he or she does not request or become embroiled in excuses when the family members describe their locus of control as being outside themselves. The therapist quickly brings the focus back to the speaker and his or her own behavior. Lengthy arguing among family members is also skirted. It is helpful to listen to the family's story and to assess how the family communicates, at what levels they perceive each other, and how realistic their goals are, but it is fruitless to allow ongoing arguing, blaming, or criticizing. Belittling statements, demeaning remarks, and the wanton expressions of anger are not regarded as helpful, and therefore are discouraged in that they are destructive to the family system. Since animosity is seen as counterproductive, the therapist intervenes to stop its expression by skillfully using the procedures described in the next session.

PRIMARY TECHNIQUES

The most basic skill and overriding technique used in reality family therapy is that of asking relevant questions. In some counseling theories, questions are discouraged, and reflective listening is encouraged, but the skilled practitioner of reality therapy asks many questions pertaining to human choice. Using the WDEP system, he or she questions family members in order to help them identify and clarify their wants and perceptions; to describe the various components of their total behavior; to evaluate their wants, behaviors, and perceptions; and to make individual and common plans to gain control and fulfill their needs.

DETERMINATION OF WANTS, PERCEPTION, LEVEL OF COMMITMENT

(W) The family members are asked what they want to derive from the counseling process. They are asked to define what they want from the family, from each other, from behaviors that are need-fulfilling outside the family. They are helped to express how they view these categories, without criticism of each other. When an inevitable attack begins, the counselor intervenes by directing the conversation to less judgmental descriptions. Practitioners of reality therapy also share their wants and perceptions by describing what they expect from the family and how they see the progress of family growth.

DESCRIPTION OF FOUR COMPONENTS OF BEHAVIOR, WITH EMPHASIS

ON DOING OR ACTING (D) Family members are asked to describe how they spend their time together and individually. The counselor acts as a TV camera viewing exactly what happened on a specific day at a precise time. This narration serves as a self-diagnosis by the family and is a prelude to evaluation and planning.

Frequently, individuals fail to have skills or activities that they perform alone that are effectively need fulfilling. They can be counseled individually or within the family sessions to develop behaviors performed alone that increase their self-esteem. When their self-esteem is elevated, they will benefit more quickly from family counseling.

The heart of this component is the use of quality time (QT), which is introduced early in therapy. This is built on effective behaviors but is strengthened simultaneously with self-esteem—enhancing behaviors that are performed alone by each family member. In other words, the counselor does not work with individuals in the family session *before* dealing with QT. To truly be called QT, the common behavior must have several characteristics:

- Requires effort. Passive behaviors, such as watching TV, do not build close relationships.

- Includes value. The behavior must be seen as important to each person.

- Involves awareness. The participants need *at least* to be aware of others. Preferably, they *need* the other persons, such as when a game is played.

- Is planned for a limited amount of time. It is best to begin with a plan to perform the activity for 10 to 15 minutes a day. If the people involved plan for a lengthy amount of time, they are less likely to follow through.

- Is done repetitively. If the QT is to have a lasting effect, it must be done repeatedly.

- Shuns criticism. This and the following characteristics are the most significant. During this time there should be no put-downs or attacks on the other person. To sustain the behavior, each individual should see it as pleasurable and need fulfilling, not as painful.

- Avoids discussions of past misery. During these precious moments, each person pledges not to bring up past conflicts, past failures, or past pain.

- Complaining is discouraged. Griping about other people creates an inner dissatisfaction and a feeling of smugness that is counterproductive to the goals of the reality therapist.

- Present or past successes are discussed. The conversation need not be phony or shallow. Nevertheless, the dialogue might be artificial at first, for families who are suffering often find it difficult to converse in ways that healthier families find easy.

- Conversation is about WDE (avoids the P). Family members can be taught how to talk to each other using the procedures of reality therapy. Over a period of time, they can learn to ask one another about wants or about how they spend their time. When they become skilled at this, they can then utilize the procedure Evaluation (explained in the next section). Wubbolding (1991) describes a conversation with a niece in which she related to him that she was assigned to read *Beowulf* over the weekend but was not going to do this painful homework. In a lengthy discussion, he asked her what she wanted to do when she graduated and whether or not reading *Beowulf* would help her get where she wanted to go. No attempt was made to push her for a plan. The next evening they spoke again briefly. Before he could say a word to her, she blurted out, "You'll be happy to know I read all my *Beowulf*." It is not always necessary to push for a plan. But it is necessary to remain nonjudgmental and accepting of the other person in order to strengthen the family system.

The marriage and family therapist helps family members increase their quality time so that they can build a storehouse of pleasant memories and perceptions. These eventually will outbalance the painful ones, creating a basis for communicating effectively, solving problems, compromising, dealing with the daily stresses of life, and getting through the inevitable crises faced by every family.

DEVELOPMENT OF SKILL IN EVALUATION (E) The therapist uses six forms of evaluation with a family (Wubbolding, 1990b, 1991). It should be noted that many family members have much difficulty with this procedure. Although the evaluation must ultimately be made and internalized by the family members, it is often futile merely to ask them evaluative questions. Chemically dependent or abusive families, for example, often are unable to make self-evaluations without the direct intervention of the counselor. The evaluations concern the following:

1. Attainability of wants. An adolescent family member may want total freedom: "I want my parents to leave me alone." The counselor helps the person ask himself or herself if this is realistic.

2. Helpfulness of perceptions. When asked how they see the child, parents might say that they see a lazy, rebellious, unkempt, unmanageable child. The therapist helps them examine if this viewpoint is really and truly helping them work out their family problems.

3. Effectiveness of behaviors. There seems to be a trait common to human beings of all cultures. Many people live by the maxim, "If it is not helping, keep doing it." For example, parents shout at their children, a behavior that rarely works for any length of time. If such behavior helped to solve problems, parents could scream once and never again need to repeat the screaming. The very reason parents yell at children is that it does not work. The practitioner of reality therapy acts as a mirror by asking the family to describe their behavior and by asking them, "Is this getting you what you want?"

4. Consequences of overall direction. This is done quickly and is not always distinguishable from 3 above. It is more general and includes such questioning as, "Is the direction and destination of this family a plus or a minus?" "Are you headed in a direction that is beneficial or destructive?" "Are the bonds that exist between you as strong as you want them to be?"

5. Level of commitment. The counselor helps each family member evaluate whether his or her respective levels of commitment to the family and to a positive direction are weak or strong commitments. An effort is made to find a common level of commitment among family members.

6. Efficacy of plans. The goal of the counseling process is to help the family make plans that result in harmonious family living. These plans should be evaluated either explicitly or implicitly. The characteristics of a plan (described next) serve as a basis of this evaluation. Effective planning results in a stronger family system.

FORMULATION OF PLANS (P) The culmination of the process is the formulation and, more importantly, the successful execution of need-fulfilling plans. Plans should be simple, realistic, precise, and firm. They should not be vague or overwhelming to the family system.

IMPORTANCE OF THE WDEP SYSTEM

The WDEP system appears to be simple, and it is indeed easy to understand because it uses clear, down-to-earth terminology. (In other words, the paucity of arcane phraseology has been based on intentionality!) Most of the jargon-free explanations are quite comprehensible to both the lay person and the professional and involve only a few Latin and Greek derivatives. But, like the skills required in a sport, these understandable skills are much more difficult to carry out in practice. The first-year student of chemistry might understand the principles of how various paints interact to form color, but only a skilled painter can then create an artistic work. And very few reach the level of Picasso, Matisse, or Warhol.

Second, the most important aspect of using the WDEP system is not the specifics of each component, but rather the concomitant learning that occurs. Families learn indirectly and as a side effect, that their wants are important, that their opinions and viewpoints are worth listening to, that their behaviors are changeable, that they are not immutably destined for failure and unhappiness, and that they have *the power and the responsibility to change for the better*. These positive and hopeful lessons are learned less by the direct statements of the therapist and more in an indirect, experiential manner. They are the result of skillful questioning by the counselor and the inner evaluations of the family members. Most importantly, the family members learn that they are a system and that systemic change is necessary if need satisfaction is to occur.

CASE EXAMPLE

The following represents part of the initial session of a family of five. Mrs. L. called to set up an appointment because of tension in the family. After she made the appointment, her son, Leon, 11, was struck by a car while walking with his brother, Bart, 13. Leon remains in critical condition in the hospital. The four remaining family members are present for the first session: mother, Wendy, 38; father, Hal, 37; daughter, Ginny, 14; and son, Bart. The segment presented here took place after the professional and ethical details were discussed: informed consent, fees, professional disclosure, limitations of confidentiality, and so forth.

Therapist: Mother, you called saying there is a lot to talk about. You said there was a great deal of turmoil in the family, and in the second call you gave me a summary of the accident and the upset that has resulted. Since you, Mother, made the call, I'd like to ask you first, Dad, what do you think about being here?

Hal: I don't really think it's necessary. We're upset, but I think we just have to handle it.

Wendy: But I made the original call for other reasons. One of them is your apathy toward the rest of us.

Hal: I don't feel that I'm apathetic.

Therapist: I'd like to ask all of you, what do you think about being here today talking with this "outsider"?

Ginny: It's OK, I guess. But I'm afraid.

Therapist: Anyone else?

Bart: It was all my fault. If I'd been paying more attention, my brother would be OK.

Hal: I've told those kids a thousand times to be careful.

Therapist: Before we go any further, I'd like to ask all of you, "What you would like to get out of these discussions, and especially what you want to get from today's session?"

Wendy: I think we better talk about the accident.

Therapist: How about you, Bart?

Bart: Yeah, it was my fault.

Therapist: Ginny, what would you like to have happen here today?

Ginny: I don't know. I'm afraid, but I'd like them to leave me alone at school.

Therapist: So far, all of you expressed some intense feelings—fear, guilt, hesitancy—about being here. We'll come back to how you feel, but first I want to ask you, Dad, "Do you want to discuss this upsetness in your family today?"

Hal: I'm not sure.

Therapist: Let's put it this way. Will your one thousandth and first lecture help solve this current crisis?

Hal: Well, I guess not!

Therapist: Can you be more definite than that? What's your judgment on it?

Hal: No, it won't help us.

Therapist: In other words, now is the time to try something different?

Hal: Yes.

Therapist: Mom, could you repeat your thoughts about being here?

Wendy: I was so upset about the fighting and bickering in the family. Hal either argues with the kids or ignores them completely and now this accident...I don't know how I can take much more.

Therapist: I'd like to ask you to think of the problem as being separate from any person. So it's not, "You are the problem." It's not, "Me against you." Rather, could you think, "It's you and I and all of us against the problem?" (They all agree they will try to think this way.)

Therapist: Do you think that this counseling can relieve some of your burden?

Wendy: I certainly hope so.

Therapist: How about the rest of you? (They all agree that they hope it will.) I hope so, too, because it is evident that you are all hurting in your own ways. Dad, do you feel any pain about this?

Hal: Yes, I sure do. It's hard to admit it, however.

Therapist: I admire you for your honesty. I want to ask you, all of you, a question. Do you want to discuss the tension and problems you had as a family previous to the accident or do you want to talk about the accident and how it has affected you?

All: The accident.

Therapist: That's exactly what I thought. But I wanted to have you define what you wanted to talk about today. We can talk again about the other problems later, OK?

All: (Nod in agreement)

Therapist: Mother, would you describe what happened, please?

Wendy: (Explains in detail how Leon and Bart were in the shopping center and left to come home, crossed the street, and how Leon was hit by a car.)

Therapist: Bart, can you add any details?

Bart: (Describes a few more details) It was all my fault. If I had stopped him, he would not be in the hospital.

Therapist: I've noticed one thing. No one has been blaming you, Bart. When you just now started to cry, your mother put her hand on your shoulder. Your dad wants all of his kids to be careful, but I didn't hear him saying it was your fault.

Hal: You didn't cause it, Bart.

Bart: It's all my fault!!

Therapist: I know you feel that way, Bart, but did you hear what your Dad said?

Bart: What?

Therapist: Dad, say it again, please.

Hal: Bart, no one is blaming you. It's not your fault.

Therapist: Would anyone else like to say anything to Bart?

Wendy: Bart, you didn't cause it.

Ginny: It wasn't your fault. You didn't expect that an accident would happen.

Therapist: Bart, you will feel guilty for a while. It's only natural. I just want you to hear what your family said. I noticed that your mother nodded in agreement. Do you understand what they said even though you don't agree with it?

Bart: Yes.

Therapist: When you hear them say what they just said, do you feel any better?

Bart: Not much.

Therapist: Do you feel any better at all, even a tiny bit?

Bart: A little bit.

Therapist: So, when they give you assurance you feel a little better even now. I'm surprised it has such a good result so quickly. I wonder if anyone else needs a little encouragement once in a while.

Wendy: We all could use it.

Therapist: Could you use it?

Wendy: Yes, I'm really upset. I told them to go to the shopping center. If I hadn't told them to go there, this wouldn't have happened.

Therapist: Does anyone blame Wendy?

Hal: No, it's not her fault.

Therapist: Dad, would you put her hands in yours as you tell her?

Hal: Wendy, you're not to blame. If anyone is to blame, it's me, for not being home enough.

Therapist: So far everyone said they are to blame except you, Ginny. Do you want to join the group?

Ginny: It's his own fault for not watching what he was doing!

Therapist: You sound angry about it.

Ginny: Yeah.

Therapist: Are you also angry, Mom? Dad? Bart?

Hal: You're damned right I am!

Wendy: I'm so upset I can't stand it.

Therapist: How about you, Bart?

Bart: Yeah. I'm plenty mad, mostly at myself.

Therapist: So, there is something that now unites this family. You're all angry, and there is some guilt among most of you about the accident. I want to ask you all a question. I have a hunch that you've been stewing about this. It's been on your mind—the self-recrimination, self-criticism, self-blame has been impossible to get away from. Is that an accurate description?

Wendy: It's been on my mind day and night.

Therapist: You lie awake at night thinking about it?

Wendy: Constantly.

Therapist: Anybody else?

Hal: I'm very distracted at work.

Therapist: Bart, how about you?

Bart: I was too sick to go to school.

Wendy: He's been vomiting and has had diarrhea.

Therapist: So, it's affected you physically. That does not surprise me.

Bart: So that's normal?

Therapist: It doesn't surprise me in the least. You witnessed the whole thing. If you weren't physically sick for a few days I'd be amazed. Ginny, how about you?

Ginny: The other kids keep asking me questions. The teachers want to know what happened. I wish they'd leave me alone. I don't want to talk about it.

Therapist: You want to keep it inside?

Ginny: I wish it would just go away.

Therapist: It would be nice if it would vanish...if you could wake up and find out it was all a nightmare?

Ginny: Yeah.

Therapist: And that's not happened?

Ginny: No, it's worse than ever.

Therapist: Ginny, have you told anyone at school the entire story as you know it?

Ginny: No. I don't want to talk about it.

Therapist: I don't blame you. It's so painful to have everyone pushing their "help" on you.

Ginny: You're right.

Therapist: On the other hand, has it helped you to keep all this bottled up in you? Has refusing to talk about it at school made the problem go away?

Ginny: I guess not.

Therapist: So there's another thing you all have in common. This accident is constantly on your minds. You think about it day and night, at work, at school. It's even affected you physically.

Wendy: We seem to have pain as a common bond.

Hal: (Nodding) Yes, we finally have something we agree on.

Therapist: Since you have pain in common as well as anger, guilt, or whatever you want to call it, would you like to lessen the pain a little bit?

Ginny: Yes…if they would only leave me alone, I'd feel better.

Therapist: Would you be interested in figuring out how to get them to leave you alone?

Ginny: Yes, I would. Can you help me do that?

Therapist: I bet I could, and the rest of the family can help, too. How about you, Bart? Would you want to leave a little piece of your guilt here, not all of it, just a part of it?

Bart: How could I do that?

Therapist: We'll try to figure that out, too. Right now, I'm wondering if you *want* to leave a little pain here when you leave.

Bart: Yes, I sure would!!

Therapist: Mom, Dad, would you like to get away from the upsetness for a few minutes each day or several times each day? You are all going to be miserable for a while. It's quite normal to be upset at a time like this. I'm only asking if you *want* to get away from it for a while?

Hal: It's like carrying a hundred-pound weight around with me. I can't set it down and I can't get away from it.

Therapist: I like how you describe it. Does it seem that way to the rest of you?

Wendy: That's a good way to describe how I feel, too.

Bart: That's it. Maybe more for me.

Therapist: Ginny, how about you? Does it feel like a weight you're carrying around?

Ginny: Yeah. It sure does.

Therapist: It feels like more to you, Bart? I want you to come back to that later. But I still need to ask you, Mother. Do you want to lessen your pain slightly?

Wendy: I sure do. If I could only set the weight down for a while…

Therapist: Is that something you would all like? To set the weight down for a while?

Hal: Does this mean this shouldn't bother us?

Therapist: No. No. No. You will always feel concern, and the weight of pain will be there for a long time. I'm merely asking if you want *some* temporary relief from the agonizing burden for a *short* and *realistic* amount of time.

Hal: I'd love to have that.

Therapist: Anyone else? Would you like to feel better for a while each day?

Bart: Sure!!

Wendy: Me, too. That would be great. Ginny, how about you?

Ginny: Yes, Mom, I'd like to go back to the way it was.

Therapist: Now we have several common bonds in this family. The accident is on your minds day and night, you are in pain about it, and each of you would like to lessen the hurt inside if you could figure out a way, and you agree on the fact that it feels like a hundred-pound weight. So, it's all of us in this room trying to solve a problem, and the problem is not a person, it's a thing! How much have you felt you had in common up to the last week when Leon was hit by the car?

Wendy: I felt we were not a family anymore.

Hal: Was it that bad?

Wendy: Yes, it was that bad.

Therapist: It sounded pretty bad to me. But today you seem to be at a fork in the road in your family life. You can make a decision to work together to help each other to handle this crisis, or you can allow this tragedy to tear your family apart by not working together to help each other. Which will it be?

Hal: Work together.

Wendy: I want to save the family and help Leon.

Ginny: I want to make our family a happy family like some of my friends have.

Bart: Me, too.

Therapist: I believe you can leave some of your pain here. I also believe you can work together to confront this problem and feel better, and help each other through it. It will, however, be necessary to take action and to do some things differently than what you have been doing. Are you willing to commit yourselves to working together with me to go down the road of less pain?

All: Yes, we are.

Therapist: How committed are you? Do you really want to accomplish those goals?

Ginny: I do.

Hal: It's OK with me. When I first came here, I thought you were going to blame me for all the family problems. I was determined you weren't going to point the finger at me. But now I see we're in this together. It really is us against a problem.

Therapist: So, changing a viewpoint can help?

Hal: Yes!

Therapist: I try to avoid doing harmful things or things that prevent progress. Besides, I don't see the problem as being caused by any one person. I see the solutions in such a way that you all could *help* work on them. I don't want to talk forever about the problems. I'd rather stress action aimed at reducing the pain and the stress. So, Dad, how committed are you to taking the road of less pain, joining together, and moving forward?

Hal: Since you put it that way, I'd sure like to do it.

Therapist: Let me help you clarify your want for this important commitment. Is it a "maybe," a "weak whim," or an "I'm going to bust my chops to do it"?

Hal: I'm firmly committed.

Therapist: Bart?

Bart: Yes, I want to work on it.

Therapist: Ginny?

Ginny: Yes, if the kids and teachers...

Therapist: (Interrupting) Let's not worry about them right now. Do you want to work hard at feeling better, regardless of anyone else at school?

Ginny: Sure.

Therapist: Wendy, how about you?

Wendy: I don't know if anything will work very well.

Therapist: Let's put it this way—I'll make an unconditional guarantee.

Hal: (Interrupting) I thought you told us it was unethical to make a guarantee.

Therapist: It is. But this is a different kind of a guarantee. If you work hard, do some things I suggest, make plans and carry them out, and if you don't feel any better, I promise I'll refund all your misery, pain, and guilt.

Hal & Wendy: (Smiling) Sounds like a deal.

Therapist: When you smiled just then, did you feel a tiny bit better?

Hal & Wendy: Yes.

Therapist: We need to work on ways to stretch that microsecond into a minute and then into 15 minutes. I'd like to ask you, Ginny, "Is there anything enjoyable that you've stopped doing at home since the accident?"

Ginny: Not at home. But I am on the girls' basketball team and I have not gone to practice since the accident.

Therapist: Do you feel better now that you've stopped going?

Ginny: Well, I guess I don't.

Therapist: I see. So, giving up basketball hasn't helped you drop part of the hundred-pound burden?

Ginny: (Hesitantly) No, it hasn't.

Therapist: What do the rest of you think? Should she give up her fun?

All: No, she should not give up fun. It won't help anyone.

Therapist: Bart, what do you think would help Ginny drop part of the weight?

Bart: She needs to get out to practice.

Therapist: You don't think she should stay at home, get sick, and feel guilty?

Bart: No.

Therapist: Would you tell that to her directly?

Bart: Why don't you go to practice? It would do you good.

Hal: I don't think it will help you, Bart, to stay home either—unless, of course, you feel physically sick. How do you feel today?

Bart: Better. I can go to school tomorrow.

Therapist: Mom, don't you think Bart should stay at home and feel as bad and as guilty as he could?

Wendy: No. Bart, you're not guilty. You're entitled to your own life at school and your music.

Therapist: You play music?

Bart: I'm in the school orchestra.

Therapist: Have you played anything since the accident last week?

Bart: No.

Therapist: Mom, in your opinion, what effect is this choice not to play having on Bart?

Wendy: It's making him feel worse.

Therapist: Ginny, what do you think?

Ginny: It's making him feel worse.

Therapist: Bart, do you agree?

Bart: I guess so.

Therapist: Ginny, would you like to hear him play his instrument?

Ginny: Yes, sometimes, I like it.

Therapist: Would you ask him to play?

Ginny: Bart, play your instrument. You don't have to give it up.

Bart: I could play for a while.

Therapist: Bart, don't overdo it. Could you play just 10 minutes?

Bart: I usually play a lot more.

Therapist: But for now could you play 10 minutes? Mom, Dad, what do you think about this?

Wendy & Hal: It would be good to hear you play again.

Therapist: Ginny, if you don't go to practice, what will happen?

Ginny: I'll get kicked off the team.

Therapist: Will that help you feel better or worse?

Ginny: Much worse.

Therapist: Dad, what do you think would help her in this situation?

Hal: There is *no* doubt about it. I think she should return to practice.

Therapist: Would you tell her?

Hal: Ginny, could you handle going to practice?

Ginny: Yes, I can.

Hal: I could come to watch your game. I haven't been to one. But this would do me good, too.

Therapist: Wow, you're volunteering to make a good plan. That's terrific. Maybe you could put some of your hurt and guilt aside for a couple of hours during the game.

Hal: I never thought of it that way.

Therapist: Would you think of it now? It's a good way to set aside the upsetness for a while. You can always come back to the hundred-pound weight after the game.

Ginny: Maybe I could drop the burden for a while, too.

Therapist: It's worth a try! Now, Mom, how about you? Do you want to leave some of it aside for a while?

Wendy: You betcha I do!

Therapist: How could you do it?

Wendy: I haven't the slightest idea.

Therapist: Let me ask you some questions. How much time have you been spending at the hospital?

Wendy: When he was in the intensive care unit, I was there 'round the clock. Now I go home to sleep.

Therapist: What effect has that had on you?

Wendy: I'm pretty exhausted. I've even neglected my aerobics.

Hal: That's unusual for you.

Wendy: These are unusual circumstances.

Therapist: Ginny and Bart, what do you think? Should your mother feel guilty if she comes home long enough to do her exercises and maybe a few other things for herself?

Bart: Who'll be there with Leon?

Therapist: About 10 nurses and doctors.

Ginny: I think you're going to get sick if you don't take care of yourself. That's what you always tell Dad and us.

Bart: Yeah, Mom, if you get sick, you'll be in bed like I was.

Therapist: Mom, are these words of wisdom for you? They even sound like your own words of wisdom coming back at you.

Wendy: Yes, I've said them many times.

Therapist: So will it help or hurt if you come home from the hospital for a few more hours?

Hal: The kids and I need you, too.

Wendy: I can't really do much at the hospital. I can get away for a while.

Therapist: This is very interesting. I hear you all wanting to help each other, telling each other to get away from the pain for a while. It sounds like you truly want to be a family and to show your love for each other.

Hal: It's hard for me to admit it, but yes, that's true.

Therapist: Is that how you look at it, Bart?

Bart: Yeah.

Therapist: Ginny?

Ginny: Uh huh.

Therapist: Mother?

Wendy: (Crying) Yes. We need each other and we need to show it.

Therapist: So you've developed some ways to set aside the hundred-pound weight for a short while. I'd like to ask you if you want to leave a small part of it here and go home a little less burdened? What do each of you think about this possibility?

Hal: How would we do this?

Therapist: First, do each of you want to do it if it could be arranged?

Wendy: Yes.

Hal: I would.

Ginny: I'd love to feel better.

Bart: Uh huh.

Therapist: I like to use symbols when I counsel and I encourage clients to do the same. I have here four pieces of paper (holds up four 8 ½ x 11" sheets of paper). Each sheet represents your pain—a hundred pounds of it. Would each of you take a sheet and describe how much of the pain you'll leave here? Tear off whatever portion you'll leave with me. Keep in mind I don't want to have all of it left here. Try to be realistic. Keep your share and take it with you and bring it back next time. Let's start with you, Bart. How much would you like to leave here?

Bart: I'd like to let you have all of it.

Therapist: No, you'll need it for a while. Just give me some.

Bart: How about half?

Therapist: Is that realistic? Can you get rid of half your pain that easily?

Bart: I guess not.

Therapist: How much can you leave here?

Bart: I'll leave 20% (tears off ⅕ page).

Therapist: Sounds good. I'll keep it in the file. What about you, Dad?

Hal: Here's 25% (tears off ¼ page).

Therapist: Ginny?

Ginny: I'll get rid of 10% (tears off ¹⁄₁₀ page).

Therapist: And you, Mother?

Wendy: I'm going to give you 40%. That will still leave me with plenty to bear.

Therapist: OK, I'll keep those in your file. If you want them back, we'll have to discuss in detail your reasons. Remember you still have pain. It is natural and healthy. But now you have just a little less. Also there is one more topic I would like to talk about with you. It is a way to relieve some distress. But as a side effect, it addresses the underlying tension due to the strained relationships—the original reason you scheduled an appointment. Would you be willing to do something together as a family? Something that helps you get away from the strain and pain? (There follows a long discussion of what they could do together. Each person presents his or her ideas. After a while they negotiate to take a 10-minute walk each night after dinner before returning to the hospital.)

Therapist: There are several guidelines that will make this time truly quality time. The most important one is that for these few moments you refrain from talking about the hospital or about any problems...*no* discussion of any past misery, *no* criticism, and *no* lectures.

Hal: What will we discuss?

Wendy: This could be a challenge.

Ginny: We could talk about my team.

Therapist: You've got the right idea—light conversation, *no* controversy. What would you like to talk about, Bart?

Bart: I could talk about school, homework, or music.

Therapist: That's it. Mom and Dad, for the first few nights could you listen and ask questions?

Hal: What good will this do?

Therapist: Tell me. Maybe you already have an idea about it.

Hal: Well, it might help us get away from our usual arguments.

Therapist: Exactly. It will help you build up pleasant memories and perceptions of each other. It will take time. And when you feel like stopping this QT, what do you need to think about?

Wendy: The tension we *used to have.*

Therapist: Yes! Are each of you willing to follow through on this plan?

All: Yes.

Therapist: Let's review what you're going to do and what you did.

Bart: I left some of my pain here today.

Therapist: You sure did!

Wendy: We're going to talk.

Hal: And we're going to listen to the kids without griping.

Therapist: And each of you has an individual plan. Do you all remember it?

All: Yes.

Therapist: We need to work on several areas in the future. I see them as (1) the pain, guilt, and anger because of the accident, and (2) the tension in the family that was there before the accident. So let's get together in one week or sooner, if there is a pressing need on your part.

All: Sounds good.

DISCUSSION OF FIRST SESSION

In the above first session, a distilled summary, the counselor used various aspects of the WDEP system. He helped each family member identify what he or she wanted from the counseling. He helped them discuss their feelings about the accident, but did not discuss these in isolation from their actions. He attempted to tie their feelings to their actions because people have more direct control over what they do than how they feel. The family members were led to make their own evaluations of the effectiveness of their own behaviors and of their attainability. Plans included individual steps to gain a better sense of inner control as well as a family strategy for helping them to function more satisfactorily as a unit. Most importantly, the therapist presented the problem as "out there." In that way the family system can deal with it more effectively and can function as a unit.

SUBSEQUENT SESSIONS

There is definitely a wealth of unfinished business for the family as a unit and for each individual. In the remaining sessions, the counselor would help the family accept the uncontrollable elements of the crisis. He or she would emphasize the use of the family QT as a way to lessen pain and increase favorable perceptions by serving as a basis for solving problems and compromising. Each person would be encouraged to develop plans for QT with each member of the family on a one-to-one basis. They would be encouraged to define what they want from each other and how they see one another. They would be asked to evaluate how they can work as a unit, provide mutual support, and use the current crisis to draw closer together. They would be encouraged to make plans to continue the closeness after the crisis has passed. The counselor would teach directly by explanations and indirectly by skillful questioning, illustrating that more effective communication can occur when they clearly converse by saying, "I want..."; "This is how I look at the situation..."; "Does this behavior help?"; "Let's make a plan." Family members would thus have alternatives to lectures, criticism, belittling, arguing, attacking and withdrawing from each other. In summary, the reality therapist uses the WDEP system with the family and teaches members to use it.

SPECIAL APPLICATIONS

The principles described in the case are applicable to special and diverse populations. The *content* of family issues is very diverse in single-parent families, minority families, families with issues such as chemical dependency, extended families, and so forth, but the *process* of reality therapy can be used with positive results. The therapist helps the family unite to solve the problem, which does not reside in a person. Members are asked to clarify their wants, to describe their behaviors, and to evaluate both their wants and their total behaviors. They are taught specific behaviors, such as how to communicate more empathically, and they are led to formulate need-satisfying plans. The WDEP system is thus a process that touches human nature at its core.

EVALUATION

Reality therapy is based on the principle that people are responsible for their behavior and that most behaviors are chosen. Some have, therefore, mistakenly seen this theory as superficial. The reverse is more accurate. Choice and degree of responsibility are never simple, and it would be a mistake to say that "choice" has exactly the same meaning for all behaviors. The theory and practice of reality therapy is an evolving system with new insights continuously emerging. For instance, in years to come, I hope to develop a more detailed taxonomy for levels of freedom subsumed under the phenomenon of human choice.

The practice of reality therapy has spread from its origin in corrections and a mental hospital to schools. Glasser (1968, 1988, 1990) has formulated ways to use it in classrooms, for drug abuse prevention, and for restructuring school itself. Wubbolding (1988, 1996b) has applied it to management and supervision as well as to self-help and probation. The ideas are universally applicable and have been taught in North America, Europe, and Asia. They aid in crossing cultures and, with skillful adjustments, not only can be used with the so-called "direct" cultures of the West, but they are quite adaptable to the "indirect" cultures of the East.

To become skillful in the use of the principles, the practitioner must recognize that endless discussion of feelings is not equivalent to dealing with them. Rather, they are treated successfully when clients change what they do. Also, the practitioner emphasizes present behavior rather than personal history, which is often interesting but beyond the current control of the family. Questioning skills are important and are appropriately used not to interrogate, but indirectly to teach and help clients develop an in-control, responsible, and need-fulfilling life style in which they live harmoniously with others. To achieve this end, the 18-month training program described earlier has been developed by the William Glasser Institute.

More information on these and other training programs can be obtained from this author at the Center for Reality Therapy, 7672 Montgomery Road, Cincinnati, Ohio 45236, phone (513) 561-1911 or fax (513) 561-3568; or, the William Glasser Institute, 22024 Lassen Street, Suite 18, Chatsworth, California 91311 phone: (818) 700-8000, fax (818) 700-0555.

RESEARCH

Among the studies showing the effectiveness of reality therapy are those related to addictions, juvenile delinquency, and self-esteem enhancement. Wubbolding (1989b) showed how it can be used in relating to a family facing nursing home decisions. It has also been researched with related family issues, but the unquestionable effectiveness from a scientific point of view still needs to be demonstrated. It has been used in family counseling, and trained practitioners testify to its usefulness. There is a wealth of research that still should be conducted to validate reality therapy as it applies to families.

SUMMARY

The proponents of reality therapy accept choice theory as a basis for the practice of reality therapy. This theory has not been discussed to any great extent in the educational, counseling, or psychological literature. Its origins are more rooted in the engineering and computer tradition. Norbert Wiener, author of *Cybernetics* (1948), was a mathematician. William Powers, a computer consultant, wrote

Behavior: The Control of Perception (1973), which has served as the basis for Glasser's efforts to ground the practice of reality therapy in solid theory.

Choice system theory teaches that human behavior is generated by inner drives that move us forward to gain what we want. We seek to mold the external world around us to match what we perceive as want and need fulfilling. The human needs are belonging, power or achievement, fun or enjoyment, freedom or independence, and survival.

Although these needs are general and universal, the wants related to them are specific and unique to each individual. In order to gain the perception of having needs met, human beings generate behaviors—acting, thinking, feeling, and physiological sensations. Consequently, behavior is *not* the result of external stimuli received from the environment, nor is it an attempt to resolve unconscious conflicts. Rather, each choice is quite purposeful and has the aim of want and need fulfillment. Thus, the practitioner of reality therapy sees acting out, depression, even psychosis and psychosomatic pain as ineffectual attempts to meet needs. These negative symptoms are a person's and a family's best attempt to fulfill wants and needs at a given moment. The counselor's work is designed to help them identify the underlying unmet wants and needs, and with appropriate questions to formulate strategies for more efficient want and need attainment.

The service delivery system, called the cycle of counseling (Wubbolding, 1996a), is made up of two general activities: (1) establishing a friendly and firm environment and (2) utilizing the procedures summarized in the WDEP system. The latter consists in helping the family members identify what they want as individuals and as a family, what they are getting, what they are not getting, how they perceive their locus of control, and how committed they are to the process of change. Family counselors using reality therapy also share their own wants and perceptions with the family in noncritical ways. Families are helped to examine what they are doing. Thus, behavioral symptoms composed of the acting component, the thinking aspect, the emotional or feeling side of behavior, and even physiological symptoms are discussed in detail, depending on each case. Individuals and families are then helped to evaluate their lives in general and in detail—the attainability of wants, effectiveness of behavior, and so forth. Finally, specific plans are built on these crucial evaluations.

As a result, families learn that they can change, that there is hope, and that they are not imprisoned in past misery. These lessons, learned by means of questioning, are most effectively taught if the therapist does not focus on direct teaching. Reality therapy is practical, easily understood, but hard to do. Nevertheless, its principles can be learned by families and used to resolve current and future problems.

ANNOTATED SUGGESTED READINGS

Ford, E., & Englund, S. (1979). *Permanent love: Practical steps to a lasting relationship*. Scottsdale, AZ: Brandt.

    A book written on building relationships between couples, but the ideas are also applicable to parent–child and friend–friend interactions.

Glasser, W. (1965) *Reality therapy*. New York: HarperCollins.

    The first significant book on reality therapy. The applications of the method in a mental hospital and in a correctional institution are discussed, stressing that change in human behavior occurs when people are held responsible and treated humanely.

Glasser, W. (1986), *Control theory*. New York: HarperCollins.
A book summarizing the brain as an input control system and how this system relates to clinical practice.

Glasser, W. (1995), *Staying together*. New York: HarperCollins.
Useful ideas on building relationships. Couples wishing to enhance their perceptions of each other and connect with each other have found the needs profile useful.

Wubbolding, R. (1988). *Using reality therapy*. New York: HarperCollins.
A thorough, practical book on how to use reality therapy. It contains specific questions on how to apply the principles and how to integrate paradoxical techniques into the practice of reality therapy.

Wubbolding, R. (1991). *Understanding reality therapy*. New York: HarperCollins.
An explanation of control theory and reality therapy through the use of metaphors. It includes a discussion of the WDEP system with specific applications.

REFERENCES

Antonius, Marcus (Aurelius). (1994). In A. Farquharson (Ed.), *The meditations of Marcus Antonius*. London: Oxford University Press.

Bluestein, J., & Collins, L. (1985). *Parents in a pressure cooker*. Albuquerque: I.S.S.

Deming, W. (1982). *Out of the crisis*. Cambridge, MA: MIT Center for Advanced Engineering Study.

Edelwich, J. (1980). *Burn-out*. New York: Herman Scievers.

Ford, E. (1974). *Why marriage*. Niles, IL: Argus.

Ford, E. (1977). *For the love of children*. New York: Doubleday.

Ford, E. (1982). Reality therapy. In A. Horne (Ed.), *Family counseling and therapy*. Itasca, IL: F. E. Peacock.

Ford, E. (1983). *Choosing to love*. Minneapolis: Winston.

Ford, E., & Englund, S. (1979). *Permanent love: Practical steps to a lasting relationship*. Minneapolis: Winston.

Glasser, N. (Ed.). (1980). *What are you doing?* New York: HarperCollins

Glasser, N. (Ed.). (1989). *Control theory in the practice of reality therapy*. New York: HarperCollins.

Glasser, W. (1961). *Mental health or mental illness?* New York: HarperCollins

Glasser, W. (1965). *Reality therapy*. New York: HarperCollins.

Glasser, W. (1968). *Schools without failure*. New York: HarperCollins.

Glasser, W. (1972). *Identity society*. New York: HarperCollins.

Glasser, W. (1976). *Positive addiction*. New York: HarperCollins.

Glasser, W. (1980). *Both-win management*. Los Angeles: Institute for Reality Therapy.

Glasser, W. (1981). *Stations of the mind*. New York: HarperCollins.

Glasser, W. (1984). Reality therapy. In R. Corsini (Ed.), *Current psychotherapies* (3rd ed.). Itasca, IL: F. E. Peacock.

Glasser, W. (1985). *Control theory*. New York: HarperCollins.

Glasser, W. (1986). *The basic concepts of reality therapy*. Los Angeles: The William Glasser Institute.

Glasser, W. (1988). *Choice drug prevention programs*. Los Angeles: The William Glasser Institute.

Glasser, W. (1990). *The quality school*. New York: HarperCollins.

Glasser W. (1992). *The quality school teacher*. New York: HarperCollins.

Glasser, W. (1995). *Staying together*. New York: HarperCollins.

Glasser, W. (1996, Summer). *The William Glasser Institute Newsletter*. Los Angeles: The William Glasser Institute.

Glasser, W. (1998). *Choice theory*. New York: HarperCollins.

Glasser, W., & Wubbolding, R. (1995). Reality therapy. In R. Corsini (Ed.), *Current psychotherapies* (5th ed.). Itasca, IL: F. E. Peacock.

Glasser, W., & Zunin, L. (1973). Reality therapy. In R. Corsini (Ed.), *Current psychotherapies* (2nd ed.). Itasca, IL: F. E. Peacock.

Kaiser, H. (1955). The problems of responsibility in psychotherapy. *Psychiatry, 18*, 205–211.

Mickel, E. (1994). Control theory and the African-centered perspective for quality management. *Journal of Reality Therapy, 14*, 49–58.

Mickel, E. (1995). Andragogy and control theory: Theoretical foundation for family mediation. *Journal of Reality Therapy, 14*, 2, 55–62.

O'Donnell, D. (1987). History of the growth of the Institute for Reality Therapy. *Journal of Reality Therapy, 2*, 2–8.

Powers, W. (1973). *Behavior, the control of perception*. New York: Aldine.

Weeks, G., & L'Abate, L. (1982). *Paradoxical psychotherapy*. New York: Brunner/Mazel.

Wiener, N. (1948). *Cybernetics*. New York: John T. Wiley.

Wiener, N. (1950). *The human uses of human beings, cybernetics & society*. Boston: Houghton, Mifflin.

Wubbolding, R. (1979). Reality therapy as an antidote to burnout. *American Mental Health Counselors Association Journal, I*, 39–43.

Wubbolding, R. (1985b). Reality management: Getting results. *Landmark, II*, 6–7.

Wubbolding, R. (1988). *Using reality therapy*. New York: HarperCollins.

Wubbolding, R. (1989b). Pictures in conflict. In N. Glasser (Ed.), *Control theory in the practice of reality therapy*. New York: HarperCollins.

Wubbolding, R. (1990b). *Evaluation*. Cincinnati, OH: Center for Reality Therapy.

Wubbolding, R. (1991). *Understanding reality therapy*. New York: HarperCollins.

Wubbolding, R. (1996a). *Cycle of counseling* (10th rev.). Cincinnati, OH: Center for Reality Therapy.

Wubbolding, R. (1996b). *Employee motivation: What to do when what you say isn't working.* Knoxville, TN: SPC Press.

Wubbolding, R. (1996c). Reality therapy: Theoretical underpinnings and implementation in practice. *Directions in Mental Health Counseling, 6*, 9, 9:3–9:17.

Wubbolding, R. (1996d). *Reality therapy training* (10th rev.). Cincinnati, OH: Center for Reality Therapy.

CHAPTER 15

Behavioral Approaches to Couple and Family Therapy

**ARTHUR M. HORNE AND
THOMAS V. SAYGER**

DEFINITION

Behavior therapy is often presented as the Second Force in psychology, with the First Force being psychoanalytic and psychodynamic therapy, and the Third Force being humanistic approaches to therapy (Nichols, 1996). The First Force places emphasis on the intrapersonal dynamics taking place within the individual as a function of biological, developmental, and parental/caretaker circumstances. The emphasis of the Third Force is on understanding the innate potential of all individuals and providing an environment in which that potential can be achieved. The behavioral approach, on the other hand, places an emphasis on behavior, though there is attention paid to affect and cognitive processes. Behavior therapy addresses the mental processes of the individual, but focuses more on the cognitions rather than the unconscious process attended to by the psychodynamic approaches. Behavior therapy has as a basic premise that *behavior is maintained by its consequences.*

Social learning is a result of the process of people learning how to relate interpersonally—literally, learning from social contacts or learning from people. It refers to learning that takes place within a social environment as one person observes, reacts to, and interacts with other people; in short, social learning is an education in human relations. People do not develop in isolation, but rather they are born into a social system, and no one is exempt from this learning experience. Within such a social matrix, children learn ways of behaving—behavior patterns—by receiving support for some ways of interacting and criticism or punishment for others. For most, this selective social exchange results in the establishment of positive ways of being in a family. A corollary can also be stated: Without the opportunity of learning to perform in a particular manner, the individual will not develop social skills in a specific area. A social-learning family treatment approach, then, attempts to provide an environment in which effective learning in the social sphere may occur: Maladaptive ways of interacting are diminished and interactional alternatives are expanded, so that families and couples may establish more effective and satisfying methods of dealing with the problems of living in close human relationships. This learning occurs in a systematic teaching-modeling-experiencing program that emphasizes learning procedures derived from psychology and related behavioral sciences.

A basic premise of social-learning family therapy is that how we behave, interact, and relate to others is learned within the family context. If those ways of behaving, interacting, and relating are fulfilling and provide the family members with satisfaction and pleasure, individuals do not seek therapy. However, when dysfunctional or unsatisfactory patterns of interaction are evident, the therapy is called for in order to learn more effective relationship and problem-solving skills.

In recent years, behavior therapy has begun to address issues of the more traditional therapies, such as the therapeutic alliance, the role of empathy in relationship development, and the problem of resistance, as well as other mainstream therapy issues. Still, the core of behavior therapy is the focus on understanding the role of behavior in the lives of people presenting for therapy.

Social-learning family theory began with the clinical application of principles derived from behaviorally oriented learning theories. Since its beginnings, social-learning theory has expanded to include elements from experimental, cognitive, and social psychology, and more recently from the broader literature of family therapy research. Whereas behavior therapy in general, and social learning in specific, began as an application of techniques derived from learning theory to the modification of discrete behavioral problems, in its evolution as a treatment discipline it has developed into a more general set of principles applicable to a wide variety of human problems. However, rather than being a series of techniques, behavior therapy is a method of inquiry for understanding and analyzing problems, for developing interventions for use within the family context, and for evaluating the effectiveness of therapy that transcends specific techniques. In its broadest sense, then, social-learning family therapy is not simply a series of techniques for treating families, but is a systematic method of understanding, working with, and evaluating change associated with families.

HISTORICAL DEVELOPMENT

Behavioral approaches to addressing human problems have been in use for several decades, and go by a number of titles: Behavior therapy, behavior modification, behavior change theory, and social learning are often used interchangeably. Behavior modification, and later behavior therapy, preceded social learning and were more restricted in both principles and applications. Behavior modification/therapy developed primarily from laboratory studies in experimental psychology, with later applications to real-life problems of people with a focus on changing specific dysfunctional behaviors. Early examples of behavior therapy applications included working with institutionalized patients, school children, and incarcerated youth. Social learning evolved from roots in behavior therapy, but has expanded upon the earlier applications—which were primarily limited to settings providing for tight control over environmental factors related to individuals, as with a child having tantrum problems in a classroom, or specific groups under treatment scrutiny, as with incarcerated adolescents in an institution that has control over reinforcers such as access to television, recreation, or even articles of clothing. Social-learning family therapy, in the last two decades, has become broader in scope and more relevant to addressing problems of living in families than the earlier behavior modification approaches. Thus, social-learning applications to family treatment are fairly recent, developing primarily since the 1970s. In part, this increased interest in family applications resulted from studies that demonstrated that a social-learning approach may be effective with a variety of populations and in diversified settings, including families (Bandura, 1969, 1986; Falloon, 1988; Horne & Sayger, 1990; Patterson, 1982; Patterson, Chamberlain, & Reid, 1982; Spiegler & Guevremont, 1998).

Whereas many models of family therapy point to a charismatic leader who forged a new approach to working with families, social-learning family therapy was developed more by a number of counselors, psychologists, and social workers interested in applications of learning principles to problems that families experienced. Early applications of behavior modification were primarily single-case studies, usually focusing upon the treatment of the disturbing behavior of a child and often involving training parents in effective methods of changing the dysfunctional behavior. Williams (1959), for example, used the learning principle of extinction (i.e., a behavior that is not reinforced tends to diminish or be extinguished) to teach parents to ignore the tantrums of a child protesting going to bed. Parents were taught to be firm, affectionate, and to ignore the child's protests. Lovibond (1963) taught parents to treat nocturnal enuresis—bedwetting—using a bell and pad system, and Risley and Wolf (1967) taught parents of autistic children methods of reinforcing speech patterns. In each case, the therapist served as a coach or expert advisor teaching parents methods of changing children's behavior. While these early attempts at helping families were often effective for addressing specific problems, they were not family therapy; for the focus was a target child—not the family—and the therapist failed to examine the interactional effects of the family members in establishing and maintaining the dysfunction, as well as the role the dysfunction may have played in the family.

The early attempts at intervention, while not family-therapy focused, were beneficial in establishing an approach to working with families that has remained a cornerstone of the model: developing observable and measurable definitions of presenting concerns, establishing methods of evaluating the impact of interventions, and an ongoing examination of the effectiveness of treatments being examined. While early studies were often simplistic, with simple counts of targeted behaviors (tantrums, for example), they led the way to today's more sophisticated and elaborate attempts to evaluate family dynamics and therapy efficacy. The research/empirical approach to working with families has provided social-learning family therapists with both clinical guidance as they use their observations and evaluations for understanding problem areas and developing interventions, as well as a means for examining the impact of change in family therapy. In an age of managed care and external evaluations of therapy efficacy, such documentation of program integrity and impact has become exceedingly important.

As behavior therapy approaches to working with children and families developed in the 1960s and 1970s there were three primary focal points that emerged: treatment of children in the family context (parent training), marital therapy, and sex therapy.

PARENT TRAINING

Gerald Patterson is identified as the person most associated with the development of social-learning treatment programs that address the treatment of problems of children in the family context. Since 1965, families with child-management and family relationship problems have been studied by therapists interested in examining effective change for the families. Patterson's project initially pursued a series of case studies for the purpose of developing a treatment methodology based upon social-learning principles, including training parents and others in the child's environment to act as agents of change. Early treatments included the use of rewards such as candy, but quickly moved toward using basic point systems, modeling, time-out, and contingent attention (Patterson & Brodsky, 1966). In the course of the project's development, a definite shift was made from the psychology lab to the natural environment in order to observe family patterns in a more realistic setting.

The process of working with these families included collecting data on child and parent behaviors and on interactions recorded by trained observers within the home setting. After observations were completed, parents were offered instruction in effective child management and relationship procedures. This was followed by additional observations in the home so that posttreatment analyses of change could be conducted. A score was derived from these analyses that identified the total number of inappropriate behaviors the individual child engaged in while being observed: the total deviant behavior score. The treatment results of this stage of family counseling research yielded a 60% to 75% reduction of inappropriate behavior from baseline to termination, with an average of 22.8 hours of professional time required per family (Patterson, Cobb, & Ray, 1973).

In addition to child problems that Patterson was treating within the family context, in-school behavior was also often a problem (Patterson & Brodsky, 1966), and so classroom procedures were developed based on social-learning theory using peers and teachers as change agents. This involved instructing teachers in the use of point systems and time-out, and the use of child-peer groups via providing peers with additional recess time when the identified child behaved more appropriately in class. Resultant changes in the child were achieved with little cost to the teacher and persisted through follow-up (Patterson, Reid, Jones, & Conger, 1975). However, as is evident from the focus on reduction of inappropriate behavior in a targeted child, treatment was primarily individualistically oriented (teach parents or teacher to change the child), and there was little attention to the interactional dynamics among the family or the role that misbehavior may have been exerting in influencing the interactional patterns of family or class members. While there was discussion of family dynamics and family structure within the clinical staffings, the literature describing the work reported only behavioral change related to the targeted child.

In 1968, Patterson initiated a new study with extremely aggressive, out-of-control boys. The children were from lower socioeconomic classes, eight from father-absent homes, and five with diagnoses of minimal brain damage and being treated with medication. Details of the procedures used were first presented by Patterson, Cobb, and Ray (1973, pp. 139–224), and later elaborated in a manual aimed at the working clinician, *A Social Learning Approach to Family Treatment* (Patterson, Reid, Jones, & Conger, 1975). During this time, the treatment procedures were refined and became more standardized. Programmed materials were given to parents, who were then tested on the materials. Before moving on to advanced-level work, parents were required to demonstrate mastery of the material presented at each level.

In the previous work, therapists working with Patterson had attempted to alter only one or two behaviors, but in the next phase of treatment they began to work with a large number of parent and child conflicts. Treatment generally encompassed all of the child's inappropriate behaviors that were of concern to the parents and referring agent. An average of 31.5 professional hours was required to produce changes in home-observed problem behaviors, and approximately two-thirds of the treated children evidenced reductions of at least 30% in their output of aggressive behavior as measured by home observations. In addition, parents provided daily reports on the occurrence of symptoms of primary concern to them. These data also showed significant reductions from a level of 63% reported at baseline to 33% reported at termination. One year of follow-up data showed persistence of the effects along both measurement dimensions. In many cases, however, brief booster treatments involving additional counseling were necessary.

In this initial work the client population did not suffer from the 56% to 70% attrition rates experienced with more traditional treatment (Overall & Aronson, 1963). Given demographic and clinical characteristics of the sample, the treatment's lower attrition and higher effectiveness were particularly encouraging. In terms of referral categories, behavior-problem and out-of-control youngsters had typically been less successful clients than their withdrawn or neurotic peers (Levitt, 1971; Robins, 1966), and in terms of client socioeconomic status, low-socioeconomic-status families were the most likely to drop out of more traditional types of treatment shortly after intake (Overall & Aronson, 1963). Family socioeconomic status and single parenthood did have an impact on treatment for the study as well as in a replication study (Fleischman, 1976), demonstrating that impoverished families and those with single mothers are more difficult to treat, require longer treatment times, and comprise a greater proportion of the failures. Generally, however, the data suggested that such families are amenable to a social learning approach.

In reviewing the phases of work completed through 1975, Patterson, Reid, Jones, and Conger (1975) found the social-learning treatment to be effective for reducing problem behaviors of the child identified as the problem in the family, and treatment also had generalized to other family members, including siblings. Further, parents began to see their child's behavior as more positive, and parents became more effective at providing positive consequences for appropriate behavior and negative consequences for acting out behaviors. Overall, mothers seemed more satisfied with their children and rated the family as happier, and fathers developed a more influential role in the family by controlling coercive actions of the child. While the focus had been on a targeted child, overall improvement in family satisfaction and happiness occurred.

At this point, it was tentatively concluded that a social-learning treatment program had been developed that alleviated some concerns of behavioral approaches to parenting. Generalization and maintenance were demonstrated, and in two control group studies—one involving assignment to a waiting period equal to the average treatment duration (Wiltz & Patterson, 1974) and the other to a placebo treatment (Walter & Gilmore, 1973)—neither of these control groups showed any reduction in their total deviant behavior.

Treatment had concentrated primarily on children who engaged in low-rate behaviors such as stealing and fire-setting (Reid & Patterson, 1976), so in 1972 Patterson began working with families who had a child who was a high-rate stealer. Family-training procedures were expanded to address these behaviors, and additional criterion measures for success of treatment were developed, including court and arrest records, as well as family support.

Parents of stealers were taught general child-management procedures for such actions as common tantrums and noncompliance. Therapists also taught parents to attend to even the mildest forms of stealing, such as unexplained borrowing or finding. When parents learned to monitor their children and to provide behavioral consequences for their mild stealing behaviors without being overly concerned about having total proof, even the low-rate behaviors became amenable to treatment. Patterson (1982) found in studying court records that misbehaving, socially aggressive children treated with a social-learning approach had almost zero police records over a two-year period, but children who were stealers presented a different picture. Approximately 30% of children who had a high offense rate for stealing and were engaged in treatment continued to steal. This rate of stealing was discouraging, but compared favorably with the 80% offense rate of stealers in an untreated control group (Patterson, 1982).

Patterson and his Oregon Social Learning Center group continue to provide leadership in research and development of interventions with families with child behavior problems. His ground-breaking research has led to a number of applications, and numerous programs have been developed to continue examining the efficacy of social-learning family therapy. Several of these are described later in this chapter.

MARITAL THERAPY

In the mid to late 1960s, a number of behavioral treatment systems were developed in the area of marriage and family therapy. Robert Weiss, in his Oregon Marital

Studies Program, was a leader in behavioral research and practice with couples. His research began in the late 1960s and has consistently led the way in assessment and evaluation of couples treatment. The Oregon Marital Studies Program produced a 10-session comprehensive program involving behavioral assessment and laboratory training for relationship skills of couples, and has maintained ongoing evaluation to examine the effectiveness of the program (Weiss, 1978).

Another behavioral treatment system for marital problems was developed in the 1960s and 1970s by Richard Stuart (1980). It, too, was based on exchange theory and was action-oriented. Its goal was smooth and efficient behavioral changes for couples. Stuart emphasized helping couples learn a "quid pro quo" approach to working with each other. "I'll do something positive for you and you do something positive for me" ("You scratch my back; I'll scratch yours"). In order to facilitate these changes, Stuart applied several steps, which included having each member of the couple make a commitment to change, have a reason to make the changes, initiate change in his or her own behavior before expecting change from the partner, record steps taken in the change process, and contract with the partner for a series of exchanges of positive or desired experiences (quid pro quo). Early in his work, Stuart used an exchange of tokens to keep track of the "bank account" to be certain that each member of the couple was giving and receiving at about equal rates. The bank account theory also provided for one member of the dyad to build up a reserve that could be used later, by banking the tokens. Stuart eventually dropped the token economy and moved toward written contracts that spouses would complete and share with each other.

Stuart has identified five intervention strategies that he advocates teaching couples:

1. To express themselves in clear, behavioral description rather than using vague and critical complaints.

2. To use positive exchange procedures rather than aversive control.

3. To develop better communication skills.

4. To create methods of sharing power and responsibility in the dyad.

5. To develop problem-solving skills that may be applied to future problems.

Robert Liberman (1970) was another of the earlier writers describing the application of behavioral methodology to the treatment of marital discord. He conducted behavioral analyses of couples coming for therapy and designed the interventions based upon his evaluations of deficits in their marital relationship. He taught the couples contingency management, a process whereby each member agreed to do something for the other in return for receiving a positive, reinforcing experience. He also taught the elements of positive communication through assisting each member of the couple to identify both problem behaviors and life goals they were willing to share with their spouse. Liberman maintained authority in the therapy and indicated that responsibility for treatment was the therapist's, and that the therapeutic interventions would be determined by an ongoing behavioral analysis, providing the therapist with information to revise and redirect treatment.

Liberman was not as detailed in his observational approach to marital work as Patterson was in working with families and children. Indeed, Liberman relied heavily upon self-reporting from the couples. His therapeutic interventions emanated from his interviewing and observations of the members of the couple, and he determined that failure to improve, as measured by his ongoing behavioral analyses, was a result of poor development and application of hypotheses based upon learning theory.

Weiss, Stuart, and Liberman shared a common grounding in social exchange theory, particularly the work of Thibault and Kelly (1959). Though they developed different approaches to marital therapy, they still shared a common grounding in theory and thus were very similar in approach. In fact, they freely borrowed and adopted techniques from one another. Social exchange theory was applied to assist couples to understand how they could replace dysfunctional and unfulfilling interactions with more rewarding and enjoyable relationships. Reciprocity—engaging in positive interactions that would result in receiving positive interactions back—was emphasized, and coercion, or the use of power or force to make the partner do what was wanted was reduced or eliminated.

During the 1970s and 1980s there was an increased emphasis on the teaching of communications skills to couples, with an awareness from the research of the time that a major difference between functional and dysfunctional couples was their communication style. There was considerable carryover from development of other behavioral interventions of the time, including assertiveness training, social skills training, and problem solving/conflict resolution methods.

Also in the 1970s and 1980s, further refinements occurred in both the practice and evaluation of social-learning couples therapy. With treatment interventions specifically oriented toward presenting problems of couples, and with clearly defined measures of efficacy, the behavioral approach to marital/couples therapy was identified as a therapy of choice (Baucom & Hoffman, 1986). Social-learning couples therapy continues to be refined and evaluated today, and it holds promise for continuing to provide an approach that is open to examination and continued development.

SEX THERAPY

Many would argue that sex therapy does not belong in a discussion of social-learning family therapy. Sex therapy did not originate from a theory of learning or the application of psychological principles, but rather from experimentation and a teaching model developed by Masters and Johnson. Also, within a family context, sexual dysfunction is often perceived as symptomatic of relationship problems and does not warrant discussion separately from the relational components. Finally, attempted treatment of some sexual dysfunctions through psychological interventions or family therapy has proven to be unsuccessful, and the dysfunctions are now recognized as physiological/medical problems, not relational or learning ones. Still, a number of areas of sexual dysfunctioning have been very amenable to social-learning therapy interventions, and there has been extensive therapy development and research that has had an important impact on the treatment of sexual dysfunctioning.

Masters and Johnson (1970) reported that many areas of sexual dysfunctioning could be addressed in a relatively straightforward manner that involved having patients learn more effective ways of performing sexually as well as ways of mastering anxiety related to sexual performance. They developed a program that entailed having patients participate in a two-week residential treatment that provided the opportunity for an extensive assessment of problems, a complete physical examination, development of a sexual history, and the development of a sexuality training program specifically individualized for the concerns of the couple. The couple would come for daily instruction and discussions about sexual activity, and then would practice, based on materials presented, outside the therapy session.

A central point of their therapy included teaching sensate focus, a process whereby patients were taught to learn to explore their own and their partner's bodies to discover more about sensate areas, but without any pressure for sexual performance or orgasm. The goal was to allow patients the opportunity of learning and exploring without the usual expectation that sexual activity would follow. This reduction of performance pressure resulted in lowered anxiety and fear of failure. The partners removed themselves from worrying about performing and being evaluated, to fully experiencing the giving and receiving of pleasure. The treatment program provided opportunities to learn more satisfying sexual responding by providing sex education, communication skills enhancement, a focus on behavioral change, and new ways of thinking about sexual activity.

Kaplan (1974) extended the work of Masters and Johnson by identifying three areas of direction for treatment: the importance of understanding individual and couple causes for sexuality problems, such as fear of failure, lack of knowledge about sexuality, and poor communication; understanding intrapsychic or early sexually traumatic events that may have influenced attitudes and beliefs about sexuality; and recognizing relationship issues that may be impeding a satisfying sexual relationship. While Kaplan continued and extended the behavioral intervention process through providing sex education, specific exercises, and sensate focus work, she also began providing a better understanding of the impact of relationships and intimacy on couples' sexual activity. She incorporated into her treatment program behavioral interventions, such as desensitization, relaxation training, and communications skills, as well as a broader approach to family therapy that included understanding the role that symptomatic behavior—sexual dysfunctioning—may play in the family system.

More recently, sex therapists have expanded upon and extended the work of earlier researchers. LoPiccolo (1977a, 1977b, 1980), for example, indicated that sex education, communications training and cognitive reframing or restructuring about sexual beliefs, and specific training in sexual technique are core elements of a behavioral approach to sex therapy. As increased sophistication of knowledge about the treatment of sexual concerns has developed, there has been a corresponding emphasis on the role of more than just the individual, and family dynamics and interactions—family systems—are an integral part of treating sexual dysfunctioning from a social-learning family therapy model.

TENETS OF THE MODEL

Social-learning family therapy focuses on understanding that how people are—how they behave and interact—is learned, is maintained, and may be changed by the interaction of the person, the behavior of the person and others, and the environment in which the person lives. Intrapersonal, behavioral, and environmental factors, then, are seen as core influences in development. The interactional pattern

FIGURE 15.1 | **INTERACTIONAL PATTERN OF FACTORS**

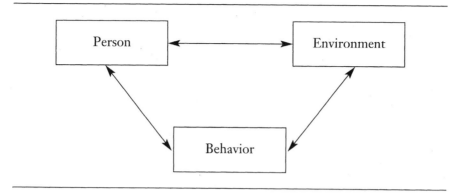

of these three factors is demonstrated in Figure 15.1; illustrating that each of the factors influences, and is influenced by, the others.

A further refinement of the interactive elements that contribute to the development of conduct problems and delinquency in children has been described by Horne, Norsworthy, and Forehand (1990) and is presented in Figure 15.2.

INTRAPERSONAL FACTORS

There are a number of intrapersonal factors that influence our development. Some factors are genetic and biological characteristics that influence how we develop. Temperament, mental ability, ethnicity, physical characteristics, and susceptibility for disease are all examples of how biological attributes may contribute to shaping and influencing our lives. We have experienced families that begin describing problems they have encountered with their children by saying "He was born that way and always has been that way," and they are likely to be accurate in their descriptions. While we don't believe that temperament or other factors predetermine a child to a particular way of behaving, the propensity is there to be influenced by other factors. Crosbie-Burnett and Lewis (1993) indicate that some of these characteristics are relatively permanent (genetic predisposition), while others change with time (physical attributes) and still others change rapidly (emotional states).

Beyond genetic and physical characteristics, other intrapersonal features influence our lives. Areas that have been examined from a social-learning orientation have included locus of control, self-efficacy, affective state, and attributions and beliefs. Of particular importance is the cognitive processing people engage in to "make sense" of their world. Not all people experience situations in the same way; for each person there are unique meanings to each situation experienced. Each person interprets the behavior of others and environmental influences differently, and how one perceives his or her level of likelihood for success or achievement, the outcome of situations, and beliefs about other people determines his or her "world view" or cognitive state, and from that the person's behavior takes meaning.

FIGURE 15.2 | **CONCEPTUAL FRAMEWORK FOR DEVELOPMENT AND PREVENTION OF SERIOUS CONDUCT DISORDERS IN CHILDREN**

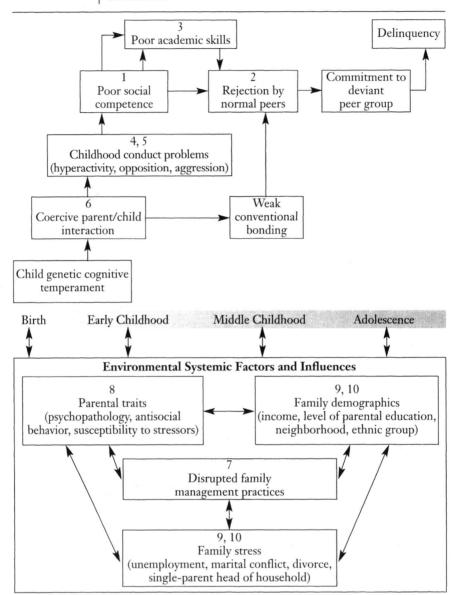

From Horne, A. (1991). Social learning family therapy. In A. Horne & J. Passmore (Eds.), *Family Counseling and Therapy* (2nd ed.). Reprinted by permission of F. E. Peacock Publishers, Inc.

BEHAVIOR

How one behaves, what one does, has impact upon others in the social realm, and also influences the individual. Behavior is the action of a person that may be observed by other people, and includes both verbal and nonverbal communications. People respond to our behavior and "make meaning" of that behavior. Behavior that is seen as warm and friendly often invites cooperation, whereas behavior that is identified as threatening or dangerous often leads to avoidance and conflict. When people engage in behavior they believe is done well, they engage in positive intrapersonal attributions about their ability and potential for achievement and success, whereas a person who does not perform well on behavioral tasks may have a sense of failure or loss. How each of these people acts, then, also influences how others will respond. People may have behavioral deficits, in that they lack skills or a repertoire of behaviors that would enable them to function more effectively in their families. Examples include not knowing about appropriate sexual activities, not having needed communications or problem-solving skills, and being unfamiliar with methods of parenting. At other times people may exhibit behavioral excesses, which may also be dysfunctional. These range from emotional behaviors, such as anger explosions or an inability to control one's temper, to physical behaviors, such as alcohol or substance abuse, overeating, or being overly demanding or controlling in relationships.

ENVIRONMENT

Environment is composed of the physical and social surroundings of a person and may be thought of as the systems in which a person is involved. Rather than thinking of systems as applying only to a family and the structure and dynamics of that family, social-learning theory posits that the environment is all the systems with which one interacts. It may be family, but it may also be the coworkers in the office. Environment also refers to broader systems that are determined by socioeconomic status (bus driver or physician); geographical boundaries (Appalachian versus Brooklynite; German or Iraqi); and culture and racial or ethnic identity.

The environment may be physical, and can include the home in which people live, the kitchen in which all members come together, the bedrooms in which each person may have private space. It may also be symbolic. Crosbie-Burnett and Lewis (1993) give the example of a hole in the wall made by a violent partner as being symbolic of the interpersonal relationships that influence the environment in which people live.

CONCEPTS

ATTRIBUTIONS People attribute certain characteristics to aspects of their environment, whether those aspects are people or physical arrangements. People develop explanations for why something has happened, and attribute to those explanations causes ("We are having to move again because my worthless father can't keep a job"). Crosbie-Burnett and Lewis (1993) indicate that causal attributions explain the locus (father in this example), the stability (we're having to move again), and globality (he never keeps a job). They also report that responsibility is another characteristic of attributions, indicating whether a person should receive blame for causing the problem (Dad never had anyone teach him how to be a good employee so it isn't his fault).

MODELING This is the process of developing a new behavior through observing others and imitating their performance. Modeling is a key component of social-learning family therapy. It is assumed that many of the dysfunctional behaviors were modeled in the family of origin or through other channels of learning such as peer groups or television, whereas more effective behaviors may be learned by modeling after persons who have the characteristics that will lead to better functioning. Therapists in social-learning treatment often model problem-solving skills, effective communication patterns, and alternative parenting methods that may be beneficial. Modeling may be in vivo, live or symbolic. Teaching families self-control skills to reduce violence in the home would likely be live; sex therapy interventions would be through the use of films and other training materials. Vicarious modeling or learning occurs through learning without direct experiencing, as through television, films, and books. The process may be very positive (learning effective problem solving via filmed models) or negative (attitudes learned through violent videos).

REINFORCEMENT A basic axiom of social-learning family therapy is that those behaviors that are positively reinforced tend to increase and reoccur, whereas those that are punished or ignored tend to reduce or extinguish. Reinforcement is a consequence immediately following and contingent upon behavior. Therefore, what may be reinforcing to one person may not be perceived as reinforcing with another. In our work with highly aggressive children we have found that social reinforcers, such as touching and smiling, are not initially reinforcing, whereas with nonaggressive children, the same behaviors are positively received. What is a reinforcer, then, is determined by the recipient, for if the desired behavior increases, it is said to have been positively reinforced. What is reinforcing is, to some extent, determined by the attributions and beliefs of the recipient of the activity.

SHAPING It is highly unusual for dysfunctional behaviors to yield to functional relationships in a brief interaction. Rather, the desired behavior is expected to be achieved through successive approximations—moving toward the desired goal. In sex therapy for treatment of orgasm disorders, it is expected that gradual progress will be made rather than an immediate change, and it is expected that tantrums of a child will gradually reduce rather than disappearing overnight.

COGNITIVE RESTRUCTURING Much of the focus of social-learning family therapy is on helping family members restructure or examine and evaluate their thoughts, beliefs, and attributions that influence how they behave. Cognitive restructuring may take several forms, including challenging irrational beliefs about how marriages "should" be, examining attributions that parents assign to children about their motivations for misbehavior, and evaluating whether effective problem solving is occurring.

COERCION Coercion is the use of power or force—aversive behaviors—to influence another person to behave a particular way. Many families presenting for social-learning family therapy have turned to coercion in order to attempt to have members behave in ways that are desired.

RECIPROCITY When relationships are reciprocal, each member gives about as much as is received: "Doing unto others as they have done unto you." This may be positive or negative, but when the relationship is balanced and reciprocal, the reinforcers or punishers are about equal between or among those involved.

RESISTANCE Resistance is a term used in most traditional therapies to indicate a reluctance on the part of people to change. In fact, an expectation in many therapies is that if change were expected to occur, it would have already done so, but since it has not, then the family is resisting change and therefore will be quite resistant in therapy. A basic tenet in systemic models is that all systems resist change. Behavior therapists, however, generally view resistance more as ineffective case management. This may take the form of the therapist's not adequately understanding the problem, a failure to present to the family the rationale for change, or an expectation of change that is inconsistent with the family—such as moving more quickly than is comfortable. Behavior therapists assume, though, that change can occur even if there is resistance and an attempt to maintain the "status quo." When the status quo becomes sufficiently painful, change is sought, and an expectation of collaborative problem solving and therapeutic movement is the norm.

SOCIAL-LEARNING FAMILY THERAPY PROBLEM DEVELOPMENT

Bateson, Jackson, Haley, and Weakland (1956) argue that the individual cannot be considered apart from the social system of which he or she is a member; the family is a system of interbehaving people. Therefore, a person identified as the problem client, such as an acting out or highly aggressive child, is seen as an individual responding to the behaviors of others within the family system. The behaviors of others within the family contribute to the deviancy of the child, and his or her deviant behavior in turn supports their behaviors. Within this framework, deviant behavior of the identified patient is not seen as dysfunctional; rather it is seen as an appropriate response to contingencies of the system and, in fact, there is a continuous reciprocal interaction between intrapersonal, behavioral, and environmental determinants: People and their environments are reciprocal determinants of each other (Bandura, 1977).

One way that people learn inappropriate behavior is through the positive reinforcement trap (Wahler, 1976). In this situation, family members may find a particular class of behaviors appealing and therefore encourage that behavior. A child who "clowns around" and is the center of attention when two years old may be a nuisance when the same behaviors are still exhibited at age six. A person who at age 20 marries another because they are "carefree, funny, and not tied down by the middle-class trap of work and wealth" may find those very features a reason for divorce 10 years later. And a man who reinforces homemaking and domestic skills for his spouse early in the marriage may find those same behaviors less appealing after several years, when he has moved to a different stage of his career development, but the spouse has not, resulting in differing values and expectations about roles in the family.

A second and much more common way of learning inappropriate behavior is through the negative reinforcement trap (Wahler, 1976). Negative reinforcement involves stopping some stimulus, which leads then to an increase in the frequency of the behavior that preceded. A parent may learn, for example, that the most effortless way to escape a temper tantrum is to provide candy or some other reinforcer. The child in the department store who engages in crying and whining for a toy or candy may usually be quieted by giving the child what was wanted. When this happens, the noxious behavior stops (temporarily), and the parent has thus been reinforced for giving the child what was wanted. Unfortunately, the child has just been reinforced for engaging in the very behavior the parent wants to stop, for the child has learned that crying can lead to positive results. Therefore, the child is likely to cry again in that situation and, since the parent has learned that giving in will cause the noise to cease, the parent will likely give the reward again in the future. This accidental learning is very powerful and, once acquired, is difficult to change. Likewise, the husband who sulks when he doesn't get his way but becomes very pleasant when his wife accedes to his demands is being taught to be an expert sulker!

Within families, accidental learning occurs frequently. Accidental learning refers to any behaviors that are developed through unintentional reinforcement or unintentional punishment. Examples of this include teaching overeating habits by having parents reward children with a clean plate award for eating everything (even when there were more calories than necessary) and acting hurt when the child leaves some food (even if the child is satiated); or, when a child fights, the father's telling him he or she shouldn't fight but that, if necessary, to always hurt the other kid more because then he or she will be "just like your old man." Other examples of accidental learning include: When a child shows off and the parents laugh and say she or he will grow up to be a movie star, they are encouraging more of the same behavior. If a child comes home from school and complains about how bad school is and the mother listens compassionately, she is reinforcing complaining behavior. When a child shows the mother a good school paper, and the mother criticizes the child's appearance, she is teaching the child to avoid seeing the mother after school.

A core concept of social-learning family counseling is that individuals strive to maximize rewards while minimizing costs. This concept, presented by Thibault and Kelly (1959) as an exchange-theory model of social psychological interaction, indicates that social behavior is maintained in a given relationship by a high ratio of rewards to costs and the perception that other possible relationships have more costs and/or fewer rewards. Conflict develops under this model when optimal behavior-maintaining contingencies do not exist (a child demands more than he or she gives; a woman finds another person more appealing than her husband) or when faulty behavior-change efforts are implemented.

Two social-reinforcement mechanisms are in operation in social-learning theory: reciprocity and coercion (Patterson & Hops, 1972). Reciprocity refers to a social-interaction exchange in which two people reinforce each other at an equivalent rate, both maintaining the relationship through positive reinforcement. In a reciprocal relationship, the probability of a rewarding encounter or outcome from the partner is more likely following the delivery of a rewarding interaction in both distressed and nondistressed couples. Coercion, on the other hand, refers to an interaction in which each person provides aversive stimuli (reactions) that control the behavior of the other, and negative reinforcement is the result of the termination of the aversiveness. Coercion in relationships leads to a reciprocal use of coercion by the other person, or as Lederer and Jackson (1968) state: "nastiness begets nastiness." Research in family counseling has clearly indicated that this phenomenon holds. The family member who delivers the highest rate of aversives also receives the highest rate of aversives from other family members (Reid, 1967). A fairly clear way of differentiating distressed from nondistressed families, in fact, is to examine the rates at which family members exchange aversive stimuli, for distressed families provide lower rates of pleasing behaviors and higher rates of punishing behaviors than nondistressed families (Birchler, Weiss, & Vincent, 1975). If inadequate positive consequences are available to family members, if there is a scarcity of positive outcomes, a distressed relationship occurs (Jacobson & Margolin, 1979; Stuart, 1980). And even if positive exchanges continue, difficulties can arise as a result of increased punishing interactions, for rewarding and punishing interchanges have been found to be independent in intimate relationships (Wills, Weiss, & Patterson, 1975). The probability of a punisher is more likely following the delivery of a punisher from the partner, particularly in distressed couples (Jacobson & Margolin, 1979).

Marital and family therapy research has carefully examined the reciprocity and coercion processes and has found that for nondistressed families, companionship with other family members is reinforcing, resulting in people enjoying being together and engaging in activities that bring them closer, whereas companionship is nonreinforcing for distressed families, resulting in people attempting to avoid one another (Jacobson & Margolin, 1979).

Gottman and his colleagues (Gottman, Markman, & Notarius, 1977; Gottman et al., 1976) describe the reciprocal interactions of family members as a "bank account" model of social exchange in which individuals have "investments" and "withdrawals" in terms of relationships with others in their family. They suggest that nondistressed families receive a relatively high rate of exchange, and inequitable exchanges are more acceptable since there is a long-term history of positive equal exchanges. This situation is not true for distressed families; instead there is considerably more attention paid to "balancing the books" on a regular basis to assure that one member does not receive an unfair share of available rewards. Reciprocity in functional, nondistressed families places greater emphasis on long-term clusters of behavior that provide rewarding experiences, whereas distressed families attend more to short-term equity within single dyadic interactions.

DEVELOPMENTAL PHASES

In studying the developmental phases of families, the understanding of reciprocity in reinforcement and punishment is very important, particularly when attempting to comprehend development of a distressed family situation. The developmental processes of a family require flexibility and an ability to adapt to change. Some families experience the meeting of two individuals, courtship, marriage, children, moving geographically, changing jobs, children leaving, changes in social and political climate, and retirement. At any point in the family's development there is the potential for the occurrence of conflict, and there are many other situations that may come along to shake the equilibrium of the family (affairs, death of a family member, in-laws moving in, illness, and so forth).

Initially when a couple meets and begins courting and then forms a union, there is a high rate of positive exchanges. There generally is a positive attraction and novelty in the relationship that each finds pleasing. Early in the relationship, couples tend to see only the positive aspects of each other, ignoring the negative, and at the same time each person attempts to present himself or herself as pleasing, and so goes to extremes to be reinforcing. During this exciting phase, individuals experience positive cognitions, entertaining only positive thoughts about each other and the future of the relationship. Thoughts generally focus on positive predictions that the future will be just like the present.

The honeymoon ends, however, in a short while for some, after a more extended period for others. When this happens, the couple may develop realistic expectations of each other and the relationship, including the development of open, clear communication. This involves couples realizing that not all aspects of the relationship will be pleasing but that by early establishment of open, clear, straightforward communication about conflict it is possible to settle relationship disagreements satisfactorily. On the other hand, the couple may maintain unrealistic expectations of each other and the relationship, leading to mutual dissatisfaction and distress in the relationship. This may result in "catastrophizing" cognitions ("I'm not in love because he isn't ideally suited to my concept of the perfect partner because if he were then he would have been more considerate; he probably doesn't love me anyway") and even the development of coercive behavior shaping through the use of punishment.

Beyond the difficulties that may be encountered in the initial stages of the relationship, each stage of the family's development process may bring additional challenges to the positive exchanges already developed. Over time, for example, it is common for the novelty of the relationship to decrease, and, as it does, each partner's potential for reinforcement is diminished, a result of habituation to each other. Habituation requires the expanding of repertoires of reinforcing behaviors in order to prevent satiation from occurring. The more widely varied the reinforcing behaviors, the less dependent the couple is on a limited menu of reinforcers; then it is less likely reinforcement erosion will occur. As sexual encounters become more commonplace, for example, and lose the excitement of novelty, couples may expand the sexual behaviors to include new and novel ways of being together. Couples who continue to interact in a routine, regular way are likely to experience boredom in the relationship and find it less rewarding. This situation may lead to distress.

Beyond reinforcement erosion, distress may develop as a result of a deficiency in family skills of the couple. Family life requires many skills, some of which the couple may have been exposed to and mastered, others of which may be new and perplexing. It becomes necessary for the couple to learn to master skills for which they are untrained, and this requires an openness and acceptance of each other as a human being (as opposed to a superperson) and the opportunity to learn, including an appropriate model, for rarely do people learn behaviors they have never seen performed by others (Bandura, 1977). Behavioral family skills include the ability of partners to communicate clearly, as well as the ability to be creative problem solvers, provide support and understanding, maintain a viable sex life, maintain a household, rear children, wash dishes, manage finances, and change with a changing world. The importance of each skill area will vary from stage to stage in the development of the relationship, and most skills may be learned as needed.

In addition to skills deficit that may lead to distress for couples, changes in the external environment may also contribute to difficulties. If alternatives outside of marriage, for example, develop more reinforcement value than is available within, the likely result will be conflict. Each individual examines the costs and benefits of a relationship and compares those costs and benefits with outside alternatives. Outside alternatives may include a third party entering the scene (an affair), career opportunities that provide increasing rewards (as the marriage may be becoming stale or commonplace, or the worker may become a "workaholic"), or people perceiving their options as greater as societal changes provide greater choices (divorce is easier, women have increased opportunities out of the house, midlife career changes have become more common). Any and all of these may lead to stress within the relationship.

APPLICATION

The definition presented of the social-learning approach to counseling families emphasized that it is a method of helping that involves analyzing problems, designing intervention strategies, and assessing change. This places responsibility upon the therapist to have the necessary skills and training to do so. These skills include:

1. Establishing a therapeutic relationship.
2. Defining concerns.
3. Developing expectancies.
4. Implementing change.
5. Following through.
6. Assessing progress.

RELATIONSHIP BUILDING

The therapist is responsible for having the basic interpersonal relationship skills to establish a therapeutic environment in which the family members will feel safe and comfortable discussing their concerns.

Families come for counseling in the midst of great discomfort. Attitudes about seeking help have changed for the better in recent years, but most families still see the need for outside assistance as a sign of weakness or inadequacy. In addition, families who come for help have genuine pains (somatic as well as physical); a dysfunctional family life is very painful. Generally it may be expected that anger is operating at some level also, for family members who hurt one another badly enough to force the family to seek help both give and receive pain, and experience significant anger. Anger may also exist as a result of an outside party, such as the school or a court, demanding that the family come for counseling against their wishes. Fear generally is operating at a high level also, and it is unknown what the family members will do if counseling is not effective.

It is imperative, therefore, that the therapist have the relationship skills necessary to understand the state of the family, to demonstrate that understanding, and to develop a sense of confidence that change is possible. This relationship is essential from the beginning, and should be maintained throughout. Family members must experience the therapist as empathic, warm, genuine, caring, and supportive.

The attitudes and beliefs of the therapist will play a large part in developing the therapeutic relationship. A belief held about each individual, each member of a family, is that the person is doing the very best he or she can given the circumstances of that person and given the previous learning experiences that person had encountered. It is important to maintain that belief, for otherwise therapists may find themselves pulling back, becoming evaluating and nonaccepting. When working with child abuse cases coming for counseling as a result of court orders, therapists have to keep in mind that even these families are doing the best—the only—thing they know how to do under the circumstances. But that is what counseling is all about—changing the circumstances by teaching people more effective methods of interacting and more satisfying ways of being with others. It is crucial that we don't "blame the victim for being the victim." Neither do we have to condone or accept the behavior that led to the referral, such as child abuse. But by understanding the families' situation and offering to provide them with alternative skills that will be more facilitative, we are demonstrating a caring and respect that can lead to the development of a rewarding relationship. It is the therapist's responsibility to accomplish this task.

The major purpose of the initial contact with the family is to set the stage for helping by developing a supportive relationship and by building positive expectancies. During the initial session, the therapist should aim to alleviate the sense of hopelessness and isolation often experienced by families. If these goals are not accomplished, then it is unlikely the family will continue in treatment. Building positive expectancies involves establishing the credibility of the treatment program. This is an important, though often neglected, step in the process. Therapist statements such as "We have worked with many families experiencing similar concerns and have had quite good success with most," "We've worked with many families that were experiencing child management problems like this," and "We've worked with many couples who have experienced similar conflicts" tend to help establish the credibility of the therapist and the program without offering promises that can't be fulfilled. It is important to provide truthful, realistic encouragement.

To facilitate establishing credibility, it is important to explain to family members what will occur during counseling. Describing the process of defining problems, developing a specific training program by which the family can deal more effectively, thus alleviating the problem, and conducting ongoing assessment of progress generally promote a sense of confidence in the program and in the therapist.

ASSESSING CONCERNS

A major element of a social-learning treatment program is assessment. Behavior therapy emphasizes assessment as a beginning activity, a baseline, of family intervention. Assessment from a social-learning approach involves examining the following components:

1. Stimulus variables, which elicit the target behavior (the situation).

2. Organismic variables, which serve as mediating factors of an individual's observable behaviors (the individual's thoughts and feelings about the situation).

3. Response variables, which are the specific behaviors (how the individual acts in response to thoughts and feelings about the situation).

4. Consequent variables, which are the changes in the environment that follow response variables and will affect the frequency of the response.

To understand the functional relationship of the variables within the family context it is necessary for the therapist to have a systematic process for observing the environmental antecedents, the behaviors, and consequences (ABCs, where A = antecedent, B = behavior, C = consequence); conduct a therapeutic intervention that is a manipulation of a condition that is functionally related to the concerns of the family; and then to again observe in order to assess change that occurred.

The selection of an intervention method is determined by what the therapist learns of factors governing problem behaviors. Critical to this understanding is a knowledge of what the problem behavior means to those involved. A family who argues a great deal because they lack effective problem-solving skills would require an entirely different intervention than a family characterized by the same frequency of arguments, but who do so because of divergent values and expectations.

INTERVENTION

Once initial contact has been made with the family, a therapeutic climate established, and initial assessment completed, it is important to develop an intervention program. The program is determined by the therapist in cooperation with family members involved.

In the following example, an intervention program for a family experiencing child-management concerns is described. The principles also apply to couples conflicts and other family dysfunctions.

SELECTING FAMILIES FOR TREATMENT The therapist should meet with the family to determine that treatment is viable at the present time. Several factors, for example, may preclude involving the family in treatment, including severe drug abuse or alcoholism, which would require treatment before beginning. Work schedules that preclude the possibility of working on tasks assigned, or anticipated moves in the very near future must be considered. This information would be determined during the initial interview with the family, which would serve the purpose also of developing a clear understanding of the amount of time required to carry out a program and to develop positive expectations of change.

BEGINNING TREATMENT During the first session, the therapist would begin collecting information about specific behaviors to be focused on in treatment, as well as the interactional sequences the family engages in related to the problem. Next, steps would begin to help parents learn effective tracking skills. Tracking means helping family members learn how to behaviorally define a problem area and then observe and count it when it occurs. For example, most parents, when entering counseling, are angry or frustrated with child-management problems and perceive their child in broad, negative terms: "He's an awful, mean bully who just doesn't love us!" This description is vague, and in teaching tracking the therapist explains to parents how to clearly define what it is that the child does, or doesn't do, that is so aggravating. Frequently, the behaviors may be redefined as noncompliance, which means the child does not do as he or she is told, or fails to complete tasks assigned by the parent. If the parent, for example, requests that a child carry out the garbage and he or she doesn't, that is noncompliance with a request, whereas if the child fails to go to bed at 8:30 as the household rules state, that is failure to comply with a household rule. Most child behavior problems may be redefined as noncompliance, and tracking has the parent observe and count the frequency of such noncompliance as a measure of the child's behavior at the beginning of treatment. Having the parent monitor this behavior also provides an opportunity to identify positive behaviors. It becomes obvious that the child does not misbehave (noncomply) 100% of the time. Therefore, it will be possible within the second session to demonstrate that the child does do what is requested a great deal of the time.

Also during the initial contact the therapist would negotiate an agreement with parents that would specify what would be expected of them and what the therapist will be doing (The therapist may say, "I will call in twice a week to report how the tracking is going; I will give at least 24 hours' notice if I have to cancel; I will...").

After completing instruction in tracking, defining the problem behaviors to be tracked, and completing a contract, the therapist will role-play several times with the parents how to do the tracking so that there is a clear understanding of what is expected.

During the next session, the therapist will review the tracking sheets completed by the parents to determine how well they are participating in the program and to identify how many misbehaviors per day occurred. During the discussion, the therapist will attempt to identify the antecedents and consequences for each behavior as a means of understanding what is maintaining the behavior within the family, remembering that the behaviors do not occur in isolation. Another activity of the therapist during this session involves helping the family identify positive events occurring as a means of helping parents have a more affirmative perception of the child. This may take the form of relabeling (The therapist may say, "In his effort to help, he spilled paint; it must be somewhat gratifying to know that, even with all the upsets you two have had recently, he still wants to help with the chores around the house"). It may also simply be identifying the positive situations and drawing the parents' attention to the fact that the child is not always messing up.

THE TREATMENT PROCESS As the therapist reviews with the parents the recordings of events during the week, the therapist responds to the environmental occurrences (when you were in the grocery store he started yelling as you passed the candy aisle), to the affective state of the parents (and you began to feel angry and explosive), and to the cognitive set of the parents (and you began thinking "This is horrible, I can't stand this, he's the most horrible kid for mistreating me like this, but I'd better give him the candy because everyone's watching and I'm afraid if he doesn't shut up I'm gonna knock the hell out of him right here in the store"). It is important that parents are aware that the therapist understands the situation, how they feel, and what they are thinking. This has already been partially completed during the initial contact, for at that time a major effort of the therapist was to develop a therapeutic relationship, but it is critical that this understanding be constantly reassessed and reviewed with the parents.

The therapist listens to the description of the weekly events with the family. When the therapist understands the situations that occurred and has demonstrated to parents that what they are experiencing is understood and clear, the therapist then begins to help parents understand that in order to develop effective parent–child relationships, particularly in conflict situations, they must have control over their own reactions. Parents need to be able to demonstrate minimally effective child-management skills. They will likely have the opposite effect if they demonstrate poor personal control. Parents must be able to handle their affective, cognitive, and behavioral reactions to the child's behavior. If parents are out of control in their reaction to a child, it is unlikely they will be able to effectively handle the conflict situations of the family.

Wording is important during this phase of counseling, for it is imperative that the parents not be identified as inept, bad, or out of control, for should the parents begin to think the therapist is labeling them as such, they are likely to terminate at that point. They have probably identified the child as the patient, and have just described in some detail how the child misbehaved while they were the victims of the child's actions. The therapist should approach the topic from a supportive, understanding framework. Examples include:

> So, when Kevin argues with you about bedtime, and then dawdles and is very slow about getting to bed, you start getting very angry, churning inside, and then you finally explode I suspect that what happens is you really tear into him, probably saying and doing things that you would prefer not to. Perhaps you later even feel guilty about what you did and then even try to make up for it. Does that happen?

> When Sharon sleeps late on the weekends and then doesn't have time to do her chores before she wants to go out and be with her friends, you get upset with her. Then, Dad, you start thinking, "By damn, if she can't help around here she won't do anything," and so you start yelling at her about being so irresponsible and selfish and always wanting her way, and then she argues back that that just isn't so, and you finally just ground her. You said last week, you've tried everything, including grounding her for a month when she talks back, but then something comes up, and she also starts behaving real nicely around the house, and you let her go—in part because you feel guilty about yelling and making such a strict grounding. It sounds as though you'd like to learn some ways to short-circuit your getting so upset that you say and do things you regret. Perhaps we can help you get better control over yourself when she messes up so that you don't get into a real battle with her, so that you can stay more reasonable and objective. That's hard to do, particularly when a kid is trying all your patience, but it may be very helpful to do. Would you like to learn some ways to keep yourself in control of the situation?

> Okay, you've said Amber teases the dog, Jessie, and gets the dog all excited and upset so that he's barking and carrying on. She usually does this right at dinner time when you're rushed and busy, and already feeling the pressure. Then you explode, go into the living room where she's acting up, and then yell and maybe even spank her. This gets you even more upset, and then you've got Amber crying, and the dog even gets upset, so that you actually get into an even worse situation. Sounds as if a way to calm

yourself down, to get a good control over yourself would be helpful, because you've already told me you know that what you do doesn't work, but you don't know what else to do. I suspect that there are lots of other things that can be done, and you even know some of them already, but you get so upset that you don't get around to using them. I'd like us to talk about ways now to un-upset yourself, to calm yourself down before taking some action. I've found that it is crucial that parents be in control of themselves before trying to get control over a child. What do you think, would that be helpful?

The first step in teaching parents to establish self-control is to reorient their thoughts. This is done by teaching them to conduct an internal dialogue problem-solving process.

I want you to say to yourself, "What am I doing?" and then to answer the question. What you are doing is starting to get upset, to blow up.

Then ask yourself, "Is it going to help me to blow up, to get into an argument with Gayle?" and then answer that question. You've already said it doesn't help, so then it will be best to do something different.

Then say to yourself, "What else can I do?" The answer is to calm yourself down, relax yourself, and then think some new thoughts, such as: "I don't like what Gayle is going, but exploding won't help. I'm going for counseling to learn better ways of getting along with her and handling the conflicts she presents. I'm doing better, and so I'll follow through now with what I've been taught."

By following through with several examples, and by utilizing a prompt card provided by the therapist, and taped to their refrigerator, parents generally can do this part fairly well, but they still need instruction in relaxation. An effective relaxation process that can be taught very quickly involves having parents close their eyes, breathe in deeply, hold their breath as they slowly count to themselves from one to ten, then exhale and again slowly count up until they need to breathe in again, then repeat the process several times. This exercise has several advantages: It can be taught quickly and can then be performed by parents in the home without their having to go through the muscle tension-relaxation process often taught; the process does slow down the bodily reactions, creating a relaxed state; and the parent breaks the pattern of thoughts that lead to anger, replacing the thoughts with counting. It may be necessary to teach parents how to instruct their child to go sit in a corner for a minute or two, or to go to their room, so that parents may have the opportunity to relax before moving into correction. It is usually helpful to point out that this relaxation and calming method may also be used with others, including employers, employees, peers, and neighbors.

FAMILY COMMUNICATIONS Once parents understand how to establish and maintain control over their reactions to the child's behavior by reorienting their thoughts, redefining their goals, and relaxing themselves, the therapist moves into instructing them on how to engage in more effective interactions with the child. Most parents who come for counseling for parent–child relationship concerns do not demonstrate an ability to communicate clearly with their children. Defining clear expectations and family guidelines is only one area of poor communications, but a crucial one for teaching parents effective parent-child conflict management. Several of the specific family communication guidelines are:

Clear commands that involve having the child's attention (eye-to-eye contact, rather than yelling from another room while the child watches television).

Polite statements ("I'd like for you to come set the table" versus "Get the hell in here now, dammit").

Clearly understood limits ("Carry out the trash now" or "Turn off the television when this program is over at 9:00").

Direct statements rather than requests ("It is time to set the table" versus "Will you please set the table?"). Don't ask if you are really telling.

Following role-playing and practicing of these skills, the therapist would assign as homework the use of each of the covered activities on a daily basis during the coming week, and would provide for two or more phone calls to check on how the program is progressing.

TEACHING DISCIPLINE During the next stage of family intervention, the therapist again reviews the weekly tracking sheets to determine how well the family has been able to give good, clear instructions and how well the family has engaged in positive family interactions. Further, the therapist is interested in whether misbehavior occurred, and if so, how well the parents have been able to maintain their own self-control instead of responding in habitual, less effective ways. Since phone contact has been made during the week, the therapist should have a good idea of how the family has been doing and if, during the week, the family had experienced difficulties, the therapist would have explained over the phone how to correct the situation, or would have scheduled a remedial meeting.

The focus of this aspect of family intervention is upon correctional procedures. A review of problems and the ways parents handle them is conducted. The parents are then taught how to provide appropriate consequences for misbehavior using a variety of correctional measures, but specifically choosing methods appropriate for problems experienced in the family. The teaching process would include reviewing these basic correctional methods:

Ignoring—for mild problems that are primarily attention-seeking.

Natural and logical consequence—for problems wherein the child is irresponsible and the consequences are nonharmful (a child who forgets where her bathing suit was left after swimming the day before may have to sit by the water while the rest of the family gets to swim).

Premack principle (grandma's law)—for problems of noncompliance as a result of which the child must complete a less enjoyable activity before being allowed to do what is wanted (eat the peas and then have the dessert; do your homework, then watch television). This establishes that the defined behavior is required before the child engages in the positive experience.

Time out—for problems in which the above correctional methods don't work, such as would occur if the natural consequence is dangerous. Time out involves removing the child from a reinforcing environment to a nonreinforcing one for a brief period (placing the child in the bathroom for five minutes or less, depending on child's age, for aggravating the dog during dinner-preparation time).

Dirty deeds—for problems for which a more serious consequence is required and when the above methods don't work. A child who misbehaves at school for eight hours wouldn't benefit from five minutes of time out. Dirty deeds involves a specific assignment that must be done (pull the weeds in this 6' x 6' plot; stack that wood by the garage; wash down all the hall walls) in a responsible time period.

Withholding privileges—for problems in which the above correctional procedures fail. A child, for example, who refuses to do dirty deeds may entice parents into a power struggle. Withholding privileges allows the parents to provide a consequence without arguing (you were told to clear the table; you didn't do it and so you were told to go to time out; you were told twice to go and refused; now there will be no bike riding for the rest of the day).

After reviewing with parents the various correctional methods, the therapist then role-plays how to present the methods to the child, including how the procedure will work, and a rationale for the activities agreed upon. Once there is confidence that parents can present the methods, the family role-plays how to actually put the procedures into action. Following that, the therapist reviews with parents all possible problems that may be expected, and then works with the family using a problem-solving approach to figure out ways of handling each barrier that the parents can foresee. Following that, parents are assigned to go home, present the new methods to the child, apply them during the week, and be in contact by phone with the therapist so that the therapist may provide coaching if necessary. This phase of counseling is crucial, and frequent phone contact (two or more times per week) is very important. It is necessary that parents experience success and not practice erroneous correctional procedures for a week before returning; as a result of erroneous procedures, the therapist will have a more difficult time correcting errors.

INCREASING POSITIVE FAMILY INTERACTIONS When the family returns for the next step in the treatment process, a review of the week's progress is conducted, followed by the next topic—procedures for developing a more enjoyable environment in the home. Whereas the purpose of the last session was to teach parents ways to decrease negative or less pleasant family experiences, the purpose of this session is to teach parents how to increase behaviors they want in their families. Some prefer to teach the positive (reinforcing) skills first, but most often parents who come in are angry, bitter, frustrated, and want help in bringing about immediate changes. Teaching parents to reinforce appropriate behavior does not respond to their immediate needs. Therefore we find that, in general, when correctional procedures are presented first, parents and other family members are much more receptive.

Reinforcement procedures address the issue of why children should behave. Previous work has addressed the fact that often when children misbehave there is a payoff in the form of some reward, but there often is no positive reward if they do behave, or what they receive is often negative, such as being ignored. As with correctional procedures, there are a variety of methods taught parents for reinforcing.

Attention: This includes verbal and nonverbal responding, ways to demonstrate interest by talking and asking questions.

Social praise: This is an extension of attention and includes ways of demonstrating approval, appreciation, and satisfaction.

Physical contact: The contact many parents have with children is of a negative or punitive method, or is nonexistent. This method of reinforcing requires teaching parents affectionate physical contact (and, as with all of the reinforcement approaches, often requires changing the parent's belief system regarding children).

Spending time: Teaching parents the importance of setting aside time on a daily basis to have contact with their children, scheduling it in if necessary.

Access to activities: This involves allowing children to do activities that are important to them, including special trips, movies, games, and other activities that are agreeable to parents and desired by the children. It allows for shared time between parents and children in a fun activity. These activities may also be in the form of work around the house or yard, or work on a project.

Points and rewards: This involves keeping a point or reward chart for the child and allowing some special activity, treat, or privilege as a result of earning sufficient points. This is presented as a last choice: Parents don't like to keep point cards, children often perceive them as punitive rather than rewarding (How many points did I lose today?), and the process is generally dissimilar to the actual home situation, resulting in more difficulty in obtaining generalization maintenance of the desired behaviors after treatment is completed. However, point systems are often very effective for creating immediate involvement and fast behavior change and can therefore be useful if effective fading is done. In addition, many children will not respond to the initial social interactions if they have demonstrated a high rate of aggressive behavior.

It is important to carefully help parents define appropriate behaviors for their child as alternatives to the negative. A child may be stopped from engaging in negative actions, but there must also be movement toward the positive. Families want to stop the pain that exists, but it is also important to work toward growth.

Again, following a review of the methods, specific applications related to the family are defined and practiced. The parents role-play implementation and ways of explaining the process to the child. Problem-solving of anticipated problems in implementation are discussed, and parents are given the assignment for the week. Phone contact is maintained but is less crucial during this phase than for previous times.

The above sessions may have been conducted in a one-hour time period each, or they may have taken several sessions covering several hours over several weeks, depending upon the speed with which the family progressed and understood what was expected. These sessions would have to be mastered one step at a time before moving on, for each session builds upon the previous one.

GENERALIZATION Most often therapy would begin with an emphasis on a problem area within the home. Parents have most control within the home and are most likely to have success initially within an environment over which they have control and in which they are at ease. After home conflicts are resolved, however, it is necessary to move into other areas. If the child is experiencing school problems, as many are, then that area should be the next targeted. It cannot be assumed that just because parents have developed the desired behavior repertoires within the home the same will be true for other environments, for generalization occurs only through building it into the program.

A school program should involve the teacher, for that professional will have a clear picture of the behaviors at school that are inappropriate. However, the role of the teacher is to teach, not discipline, and therefore it is not necessary to go over the disciplinary and reinforcement methods, as has been done with the parents, though this may be done if the teacher and the school are willing and interested in applying the procedures within the classroom, as many indeed are. Instead, it is important to instruct the teacher to effectively define problem behaviors and track these behaviors. The teacher then tracks the child's behavior at school and completes a daily report card for each behavior area, which the child takes home to the parents, and the parents provide a consequence. This can be highly effective for the teacher who has fewer disciplinary responsibilities and is likely to find the project agreeable. The parent has previously developed correctional and reinforcing properties and therefore is prepared to provide correctional procedures, and the child has clearly defined expectations, which improves the likelihood that the opportunity will be successful.

Generalizing to other areas is also important. Any other problems should be systematically treated just as home and school problems were. These may include neighborhood conflicts, shoplifting and stealing, and other activities not acceptable within a family structure.

MAINTAINING CHANGE AND CLOSING TREATMENT Following generalization training for the family, it is important to move into training that will provide for maintenance of the acquired skills. This includes systematic training in family problem-solving skills and family communication, with the expectation that the family will engage in considerable practice. One week or several may be involved, depending upon the understanding level of the family and the degree to which they practice the skills. A skill area that is more fully developed during this phase of treatment is communications skills training. This includes continued work on presenting expectations and requests, effective reinforcing and praising, and playing and shared activities, and it also expands into negotiation skills, family conference methods, and family management skills for handling difficult situations.

Much of the research and applied work that has been done using a social-learning treatment approach has involved seeing the parents and having them work with the child at home. This method works and is particularly helpful to therapists who have tight time schedules or who have less experience working with families. It is also a useful approach the first few times a therapist attempts to implement a program such as the one described. However, it is recommended that the entire family be involved in treatment and that the problem be defined as a family problem rather than as a child-behavior or child-management concern. As has been defined earlier, the child is functioning within a family unit and the behavior is learned and maintained within that family setting. By having all members present it is possible to teach the skills involved to all family members, to have input from the child about what parents do that is helpful and what is not, and to provide a model for the activities being covered. It is possible, for example, to point out when the parents say that "He never behaves himself" to say, "Well, let's say some of the time he doesn't because, we can see, he is behaving now. I wonder why he is willing to behave now, while I'm around, when he doesn't other times? Do you think that you might help us understand that?"

The model presented has placed emphasis on child-management concerns within the family. The same procedures would be applied, though, regardless of the family conflicts occurring. For example, similar methods are used for marital concerns, counseling families with adolescents who are rebelling, and other problems that families experience as they develop from young married, to mature, and even to retirement phases of relationships. For examples of two approaches to treating marital conflicts, see Jacobson and Margolin (1979) and Stuart (1980). For a treatment of child-management problem areas, see Fleischman, Horne, and Arthur (1982) and Horne and Sayger (1990).

CASE EXAMPLE

Dan and Kim were referred for counseling by the elementary counselor in their son Kevin's school. Kevin was a sixth-grader who had a poor school record over several years and had been in frequent difficulties in school, including being expelled for fighting and truancy. Kevin was described by the school counselor as a child with a chip on his shoulder who would fly off the handle with the teacher or other kids.

When Kim made the contact, she asked if she could bring Kevin in to be seen for his school behaviors. She was somewhat surprised when she was asked if she, her husband, Kevin, and any other siblings might be able to come in for a conference. She explained that Kevin had the problem, that the two younger siblings were not having any problems, and that Dan would not come. It was explained to her that it was important to meet with the entire family in order to see how Kevin got along with the people in his family and to learn from each family member how they saw Kevin getting along. It was also intimated that Kevin couldn't be seen if the whole family couldn't make it to the initial session.

By arranging the first session in the late afternoon to accommodate Dan's schedule, it was possible for all to attend. The two younger siblings and Kevin were asked to play for a while in the playroom while the parents met with the two cotherapists. (Cotherapists are often used since families present so much during interviews it is often helpful to have one doing the primary work while the other serves as a process observer and occasional rescuer.)

Dan indicated resentment at being at the session and that he didn't like the school interfering into his family life. He indicated that the school had the problem, because he could handle his children but the school couldn't. In the process of talking with Dan, he indicated that when Kevin misbehaved he would just "knock the hell out of him" and Kevin would straighten up very quickly. Dan was asked to describe a few times when that was necessary, and he was able to tell about a couple incidents within the last few weeks.

Kim was also asked about how she perceived the situation, and she agreed with Dan. She felt that it was mostly the school's problem, because when she couldn't handle Kevin she would just tell Dan when he got home from work and then Dan would straighten the situation out very quickly.

As each talked it was obvious that some behavioral problems did exist within the home, and that the father was the major back-up enforcer when Kim's efforts failed. Frequently parents deny or ignore child-management problems until an outside agency intervenes and demands that changes be made, as was true in this case. When this occurs, it is frequently good to work toward developing a collaborative set between the parents and with the therapist in order to work cooperatively to remove the source of conflict.

Therapist: It seems that over the years you two have had some difficulties with Kevin in that he misbehaves a good bit, but you have been able to handle him to your satisfaction. Kim, you pretty much are able to get Kevin to do what is expected, but when you can't, you have Dan to back you up, though sometimes it takes a while before he gets home. Kevin has had problems at school for a long time—pretty much ever since he got started—but you have figured that's the school's problem, that they should be able to handle Kevin.

Dan: Damned right. That's what they are there for. I was a lot like Kevin and they certainly handled me.

Therapist: Right. They should be able to handle the kids at school, but at times things aren't the way they should be. I think this is an example of that situation because, I think, you pretty clearly have a kid who is more than the school can handle. He's a real expert at what he does, which is messing up. And the teachers haven't been able to get through to him, nor has the principal, and so far, no one else has, and so the school is throwing it back into your lap.

Kim: That isn't fair, we can't go to school and sit by him all the time, and we sure can't beat him all the time for coming home in trouble. That hasn't worked.

Therapist: I'm glad you see that. What we do here is to work with families who are having troubles. Some of the troubles may involve getting along in the home, sometimes it is troubles such as shoplifting and stealing, sometimes it's marriage problems, and sometimes it's problems like Kevin has, getting along in school. What we do is teach parents how they can work with the school to bring about the changes that the school needs and that help Kevin become a better student, while at the same time developing a happier way of being with others. I know you don't want to be here, that seeing a counselor isn't your idea of fun, but what we can do, if you are willing, is work together toward the changes the school wants so that they will reduce their pressure on you. I think we can do that fairly quickly if you are interested in working with us here, but it does involve some real intensive work for a while, and will require that you put in some time on exercises I'll assign you. It won't be easy, and, in fact, will be a nuisance a lot of the time. On the other hand, what we find is that generally families get along a lot better with fewer arguments and less hassle after we work together, which may mean your family life will be even happier than it is now. Also, you've got to do something about the school situation or they will take legal action of some sort, which nobody wants; I'll work with you to get the school to back off if you want. You've got to keep in mind, also, that Kevin is getting to be older and bigger, and if there are problems with him now, they'll likely just get worse over the next few years...someday he's likely to be bigger and stronger than either of you, and if he hasn't learned how to take care of himself on his own, by that time it may be too late. Do you think you'd like to work with us?

Dan: Well, maybe Kim should, she's the one who has the problems around the house, not me.

Therapist: That's a good point, Dan, and I'm glad you brought that up. You see, dads generally do have less trouble than moms do. At least when the children are smaller, they often have less conflict because they are bigger and more powerful. Also, traditionally the parenting role has fallen mainly on moms. But, as I look at Kim I see a person who can use some support, some collaborative parenting. Since you have fewer problems with Kevin it will be important for you to work with us, to help with the program we have here, in order to give Kim the support and backing she needs. You see, the way we look at family situations is that all of you are in this together, and if one person is having some problems, then all people in the family experience the consequences. It is up to the rest of the family to pitch in and help out, learn to be supportive of the whole family. Are you willing to do that?

Dan: Well, I'll help out, but I don't see that *I* need the help.

Therapist: As I said, we see that all family members are involved in the welfare of the whole family. Kevin didn't get to be the way he is without all of the family being involved, and in order to make some changes the family will have to work together. Just as what you do affects Kevin, and what Kevin does affects you, the same is true for you and Kim, and Kim and you. Each member of the family influences each other member, and it is necessary for all to see this as a family project if change is to occur. That's why I asked that the whole family come, so that we could all spend some time with each other and so that we can work out an agreement with even the youngest member of the family to join in. It's a lot more helpful if everyone is working together, and the changes in the family will progress much more quickly. We're not excited about taking the time that will be necessary if just one parent works with one child, since the changes will be much slower and a lot less effective. We're asking for the family to work as a team with us. Okay?

At this point the parents agreed to work together and to take shared responsibility for family treatment. The children were then invited to join the session. As the family talked, it became obvious that discipline problems existed for all of the children—both in the school and in the home. The parents were quick to blame the children for misconduct, but the children were equally adept at accusing the parents of being too lax at times and too strict at other times. The children were able to give a fairly clear picture of parents who ignored conflicts until they became extreme, and then responded with a heavy hand and much yelling and screaming. The parents would allow the children to get by with many minor infractions and some serious acts and then at a very unpredictable time the parents would explode. Often they would feel guilty afterwards, and the children most often felt angry and wanted revenge for how they had been treated. Thus the conflict was likely to escalate into a full-scale family confrontation over a few days' time until the parents finally pulled out all reserves and finished the battle…for the time being.

Following the family discussion, one cotherapist went into another room with the children to begin asking for specific problems they saw within the family while the other therapist continued meeting with the parents to complete several inventories and begin defining specific goals as well as problems and changes sought. During the interview with the children, they indicated that they would like for the parents to stop yelling and stop spanking them. They also indicated that often they did not understand what was expected of them (vague commands), and that sometimes they were expected to do things they did not know how to do (skills deficits), or were not allowed to do things they did know how to do.

In completing specific checklists and inventories with the parents, the therapist learned that, as suspected, there were problems with Kevin and with the siblings around the house. The father, however, had ignored the problems, since he was at work most of the day and could use his power of punishment and threat when at home to get the peace he wanted. The mother, on the other hand, was quite angry and depressed about the situation; angry that she was in such a situation and depressed because she saw no way out. Beyond the child-management concerns there was also a major disagreement of perceptions as reflected on a marital adjustment scale. When questioning about this, the therapist learned that, indeed, there were strong marital conflicts, and the question of divorce had been frequently discussed in recent months. The therapist discussed this topic with the parents to determine their current standing and learned that the marriage was tenuous and could easily go either way. This being the case, the therapist inquired about whether the marriage was stable enough at this point to center upon the child-management concerns, or if they should be tabled while attending to the marital conflict. It is possible to attend to both at once, but the family has to have a strong commitment and be open to major input, and therefore it is generally best to work on one area at a time if possible. It often turns out that marital conflict is less a problem after child-management concerns are resolved, for often the marital issues are directly affected by the child problems. A family with severe child problems is not fun or pleasant—in short, not reinforcing—and therefore, both parents want to escape. The behaviors of the child are aversive, and each parent wants to blame the other for not being a better parent; child problems frequently tie up so much time and energy that there is little left for affection between adults—the child gets all of the attention. Similarly, child-discipline problems can be a result of marital concerns when the children see the strife and fighting between adults and realize there is no time or energy left for them. This did not seem to be the case with Kim and Dan, as the child-management problems had been going on since Kevin was very young, but the marital concerns had occurred only in the last year.

The family all came back together and the cotherapists reviewed the goals of treatment that had been established. A brief review of the treatment program was presented, including the number of anticipated sessions, the necessity for homework assignments and phone calls, and costs involved. It is best that all members of the family know in advance about the degree of commitment required. It is better to have a clear and informed decision as to whether or not the family is willing to participate in treatment than for them to drop out three or four weeks down the road. One commitment that is specified is that stopping treatment by being a "no show" is not allowed: The family has to come in for a termination session. At that time, if it is determined that the treatment program presented is not meeting the needs of the family, it may be varied or, if it cannot be varied, then an alternative resource is found for the family. There exists a professional concern for the welfare of the families, and they have a right to referral if necessary.

After understanding was reached, each member of the family was asked to sign an agreement indicating support and understanding of the treatment program as outlined and specifying what family issues would be initially targeted for attention. The family was then given a brief explanation of tracking, the parents practiced tracking child-behavior problems, and the children practiced tracking parent requests and consequences. The family was then given their homework assignment and the session ended.

Kevin's school was contacted and the elementary school counselor was informed that the family would participate in treatment, but that a school program would not begin for several weeks as the goal of treatment initially was to obtain the desired changes in the home and then generalize to the school.

As the program progressed with the family, child-behavior problems became less frequent and parent disciplinary methods became more consistent and less aversive. The program generalized to the school within three weeks, and change was effected there as well. The parents met individually with the therapist for several sessions when the school program was developed in order to work on marital concerns. This involved developing a problem-solving and communications training segment for them and making specific homework assignments, which included weekends together once a month, "love-evenings" (see Stuart, 1980) once a week, and renegotiation of traditional roles each had accepted in the past, but were not fulfilling in the present.

The family terminated treatment after a four-month period of involvement, at which time there was clear evidence that within the home and school conflicts had subsided and more desirable interactions were occurring. It was necessary to have three "booster sessions" after about six months when a new school year began and Kevin reverted to his previous behavior in the classroom. By introducing the school program to his new teacher, and reinstituting the program with his parents, the behavior changed quickly.

EVALUATION

Empirical research has been a major element of social-learning treatment since its inception. The definition presented at the beginning of this chapter even presented the model as a system of inquiry rather than a collection of techniques. Comprehensive reviews of marital and family therapy literature have indicated that behavior therapy is the school that has most rigorously assessed the effectiveness of its procedures. The historical review presented earlier in this chapter reports that behavioral family counseling is effective for bringing about change in approximately two out of three families (Patterson, Reid, Jones, & Conger, 1975). Further, a review of behavioral marital therapy (Jacobson & Margolin, 1979) reports that the treatment is more effective than a baseline control and more effective than a placebo. In the last decade, considerable support has been developed for the approach, but the relative effectiveness of behavior therapy in relation to other therapies is still to be determined.

ANNOTATED SUGGESTED READINGS

Falloon, I. R. H. (1988). *Handbook of behavioral family therapy*. New York: Guilford Press.
An edited text describing behavioral interventions in the family context. Covers many
different types of behavioral treatments for specific problem areas.

Fleischman, M. J., Horne, A. M., & Arthur, J. L. (1983). *Troubled families: A treatment program*. Champaign, IL: Research Press.
A comprehensive treatment protocol is provided for the implementation of a social-
learning family therapy model. Therapist agendas, homework assignments, and comprehensive directions on a session-by-session format are provided to direct the
therapist through the implementation of the model. Sessions include setting up for
success, discipline, reinforcement, communication, generalization and maintenance,
and self-control, among others.

Horne, A. M., & Sayger, T. V. (1990). *Treating conduct and oppositional defiant disorders in children*. Boston: Allyn & Bacon.
This clinically focused book provides a theoretical understanding of the development
of behavior disorders in children and then outlines a social-learning model of family
therapy as an early intervention procedure to reduce dysfunctional behavior. Chapters
include family assessment, preparing for success, self-control, family communication,
and family–school collaboration. Discussion is provided on conducted research using
the model outlined in the book.

Patterson, G. R., Reid, J. B., Jones, R. R., & Conger, R. E. (1975). *A social learning approach to family intervention, Volume 1: Families with aggressive children*. Eugene, OR: Castalia.
This book provides an overview of the socially aggressive child, clinical research, and
procedures for working with families of aggressive children. Included in this overview
are the referral process, the intake interview, contracting, interventions in the classroom, marital conflicts, and therapist behaviors.

Sanders, M. R., & Dadds, M. R. (1993). *Behavioral family intervention*. Boston: Allyn &
Bacon.
This book includes an overview of the nature and causes of behavioral disorders in
children, clinical assessment, and the communication of assessment findings. Additionally, details of family intervention procedures are provided, including positive
parenting, generalization and maintenance, management of home- and school-related problems, and assessment and treatment of marital problems. Issues and future
directions of behavioral family therapy are also presented.

Schwebel, A. I., & Fine, M. A. (1994). *Understanding and helping families: A cognitive-behavioral approach*. Hillsdale, NJ: Lawrence Erlbaum Associates.
This book provides a theoretical and conceptual perspective from a cognitive-
behavioral approach to understanding family health, assessment, and cognitions within the family schema. Theoretical applications including the five-step process model
of cognitive-behavioral family therapy and family life education are provided.

REFERENCES

Bandura, A. (1969). *Principles of behavior modification*. New York: Holt, Rinehart & Winston.

Bandura, A. (1977). *Social learning theory*. Englewood Cliffs, NJ: Prentice-Hall.

Bandura, A. (1986). *Social foundations of thought and action: A social cognitive theory*. Englewood Cliffs, NJ: Prentice-Hall.

Bateson, G., Jackson, D. O., Haley, J., & Weakland, J. (1956). Toward a theory of schizophrenia. *Behavioral Science, 1*, 251–264.

Baucom, D. H., & Hoffman, J. A. (1986). The effectiveness of marital therapy: Current status and application to the clinical setting. In N. S. Jacobson & A. S. Gurman (Eds.), *Clinical handbook of marital therapy* (pp. 597–620). New York: Guilford Press.

Birchler, G., Weiss, R., & Vincent, J. (1975). A multimethod analysis of social reinforcers exchange between maritally distressed and nondistressed spouse and stranger dyads. *Journal of Personality and Social Psychology, 31*, 349–360.

Crosbie-Burnett, M., & Lewis, E. A. (1993). Theoretical contributions from social and cognitive-behavioral psychology. In P. G. Boss, W. J. Doherty, R. LaRossa, W. R. Schumm, & Suzanne K. Steinments (Eds.), *Sourcebook of family theories and methods: A contextual approach* (pp. 531–558). New York: Plenum.

Falloon, I. R. H. (1988). *Handbook of behavioral family therapy.* New York: Guilford Press.

Fleischman, M. J. (1976). *The effects of a parenting salary and family SES in the social learning treatment of aggressive children.* Unpublished doctoral dissertation, University of Oregon, Eugene.

Fleischman, M. J., Horne, A. M., & Arthur, J. (1982). *Troubled families.* Champaign, IL: Research Press.

Gottman, J., Markman, H., & Notarius, C. (1977). The topography of marital conflict: A sequential analysis of verbal and nonverbal behavior. *Journal of Marriage and the Family, 39*, 461–477.

Gottman, J., Notarius, C., Markman, H., Bank, S., Yoppi, B., & Rubin, M. (1976). Behavior exchange theory and marital decision making. *Journal of Personality and Social Psychology, 34*, 14–23.

Horne, A. M., Norsworthy, K. L., & Forehand, R. (1990). A conceptual framework for the development of delinquency. Unpublished manuscript, University of Georgia, Athens.

Horne, A. M., & Sayger, T. V. (1990). *Treating conduct and oppositional defiant disordered children.* New York: Pergamon Press.

Jacobson, N., & Margolin, G. (1979). *Marital therapy: Strategies based on social learning and behavior exchange principles.* New York: Brunner/Mazel.

Kaplan, H. S. (1974). *The new sex therapy: Active treatment of sexual dysfunction.* New York: Brunner/Mazel.

Lederer, W., & Jackson, D. (1968). *Mirages of marriage.* New York: Norton.

Levitt, E. (1971). Research on psychotherapy with children. In A. Bergin & S. Garfield (Eds.), *Handbook of psychotherapy and behavior change* (pp. 474–494). New York: Riley.

Liberman, R. P. (1970). Behavioral approaches to family and couple therapy. *American Journal of Orthopsychiatry, 40*, 106–118.

LoPiccolo, J. (1977a). Direct treatment of sexual dysfunction in the couple. In J. Money & H. Musaph (Eds.), *Handbook of sexology.* New York: Elsevier/North Holland.

LoPiccolo, J. (1977b). From psychotherapy to sex therapy. *Society, 14*, 60–68.

LoPiccolo, J. (1980). Methodological issues in research on treatment of sexual dysfunction. In R. Green & J. Weiner (Eds.), *Methodological issues in sex research* (pp. 100–128). Washington, DC: U.S. Government Printing Office.

Lovibond, S. H. (1963). The mechanism of conditioning treatment of enuresis. *Behavior Research and Therapy, 1*, 17–21.

Masters, W. H., & Johnson, V. E. (1970). *Human sexual inadequacy.* Boston: Little, Brown.

Nichols, W. C. (1996). *Treating people in families: An integrative framework*. New York: Guilford Press.

Overall, B., & Aronson, H. (1963). Expectation of psychotherapy in patients of lower socioeconomic class. *American Journal of Orthopsychiatry, 33*, 421–430.

Patterson, G. R. (1982). *Coercive family process*. Eugene, OR: Castalia.

Patterson, G. R., & Brodsky, A. (1966). A behavior modification programme for a child with multiple behavior programs. *Journal of Child Psychology and Psychiatry, 7*, 277–295.

Patterson, G. R., Chamberlain, R., & Reid, J. B. (1982). A comparative evaluation of a parent-training program. *Behavior Therapy, 13*, 638–650.

Patterson, G. R., Cobb, J., & Ray, R. (1973). A social engineering technology for retraining the families of aggressive boys. In H. Adams & I. Unikel (Eds.), *Issues and trends in behavior therapy* (pp. 139–224). Springfield, IL: Charles C. Thomas.

Patterson, G. R., & Hops, H. (1972). Coercion: A game for two. Intervention techniques for marital conflict. In R. Ulrich and P. Mountjoy (Eds.), *The experimental analysis of social behavior*. New York: Appleton-Century-Crofts.

Patterson, G. R., Reid, J., Jones, R., & Conger, R. (1975). *A social learning approach to family intervention*. Eugene, OR: Castalia.

Reid, J. (1967). *Reciprocity and family interaction*. Unpublished doctoral dissertation, University of Oregon, Eugene.

Reid, J., & Patterson, G. R. (1976). The modification of aggressive and stealing behavior of boys in the home setting. In A. Bandura & E. Ribes (Eds.), *Behavior modification: Experimental analyses of aggression and delinquency* (pp. 123–145). Hillsdale, NJ: Lawrence Erlbaum Associates.

Risley, T. R., & Wolf, M. M. (1967). Experimental manipulation of autistic behaviors and generalization into the home. In S. W. Bijou & D. M. Baer (Eds.), *Child development: Readings in experimental analysis* (pp. 184–194). New York: Appleton-Century-Crofts.

Robins, L. (1966). *Deviant children grown up: A sociological and psychological study of psychopathic personality*. Baltimore: Williams & Wilkins.

Spiegler, M. D., & Guevremont, D. C. (1998). *Contemporary behavior therapy* (3rd ed.). Pacific Grove, CA: Brooks/Cole.

Stuart, R. B. (1980). *Helping couples change*. New York: Guilford Press.

Thibault, J., & Kelley, H. H. (1959). *The social psychology of groups*. New York: Wiley.

Wahler, R. (1976). Deviant child behavior within the family. Developmental speculations and behavior change strategies. In H. Leitenberg (Ed.), *Handbook of behavior modification and behavior therapy*. Englewood Cliffs, NJ: Prentice-Hall.

Walter, H., & Gilmore, S. (1973). Placebo versus social learning effects in parent training procedures designed to alter the behavior of aggressive boys. *Behavior Therapy, 4*, 361–374.

Weiss, R. I. (1978). The conceptualization of marriage from a behavioral perspective. In T. J. Paolino & B. S. McCrady (Eds.), *Marriage and marital conflict* (pp. 165–239). New York: Brunner/Mazel.

Williams, C. D. (1959). The elimination of tantrum behaviour by extinction procedures. *Journal of Abnormal and Social Psychology, 59*, 269.

Wills, T., Weiss, R., & Patterson, G. R. (1975). A behavioral analysis of the determinants of marital satisfaction. *Journal of Abnormal and Social Psychology, 42*, 802–811.

Wiltz, N., & Patterson, G. R. (1974). An evaluation of parent training procedures designed to alter inappropriate aggressive behavior in boys. *Behavior Therapy, 5*, 215–221.

CHAPTER 16

Rational-Emotive Behavior Marriage and Family Therapy

ALBERT ELLIS

DEFINITION

Rational-emotive behavior family therapy follows the principles and practice of rational-emotive behavior therapy (REBT), a theory of personality and a method of psychotherapy developed by clinical psychologist Albert Ellis in the 1950s. REBT holds that when family members become emotionally disturbed or upset (for example, anxious, depressed, hostile, self-pitying, or behaviorally dysfunctional) at point C (emotional and behavioral consequence) following a significant activating experience or adversity (point A), A may significantly contribute to—but actually does not "cause"—C. Instead, disturbed consequences (in individuals and in families) are largely (though not exclusively) created by B—the family members' *belief system*. When undesirable or disruptive consequences (C) occur, these can largely include people's irrational beliefs (iBs)—absolutistic, *mus*turbatory, unrealistic demands, commands, or expectations on (1) themselves, (2) others, and/or (3) environmental conditions. When these irrational beliefs (iBs) are effectively disputed (at point D) by challenging them logically, empirically, and pragmatically, the disturbed consequences are minimized and are less likely to recur (Ellis, 1957, 1988, 1994b, 1996; Ellis & Dryden, 1997; Ellis & Harper, 1997).

HISTORICAL DEVELOPMENT

Ellis is the father of REBT and the grandfather of cognitive behavior therapy (CBT). Ten years and more after Ellis started practicing, speaking, and writing about REBT in 1955, several other cognitive behavior therapists began practicing various kinds of CBT—especially Albert Bandura, Aaron T. Beck, Marvin Goldfried and Gerald Davison, Neil Jacobson, Arnold Lazarus, Michael Mahoney, Maxie Maultsby, Jr., and Donald Meichenbaum. General REBT and CBT are similar, but preferential REBT differs from CBT in that it is more forceful, more emotive, more multimodal, and more philosophic than CBT (Ellis, 1994b, 1996; Ellis & Dryden, 1997)

PRECURSORS

The philosophic origins of REBT go back partly to stoic philosophers, particularly Epictetus and Marcus Aurelius. Although most of the early Stoic writings have been lost, their main gist comes through Epictetus, who in the first century of the Christian Era wrote in *The Enciridion* (or *Manual*): "People are disturbed not by things, but by the view which they take of them." His disciple, the Roman Emperor Marcus Aurelius, advanced Stoicism in his famous *Meditations.* Several ancient Taoist and Buddhist thinkers also emphasized two of its main points: Human emotions are integrated with ideas; and to change disturbed feelings, one had better strongly think and act differently.

The principal therapist who anticipated REBT theory and practice was Alfred Adler (1964), who wrote: "I am convinced that *a person's behavior springs from his ideas*" (p. 19). This states some of the tenets of REBT succinctly and accurately.

In addition, a number of therapists during the early 1950s, when REBT was first being formulated, independently began to arrive at theories and methods that significantly overlap with the methods outlined by Ellis. These include Eric Berne, George Kelly, Abraham Low, Julian Rotter, and Joseph Wolpe.

BEGINNINGS

Ellis started to develop marriage and family therapy during the late 1940s and to create REBT in the early 1950s, after he practiced classical psychoanalysis and analytically oriented psychotherapy and found them inefficient. He saw that, no matter how much insight his clients gained—especially about their early childhood—they only partly improved and still retained strong tendencies to create new symptoms. This was because they were not merely indoctrinated with self-defeating ideas but also actively *invented, accepted,* and *kept reindoctrinating themselves with* these dysfunctional beliefs.

Ellis also discovered that his clients often resisted changing their irrational philosophies, because they *naturally* tended to musturbate; to absolutistically demand (1) that they *must* do well and win others' approval, (2) that other people *had to* act considerately and fairly, and (3) that environmental conditions *ought not* be frustrating and ungratifying. Ellis concluded that humans, just because they are humans, are naturally constructivist and problem solving. But they also have innate and acquired tendencies to construct strong dysfunctional ideas and often take their healthy preferences—such as desires for love, approval, success, and pleasure—and irrationally define them as "needs" or "necessities." They especially tend to do this when they live intimately, in marital or family groups; and therefore their disturbed interactions are partially intrinsic to family living but are also part and parcel of the easily held premises that they frequently bring to intimate relationships (Ellis, 1957, 1988, 1994b, 1996; Ellis & Dryden, 1997; Ellis & Harper, 1997; Ellis, Sichel, Yeager, DiMattia, & DiGiuseppe, 1989).

By experimenting with different therapeutic procedures, Ellis also discovered that deep-seated human irrationality is rarely changed by most therapy techniques because individuals and family members are so strongly habituated to their dysfunctional thinking and dysfunctional behavior that they weakly challenge them, and this is unlikely to work. Passive, nondirective methodologies rarely help them change. Warmth and support often enable clients to live more "happily" with unrealistic notions. Suggestion or "positive thinking" sometimes encourages them to cover up and live with basic self-devaluations but seldom helps them remove these notions. Abreaction and catharsis enable them to feel better but often reinforce their unrealistic demands. Behavioral desensitization sometimes relieves clients of anxieties but does not change their anxiety-arousing basic philosophies (Ellis, 1988, 1994b, 1996).

What works more effectively, Ellis found in the early days of REBT, is an active-directive, cognitive-emotive-behavioral challenging of clients' self-defeating assumptions. Effective psychotherapy, in group, family, and individual settings, includes full tolerance of people *as individuals* combined with showing them how to campaign against their dysfunctional *ideas, traits,* and *performance.*

When still using psychoanalysis, Ellis began to do conjoint marital counseling and family therapy and found that these methods were more efficient and briefer as he replaced analysis with REBT. For REBT, marriage and family therapy not only gets to the fundamental premises that underlie people's disillusionment with themselves and their family arrangement, but also uses cognitive, emotive, and behavioral methods of teaching them communication, sexual, relating, and other skills that will help them enhance their associations.

CURRENT STATUS

The Albert Ellis Institution for Rational Emotive Behavior Therapy, a not-for-profit scientific and educational organization, was founded in 1959 to teach the principles of rational living and to train therapists. With headquarters in New York City and branches in several cities in the United States, as well as in Italy, Holland, France, Germany, Canada, Mexico, Australia, and other countries, the Institute disseminates the REBT approach, including (1) adult education courses; (2) postgraduate training programs for professionals; (3) moderate cost clinics for individual, group, and marital therapy; (4) special workshops, seminars, practica, intensives, and marathons for professionals and the public given regularly in various parts of the world; and (5) the publication and distribution of books, monographs, pamphlets, recordings, and the *Journal of Rational-Emotive and Cognitive-Behavior Therapy.*

The Institute has a register of psychotherapists who have received training certificates in REBT, including marriage and family therapy. In addition, other therapists mainly follow REBT principles, and a still greater number use major aspects of REBT in their individual, group, and family work. Cognitive restructuring, employed by almost all cognitive-behavior therapists (and many other therapists), consists mainly of REBT.

RESEARCH STUDIES Many articles and books evidence the effectiveness of REBT and related cognitive-behavior therapies with many kinds of disturbed individuals. REBT already has led to the publication of several hundred outcome studies, most of which have shown that it helps clients improve significantly more than other modes of therapies or no-therapy control groups (Hajzler & Bernard, 1991; Lyons & Woods, 1991; McGovern & Silverman, 1984; Silverman, Mc-Carthy, & McGovern, 1992).

In addition, hundreds of controlled experiments have been done that lend support to the main theoretical principles of REBT as well as to its most important clinical hypotheses. Following Ellis's lead, a number of closely related cognitive-behavioral therapies have been devised, and hundreds of studies confirming their effectiveness have now been published (Hollon & Beck, 1994).

REBT and CBT have been investigated and found to be effective in family relationships in a number of research studies that have been summarized by Baucom & Epstein (1990), Beck (1988), Hayes, Jacobson, Follette, & Dougher, 1994.

The first major books applying the principles of REBT to marriage and family problems were *How to Live with a "Neurotic": At Home and at Work* (Ellis, 1957) and *A Guide to Successful Marriage* (Ellis & Harper, 1961). Subsequently, a large number of articles and books have been published that demonstrate how REBT can be efficiently applied to marriage and family therapy and to parenting problems.

In the specialized area of sex therapy, REBT has been one of the prime influences in the treatment of sexual problems. Even before William Masters and Virginia Johnson published their notable work on sex therapy, the cognitive behavioral approach to sex problems was pioneered by Ellis in the 1950s and 1960s in such books as *The Art and Science of Love* (1960) and *Sex and the Liberated Man* (1976b, original edition, 1963). As the twentieth century draws to a close, the REBT and CBT approaches to the treatment of sex problems have led to considerable outstanding work in sex therapy, including that of Arnold Lazarus, Joseph LoPiccolo, Lonnie Barbach, Janet L. Wolfe, and Bernie Zilbergeld.

TENETS OF THE REBT MODEL

BASIC CONCEPTS

REBT is one of the most integrative therapies because it has several unique theories, but they include the proposition that many cognitive, emotive, and behavioral methods, a number of which are also used by other systems of therapy, are important—and sometimes crucial—for personality change. It was distinctly multimodal even before Lazarus (1989) adopted that term, and is more emotive and behavioral than most other cognitive behavior therapies. Its basic theory includes the following hypotheses about human "nature" and how it can lead to individual and family disturbance and to personality change.

BIOLOGICAL AND SOCIAL INTERACTIONISM Humans are born with strong biological predispositions, including the powerful tendency to be gregarious, to have sex–love relationships, and to live in some kind of family groups. One of the strongest of their innate tendencies is to be teachable or suggestible and to easily pick up, from their early childhood onward, the customs and traditions of significant others, especially the family members with whom they are reared. Once they learn certain "correct" social standards and preferences (for example, to eat, dress, and relate in "proper" family ways) they have strong inherent tendencies to follow these ways and also to raise their preferences into absolutistic, perfectionistic demands and musts. They easily accept the *must*urbatory thinking of others; but they also have their own creative tendencies to overgeneralize and absolutize. They finally behave, in self-helping and self-defeating ways, because of their biological predispositions *and* their (also partly innate) susceptibility to early and later environmental influences.

VULNERABILITY TO DISTURBANCE Virtually all people are easily disturbable. They frequently think, emote, and behave in ways that are against their own chosen interests and that sabotage the social groups in which they choose to live. Their main goals are to stay alive and to enjoy themselves, vocationally and recreationally, when they are alone, with others, with a few intimates. They frequently sabotage some or all of these major goals, however, by their own grandiose, unrealistic, absolutistic thinking and by the unhealthy feelings and behaviors that accompany this thinking.

COGNITIVE-EMOTIVE-BEHAVIORAL INTERACTIONISM Humans rarely have pure thoughts, emotions, or behaviors that do not interact or transact with each other. What we call their "thinking" is profoundly related to and influenced by their desiring (for example, to stay alive and to feel happy) and their behaving (eating, living with others, and working). What we call their "emoting" is strongly influenced by their cognitions (e.g., evaluating the way others treat them as "good" or "bad") and by their actions (e.g., exercising or not exercising). What we call their "behavior" is importantly guided by their thoughts (e.g., "I think that I am doing the wrong thing and that is horrible!") and by their emotions (e.g., feelings of love or hatred for a person or an event). When we therefore call the members of a family "emotionally disturbed," we really mean that they have dysfunctional feelings, thoughts, and actions.

CHOICE IN DISTURBANCE AND IN PERSONALITY CHANGE In spite of the fact that human behavior is partly "caused" or "determined" by innate factors (hereditary predispositions) and by external conditions (environmental influences) that are beyond anyone's full control, people seem to be born with a good degree of potential self-determination, choice, or will. Whether they are aware of it or not, they to some extent choose to listen to and be influenced by early environmental situations; and as they grow older they develop greater abilities to choose the kinds of thoughts, feelings, and behaviors that they prefer and to avoid or minimize the kinds they dislike (Ellis, 1988, 1994b, 1996). Because of their innate and acquired tendencies to change themselves, psychotherapy is feasible, and one of the main goals of marriage and family therapy is to help people see that they can change their reactions to themselves and to other family members.

Rational-emotive behavior family therapy shows them how to maximize their "free will" and to use their inherent abilities to become more self-actualizing.

DEFINITION OF RATIONALITY In rational-emotive behavior family therapy, rationality does not mean behavior that is mainly logical, unemotional, or detached. Rational, instead, means people's choosing certain values, purposes, or goals, and then using efficient, flexible ways of trying to achieve them. REBT therapists do *not* show clients' basic aims and purposes. They accept clients' social, ethnic, religious, political, and other values; and they collaborate with clients in discovering what these fundamental goals are and how the clients think, feel, and behave in ways that interfere with their goals. They explore how these clients can efficiently and flexibly get more of what they want and less of what they don't want in their lives.

IMPORTANCE OF COGNITION IN PERSONALITY CHANGE As noted above, REBT takes an interactional approach and stresses that cognition, emotion, and behavior greatly influence each other. But although it points out that a significant change in people's feelings or actions often brings about important philosophic change, it particularly emphasizes that a major change in their philosophy can help bring about profound changes in their emotions and behaviors. This is because humans are uniquely thinking or symbolizing animals. They not only think in complex ways but have the unique ability to think about their thinking—and at times to think about thinking about their thinking. Consequently, REBT—more so than any of the other schools of marriage and family therapy—employs a large number of cognitive methods (which will be outlined below). It is a highly depth-centered and philosophically oriented system of personality change and tries to help all the individual family members, as well as the family enclave, make far-reaching changes in their basic attitudes (Ellis, 1962, 1988).

REBT holds that people's disturbance-creating philosophies are often tacitly held, usually just below the surface of consciousness, but that they can be fairly easily revealed and disputed by several techniques (Ellis, 1988, 1994b, 1996; Ellis & Dryden, 1997; Ellis & Harper, 1997; Ellis, Sichel, Yeager, DiMattia, & DiGiuseppe, 1989).

THE ABCS OF EMOTIONAL DISTURBANCE REBT hypothesizes that when family members feel upset about anything or behave dysfunctionally at point C (emotional or behavioral consequence), C is usually preceded by A (an activating experience or adversity) such as a family member's failing at some important task or being rejected by someone whose love he or she seeks. When A occurs, it does not directly "cause" or create C, although it may indirectly contribute to it. Instead, B (the family member's belief system *about* what is occurring at A), more directly "causes" C.

More specifically, REBT hypothesizes that if, say, a husband feels upset about almost anything at point C (consequence), he has both rational beliefs (rBs) and irrational beliefs (iBs) about what the other family members are doing (or supposedly doing) to frustrate or bother him at point A (activating experience). His rational beliefs at B take the form of wishes, wants, and preferences—for example, "I would like to be a good husband and have my wife love me. I don't like failing as a father or mate and having her despise me." These rational beliefs (rBs) almost invariably lead him to feel healthy emotional consequences, such as sorrow, regret, or annoyance, when he fails and gets rejected at A.

If this husband stayed rigorously with rational beliefs, REBT contends, he wouldn't feel and act in a disturbed manner when adversities (As) occurred. He would rationally tell himself, at point B, something like: "Too bad! I have not yet succeeded in being a good husband and having my wife love me. Tough! I'll try harder to succeed and thereby to feel better about my family life. But if I can't, I can't. That's unfortunate, but hardly the end of the world! I can still be a happy, though not quite so happy, person."

Sadly enough, however, this husband often adds to his rational beliefs (rBs) a set of irrational beliefs (iBs) along these lines: "I *must* be a good husband and have my wife love me! How *awful* if I don't succeed in these respects. I *can't stand* failing and being rejected by my family! What a *rotten person* I am for doing so badly!" As a result of these irrational beliefs (iBs) and not merely as a result of his failing and being rejected at point A, this husband tends to feels the consequences (C) horror, low frustration tolerance, and self-downing, and he thereby becomes what we often call "emotionally disturbed." Also, at C, he may resort to dysfunctional behavior, such as abusing his wife and children, alcoholism, staying away from home, or a hasty divorce.

The ABC theory of REBT, then, states that the "causes" of disturbed emotional consequences (C) in family life are not merely the activating experiences that happen in the family at A but also include the spouses' and children's irrational beliefs (iBs) about these As. Although people can theoretically have a large number of irrational beliefs, these are subheadings under three major absolutistic *musts*. These are (1) "I *must* (or *should* or *ought to*) perform well and/or be approved by significant others. It is *awful* (or *horrible* or *terrible*) if I don't. I *can't stand it*! I am a pretty rotten *person* when I fail as I *must* not!"; (2) "Other people *must* treat me considerately and fairly. It is *horrible* if they don't! When they fail me, they are *bad individuals* and I *can't bear* them and their crummy behavior!"; and (3) "Conditions *must* be the way I want them to be, and it is *terrible* when they are not! I *can't stand* living in such an awful world! It is an *uttterly abominable place*!" (Ellis, 1988, 1994b, 1996; Ellis & Dryden, 1997; Ellis & Harper, 1997).

If family members subscribe to one or more of these three basic *musts* and their various derivativisms, they will often create emotional disturbances and dysfunctional behaviors. If they clearly see their absolutistic and unrealistic commands on themselves, on others, and on the universe, and if they work hard at replacing them with strong preferences, they will rarely disturb themselves about life's adversities, although they will still often have strong healthy negative feelings of displeasure, frustration, disappointment, and sorrow (Ellis, 1988).

INSIGHT AND REBT While REBT emphasizes cognition, it holds that psychodynamic insight seldom leads to profound personality change and, instead, is usually wasteful and sidetracking. It rarely discovers and disputes people's dysfunctional philosophies. Instead, REBT stresses a number of rational-emotive insights.

Thus, REBT shows how family problems often lead to interrelated ABCs. When a husband criticizes his wife at point A, she may believe, at point B, "He *must* not do this to me and is a rotten person if he does what he absolutely *should* not do!" and may thereby create the consequence (C) of rage. But he then may take her rage (C), make it into his own activating event (A), then tell himself at B, "I *must* not make her angry! What a worm I am for doing what I *must* not do!" He may thereby make himself guilty and depressed at C (consequence).

Then the wife may take her husband's consequence (C), make it into her own activating event (A), tell herself, "He *must* not be depressed! I can't stand it!" at point B and thereby bring about her own consequence (C) of self-pity and low frustration tolerance.

So in all close relationships, one person's Cs may easily be used or interpreted to produce another's As. That is why in REBT family therapy we try to help reduce the emotional and behavioral disturbances (Cs) of *all* the interrelated individuals (Ellis & Dryden, 1997; Ellis, Sichel, Yeager, DiMattia, & DiGiuseppe, 1989). The three main insights that clients had better achieve include:

Insight No. 1: The "causes" of family members' practical problems may lie in environmental situations (As) but the "causes" of their emotional problems mainly lie in their irrational beliefs (iBs) about family adversities (As).

Insight No. 2: Regardless of how family members originally became (or made themselves) disturbed, they feel upset today because they are *still* indoctrinating themselves with the same kinds of iBs that they held in the past. Even if they learned some of these iBs from their parents and other early socializing agents, they *keep* repeating and retaining them today. Therefore, their present *self*-conditioning is more important than their early external conditioning.

Insight No. 3: If family members achieve Insights No. 1 and 2 and thereby fully realize that they have largely created and keep carrying on their own disturbed feelings, these two insights will not automatically make them change their irrational beliefs. Only if they constantly *work* and *practice*, in the present as well as in the future, to think, feel, and act *against* these iBs are they likely to change them and make themselves significantly less disturbed (Ellis, 1988, 1994b, 1996).

HUMANISTIC OUTLOOK REBT takes the humanistic and existentialist position that family members largely create their own world by the phenomenological *views* they take of what happens to them. It also accepts the philosophy that people had better define their own freedom and cultivate a good measure of individuality—but at the same time, especially if they are to live successfully in family ways, adopt an attitude of caring, sharing, and social interest (Ellis, 1994b, 1996). In accordance with its humanistic outlook, REBT especially emphasizes what Carl Rogers calls unconditional positive regard and what Ellis terms unconditional self-acceptance (USA) and unconditional other-acceptance (UOA) (Ellis, 1988; Ellis & Harper, 1997; Ellis & Tafrate, 1997). As a consequence, REBT takes the unusual stand that we'd better not rate ourselves, our essence, or our being but only our deeds, acts, and performances. We can choose to do this limited kind of rating not in order to *prove* ourselves—that is, to strengthen our ego and self-esteem—but in order to *be* ourselves and *enjoy* ourselves (Ellis, Sichel, Yeager, DiMattia, & DiGiuseppe, 1989).

BEHAVIORAL OUTLOOK REBT holds that family members are easily disturbable and that, even when they have persuaded themselves to give up irrational beliefs, they easily fall back into self-defeating pathways. It sees people as being biologically and socially prone to dysfunctional behaviors and to resisting giving up these activities. It therefore employs a great deal of behavior modification or retraining experiences. In fact, REBT practitioners often use more operant conditioning and in vivo desensitization procedures than do many classical behavior therapists. Along with the usual behavior therapy methods, however, REBT almost always employs many cognitive and emotive approaches.

Therefore, it is intrinsically a form of what Lazarus (1989) calls "multimodal behavior therapy" (Ellis, 1996; Ellis & Dryden, 1997).

DISTURBANCE ABOUT DISTURBANCE REBT has always emphasized the self-talking or self-indoctrinating aspect of human disturbance and family malfunctioning. In addition, it particularly stresses that individuals and family members frequently have secondary as well as primary symptoms of disturbance. Thus, a wife may, at point A, experience criticism from her husband, tell herself, at point B, "I must not be criticized so severely! I am sure that there is something very wrong with what I am doing!" At C (emotional consequence) she then feels depressed. But, being human and having self-downing tendencies, she then makes C into another A and notes to herself, at her secondary B: "I see that I am depressed. I must not be depressed! It's foolish for me to depress myself! I'm a stupid worthless individual for being depressed!" She then is depressed about her depression; and her secondary symptom may be more intense and prolonged than her primary one.

RATIONAL-EMOTIVE BEHAVIOR FAMILY THERAPY AND OTHER SYSTEMS OF FAMILY THERAPY

There are many systems of family therapy today, but the main (or at least most popular) ones seem to be the psychoanalytic, systems, and behavioral schools. Here, briefly, is how rational-emotive behavioral family therapy overlaps with and differs from psychoanalytic and systems schools.

REBT AND PSYCHOANALYTIC FAMILY THERAPY REBT differs considerably from classical Freudian analysis and also from object-relations theories and practices, because both of these systems overstress deeply hidden and repressed unconscious states; exaggerate the crucial importance of early childhood experiences in causing adult disturbances; deify the automatic health-producing qualities of insight into one's past; and encourage intense transference and countertransference relationships between clients and therapists. REBT is highly skeptical of these theories and practices.

REBT reveals family members' unconscious thinking—especially when they are unaware of their hidden musts and demands—but quickly shows that most of it is just below the surface of awareness and is only occasionally deeply repressed. It helps clients see that their early experiences were traumatic because they partly told themselves awfulizing philosophies about them. It gives family members insight into their self-damaging beliefs about their histories rather than an obsessive review of their happenings. It provides clients with unconditional acceptance by their therapists but does not make their relationship with him or her an intensive love-hate part of their lives. In many ways, rational-emotive behavioral family therapy is much more present-centered, philosophically oriented, and more realistic and problem-solving than is psychoanalytic therapy.

REBT AND SYSTEMS FAMILY THERAPY REBT largely goes along with a great deal of the "systems theory" perspective, including these propositions: (1) In studying families and family therapy, we had better pay attention not only to interpretation of individual thoughts, feelings, and behaviors but also to wholeness, organization, and relationship among family members. (2) We had better also seriously consider general (as well as reductionist) principles that might be used to explain biological processes that lead to increasing complexity of organization (for the organism). (3) We had better concentrate on patterned rather than merely on linear relationships and to a consideration of events in the context in which they are occurring rather than an isolation of them from their environmental context. (4) The study of communication among family members often shows how they become disturbed and what they can do to ameliorate their disturbances.

While agreeing with these basic views of systems theory–oriented family therapy, REBT would offer a few caveats as follows: (1) Focusing on wholeness, organization, and relationships among family members is important, but can be overdone. Families become disturbed not merely because of *their* organization and disorganization but because of the serious personal problems of the family members. Unless, therefore, these are considered and dealt with, too, any changes that are likely to occur through changing the family system are likely to be superficial and unlasting. (2) Family systems therapy tends to require an active-directive therapist who makes clear-cut interventions and who engages in a great deal of problem solving. REBT is highly similar in these respects. But family system therapists often ignore the phenomenological and self-disturbing aspects of family members' problems and mainly deal with the system-creating aspects (Ellis, Sichel, Yeager, DiMattia, & DiGiuseppe, 1989). In REBT terms, they often focus on solving A-type (activating events–type) family problems and *not* on the more important B-type (belief system–type) problems. REBT *first* tends to show family members how they philosophically disturb themselves *about* what is happening to them at point A and how, at B, *they* basically create their family and personal problems at C. Its approach is double-barreled rather than single-barreled in this respect (Ellis, 1994b; Ellis & Dryden, 1997). (3) Family therapists often miss the main reasons behind most people's emotional problems: namely, their absolutistic *musts* and *shoulds* and their own and other family members' behaviors (Ellis, Sichel, Yeager, DiMattia, & DiGiuseppe, 1989; Huber & Baruth, 1989).

Systems therapy, as Bowen (1978) has indicated, covers many widely differing "systems," many of which significantly differ from each other and had better be given specific names. Some of them, like Bowen's (1989) and Haley's (1989) are quite cognitive-behavioral and significantly overlap with, and may easily be integrated with, REBT (Ellis, Sichel, Yeager, DiMattia, & DiGiuseppe, 1989; Huber & Baruth, 1989).

REBT AND BEHAVIORAL FAMILY THERAPY REBT subscribes to virtually all the main principles of behavior-oriented family therapy, since it is a form of behavior therapy itself and (as noted above) invariably uses many behavioral theories and methods. However, it uses behavioral techniques mainly to help family members change their basic philosophic assumptions and to make an "elegant" change in their thinking, feeling, and acting, rather than the symptomatic change that some of the "pure" behavior therapist, such as Joseph Wolpe, aim for. And it recognizes that some behavioral methods of individual and family change—such as social reinforcement and gradual desensitization of fears—not only have distinct limitations but also have profound philosophic implications that may lead to antitherapeutic results. Thus, if therapists reinforce family members' changes by giving them social approval, these clients may become overdependent on the therapist and may increase rather than decrease their dire needs for approval, which are often one of the main sources of their disturbances (Ellis & Dryden, 1997).

APPLICATION

CLIENTS AND PROBLEM AREAS FOR WHICH RATIONAL-EMOTIVE BEHAVIOR FAMILY THERAPY IS ESPECIALLY EFFECTIVE

All forms of therapy seem to be especially effective with clients who are young, intelligent, verbal, and not too seriously disturbed (Garfield & Bergin, 1978); and REBT, too, works best with family clients who are in this range. However, it is one of the few forms of treatment that also is effective with what I call DCs (difficult customers)—that is, individuals who are psychotic, personality disordered, organic, or mentally deficient. Naturally, it does not work *as well* with these DCs as it does with less disturbed clients. But it particularly helps them to accept themselves for being handicapped. It also shows them how to achieve higher frustration tolerance, to react better in difficult family situations, and to train themselves to be less disturbed than they would otherwise be (Ellis, 1994a, 1994b, 1994c, 1996).

Moreover, rational-emotive behavior family therapy particularly helps less seriously disturbed family members fully accept and nicely put up with more aberrated members. If children have attention deficit disorder, hyperactivity, dyslexia, or severe personality disorders—as they sometimes do—REBT shows their parents that although they may have significantly contributed to these children's disturbances, they usually did not directly *cause* them. It teaches such parents that there are almost inevitably strong biological factors in their children's overresponsiveness or underresponsiveness and that they, the parents, are hardly to blame for such factors. It also shows parents how to fully accept their emotionally or physically handicapped offspring and how to try to help them to be less (though not necessarily non-) disabled (Ellis, 1978).

At the same time, REBT shows children how to accept their disturbed parents with *their* handicaps; and how to stop seriously upsetting themselves because these parents are not the way they supposedly *should* be. Thus, in the case of 14- and 12-year-old sons who were extremely incensed about their alcoholic father's irresponsibility and their mother's neglecting them for a young lover, they were able to see, after only a few sessions of family therapy using REBT, that both their parents were acting in a highly irresponsible manner but that they, like all humans, had a *right to be wrong*; that they were fallible, disturbed individuals who decided to act the way they did but who could be accepted and forgiven in spite of their antifamily behaviors. Once these two youngsters learned, in family therapy, to accept their parents *with* their irresponsible behaviors, they were able to maintain reasonably good and loving relationships with them, and to focus on what they themselves could do to thrive in this poor family environment. Their schoolwork and their relations with their own friends considerably improved, and they were even partly able to help their parents face their problems and to act somewhat more responsibly. This is a main goal of rational-emotive family therapy: By showing family members how to rate only the poor *behaviors of* other members, parents or children are then able to help these others to improve their dysfunctional actions.

GOALS OF THE THERAPEUTIC PROCESS

The main goals of rational-emotive behavior therapy include:

1. Helping all the family members, if feasible, to see that they largely disturb themselves by taking the actions of the other members *too* seriously, and that they have the choice, no matter how these others behave, of *not* seriously upsetting themselves about their misbehaving.

2. Helping the members continue to keep, and even augment, their desires, wishes, and preferences but to become keenly aware of and to revise their absolutistic *musts*, demands, and commands that others in the family act the way they would prefer them to act.

3. Encouraging parents and children to feel strongly sad, regretful, frustrated, annoyed, and determined to change things when they are not getting what they want in and out of the family setting; but clearly differentiating these healthy negative feelings from their unhealthy feelings of severe anxiety, depression, hostility, self-pity, and low frustration tolerance; and minimizing the latter while still feeling the former emotions.

4. Pinpointing and being closely in touch with their irrational beliefs—their absolutistic shoulds, oughts, and musts—that usually underlie their neurotic feelings and dysfunctional behaviors, and continuing to dispute and challenge these ideas and replace them with more flexible and effective philosophies of living.

5. Learning a number of cognitive, emotive, and behavioral techniques that will reduce their self-defeating and family-defeating behaviors, and encouraging them to think, feel, and behave more sensibly and self-enhancingly.

6. Working at solving practical problems that may be preventing them and other family members from being as happy and effective as they would like to be, as they change their basic disturbance-prone attitudes. In REBT terms, as they work at changing irrational beliefs (iBs) clients also work at changing their As (adversities) that contribute to these Bs and that also contribute to their Cs (dysfunctional consequence).

7. Not only learning to deal effectively with the present crises in their families but also realizing that in the future they can accept adversities, refuse to unduly upset themselves about them, and work at achieving both practical and emotional solutions to their family (and other) problems.

CLIENTS' PRIMARY RESPONSIBILITIES

Family members are shown that if they really want to be responsible to themselves and to other members, they had better decide, and act upon their decision, to *work and practice* at helping to change themselves and others. They are shown that there is no free lunch, and that desirable behaviors do not arise automatically, but result from strong determination plus hard work to change.

In rational-emotive behavior family therapy, therefore, each family member is given responsibility for his or her inner changing and for trying to improve practical family problems. As in the family counseling methods of Dreikurs (1967), it is recommended that children be given a chance to set family policies, along with their parents and other adults; but they also are to take responsibility for their actions and try not to cop out by blaming others for what they do. Adult family members, too, are shown how to acknowledge their own feelings and actions and take responsibility for them—even when other individuals in the family are acting badly and are contributing to difficulties. It is emphasized that one family member has little ability to change others (though he or she can encourage such changes) and that changing oneself largely depends on one's own attitudes and efforts, and not on the manner in which others treat one.

Clients are held to be responsible for their attendance at family therapy sessions and for doing their homework assignments. If they do not like what is happening during the therapy, they are encouraged to speak up about their feelings and to object to what is going on. They are also encouraged to speak up about their feelings about other family members and to voice clearly what they would like, and would not like, to see accomplished within the family system.

Clients are responsible for their own change—since no therapist can really change them. They can only modify their own behavior (or refuse to do so) and they are never blamed for choosing not to change. They are consistently shown that they are in control of their own emotional destiny, because they have the power to alter their own thinking, emotion, and behavior. But if they stubbornly persist at self-defeating actions, they are undamningly shown that this is their way and that they are fully entitled to keep it, but that they still have real options to change.

THERAPIST'S ROLE AND FUNCTION

REBT is one of the most active-directive therapies, and this applies, too, to rational-emotive behavior family therapy. The therapist is a highly trained individual who understands how people needlessly upset themselves and what they can usually do to stop doing so. REBT therapists, therefore, are authoritative without being authoritarian; they bring up discussions of basic values without foisting there own personal values onto clients; and they push, coach, persuade, and encourage—but never command!—clients to think and act against their own self-sabotaging tendencies.

Some of the specific skills that REBT practitioners display in family therapy include: (1) They empathize with clients' thinking and feeling and *also* with their basic disturbance-creating philosophies. (2) They monitor clients' reactions to other family members and to the therapist and show them how to become highly involved but not overinvolved and dependent on others (including the therapist). (3) They show clients how they are relating well and poorly and teach them communication skills. (4) They teach general principles of nondisturbance and self-help and instruct clients how to use these with themselves and other family members. (5) They confront clients with their avoidance, defensive, and resistant behaviors show them the irrational beliefs behind these behaviors; and help them change these beliefs and become much less defensive. (6) They at times are questioning, forceful, and action-encouraging, just as a successful teacher of children or adults would be. (7) They reveal their own feelings and ideas, and show clients how they are not afraid to express themselves and to take risks during therapy sessions. (8) They teach sex, love, relating, and other skills as these seem appropriate for different clients. (9) They specifically focus on teaching themselves and clients several unique REBT-oriented skills, such as (a) actively listening for, probing, and discovering what clients are telling themselves (their rational and irrational beliefs); (b) showing clients the connections between thinking and emoting—between B (their belief systems) and C (the emotional and behavioral consequences) of this thinking; and (c) disputing (D) clients' irrational beliefs (iBs) and showing them how they can do so on their own (Ellis, 1988, 1994b, 1996; Ellis & Dryden, 1997; Ellis, Sichel et al., 1989).

PRIMARY TECHNIQUES USED IN RATIONAL-EMOTIVE BEHAVIOR FAMILY THERAPY

COGNITIVE TECHNIQUES Clients are shown how to discover their dysfunctional beliefs and how to realistically, logically, and pragmatically *dispute* these beliefs. They are shown how to replace them with rational coping statements, such as "I am a *fallible* human who doesn't *have to* behave competently!"; "Others will do what *they* want and not necessarily what is right or what *I* want!"; and "I do not *need* what I desire and can still be a reasonably happy human when frustrated or deprived!" They are taught to use some of the principles of general semantics, promulgated by Alfred Korzybski (1933), to interrupt their all-or-none thinking when they make such statements as "I *always* fail," "I *can't* change," and "I'll *never* get what I want." They are given several different forms of cognitive homework to do, such as to look for their absolutistic *shoulds* and *musts* and to steadily fill out the *REBT Self-Help Report Form* (Sichel & Ellis, 1984). They are shown special cognitive methods, such as *Disputing Irrational Beliefs (DIBS)* (Ellis, 1974), which they can use on their own. They are helped to figure out several choices and actions that are better alternatives to the ones that they are now using. They are encouraged to use rational self-statements, such as "Nothing is awful—only highly inconvenient!" and "There's no gain without pain!" and the philosophies of tolerance, flexibility, humanism, and unconditional acceptance of themselves and others. They are shown some of the evil consequences of their self-defeating behaviors and how they will distinctly suffer from their low frustration and short-range hedonism. They are taught imaging techniques that will help them in their marital and sex lives. They are shown how to use cognitive distraction, such as Edmund Jacobson's progressive relaxation technique or Masters and Johnson's sensate focus, to divert them from their anxiety and depression (Ellis, 1988).

EMOTIVE TECHNIQUES Rational-emotive behavior family therapy employs many emotive, evocative, and dramatic techniques that are also designed to show people how they feel and think and to help them to change their unhealthy feelings to healthy ones. REBT practitioners use rational emotive imagery (Maultsby & Ellis, 1974) to help clients get in touch with their worst feelings, such as horror, despair, and rage, and to change them to healthy negative feelings, such as disappointment, sorrow, and annoyance. They use role-playing methods to show clients how to express and work through some of their self-sabotaging feelings and behaviors. The employ shame-attacking exercises to induce clients to deliberately bring on and then surrender their feelings of intense shame and self-downing. They resort to dramatic and evocative confrontation, especially with clients who refuse to acknowledge or work through some of their feelings. They often use forceful language to help loosen people up and get them to face some of their "unfaceable" problems and emotions. They get clients to vigorously and powerfully repeat to themselves, in a highly emotive manner, sensible statements, such as "I do NOT need what I want!"; "I never HAVE to succeed, no matter how DESIRABLE it may be to do so!"; and "People SHOULD sometimes treat me badly!—for that's the way they naturally behave!" They often use humor and paradoxical intention to strongly attack some of their clients' irrational beliefs and to show how silly they are (Ellis, 1977). They give clients, as noted above, unconditional acceptance, and thereby show them that they *can* accept themselves, even when their behaviors are abominable.

BEHAVIORAL TECHNIQUES REBT has always been exceptionally behavioral as well as cognitive—more so in some ways than the behavioral therapies of some of the main behavior therapists, such as Wolpe. Some of the behavioral techniques it frequently utilizes are these: It gives clients activity homework assignments, most of them to be done in vivo rather than merely in these clients' imaginations. Frequently, these assignments consist of clients staying in an unpleasant marital or family situation until they make themselves unupset about it—and then, perhaps leaving it. REBT also uses operant conditioning and contracting methods: helping family members to contract with other members to do one thing (such as communicate more often) if the other will also do something else (such as be more tidy around the house). Parents are also frequently shown how to use operant techniques to help their children change their undisciplined or other self-defeating behaviors. Skill training—such as assertion training—is often taught, cognitively and behaviorally. Other deconditioning and reconditioning methods are also used in rational-emotive behavior family therapy, including covert desensitization, emotional training, sexual resensitization, and flooding (Ellis, 1978). In vivo implosion or flooding is recommended for some clients, as it has been found to be one of the most effective means to help them overcome long-standing phobias, compulsions, and obsessions that seriously interfere with their marital and family lives (Ellis, 1994a, 1994b, 1994c, 1996; Ellis & Abrams, 1994; Ellis & Velten, 1992).

CASE EXAMPLE

The following is a typescript of part of the initial family treatment session with a mother, father, and their 15-year-old daughter, Debbie. The mother, 45 years of age, is a housewife who has done a little professional dancing during the last few years. The father is also 45 and runs his own business in New York's garment district. They have 21-year-old and 17-year-old sons, both of whom are doing well in school and without serious difficulties; and they are both very upset about their daughter because she has always shown herself to be quite bright—has an IQ of 140 on regular intelligence tests—but she doesn't do her schoolwork, refuses to cooperate with family chores, doesn't look for a job when she promises to do so, fights with her brothers, steals from her family and from the neighbors, and is otherwise disruptive. She acknowledges some of these failings but makes innumerable excuses for them.

At the beginning of the first family therapy session, Debbie admits that she is a "kleptomaniac" and that she uncontrollably steals money. But she denies using it for alcohol and marijuana, which she also denies using regularly. She and her parents agree that she had two good years, in the seventh and eighth grades, when she was in a strict Catholic school. But she has now lost her goal in life—which was to be a lawyer and a politician—and feels purposeless and hopeless and has no incentive to work at school or anything else. Early in the first session, she notes that she had a purpose during the two years she did well: "I knew I wanted to be a lawyer."

Therapist: Yes?

Debbie: And I worked on that.

Therapist: But you've now given that up?

Debbie: Yeah.

Therapist: Why did you give that up?

Debbie: Because I really wanted to become a politician.

Therapist: And you don't want to become a politician anymore?

Debbie: No. They have bad practices and stuff.

Therapist: So that's out of the window?

Debbie: Yes, I have no goal.

Therapist: You're right. If you had a goal in life that would probably help you be happier and avoid the trouble you're getting in. But if you no longer want to be a politician, what stops you from picking some other profession and working toward that?

Debbie: Well, I usually only pick one goal and don't think of other things.

Therapist: Well, you could still choose to be a lawyer, even if not a politician. And there are lots of other things that you could pick that you are capable of doing. Do you think you're capable of doing what you really want to do?

Debbie: For the most part, yes.

Therapist: You had really better give some more thought to that. When bright people like you screw up and give up on goals, they frequently feel that they're incapable of succeeding at them. So perhaps you are in that category, too.

Debbie: Maybe.

(The therapist's main hypotheses, which he theorizes in many cases like Debbie's, are: (1) she has low frustration tolerance and refuses to do things, such as disciplining herself, which are hard and uncomfortable; and (2) she has severe feelings of inadequacy, which block her from trying hard to achieve anything and encourage her to cop out at tasks at which she thinks she might not do well enough. The therapist tries to help her bring out information to back these hypotheses and only partly succeeds in doing so. But the manner in which she replies to him and to her parents, who are present during the entire session, leads him to believe that his hypotheses are plausible.)

Therapist: Do you want to keep getting into the kind of trouble that you're in, with your parents, with the school, and with your brothers?

Debbie: No.

Therapist: Why do you think you steal?

Debbie: 'Cause I can't control myself.

Therapist: That's a nutty conclusion! You have *difficulty* controlling yourself. But that doesn't mean the you *can't*. Suppose that every time you stole, the authorities cut off one of your toes. How long do you think you'd continue to steal?

Debbie: (Mumbles something like "Many times")

Therapist: Many times? Well. That's a strong belief you have—but it's not true. You most probably wouldn't. You would then have a powerful *impulse* to steal; but you don't have to give in to your impulses. For two years you weren't doing self-defeating things and did well at school and at home; you didn't steal. Doesn't that show that you're *able* to control your impulses?

Debbie: Yes, to some degree.

Therapist: Yes, for two whole years you were apparently okay. You were obviously able to control yourself.

Debbie: Because I had a purpose. And I was working on that purpose.

Therapist: Yeah. And that was fine. If you have a purpose, you'll use your energies in that direction, and then you will rarely use them in self-defeating ways.

[Although it is quite early in the first session, the therapist tries to show Debbie and her parents that, in REBT terms, activating events or adversities (A) do not directly cause emotional consequences (C). Instead, they are importantly accompanied by beliefs (B). So he tries to help Debbie to see that just before she gives in to her urge to steal she is telling herself something; and that this set of beliefs (B) is a main cause or contributing factor to her dysfunctional consequences (C).]

Debbie: I want it.

Therapist: You mean, "I want the money I take?"

Mother: I think the main thing she wants is to buy liquor or dope with the money.

Therapist: That may be. But let's go along with Debbie's views. You're saying that you want the money. Right?

Debbie: Yes.

Therapist: But if you only stuck to that belief—"I want the money"—you probably wouldn't steal. Do you know why?

Debbie: Because I'd see that I often get caught and wouldn't want to get caught stealing it.

Therapist: Right! Whenever we have a want or a wish, we tend to see the consequences of having it, and we often reject it. So you're probably saying something much stronger than "I want the money" when you steal. Do you know what that stronger belief probably is?

Debbie: No. Uh, maybe: "I need it."

Therapist: Correct! "I need the money that I want! I MUST have it because I want it!" And that NEED and that MUST will often drive you to steal, even when you know you may get caught and suffer poor consequences. But is your NEED or MUST true? MUST you have the money? Or MUST you have what you get with the money—alcohol, pot, or anything else?

Debbie: No.

Therapist: That's right: No! But if you keep insisting that you MUST have the money (or anything else), you're probably going to feel not only uncomfortable but horrible, off the wall, when you don't have what you think you MUST. Then, when you feel exceptionally uncomfortable, you may well go on to another MUST: "I MUST not feel uncomfortable. I CAN'T STAND this discomfort of not having what I MUST have!" Is that what you're saying, too?

Debbie: Yes. I CAN'T stand it. I CAN'T!

Therapist: Stop a minute, now! CAN'T you really stand it? CAN you actually bear the discomfort of being frustrated and not getting exactly what you want at this very moment that you want it?

Debbie: I don't like it.

Therapist: Right. But you're not merely sticking to, "I don't like it." That would be fine, if you did. I hear you saying, "BECAUSE I don't like it, I CAN'T STAND it! It's AWFUL if I don't have it!"

Debbie: But I really want it!

Therapist: Yes, of course. But your want is not what drives you to stealing. Your basic belief, "I MUST HAVE what I want!" is what does so. And we call that attitude and the feeling that goes with it low frustration tolerance. You're apparently telling yourself, "I WANT, and MUST HAVE, what I want right now! I CAN'T BEAR frustration and deprivation." Isn't that what's really going on in your head?

Debbie: Yes, I CAN'T stand it!

Therapist: Well, as long as you have that basic philosophy—"I absolutely NEED what I want and I CAN'T STAND not having it!"—you'll be driven, driven by those beliefs, to steal, fight with your family, break things, goof at school, and do other things that tend to get and keep you in trouble. But you could have, instead, the philosophy: "I want what I want and am determined to try to get it. But if I don't get it right now, tough! So I don't! I do not NEED everything I immediately want!" But you are saying to yourself, as far as I can see, "I DO need it!"

Debbie: Well, perhaps I'm doing it because I'm escaping.

Therapist: Escaping from what? What are you escaping from? Feelings of inadequacy, you mean? The feeling that you haven't the ability to get some of the things that you want and think you need?

Debbie: That could be one.

Therapist: Let's talk about those inadequacy feelings for a moment. What are they? Are you willing to talk about them in front of your parents?

Debbie: It doesn't matter.

Therapist: Well, what do you feel inferior about?

Debbie: I'm confused. I haven't figured out what's the purpose of it all. I don't see how to react to certain problems.

Therapist: Such as?

Debbie: Well, some domestic problems. And I just don't get along with people. I like them but I don't understand them.

Therapist: And you think that you SHOULD, you MUST understand them?

Debbie: Yes. And that's why I often try to get high.

Therapist: And do you blame yourself, then, for getting high?

Debbie: Yes, sometimes.

Therapist: Well, let's assume that getting high won't solve things or make you understand people better, and it's therefore something of a mistake. And let's suppose you're not yet very good at understanding and getting along with people. Why do you put yourself down for these failings?

Debbie: Because I know that it's not right.

Therapist: Yes, well let's assume that. Suppose what you're doing is wrong. How does that make you a worm, that wrong behavior?

Debbie: (Silence)

Therapist: Suppose your mother and father do something wrong. Are they worms for doing that wrong thing?

Debbie: No.

Therapist: Then why are you?

Debbie: Because then I'm a wrong person.

Therapist: But you're NOT a wrong person! That's your nutty thinking! That's what we call an overgeneralization. If we can help you to give up that kind of irrational thinking, and get you to completely accept YOURSELF, even when you are doing the WRONG THING, then you can usually go back and correct your error. But if you put YOURSELF down and define yourself as a no-goodnik for acting wrongly, there's no good solution to the problem! For how can a worm be dewormified? (Debbie and her parents all laugh fairly heartily at this statement.) Your feelings of inadequacy don't come from doing the wrong thing. They come from CONDEMNING YOURSELF for doing it—putting yourself into hell. That makes things much worse.

Debbie: Yes, it does.

Therapist: But do you really see all of what's going on here? You first do badly—or think that you will do badly at something. Then you put yourself down, MAKE YOURSELF feel inadequate as a person. Then you tend to do something like drink or smoke pot, to make yourself relax temporarily and feel a little better. But then you get into more trouble, because of the alcohol or pot or the stealing that you did to get the money for it, and then you blame yourself more and go around and around in a vicious self-damning circle.

Debbie: I guess I do. I keep thinking that I'm really no good. And then things get worse.

Therapist: Right!

Debbie: But how can I stop that?

Therapist: The best solution is to see very clearly what I said before: that some of your acts are wrong and self-defeating but that YOU are not a worm for doing them. If we could get you to fully accept YOURSELF, your BEING, your TOTALITY, even when you are screwing up and acting stupidly or badly, then we could get you to go back and work on avoiding your screwups. And you could change most of them, which you are quite capable of doing—if you weren't wasting your time and energy and making things worse by your self-damning. That isn't going to work.

Debbie: It doesn't. I just feel worse. And then I think that I have to keep repeating this, uh, inadequate behavior.

Therapist: Right! The more you condemn YOURSELF for your poor BE-HAVIOR the more you lose confidence in your ability to correct that behavior.

Debbie: (Smiling) A worm can't be dewormified!

Therapist: Exactly! If you are, to your core, a thorough turd, how can you change your turdiness? No way!

Debbie: But how do I stop blaming myself?

Therapist: By changing your fundamental MUSTS. For, at bottom, you seem to be saying: "I MUST, I HAVE TO do well." Not, "I'd LIKE or PREFER to do well." And you're also saying to yourself, and very strongly, "I MUST NOT suffer inconveniences. It's AWFUL if I do." You could tell yourself, instead, "I'd LIKE to avoid inconveniences. But if I don't, I don't! I can experience them—and still be a happy human!"

Debbie: I see what you mean. But how am I going to keep seeing that and believing it?

Therapist: By darned hard work! By continuing *to think about* what you say to yourself and do. And by changing your perfectionistic demands into preferences and desires.

(The therapist, without having the full details of the history of Debbie and her parents, uses some data that he quickly discovers from them and hypothesizes from REBT theory that she *demands* that she perform well and *insists* that the universe treat her kindly. He tests these hypotheses with Debbie, gets some evidence to support them, and then quickly and forthrightly challenges her unrealistic, irrational beliefs. He also show her that she can do this herself, and can change these beliefs and create better emotional and behavioral results. As he talks to Debbie, he from time to time shows her parents that they, too, have MUSTS about Debbie, and that they are unrealistically *demanding* that she act well and are condemning her and upsetting themselves when she doesn't. So he favors their listening to his disputing of Debbie's irrational beliefs (iBs). But he also indicates that they often think the same way as she does, that they also have iBs—and that they do not have to perpetuate them. Toward the end of the session the therapist speaks to Debbie and then to her parents.)

Therapist: If I can help you, Debbie, to keep your desires and to give up your MUSTS, you'll begin to feel and act better. By so doing, you'll most probably get more of what you want and less of what you don't want. But you won't get *everything* you want! No one does. (To Debbie's parents): She has many healthy preferences, but then she tells herself, "I MUST, I MUST fulfill them!" And: "I MUST get what I want IMMEDIATELY!" Now, if I can get all of you, including her, to look for the SHOULD, look for the MUST, which you are all bright enough to do, and if I can persuade you to tackle these *demands* and change them to healthy *wants*, you will all upset yourselves much less and tend to solve your problems of getting along together and living happily in this difficult world. (To Debbie, again): If I can help you do *that*, then you'll get along with your parents and siblings and live more successfully. What you now often do is to overwhelm your desires with impractical MUSTS. "I MUST do this and MUST do that! But maybe I won't. And that would be TERRIBLE!" Then you feel depressed and anxious and start copping out. Then you blame yourself for acting badly and feel more anxious and depressed. A very vicious circle! Have you read any of my writings on this?

The therapist closes the session by assigning all three of them, Debbie and her parents, to read a group of pamphlets on REBT that the Albert Ellis Institute gives to clients at its clinic in New York, and also to read *A Guide to Rational Living* by Ellis and Harper (1997), which many clients find helpful. Debbie and her parents are to make another appointment, next week; and in between, to make a note of all the times they feel upset during the week, especially about each other, and what is happening in the family. They are to look for the absolutistic SHOULDS and MUSTS that accompany these feelings, to try to dispute them, and to bring them up during the next session, to see how they are doing at discovering and challenging them.

Following this first session, Debbie and her parents were seen once a week for a total of 16 weeks. Debbie was seen primarily for individual sessions by herself, although usually one or both parents were also seen with her for a half hour, while she was seen by herself for an additional half hour. On a few occasions, her parents were also seen by themselves to deal with their anger and other feelings of upsetness about her "rotten" behavior and about their own problems with each other and with outsiders—especially, her father's problems with his business associates and her mother's problems with her women friends. A number of rational-emotive behavior family therapy techniques were used with Debbie and her parents during these sessions.

It would have been preferable as a part of their therapy to see her two brothers, too, for some of the sessions. But the parents insisted that the brothers had no problems and might be harmed by participating in therapy. The brothers themselves also resisted coming, as they thought that Debbie had a serious emotional problem, but that they did not. Under more usual conditions, the brothers would have been seen along with the other members of the family. Here are some of the REBT methods that were employed:

COGNITIVE METHODS

Whenever Debbie or her parents showed any feelings of anxiety, depression, anger, or self-pity (which they frequently did) or when Debbie continued her antisocial behavior, they were shown the ABCs of REBT: That their Cs (emotional consequences) did not merely stem from their As (adversities) but also from their own iBs (irrational Beliefs) *about* these As. They were shown their absolutistic *shoulds* and *musts* and how to dispute them. They were given the cognitive homework of doing the rational self-help report form published by the Institute (Sichel & Ellis, 1984), and these were gone over with them and discussed with the therapist. They were given, as noted above, bibliotherapeutic materials on REBT to read and discuss—particularly *A Guide to Rational Living* (Ellis & Harper, 1997), *How to Live with a "Neurotic": At Home and at Work* (Ellis, 1957), *How to Stubbornly Refuse to Make Yourself Miserable About Anything—Yes, Anything* (Ellis, 1988), and *How to Stop People from Pushing Your Buttons* (Ellis & Lange, 1994). They were also encouraged to listen to some of the cassette recordings distributed by the Institute, such as *Conquering Low Frustration Tolerance* (Ellis, 1976a) and *Unconditionally Accepting Yourself and Others* (Ellis, 1992). They also participated in some of the four-hour workshops on parent-child relationships and overcoming depression that the Institute held.

Cognitively, too, the members of this family, especially Debbie, were given useful suggestions on how to solve certain practical problems that arose (such as how Debbie could get and keep a job, in spite of her poor reputation in the community). They were shown how to write down and focus on the real disadvantages of their avoidant behaviors. They were taught some of the principles of general semantics dealing with overgeneralization and allness. They were shown how to use cognitive distraction methods, such as Edmund Jacobsen's muscular relaxation methods, when they wanted to temporarily calm themselves down. The therapist sometimes used humor and paradoxical intention with them—for example, he encouraged Debbie to deliberately fail at certain tasks, to prove to herself that the world did not come to an end when she did—and he helped her to see the humorous side of her taking things too seriously and of blaming herself for her poor behavior. They were continually taught how to accept themselves fully, and to stop condemning themselves for anything, even when they obviously made stupid mistakes.

EMOTIVE METHODS

Emotively, even though the therapist pulled no punches in showing Debbie how she was being irresponsible to herself and others, she could always see that he fully accepted her, as a human, in spite of her failings and that he had confidence that she definitely could—if she would—change. He also helped her to do rational-emotive imagery as homework assignments: to imagine that she really did very badly, at work or socially; that others despised her for her poor behavior; to first allow herself to feel very depressed about this image; but then to make herself feel only sorry and disappointed rather than self-downing. The therapist did role-playing, with her and her parents, let her confess to them some of the things she hadn't yet told them, and then persist at the confessions and work through the shame she felt about their shocked responses. He encouraged her to do out-of-session REBT shame-attacking exercises—such as to wear very "loud" clothing—and to work at not making herself feel embarrassed or humiliated when she did this. He helped her to write out some rational self-statements—such as, "I do not need immediate gratification, no matter how much I really want it!"—and to repeat these to herself very vigorously 10 or 20 times a day until she strongly agreed with them. The therapist used George Kelly's (1955) fixed role-playing method with both Debbie and her parents, and had them write scripts about the kind of people they would like to be and then enact these scripts for a week, until they became used to acting in that unfamiliar way.

BEHAVIORAL METHODS

With Debbie in particular, the therapist used several behavioral methods and taught her parents how to use them with her. Whenever she spent at least two hours a week looking for a part-time job, she was permitted to socialize with her friends or do other things she enjoyed. And whenever she lied or stole, she was confined to her room for several hours at a time. When her parents criticized her in an angry, damning manner, they were also to refrain from socializing with their friends for that day. These reinforcements and penalties worked fairly well— as long as they were enforced. But her parents had to keep after Debbie and she, to some extent, had to keep after them to actually carry out their reinforcements and penalties.

Debbie was encouraged to take several different kinds of activity homework assignments—including looking for a job, doing various family chores, and behaving in a cooperative instead of disruptive manner with her parents and her siblings. Some of these she quickly carried out, and benefited from seeing that she was able to do them and was not totally out of control, as she often said she was. Other assignments, such as the chores, she did sporadically but still seemed to derive some benefit from doing them.

At the end of 16 weeks of rational emotive bahavior family therapy, Debbie was doing her school work regularly, had ceased stealing, and was getting along much better with her family members. Even more than this, she was distinctly accepting herself with her imperfect performances. Her mother and father were considerably less angry at her, even when she fell back into her old disruptive behavior; and they used some of the rational ideas and procedures we were discussing and began to feel much less angry at one another and to behave more cooperatively. Their sex life also improved considerably, mainly because of their better relationships with themselves and with Debbie. The father returned for several therapy sessions a year and a half later, because he was avoiding some of his office work and was putting himself down for this; and at that time it was ascertained that Debbie was still acting remarkably better and that much more family harmony existed.

EVALUATION

As noted in the section on research studies, REBT has an unusually detailed and good record as far as research into its basic personality hypotheses and its claims for clinical effectiveness are concerned. In the field of marriage and family therapy in particular, reviews of a number of outcome studies favorable to it have been published (as also previously noted). Clinically, it appears to work very well, whether clients are seen separately or conjointly; and it is useful in premarital, marital, and divorce cases (Ellis, 1978, 1994b; Ellis & Harper, 1997). Case studies and anecdotal reports of the effectiveness of any form of therapy, especially family therapy, are highly suspect, however, and more controlled research is much desired.

SUMMARY

Rational emotive behavior family therapy is a special form of REBT and follows the general principles it uses in individual and group therapy. It overlaps with behavior therapy and with systems therapy in many of the techniques that it uses, but it is a form of cognitive behavior therapy (CBT) that includes the following unique features: (1) It importantly stresses the cognitive or philosophic aspects of emotional disturbance and of family disruption. (2) It teaches family clients that they importantly choose to disturb themselves and that they can effectively refuse to continue to do so. It is one of the main constructivist therapies that emphasizes the unique ability of people to disturb and to undisturb themselves. (3) It employs a number of cognitive, emotive, and behavioral techniques, not merely to achieve symptomatic change but to help family clients achieve a profound philosophic reconstruction that will hopefully lead to elegant and permanent change. It aims to show people how to make themselves significantly less disturbed—and preferably remarkably less disturbable (Ellis, 1996). (4) It clearly acknowledges the biological as well as the sociological bases of individual and family disturbance and therefore stresses vigorous and forceful, active-directive methods that will impinge upon and help alter the strongly held disturbances that family members frequently experience. (5) It favors a scientific and highly humanistic outlook in both its theory and its practice. (6) It stresses a phenomenological, intrapsychic, and depth-centered approach to understanding and tackling human disturbance but at the same time uses practical problem-solving and skill-training methods of changing family situations and interactions.

ANNOTATED SUGGESTED READINGS

Ellis, A. (1975). *How to live with a "neurotic."* North Hollywood, CA: Melvin Powers.
> The first book on REBT, originally published in 1957, showing how readers can cope with and help difficult individuals, and especially showing married and mated individuals how they can live successfully with difficult partners.

Ellis, A. (1994). *Reason and emotion in psychotherapy.* Revised and updated. Secaucus, NJ: Birch Lane Press.
> Revised edition of the first book presenting REBT in textbook form, mainly written for therapists and counselors but also widely used by those who want to help themselves overcome their emotional problems.

Ellis, A. (1996). *Better, deeper, and more enduring brief therapy.* New York: Brunner/Mazel.
> Shows how REBT can be used in brief therapy with neurotic and personality-disordered individuals.

Ellis, A., & Dryden, W. (1997). *The practice of rational emotive behavior therapy.* (Rev. ed.). New York: Springer.
> Brings REBT theory and practice up to date and specifically shows how it is practiced in different kinds of settings, including individual, group, couples, and family therapy settings.

Ellis, A., Sichel, J., Yeager, R., DiMattia, D., & DiGiuseppe, R. (1989). *Rational-emotive couples therapy*. New York: Pergamen.

Gives in detail the REBT theory and practice of couples and family therapy.

REFERENCES

Adler, A. (1964). *Social interest: A challenge to mankind*. New York: Capricorn.

Baucom, D. H., & Epstein, N. (1990). *Cognitive-behavioral marital therapy*. New York: Brunner/Mazel.

Beck, A. (1988). *Love is not enough*. New York: Harper and Row.

Bowen, M. (1978). *Family therapy in clinical practice*. New York: Aronson.

Dreikurs, R. (1967). *Psychodyanamics, psychotherapy and counseling*. Chicago: Alfred Adler Institute.

Ellis, A. (1957). *How to live with a "neurotic": At home and at work*. New York: Crown. Rev. ed.: Hollywood, CA: Wilshire Books, 1975.

Ellis, A. (1960). *The art and science of love*. Secaucus, NJ: Lyle Stuart.

Ellis, A. (1962). *Reason and emotion in psychotherapy*. New York: Citadel Press.

Ellis, A. (1963). *The intelligent woman's guide to manhunting*. New York: Lyle Stuart and Dell. Rev. ed.: *The intelligent woman's guide to dating and mating*. Secaucus, NJ: Lyle Stuart, 1979.

Ellis, A. (1974). *Disputing irrational beliefs*. New York: Institute for Rational-Emotive Therapy.

Ellis, A. (Speaker). (1976a). *Conquering low frustration tolerance* (cassette recording). New York: Institute for Rational-Emotive Therapy.

Ellis, A. (1976b). *Sex and the liberated man*. Secaucus, NJ: Lyle Stuart.

Ellis, A. (1977). Fun as psychotherapy. *Rational Living, 12*(1), 2–6. Also: Cassette recording. New York: Institute for Rational-Emotive Therapy.

Ellis, A. (1978). Family therapy: A phenomenological and active-directive approach. *Journal of Marriage and Family Counseling, 4*(2), 43–50. Reprinted: New York: Institute for Rational-Emotive Therapy.

Ellis, A. (1988). *How to stubbornly refuse to make yourself miserable about anything—yes, anything!* Secaucus, NJ: Lyle Stuart.

Ellis, A. (Speaker). (1992). *Unconditionally accepting yourself and others* (cassette recording). New York: Institute for Rational-Emotive Therapy.

Ellis, A. (1994a). Rational-emotive behavior therapy approaches to obsessive-compulsive disorder (OCD). *Journal of Rational-Emotive & Cognitive-Behavior Therapy, 12*, 121–144.

Ellis, A. (1994b). *Reason and emotion in psychotherapy*. Revised and updated. Secaucus, NJ: Birch Lane Press.

Ellis, A. (1994c). The treatment of borderline personalities with rational-emotive behavior therapy. *Journal of Rational-Emotive & Cognitive Behavior Therapy, 12*, 101–119.

Ellis, A. (1996). *Better, deeper, and more enduring brief therapy*. New York: Brunner/Mazel.

Ellis, A., & Abrams, M. (1994). *How to cope with a fatal illness*. New York: Barricade Books.

Ellis, A., & Dryden, W. (1997). *The practice of rational-emotive behavior therapy* (Rev. ed.). New York: Springer.

Ellis, A., & Harper, R. A. (1961). *A guide to successful marriage* (1st ed.). North Hollywood, CA: Wilshire Books.

Ellis, A., & Harper, R. A. (1997). *A guide to successful marriage* (3rd ed.). North Hollywood, CA: Wilshire Books.

Ellis, A., & Lange, A. (1994). *How to keep people from pushing your buttons.* Secaucus, NJ: Carol Publishing Group.

Ellis, A., Sichel, J., Yeager, R., DiMattia, D., & DiGiuseppe, R. (1989). *Rational-emotive couples therapy.* New York: Pergamon.

Ellis, A., & Tafrate, R. C. (1997). *Anger—How to live with and without it* (Rev. ed.). Secaucus, NJ: Carol Publishing Group.

Ellis, A., & Velten, E. (1992). *When AA doesn't work for you: Rational steps for quitting alcohol.* New York: Barricade Books.

Garfield, S., & Bergin, A. E. (Eds.). (1978). *Handbook of psychotherapy and behavior change* (2nd ed.). New York: Wiley.

Hajzler, D., & Bernard, M. E. (1991). A review of rational-emotive outcome studies. *School Psychology Quarterly, 6*(1), 27–49.

Haley, J. (1989). *Problem-solving therapy* (Rev. ed.). San Francisco: Jossey-Bass.

Hayes, S. C., Jacobson, N. S., Follette, V. M., & Dougher, N. J. (1994). *Acceptance and change.* Reno, NV: Context Press.

Hollon, S. D., & Beck, A. T. (1994). Cognitive and cognitive-behavior therapies. In A. E. Bergin & S. L. Garfield (Eds.), *Handbook of psychotherapy and behavior change* (pp. 428–463). New York: Wiley.

Huber, C., & Baruth, (1989). *Integrating rational-emotive and systems family therapy.* New York: Springer.

Kelly, G. (1955). *The psychology of personal constructs* (2 vols.). New York: Norton.

Korzybski, A. (1933). *Science and sanity.* San Francisco: International Society of General Semantics.

Lazarus, A. A. (1989). *The practice of multimodal therapy.* New York: McGraw-Hill.

Lyons, L. C., & Woods, P. J. (1991). The efficacy of rational-emotive therapy. *Clinical Psychology Review, 11,* 357–369.

Maultsby, M. C., Jr., & Ellis, A. (1974). *Technique for using rational-emotive imagery.* New York: Institute for Rational-Emotive Therapy.

McGovern, T. E., & Silverman, M. S. (1984). A review of outcome studies of rational-emotive therapy from 1977 to 1982. *Journal of Rational-Emotive Therapy, 2*(1), 7–18.

Sichel, J., & Ellis, A. (1984). *REBT self-help report form.* New York: Institute for Rational-Emotive Therapy.

Silverman, M. S., McCarthy, M., & McGovern, T. (1992). A review of outcome studies of rational-emotive therapy. *Journal of Rational-Emotive & Cognitive-Behavior Therapy, 10,* 111–186.

CHAPTER 17

Feminist Family Therapy

KATHRYN L. NORSWORTHY

When those who have the power to name and to socially construct reality choose not to see or hear you, whether you are dark-skinned, old, disabled, female, or speak with a different accent or dialect than theirs; when someone with the authority of a teacher, say, describes the world and you are not in it, there is a moment of psychic disequilibrium, as if you looked into a mirror and saw nothing.

– Adrienne Rich

DEFINITION

Feminist family therapy stands on the frontier of the family therapy field as an important meta-model for centralizing diversity and concepts of power in the understanding of family relationships. Feminist and multicultural principles are foundational in the much-needed revision and reconstruction of contemporary theories of family therapy. We are beginning to understand the necessity of recognizing the ways in which race, class, gender, sexual orientation, spiritual tradition, age, physical ability, language, and other variables interact, organize, and influence the experiences of each of us. Now we also must acknowledge the fundamental nature of these identities as social constructions in understanding families and their social and political contexts. From a feminist perspective, Adrienne Rich poses the most pressing challenge to the family therapy field as we approach the new millenium. **515**

She explains the need to rewrite and reorganize family theories and practices to reflect the lived experiences of this multicultural, diverse society in which we live—to reflect more inclusive and realistic pictures of families from diverse backgrounds, with multiple identities, and based on broader definitions.

Feminist theory, whether applied to understanding the individual, the group, the family, or larger social, cultural, and political systems, is a theory of liberation. Feminist family therapy identifies the important interrelationships in the personal and political spheres of family life. The location of the family in these larger "systems," and the ways members' thoughts, feelings, actions, and relationships are imbedded in and influenced by social, political, and cultural factors, become the central focus of a feminist family therapy meta-theory. As an agent of social change, the feminist family therapist challenges the inequities within the family based in power imbalances and oppression, and works to help all members find their voices and trust themselves as important sources of information and authority within the family. The personal becomes political.

HISTORICAL DEVELOPMENT

As feminist scholars and practitioners are keenly aware, "history" is usually created and reported in the service of those holding privilege and power in the culture. I want to acknowledge that this account of "herstory"—the development of the field of feminist family therapy—is reflective of my values and beliefs and those of feminist colleagues with whom I consulted regarding the significance attached to particular events and scholarly works mentioned in this section. I use the term "herstory" because this theoretical perspective is borne almost exclusively of the work of women.

The roots of feminist family therapy in the United States extend across disciplines and reflect influences from a diverse group of women. Women of color and white women have been voicing and writing about their struggles and challenges within the contexts of gender, race and ethnicity, class, and sexual orientation for centuries. According to Deborah Luepnitz (1988), "Modern feminism, born of Enlightenment ideals of democracy and energized by American Reconstructionist passion, has existed in the United States since the 1850s."

For the purposes of this chapter, we will turn our attention to the early 1960s when the "second wave" of middle-/upper-class white feminism emerged within the context of the civil rights movement in this country. During this period, gender, for white women, and race, for African Americans, were launched as central factors in organizing the human experience, and the study of sexism and racism in U.S. society emerged. Betty Friedan (1963) pioneered the discussion on gender by raising the issue for women in her well-known book *The Feminine Mystique*. Nancy Chodorow (1978), Dorothy Dinnerstein (1976), and Adrienne Rich (1976) provided important leadership in theorizing and conceptualizing how gender is constructed in the family and larger sociocultural contexts. However, this movement was devoted almost exclusively to the study of white, heterosexual women and their families.

Women of color were concurrently and independently giving voice to their experiences through the lens of race, ethnicity, and the accompanying oppression.

For example, Angela Davis (1981), Bell Hooks (1984), and Audre Lorde (1984) all contributed powerful accounts of the complex historical and contemporary challenges facing African American women. They were also noting that the white feminist perspectives were not representative of their experiences, and they expressed concern about the ways that white middle- and upper-class feminists placed gender at the center of feminist theory and made sweeping generalizations about the applicability of white feminism to all women, regardless of their race, ethnicity, class, sexual orientation, and other diverse characteristics.

The advent of the family therapy movement over 35 years ago brought a radically different way of conceptualizing individual and family distress, taking it out of the intrapsychic realm and framing it within a systems context. Most of the original pioneers in the family systems movement were white men, and even as more women, again mostly white, entered the field, the focus until the late '70s remained on the cybernetic-based model of family functioning. As we have discussed earlier, the major theories described a white, masculinized model of family reality and "health."

Then, in 1975, the American Psychological Association Task Force on Sex Bias and Sex Role Stereotyping in Psychotherapeutic Practice identified the prevalence of sex-role sterotyping, sexist bias, and the privileging of men's needs and activities over women's in the practice of counseling and psychotherapy (American Psychological Association, 1975). This effort effectively brought to light the disadvantaged position of women, even in the therapeutic relationship.

Concurrently, a number of women in the family therapy field, profoundly influenced by the women's movement and the proliferation of feminist literature, were thinking independently or in small groups about how to modify, integrate, or reconcile the feminist and the family systems perspectives. Marianne Walters describes the paths that she and her feminist family therapist colleagues, Peggy Papp, Betty Carter, and Olga Silverstein, followed, beginning in the mid-'70s, in bringing feminist theory and practice to the practice of family therapy (Walters, Carter, Papp, & Silverstein, 1988). "When the four of us met together the first time in the summer of 1977 to discuss ways to bring women's issues and feminist consciousness into the mainstream of family therapy, we were struck with how much the women's movement had already begun to affect our lives and our thinking" (p. 6). This group, which began to conduct trainings on women's issues in family therapy, was met with great enthusiasm, and quickly formed the Women's Project in Family Therapy. Their 1988 book, *The Invisible Web*, represents a seminal contribution based on their hard work and dedication to bringing the issue of gender to light as a critical factor in working with families.

One of the first public signs of feminist questioning of the dominant voices in the field of family therapy emerged when Rachel Hare-Mustin (1978) wrote a provocative article for the mainstream family therapy journal *Family Process*, entitled "A Feminist Approach to Family Therapy." She challenged the role of family therapy in reinforcing stereotyped sex roles within the family, and the lack of theoretical consideration of the larger social context of the family and its members, particularly women. Continued contributions on the topic of gender and family therapy theory and practice came from Hare-Mustin (1979, 1980, 1989) as other powerful voices emerged. And they were not always fully embraced by their colleagues.

Monica McGoldrick, Carol Anderson, and Froma Walsh (1989), in the first chapter of their seminal work, *Women in Families*, describe their painfully humorous experience in 1984 of assembling a group of women "at the cutting edge of family therapy training, theory, and research" (p. 3) at Stonehenge, Connecticut, to discuss the issues of women in families and family therapy. Initial reactions from the attendees ranged from not seeing the point of meeting with other women, feeling that meeting with other women would be boring, and not viewing gender as a significant factor in relationships to being concerned that male colleagues would not approve of their attending such a meeting. Apparently men also reacted strongly. "The meeting was compared to a coven of witches. Women who were interested in attending were called radicals, men haters, and—the worst of all possible insults—'non-systemic thinkers'" (p. 4). Much to their credit, McGoldrick, Anderson, and Walsh followed through with their commitment to hold the landmark colloquium, called the Stonehenge conference, and women scholars and family therapists continued the process of describing the integral role of gender in organizing the human experience.

Subsequent contributions, such as the books *Feminist Family Therapy* by Thelma Jean Goodrich, Cheryl Rampage, Barbara Ellman, and Kris Halstead (1988) and *Women and Family Therapy*, edited by Marianne Ault-Riché (1986), along with the 1989 development of *The Journal of Feminist Family Therapy*, first edited by Lois Braverman, are examples of the expansions of the field of feminist family therapy. In 1986, Judith Myers Avis contributed the first chapter, entitled "Feminist Issues in Family Therapy" (Avis, 1986), to a family therapy text, *Family Therapy Sourcebook*, edited by Piercy, Sprenkle, and Associates. This chapter now appears in an updated version in the second edition of the text.

Within the past 10 years, important expansions of feminist family therapy have come from explorations of race, ethnicity, culture, class, sexual orientation, disability, and religion and spirituality. Among others, Ruth Hall and Beverly Greene (1994) have issued a wake-up call to family therapy theorists and practitioners to develop cultural competence that expands beyond gender in the ethical practice of feminist family therapy. Nancy Boyd-Franklin and Nydia Garcia-Preto (1994) offer a thorough discussion of the importance of addressing cultural factors in family therapy with African American and Hispanic clients. Rhea Almeida (1994), in her book *Expansions of Feminist Family Theory Through Diversity*, challenges clinicians by addressing the question "How do race, class, culture, and gender socially construct varying dimensions of social inequality that in turn organize different forms of family life?" (p. 1).

Also important to mention here is the work of Leonore Tiefer (1995), feminist sexologist and author of the witty and provocative book *Sex Is Not a Natural Act*. Tiefer's groundbreaking feminist critique of human sexuality research, and of contemporary theories and practices in sex therapy, challenges normative models of conceptualizing human sexuality and the dominant frameworks for sex therapy.

TENETS OF THE MODEL

INTRODUCTION

In discussing the theoretical foundations of feminist family therapy, I find myself with a challenging task. Feminist theories and practices have often been conceptualized in response to the dominant models of personality development and individual and family counseling theory that do not represent the experiences of large segments of society (Morawski & Bayer, 1995). This chapter offers a stimulating opportunity to centralize the basic tenets and practices of a feminist family therapy meta-model in our practice, teaching, and research. Feminism comes in many forms, with varied and complex intellectual and contextual roots. Presented here are my efforts as a white, middle-class (with working-class roots), able-bodied, feminist, academic psychologist and clinician to synthesize the ideas of many brilliant and talented feminist scholars and practitioners with my own into a discussion of feminist family therapy theory. In keeping with the spirit of feminist thought, I want to acknowledge that, in the writing of this chapter, I am both informed and limited by my own location and context, and that a particular version of feminist family therapy theory and practice will be described. Others in the field would possibly offer similar or perhaps radically different points of view. Most important to me is to attempt not to repeat the mistakes of the past involving the promotion of a theory as all-inclusive, thereby rendering invisible large segments of the population about whom the theories are supposed to apply. In this chapter, I will deliberately attempt to make room for the integral impact and interactions of multiple cultural identities of the clients and the therapist. For the purposes of this chapter, culture is defined as gender, race, ethnicity, sexual orientation, class, spirituality, physical ability, age, language, and other factors that serve to organize the human experience.

DEFINITION OF THE FAMILY

In the United States, the dominant social and political definition of the family has been a man, a woman, and one or more children, and this definition has been codified into law and promoted by the majority of religious institutions and the psychotherapy community. When we apply feminist principles of analysis to this dominant definition, a very large constituency of groups of individuals who consider themselves families are left out, including single-parent families, gay and lesbian families, cohabitating couples with or without children, many families of color, and single people within close friendship circles. As McGoldrick (1994) observes, "Our entire society is organized to accommodate a type of family structure that represents only 6% of the U.S. population—nuclear family units with an employed father and a homemaker mother, who devotes herself to the care of her husband and children" (p. 130).

A feminist definition of family is one that is defined by the individual, is based on psychological connections, and includes the subjective experiences of the family members. Bloodlines may or may not be important, and the person's perceptions of who is family may be fluid and contextual. This model allows for changing boundaries that need not be rigidly drawn and maintained into perpetuity. Using feminist guiding principles, the family is defined by each one of us at any given point in time, and that definition may change for many reasons—sometimes legal ones such as divorce—but more often as a result of changes in life circumstances, quality of relationships, or other contextual factors.

FAMILY DEVELOPMENT PROCESS

If the family is defined by its members, is there anything to be said from a feminist perspective about family development or a family life cycle? Clearly, in using a more inclusive definition, taking into account many configurations that change over time, the developmental process of a family will be highly contextually and culturally determined. What is most predictable in the life span of a particular family is that there will be periods of relative stability and periods of transition that may be spawned by such factors as developmental transitions of individual family members, changing family membership, job changes of one or more members, family relocation, or the aging, illness, or death of a member. Following a feminist framework, we would not attempt to map a model of family development or a family life cycle that would apply to the many kinds of family constellations that exist in our society. There is no feminist "standard" by which families are measured to determine their validity, level of "health," or legitimacy. The yardstick involves an examination of each member and whether the family is serving to facilitate and support his or her developmental process, that is, each member's efforts to fulfill his or her full potential as a human being in terms of developing a degree of autonomy while remaining in connection. This balance of individualism and connection is highly subjective and determined by culture, race, class, sexual orientation, gender, spiritual system, and any of the other salient factors of human experience within the context of the family at any given point in time.

IMPACT OF PATRIARCHY

Feminist family therapy offers us a way of viewing ourselves and the families with whom we work as profoundly impacted by the patriarchal societal structures into which we are enculturated (Imber-Black, 1986). Not only does this model of family therapy theory consider the external impact of the social and political forces in our cultures that shape and influence our lives, but it also emphasizes "the invisible and sometimes nonconscious ways in which patriarchy has become embedded in everyone's daily life—in our identities, our manners of emotional expression, and our experiences of personal power and powerlessness—to our profound detriment" (Brown, 1994, p. 17). Patriarchy has been defined as the privileging of the male gender and that which is defined as masculine within the culture, leading to male domination and the oppression, subjugation, and inequality of women and that which is defined culturally as female or feminine. Both men and women internalize patriarchal values and are adversely affected by them. Thus, principles of patriarchy tend to be enacted within the context of family relationships, often outside the conscious awareness of family members.

THE ROLE OF CULTURE

Recently, feminist family therapy has also recognized the centrality of client cultural identities in understanding how families operate, as well as the importance of the "culture of the therapist" in her or his relationships with the families with whom she or he works (Comas-Diaz, 1994; Enns, 1993; Espin, 1993, 1994). Inherent in this world view is that these factors also are linked with oppression; thus, this model incorporates the idea of interlocking oppressions (Frye, 1995) as critical sources of understanding of the family experience and those of the individual members. In other words, racism, sexism, homophobia, classism, and other forms of oppression inevitably impact on the functioning of the family and the development of its individual members (Brown, 1990, 1995; Greene, 1994; Hardy & Laszloffy, 1994; McGoldrick, 1994).

HIERARCHY AND POWER IN FAMILY LIFE

Hierarchy is a central feature of a patriarchal system. The implication of this observation is that various members of a family hold differing degrees of power, and have differing degrees of control over how their lives are defined and lived. From a feminist theoretical framework, how the power structure within the family operates is critical in understanding overall family functioning and the well-being, or lack thereof, of individual members.

Gender has been widely discussed as an index for understanding power differentials (Barber & Allen, 1992; Kliman, 1994; Taggart, 1989; Walters, Carter, Papp, & Silverstein, 1988). Therefore, whose needs are met and whose are sacrificed in family life are central concepts to a feminist family theoretical mode. The startling, yet overlooked, results of the Timberlawn studies (Lewis, Beavers, Gossett, & Phillips, 1976) revealed that in middle-class, U.S. families that are held up as "adequate," the men were satisfied, relatively symptom-free, and well functioning, while the women were overwhelmed, dissatisfied with their sexual relationships, and symptomatic. Within the context of a society dominated by patriarchal values, as Ellyn Kashak (1992) points out, the one who holds the power determines reality and what can be expressed and what must be held in silence. She goes on to say, "Since the context of our culture is patriarchal, masculinized, and misogynist, it can and often must be unconscious in order for females to function, but it leads them to contain within themselves the pains and wounds to which they are subjected. For males, to whom it is not likely to be as jarring or debilitating, it can more comfortably remain outside of awareness" (p. 31). In other words, the silencing of women's voices and that which is culturally defined as feminine or female is an insidious, generally covert process within this culture, with costs to women and men alike.

Other kinds of power differentials may enter into the family picture, and impact on how entitled a family member may feel to voice a need or desire, set a limit, or claim rights to define his or her own experience within the family. Economic imbalances among members of the family—who brings home the bulk of the family income—lead to power differences when one family member earns substantially more than others. How each member of the family locates herself or himself from a class perspective may also influence a member's sense of agency. For example, many working-class people were enculturated as children with little sense of entitlement. This organizing principle of "I am not enough; I don't deserve much in life" may be carried into their middle-class adult family and social experiences. Race or ethnicity can also serve to organize family relationships along the power dimension. For example, the gay Cuban-American immigrant who has experienced significant prejudice and oppression in dominant Anglo culture may struggle to find his voice with his white partner.

THE FAMILY AS AN AGENT OF THE DOMINANT CULTURE

Recognition of dominant patriarchal values in the culture leads to a recognition of the role of the family as an agent of the dominant culture in the socialization of its members. From this point of view, throughout the life span each family member "takes in" or internalizes values, roles, and individual and interpersonal ways of being that are defined by the dominant culture as appropriate for men, women, boys, girls, African Americans, Asian Americans, Euroamericans, homosexuals, Christians, or any other group. The ways in which this internalization process takes place may differ from one person and family to the next. The process is especially impacted by those aspects of the individual that place him or her in a dominant group, such as white or male, and the aspects of the person that fall outside the privileged group or characteristic, such as woman, "of color," homosexual, or poor. This same phenomenon is of importance when members of the same family hold memberships in different groups and enact within-family oppression.

HISTORY/HERSTORY

Another essential factor in examining the context of the family and its individual members from a feminist position involves an understanding and consideration of historical contributions to the present-day situation. History, as it is written and reported, shapes the way in which we have come to see ourselves, the way we make sense of our experiences, and how empowered we believe we are to change the circumstances of our lives. It serves as the "backdrop," the ground for the emerging figure of how a family operates: who has the power and authority, who decides what is important, and whose needs the family structure centers around.

To illustrate the centrality of history in understanding family relationships and the links between current family functioning and historical factors, several examples come to mind. The African American family and experience come out of a history of having been involuntarily brought to this country and forced into slave labor. Families were separated, men and women were not allowed to marry, and African American people were relegated to nonhuman status. These experiences had a severely disruptive effect on each man, woman, and child individually; on their traditional family structure and way of operating; and on their freedom to engage in their indigenous cultural practices. Coping and adaptation in the face of the oppressive conditions in which they lived were inherent in the African American experience during this period in history. Even though antislavery laws were passed, and citizenship and voting rights legislated, racism continues to be a very real experiences for blacks in the United States. The legacy of African Americans as "the other" in the minds and hearts of dominant white culture leads to the continuation of the oppression of this group. How can the African American family not be affected by the experience of living in a society in which people are hated simply because of the color of their skin? It is a testimony to the resilience and tremendous strength of the African American community that the family has not only survived, but continues to play a central role within the culture today.

Gay and lesbian families also reflect the impact of a history of having been pathologized, denigrated, and rendered invisible by the church, the U.S. political system, and, ironically, by the psychiatric and psychotherapy community. We can still remember well the inclusion of homosexuality as a mental disorder in the DSM and the lack of legal protection against discrimination in any state in this country. These beliefs and practices both continue into the present and profoundly impact on gay and lesbian family relationships, since homosexual families are still not legally acknowledged, gay hate crimes are on the rise, and the internalization of this homoprejudice poses a significant challenge to gays and lesbians in forming and maintaining close, loving relationships.

Luepnitz (1988) eloquently writes about the historical roots of contemporary gender roles in white, middle- and upper-middle-class heterosexual U.S. families. She astutely notes the little-discussed notion that women were not identified as "natural nurturers" until the eighteenth century, when the French philosopher Rousseau, disturbed by the rampant maltreatment and neglect of children, began to write about the importance of encouraging women to fulfill their "inherent, essential nature" by focusing their complete attention to the duties of child-rearing. This position was soon adopted by the bourgeois class of that period. Women were essentially "sent home" out of the public sphere to do the invisible work of taking care of the home and children, while men continued to go out into the public domain, and support the family in matters of politics, society, and economics. Obviously, this "gendered" family structure, which spread to other parts of Europe and the United States, along with the continuing dominant belief that women are best suited to raise the children and take care of the household, permeates the U.S. white, middle- and upper-middle-class heterosexual family today—even as increasing numbers of women once again return to the workforce.

THE PERSONAL AS POLITICAL

A hallmark of feminist philosophy and practice is the emphasis on the personal as political and the importance of deprivatizing experience and placing it in a social and political context. In the case of feminist family therapy, the experiences of individual family members and the interrelationships among members may have unique meanings that do not represent a larger social, political, and/or cultural perspective; however, particularly in the case of experiences of oppression or "gendered" ways of relating or operating in the world, the personal undeniably represents a political and social reality firmly rooted in patriarchal structures.

THE CONCEPT OF "VOICE"

The concept of "voice" is central to a feminist orientation to family therapy. From a feminist perspective, the narrative self-reports of the individual represent a valid source of information about reality. Each person serves as a central and legitimate source of authority about her or his life and possesses the capacity and agency to decide what is best for her or him. Within a family context, the implication is that each member has a unique understanding of how the family operates. All members can offer valid commentary on what is going right and wrong and what is the best direction for the family facing a life challenge. Of course, this perspective of the individual as a source of authority and agency to be reckoned with leads to the development of family solutions in which "effective family functioning" is not at the expense of particular members. This is especially relevant for women, whose voices are typically engulfed, subsumed, and silenced by patriarchal cultural values and practices.

HOLISTIC PRINCIPLES

Kaschak (1992) describes a feminist epistemology as one that acknowledges the interconnections and interrelationships among all aspects of experience. She notes that one's cognitions, feelings, physical sensations, and abilities, as well as one's interpersonal interactions and cultural and evaluative experiences operate in unity rather than as separate entities in our daily lives. "Feminist thought acknowledges multiple realities and, therefore, multiple, complex, and variable models of psychological functioning" (Kaschak, 1992, p. 32). Implied in these words is that feminist family therapy must be a holistic approach to family work. We must find a way to address the family in its complexity rather than segmenting off aspects of the family experience for understanding and intervention. The individual members, the family as a system and a set of interrelationships, and the family and its members embedded in a larger social, political, and cultural system are all inseparable aspects of a conceptualization of feminist family therapy theory and practice.

USE OF LANGUAGE

The use of language in reference to how family and individual concerns and distress are defined is crucial within a feminist family world view. The power of language in determining reality and influencing how knowledge and history are formulated is not underestimated. For example, traditionally in the family therapy world descriptors such as "overinvolved mother" and "peripheral father" have been used to describe roles and behaviors of family members centered around heterosexual couples. What a powerful difference it would be to describe the family issue as "the parents are responding to powerful social and political roles ascribed by contemporary dominant white middle-class cultural norms." We can see the difference in where the responsibility for the "problem" is assigned, and therefore, what might be done to address the family in a therapeutic setting. People with disabilities understand the powerful implications of the use of the term "disabled people" versus the more empowering "differently abled" terminology. A core consideration when examining the issue of language involves whether or not the questions asked or the references used individualize or marginalize distress that is actually created and perpetuated by the larger social systems in which families operate. We must also continuously question whether the language we use serves to further reinforce limiting stereotypes about the family and its members—thus, colluding with society to enforce rigid standards of behavior and ways of being. For example, saying to a tall black teenage boy that he must be good at basketball, rather than inviting him to express his own opinion about what he is good at, exemplifies this kind of collusion with the dominant cultural belief system through the use of language.

FAMILY SYSTEMS THEORY AND FEMINIST THEORY: COMMON GROUND

While there are certainly other theoretical frameworks represented in the field of family therapy theory, family systems theory, based on Bateson's (1972, 1980) cybernetic model, represents the fundamental conceptual framework from which most of the dominant theories were developed. Probably the most obvious common ground between a family systems model and a feminist-based model of family therapy is in depathologizing family concerns. Both perspectives hold that family distress is not based in illness, though this may be the point at which the departure begins, for each theoretical orientation would then go on to explain and place emphasis on differing causative factors.

Family systems theory and feminist theory each acknowledge the importance of the contexts of human behavior—that individuals are best understood by examining the systems in which they are located. Though family systems models, in theory, recognize that the family dwells in a larger context, few of the major theoretical perspectives really consider these larger systems in actual practice. Feminist family therapy, on the other hand, posits that it is only by viewing the family through the lens of the larger systems in which it is embedded that a skillful assessment and effective, well-informed therapy can take place (Imber-Black, 1986). This position is reflected in Harriet Goldhor Lerner's (1988) article entitled "Is family systems theory really systemic? A feminist communication."

The emphasis on the relationships in the family is a shared principle between the two theories. Both view the family as a collection of relationships, and recognize that understanding the nature of the relationships and changing aspects of the relationships is a focal point for intervention. The two perspectives differ in substantial ways, however, on how to conceptualize a relationship or family that is working well, as well as the characteristics of the individual's behaviors that define effective functioning. This will be discussed in detail in the following section.

APPLICATIONS AND TECHNIQUES

PROCESS OF THERAPY

It must be said that, while modern feminist philosophy, politics, and even clinical practice predate family systems theory and practice by over 75 years, the field of family therapy has been slow to loosen its boundaries to feminist influences (Porter & Yahne, 1994).

Many of the "traditional" family theories—such as Bowenian, strategic and communications models, structural, and psychoanalytically based models, for example, object relations—have been critiqued by feminist therapists. Their efforts have been devoted to challenging the theoretical formulations and key concepts of these theories, and demonstrating the problems in the practice of these major theories from the feminist point of view. Some authors have reworked aspects of the theories (Bograd, 1988; Luepnitz, 1988; MacKinnon & Miller, 1987; Skerret, 1996), while others have wondered whether feminism and family systems theories are compatible at all (Braverman, 1988; Goldner, 1985b).

Most of those who have written about the integration of feminist philosophy and practice with various models of family therapy theory have used one of the major theoretical approaches as their starting points (Walsh & Scheinkman, 1989). In other words, most of the work thus far has been devoted to a feminist reworking or critiquing of existing theories of family therapy, rather than constructing a theory and practice of feminist family therapy.

This leads to the rather obvious question of "What does the process of feminist family therapy look like?" The answer is still evolving, and is best discussed in terms of how to centralize feminist meta-theory in family therapy theory and application. Clearly, any conceptualization done here is "a work in progress," and I invite the reader to use this effort as a starting point from which to add, modify, argue, and challenge in continuing this exciting process.

Laura Brown (1994), in *Subversive Dialogues*, says, "A feminist theory of therapy must, to maintain integrity, be based on a model of antidomination and diversity" (p. 72). For the feminist family therapist, this means working with a family to become more aware of the ways in which each member has internalized and is enacting oppressive societal values that serve to limit their options as individuals and their relationships within and outside the family. The process of teasing out how a family and its members are impacted by oppression and domination, especially when multiple oppressions are involved, is complex. How family members and the family as a whole have attempted, successfully or with difficulty, to cope with daily experiences of social and politically based experiences of oppression would be foundational in understanding and working with a family. These experiences form the basis for organizing and determining, to a significant degree, how members relate to one another within the family and how they carry on their business in the world at large.

For example, how does gender socialization impact on the roles taken by different family members, adults and children? How is each member's sense of agency and his or her entitlement both to be treated with respect and to have needs met within the family relate to socially constructed gender roles? For the family of color, how might the shade of skin color relate to the degree of respect given each member?

The family as a whole is also invited to examine how these dominant social and political paradigms impact on their sense of pride in their particular kind of family structure and successful navigation of the dominant landscape. A family located in the so-called lower-class segment of the social hierarchy may include several generations living together, with older children contributing to the family's economic survival. The family may be functioning effectively within its own context, yet members may feel a sense of shame or failure because of "not mea-suring up" to the Ward and June Cleaver model of the U.S. family success story.

Every family, and each member within the family, must define for them-selves whether and which aspects of domination and oppression are most salient. The feminist family therapist remains aware of the importance of each family member's finding her or his own voice and sense of authority in naming the source and kinds of oppression, and recognizes that this is the client's call. A woman of color may be much more concerned and feel much more impacted by racism and classism than by sexism, and it is critical that the therapist not make assumptions placing gender as the most salient variable in the lives of the fami-ly members.

Membership in dominant groups and the impact of that membership with-in the family is the other side of the coin in helping a family sort out the impact of societal oppression. While a Cuban-American man may be a minority group member in the larger U.S. culture, he is a member of the dominant "male" group, within both Anglo society and many segments of Cuban culture. An im-portant part of a feminist therapeutic process for the family would almost cer-tainly include an effort to examine and change how this man may be using his male privilege in ways that restrict and limit other members of the family, thus, negatively impacting his ability to have satisfying emotional connections with his partner and children, and how this dynamic is supported in the larger soci-ety, while also exploring the effects of his experiences of racism outside the family context.

A model of diversity as the foundation of theory and practice of feminist family therapy is an exciting and challenging proposition. Feminist scholars and clinicians in the family therapy field have raised the problem of the bias in most major family therapy theories toward dominant values and models of "normalcy." A process of family therapy coming out of a feminist framework requires the therapist to reevaluate all her or his previous training and assumptions about what is a family, effective family functioning, goals of therapy, and the very ways in which most of us have been taught to work with our clients. To quote Shunryu Suzuki (1970), a wise and respected Japanese teacher of Zen Buddhism here in the United States, we must approach our clients with a "beginner's mind." That is, first we recognize that the dominant models of family therapy theory and practice hold up "mythical norms" embedded in white middle- and upper-class patriarchal social structures and values. Then we acknowledge the family and its members as valid, authoritative sources of knowledge about what is appropriate for them within their contexts and lived experiences. We look to the family members as col-laborators in their journey toward change and transformation. We help each fam-ily member develop a voice—an authentic, expressed discourse about his or her own experience in the family and the accompanying needs, wants, likes, dislikes, thoughts, and feelings. This implies working with the family to cultivate a context of respect and capacity to listen to one another.

Another important aspect of the therapy may be to enlist the family in ex-amining the ways that the U.S. "myth of self-sufficiency" may be affecting how the family operates. Are family members viewing the ways they depend on one another, on extended families, and on other systems outside the immediate house-hold negatively thus leading to self-criticism, shame, and conflictual or distant family relationships? Or are they isolating themselves from available support based on a belief that to do otherwise symbolizes weakness or inadequacy? Untangling the beliefs around dependence and independence and supporting the family in developing the level of interdependence that fits within their own circumstances and cultural identities are important directions in feminist family therapy. McGoldrick (1994) eloquently writes about this predominant myth about the "well-functioning family":

> Most family therapy, like our dominant social ideology in general, has tended to be oriented toward a view of families as traditional self-sufficient units, usually nuclear units....Poor families in the dominant view are seen as deficient, because they are obviously and critically dependent on systems beyond themselves for their survival. But we are all dependent for our survival on systems beyond ourselves and our nuclear families. It is just that those of us who are of the dominant groups fail to realize this, because we take the invisible ways the government supports us and our needs for granted. Schools, courts, the police, and all the other institutions of the society operate for the protection and benefit of the dominant groups. Thus, the dominant groups, who make the rules and definitions, are kept blind to their dependence on those who take care of them." (p. 131)

Within the context of interdependence emerges the issue of belonging. McGoldrick (1994) has urged family therapists to encourage our clients to develop multiple group identities in order to nurture the multifaceted nature of human identity and to foster a sense of belonging. By affiliating with different groups, we can find homes for the many diverse aspects of ourselves rather than expecting one group, especially the immediate family, to provide for all of the diverse needs of its members. A diversity of affiliations outside the family promotes flexibility and appreciation of difference in addition to its important function of providing a place of belonging. Again, cultural values may significantly influence the salience of this issue in family life.

Implicit in the discussion of developing group identities is the assumption that family members will appreciate and value difference. However, we know that this is often not the case and can be the issue that leads a family to seek counseling. From a feminist perspective, the process of therapy involves helping family members confront their attitudes about differences in their family, and to begin to understand and (if it is beneficial) change their perspectives. Of course, fear, inadequacy, or lack of information can explain difficulties in changing negative attitudes toward differences. Internalization of dominant values that render differences substandard, abnormal, or unacceptable may also explain intolerance with the family—thus, becoming a focal point of the therapeutic process. The white heterosexual couple who struggle to accept their gay child represents this kind of therapeutic challenge, as the counselor seeks to assist them in addressing their societally based homoprejudice as well as the accompanying feelings of sadness and loss of their expectations, hopes, and dreams. Another example of this process might involve working on internalized racism with a family in which the lighter-skinned Mexican-American father and son have negative feelings about the darker skinned daughter/sister.

ROLE OF THE THERAPIST

One of the hallmarks of a feminist model of family therapy is the emphasis on demystification of the therapy process. From this perspective, it is in the best interest of the family for the therapist to work as collaboratively as possible and to share information about the therapy process with them. Further, while there is clearly a power differential between the therapist and the clients, and while the feminist family therapist recognizes and takes responsibility for her or his power seriously, efforts are made not to exacerbate or unnecessarily inflate the power imbalance, particularly by withholding information about the therapy process.

From the vantage point of the feminist family therapist, therapeutic neutrality is a myth. The therapist must always hold in her or his mind that liberation from constraining social and political influences is central to the work with the family. Every interaction is carefully scrutinized in an effort to avoid perpetuating constraining social and political stereotypes and promulgating dominating or subordinate roles with the family. It is critical that the therapist acknowledge the dominant social and political structures in effect in the lives of the families with whom we work and in our own lives. From the position of social activist, the therapist maintains a goal of working to end the social and political conditions that lead to power imbalances and oppression within the family. Within the context of therapy, the feminist family clinician works with the family to examine how domination and oppression by the family's cultural framework are enacted within the family to the detriment of each member.

Within the relationship between the client family and the feminist family therapist, an atmosphere of respect and an appreciation for the strengths and resources of the family are valued and fostered. The concept of power is redefined from the patriarchal definitions of "power over" to the language of connection and relationship. Brown (1994) discusses the concept of nurturance and presence as sources of power in the therapeutic relationship. According to Brown, both of these therapeutic capacities are important "sources of impact, influence, and ultimately of authority" (p. 109). This is a powerful idea, since both of these qualities have been devalued in dominant U.S. culture, and feminist family therapist are reclaiming their importance in their work with families. Another ingredient in the therapeutic relationship is mutuality, the "passionate engagement" between the therapist and the family members whereby each is affected by the other (Surrey & Heyward, 1990, as discussed by Brown, 1994). This type of mutuality is encouraged within the family relationships as well.

Feminist theory also has strong roots in democratic principles. The feminist family therapist makes every effort to develop a relationship that is respectful of the voices and opinions of each member—thus reflective of democratic values.

CASE EXAMPLES

Selection of material for a case example is in itself problematic when attempting to apply feminist family therapy principles. First, as we discussed earlier, feminist philosophical perspectives have been integrated into the work of feminist family therapists practicing a wide range of family therapy approaches. Additionally, in the construction of a case example, the choices of family structure, race/ethnicity of members, sexual orientation, class, physical ability, language, spiritual traditions, and the like all convey important messages about the perception of "family." In order to avoid setting up a particular family form as the norm, I would like to discuss two shorter case vignettes representing different family structures and member characteristics. The core values of feminist family therapy will be addressed through these examples, leaving room for the clinician to incorporate a range of family therapy theoretical constructs. However, my hope is that readers will consciously question the values of the constructs and theoretical principles of their preferred family therapy theories as they apply to diverse family structures, within the social and political realities of oppression, and from the perspectives of gender, race/ethnicity, sexual orientation, class, spiritual tradition, physical health and ability, and other important aspects of humanity. The case examples were intentionally developed to include a first-person account of the therapy process and outcome in the spirit of valuing the "voice" of the client.

FAMILY 1

My name is Gloria, and I am a 39-year-old African American single mother of two children, Bobby, age 17, and Rosalyn, age 14. My husband, Will, died three years ago, and, though I receive a small monthly pension from his job as a city employee, I have had to take on a job in nursing to support my family. Five years ago I had stopped working outside the house at the office of one of our doctor friends because we moved to a new neighborhood and the kids needed someone around to watch after them. I wanted to do it and Will was making enough to support the family. It was working out fine for everybody.

Our family has been seriously stressed by Will's death. Both kids had been very active in school before their father died, but gradually they disconnected from their old friends. Bobby began running with a tough group and missing school, even though he had been a very good student up until this year. Rosalyn went to school but was coming home right away to do the housework for me. She didn't seem to have as many friends as she used to and became very quiet and withdrawn. As for me, I hardly had time to think because I was trying to make ends meet, working as much overtime as I could. Before counseling, I was very worried about my children and myself because the family seemed to be falling apart.

When we first began therapy (at the suggestion of the school guidance counselor), the children and I were wondering how it would go since the only counselor available was a white woman. Early on, she asked us all how we felt about working with her and also asked us about our experiences of racism in our lives. This helped because we then told her that we were apprehensive about working with her, and she listened and didn't get defensive. She seemed to understand our concerns and repeatedly asked us to let her know at any time if we were feeling like she was not understanding us or like she had offended us in some way. She told us that she had been working for a long time on getting rid of her own racism, but she knew it was a lifelong process. While she didn't expect us to educate her—she said that was her job—she knew that she didn't know everything, and that every family was different and had different ways of dealing with things. It seemed like she would be alright, and, as it turned out, she was. While I think we still would have preferred to work with a black counselor, we did find her very helpful and open to any feedback we gave her, even when we let her know she was "offbase" about something.

We each talked about our lives during counseling, and I was not really suprised to hear the children talk about the racist attitudes in their predominantly white school and what they were going through with teachers and other students. I realized that we had each been trying so hard in our own way to cope with all the changes that we just weren't talking like we used to. I got some insight into why Bobby was avoiding classes and getting involved with a group of boys who were so defiant. Rosalyn was also trying to deal with being told by one of her teachers that girls were not good in math even though it was her favorite and best subject. She ran into the same thing in sports—both boys and girls made fun of her because she is an excellent athlete in soccer and softball.

Both children said they really missed me and the time we used to spend together. They said they felt like they lost me when their lost their dad, as well as the bigger family of grandparents, aunts, uncles, and cousins. I began to realize that they were right, that I was working so hard and had been so upset by Will's death that I shut off from my children and other family members who could be there to help and support us. I felt the pressure to "do it all," a feeling common to many black women I know. It also became clear that I was more vulnerable to racism and sexism myself when I was more isolated from my people, as I had been since Will's death.

The family seems to be doing better now. We have moved in with my aging parents, who have a bigger house, and my children get a lot of attention from them and the other relatives and friends who live in the neighborhood. Since we moved, I was able to quit my nursing job at the hospital and eliminate that major source of stress for me. I am now working part-time in a small clinic close to home. It has done me good to get back to my family, even though it's not always easy living with my parents. The kids and I talk more about what is going on every day, and I, along with their other relatives, can pass along lots of advice and help on how to deal with the prejudices and other problems they face in their lives. Life is still not easy, but we get a lot of strength from each other, and I feel like a family again. Sooner or later, we will probably move into our own house, but for now this seems like the right place to be.

FAMILY 2

Sara and Joseph, a white couple, ages 40 and 43 respectively, came to family therapy with their son, Aaron, age 7. Sara, who primarily works in their home, also holds a part time job as a teacher assistant. Joseph earns the greater income in his job as a plumber. The couple reported increased tension within the relationship over the past several years, with depression and anxiety as Sara's primary individual concerns, and "a short fuse" reported by Joseph as his biggest challenge. When the family began counseling, Aaron had begun to experience a drop in grades and had anxiety about going to school. The couple reported having difficulty communicating with one another other than through fighting. The fights seemed to center around finances and parenting of Aaron.

In assessing the family, the therapist asked them to explore their cultural backgrounds, including areas such as race/ethnicity, class, religious affiliations, and gender roles prescribed by these "cultural institutions." Sara learned through discussions with her parents that their roots were in England on both sides of the family, and that the families had come to the United States during the 1700s and settled in the southeastern United States. Joseph's family arrived later, in the late 1800s, from Ireland, also settling in the Southeast. Historically, both families have been and continue to be working-class Protestants, with strong traditional gender roles prescribed both within their families and in their small southern community. A family rule on both sides of the family seems to be the proverbial "Behind every good man is a good woman."

During counseling, Sara revealed that she was a very good student in high school, graduating second in her class of over 500. She indicated that she ruled out college because no one in her family had ever attended, and she was expected to get married and begin a family as soon as she graduated. She did marry at 19, but did not have a baby for 12 years, instead working in a retail store where she was quickly promoted to manager because of her talents and responsible attitudes. She resigned her job when Aaron was born, and only returned to part-time employment (at Joseph's objection) within the past two years. Joseph said that he came from a long line of skilled workmen who always supported their families, and did whatever it took to make a living, even during the depression era. He said that all of the men in his family have been hard drinkers and quick-tempered. While he does not drink a lot, he stated that he does "fly off the handle too quickly." He indicated that he really gets angry with Sara for being so soft with Aaron, and trying to "turn him into a pansy." Sara, in turn, reported that she worried continuously that Joseph would lose his job due to his temper, and also got frustrated because he "gave her hell" every time she bought anything for herself or that he didn't think they needed.

Counseling took place over the course of 13 months, and was hard, but rewarding, work for the family. Sara reported the following:

> When we came in, I thought that it was all me, that I was the problem because I was crying all the time and feeling like my marriage was in deep trouble. The counselor helped us look at the ways our family traditions throughout the generations are played out in our relationships, especially the roles of men and women, and the ways we communicate and solve problems. I could also see that I took in a lot of what I saw on television and in magazines about what a "good wife" should be like, even though I believe I was very unhappy trying to be a way that did not fit for me. I began to feel better as I discovered what I really thought and felt as a strong, intelligent, capable woman, and began to express myself to Joseph and in my outside activities, rather than trying to conform to a standard that didn't feel comfortable. It was helpful to talk about how I feared Joseph's temper, and how I was silenced by the threat of violence, even though Joseph had never hit me or Aaron.

Joseph also reported a positive outcome from the counseling process:

> I really didn't want to go to counseling. I thought it was sissy stuff, and that I didn't need it because I wasn't the one with the problem. It was amazing to find out how much about being a man I learned from my family, and how negative the impact of not controlling my temper was having on the people I love the most, Sara and Aaron. We have been getting a lot closer over the past year, and I can even feel good about hugging Aaron and showing him that strong men do that with other guys. Before counseling, I thought that only weak men showed their tender sides, and that I should be less of a man if I cried or showed any feelings other than anger. I realized that I often used my size and power to intimidate Sara when I felt inadequate or inferior. It was also helpful to see that I have carried some shame about being a working-class man, because where we live you are looked down on by a lot of people in the professional community if you are in the trades. It was great to go back and look at the strengths of the men and women in my family, and what I got from them. Sara and I both did this, and we found out that we could decide what things we wanted to keep in our own family and what rules and roles did not work for us in the kind of marriage we wanted—an equal partnership where we love and respect one another, and work to help each other be the best we can be. By the way, Aaron is speaking his mind more these days, and doing a lot better in school. We all found out that, in getting to know

ourselves better, and finding ways to respectfully say what we want and what we need to say, we feel good about who we are individually and as a family.

EVALUATION OF THE THEORY

As a new voice in the field, feminist family therapy theory is still being created, and is largely based in a philosophical perspective supported by multidisciplinary research on sex differences, women's development and mental health, and research in the multicultural counseling literature. Portions of this research have further clarified the problematic issue of theory construction based on masculinized values and generalizing the theories to larger populations for whom they don't apply, and whom they thus pathologize (Gilligan, 1982; Caplan, 1985). Sex-difference research has delineated the clear disadvantaging of women in U.S. society based on gender. This body of work has demonstrated how gendered communication styles have served to maintain gender hierarchy (Fishman, 1978; Henley, 1977), and documented high rates of depression (Bart, 1971; Weissman, 1980), poorer adjustment and marital satisfaction (Bernard, 1972), and lower self-esteem (Feldman, 1979) among women who adhere to more stereotypic gender roles in marital relationships. Significant power imbalances in favor of men among white heterosexual couples have also been identified (Treiman & Hartmann, 1981) along with a greater vulnerability for women to psychological distress due to sociocultural stressors such as sexism and misogyny (Veroff, Douvan, & Kulka, 1981). The classic study by Broverman, Broverman, Clarkson, Rosenkrantz, and Vogel (1970) reveals the sex-role stereotyping by mental health professionals in their assessing of stereotypical masculine behavior as adult and preferred, and stereotypical feminine behavior as nonadult and nonpreferred. These data reveal the double bind for women of having to choose between behaving in a manner that is "nonfeminine and adult" or "feminine and nonadult."

In critiquing dominant contemporary models and practice of family therapy, feminists have noted that family therapists intentionally or unintentionally interact in ways that encourage and support stereotypical male and female roles and behaviors in men and women (Gurman & Klein, 1984; Jacobson, 1983). Even the professional literature has reflected a bias that disadvantages women and holds them responsible for family problems. Caplan and Hall-McCorquodale (1985), in a survey of nine major clinical journals, including *Family Process*, during 1972, 1976, and 1982, documented that two-thirds of the authors blamed mothers for 72 kinds of behavioral and emotional problems in their children while tending to describe fathers only in positive terms whereby they were not implicated in their children's problems.

The multicultural family literature describes the differing gendered roles and behaviors of men and women across cultures and the role of ethnicity in understanding families from diverse backgrounds. For example, in their excellent volume *Ethnicity and Family Therapy*, McGoldrick, Giordano, and Pearce (1996) offer a wealth of information regarding theory and research with families from a range of ethnic backgrounds. Additionally, Barbara Okun (1996) presents a valuable review of research, theory, and practice issues with diverse family groups such as homosexual families, multiracial families, and adoptive families. Further, McGoldrick and Rohrbaugh (1987) described continuing cultural and gender-role stereotypes several generations after immigration in an interesting study of the ethnic patterns of the families of family therapists.

An important focus for future research now lies in continuing to validate the use of a feminist model of family therapy with diverse client populations. While quantitative studies are valuable in verifying the utility of specific feminist family therapy interventions, it is necessary also to value multiple methods of inquiry—such as qualitative research contributions that describe the process aspects of feminist work with families (Giblin & Chan, 1995), case studies, and naturalistic studies—in survey research. Additionally, we are only beginning to recognize and call for the feminist family therapist to receive training that focuses on her or his own identity-development process, resolving issues related to those majority group identities and the associated privilege, and successfully negotiating minority identities that impact on how she or he relates to clients (Ault-Riché, 1988; Korin, 1994; Libow, 1986). Further, how to train feminist family therapists in ways that do not encourage internalization of patriarchal, masculinized views of human behavior and development is an important research question for continued attention.

SUMMARY

Feminist family therapy is an exciting new voice in the field of family therapy theory. In many ways, it is more a meta-model of family counseling based in philosophical ideals than a theory with clear techniques. Therapists using a feminist model of family work must evaluate their current theories of choice to determine whether the principles and applications are compatible with feminist principles. It is useful to look carefully at the work of feminist family therapists who have given careful thought to the integration of these ideas with the major family therapy theories (Ault-Riché, 1986; Avis, 1985, 1986, 1988; Bograd, 1986, 1988; Goldner, 1985a & b; Libow, Raskin, & Caust, 1982; MacKinnon & Miller, 1987). Researchers and clinicians are also beginning to discuss ethical issues and training guidelines for feminist family therapists and supervisors (Costa & Sorenson, 1993; Porter & Yahne, 1994; Snyder, 1994; Weingarten & Bograd, 1996). Following is an annotated list of some of the important contributions made by feminist family therapists and researchers working from a range of theoretical models of feminist family therapy.

ANNOTATED SUGGESTED READINGS

Almeida, R. V. (Ed.). (1994). *Expansions of feminist family theory through diversity*. New York: Harrington Park Press.
> Rhea Almeida presents an exciting and challenging group of family therapy theoretical and applied articles on issues of diversity in feminist family therapy. This is a must read for understanding the critical need to include diversity as a foundation of family therapy theory and practice.

Braverman, L. (Ed.). (1988). *A guide to feminist family therapy*. New York: Harrington Park Press.
> This volume is a pioneer effort in the integration of feminist theory and practice with family therapy theory, research, and training. Lois Braverman is the founding editor of the journal, *Feminist Family Therapy*.

Luepnitz, D. A. (1988). *The family interpreted: Psychoanalysis, feminism, and family therapy*. New York: Basic Books.

> Deborah Luepnitz offers a sophisticated feminist critique of the major theories of family therapy, including a section on Bateson's cybernetic model. She also includes a provocative review of the "herstory" of white, middle-class families and African American families, and an interesting feminist reworking of object relations family therapy.

McGoldrick, M., Anderson, C. M., & Walsh, F. (Eds.). (1989). *Women in families: A framework for family therapy*.

> This collection offers a thorough treatment of the diverse issues of women in developing a theory and practice of feminist family therapy. Training and supervision of feminist family therapists is also discussed.

Snyder, M. (Ed.). (1994). *Ethical issues in feminist family therapy*. New York: Haworth Press.

> Maryhelen Snyder offers the following quote in her introduction to this excellent volume: "Every human act has an ethical meaning because it is an act of constitution of the human world" (Maturana & Varela, 1987, p. 247). The contributing authors in this book issue family therapy professionals a wake-up call to the reality of these words.

REFERENCES

Almeida, R.V. (Ed.). (1994). *Expansions of feminist family theory through diversity*. New York: Haworth Press.

American Psychological Association. (1975). Report of the task force on sex bias and sex role stereotyping in psychotherapeutic practice. *American Psychologist, 30*, 1169–1175.

Ault-Riché, M. (1986). A feminist critique of five schools of family therapy. In M. Ault-Riché (Ed.), *Women and family therapy* (pp. 1–15). Rockville, MD: Aspen Systems.

Ault-Riché, M. (1988). Teaching an integrated model of family therapy: Women as students, women as supervisors. In L. Braverman (Ed.), *A guide to feminist family therapy* (pp. 175–192). New York: Haworth Press.

Avis, J. M. (1985). The politics of functional family therapy: A feminist critique. *Journal of Marital and Family Therapy, 11* (2), 127–138.

Avis, J. M. (1986). Feminist issues in family therapy. In F. P. Piercy, D. H. Sprenkle, and Associates (Eds.), *Family therapy sourcebook* (pp. 213–242). New York: Guilford Press.

Avis, J. M. (1988). Deepening awareness: A private study guide to feminism and family therapy. In L. Braverman (Ed.), *A guide to feminist family therapy* (pp. 15–46). New York: Haworth Press.

Barber, K. M., & Allen, K. R. (1992). *Women & families*. New York: Guilford Press.

Bart, P. B. (1971). Sexism in social science: From the iron cage to the guilded cage, or, the perils of Pauline. *Journal of Marriage and Family Therapy, 33*, 734–745.

Bateson, G. (1972). *Steps to an ecology of mind*. New York: Ballantine.

Bateson, G. (1980). *Mind and nature*. New York: Dutton.

Bernard, J. (1972). *The future of marriage*. New York: Bantam.

Bograd, M. (1986). A feminist examination of family therapy: What is women's place? *Women & Therapy, 5*(2 & 3), 95–106.

Bograd, M. (1988). Enmeshment, fusion or relatedness? A conceptual analysis. In L. Braverman (Ed.), *A guide to feminist family therapy* (pp. 65–80). New York: Haworth Press.

Boyd-Franklin, N., & Garcia-Preto, N. (1994). Family therapy: A closer look at African American and Hispanic women. In L. Comas-Diaz & B. Greene (Eds.), *Women of color: Integrating ethnic and gender identities in psychotherapy* (pp. 239–264). New York: Guilford Press.

Braverman, L. (1988). Feminism and family therapy: Friends or foes. In L. Braverman (Ed.), *A guide to feminist family therapy* (pp. 5–14). New York: Haworth Press.

Broverman, I., Broverman, D., Clarkson, F., Rosenkrantz, P., & Vogel, S. (1970). Sex role stereotypes and clinical judgments of mental health. *Journal of Consulting and Clinical Psychology, 34,* 107.

Brown, L. S. (1990). The meaning of a multicultural perspective for theory-building in feminist therapy. In L. S. Brown & M. P. Root (Eds.), *Diversity and complexity in feminist therapy* (pp. 1–21). New York: Haworth Press.

Brown, L. S. (1994). *Subversive dialogues.* New York: Basic Books.

Brown, L. S. (1995). Cultural diversity in feminist therapy: Theory and practice. In H. Landrine (Ed.), *Brining cultural diversity to feminist psychology: Theory, research, and practice* (pp. 143–161). Washington, DC: American Psychological Association.

Caplan, P. J. (1985). *The myth of women's masochism.* New York: Dutton.

Caplan, P. J., and Hall-McCorquodale, I. (1985). Mother-blaming in major clinical journals. *American Journal of Orthopsychiatry, 55*(3), 345–353.

Chodorow, N. (1978). *The reproduction of mothering: Psychoanalysis and the sociology of gender.* Berkeley: University of California Press.

Comas-Diaz, L. (1994). An integrative approach. In L. Comas-Diaz & B. Greene (Eds.), *Women of Color: Integrating ethnic and gender identities in psychotherapy* (pp. 287–318). New York: Haworth Press.

Costa, L., & Sorenson, J. (1993). Feminist family therapy: Ethical considerations for the clinician. *The Family Journal: Counseling and Therapy for Couples and Families, 1*(1), 17–24.

Davis, A. (1981). *Women, race and class.* New York: Vintage.

Dinnerstein, D. (1976). *The mermaid and the minotaur.* New York: Harper and Row.

Enns, C. Z. (1993). Twenty years of feminist counseling and therapy: From naming biases to implementing multifaceted practice. *The Counseling Psychologist, 21*(1), 3–87.

Espin, O. (1993). Feminist therapy: Not for or by white women only. *The Counseling Psychologist, 21*(1), 103–108.

Espin, O. (1994). Feminist approaches. In L. Comas-Diaz & B. Greene (Eds.), *Women of color: Integrating ethnic and gender identities in psychotherapy* (pp. 265–286). New York: Guilford Press.

Feldman, L. (1979). Marital conflict and marital intimacy: An integrative psychodynamic-behavioral-systemic model. *Family Process, 18,* 69–78.

Fishman, P. (1978). Interaction: The work women do. *Social Problems, 25,* 397–406.

Friedan, B. (1963). *The feminine mystique.* New York: Norton.

Frye, M. (1995). Oppression. In P. Rothenberg (Ed.), *Race, class, and gender in the United States: An integrated study* (3rd ed., pp. 81–84). New York: St. Martin's Press.

Giblin, P., & Chan, J. (1995). Research: A feminist perspective. *The Family Journal: Counseling and Therapy for Couples and Families, 3*(3), 234–238.

Gilligan, C. (1982). *In a different voice.* Cambridge, MA: Harvard University Press.

Goldner, V. (1985a). Feminism and family therapy. *Family Process, 24,* 31–47.

Goldner, V. (1985b). Warning: Family therapy may be hazardous to your health. *The Family Therapy Networker, 9*(6), 19–23.

Goodrich, T. J., Rampage, C., Ellman, B., & Halstead, K. (1988). *Feminist family therapy*. New York: Norton.

Gurman, A. S., & Klein, M. H. (1984). Marriage and the family: An unconscious bias in behavioral treatment? In E. A. Blechman (Ed.), *Behavior modification with women*. New York: Guilford Press.

Greene, B. (1994). Diversity and differences: The issue of race in feminist therapy. *Women in context: Toward a feminist reconstruction of psychotherapy* (pp. 333–351). New York: Haworth Press.

Hall, R., & Greene, B. (1994). Cultural competence in feminist family therapy: An ethical mandate. In M. Snyder (Ed.), *Ethical issues in feminist family therapy* (pp. 5–28). New York: Haworth Press.

Hardy, K.V., & Laszloffy, T. A. (1994). Deconstructing race in family therapy. In R.V. Almeida (Ed.), *Expansions of feminist family theory through diversity* (pp. 5–34). New York: Harrington Park Press.

Hare-Mustin, R. T. (1978). A feminist approach to family therapy. *Family Process, 17*, 181–194.

Hare-Mustin, R. T. (1979). Family therapy and sex role stereotypes. *The Counseling Psychologist, 8*, 31–32.

Hare-Mustin, R. T. (1980). Family therapy may be dangerous to your health. *Professional Psychology, 11*, 935–938.

Hare-Mustin, R. T. (1989). The problem of gender in family therapy theory. In M. Mc-Goldrick, C. M. Anderson, & F. Walsh (Eds.), *Women in families: A framework for family therapy* (pp. 61–77). New York: Norton.

Henley, N. (1977). *Body politics: Power, sex, and nonverbal communication*. Englewood Cliffs, NJ: Prentice-Hall.

Hooks, Bell (1984). *Feminist theory: From margin to center*. Boston: South End Press.

Imber-Black, E. (1986). Women, families, and larger systems. In M. Ault-Riché (Ed.), *Women and family therapy* (pp. 25–33). Rockville, MD: Aspen Systems.

Jacobson, N. S. (1983). Beyond empiricism: The politics of marital therapy. *American Journal of Family Therapy, 11*, 11–24.

Kaschak, E. (1992). *Endangered lives: A new psychology of women's experience*. New York: Basic Books.

Kliman, J. (1994). The interweaving of gender, class, and race in family therapy. In M. P. Mirkin, *Women in context: Toward a feminist reconstruction of psychotherapy* (pp. 25–47). New York: Haworth Press.

Korin, E. C. (1994). Social inequalities and therapeutic relationships: Applying Freire's ideas to clinical practice. In R. V. Almeida (Ed.), *Expansions of feminist family theory through diversity* (pp. 75–98). New York: Harrington Park Press.

Lerner, H. G. (1988). Is family systems theory really systemic? A feminist communication. In L. Braverman (Ed.), *A guide to feminist family therapy* (pp. 47–63). New York: Haworth Press.

Lewis, J. M., Beavers, W. R., Gossett, J. T., & Phillips, V. A. (1976). *No single thread: Psychological health in family systems*. New York: Brunner/Mazel.

Libow, J. A. (1986). Training family therapists as feminists. In M. Ault-Riché (Ed.), *Women and family therapy* (pp. 16–24). Rockville, MD: Aspen Systems.

Libow, J. S., Raskin, P. A., & Caust, B. L. (1982). Feminist and family systems therapy: Are they irreconcilable? *American Journal of Family Therapy, 10*(3), 3–12.

Lorde, A. (1984). *Sister outsider: Essays and speeches*. New York: Cross Press.

Luepnitz, D. A. (1988). *The family interpreted: Psychoanalysis, feminism, and family therapy.* New York: Basic Books.

MacKinnon, L. K., & Miller, D. (1987). The new epistemology and the Milan approach: Feminist and sociopolitical considerations. *Journal of Marital and Family Therapy, 13*(2), 139–155.

Maturana, H., & Varela, F. (1987). *The tree of knowledge: The human biological roots of understanding.* Boston: New Science Library.

McGoldrick, M. (1994). Family therapy: Having a place called home. In R.V. Almeida (Ed.), *Expansions of feminist family theory through diversity* (pp. 127–156). New York: Harrington Park Press.

McGoldrick, M., Anderson, C. M., & Walsh, F. (1989). Women in families and in family therapy. In M. McGoldrick, C. M. Anderson, & F. Walsh (Eds.), *Women in families: A framework for family therapy* (pp. 3–15). New York: Norton.

McGoldrick, M., Giordano, J., & Pearce, J. K. (1996). *Ethnicity and family therapy* (2nd ed.). New York: Guilford Press.

McGoldrick, M., & Rohrbaugh, M. (1987). Researching ethnic family stereotypes. *Family Process, 26*(1), 89–99.

Morawski, J. G., & Bayer, B. M. (1995). Stirring trouble and making theory. In H. Landrine (Ed.), *Bringing cultural diversity to feminist psychology: Theory, research, and practice* (pp. 113–137). Washington, DC: American Psychological Association.

Okun, B. F. (1996). *Understanding diverse families: What practitioners need to know.* New York: Guilford Press.

Porter, N., & Yahne, C. (1994). Feminist ethics and advocacy in the training of family therapists. In M. Snyder (Ed.), *Ethical issues in feminist family therapy* (pp. 29–47). New York: Haworth Press.

Rich, A. (1976). *Of woman born: Motherhood as experience and institution.* New York: Norton.

Skerrett, K. (1996). From isolation to mutuality: A feminist collaborative model of couples therapy. *Women & Therapy, 19*(3), 93–106.

Snyder, M. (Ed.). (1994). *Ethical issues in feminist family therapy.* New York: Haworth Press.

Suzuki, S. (1970). *Zen mind, beginner's mind.* New York: Weatherhill.

Taggart, M. (1989). Epistemological equality as the fulfillment of family therapy. In M. McGoldrick, C. M. Anderson, & F. Walsh (Eds.), *Women in families: A framework for family therapy* (pp. 97–116). New York: Norton.

Tiefer, L. (1995). *Sex is not a natural act & other essays.* Boulder, CO: Westview Press.

Treiman, D., & Hartmann, H. (1981). *Women, work, and wages.* Washington, DC: National Academy of Sciences Press.

Veroff, J., Douvan, E., & Kulka, R. A. (1981). *The inner American.* New York: Basic Books.

Walsh, F., & Scheinkman, M. (1989). (Fe)male: The hidden gender dimension in models of family therapy. In M. McGoldrick, C. M. Anderson, & F. Walsh (Eds.), *Women in families: A framework for family therapy* (pp. 16–41). New York: Norton.

Walters, M., Carter, B., Papp, P., & Silverstein, O. (1988). *The invisible web: Gender patterns in family relationships.* New York: Guilford Press.

Weingarten, K., & Bograd, M. (Eds.). (1996). *Reflections on feminist family therapy training.* New York: Haworth Press.

Weissman, M. M. (1980). Depression. In A. M. Brodsky & R. T. Hare-Mustin (Eds.), *Women and psychotherapy.* New York: Guilford Press.

CHAPTER 18

Integrative Family Therapy

WILLIAM C. NICHOLS

…the boundaries between the intrapersonal and the interpersonal are subtle.

– **Alan S. Gurman and David P. Kniskern,** *Handbook of Family Therapy*

DEFINITION

Integrative family therapy focuses on the treatment of persons in their primary contexts. It emphasizes developmental, contextual, and interactional dimensions of human life. Integrative family therapy is concerned with integrating theories pertaining to human development and behavior with theories dealing with the contexts in which human beings function. The particular approach that I have developed over four decades and continue to refine embraces and draws from theoretical stances and empirical materials pertaining to both human persons and human systems, and specifically with psychodynamic (object relations) systems, and behavioral (cognitive-behavioral and social learning) theories.

Therapy itself is concerned with human personality. The ultimate objective in therapy is, or ought to be, the healing, growth, and development of individuals. My assumption is that understanding personality is not possible without comprehending the context in which it is formed and sustained as a system and as a subsystem in a hierarchy of systems (Nichols, 1996, p. 11). As is the case with most approaches to family therapy, integrative family therapy, therefore, works with the client's significant systems and subsystems. At the same time, I assume that working with human behavior means dealing with "living, feeling, anxious, fearing, desiring human beings" (Nichols, 1996, p. 11), who are unique persons as well as members of systems. Hence, I consider it important to understand and to give heed to important intrapsychic issues in the processes of assessment and treatment, emphasizing that intrapsychic processes do not exist in a vacuum but for the most part are interactional.

Personality, in other words, has both "inside" and "outside" aspects. Ongoing assessment provides guidance for determining when, where, and how to intervene in the lives of clients and their contexts. The test of where to intervene and how to proceed, whether going "inside" the psyche or dealing with the context in which the person exists and functions, often is basically a pragmatic one. How necessary is it to seek to uncover the individual's unconscious thoughts and conflicts and, on the other hand, how essential is it to attempt to bring about systemic change in families and in other important systems such as school and work situations in order to effect desired change in the life of the person(s) with whom one is working?

As with many other family systems approaches, integrative family therapy requires the therapist to "think systems" at all times, even when one is seeing only one member of a family in therapy. It is not the number of persons present but the orientation of the therapist that determines whether the treatment involves a systems approach.

This chapter deals with integrative family therapy, which is not to be confused with eclecticism. Despite the ironic and unfortunate fact that integration is often confused with eclecticism or technical integration, these are two quite different approaches, whose differences need to be appreciated. As Norcross and Newman (1992) have spelled out, the differences between eclecticism and integration in psychotherapy can be stated as follows:

ECLECTICISM IS CONCERNED WITH:	INTEGRATION IS CONCERNED WITH:
Technical blending	Theoretical blending
Differences in therapies	Similarities in therapies
Applying the parts of therapy	Unifying the parts of therapy
Applying what is	Creating something new
Focusing on the sum of parts	Focusing on an entity that is more than (different from) the sum of its parts

AND IS:	AND IS:
Atheoretical	More theoretical than empirical

The latter characteristic should not be construed as implying that integrative family therapy is not empirical, because the model presented here is not only theoretically driven, but also empirically driven to the extent that it cuts across theoretical grounds.

Integrative family therapy is not concerned with pulling and meshing techniques from various treatment models or with proving or advocating the superiority of a given model but with blending our theoretical understanding, unifying theory where possible, and engaging in an always unfinished process of working with the complexities of human personality and behavior.

While not indifferent to techniques, integrative family therapy does not give anything resembling top priority to techniques. Rather, clinical experience, empirical research (e.g., the outcome studies of Gurman, 1973; Gurman & Kniskern, 1981; Gurman, Kniskern, & Pinsof, 1986), and systems theory itself all support the notion that many different techniques can be effective. The systems concept of equifinality—that is, the notion that one can reach the same goal from several or sometimes many different starting points—provides a theoretical basis for the clinician's confidence that more than one approach can be useful and effective.

The integrative family therapy described in this chapter is not an "either/or" approach in which the focus is either on the individual or on family systems but a "both/and" orientation. Best described in Nichols (1996, p. 22), it takes into account:

- Individuals, including attention to intrapsychic processes, as these are part of development and functioning; how they are attracted to and relate to others, particularly entry into and continuation in voluntary relationships of intimacy such as mate selection and marriage; and how they learn and how their behavior is changed.

- Systems and subsystems, especially the family system and the family's subsystems—marital, parental, sibling, and individual.

HISTORICAL DEVELOPMENT

In writing this section I am aware of two streams of integration in family therapy. One involves the work of Ackerman (1958), Charny (1966), Sander (1979), Duhl and Duhl (1981), Pinsof (1983, 1995), Kirschner and Kirschner (1986), Wachtel and Wachtel (1986), and Feldman (1985, 1992), as well as the movement toward integration in psychotherapy generally (Norcross & Goldfried, 1992).

The second stream and the one featured in this chapter is my own work, which has been summarized best in Nichols and Everett (1986), and Nichols (1988, 1996), and illustrated in various clinical descriptions (e.g., Nichols 1985; Nichols, 1998). Unlike several of the models mentioned above, my integrative approach attempts to maintain a consistent focus on human personality and the complexities of its development and functioning and that of its significant systems and subsystems rather than focusing on bringing together different modalities of interviewing such as individual sessions and conjoint sessions involving a marital couple or a total family. Also, some of the first-stream approaches mentioned above appear to be closer to "technical integration" or eclecticism than to genuine integration of theory.

From the beginning of my struggles to develop an integrative framework for understanding and working with people therapeutically, I have been exposed to a wide variety of studies pertaining to human development and behavior, particularly those in the social and cultural areas as well as in psychology. My own psychological need to be as complete as possible in my understanding and the accompanying inability to be a "true believer" satisfied with a unilateral approach inevitably have resulted in a career-long effort to be integrative. At the same time, I have recognized that remaining open to information from different sources requires one to tolerate ambiguity, that is, to be able to hold conflicting pieces of information simultaneously, acknowledging that both or all are valid although they may appear to be contradictory. Thus the approach described here involves forming a framework into which a variety of types of interventions may fit rather than a blueprint or treatment manual approach to therapy.

The first conscious focus on integration came when I became a family therapist, before I had ever heard the term. My epiphany experience—the sudden manifestation of the meaning of the personality/context issue—occurred four decades ago when I witnessed the removal of the fence around a state mental hospital. Realizing that major tranquilizing medications could alter the behavior of even highly disturbed individuals so that they could be released from incarceration in hospitals, I also recognized that the family and other parts of the person's significant environment required alteration as well if many of the former patients were to hold their medication-induced gains. (The epiphany experience and some of the subsequent developments and implications associated with it are described in Nichols, 1990.)

Prior to that time I had already encountered the work of Harry Stack Sullivan (1953, 1954). Thus entered a major influence into my integrative efforts. Sullivan, who was influenced by the integrative, synthesizing milieu of the University of Chicago, brought together many diverse streams of knowledge to explain the development and functioning of human personality. I found the orientation—openness to data from assorted sources and melding of that material into new and developing constructs—both stimulating and illuminating. Sullivan's approach was refreshingly different from that of classical psychoanalysis, which was another part of my early orientation. Eventually it seemed clear to me that many of the tenets of psychoanalysis and psychoanalytic psychotherapy were more matters of faith and belief than solidly based on fact. Modifications of psychodynamics to include aspects of culture and group life made sense to me. This was done without throwing out everything that psychodynamic psychology has to contribute. As implied above, the outcome was the stance that the issue is not whether unconscious processes exist, whether transference, countertransference, and other constructs can be found, but rather how significant they are in a given case, and whether it is important and necessary to address them directly. Most important of all, however, in Sullivan's influence has been the support his work has given to the idea that integrating information and understandings and devising a therapeutic orientation constitute an ongoing process.

Philosophically, Heraclitus's conclusion that "all is flux," that everything is always in a state of change, fits well will Sullivan's work and with mine. I began to teach student therapists to make careful initial assessments and to continue to make assessments as they worked with clients. As they did so, I urged them to "hold your constructs and conclusions both tightly—so that you have some basis for dealing therapeutically with clients—and loosely, so that you do not become intellectually rigid and frozen but remain open to new information and growth and can continue to change."

One of the ironies of the family therapy field is that many of those who were highly influenced by Sullivan's emphasis on personality as a process and on social and cultural contributions to personality formation absorbed only part of his approach. While they were quick to accept his rejection of classical psychoanalytic impulse theory and heralded systems theory as part of their epistemology, they typically have not identified with his synthesizing and integrating emphases. Salvador Minuchin (1982) has long since decried the tendency of some family therapists to rigidify their thinking and therapy modalities, erecting "castles" behind the ramparts and moats over which they reign as gurus. Minuchin said that when people came to his "castle" he would not be there, implying that he would have moved on to new fields.

Another early influence on my thinking and approach to clinical work was Nathan W. Ackerman's (1958) biopsychosocial model of personality. Sullivan's "one genus postulate," in which he proclaimed that "we are all more simply human than otherwise," had already symbolized for me that we could assume more similarity than variability among the representatives of homo sapiens. This bias supported my inclination to search more assiduously in the social, cultural, and psychological spheres than in the physical for understanding of group variations in human personality and behavior.

Four years of teaching basic social science, family courses, social psychology, and general and cultural anthropology, and some postdoctoral studies in anthropology, reinforced my need to try to integrate theoretical constructs dealing with nonbiological factors. The study of culture and physical anthropology helped to continue sensitizing me to the physical commonalities among homo sapiens and to the plasticity and manifold characteristics and adaptations of human personality. Much of my subsequent writing (Nichols, 1988, 1996; Nichols & Everett, 1986) has included reference to Kluckholn and Murray's (1956) four determinants of personality formation, which I have characterized as constitutional, group membership, role, and idiosyncratic experiential determinants, and to the interaction of those determinants.

TENETS OF THE MODEL

This integrative approach embodies the assumption that one cannot either deal with the individual alone and ignore systems or deal with a system alone and ignore the individual person and be an efficacious therapist, except in a quite limited sense. What I observed four decades ago—that many of the mental hospital patients who were released after medication and individual treatment did not maintain their gains unless changes were made in their family and their environment—and many observations since, remind me that both aspects, person and system, need to be considered in therapy.

Whereas psychoanalysis and psychodynamic approaches to human beings often overemphasized intrapsychic processes and treated individuals as if they were closed systems affected primarily by internal impulses, swinging the pendulum to the other extreme and dealing with individuals as if what they think and feel internally is irrelevant also has its limitations. The "black box" stance taken by some pioneering family therapists in the 1950s—in which it was regarded as unnecessary to seek to deal with intrapsychic processes—was understandable as a reaction to the rigidity and excesses of much of the reigning psychoanalytic thought and practice. To conclude that one can work only with systems and thereby produce therapeutic effects for individuals can be as erroneous as the approach against which those early family therapists reacted.

Another assumption is that three major orientations in psychotherapy have "won their spurs" as ways of conceptualizing human behavior and offer important theoretical bases for understanding human personality and devising meaningful interventions into human problems: psychodynamic psychotherapy, behaviorism, and systems theory. A further assumption is that these three theoretical orientations can be integrated to a workable degree so that they form an integrative framework for therapy. (See Nichols, 1996, pp. 21–56, for a more extensive discussion of the materials that follow on psychodynamic psychotherapy, behaviorism, and systems and general system theory.)

PSYCHODYNAMIC PSYCHOTHERAPY

The parts of dynamic psychotherapy that I consider adequately durable and appropriate for integration come from among those theorists who have abandoned Sigmund Freud's instinct (drive) theory and who have attempted to comprehend personality in relation to cultural and social forces. The major contributors include Sullivan, with his interpersonal theory, and W. R. D. Fairbairn (1952, 1954, 1963), with his version of "British object relations" theory. Sullivan, with his emphasis on the interpersonal setting, cultural content, and crucial role of communication processes in human development and interaction, gives an "outside" perspective. Fairbairn, with his version of object relations theory, gives an important "inside" view with more specificity than Sullivan on the internal organization of the person.

Object relations theorists typically emphasize that internalized residues of one's early interactional experiences with important persons (or "objects") and the patterns of relating that are learned in those early experiences, as subsequently evolved and developed, furnish the basis for later intimate relationships. Carrying those experiences in our mind either as internal objects or memories, we form some guidelines for reacting to and dealing with the present, according to this theory.

SIGNIFICANCE OF THE UNCONSCIOUS Not the least of the contributions that psychodynamic psychology offers integrative family therapy is an appreciation for the significance of mental activity that occurs outside our awareness. In addition to sensitizing us to the presence and role of self-deception, this perspective also gives us guidelines for searching out experiences and tendencies that are being disavowed (Wachtel & McKinney, 1992). Many therapists who do not consider themselves psychodynamically oriented nevertheless recognize the presence of "anniversary reactions" and some of their potential for explaining current emotional reactions on the basis of past experiences that took place on a calendar location similar to the present date (e.g., losing a loved one at today's approximate day or month at some time in the past).

Some of object relations' most helpful theoretical concepts (adapted from Nichols, 1996, pp. 29–34) include splitting, introjection, projection, projective identification, and collusion. These five unconscious process concepts pertain basically to how persons perceive and relate to other persons with whom they have contact.

SPLITTING In this primitive defense, an individual splits the good from the bad in an external object (person) and retains the split perception internally. The result is a subsequent interactional style in which negative and positive thoughts and feelings are split and experienced in isolation from each other and play significant roles in loving and trusting another person.

INTROJECTION This is a process in which we incorporate the picture of another person as we perceive him or her to be and then transfer affect from the actual person to our psychic picture. We can, for example, idealize a person and fall in love with the idealized picture of the person rather than with the real person, a process that is frequently seen.

PROJECTION In projection we externalize or "throw out" undesired aspects of oneself and place them on another person or persons in the external world. For example, a man who is in love with a woman can attribute to her feelings of love toward himself.

PROJECTIVE IDENTIFICATION This process involves externalizing an aspect of one's psychic processes onto another person, identifying with this projected part as it is perceived and experienced in that person, relating to that part as we would if it were inside oneself, and attempting to pull that person into collusively acting in the way in which he or she is perceived.

COLLUSION Projective identification is an interactive process that calls for the object of one's projective identification to accept the projection and to act accordingly. Henry V. Dicks (1967) has described one form of collusive process in marriage as consisting of an unconscious agreement between spouses that, "I will regard you as not sexual, if you will regard me as not aggressive." Don D. Jackson (Watzlawick, Beavin, & Jackson, 1967) analyzed in family therapy terms an implicit, conscious-level collusion between George and Martha to maintain a marital myth in *Who's Afraid of Virginia Woolf?*

BEHAVIORISM

Behavioral theory and concepts are helpful in relation to learning. Social learning theory has been used for several decades in behavioral family therapy, especially with regard to parent–child problems and issues. Behaviorism perceives symptoms as learned responses that are not adaptive to the needs and situations of the person. Much of its theory emphasizes reciprocal interaction with other persons. The emphasis of the cognitive-behavioral approach is on the mental process of individuals, specifically on their cognitions. This emphasis blends well with the emotional emphasis of psychodynamic psychology and is used extensively in integrative family therapy, especially in marital therapy.

Reciprocity lends itself to the formation and use of contracts between individuals, especially in marital interaction. Two kinds of such contracts are the "quid pro quo" (literally, "something for something") and the "good faith" contract. The integrative family therapy described here makes frequent use of "good faith" contracts.

SYSTEMS THEORY

The most relevant concepts from systems theory for integrative family therapy include:

SYSTEM A system is something put together so that whatever affects one part also affects other parts. A family, for example, is a system composed so that what affects one part also affects others, much in the manner of a human body in which an injury to one part results in the other parts responding protectively.

ORGANIZATION All systems are organized. A family may be organized around an alcoholic husband–father, a co-dependent wife–mother, and a group of compliant or rebellious children, for instance. Conversely, the family can be organized in a functional and healthy fashion.

SUBSYSTEM Subsystems conduct particular processes in a system. Within the family, the major subsystems are the spousal, parent–child, and sibling. Each subsystem will have its own organization, patterns of interaction, and boundaries. In some instances, therapy may be focused primarily on one subsystem, such as the spousal, in order to benefit another subsystem such as the sibling or the individual subsystem of a symptomatic child.

WHOLENESS AND BOUNDARIES These concepts are part of the larger concept of organization. Systems theory emphasizes patterns rather than reductively analyzing organizations in terms of their parts. Gregory Bateson (1979) spoke of "the pattern which connects." Finding the pattern that connects enables the therapist to determine how and where to intervene in order to effect change in the family system. The concept of boundaries identifies who is to be included in a system and who is to regulate the flow of information and feedback to the system.

OPEN SYSTEMS AND CLOSED SYSTEMS An open system exchanges information with the external environment and other systems. A family as a relatively open system has a balance of protecting and engaging mechanisms that enable family members to come and go in a functional fashion, influencing and being influenced by schools, community, and various other entities in the environment. A closed or relatively closed system would have little interchange with the environment and would likely be dysfunctional. Living systems maintain a "steady state" in which their mechanisms help them to fluctuate between behaviors that maintain the status quo and behaviors that help them deal with new challenges in the environment. For example, a family works to engage its teenagers' participating in the family at the same time that it permits them to spend time with their peers and to engage in behaviors that are different from family patterns.

EQUIFINALITY The same results can be secured by starting from different points and by using different means. The parental subsystem can perform "good parenting" in a variety of different ways, for instance. As will be noted again later, one practical implication of the concept of equifinality is that similar therapeutic outcomes can be obtained by different methods and from different beginning points. "Circular causality," as contrasted with "linear causality," is one of the more widely valued ideas in systems theory.

FEEDBACK Systems have two channels conveying information, so that one loops back from the output to the input, bringing back information that affects subsequent outputs from the system. This pattern permits self-correcting behavior on the part of the system. "Positive" feedback causes change. "Negative" feedback cancels out errors and helps the system to maintain a steady state.

NONSUMMATIVITY "The whole is different than the sum of its parts" is a succinct expression of nonsummativity. A family is different than the sum of its parts. To assess and understand a family, a clinician must view the family as a whole; a different picture emerges when the clinician sees four family members separately than when he or she seems them together.

COMMUNICATION Systems theorists consider all behavior as communication; hence, one cannot not communicate because one cannot not behave. Communication determines the relationships and establishes the roles in a family. Patterns of nonverbal and verbal communication not only shape the behavior of members but also reveal to the clinician the relative openness of family boundaries and thus the availability of the family to therapeutic interventions and change.

It is exceedingly important to recognize that the family is a particular kind of system and that it is as necessary to "think family" as it is to "think systems" (Nichols & Everett, 1986). Rather than being simply a system, the family is a system with a history, as contrasted with ad hoc therapy groups composed of previously unrelated individuals. The family as a system has a life cycle that faces its members with particular tasks that need to be accomplished at various stages in the family's life. Some family therapists have emphasized that the failure to achieve successful completion of a major task causes the family to become "stuck" and to produce symptoms, usually in one member who is frequently labeled "the identified patient." The transitions between one stage of the cycle and another have been identified by some (e.g., Carter & McGoldrick, 1988) as being particularly problematic for families. My integrative approach emphasizes the importance of successfully accomplishing core tasks within a given stage as well as negotiating the transitions between stages (Nichols, 1996). Not handling tasks within a stage does not result in as spectacular a dysfunction as failure to effect the transitions between stages successfully but it still makes for problematic functioning. In addition to the family life cycle, the therapist needs to be aware of and deal with the marital life cycle of the spouses (Nichols & Pace-Nichols, 1993) and the individual life cycles of the individual members (Nichols, 1996).

Family systems are composed of people, whose development and functioning are affected by the family both while they are living in the nuclear/extended family setting that launches them into the world and long after they have departed. Everett and I (Nichols & Everett, 1986) have described the family as integrative because those family processes work over several generations. This has what should be rather obvious implications for dealing in therapy with intergenerational patterns of relating and results in a noticeable amount of family-of-origin work with clients.

The family also is a system that one enters involuntarily, except in the case of marriage. Marriage, as the lone voluntary relationship in a family, is the most tenuous of family relationships, the "fragile bond" as Napier (1988) has termed it. As such, it demands particular attention to the forms of attachment between the spouses and to the kind and degree of commitment held by both partners.

THE FIVE "Cs"

Marriage, the nexus of the nuclear family, involves certain core or central internal relationship tasks that prove exceedingly useful as information guidelines in assessing the condition of the marital relationship. Constructed nearly two decades ago from an analysis of 100 consecutive marital cases in my case load, the five Cs have been refined and have proved their pragmatic worth in the intervening years. They also have the value of being understandable and usable to clients in assessing their own program in treatment (Nichols & Everett, 1986; Nichols, 1988, 1996). They are:

COMMITMENT This refers to how and to what extent the spouses value their relationship and their intentions with regard to its maintenance and continuation. Commitment also can be assessed with regard to the clients' commitment to therapy and change.

CARING This pertains to the kind of emotional attachment that ties the partners to each other. The term is used instead of the more ambiguous term "love," for which it is a reasonably close synonym that does not carry the problematic connotations of love.

COMMUNICATION This concerns the ability to communicate verbally and symbolically, to share meanings.

CONFLICT/COMPROMISE This refers to the ability to recognize, acknowledge, and deal with the conflicts and disagreements that are inevitable in any intimate relationship.

CONTRACT "Contract" is the title for the set of expectations and explicit, implied, or presumed agreements held by marital partners. (Following an approach described by Sager, 1976, these expectations and agreements may be conscious and verbalized, conscious but not verbalized, or outside the level of awareness.)

(An extensive description of the use of the five Cs construct with a normal, fairly typical marital therapy case involving no serious pathology can be found in Nichols, 1998.)

A NOTE

Incidentally, the emergence of systems consultation (Wynne, McDaniel, & Weber, 1986), one of the important trends of the time, should be regarded as what it is, an extension of systems theory to altering systems, not as a further development of therapy. Systems theory can be applied to various kinds of systems, such as schools and workplaces, but effects on individuals are likely to be more preventive and effects on the system more metaphorical than therapeutic (healing).

ASSUMPTIONS AND VALUES IN THE APPROACH

Beyond the theoretical concepts derived from the three theoretical approaches described above, there are some assumptions and values accompanying my integrative family approach that merit the label of tenets (Nichols, 1996, pp. 75–83). Most of them in some form probably are shared with the majority of therapists. Briefly stated, they are:

THE CLIENT SYSTEM Briefly put, the clinician can affect the family system by working with the entire unit or with one member and, conversely, can affect the person by working with the system as a system. The term *client* is preferred rather than *patient*, which implies passivity. The goal of systems intervention is to secure change so that the system no longer operates pathologically or ineffectively, thus producing symptoms in a member or members.

RESPECTFUL TREATMENT OF CLIENTS Clients are enlisted as collaborators in the therapy process and are encouraged to exercise their right to self-determination within the therapy framework. In this process, the therapist attempts to maintain an appropriate balance between the rights of individual family members and family system/subsystem rights and needs. Equitable behavior on the part of the therapist sometimes involves taking a stand against certain behaviors such as child or spousal abuse.

THE RELATIONSHIP AND ALLIANCE WITH CLIENTS Closely associated with the foregoing is the importance of the establishment of a relationship of trust and the formation of a therapeutic alliance with clients. Techniques in integrative family therapy are, as noted, secondary to the clinician's ability to form such relationships, to relate sensitively, empathically, and sensibly with the client system.

DIRECT AND INDIRECT INTERVENTION WITH CLIENTS Again stating a matter briefly, I am in agreement with Donald Williamson (1991, p. 81), that "paradox [an indirect approach] is always the second choice [in psychotherapy]. It is always preferable to deal with clients in a straightforward way." When paradox is considered necessary, Williamson prefers to be playful and to have both parties "on the inside of the joke" instead of intentional paradox, which is viewed as antithetical to intimacy.

THE RESPONSIBILITY FOR CHANGE "I have never changed anybody, and neither has anybody else. I have helped a lot of people to change." That is a succinct reference to the belief that the role of the therapist is to serve as a facilitator, rather than one who is totally responsible for change. Providing a genuine relationship and respectfulness, accompanied by realistic and appropriate hope, is the role of the therapist, who helps the client system to change as it is willing and able to do so. This role lies between the stance of those who would assign no responsibility to the therapist and those who would give total responsibility to the clinician.

THE MOTIVATION OF CLIENTS Just as we do not change others, we do not motivate others. Even one of the most vocal proponents of the idea that the therapist is responsible for change indicates that when he is talking about motivating people he is actually persuading clients to take action (Haley, 1976, p. 54). Therapy is a persuasion or social influence process. The motivational element shows up as a crucial factor in the client system's commitment to therapy, commitment to change, and commitment to the partner and the marital relationship. While the therapist can create supportive and confrontive conditions, as well as conditions of hope, most therapy is not likely to be more effective than the motivation of the client system.

THE PRINCIPLE OF LEAST PATHOLOGY This concept, which also has been articulated quite effectively by William Pinsof (1983), involves an initial determination of whether the client problems can be dealt with in a simple, straightforward manner, or whether more long-term and more depth-oriented approaches need to be taken. If direct observations, suggestions, or recommendations, including proffering of information, bring about desired change, additional therapeutic work may not be needed. Quite early in my career, I recommended a typical psychodynamic course of therapy for a man plagued with alcohol abuse. Instead of entering therapy, the man and his wife consulted their clergyman, who told the man to stop drinking. He followed that advice and was still abstaining a decade later. While not all problems are resolved that easily, some can be, and it makes sense to try direct common-sense approaches in many instances.

THE EDUCATION OF CLIENTS Similarly, clients sometimes need information and need to know what can be done and what is required of them. Part of the therapist's role is determining what else is necessary in order to assist clients to do what needs to be done. This may include providing skill training in communication, for example, or working with their family of origin, as well as helping to free them of crippling anxiety that restricts their competence.

GENDER CONSIDERATIONS AND ETHNICITY CONSIDERATIONS Family therapy in recent years has been compelled to reexamine its perceptions of both gender—issues pertaining to femininity and masculinity—and ethnicity—basic dimensions of humankind as marked by common history, language, characteristics, and customs. Race and racial issues frequently are included under the general rubric of ethnicity, but deserve separate recognition and treatment. Attempts are made in the integrative family therapy approach described here to give appropriate and sensitive attention to the characteristics typically found in members of a minority category and to specific individual, idiosyncratic characteristics of persons.

The foregoing sets the stage for tailoring treatment to the needs of the person and the situation rather than collecting treatment techniques and strategies applicable to a broad range of problems.

APPLICATIONS AND TECHNIQUES

Treatment in the integrative approach featured here is flexible. This follows logically from the nature of this integrative modality in which the focus is on using theory to provide understanding of the personality or personalities in the client system with which one is working. Using different theoretical stances to comprehend personality, context, and problems rather than attempting to put together techniques leaves the path open for therapists to devise strategies that are consistent with their comprehension of the issues as residing mainly in the psychodynamic, systems, and/or social learning spheres. A number of different interview formats—conjoint, individual, subsystem, total nuclear family system—may be employed. The focus may change as developments occur during the process of therapy (Nichols, 1996) and as immediate goals are met on the way to reaching outcome goals (Nichols, 1985).

There is no intent in my integrative family therapy to provide a treatment manual approach in which specific interventions are to be made for specified conditions or syndromes. The reality is, as noted, that many different techniques can be used effectively, that "many different roads lead to Rome," as it were. This does not mean that "one approach is as good as any other." Rather, the techniques of intervention used should be consistent with the developmental, cognitive-intellectual, and motivational characteristics of the client system and the symptomatology as well as the particular life cycle(s) with which one is working—total family, marital, and individual.

Neither is there any ambition associated with this approach to find or develop anything resembling a universal treatment technique or set of techniques that can or should be applied to all cases. Communication is no panacea, for example. Total reliance on communication to resolve problems would ignore the reality that people can communicate clearly and disagree absolutely; more typically the need is for the ability to resolve the conflicts that clear communication can uncover. For another example of the fact that finding universal answers frequently proves illusory, we need to recall that it was necessary to abandon the early high hopes in family therapy that double-bind theory (Bateson, Jackson, Haley, & Weakland, 1956) could explain schizophrenia and that improved communication could prevent the development of the condition. Finding a "key" or "the key" to successful therapy continues to be a common activity nevertheless; among the latest developments being the recent recognition by some that narrative approaches have value and their elevating them to a major position in family therapy.

ASSESSMENT IN FAMILY THERAPY

Assessment can follow either a standardized or a tailored path. A standardized approach systematically assesses all categories of client systems in the same manner (e.g., using structured interview guides, using formal assessment devices, and including the same points with all client systems in a given category). Data collection thus can involve using standardized assessment devices, interviewing, observing, and securing reports from outside sources such as previous therapists, schools, physicians, and other professionals. Among the clinically more helpful formal assessment devices are the Family Assessment Device (Miller, Kabacoff, Epstein, Bishop, Keitner, Baldwin, & van der Spuy, 1994) and the Beavers Family Systems Model (Beavers & Hampson, 1990).

The integrative family therapy approach described here relies heavily on interviews, the most widely used way of performing clinical assessment. Conjoint family sessions or conjoint marital sessions provide an opportunity to learn about how the system operates, as well as how individual members function in the system or subsystem. They also permit the clinician to begin forming a therapeutic alliance from the outset. Assessment and therapy thus coexist from the outset. Individual interviews are sometimes used on a prescriptive basis. Using individual interviews sometimes provides information not otherwise available, but carries the drawback of potentially creating practical and ethical dilemmas, thus making it crucial for the clinician to set forth clear, explicit guidelines on confidentiality at the beginning (Feldman, 1985). Genograms (McGoldrick & Gerson, 1985) are used on occasion, although not routinely as is the case with many family therapists. Much of the same kind of information obtained through use of a genogram can be secured by using a background information form that I have used for nearly 30 years along with pertinent, focused questions (Nichols, 1988, pp. 110–111; 1996, pp. 108–109).

TREATMENT PLANNING AND INTERVENTION

Treatment planning and interventions are related to the nature of the presenting complaints/problems as well as to problems discovered during the subsequent course of therapy and the state of development of the family, marriage, and individuals. Clinically, it has proved useful to conceptualize families in terms of a broad approach, as families in formation, expanding families, contracting families, and postparental families. For families experiencing reorganization, the conceptualization views families as families in transition; divorce and families in transition; and remarriage (Nichols & Everett, 1986; Nichols, 1988, 1996). Using such a general developmental framework and considering the family life cycles that apply provides a basis for deciding how to conceptualize and deal with issues of sequence and causation (Wilkinson, 1993; Nichols, 1996). If we are seeing, for example, a family that is in the contraction stage, we would need to consider the extent to which the family unit is releasing family members appropriately and incorporating new members by marriage; how well the individual members who are in middle adulthood (i.e., the marital-parental pair) are dealing with the possibility of assuming responsibility for their own parents; and other issues related to this stage of family development and functioning. These life cycle and developmental issues provide a focus for beginning to assess the difficulties and competencies of the clients and for deciding where we may need to make interventions into the family system.

In addition to those factors, the nature and form of therapeutic intervention are influenced by the nature and severity of the symptoms and problems manifested initially and subsequently, the strengths and current functioning of the client system, including contributory historical issues, and the therapist's orientation and ability, including the kind of therapeutic alliance he or she is able to form with the client system (Nichols, 1996, p. 55).

If intervention is needed, the goal is to solve problems and seek change in the presenting problems of the identified client system—which often is an identified individual—as well as to secure appropriate alteration in each of the other systems levels. The levels and symptoms/presenting problems can be described in terms of individual symptoms, as in *Diagnostic and Statistical Manual of Mental Disorders IV* (American Psychiatric Association, 1995), in terms of marriage-marital problems, parent-child-parent-child problems, and family-nuclear family and extended family problems. Each level is likely to require its own specific treatment goals (Nichols, 1996, p. 119).

A wide range of individually diagnosable conditions are successfully treated today by marital therapy, and the number and types continue to expand. Some of these and sources of additional information on them are described in Nichols (1988, pp. 76–80). They include agoraphobia, alcoholism, depression, eating disorders, narcissistic disorders, sexual disorders, children's disorders, and paranoid reactions.

GUIDELINES FOR TREATMENT PLANNING AND THERAPEUTIC INTERVENTIONS

The point of initial intervention and the techniques selected should depend basically on the nature of the problem being addressed. In all candor, observation and experience indicate that the preferences of the therapist, including his or her degree of comfort with a particular technique, often play a major role in the techniques selected (Nelson & Trepper, 1993). Stringent attempts are made in integrative family therapy to intervene in ways that are consistent with the situation and needs as informed by the major theoretical orientations in the framework.

BEHAVIORAL INTERVENTIONS Problems that are discrete and specific in nature are more likely than those that are complex or somewhat nebulous to be amenable to direct behavioral approaches. Similarly, if the assessment indicates that learning issues are involved, social learning theory principles can be employed. Behaviorism views symptoms as learned responses that are not appropriate or not adaptive to the current situation. Behavioral and educational approaches typically can be applied to many communication problems. Specific behavioral methods, including behavioral marital therapy, sexual therapy, divorce mediation, parent training, problem-solving skill training, and conflict resolution training, have been designed for given problem areas (Falloon, 1988). Following the principle of least pathology mentioned above, overt approaches—including the use of educational interventions and straightforward recommendations that the client system take specified steps—often can be used with a high chance of successful outcome. When they do not produce desired results, it typically is appropriate for the therapist to move to the next level of system intervention.

Cognitive-behavioral interventions (Baucom & Epstein, 1990), dealing as they do with cognition and action, are useful at all levels of intervention, sometimes as the sole method of intervention and sometimes as adjunctive to psychodynamic or systems interventions. Incidentally, it appears from observation and supervision/consultation with therapists from many different official theoretical persuasions that many, perhaps the majority, use cognitive-behavioral approaches fairly frequently, often without recognizing or acknowledging that they are doing so.

PSYCHODYNAMIC INTERVENTIONS Psychodynamically informed interventions are likely to be the first therapeutic choice when the problems facing the clinician pertain essentially to attachment between persons. These include, in particular, problems with mate selection; with various aspects of attachment, especially problems in the nature of the attachment; and with patterns of personality needs such as patterns of self-deceptive behavior that appear to lie outside the awareness of the individual. Object relations theorists and clinicians have developed theories, including typologies, that are exceedingly useful in explaining not only the selection of a mate and the continuation of a marriage but also the relationship of specific family transactional patterns to specific forms of psychopathology in an individual in the family (Slipp, 1988).

Certain parts of object relations issues can be inferred from the statements and behaviors of clients quite early in the initial session(s) with them. It often is not difficult, for example, to discern that a client who "just has to have" the love and attention of another person is operating at a need-gratification level in which persons are interchangeable, in which the need is more important than the person sought. As contrasted with individuals functioning at a more mature object constancy level, the need-gratification individual predictably is much less likely to be able to be able to maintain the kinds of commitments that therapy and marriage require, or to tolerate the occasional emotional deprivations that are required in marriages where there are children and the spouse's attention has to be shared. Specific needs in marital complementarity and marital collusion have been described and illustrated extensively by Dicks (1967) and Willi (1982, 1984, 1992).

Psychodynamic interventions based on the therapist's assessment of indications of repression, distorted perceptions, various defense mechanisms, and transferentially based feelings and actions can be used effectively in many instances, especially for the purpose of treating individual problems through marital therapy (Sager, 1967, 1976).

SYSTEMS INTERVENTIONS Systems theory gives us some of the best constructs, explanations, and understandings uncovered to date for comprehending how individuals function in their own contexts and the part that one's sociocultural context plays in the shaping of human interaction. No longer can we responsibly deal with human beings as if they were lone individuals or atoms bumping around without regard to the shaping processes of their context. One gets quite different results from working individually with a family member as if he or she were a lone individual and intervening with the family system or with relevant subsystems. Some illustrations of the effects of systems interventions will be given in the next section.

Interventions in an integrative approach, as perhaps in much therapy, typically must be juggled, as noted above. On the basis of the initial assessment, for example, decisions must be made to focus on selected areas for initial, active intervention—on the crisis, or "hot spots" in other words. While this is being done, the therapist holds in abeyance family system interventions that will affect broader issues such as the functioning of the family and the symptoms manifested by individuals. As treatment proceeds, there may be a shifting back and forth of the focus and active interventions from one area to another. This can be in terms of giving attention to individual, marital, and parental concerns in a flexible and planned manner, or in other fashions such as focusing primarily on work concerns with an individual while putting social/personal relationships temporarily on "the back burner" and returning to them later.

CASE EXAMPLE

Rather than using a single case example that would limit the scope of issues to be covered, I have chosen to draw from several different cases in order to describe some diverse treatment issues and approaches.

A DIFFERENTIATING COUPLE: SOME TRANSGENERATIONAL ISSUES IN MARITAL THERAPY

The first case in this section is both typical and atypical. More fully described elsewhere (Nichols, 1985), it was typical in that it was concerned with systems and dynamics, used various modalities of interviewing—conjoint marital, individual, and family-of-origin sessions—flexibly, and used various roles and tactics—teaching, uncovering, support, confrontation—flexibly. It was atypical in that it lasted more than two years, and the difficulties of one spouse received more time and attention than is usual in a marital therapy case.

The Browns (pseudonym) were a couple in their late twenties who had been married for six years and had daughters ages four years and 18 months respectively. The presenting complaints were marital and individual. They agreed that they had trouble in "relating" and in communicating. Individually, Carol was troubled by fantasies about males whenever she became emotionally close to a member of the opposite sex. Subsequently it became clear that her fears and fearfulness were major sources of concern. Exploration disclosed that the family of each attempted to keep both partners from differentiating and living as reasonably emancipated adults. Not surprisingly, both Paul and Carol were anxious that the other was not committed to them. Both partners were functioning essentially at the object constancy level. Carol was diagnosed as troubled by Personality Disorder Not Otherwise Specified. Paul had features meeting the Dependent Personality Disorder and some compulsive features. Both came from mid-range families (i.e., families that tend to hold on to their children and produce neurotic disorders), as assessed by the Beavers Systems Model (Beavers & Hampson, 1990).

Following the initial assessment, I recommended for the foreseeable future a pattern of individual appointments for Carol with conjoint marital sessions in lieu of an individual meeting every three to four weeks. Later, the pattern was reversed, with Paul being seen individually in conjunction with periodic conjoint sessions. This "phase-oriented approach to treatment," so succinctly described by Wynne (1983) for use with seriously mentally ill clients, worked very well with the Browns.

With Carol, the movement in individual sessions was back and forth between past and present, and the focus was on her as an individual and on her marital and family systems. Having been indoctrinated by her mother regarding how holy and great sex was and simultaneously conditioned to accept traditional gender roles that made females dependent on males, Carol had developed a growing idea that males were the source of acceptance, touching, and love in general. As she came to understand the adaptational nature of the fantasies and increased her ability to discriminate and cope more effectively in social situations, Carol's problems with sexual fantasies and fears began to diminish. This, in turn, increased pressure on the marriage as she began to expect more from Paul. We also worked on Carol's difficulties with her older daughter, leading to her recognition of the transgenerational nature of those problems.

After a pattern of several conjoint meetings in which we established additional clarity regarding the expectations each partner had for the marriage, the pattern reversal was established in which Paul, instead of Carol, was seen individually. I worked initially with Paul in logical, "structural" terms that fit well with his engineering outlook on life. After several weeks of individual with periodic conjoint sessions, we began to focus on the family-of-origin relationships of each partner. The ability to differentiate themselves was made an explicit treatment goal. Each was enlisted in helping the other to restructure relationships with their family of origin. They established some family-to-family contacts with Paul's family of origin to replace his family's pattern of seeking to involve him in its ongoing problems and relationships, as had been the case when he was still living at home. An outcome of this was the exposure of Paul's reluctance to make decisions either at work or at home, a carryover from his need to "walk the line" and try to avoid becoming triangulated by his parents when he was growing up. Focusing on his work, his current family, and his family of origin, we examined a number of social situations carefully, looking at what had happened or could be expected to happen, and role-played situations, "building up behavioral muscles" as we had done with Carol earlier.

Success in these endeavors enabled us to rework some earlier problems and unresolved issues from the Browns' marriage. In addition to working on parenting understanding and skills, I referred the Browns to a developmental child psychologist who had a strong background in family work. She found the child about whom the Browns were concerned essentially free of psychopathology and functioning well within a normal range. She reported that the Browns were starved for information and help about normal child-rearing and "soaked it up like sponges."

The use of family photographic slides and subsequent exploration of the observations and feelings elicited from Carol a memory of a family secret involving the accidental killing of a child by a grandmother and the woman's subsequent "nervous breakdown" and lifelong hospitalization. The secret surrounding those events had by that time affected four generations. Use of the concepts of "nongenetic transmission" and "nonverbal transmission" helped Carol to diminish her fears about herself and her older daughter.

Family-of-origin sessions with Carol and her nuclear family, patterned after James Framo's two-session weekend model (Framo, 1981), were helpful to Carol in extending her ability to differentiate and to focus her attention and commitment more fully on her current nuclear family. As Carol and Paul were assisted in pulling away from the sometimes almost overwhelming centripetal pull of her family, they were able to increase their ability to face more squarely the issues of commitment and appreciation of one another.

This is necessarily a brief and somewhat skimpy description of the Brown case because of space limitations. The original printed description covered space equivalent to this entire chapter, but this summary should give something of the flavor of the flexible and integrative family/marital therapy.

A CASE OF OVEREATING: USE OF INDIRECT AND DIRECT INTERVENTIONS

Both direct treatment approaches (direct in terms of psychodynamic work) and indirect treatment approaches (paradoxical directives) can be used together. Direct approaches involve exploration and elucidation of problems, active feedback and sharing with the client system, education, and persuasion. Indirect methods employ paradoxical strategies and interventions, including metaphors and directives that appear contradictory to the aims of therapy.

The following case (Nichols & Everett, 1986, pp. 135–136) involved Janet, a 28-year-old professional woman who had struggled with obesity and problems of overeating for half of her life. Diets, hypnosis, Overeaters Anonymous, and several different therapists had been tried without success. Early on, the client and I established that she was an "angry" overeater and a "sneak" eater. Her anger overflowed and seemed to be displaced into her marriage, where she would on occasion go into a rage and physically attack her husband. I worked with her, teaching her to leave the scene and go for a walk when she got angry and was losing control. The focus on controlling her anger was essentially a cognitive behavioral type of intervention.

Her use of leaving the scene and walking until she cooled down had at least three consequences: (1) It prevented/stopped the unfortunate confrontations and physical combat between the spouses. (2) It demonstrated to the client that she could control her anger. She later confided, "I never knew it was possible to control my anger until you had me leave and take a walk until I could calm down." She had grown up in a family in which the members were either totally calm and rational (denying any anger) or exploding, with no intervening gradations. Leaving the scene and not acting on her upset gave her the new experience of being in control, something that she had not even considered possible for most of her life. (3) It enabled her to control the externalizing behavior and to concentrate on therapy and on changing.

The directive that I gave her indicated that she did not have to sneak food, that she could eat at times and places where it was pleasurable and enjoyable—at her dining room table with a tablecloth and best china and silver, rather than in her automobile or hiding in the basement. I made it explicit that we were not going to be concerned with what she ate or how much, but did ask that she keep a record for the following week so that we could know whether she was eating only when it was pleasurable, promising that if she were not, we would try to make some changes so that eating was enjoyable.

The behavioral changes and the therapeutic relationship led to a rather dramatic breakthrough. The bingeing stopped within two days. At the next therapy session the client recalled a high school incident in which the great social rewards promised by her mother if she had lost weight had not materialized. An examination of the long-repressed anger at her mother's promised rewards and extended nagging that emerged in that session led to some working through and coaching. The result was that she went back home on several occasions to deal with her mother regarding some old unresolved matters between them. Except for one brief period a few months later in which Janet acknowledged that she was "testing things" with her parents, she did not return to bingeing. Janet lost 80 pounds and had maintained the loss and a new "think thin" attitude at a follow-up session two years later.

FAMILY-OF-ORIGIN WORK IN A "STUCK" CASE

Family-of-origin members can—and in this approach, should—be brought in for a session or sessions with the client in which he or she is "stuck" because of significant unresolved issues, and clinical judgment indicates that the members can contribute to helping liberate the client and open up the path to therapeutic progress. The decision as to whether to include the entire nuclear family or a subsystem is made prescriptively and depends in large measure on the nature of the issue/issues behind the "stuckness." Where there is a variety of issues involving several members, the decision typically is to work with the entire family unit as in the case of Carol. When the problem is more circumscribed and specific, the option may be to send the client home to work with the issues, as in the case of Janet, or to invite a subsystem in, as was done with Ted in the following example.

Among the hindering emotions that were hampering this young adult's vocational, personal relationship, and marital interaction were reactions of fear, sometimes paralyzing in nature, of his intense, highly successful executive father. In a session with Ted's parents, we explored the father's feelings about his work. Ted learned for the first time how driven his father was to avoid failure and how frightened his father was. A dramatic and pivotal event occurred when I asked the father what his own father (Ted's grandfather) was like. He exploded that his father was a dictator, a tyrant, a Prussian. Ted, who saw his grandfather as a powerful man but was not the least frightened of him, was stunned. Right in front of him Ted could see his father not as a frightening figure but, rather, as "a frightened little boy," panic-struck at the thought of Ted's "grandpa."

Consequently, as we worked through Ted's feelings in later sessions, it was possible to watch him being released from his old fears and anxiety regarding his father. The "live" experience was the turning point in Ted's movement into change and growth, out of being stuck in a morass of crippling emotions.

SESSIONS WITH SIBLINGS

Several different kinds of sessions with sibling subsystems are used in this integrative approach. One such approach was used, for example, with a woman who had been widowed more than 20 years earlier, and her three adult children. All three of the children, who ranged up to 42 years of age, had been in therapy intermittently during their adult years. The mother had remained single. The clue that something was changing came when the mother, in an exchange of letters with a daughter who was beginning to ask some questions about her father and the family, disclosed that she had changed her hair style and was no longer keeping it colored and styled as she had 20 years earlier. Three sessions with the surviving family members resulted in further movement on the mother's part. Putting things briefly, the long-widowed woman began to deal with her long-denied feelings of loss and gave her children tacit, and then overt, permission to grieve the loss of their father. As she was able to give him up and get on with her life, she gave her children license to do the same thing. The results were not dramatic and spectacular but were clearly evident, and the individual's growth began to gain momentum over the following months.

A second pattern of sibling subsystem sessions was used in a family situation in which the parents and two daughters, ages 17 and 19, were first seen together, the initial complaint being the 17-year-old's "rebellion, poor grades, and totally unacceptable boyfriend." Deciding that the bond between the two daughters was strong and that the older apparently also was uncomfortable with the family patterns and would be supportive of her sister, I introduced the idea of sibling sessions to the family. Recognizing the efforts all had made and the communication difficulties that prevailed at home and in my office, I suggested that if the daughters could start talking out of the parents' presence, it might be easier for all of us to come back together after a few sessions and open up communication so that the family could "talk better and more comfortably" (Nichols, 1996, pp. 211–213).

In three sessions with the siblings, I listened to their complaints over being compared, which pushed them apart, and to their concerns over their parents holding onto them. When they expressed apprehension about how their mother and father would fare when both of them left home, we explored the questions of what they thought they could do to improve the home situation. Through interpretation of their parents' anxieties and normalizing the parental concern over being left without children at home, the question was posed as to whether they thought if would be helpful for them to ask their parents how they felt about their leaving home. When total family sessions were reinstated, the daughters used the coaching we had been through to address their concerns directly to their parents and to listen in turn to what came back from their parents. This led into family problem-solving around daily concerns and for assumption on the part of all four of responsibility for making this coming transition smoother. Some marked changes emerged in the behaviors of the 17-year-old. Subsequently, a final phase of therapy consisted of marital therapy, including some work on helping this middle-aged couple to differentiate more fully from their own families of origin and concerns over parental approval/disapproval of their childrearing. A fourth sibling session at the time the teenagers left treatment helped to consolidate gains and to clear the way for more effective marital work with the parents.

Transitions around divorce and family reorganization also provide opportunities for the effective use of sibling sessions.

EVALUATION OF THE THEORY

Integrative family therapy has not, to my knowledge, been subjected to rigid, carefully controlled empirical research. Various parts of the theoretical constructs that underlie this approach have been researched. The behavioral aspects, for example, have been highly researched, research being one of the hallmarks of behavioral therapy. One of the appealing elements of behavioral theory for me has been the fact that its adherents have been so committed to research, measurement, and obtaining sound empirical results. Some of the results from research can be used with most clients in quite practical ways. For example, I frequently point out to clients that researchers have found that "If you wish to stop (extinguish, in the jargon) behavior, you do not reward it. Any response is a reward." This idea eventually makes sense to most clients with whom I work, and leads to efforts to change rewarding behaviors that lead to nondesired outcomes.

As noted above, this integrative approach is concerned with learning and with cognitive behavioral therapy. My observation, as frequently noted, has been that many therapists, and perhaps most, at times use cognitive behavioral behaviors and seem to operate at least implicitly with cognitive-behavioral assumptions.

Various parts of systems theory have been researched, but not (again to my knowledge) specifically in relation to the integrative family therapy described in this chapter. Psychodynamic concepts, including object relations, have been difficult to quantify, and many psychodynamic ideas and attempts to study them by means of projective testing have been impressive much more to clinicians than to empirical researchers.

Recently, I encountered some indications in reviewing an article submitted to a journal that Spanier's Dyadic Adjustment Scale (DAS) (Spanier, 1976) had been tentatively compared with the five "Cs" of commitment, caring, communication, conflict and compromise, and contract as described in Nichols and Pace-Nichols (1993). Various scales in the DAS appear to offer promise of measuring some of these "Cs," which have proven quite valuable as "rule-of-thumb" guides in assessing couples' adjustment and adaptation. Measuring the adjustment of couples by means of the DAS scales and comparing the results with clinicians' assessment from interview and observation conclusions could be quite helpful in my judgment, particularly if it could be established that alteration of some of Spanier's scales would produce results that would result in the saving of clinical interview time.

Perhaps the major promise of advancement in the sphere of integrative family therapy stems from the fact that a few clinicians in several population centers across the country, from New York to Chicago to Atlanta to California, have offered their explorations and efforts to integrate theory during the 1980s and 1990s. My own therapeutic work and teaching integrative efforts have been around for several decades, and three books (Nichols & Everett, 1986; Nichols, 1988, 1996) and some book chapters (e.g., Nichols, 1998) have offered illustrations in the past decade. This approach is not easily taught and tends to be more readily developed by a clinician at mid-point or later in his or her career.

Apart from the movement, admittedly not very large, to develop integrative family therapy, there has been a significant and growing effort to achieve integration in psychotherapy generally. The best summary with which I am well acquainted at this time is the volume edited by Norcross and Goldfried (1992), which not only offers summaries of work in this area but also provides constructs that can be useful to clinicians and researchers alike. It is to be hoped that scientist–practitioners from systems perspectives will be more active in the integrative arena than seems to have been the case to date.

As a clinician, I am well-satisfied that the integrative approach that I use in my practice is useful, helpful, and, in brief, passes pragmatic tests. I cannot ask others to take this on faith. I certainly do not and would not claim that it is better than other approaches but at the same time am not willing to accept readily any claims that any other approach is superior. The evidence seems too strong that it is not necessarily the theoretical ideas that one espouses or the therapeutic techniques that one uses that result in positive therapeutic outcomes, but that other factors, including, in particular, the kind of relationship one forms with a client system, strongly affect the outcome. A homey description of a great football coach that "He'll take hisn (players) and beat yourn (players)" and "He'll take yourn and best hisn" perhaps can be applied to therapists and therapy. The factors referred to here help to make it difficult to perform meaningful research on therapy, particularly to do worthwhile process research pertaining to theory.

SUMMARY

The study of human personality in its normal and abnormal manifestations within a given culture and across cultures, ethnic groupings, and genders is a concern that has driven my intellectual efforts for most of my professional career. The need to tailor the interventions we make to the needs, mentality, motivation, ability, and desires of clients is, as noted, an essential concomitant of an attempt to understand human personality in both its commonalities and its uniqueness. "One size does not fit all."

   This chapter has been concerned with an effort to describe and illustrate, as well as possible within a short span of pages, an integrative theoretical approach that I consider helpful to the understanding and therapy of human beings. I am reminded of the advice Hall and Lindzey (1957) provided students in their classic book on theories of personality, namely, to take one theory and immerse themselves in it and then to learn others later. That approach to learning about personality theory and about therapeutic theory and practice has some advantages. It is not advice that I have been able to follow, and I invite those who similarly cannot be content with one approach to turn themselves loose in the ambiguous field of integrative work. It is frustrating for most of us to have to admit that we cannot put a label on everything and account for all of the factors and dynamics in a situation, but it would be more frustrating for some of us to be restricted to a single framework. The challenge is, again, to hold major moving assumptions tightly and yet remain open to changing them as the data change, to be able to tolerate what I have called "lumps in the oatmeal," conflicting ideas and pieces of knowledge that we cannot reconcile, to engage continually in clarifying and integrating as we can.

ANNOTATED SUGGESTED READINGS

Dicks, H. V. *Marital tensions.* New York: Basic Books.
   A pioneering work in object relations marital therapy, this book provides many clear case illustrations of marital complementarity and neurotic interaction. It is still one of the better books on "can't live with and can't live without" marriages.

Feldman, L. B. (1992). *Integrating individual and family therapy*. New York: Brunner/Mazel.
  A short book that succinctly describes how intrapsychic and interpersonal approaches to therapy can be combined. As does Nichols, Feldman strongly emphasizes the tailoring of therapy to the needs of the client.

Nichols, W. C. (1988). *Marital therapy: An integrative approach*. New York: Guilford Press.
  An attempt to sketch out an integrative approach involving systems, psychodynamic object relations, and behavioral theories and interventions in the assessment and treatment of marital discord.

Nichols, W. C. (1996). *Treating people in families: An integrative framework*. New York: Guilford Press.
  Extends the integrative approach involving systems, psychodynamic object relations, and behavioral theories and interventions described in Nichols (1988) to involve therapy with entire families, as well as couples and individuals. Much attention is given to the interlocking of family life, marital, and individual life cycles and their values in therapy.

Norcross, J. C., & Goldfried, M. R. (Eds.). (1992). *Handbook of psychotherapy integration*. New York: Basic Books.
  A basic reference on contemporary efforts to secure integration in psychotherapy. Not always easy reading, but recommended for the serious professional.

Pinsof, W. M. (1995). *Integrative problem-centered therapy: A synthesis of family, individual, and biological therapies*. New York: Basic Books.
  Probably the most broadly based of the integrative approaches, this Pinsof work strongly and effectively challenges the idea of matching treatments to disorders, showing that the crucial factors in determining treatment process and outcome are the structures that maintain the problem.

REFERENCES

Ackerman, N. W. (1958). *The psychodynamics of family life*. New York: Basic Books.

American Psychiatric Association. (1995). *Diagnostic and statistical manual of mental disorders* (4th ed.). Washington, DC: Author.

Bateson, G. (1979). *Mind and nature*. New York: Bantam Books.

Bateson, G., Jackson, D. D., Haley, J., & Weakland, J. (1956). Toward a theory of schizophrenia. *Behavioral Science, 1*, 251–264.

Baucom, D. H., & Epstein, N. (1990). *Cognitive-behavioral marital therapy*. New York: Brunner/Mazel.

Beavers, W. R., & Hampson, R. B. (1990). *Successful families: Assessment and intervention*. New York: Norton.

Carter, B., & McGoldrick, M. (1988). *The changing family life cycle: A framework for family therapy*. New York: Gardner Press.

Charny, I. W. (1966). Integrated individual and family psychotherapy. *Family Process, 5*, 179–198.

Dicks, H. V. (1967). *Marital tensions*. New York: Basic Books.

Duhl, B. S., & Duhl, F. J. (1981). Integrative family therapy. In A. S. Gurman and D. P. Kniskern (Eds.), *Handbook of family therapy* (pp. 483–513). New York: Brunner/Mazel.

Fairbairn, W. R. D. (1952). *Psychoanalytic studies of the personality*. London: Routledge & Kegan Paul.

Fairbairn, W. R. D. (1954). *An object relations theory of the personality*. New York: Basic Books.

Fairbairn, W. R. D. (1963). Synopsis of an object-relations theory of the personality. *International Journal of Psycho-Analysis, 44*, 224–225.

Falloon, I. R. H. (1988). Behavioural family therapy: Systems, structures, and strategies. In E. Smith & W. Dryden (Eds.), *Family therapy in Britain* (pp. 101–126). Philadelphia: Milton Keynes.

Feldman, L. B. (1985). Integrative multi-level therapy: A comprehensive interpersonal and intrapsychic approach. *Journal of Marital and Family Therapy, 11*, 357–372.

Feldman, L. B. (1992). *Integrating individual and family therapy*. New York: Brunner/Mazel.

Framo, J. L. (1981). The integration of marital therapy with sessions with family of origin. In A. S. Gurman & D. P. Kniskern (Eds.), *Handbook of family therapy* (pp. 133–158). New York: Brunner/Mazel.

Gurman, A. S. (1973). The effects and effectiveness of marital therapy: A review of outcome research. *Family Process, 12*, 145–170.

Gurman, A. S., & Kniskern, D. P. (1981). Family therapy outcome research: Knowns and unknowns. In A. S. Gurman & D. P. Kniskern (Eds.), *Handbook of family therapy* (pp. 742–745). New York: Brunner/Mazel.

Gurman, A. S., Kniskern, D. P., & Pinsof, W. N. (1986). Research on the process and outcome of family therapy. In S. L. Garfield & A. E. Bergin (Eds.), *Handbook of psychotherapy and behavior change* (pp. 525–623). New York: Wiley.

Haley, J. (1976). *Problem solving therapy: New strategies for effective family therapy*. San Francisco: Jossey-Bass.

Hall, C. S., & Lindzey, G. (1957). *Theories of personality*. New York: Wiley.

Kirschner, D. A., & Kirschner, S. (1986). *Comprehensive family therapy: An integration of systemic and psychodynamic treatment models*. New York: Brunner/Mazel.

Kluckhohn, C., & Murray, H. A. (1956). Personality formation: The determinants. In C. Kluckhohn, H. A. Murray, and D. M. Schneider (Eds.), *Personality in nature, society, and culture* (2nd ed., pp. 53–67). New York: Knopf.

McGoldrick, M., & Gerson, R. (1985). *Genograms in family assessment*. New York: Norton.

Miller, I. W., Kabacoff, R. I., Epstein, N. B., Bishop, D. S., Keitner, G. I., Baldwin, L. M., & van der Spuy, H. I. J. (1994). The development of a clinical rating scale of the McMaster Model of Family Functioning. *Family Process, 33*, 53–69.

Minuchin, S. (1982). Reflections on boundaries. *American Journal of Orthopsychiatry, 52*, 655–663.

Napier, A. Y. (1988). *The fragile bond*. New York: Harper and Row.

Nelson, T. S., & Trepper, T. S. (Eds.). (1993). *101 interventions in family therapy*. New York: Haworth Press.

Nichols, W. C. (1985). A differentiating couple: Some transgenerational issues in marital therapy. In A. S. Gurman (Ed.), *Casebook of marital therapy* (pp. 198–228). New York: Guilford Press.

Nichols, W. C. (1988). *Marital therapy: An integrative approach*. New York: Guilford Press.

Nichols, W. C. (1990). Tear down the fences: Build up the families. In F. W. Kaslow (Ed.), *Voices in family psychology, 1* (pp. 171–191). Newbury Park, CA: Sage.

Nichols, W. C. (1996). *Treating people in families: An integrative framework*. New York: Guilford Press.

Nichols, W. C. (1998). Integrative marital therapy. In F. M. Dattilio (Ed.), *Integrative cases in couples and family therapy: A cognitive-behavioral perspective* (pp. 233–256). New York: Guilford Press.

Nichols, W. C., & Everett, C. A. (1986). *Systemic family therapy: An integrative approach*. New York: Guilford Press.

Nichols, W. C., & Pace-Nichols, M. A. (1993). Developmental perspectives and family therapy: The marital life cycle. *Contemporary Family Therapy, 15*, 299–315.

Norcross, J. C., & Goldfried, M. R. (Eds.). (1992). *Handbook of psychotherapy integration*. New York: Basic Books.

Norcross, J. C., & Newman, C. F. (1992). Psychotherapy integration: Setting the context. In J. C. Norcross & M. R. Goldfried (Eds.), *Handbook of psychotherapy integration* (pp. 3–45). New York: Basic Books.

Pinsof, W. M. (1983). Integrative problem-centered therapy: Toward the synthesis of family and individual psychotherapies. *Journal of Marital and Family Therapy, 9*, 19–35.

Pinsof, W. M. (1995). *Integrative problem-centered therapy: A synthesis of family, individual, and biological therapies*. New York: Basic Books.

Sager, C. J. (1967). Transference in conjoint treatment of married couples. *Archives of General Psychiatry, 16*, 185–193.

Sager, C. J. (1976). *Marriage contracts and couples therapy*. New York: Brunner/Mazel.

Sander, F. M. (1979). *Individual and family therapy: Toward an integration*. New York: Jason Aronson.

Slipp, S. (1988). *The technique and practice of object relations family therapy*. Northvale, NJ: Jason Aronson.

Spanier, G. B. (1976). Measuring dyadic adjustment: New scales for assessing the quality of marriage and similar dyads. *Journal of Marriage and the Family, 38*, 15–28.

Sullivan, H. S. (1953). *The interpersonal theory of psychiatry*. New York: Norton.

Sullivan, H. S. (1954). *The psychiatric interview*. New York: Norton.

Wachtel, P. L., & McKinney, M. K. (1992). Cyclical psychodynamics and integrative psychodynamic therapy. In J. C. Norcross & M. R. Goldfried (Eds.), *Handbook of psychotherapy integration* (pp. 335–370). New York: Basic Books.

Wachtel E. F., & Wachtel, P. L. (1986). *Family dynamics in individual psychotherapy: A guide to clinical strategies*. New York: Guilford Press.

Watzlawick, P., Beavin, J., & Jackson, D. D. (1967). *Pragmatics of human communication: A study on interactional patterns, pathologies and paradoxes*. New York: Norton.

Wilkinson, I. (1993). *Family assessment*. New York: Gardner Press.

Willi, J. G. (1982). *Couples in collusion*. New York: Jason Aronson.

Willi, J. G. (1984). *Dynamics of couples therapy*. New York: Jason Aronson.

Willi, J. G. (1992). *Growing together, staying together*. Los Angeles: Jeremy P. Tarcher.

Williamson, D. S. (1991). *The intimacy paradox: Personal authority in the family system*. New York: Guilford Press.

Wynne, L. C. (1983). A phase-oriented approach to treatment with schizophrenics and their families. In W. R. McFarlane (Ed.), *Family therapy in schizophrenia* (pp. 251–265). New York: Guilford Press.

Wynne, L. C., McDaniel, S. H., & Weber, T. T. (1986). *Systems consultation: A new perspective for family therapy*. New York: Guilford Press.

CHAPTER 19

The Ethical Practice of Marriage and Family Therapy

JOSEPH J. SCALISE

Traditionally, codes of ethics have represented a collection of philosophical and behavioral guidelines developed by professional associations and adhered to by the association's membership. Mappes, Robb, and Engels (1985) offer several specific reasons for establishing a code of ethics: to protect clients, to provide guidance to professionals, to ensure the autonomy of professionals, to increase the prestige of the profession, to increase clients' trust and faith in the members of the profession, and to specify desirable conduct between professionals (p. 246). Other authors have identified additional goals for professional codes of ethics. Mabe and Rollin (1986, 1990) believe that a code of ethics serves as a basis for how a professional behaves, helps to establish a professional identity, and can be viewed as part of the maturation process of a profession. Brock (1994) states that a code of ethics can be a vehicle to enforce existing professional guidelines; to describe the manner in which a professional should conduct a safe and effective practice; and to indicate to the members of the association, to their clients, and to others that the primary concern is the client's interest and well-being.

Throughout the past 50 years, the leading professional associations in the field of mental health have developed, revised, and refined their ethical codes (American Association for Marriage and Family Therapy, 1991; American Counseling Association, 1995; American Psychiatric Association, 1993; American Psychological Association, 1992; National Association of Social Workers, 1996;

National Board of Certified Counselors, 1987; National Federation of Societies for Clinical Social Work, 1988). With each periodic update, changes are made in response to new legal decisions, the rapidly evolving practice milieu, as well as the questions and demands of members. For example, the American Psychological Association published *Ethical Principles of Psychologists and Code of Conduct* (1992), the American Counseling Association instituted its *Code of Ethics and Standards of Practice* (1995), and the National Association of Social Workers recently enacted a significantly revised *Code of Ethics* (1996). All of these changes were promulgated in an attempt to provide more specific guidelines for their members.

Anyone reading the professional literature of the various mental health disciplines can easily find hundreds of articles, monographs, chapters, and books about ethical and legal practice (see Scalise, 1989, 1995a). However, there still remain serious questions, conflicts, and debates about the parameters of appropriate professional behavior. In some instances, practitioners encounter what they perceive as the requirements of a code of ethics that conflicts with their own personal values, with their theoretical orientation, with the licensing laws in their own states, or perhaps with the policies of their work settings. Most recently, practitioners have also felt the changing demands of working with insurance and managed care companies, the expanded scrutiny of their professional conduct through state licensure, increased complaints to regulatory boards by consumers, and a more frequent interface with the legal system. As a result, practitioners have increasingly called for more specific guidelines as to how to establish and maintain an ethical and legal practice.

Historically, the typical professional association's code of ethics is based upon a model of individual psychotherapy. Marriage and family therapy practitioners, given their particular theoretical orientation, have felt that these guidelines did not always adequately address their concerns (Green & Hansen, 1989; Hines & Hare-Mustin, 1978; Huber, 1994; Margolin, 1982; Miller, Scott, & Searight, 1990; Vesper & Brock, 1991). The rapid growth and recognition of marriage and family therapy as a distinct profession has helped to spur the evolution of several associations specifically for professionals who are recognized as marriage and family therapists. In response to the needs of the membership and to provide some basic ethical guidelines, the two largest international marriage and family therapy associations, the American Association for Marriage and Family Therapy (AAMFT) and the International Association for Marriage and Family Counseling (IAMFC), have both promulgated codes of ethics. AAMFT published its first code in 1962 and revised it in 1975 and several other times subsequently, with the last revision in 1991 (Brock, 1994). For over 30 years it was the only code of ethics to exclusively address the practice of marriage and family therapy (Huber, 1994). Recently, IAMFC, a rapidly growing division of the American Counseling Association, published a code of ethics (IAMFC, 1993) for its members. The main content areas of each of these codes of ethics are listed below:

AAMFT CODE OF ETHICS	IAMFC CODE OF ETHICS
(1) Responsibility to clients	(1) Client well-being
(2) Confidentiality	(2) Confidentiality
(3) Professional competence and integrity	(3) Competence

(4) Responsibility to students, employees, and supervisees

(4) Assessment

(5) Responsibility to research participants

(5) Private practice

(6) Responsibility to the profession

(6) Research and publications

(7) Financial arrangements

(7) Supervision

(8) Advertising

(8) Media and public statements

A comparison of these two codes, not surprisingly, reveals a number of similarities. Both emphasize a strong responsibility to the client's welfare and well-being, a recognition of the critical importance and uniqueness of the confidential relationship within marriage and family therapy, a demand for professional competence and integrity, and some guidelines concerning research participants. Some minor differences do exist, though they are more a matter of form than substance. The AAMFT code, in addition to containing specific sections about financial arrangements and advertising, includes individual sections about the members' responsibility to students, employees, supervisees, and to the profession in general. In contrast, the IAMFC code contains a separate section about assessment, supervision, and the responsibilities of interacting with the media, as well as some specific guidelines to be observed when making public statements. However, as noted above, the careful reader of these two codes will find the standards to be highly compatible and, in many instances, almost interchangeable.

There are two other major professional groups primarily interested in the practice of marriage and family therapy, the American Family Therapy Association (AFTA) and Division 43 (Family Psychology) of the American Psychological Association (APA). However, neither of these groups has addressed the needs of their members, who practice marriage and family therapy, through a specific code of ethics. AFTA does not have a specific code of ethics for its members, and Division 43 continues to be governed by the provisions of the *Ethical Principles of Psychologists and Code of Conduct* (American Psychological Association, 1992) that was developed primarily based upon a one-to-one therapeutic relationship.

However, perhaps the most significant change that has occurred during the last 15 years in the practice of marriage and family therapy has been the rapid expansion of the state licensing and certification. As of May 1998, 41 states were licensing or certifying marriage and family therapists (MFTs) (L. P. Bergen, personal communication, May 16, 1998). This legal recognition of the profession has directly resulted in a greater acceptance of marriage and family therapy as a separate and distinct mental health profession and has prompted insurance and managed care companies to include licensed MFTs as providers in many states. It has also greatly expanded the ethical and legal scrutiny faced by MFTs. Routinely, a state legislature will include provisions for the protection of the public as part of any licensing or certification law. As a result, state regulatory boards charged with licensing or certifying MFTs are typically mandated to establish a code of ethics, to set minimal standards of practice, and to establish specific disciplinary procedures to monitor and govern the behaviors of licensees. This means that, in those states with licensing or certification laws, MFTs are subject to not only the disciplinary actions of their professional association, but also a state licensing board and, quite possibly, the criminal justice system. In fact, a licensed MFT may risk losing his or her privileges to practice for violating the board's code of ethics.

As the MFT licensure movement spread across the country and each state established its own regulatory board, these various state boards joined together to form their own association, the Association of Marital and Family Therapy Regulatory Boards (AMFTRB). To assist new state boards, one important task undertaken by AMFTRB was to develop a model code of ethics (AMFTRB, 1993). This code was designed either to be utilized as it was written or to serve as a basis for an individual state licensing board to write its own code of ethics. AMFTRB's (1993) model code of ethics is considerably less specific than the code of ethics of any professional associations or most state boards. The code includes the following sections: (1) Professional Competence and Conduct; (2) Responsibility to Clients; (3) Confidentiality and Data Privacy; and (4) Responsibility to the Profession. To date three state boards, Arkansas, Massachusetts, and North Carolina, have adopted this model code of ethics (Rich, 1996).

For many years, authors who have focused on the ethical dilemmas faced by marriage and family therapists (Green & Hansen, 1989; Hines & Hare-Mustin, 1978; Huber, 1994; Margolin, 1982; Miller, Scott, & Searight, 1990; Vesper & Brock, 1991) have noted that too often the available guidelines are too general and lack the specificity needed by practitioners. In addition, the swift expansion in the number of states licensing MFTs, the ever growing acceptance of the services provided by MFTs by both insurance and managed care companies, as well as the expanding vulnerability to malpractice suits and disciplinary action by state regulatory boards have served to increase the demand by practitioners for practical guidelines for ethical practice. Despite the changing requirements in the field of marriage and family therapy, the codes of ethics of professional associations simply have not kept pace with the demand from practitioners for more guidance.

In my experience, the ethical dilemmas that I am most frequently asked about by MFTs, and that generate the most anxiety, are in the following practical areas: informed consent procedures; fees, billing, and collections policies; establishing and maintaining clinical and financial records; privacy, confidentiality, and privileged communications; the duty to warn, protect, and report; avoiding malpractice; and dual relationships.

Quite possibly, it is impractical and unrealistic to expect that the codes of ethics can respond to the ever changing professional environment faced by MFTs and to provide the specificity needed. I strongly believe, however, that there is an accrued body of knowledge available that provides the "practical ethical" guidelines being asked for and needed by marriage and family therapy practitioners. Please note that the following information is not intended as a substitute for a thorough knowledge of a state licensing board's requirements, a professional association's code of ethics, consultation with other professionals, or any specific legal advice provided by an attorney. Rather its purpose is twofold—first, to call attention to some of the most puzzling dilemmas being encountered by MFTs; and second, to help avoid some of the common pitfalls by providing some "answers" to the most frequently asked questions.

INFORMED CONSENT

The concept of informed consent as it now applies to psychotherapy clients is rooted in the history of the medical profession. Various judicial decisions, dating back to the mid-eighteenth century, have served to significantly shape the informed consent procedures that are utilized today. Over the past several decades, the requirements of informed consent have been applied to the practice of individual, group, and marriage and family therapy. While many psychotherapists utilize some form of informed consent, their procedures often are simply too haphazard. Even today, many MFTs remain unclear as to exactly what is informed consent and how to implement it in their practice.

Informed consent is based upon an individual's right to make a decision about submitting to any treatment procedure. In addition, the individual has the right to refuse, except under certain limited circumstances (e.g., the individual is judged incompetent), any treatment without his or her voluntary consent.

As a legal concept, informed consent generally consists of three elements: competence, information, and voluntariness (Bray, Shepherd, & Hays, 1985; Corey, Corey, & Callanan, 1993; Everstine, Everstine, Heymann, True, Frey, Johnson, & Seiden, 1980). *Competence* refers to an individual's ability to make a qualified decision about some life-affecting event; *information* implies that the individual, prior to making a treatment decision, has been provided with all of the necessary data; and finally, *voluntariness* indicates that the individual was free from any coercion or influence during the decision-making process.

In addition to the three components listed above, Meisel, Roth, and Lidz (1982) add two additional elements—understanding, and the decision itself. *Understanding* refers to the fact that the individual making the decision actually comprehends the information being provided. It is assumed that an individual who is provided with adequate information and who is competent will grasp the information and be able to make a reasonable decision concerning the course of treatment. Although, generally, practitioners are not obligated to ascertain the level of the understanding of the client, it is certainly prudent to make every effort to ensure that the client understands the treatment procedures. The most common legal standard that has been applied is that "as long as a reasonable person would have understood the information" (p. 196), then the consent was informed. The remaining step in the process is the actual rendering of the *decision*, either to consent or to refuse treatment.

Doverspike (1996) recommends one additional component, the appropriate *documentation* of the consent. For example, in addition to simply documenting the discussion of informed consent procedures in the case notes, he states that the therapist should have the client sign a form during the intake procedure or during the first session indicating that he or she was provided with the appropriate information, that all questions were answered, and that consent to treatment was freely given.

In order to be able to consent to treatment, an individual must be of minimum legal age to give consent; must be able to engage in rational thought to a sufficient degree to make a competent decision; and may not have been declared legally incompetent. *Direct consent*, also known as express (actual) consent (Bray et al. 1985), should be obtained from all competent persons. If the client has been judged legally incompetent or is a minor, then *substitute consent* should be obtained from a parent, guardian, or court-appointed conservator. In those situations involving a client who, for whatever reasons is incompetent to give consent, and even though it may not be legally necessary, it is advisable (and therapeutically prudent) to obtain both *substitute* consent and the client's assent. *Assent* (Bray et al., 1985) is an affirmative agreement by one who lacks the legal capacity to provide consent (e.g., a minor child).

Some writers have discussed the concept of *apparent* consent (Bray et al., 1985). Though debatable, it has been asserted that under certain circumstances, even the client who does not verbally articulate a decision may imply consent through his or her conduct (e.g., accepting treatment). This suggests that if a client does not object to a procedure, then he or she has tacitly consented to the treatment. This would be, at best, a questionable ethical stance and, in my opinion, indefensible.

Under very limited circumstances, there is also *consent implied by law* (Bray et al., 1985). This form of consent allows treatment necessary to save a person's life or for some other fundamental interest. For this consent to apply, four conditions must be met: (1) the client is unconscious and otherwise unable to grant or withhold consent; (2) an immediate decision is imperative; (3) a reasonable person in the client's position would consent; and (4) there is no reason to believe that the client would not give consent if he or she could. While this type of consent obviously has somewhat limited use for psychotherapists, it is important to be aware of the concept.

Bray et al. (1985) state that "consent, to be effective, must stem from a knowledgeable decision based upon adequate information about the therapy available, the available alternatives, and the collateral risks" (p. 53), although therapists continue to wonder just how much information must be disclosed. Historically, case law has applied the "reasonable and prudent person" standard, meaning that the therapist must provide sufficient information so that a "reasonable and prudent person" can decide whether to consent to or to continue therapy (p. 54). However, it is still the responsibility of the therapist to decide exactly what type and how much information to provide.

While the literature does offer some suggestions, there remains some confusion among practitioners as to exactly how to implement an informed consent-to-treatment procedure. In addition, certain professionals, such as group and marriage and family therapists, face some unique problems. Hare-Mustin, Marecek, Kaplan, and Liss-Levinson (1979) state that the client must be provided with detailed information about "the procedures, goals, and possible side effects of therapy; the qualifications, policies and practices of the therapist; and the available sources of help other than therapy" (p. 5). A more extensive list of topics to be discussed is provided by Corey, Corey, and Callanan (1993). These authors believe that the therapeutic process, the background of the therapist, the costs involved, the length of therapy and termination, whether any consultation with colleagues will occur, possible interruptions in therapy, the clients' right of access to their own files and rights pertaining to their diagnosis, the nature and extent of confidentiality and privileged communications, the recording of sessions, dual relationships, benefits and risks, and alternatives to the proposed treatment should be discussed as part of the informed consent procedure.

Therapists should plan to devote part of the first session (as needed) to ensure that each client is thoroughly informed about—and understands the process and procedures of—therapy and is, therefore, able to give an informed consent.

This step is particularly important in family therapy where it is quite common to have family members of different ages and levels of intellectual and emotional maturation.

One frequent complaint by therapists is their concern about having to devote time during a session to obtain informed consent, particularly with the number of sessions being subject to control by insurance and/or managed care companies. However, dedicating time to acquire an appropriate consent from all family members is a critical investment in developing the therapeutic relationship. While one way to save time is to provide some of the necessary information in writing, it is inappropriate to assume that a written presentation of this information is sufficient. It is the explicit responsibility of the therapist to take all appropriate steps to ensure that the client possesses and understands all of the information necessary to make an informed decision. It is also critically important to use language that will be easily understood by the client(s). The following topics (Everstine et al., 1980; Vesper & Brock, 1991) can serve as a guideline as to what should be discussed with all clients as part of an informed consent procedure prior to initiating treatment:

1. Provide a detailed explanation and rationale of all the treatment procedures (e.g., a description of the methods of therapy, goals, frequency and duration of session; length of treatment, etc.).

2. Offer an explanation of the role and professional qualifications of the individual(s) providing the treatment (e.g., academic degree(s) and any specialized training and skills; description of professional experience(s); licensure status, etc.).

3. State the limits of confidentiality and, if applicable, privileged communications (e.g., legal limits in effect in your state; requirements of third-party payors for diagnosis and records; possible case consultation with colleagues, etc.).

4. Explain any possible risks or expected discomforts (e.g., that family secrets might be revealed).

5. Enumerate any benefits that can be reasonably expected; be careful not to make any guarantees about outcomes.

6. Explain the availability of any alternative treatments of similar benefits (e.g., self-help groups, such as AA, NA, etc.).

7. Discuss office policies and procedures (e.g., payment and collection procedures; charges for missed appointments; emergency/after-hours policies, etc.).

8. Explain to the client that you will answer any questions about the treatment at any time.

9. Ensure that the client understands that the consent can be withdrawn at any time and treatment discontinued.

10. Have all client(s) sign the informed consent to treatment form and give a copy to the client(s).

Some therapists have argued that to discuss information with clients in the manner required by law compromises the effectiveness of treatment. To the contrary, some recent research (Walters & Handlesman, 1996) has indicated that clients are more trusting of the treatment after having been provided specific information during the informed consent procedure. In addition, the law is clear that the presence of a mental disorder does not ipso facto (by the fact itself) eliminate the need for disclosing information about treatment.

There are two other important caveats to remember about informed consent. First, informed consent cannot be used as a defense for unethical, unprofessional actions. Secondly, when the treatment involves a minor, it is important to bear in mind that, generally, children do not have the right to consent to treatment. Therefore, before starting treatment, one must obtain consent from a parent or guardian (Margolin, 1982). Usually the consent of either parent will allow for the treatment of a minor child, but if there is any question about the custody of the child, a copy of any legal documents pertaining to custody issues should be carefully reviewed. I would also recommend that the assent of the child be obtained because the child's cooperation aids treatment and outcomes.

While the specific legal requirement of obtaining informed consent before beginning diagnosis and treatment generally applies only to the person(s) in direct contact with the therapist, systems-oriented practitioners are aware that any treatment may have an impact well beyond that of the identified patient. Therefore, MFTs must pay particular attention to the effects that treatment may have on all members of the family system. As Vesper and Brock (1991) have noted, "a clinician must inform a client of the benefits and possible risks encountered in pursuing therapy (e.g., marital disharmony, arguments and misperceptions between family members and at times the therapist, and the heightening of emotional sensitivity)" (p. 53).

There are a number of other concerns about how informed consent procedures apply to the practice of marriage and family therapy. Some authors (Hines & Hare-Mustin, 1978; Huber, 1994; Margolin, 1982; Miller et al., 1990) have noted that it is important to recognize that not all family members may benefit from the therapy equally, and, under certain circumstances, family therapy may be actually viewed as detrimental for individual family members. Examples are when only one spouse is in therapy and decides, contrary to the wishes of the other, to end the marriage, or if the therapist promotes the disclosure of information that may be perceived as further harming the marital relationship or that may be used at a later date by the more powerful partner. Another very important issue to be considered is the extent of the voluntariness of the consent of each of the family members. In a quite common scenario, not all family members are equally eager for therapy, and if the therapist refuses to treat the family unless all members are present, does this ideological stance deny an individual family member the right to refuse treatment? According to Doherty and Boss (1991) and Miller et al. (1990), this might be interpreted as a form of coercion. The issue is whether one family member is allowed to exercise the right to refuse treatment by making the decision not to participate. The MFTs must always remember that each family member who is legally able is responsible for his or her own decision and that no individual member can give informed consent to treatment for the entire family.

Competency is also a critically important part of the informed consent procedures for MFTs. This is particularly important in those situations involving a family who may be trying to cope with a parent who is aging or senile, a spouse who is mentally disabled, or a minor child or children in need of treatment (Vesper & Brock, 1991). The important issue to address is whether or not the individual can actually give an informed consent to treatment. Does this person understand the information being presented concerning the possible risks, the alternative treatment options, and any other information necessary to make a decision whether to accept or reject treatment? A possible guide for family therapists might be to disclose a risk when the client would find it important in deciding whether or not to consent to the therapy (e.g., what would a reasonable person who finds himself or herself in the position of the client need to know?).

Another area in which informed consent procedures are important is the supervision of MFTs. The supervisor is responsible for ensuring that, prior to the client's giving any consent to treatment, nothing about the supervisory relationship is withheld and that the client is aware of the nature and extent of the supervisory relationship. During the initial session, the client should be informed that the therapist is being supervised, as well as the purpose of the supervision (e.g., acquiring experience for licensure, development of specific skills, or as a result of some disciplinary action), the name and credentials of the supervisor, and the provisions for maintaining confidentiality; all other aspects of the supervisory relationship (e.g., if the sessions are being taped, if anyone will be observing, etc.) should be thoroughly discussed. The supervisor should also be available to meet with the client to discuss the supervisory process and to ensure that there has been no misrepresentation of the circumstances of the supervision (e.g., the issue of intervention when necessary).

FEES, BILLING, AND COLLECTIONS

The issues of setting a fee, discussing fees with a client, billing, and later collecting the money owed for services are, for many therapists, some of the most troublesome aspects of a practice. There seems to exist, for many in the helping professions, a real mental dichotomy between being a therapist and recognizing and accepting that what we do is also a business. While this is rarely discussed in most training programs, one must remember that this is how a living will be made. When a client seeks services and you agree to provide treatment, a business contract has been established with that person: That client is agreeing to pay a fee for your services.

Establishing and maintaining proper business practices is also an ethical issue. Therapists have an obligation to their clients to have clearly established financial procedures that are explained in detail and understood by the client. There should be well-defined procedures for all of the financial aspects of the practice; business policies and procedures should be clearly delineated and, whenever possible, presented in writing to the client, as well as should the cost of each service provided (e.g., fees for therapy, missed appointments, phone calls, preparation of reports, copying of files, consultation with family members or employers, billing, filing insurance claims, collections, etc.).

For many therapists, the initial feelings of uncomfortableness that this is a business are first felt when trying set a fee for their services. As noted above, the idea that the therapist is a "paid" helper, "selling" knowledge and expertise for a fee, is one of the most difficult and uncomfortable realizations that a therapist encounters. Generally, this is more of a problem for the therapist than for the client. Clients expect to pay a fee, and since many have already shopped around, they typically have some idea about the prevailing fees in the area. However, answers to any questions about fees should be provided in a nonapologetic, honest, and straightforward manner.

As you begin to think about setting or raising your fee, perhaps the most basic question to ask yourself is: How much do I value what I do? (Beigel & Earle, 1990, p. 136). But this is not the only question to consider. Some of the other important questions to ask are: What is a reasonable and fair fee? What factors should I consider? What about a sliding scale? What do I do when a client's insurance benefits are exhausted, or if the client loses benefits? What about offering the first session free? What about bartering? What about waiving copayments? Do I have to file insurance claims for my clients? Will clients equate my fee with perceived quality? Can I charge for missed appointments or for any adjunctive services that might be provided?

The first step in this process is to gather some data about the fees being charged in the local area. There are numerous ways to do so. For instance, you might want to consider conducting an informal telephone survey of fees in your area. First, identify other therapists who possess similar educational backgrounds, levels of experience, and who hold equivalent licensure and/or other credentials, and ascertain what they are charging for similar services. Another resource to consult is your state and national professional associations. These groups, however, are often very reluctant to report or even collect such data so as to avoid being accused of price fixing. Under no circumstances, as Knapp and Vande-Creek (1993) note, should a professional association ever tell or even recommend a specific fee. Occasionally, some popular magazines, such as *Newsweek, Time*, or *Consumer Reports*, will publish this information as part of a feature article. At other times, regional and national fee survey data may be contained in an article in a professional publication (e.g., *The Marriage and Family Therapy News, The APA Monitor, ACA's GuidePost*, or *Psychotherapy Finances)*. Other resources may be a your state government, the consumer protection office, or the insurance commissioner's office.

Another potential source of information is to contact various third-party payors (e.g., insurance companies, employee assistance programs, and managed care companies) to ascertain both the maximum allowable fee as well as the "usual and customary" charges in your area. However, do not be surprised if these groups are, at best, reluctant to share these data or simply refuse to reveal this information.

It is also important to consider the geographical location of the practice. Factors such as cost of living, economic conditions, office expenses, any special training or skills possessed, and even competition are also some of the important factors to consider when establishing fees (Woody, 1988). It is quite common to find that fees charged in the city are higher than those changed in rural areas.

Some practitioners decide to use a sliding-fee scale. While this is neither unethical nor illegal, you must be very careful in implementing such a procedure. It is absolutely essential that the financial arrangements (the fee for services, billing, copayments, collection policies, etc.) for all clients that you see in your practice be the same. For example, a fee schedule based upon individuals' ability to pay must be applied identically to all clients. A therapist who charges clients with insurance one fee and those without insurance a different fee is committing insurance fraud. There are various state laws as well as federal racketeering statutes that prohibit such practice. In addition, one may not "lower" a fee for clients by forgiving a co-payment, not collecting a copayment, and/or billing the insurance company a higher fee to "recover" the "forgiven" copayment. Such practices are illegal, and insurance companies legally can and will seek to reclaim any monies paid for these fraudulently billed services. Additionally, such fraudulent billing practices will also be subject to the disciplinary action of the state licensing board and professional association and, quite probably, will result in criminal prosecution. Also remember that it is your responsibility to make a "good faith effort" to bill for and collect all copayments that are due.

The problems noted with using a sliding-fee scale often prompt practitioners to ask how or if they can provide services at a reduced cost, or even pro bono. Often, such a question is motivated by the most noble of motives and/or due to the encouragement of their professional associations. For example, the IAMFC code, Section V, (C), states that "members in private practice provide a portion of their services at little or no cost as a service to the community" (p. 76), while the AAMFT code, Section 6.5, stipulates that members should devote "a portion of their professional activity to services for which their is little or no financial return" (p. 8). To do so within the context of your private practice is, in my opinion, at best, legally suspect. Remember the caution noted above—fees, billing, and collection procedures must be the same for all clients in the practice. Therefore, providing services in your practice for certain individuals or families at little or no cost risks violating the law. To fulfill this ethical obligation, find some alternative ways (e.g., volunteer your time at an agency that provides services at little or no cost).

The above caveat does not apply to various managed care, Employee Assistance Programs (EAP), or other particular contracts that are negotiated with a specific entity. The difference is that those contracts are administered by a disinterested third party, and to receive the services, individuals must belong to that program. In effect, the therapist and the company have negotiated a set fee, generally lower than usual, to provide services to the members of that group.

Another important issue arises when you consider increasing fees. While raising fees is neither illegal nor unethical, unless handled properly, it can be problematic. Therefore, when deciding to raise fees, provide clients with reasonable notice, perhaps as long as three or four months. This allows clients to adjust their budgets, will help to reduce resistance, and may well prevent some clients from dropping out of therapy. In some practices, therapists have a policy that maintains the fee for current clients and raise fees for "new" clients. Beigel and Earle (1990) caution that such a policy may create significant bookkeeping and collection problems. Instead they recommend that, with appropriate notice, that the increase in fees be applied to all clients.

There are several other important things to remember about financial matters. Do not allow clients to run up a large balance or a bill to go uncollected. Generally, the longer a bill goes uncollected, the less likely it is that it will ever be paid. Trying to collect a large bill often leads to an angry response from the client and is a contributing factor in the filing of complaints.

Never "barter" with clients as a means of paying for services. Though some ethical codes condone such arrangements under certain circumstances, bartering has so many inherent problems that it should be avoided. A few of the possible problems of such an arrangement are: It may constitute a dual relationship; it is very difficult to determine the fair market value of such goods and services and this may lead to a dispute between you and the client; and the bartered goods or services, for tax purposes, must be declared as income and if there is an audit, it may prove difficult to substantiate the assessed value.

Take the time to be sure that clients understand the billing procedures. Most practitioners would agree that the simplest policy is that payment is expected at the time services are rendered, but that is becoming less common with the usual involvement of a third-party payor. In either case, be sure to keep accurate records of who was seen, when, how much was charged, and the amount paid. If the client pays in cash, provide a receipt; if you agree to monthly billing, decide in advance just how much indebtedness will be allowed to accrue. If charges for any other services (e.g., telephone consultations, writing reports, etc.) are assessed, be sure that the client is aware of and understands in advance who is responsible for payment.

Establish a clear, concise policy concerning missed appointments and/or no-shows; inform your clients and then stick to it. Also, it is important to remember that insurance and managed care companies almost never allow billing for missed or canceled appointments. Don't do it without written authorization; it is fraud.

If given a "bad" check, take prompt action. Contact the client immediately and request that a another viable check be provided or that a cash payment be made. Clients should have been told in advance that they will be responsible for paying any expenses incurred as a result of the returned check. If this problem persists, then require that payment be made in cash or with a money order.

Establishing and then actually implementing a collection policy for delinquent accounts is typically another problem for many practitioners. The first step in preventing this problem should have been taken before any services were ever provided. As part of the informed consent procedures, carefully explain the fees; when payment is due (e.g., at the beginning or end of session); whether insurance claims will be filed for the client or if the client is responsible for filing them; that any copayment is due at the time of services; if cash, checks, or credit cards are accepted; billing procedures (e.g., monthly); and collection procedures. Finally, make sure that the client completely understands the policies.

It is important to decide, in advance, how long a debt will be carried on the books. Remember, do not allow large balances to accrue. If after exhausting all normal procedures (e.g., sent regular statements, called and discussed the situation with the client, offered to establish a monthly payment plan, etc.), you have been unable to collect the amount owed, you may want to utilize a collection service. However, be very cautious and selective about the collection service utilized and pay particular attention to the collection procedures that are employed. Ask for a detailed explanation about any and all procedures utilized and have a written contract to ensure that clients are not threatened or harassed.

RECORDS

Perhaps the single most neglected aspect of ethical practice is the area of record keeping. The importance and absolute critical nature of maintaining good records is often not appreciated until there is some type of a crisis (Mitchell, 1991). For example, an emergency situation involving a client occurs when you are unavailable and a colleague is required to provide an intervention, or a lawsuit is filed alleging malpractice and the treatment records are needed to substantiate the necessity and efficacy of the treatment; or perhaps an insurance company demands a refund of payment alleging that billing has been submitted for services not performed. In all of these situations, the treatment records can demonstrate that appropriate and reimbursable services were provided to the client. Too often, it is only after one of these situations, or any number of others have occurred, that therapists understand the importance of record keeping. Even an appointment book is a very valuable clinical record. If there is any question about if and when a client was seen, it can be very useful in reconstructing the schedule or even helpful in establishing payment and other financial records.

Some therapists argue, in an attempt to defend negligent record keeping, that since they are the only person who has access to the record, any manner of record keeping that they deem "useful" is sufficient. This is a totally spurious statement. Nobody can predict, with any degree of certainty, who may gain access to the treatment record and how the services provided will be interpreted. Different people have different reasons for wanting access to the records. A colleague may read the records as a basis for additional treatment; an attorney may want to confirm negligence or to defend the treatment in a malpractice suit; an auditor may want to try to determine a level of compliance with laws/regulations; or a client may simply want to read what has been written about him or her.

In the past, on some occasions, it has been recommended that therapists keep what have been labeled as "shadow" or "unofficial" records. Simply explained, this means that two separate files are kept. One set is the "official" office record in which there is only the bare minimum of information, while in the other record, more complete information is stored. This is essentially a waste of time, unethical, and perhaps illegal. This also does not help to hide any information from an attorney. Any competent attorney will ask if the record presented is complete, and if the question is not answered truthfully, it is perjury. Some others have also suggested that no records or, at best, that sketchy records be kept in hopes of avoiding having to turn over any records to the courts. This idea is absolutely foolish. How do you explain sketchy records or the lack of records in court? You cannot avoid accountability for maintaining poor records.

The purpose of the clinical record is to document that the treatment provided was necessary and met a reasonable standard of care (Fowler, 1979). For instance, if the record does not show evidence that a diagnostic interview was conducted, how was the diagnosis that is listed on the insurance claim form determined? Or if the treatment plan or progress notes are illegible, vague, missing, or even nonexistent, then it may be reasonably judged that you have failed to provide any confirmation that treatment was necessary and met a reasonable standard of care.

Typically, the first contact is initiated by the client with a telephone call to the office seeking information or wanting to set an appointment. The responsibility of record keeping begins at that moment (Mitchell, 1991). It is important when a client sets an appointment that certain basic information be ascertained. This can be easily accomplished by utilizing a "telephone intake form." This allows specific data about the client—such as name, address, telephone number, referral source, brief idea of presenting problem(s), insurance or managed care company information, and a record of first appointment date—to be collected in a systematic manner and serves as the beginning of the record. The importance of gathering information about the insurance coverage at this time is that it will allow you to be aware of and to provide the client, as part of the informed consent procedure, appropriate information about possible coverage or the lack thereof.

At the first session, a "formal" intake interview should be conducted. Important information to obtain is complete demographic data (name, address, gender, occupation, date and place of birth, religion, etc.), employment history, family history, medical history, prior treatment history—both inpatient and outpatient, educational history, emergency contact person(s) and their phone numbers, and insurance/managed care information, including a copy of any identification card. In addition, a written record of the client's consent to treatment should be obtained, as well as a signed acknowledgment that he or she has received in a written format, understands, and has had an opportunity to discuss and/or ask questions about office policies and procedures (e.g., emergencies, charges for canceling or missing appointments, billing and collection policies, phone calls, etc.)

As indicated, the first session is also an appropriate time to provide the client with any information obtained from his or her insurance company concerning benefits. This allows the client and the therapist to discuss any financial arrangements that may need to be made. Also, have the client sign the assignment of insurance benefits form so that any insurance payments can be sent directly to the practice. A policy such as this can often help to avoid payment problems later. Be sure to document all of this in the treatment record.

The initial session is typically designed to provide an opportunity to evaluate the client and presenting problems. In addition, time should be allotted to ensure that you have the client's informed consent and have answered any and all questions. The record should indicate that the following information was discussed with the client: limits of confidentiality/privileged communications, presenting problem, why the client is coming to therapy at this time, client's goals for treatment, all relevant historical data and development of complaint, any previous treatment and/or details of the client's attempt to resolve the problem(s), how both you and client see the specific problem(s), diagnostic impressions, initial treatment plan, answers to any questions the client might have, a signed release to obtain previous treatment history, if available, and who referred the client.

A treatment plan, developed in conjunction with the client, should also be in the files. The purpose of the treatment plan is to document the need for service. It should be written in a manner that is easy to understand and must contain information that is consistent with the assessment of problem(s) identified during the diagnostic interview. Do not collude with the client to treat problems that have not been documented in the records.

According to Woody (1991) and Mitchell (1991), the individualized treatment plan should contain the following components: a statement of the problem(s) (e.g., identify the specific problem(s) and the specifier); any clinical impressions and diagnoses; a statement of short- and long-term goals (e.g., What is the course of treatment? What specifics will result from treatment? What is the expected date of achievement of goals?); a listing of the strengths (e.g., What will help client achieve goals?); a listing of deficits (e.g., What might hinder achievement of goals?); specific interventions utilized; a specific date to review the treatment plan; a plan for termination of services; and, after treatment is completed, a case summary.

Another important part of the case record is the progress notes. These notes document the specific interactions, interventions, problems, and changes that occurred over the course of therapy. Therefore, it is critically important that these notes be completed as close to the actual session as possible. Progress notes represent the history of the treatment and your role in it. Therefore, certain information generally appears in the progress notes: date of each session; who attended the session; the content of session; a report about the status of identified problems; the results of any mental status exam that was conducted; any subjective information gathered during the session, supported by clinical observations; any behavioral observations (especially noncompliant behaviors); any recommendations/interventions made during the session; any homework that was assigned; and the date and time of the next appointment. It is also helpful to use relevant quotes whenever possible.

Other important information that should be kept in the clinical records is: a record of any telephone calls from or to the client, or from or to anyone else about the client; copies of any correspondence or communications to, from, or about the client; copies of any reports (e.g., testing, medical records, etc.); records of referrals to adjunctive therapies; records of previous treatment; financial information (though these records may be kept in a separate file, they should be readily accessible); and a termination summary, and, if needed, an aftercare plan.

One frequently asked question is how long should records be kept? In the literature, the recommendations vary, but I would suggest a minimum of seven years. If the treatment involves a child, it is a good idea to maintain the complete file for a minimum of three years after the child reaches legal age (Committee on Professional Practice and Standards, American Psychological Association, 1993). Furthermore, even after the time limit has expired, I would suggest that you keep a case summary forever.

Another common question is what do I do if the client wants a copy of the records? Clients have a legal right to their records, and while they must be provided (Remley, 1990), records should not be released without written permission. The limits of confidentiality and privileged communications for your state should have been carefully explained during the informed consent procedures and should be followed carefully. In some cases you may be reluctant to release the records because in your judgment, the client might not understand or be harmed by the information contained in the records. Generally, unless there is a very compelling reason why the client should not see the record, a copy should be provided if requested and the appropriate release of information completed. Also note that it is quite probable if you have refused to release the record, and the client goes to court, that you will be ordered to release the record.

An important point for MFTs to remember is that, since the treatment often involves multiple clients, records cannot be released without the written consent of all of the clients legally able to provide consent. Therefore, if one family member asks for a copy of the records, the complete record should not be released without the appropriate consent of all.

At some point you will probably receive a subpoena calling for the release of treatment records. Often the subpoena is asking for records for a client who has not given written permission their release (e.g., in a divorce, the attorney for one side issues the subpoena). Therefore it is important to take the time to become familiar with the laws governing privileged communications in your state, as well as the state licensing board of ethics. It is also important to remember that there are many types of subpoenas. Upon receiving one, contact your attorney for advice on how to respond since, as Haas and Malouf (1995) note, "attorneys who have no legitimate right to the records will sometimes bluster and threaten, hoping that the clinician will be sufficiently intimidated to release the information" (p. 131).

PRIVACY, CONFIDENTIALITY, AND PRIVILEGED COMMUNICATIONS

Confidentiality has long been considered the cornerstone of a successful psychotherapy relationship. While clients typically assume that whatever they disclose during the course of therapy will not be revealed without their consent, the reality is that neither confidentiality nor privileged communications are absolute. There are, in fact, certain circumstances in which a therapist must break the confidences of a client, and there are numerous other times during which the idea of the absolute confidentiality of the therapeutic relationship is, at best, compromised (Lakin, 1991).

The origin of confidentiality in the helping professions can be traced back to the physician–patient relationship beginning in the sixteenth century (Denkowski & Denkowski, 1982). Over the years it has become an accepted part of the relationship between health care professionals and their clients. During the last century, as the field of psychotherapy began to grow and gain widespread acceptance, all professional associations included the requirement of maintaining confidentiality as part of their ethical codes. Today, regardless of professional training and/or theoretical orientation, psychotherapists are well versed in the important role that confidentiality plays in the therapeutic relationship. In addition, despite the long-established legal precedent that testimony should be heard from any and all witnesses, courts have frequently refused to force a therapist to reveal communications that occurred during the course of therapy unless the benefits to society outweigh the need for confidentiality. Perhaps it is for this reason that confidentiality is considered to be "the single most widely recognized ethical issue in the practice of psychotherapy" (Huber, 1994, p. 18).

While most therapists readily acknowledge the importance of confidentiality, the literature has sometimes served to confuse the issue by using the terms *privacy*, *confidentiality*, and *privileged communications* interchangeably, when they are distinctly different (Scalise, 1989, 1995b; Scalise & Ginter, 1989). A clear explanation of the differences is provided by Shah (1969, 1970). Briefly, confidentiality "relates to matters of professional ethics" and "protects the client from unauthorized disclosures" (Shah, 1969, p. 57). Privacy, a much broader concept, "recognizes the freedom of the individual to pick and choose for himself the time, circumstances and particularly the extent to which he wishes to be protected from unwarranted intrusions" (Shah, 1970, p. 243). Privileged communications is "the legal right which exists by statute and which protects the client from having his confidences revealed publicly from the witness stand during legal proceedings without his permission" (Shah, 1969, p. 57).

During the past 25 years, these concepts have become increasingly important as therapists have attempted to balance client rights with the accelerating demands of various third parties wanting access to confidential information. Clients are typically informed at the beginning of treatment that anything revealed will be held confidential and, in those states with such statutory protection for clients, privileged. However, at almost the same time, clients are asked to sign a broad release-of-information form allowing their insurance or managed care company access to their records. The client who refuses to sign the release will quite likely be unable to utilize the mental health coverage provided as part of his or her general health insurance policy. This is a dilemma faced each day by clients, and later by therapists who may be reluctant to release any more information than deemed necessary to submit an insurance claim. Therefore, as part of the informed consent procedure, it is critically important that clients are made aware of the limits of both confidentiality and, if applicable, privileged communications.

Smith-Bell and Winslade (1994) note that the client's rights to privacy and confidentiality, though limited, are important and that therapists must strive to protect these rights to the fullest extent allowed by law and required by professional ethical standards—while also recognizing the legitimate right of third parties to have access to certain information. Therefore, the critically important question for the therapist is how to ethically and legally balance these sometimes conflicting demands.

As noted above, confidentiality has for many years been embodied in the codes of ethics of various professional associations and later, as state governments began to regulate the various helping professions, it was quite common for confidentiality to be included as part of the required professional behavior of licensees. The result is that therapists are bound by professional, ethical, and moral obligations to maintain client's confidences that were revealed as part of the therapeutic relationship. Where once the concept of privileged communications was limited to relationships such a lawyer–client, physician–patient, and priest/minister–penitent, during the last three decades, the clients of other helping professionals (e.g., MFTs, counselors, social workers, and psychologists) have also been granted such statutory protection. "Such privilege statutes indicate that the state's legislative bodies consider the trust relationship between helper and client to be more important than the need of the courts to have access to all information potentially usable as evidence" (Haas & Malouf, 1995, p. 35). However, not all states have enacted such legislation, so it is important to check individual state laws to determine if the communications between therapists and clients are privileged.

It is also important to note that typically the federal courts have not recognized the existence of such a privilege. However, recently the United States Supreme Court, in the case of *Jaffee v. Redmond* (1996), has affirmed the existence of privileged communications between licensed clinical social workers and their clients. At this point it is not known whether this ruling will be applicable to other mental health professionals, though Wolfe (1996) opined that "future decision will extend the privilege to other types of therapists" (p. 19).

Despite the numerous discussions and writings about confidentiality and privileged communications (see Scalise, 1989, 1995a), there still remain many troublesome areas that therapists frequently encounter and to which they must respond, sometimes very quickly. What we do know for sure is that the privilege belongs to the client, not the therapist, and as such, only the client can waive it. We also know that neither confidentiality nor privileged communications are absolute. For example, all 50 states now require therapists to report suspected cases of child abuse regardless of confidentiality or privilege. Also, as noted by Haas and Malouf (1995), it is important to remember that "judges are the ultimate interpreters of how and when privilege applies and judges seem to differ in terms of the extent to which they honor privilege" (p. 36).

Another exception to the confidentiality/privilege rule occurs when the therapist believes that the client is suicidal or is a threat to harm a third party. In most states, under these circumstances, the therapist must break confidentiality and/or privilege and take the appropriate steps to warn and protect (see next section). In some other states, other exceptions exist. Some of these exceptions (Huber, 1994; Reynolds, 1976; Vesper & Brock, 1991) are when the client has sought treatment for the sole purpose of having the therapist assist in the commission of a crime; when the treatment is part of a workmen's compensation claim; when the client alleges malpractice against the therapist; when the treatment or evaluation was pursuant to a court order; in child custody cases; or when the client is charged with a crime.

In addition to the above, there are several other areas that are often problematic for therapists. If you practice for any length of time, you will eventually receive a subpoena for case records. For most therapists, the first time this happens, it is a daunting experience. However, the simple fact that you have been served a subpoena does not mean that the information requested must be immediately released nor does the existence of a privileged communications statute mean that the subpoena can be ignored (Haas & Malouf, 1995). In this situation, the first step should be to ascertain if the client wants the information released. If he or she does and signs the appropriate release of information form, then release the records.

However, if the client does not grant permission to release the records, the therapist must then determine how to respond to the subpoena. In a state where clients have been granted the protection of privileged communications, the therapist can assert the privilege on behalf of the client. Absent any statutory privilege, as a licensed professional, consult the state licensing board's code of ethics to determine the requirements for maintaining confidentiality. Also, if you are a member of a professional association, then typically that group will have promulgated a code of ethics that requires maintaining confidentiality. Finally, be sure to contact your own personal attorney for advice as to how to respond.

While a subpoena is "simply an order filed with the court by an attorney requesting information or testimony" (Huber, 1994, p. 193), do not ignore it. If the subpoena requires you to appear in court, appear at the specified time and place. When called upon to present records or to testify, assert privilege and confidentiality on behalf of the client. At that point, the judge may honor the assertion of privilege, or order you to testify or to turn over the requested records. Without the legal protection of a privileged communication statute, you must comply with the judge's order or face sanctions. If there is a privileged communications statute, as an included professional, assert the privilege on behalf of the client. The judge may choose to honor the privilege or order you to testify. If so ordered, then in consultation with your attorney, decide what will be the appropriate response.

For those therapists whose practice includes working with multiple clients (e.g., MFTs), the issue of maintaining confidentiality and privileged communications presents some additional unique challenges. This is due, at least in part, to the fact that the historical view of psychotherapy has been the individual therapy model. Therefore, the complex and complicated nature of marriage, family, and other therapy modalities that involve multiple clients has not been adequately addressed in relation to confidentiality and privileged communications.

One issue that therapists are almost certain to encounter is a request for the release of clinical records. Since the communications between a therapist and a client are recorded in the clinical record, it is normally assumed that this information is confidential and/or privileged. However, the courts have not always uniformly upheld the protected nature of the case record. In some instances, the courts have ruled that the records must remain confidential, but in other cases, the courts have demanded that the records be presented in court or, at least, for an examination to determine if the records contain information that should be available to the court.

Additionally, when the treatment involves a couple or family, determining who exactly owns the record and who may authorize its release is further complicated. Many marriage and family therapists assert that the family system is the client, not any single family member, and while systems theory may support this viewpoint, legal support for this contention is, at best, unclear (Huber, 1994). Therefore, carefully investigate any legal precedents and case law in your state to determine to what extent the communications that take place during marriage and family therapy are protected.

One possible way to handle this type of dilemma (Haas & Malouf, 1995; Huber, 1994; Scalise, 1996) is to obtain a written, pretreatment contract, signed by all participants, not to seek the case records, nor to attempt to compel the therapist to divulge the contents of the records or the communications that occurred during treatment as part of any legal (e.g., divorce) proceedings. Though such a contract may not be legally binding, it may serve to discourage attempts to obtain case information and/or illustrate to the courts that the therapy had been conducted based upon an agreement of confidentiality.

However, it is important to remember that if all therapy participants sign a valid release, the records must be released. In addition, as noted earlier, neither confidentiality nor privileged communications are absolute. Typically, it is very important to become familiar with the legal exceptions in your state that require the release of records when so mandated. While a subpoena generally does not constitute such an exception, an order by the court does require compliance (Huber, 1994; Vesper & Brock, 1991).

Child custody cases represent another situation in which courts have frequently decided that the best interests of the child supersede the importance of maintaining confidentiality and privileged communications. Again, it is incumbent upon the therapist treating a family or a child where custody is or may become an issue to inform the participants prior to starting treatment about the limits of confidentiality and privilege. As suggested above, a pretreatment agreement may be a reasonable approach in such situations.

Hines and Hare-Mustin (1978), Margolin (1982), and Huber (1994) discuss another potential problem—how to handle family secrets—that MFTs are likely to encounter. At one extreme are those therapists who espouse the position that the disclosures of each individual family member will be treated as if he or she were a client in individual therapy. Other therapists maintain the unyielding position of not keeping any secrets from other family members and, of course, there are many variations in between these two positions. Regardless of the stance you take, it is important that you are aware of the requirements for maintaining confidentiality and privileged communications in your state and that these policies are clearly explained and understood by all participants prior to the beginning of treatment.

DUTY TO WARN, PROTECT, AND REPORT

During the past two decades, mental health professionals, including MFTs, have been explicitly charged with the task of attempting to predict the dangerousness and the potential for violence of their clients and to then take appropriate action to protect third parties from harm (Dickson, 1995). On July 1, 1976, in one of the most important decisions to affect mental health practice ethics this century, the Supreme Court of California issued a decision in the *Tarasoff* (1976) case and created a legal duty for psychotherapists to both warn and protect third parties. While this decision was applicable only in California, this precedent has subsequently been extended to many other jurisdictions in the United States and has resulted in the establishment of a generally accepted policy that a therapist has a duty to warn and protect a third party from harm (Haas & Malouf, 1995). While the question of whether this is clinically feasible with any degree of certainty is frequently the subject of debate, this has not deterred other courts from adopting a similar position or some state legislatures from legally establishing such a responsibility.

Needless to say, the *Tarasoff* decision and all that has occurred since 1976 has been the subject of considerable discussion in the professional literature. Numerous articles, monographs, and books (see Scalise, 1995a) have been published warning therapists about the magnitude of this responsibility. For example, Bersoff (1976) likened this "new" role for the therapist as being one of both a protector and law enforcer, while Stone (1976) posited that any attempt to increase therapists' responsibilities to include warning potential victims would be counterproductive and, in fact, such a policy would increase the risk of violence within society.

However, despite these dire predictions, the duty to warn and protect has gained almost universal acceptance among therapists. But this does not mean that there is a uniform understanding of how and when the duty to warn and protect is to be implemented in all situations. There still remain many questions, contradictory legal decisions, and too few definitive answers. For example, some judges have applied the duty to warn and protect to foreseeable victims, while in other jurisdictions, the courts have limited the duty only to cases where there is a specific foreseeable victim. To further confuse the matter, as Gehring (1982) points out, to meet the test of a foreseeable victim, it is not necessary for the therapist to know the exact identity of the intended victim. The simple "knowledge of the class of individuals to whom there is a risk is sufficient to met the test of a foreseeable victim" (Gehring, 1982, p. 209).

Still other courts, while continuing to utilize the concept of a foreseeable victim, have done so with some modifications. Herlihy and Sheeley (1988) report that the duty to warn and protect has been extended to include those "who may not be readily identifiable by the therapist but who would be likely targets if the clients became violent" (p. 206). To further compound the confusion, some courts have interpreted the duty to warn and protect to include situations in which there is a "serious threat of substantial damage to real property" (p. 206). Perhaps Dickson (1995) summarizes the confusing and sometimes conflicting decisions best when he writes, "in some states, third parties must be identifiable, in others this is not required. Some have no requirements for protecting a third party in danger. Some have apparently rejected the duty to protect doctrine" (p. 140). Nevertheless, in spite of any controversy and regardless of your own personal beliefs about whether a therapist has a duty to warn, protect, and report, it is quite clear that, in most situations, such an obligation does, in fact, exist (Dickson, 1995; Herlihy & Sheeley, 1988; Huber, 1994; VandeCreek & Knapp, 1984; Vesper & Brock, 1991).

While this may seem an impossible responsibility to fulfill, the courts have demonstrated that they are aware of the difficulty of such a task. Generally, therapists are not required to interrogate their clients or to conduct any investigation (VandeCreek & Knapp, 1984). Neither must every utterance a client makes about violence be reported, nor must every client who talks about suicide be hospitalized. What one must do is to be cognizant of your responsibilities and to exercise your best clinical judgment. To do so you must possess the skills necessary to make an accurate assessment and, subsequently, a judgment about each client. Furthermore, you must demonstrate that you are "aware of the balance between immediate client welfare and the best interests of society" (Gross & Robinson, 1987, p. 341) and behave in a manner that reflects the "standard of what a reasonable professional in the community would do under similar circumstances" (Corey, Corey, & Callanan, 1993, p. 118). In addition, it is important to understand that you will not be held "liable for failure to warn when the propensity toward violence is unknown or would not be known by other psychotherapists using ordinary skills" (Knapp & VandeCreek, 1982, pp. 514–515).

The duty to warn and protect also extends to clients who may be suicidal (Corey, Corey, & Callanan, 1993; Vesper & Brock, 1991). Though some clients and some therapists might argue that a client has a right to take his or her own life, if in your best clinical judgment you conclude that an individual poses a serious personal threat, there is a duty to warn and protect. While the exact course of action will depend on the assessment of the immediacy of the threat, you will be expected to use a "reasonable standard of care in the diagnosis of suicidal intent and the development and implementation of a treatment plan" (VandeCreek & Knapp, 1993, p. 26).

If it is determined that the client is not an immediate threat to self-harm, the therapist may chose to have the client sign a contract stating that he or she will not harm himself or herself and will contact the therapist if the threat becomes greater. Other options are to seek permission from the client to contact family members or friends to serve as a social support system and/or to increase the frequency and intensity of treatment. A voluntary admission to a psychiatric hospital is another option, and as a last resort, the therapist can seek an involuntary commitment.

The rapid spread of AIDS has also presented therapists with some unique ethical dilemmas concerning the duty to warn and protect. In many ways, assessing danger in these situations may be more difficult than attempting to predict dangerousness and the potential for violent behavior with other clients. What makes the accurate assessment of danger to others so difficult concerning AIDS is that many of the risk factors may not yet have been identified. Additionally, there is very little guidance available from case law to help resolve the conflict between the rights of the HIV-positive individual and the rights of those with whom he or she might have sexual contact (Vesper & Brock, 1991). Nevertheless, when the therapist becomes aware of the client's HIV-positive status, it is imperative that any concerns be discussed and a plan be jointly developed to ensure the safety of those at risk, while maintaining the confidentiality of the client.

The therapist should help the client to understand the importance of informing past and present sexual partners of the HIV-positive status. If the client refuses, "the therapist may wish to consider notifying any identifiable person who may be in danger of contracting the disease" (Vesper & Brock, 1991, p. 62). However, before taking any action, the therapist should seek appropriate legal and professional counsel. As VandeCreek & Knapp (1993) state, "although psychotherapists have a responsibility to treat HIV-positive patients with compassion and understanding, they cannot ignore the threat to the public" (p. 32).

A closely related responsibility is the duty to report. This duty is "based upon the belief that certain conditions are considered by the state to be so dangerous, either to the public or to specific individuals, that reports of their existence must be made regardless of the potential harm to the treatment process" (Haas & Malouf, 1995, p. 38). Perhaps the clearest example of the duty to report involves suspected cases of child abuse and neglect. Every state now requires health care professionals, including therapists, to file a report of suspected child abuse with the appropriate state agency. In addition, some states also require the reporting of elder abuse. Understandably, the specific requirements for reporting abuse vary from state to state. Therefore, it is critically important to be aware of one's individual responsibilities.

MALPRACTICE

Marriage and family therapists have grown increasingly concerned about possible civil liability due to allegations of malpractice as a result of services they have provided. Defined in the broadest of terms, malpractice includes any and all forms of misconduct by a professional (Dickson, 1995). More specifically, malpractice is a matter of the competence of the therapist, whether the treatment met a reasonable standard of care as compared to other similar professionals, and if the treatment resulted in some injury to the client (Dickson, 1995; Knapp, 1980). Legally, malpractice "consists of departing from usual practice or not exercising due care in fulfilling one's responsibility" (Corey, Corey, & Callanan, 1993, p. 129), as well as negligence, including unintentional harm. When malpractice is alleged, the client's normal recourse is to seek damages through the courts.

Malpractice litigation is based on the concept of "torts." A tort is defined as "harm done to an individual in such a way and of such type that the law will order the person who did the harm to pay damages to the injured party" (Krauskopf & Krauskopf, 1965, p. 227). Since tort law provides for monetary awards for clients of professionals whose behavior violates their professional duty as established by law, it is very important to understand the concepts of duty and fiduciary relationships. The relationship developed between a mental health professional and a client is deemed a fiduciary relationship because it is one that fosters trust and confidence. The professional has a responsibility to nurture this relationship so that it benefits the client, thereby establishing a duty to the client. The client has a right to expect "good professional care," and the therapist has the responsibility to provide that standard of care. This means that the practitioner will be held to the level of performance of the ordinary practitioner of the profession. Therefore, if one holds oneself out as an expert in a particular discipline, the prevailing standard of care in that area must be met. It is also important to remember that the concept of malpractice applies not only to licensed professionals, but also to unlicensed professionals who provide similar services.

This type of relationship also contains some elements of contract law. For example, there is an offer (the client calls or comes to the office); an acceptance of the offer (the therapist listens to the problem and agrees to start a therapeutic relationship with that client); and a mutuality of understanding exists (therapist informs the client about the nature of therapy and client gives consent to participate in order to alleviate the presenting problem). However, despite the above, the use of contractual liability as a source of litigation against therapists is rare (Huber, 1994).

According to Huber (1994) and Corey, Corey, and Callanan (1993), the client/plaintiff must allege and prove four legal elements to sustain a complaint of malpractice. First, that the therapist/defendant owed a legal duty to the client/plaintiff (e.g., the therapist–client relationship was established); second, the therapist/defendant's conduct violated that duty by failing to conform to a legal standard established to prevent unreasonable risk or harm; third, that there was sufficient causal connection between the conduct of the therapist/defendant and the harm suffered by the client/plaintiff; and finally, that the harm to the client/plaintiff is an actual personal injury that can be measured in economic terms.

The simplest of these elements to prove is that a professional relationship existed. Generally, all that is needed is a billing statement or a clinical record. Proving the second element—that the therapist failed to maintain an acceptable standard of care—is more difficult. One major obstacle in proving that the care was substandard is that there are so many different and distinctive ways to approach the treatment of a particular presenting problem. It is quite rare that there exists conclusive evidence supporting that there is one, and only one, method of treatment. For example, "marriage and family therapists who adhere to a particular school carry less liability in that the scope of a standard of care is clarified" (Huber, 1994, p. 153). However, there is also an inherent risk in such close adherence to any certain model, since any deviation from the proscribed method may be viewed as outside the tenets of that particular school, and as such possibly judged below the acceptable standard of care. This, however, does not mean that any and every type of behavior will be judged acceptable as appropriate treatment.

The third element that the client must prove, that an injury or harm occurred as a result of the treatment, may also present some difficulty. It is easiest to prove if the injury is of a physical nature, while it is much more difficult to substantiate psychological or emotional harm (e.g., psychological distress from a divorce following "failed" marriage therapy). Finally, even in those cases where there has been some injury, the client is still required to prove that the treatment was the direct or proximate cause of the injury. Dickson (1995) presents a very clear example of a case of direct or proximate cause: "a patient in therapy threatens suicide in such a way that a reasonable professional would believe the threat valid and would have taken steps to protect the patient, but no action was taken and the patient left the office and before anything else occurred, attempted suicide and was injured or killed" (p. 524). In this scenario, it is highly likely that the care provided by the therapist would be judged as below standard.

In addition to the above, there are many other types of "injuries" that may also be the subject of malpractice claims. Strupp, Hadley, and Gomes-Schwartz (1977) cite the intensification of the presenting problem, the development of new symptoms or problems, dual relationships, and inappropriate therapeutic directions as possible injuries that clients may claim they sustained in the course of therapy. Other possible "injuries" that clients might also allege were caused by treatment are divorce, loss of affection, estrangement from loved ones, loss of a job, and emotional pain and suffering.

As Dickson (1995) notes, "monetary awards for malpractice are generally in the form of compensatory damages to the individual for losses suffered because of malpractice" (p. 525). In addition, the therapist could also be required to pay other monetary damages in the form of lost earnings, additional treatment, and damages awarded to "others related to the injured party" or "in the event of a fatality, wrongful death" (Dickson, 1995, p. 525).

According to the literature (Corey, Corey, & Callanan, 1993; Dickson, 1995; Hall, 1994; Huber, 1994; Krauskopf & Krauskopf, 1965; Lenson, 1994; Reaves & Ogloff, 1996; Smith, 1991; Vesper & Brock, 1991), the most common causes for malpractice litigation are: treatment without informed consent; sexual misconduct; failure to warn; breach of confidentiality/privileged communications; misuse of therapy (dual relationships); failure to advise client of the risks of therapy; false imprisonment (holding client against his or her will in a hospital); practicing beyond scope of education/training/competence; misdiagnosis and inappropriate treatment; failure to prevent suicide; confining or not confining a client to an institution (client kept in hospital based upon inaccurate or false information from therapist or if client is erroneously discharged from hospital based upon information from therapist); inappropriate termination and abandonment; assault and battery (usually threats or physical confrontation with clients); defamation (communicating something injurious either verbally or written about client); and failure to collect payment in an appropriate manner (behaviors that harass the client).

There are several other areas of possible malpractice allegations or ethical complaints. One issue of particular importance that is all too often neglected is the therapist's responsibility to ensure that all employees, and/or colleagues, including someone who simply utilizes office space, maintain the same legal and ethical standards (e.g., confidentiality of records). Another area of potential liability for the therapist involves the actions of any professional or trainee under his or her supervision. Additionally, therapists, like any other business person, are subject to the liability of "employer-employee claims and suits involving charges of sexual harassment and age and gender discrimination" (Reaves & Ogloff, 1996, p. 135).

As noted above, the most frequent and most successful malpractice cases are for sexual misconduct (Dickson, 1995; Vesper & Brock, 1991). Since all codes of ethics prohibit sexual relationships with clients, in such a circumstance it is quite easy to prove that the care did not meet an acceptable standard. In addition, there is also a substantial body of literature (Brown, 1988; Knapp, 1980; Pope, 1994; Reaves & Ogloff, 1996; Streane, 1993) that documents the harm done to clients as a result of therapist–client sexual relationships, thus allowing the client/plaintiff to prove that there was harm. Proving proximate cause may be slightly more difficult, particularly in those cases where there has been a lengthy period of time between the harmful action and the suit.

There are numerous ways, however, that a therapist can minimize the likelihood of a lawsuit or ethical complaint. Many authors (Corey, Corey, & Callanan, 1993; Laurence, 1990; Reaves & Ogloff, 1996; Robinson, 1989; Vesper & Brock, 1991) have offered specific advice that can be very helpful. Collectively, their suggestions are: Maintain a good, honest relationship with clients; do not enter private practice unless you have sufficient education, training, and clinical experience; have a good rationale for what you are doing; maintain good records; respect your clients' beliefs; do not identify yourself as a specialist unless you have the specialized training, certifications, and expertise; warn potential victims of violent patients; terminate noncompliant clients; don't abandon clients without referral; make no guarantees; keep current with the professional literature; avoid hugging or kissing clients; maintain your liability insurance; be aware of ethical issues; seek consultation and supervision; and maintain confidentiality.

It is important to note that there are no absolute ways to guarantee that a malpractice lawsuit or an ethical complaint will never be filed against you. However, if faced with a malpractice suit or an investigation of a possible ethical violation, the first action to take is to consult your personal attorney, then follow the advice offered by Laurence (1990): "(1) Do not change your records in any way; (2) Do not try to transfer your assets; (3) Do not discuss the case with anyone (except your attorney or malpractice insurance claims representative); (4) Do not talk to (or argue or attempt to reason with) the client, the client's family, friends or attorney; (5) Do not talk with the media; (6) Do not overreact to the summons or subpoena that starts the case; (7) Do not be hostile to your insurance claims representative or defense attorney; and (8) Do not expect that a counterclaim against the client or client's attorney for malicious prosecution will be successful" (pp. 248–249).

Remember that simply because you are sued or have an ethical complaint filed against you does not mean that you actually committed malpractice. In our litigious society, anyone can sue anyone at almost any time.

DUAL RELATIONSHIPS

The ethical codes of every major mental health professional association and state licensing or certification agency include some discussion about dual relationships. They are also a frequent topic of considerable interest at ethics workshops or whenever professional issues are discussed. Dual relationships are also the subject of considerable conjecture and misunderstanding. A dual relationship occurs when the therapist establishes a second relationship with a client, and the relationship occurs at the same time or in very close proximity to the first (e.g., therapist and business partner). Most, if not all, professionals would agree that it is not possible to avoid all dual relationships or that are all dual relationships are inherently harmful. However, there are certain, readily identifiable dual relationships that are harmful and are strictly prohibited. One factor that denotes a harmful dual relationship is that the client is exploited. This type of relationship also impairs clinical judgment, blurs critically important boundaries and roles of the participants, and corrodes the therapeutic relationship.

Since the power of the therapeutic relationship is, by nature, imbalanced in favor of the therapist, the existence of a dual relationship increases the likelihood that an abuse of power will occur. While most therapists are very cognizant of the power differential and strive to ensure the safety of the client, once the boundaries have been violated, the commonly accepted behavioral guidelines no longer apply and neither the therapist nor the client knows how to respond to the changes. As noted above, what makes this so problematic is that while the therapist's power generally remains intact, so does the client's vulnerability.

Perhaps the clearest example of an exploitive, abusive relationship is the occurrence of sexual intimacies between the therapist and the client. Unfortunately, a number of reports (George, 1983; Huber, 1994; Kagle & Giebelhausen, 1994; Pope, 1994; Skelly, 1993; Vesper & Brock, 1991) indicate that this is the most frequent ethical violation encountered by both the ethics committees of professional associations and professional liability insurance companies. The frequency of this violation may be somewhat surprising, given the clear and decisive prohibition against such behaviors. Without exception, codes of ethics of state licensing boards and professional associations strictly prohibit this type of dual relationship. Also, in many states, it is a crime punishable by a fine and imprisonment.

The harmful effects of such a relationship are well documented (Brown, 1988; George, 1983; Haas & Malouf, 1995; Pope, 1994; Pope, Levenson, & Schover, 1979; Pope, Sonne, & Holroyd, 1993). Both Brown (1988) and Pope (1994) provide specific information about the harmful effects of sexual intimacies between a therapist and a client. Brown (1988) notes the following effects on clients: feelings of abandonment, rage, grief, and loss of safety. Pope's (1994) list of possible client reactions includes: guilt, an impaired ability to trust, ambivalence, feelings of emptiness and isolation, emotional liability, suppressed anger, sexual confusion, increased risk of suicide, role reversal and boundary disturbances, and cognitive dysfunction.

While sexual dual relationships are generally considered to be the most egregious, there are other types of dual relationships that are also exploitive and harmful. Entering into a business relationship with a client is a dual relationship that may take many different forms—such as seeking advice about investments, hiring the client to perform various services, bartering for goods or services to pay for therapy, starting a business or purchasing property together, or hiring a client's family member. Again, in this type of relationship, due to the imbalance of power and the vulnerableness of the client, the potential for exploitation is ever present.

Another example of a common but harmful dual relationship occurs when the therapist establishes a close personal relationship with the client. The temptation to establish such a relationship is often quite natural and may even be rationalized in that this situation is unique and serves the needs of the client (Kagle & Giebelhausen, 1994). However, the dynamics of this type of relationship are similar, in some very important ways, to the sexual dual relationship previously discussed and therefore preclude any possibility of developing an equal relationship.

Some may argue that a client and therapist, particularly after the therapeutic relationship has been terminated, are free to establish a friendship with anyone they chose and that to deny this opportunity is unfair. However, the same issues that existed during the therapeutic relationship will continue posttermination. While trust, intimacy, and self-disclosure are important elements in both friendships and the client–therapist relationship, there are crucial differences. In the client–therapist relationship, the information generally flows one way, and there is an imbalance of power, as well as a significant difference in the degree of self-disclosure. The client–therapist posttermination relationship will be distorted by—and will, more than likely, continue to be based upon—the client's unrealistic expectations of the therapist. The assumption that some transformation, of near magical proportions, occurs in the relationship after termination that then allows the creation of what Brown (1988) terms an "equality of relationship" (p. 251) is spurious, at best.

In addition to the client–therapist dual relationships noted above, other types of relationships may also become exploitive. One example is the professional supervisory relationship. All therapists, as part of their training, are required to practice under the supervision of a more skilled and experienced therapist. Again, due to the imbalance of power, the potential for exploitation is present. Interestingly, Vesper and Brock (1991) contend that the theoretical orientation of the therapist involved is a critical issue. They note that it is the accepted method for the psychoanalytically trained therapist to obtain treatment and supervision from the same analyst. However, for the systems-oriented practitioner, "supervision and therapy must be administered by two different therapists" (p. 18). Realistically, though, in many situations the marriage and family therapy supervisor also may have other relationships with the trainee. This is particularly true in educational situations where the supervisor may also be professor and academic advisor, but this condition may readily occur in an agency where the supervisor may be the employer as well. In all such situations, the boundaries must be clearly established and maintained and there must be adequate provisions in place for the protection of all parties.

As noted at the beginning of this section, dual relationships are quite common, are not inherently wrong, and in many situations cannot be avoided. However, in all situations, therapists should take appropriate professional precautions to ensure that their judgment is not impaired and no exploitation occurs. It is always the responsibility of the therapist to maintain the boundaries and to prevent the exploitation of the client.

ANNOTATED SUGGESTED READINGS

Corey, G., Corey, M. S., & Callanan, P. (1993). *Issues and ethics in the helping professions* (4th ed.). Pacific Grove, CA: Brooks/Cole.
An easy-to-read, general treatment of ethical issues for all mental health practitioners.

Dickson, D. T. (1995). *Law in the health and human services.* New York: The Free Press.
Comprehensive source that emphasizes the legal aspect of mental health practice. Well written, but it is helpful if the reader has some prior familiarity with the topics.

Haas, L. J., & Malouf, J. L. (1995). *Keeping up the good work: A practitioner's guide to mental health ethics*. Sarasota, FL: Professional Resource Press.

> Provides good advice concerning record keeping, the financial and public (e.g., advertising) aspects of practice, testing, as well as confidentiality, informed consent, and dual relationships. Additional chapters about the therapist's power, loyalty conflicts, and relationships with colleagues are also important reading.

Huber, C. H. (1994). *Ethical, legal and professional issues in the practice of marriage and family therapy* (2nd ed.). New York: Macmillan College Publishing.

> Written in a textbook style. Includes three chapters on legal and professional issues specifically for marriage and family therapists.

Koocher, G. P., & Keith-Spiegel, P. C. (1990). *Children, ethics & the law*. Lincoln, NE: University of Nebraska Press.

> Family therapists and anyone working with children should read this. One of the few books devoted to ethical issues of working with children. [Currently under revision].

Pope, K. S. (1994). *Sexual involvement with therapists*. Washington, DC: American Psychological Association.

> A comprehensive overview. Particularly helpful for therapists that treat clients who have been sexually involved with their former therapists.

Pope, K. S., Sonne, J. L., & Holroyd, J. (1993). *Sexual feelings in therapy*. Washington, DC: American Psychological Association.

> Very helpful. Important topic that is too often neglected in both training programs and among practitioners.

Rave, E. J., & Larsen, C. C. (Eds.). (1995). *Ethical decision making in therapy: Feminist perspectives*. New York: Guilford Press.

> Presents ethical issues from a feminist perspective. Experienced feminist therapists provide personal reactions to the various case scenarios.

Vandecreek, L., & Knapp, S. (1993). Tarasoff *and beyond: Legal and clinical considerations in the treatment of life-endangering patients* (Rev. ed.). Sarasota, FL: Professional Resource Exchange.

> A brief, well-written, and understandable update about both the legal and clinical considerations for therapists who work with life-endangering client. Substantial reference list includes specific court cases.

Woody, R. H. (1988). *Fifty ways to avoid malpractice*. Sarasota, FL: Professional Resource Exchange.

> Sensible, practical, and easy-to-understand guidelines. However, the book was published in 1988, before the drastic changes brought in the mental health field.

Woody, R. H. (1997). *Legally safe mental health practice: Psycholegal questions and answers*. Madison, CT: Psychosocial Press.

> Easy-to-read question-and-answer format. Information provided, based upon author's experiences, is helpful as an overview. Lacks any references, but does include a short list of recommended readings.

REFERENCES

American Association for Marriage and Family Therapy. (1991). *Code of ethics*. Washington, DC: AAMFT.

American Counseling Association. (1995). *Code of ethics and standards of practice*. Alexandria, VA: ACA

American Psychiatric Association. (1993). *The principles of medical ethics with annotations applicable to psychiatry.* Washington, DC: APA

American Psychological Association. (1992). *Ethical principles of psychologists and code of conduct.* Washington, DC: APA

Association of Marital and Family Therapy Regulatory Boards. (1993). *Model code of ethics.* AMFTRB Home Page. [On Line]. Available http://AMFTRB.org.

Beigel, J. K., & Earle, R. H. (1990). *Successful private practice in the 1990s: A new guide for the mental health professional.* New York: Brunner/Mazel.

Bersoff, D. H. (1976). Therapists as protectors and policemen: New roles as a result of Tarasoff? *Professional Psychology, 7*(3), 267–273.

Bray, J. H., Shepherd, J. H., & Hays, J. R. (1985). Legal and ethical issues in informed consent to psychotherapy. *The American Journal of Family Therapy, 13*(2), 50–60.

Brock, G. (Ed.). (1994). *American Association for Marriage and Family Therapy: Ethics casebook.* Washington, DC: AAMFT.

Brown, L. S. (1988). Harmful effects of posttermination sexual and romantic relationships between therapists and their former clients. *Psychotherapy, 25*(2), 249–255.

Committee on Professional Practice and Standards, American Psychological Association (1993). Record keeping guidelines. *American Psychologist, 48*(9), 984–986.

Corey, G., Corey, M. S., & Callanan, P. (1993). *Issues and ethics in the helping professions* (4th ed.). Pacific Grove, CA: Brooks/Cole.

Denkowski, K. M., & Denkowski, G. C. (1982). Client-counselor confidentiality: An update of rationale, legal status, and implications. *The Personnel and Guidance Journal, 60*(6), 371–375.

Dickson, D. T. (1995). *Law in the health and human services: A guide for social workers, psychologists, psychiatrists, and related professionals.* New York: The Free Press.

Doherty, W. J., & Boss, P. G. (1991). Values and ethics in family therapy. In A. S. Gurman & D. P. Kniskern (Eds.), *Handbook for Family Therapy* (Vol. II, pp. 606–637). New York: Brunner/Mazel.

Doverspike, W. F. (1996). Informed consent for psychological services, Part I: Clinical Services. *Georgia Psychologist, 50*(2), 56–58.

Everstine, L., Everstine, D. S., Heymann, G. M., True, R. H., Frey, D. H., Johnson, H. G., & Seiden, R. H. (1980). Privacy and confidentiality in psychotherapy. *American Psychologist, 35*(9), 828–840.

Fowler, D. R. (1979). Clinical record. In R. M. Pressman (Ed.), *Private practice: A handbook for the independent mental health practitioner* (pp. 85–98). New York: Gardner Press.

Gehring, D. D. (1982). The counselors' "Duty to Warn." *The Personnel and Guidance Journal, 61*(4), 208–210.

George, J. C. (1983). Psychotherapist-patient sex: A proposal for a mandatory reporting law. *Pacific Law Journal, 16*, 431–459.

Green, S. L., & Hansen, J. C. (1989). Ethical dilemmas faced by family therapists. *Journal of Marital and Family Therapy, 15*(2), 149–150.

Gross, D. R., & Robinson, S. E. (1987). Ethics, violence, and counseling: Hear no evil, see no evil, speak no evil? *Journal of Counseling and Development, 65*(7), 340–344.

Haas, L. J., & Malouf, J. L. (1995). *Keeping up the good work: A practitioner's guide to mental health ethics* (2nd ed.). Sarasota, FL: Professional Resource Press.

Hall, J. E. (1994, November 17). Sexual relationships with clients. Proceedings of symposium: Therapeutic Malpractice, pp. 25–46, Atlanta, GA.

Hare-Mustin, R. T., Marecek, J., Kaplan, A. G., & Liss-Levinson, N. (1979). Rights of clients, responsibilities of therapists. *American Psychologist, 34*(1), 3–16.

Herlihy, B., & Sheeley, V. L. (1988). Counselor liability and the duty to warn: Selected cases, statutory trends, and implications for practice. *Counselor Education and Supervision, 27*(3), 203–215.

Hines, P. M., & Hare-Mustin, R. T. (1978). Ethical concerns in family therapy. *Professional Psychology, 9,* 65–71.

Huber, C. H. (1994). *Ethical, legal and professional issues in the practice of marriage and family therapy* (2nd ed.). Upper Saddle River, NJ: Prentice-Hall.

International Association for Marriage and Family Counseling. (1993). Ethical code for the International Association for Marriage and Family Counseling. *The Family Journal: Counseling and Therapy for Couples and Families, 1*(1), 72–77.

Jaffee v. Redmond (1996). U.S. 116 S. Ct. 1923.

Kagle, J. D., & Giebelhausen, P. M. (1994). Dual relationships and professional boundaries. *Social Work, 39*(2), 213–220.

Knapp, S. (1980). A primer on malpractice for psychologists. *Professional Psychology, 11*(4), 606–612.

Knapp, S., & VandeCreek, L. (1982). *Tarasoff*: Five years later. *Professional Psychology, 13*(4), 511–516.

Knapp, S., & VandeCreek, L. (1993). Legal and ethical issues in billing patients and collecting fees. *Psychotherapy, 30*(1), 25–31.

Krauskopf, J. M., & Krauskopf, C. J. (1965). Torts and psychologists. *Journal of Counseling Psychology, 12*(3), 227–237.

Lakin, M. (1991). *Coping with ethical dilemmas in psychotherapy.* New York: Pergamon Press.

Laurence, K. (1990). Reacting and minimizing the likelihood of a malpractice suit. In G. Seiler (Ed.), *The mental health counselor's sourcebook* (pp. 247–260). New York: Human Sciences Press.

Lenson, E. S. (1994). *Succeeding in private practice.* Thousand Oaks, CA: Sage.

Mabe, A. R., & Rollin, S. A. (1986). The role of ethical standards in counseling. *Journal of Counseling and Development, 64*(5), 294–297.

Mabe, A. R., & Rollin, S. A. (1990). The role of a code of ethical standards in counseling. In G. Seiler (Ed.), *The mental health counselor's sourcebook* (pp. 91–102). New York: Human Sciences Press.

Mappes, D. C., Robb, G. P., & Engels, D. W. (1985). Conflict between ethics and law in counseling and psychotherapy. *Journal of Counseling and Development, 64*(4), 246–252.

Margolin, G. (1982). Ethical and legal considerations in marital and family therapy. *American Psychologist, 37*(7), 788–801.

Meisel, A., Roth, L. H., & Lidz, C. W. (1982). Toward a model of the legal doctrine of informed consent. In R. B. Edwards (Ed.), *Psychiatry and ethics* (pp. 192–211). Buffalo, NY: Prometheus Books.

Miller, T. R., Scott, R., & Searight, H. R. (1990). Ethics for marital and family therapy and subsequent training issues. *Family Therapy, 17*(2), 163–171.

Mitchell, R. W. (1991). *Documentation in counseling records.* The AACD Legal Series, Vol. 2. Alexandria, VA: American Association for Counseling and Development.

National Association of Social Workers. (1996). *Code of ethics.* Washington, DC: NASW.

National Board of Certified Counselors. (1987). *Code of ethics.* Alexandria, VA: NBCC.

National Federation of Societies for Clinical Social Work. (1988). *Code of ethics.* Arlington, VA: NFSCSW.

Pope, K. S. (1994). *Sexual involvement with therapists.* Washington, DC: American Psychological Association.

Pope, K. S., Levenson, H., & Schover, L. R. (1979). Sexual intimacies in psychology training programs: Results and implications of a national survey. *American Psychologist, 34*(8), 682–689.

Pope, K. S., Sonne, J. L., & Holroyd, J. (1993). *Sexual feelings in psychotherapy.* Washington, DC: American Psychological Association.

Reaves, R. P., & Ogloff, J. R. P. (1996). Liability for professional misconduct. In *Professional conduct and discipline in psychology* (pp. 117–142). Washington, DC: American Psychological Association; and Montgomery, AL: Association of State and Provincial Psychology Boards.

Remley, T. P. (1990). Counseling records: Legal and ethical issues. In B. Herlihy and L. Golden (Eds.), *AACD ethical standards casebook* (4th ed., pp. 162–169). Alexandria, VA: AACD.

Reynolds, M. M. (1976). Threats to confidentiality. *Social Work, 21*(2), 108–113.

Rich, F. (1996, October 17). Report of the ethics committee to the annual meeting of the Association of Marital and Family Therapy Regulatory Boards, Toronto, Canada.

Robinson, S. (1989). Counselor competence and malpractice suits: Opposite sides of the same coin. *Counseling and Human Development, 20*(9), 1–8.

Scalise, J. J. (Ed.) (1989). Respect for the client: Issues in confidentiality and privileged communications. *The Professional Reader, 1*(2) [Entire Issue].

Scalise, J. J. (1995a). *An ethics bibliography for counseling, marriage and family therapy, social work and psychology.* Athens, GA: Author.

Scalise, J. J. (1995b, May-June). From confidentiality to privileged communication: Part 1. *Georgia Association for Marriage and Family Therapy Newsletter*, pp. 3–4.

Scalise, J. J. (1996, April 12). Practical ethics. Professional workshop. Athens, GA.

Scalise, J. J., & Ginter, E. J. (1989). Confidentiality and privileged communications: An overview. *The Professional Reader, 1*(2), 37–38.

Shah, S. A. (1969). Privileged communication, confidentiality, and privacy: Privileged communications. *Professional Psychology, 1*(1), 56–69.

Shah, S. A. (1970). Privileged communications, confidentiality, and privacy: Confidentiality. *Professional Psychology, 1*(2), 159–164.

Skelly, F. J. (1993, July 5), Boundary crossings. *American Medical News*, pp. 11, 13–14.

Smith, R. S. (1991, May 17). Avoiding malpractice. Presentation at Inner Harbor Hospital, Ltd. Douglasville, GA.

Smith-Bell, M., & Winslade, W. J. (1994). Privacy, confidentiality, and privacy in psychotherapeutic relationships. *American Journal of Orthopsychiatry, 64*(2), 180–193.

Stone, A. A. (1976). The *Tarasoff* decisions: Suing psychotherapists to safeguard society. *Harvard Law Review, 90*, 358–378.

Streane, H. S. (1993). *Therapists who have sex with their patients.* New York: Brunner/Mazel.

Strupp, H. H., Hadley, S. W., & Gomes-Schwartz, B. (1977). *Psychotherapy for better or worse: The problem of negative effects.* New York: Jason Aronson.

Tarasoff v. Regents of University of California, (1976). 551 P.2d334, 131 Cal Rptr. 14.

VandeCreek, L., & Knapp, S. (1984). Counselors, confidentiality and life-endangering clients. *Counselor Education and Supervision, 24*(1), 51–57.

VandeCreek, L., & Knapp, S. (1993). Tarasoff *and beyond: Legal and clinical considerations in the treatment of life-endangering patients* (Rev. ed.). Sarasota, FL: Professional Resource Press.

Vesper, J. H., & Brock, G. W. (1991). *Ethics, legalities and professional practices issues in marriage and family therapy.* Boston: Allyn and Bacon.

Walters, M. I., & Handlesman, M. M. (1996). Informed consent for mental health counseling: Effects of information specificity on clients ratings of counselor. *Journal of Mental Health Counseling, 18*(3), 265–274.

Wolfe, T. W. (1996, October). The evidentiary privilege as applied to psychological counseling. *Georgia Bar Journal,* 16–20.

Woody, R. H. (1988). *Fifty ways to avoid malpractice.* Sarasota; FL: Professional Resources Exchange.

Woody, R. H. (1991). *Quality care in mental health.* San Francisco: Jossey-Bass.

NAME INDEX

Abrams, M., 503
Ackerman, N., 17, 142, 301, 541, 543
Adler, A., 13, 16, 27, 64, 333, 366–81, 382,
    383, 384, 385, 386, 387, 388, 389, 390,
    391, 393, 396, 397, 399, 401, 403, 404,
    405, 490
Adler, K., 370, 373, 386
Allen, K., 521
Allman, L., 18
Allred, G., 411
Almeida, R., 518
Andersen, T., 223
Anderson, C., 517
Anderson, H., 212, 216, 229
Anderson, W., 352
Andolfi, M., 150
Ansbacher, H., 376, 377, 381, 382, 385, 391,
    397, 402, 406, 409
Ansbacher, R., 376, 385, 391, 397, 402, 406,
    409
Aponte, H., 141, 150
Appelgate, J., 315
Aronson, H., 458
Arthur, J., 42, 47, 481
Ascher, L., 55
Aspy, D., 357
Auerswald, E., 35
Ault-Riché, M., 518
Auw, A., 336
Avis, J., 30, 238, 518

Baker, L., 143, 165
Bakhtin, Mikhail, 214
Baldwin, L., 552
Baldwin, M., 64, 72, 74, 78, 79, 80, 81, 82
Balint, M., 304
Bandura, A., 456, 467, 470, 490
Banmen, J., 64, 82

Barbach, L., 492
Barber, K., 521
Barcai, A., 143
Barnard, C, 302
Barrett-Lennard, G., 357
Bart, P., 533
Barthes, R., 214
Baruth, A., 498
Baruth, L., 403
Bateson, G., 15, 17, 64, 170, 172, 174, 216,
    233, 246, 358, 467, 525, 546, 551
Baucom, D., 461, 492, 553
Bayer, B., 519
Beavers, W., 45, 521, 552, 555
Beavin, J., 43, 45, 212, 545
Beck, A., 490, 492
Becvar, D., 30
Becvar, R., 30
Beigel, J., 574, 575
Bell, James, 16
Bell, John, 17
Bell, N., 309
Belove, L., 403
Berg, I., 247, 258
Berg-Cross, L., 13, 21
Bergen, L., 567
Berger, H., 150
Bergin, A., 499
Bernard, M., 492
Berne, E., 64, 490
Bernhard, Y., 73
Bersoff, D., 584
Betof, N., 150
Bion, W., 306
Birchler, G., 469
Bishop, D., 552
Bitter, J., 64, 81, 82, 386
Blanck, G., 315, 324

SUBJECT INDEX